THE

County Council

Published in 2023 by Times Books

An imprint of HarperCollins Publishers
Westerhill Road
Bishopbriggs
Glasgow G64 2QT
www.harpercollins.co.uk
times.books@harpercollins.co.uk

HarperCollins Publishers
Macken House, 39/40 Mayor Street Upper,
Dublin 1, D01 C9W8, Ireland

First published in 1993. Twenty-ninth edition 2023

© Times Media Ltd 2023

The Times® and The Sunday Times® are registered trademarks of Times Media Ltd

ISBN 978-0-00-858785-7

Main league table and individual subject tables compiled by UoE Consulting Limited.

Please see Chapters 1 and 12 for a full explanation of the sources of data used in the ranking tables.
The data providers do not necessarily agree with the data aggregations or manipulations appearing
in this book and are also not responsible for any inference or conclusions thereby derived.

Text: Zoe Thomas with contributions from John O'Leary
Data and editorial consultant: Nick Rodrigues
Project editor: Anna Brüning
Design and layout: Davidson Publishing Solutions

The contents of this publication are believed correct at the time of printing. Nevertheless the
publisher can accept no responsibility for errors or omissions, changes in the detail given or for any
expense or loss thereby caused.

HarperCollins does not warrant that any website mentioned in this title will be provided
uninterrupted, that any website will be error free, that defects will be corrected, or that the website
or the server that makes it available are free of viruses or bugs. For full terms and conditions please
refer to the site terms provided on the website.

A catalogue record for this book is available from the British Library.

Printed and bound in the UK using 100% Renewable Electricity at CPI Group (UK) Ltd

MIX
Paper | Supporting
responsible forestry
FSC™ C007454

This book is produced from independently certified FSC™ paper
to ensure responsible forest management.

For more information visit: www.harpercollins.co.uk/green

Contents

About the Author

Zoe Thomas is a journalist and education writer. She has worked on *The Times and Sunday Times Good University Guide* since 2005 and is a former staff journalist for the Sunday newspaper. For the past 13 years, she has written extensively for the *Guide*, both its UK and Irish editions, and its sister publication *The Sunday Times Schools Guide, Parent Power*, the annual review of Britain's leading primary and secondary schools. She has a degree in media studies from the University of Sussex.

Acknowledgements

We would like to thank the many individuals who have helped with this edition of *The Times and Sunday Times Good University Guide*, particularly Nick Rodrigues and Alastair McCall, editor and former editor respectively of *The Sunday Times Good University Guide*, John O'Leary, journalist, education consultant and the former author of this *Guide*, and Anna Brüning, project editor. Thanks also go to Harley Griffiths, Jethro Lennox, Keith Moore, Amy Townsend-Kennedy and Rachel Weaver at HarperCollins Publishers, and to Catherine North, Sophie Bradford, Fiona Kugele, Nicki Horseman and Andrew Farquhar at UoE Consulting Limited, which has compiled the main university league table and the individual subject tables for this *Guide* on behalf of *The Times*, *The Sunday Times* and HarperCollins Publishers.

To the members of *The Times and Sunday Times Good University Guide* Advisory Group for their time and expertise: Christine Couper, Director of CouperJones higher education consultants; James Galbraith, Senior Strategic Planner, University of Edinburgh; Josh Gulrajani, Bath Spa University; Daniel Monnery, Director of Corporate Strategy, Northumbria University; Jackie Njoroge, Director of Strategy, University of Salford; Steve Walsh, Head of Planning, Aberystwyth University; David Totten, Head of Planning, Queen's University, Belfast; Jenny Walker, Senior Planning Officer, Loughborough University; to Emily Raven, Denise Jones, Kathryn Heywood and Jonathan Waller of HESA for their technical advice; also to Richard Puttock, Director of Data, Foresight and Analysis, Office for Students. To Katie Meynell and Blanca Schofield for their contributions to the book. We also wish to thank all the university staff who assisted in providing information for this edition.

Timeline to a University Place

Making an application to university is one of life's big events. It is worth getting organised and ticking off the actions that punctuate the journey from sixth form to Freshers' Week in good time. Being prepared for each step as it comes will give you greater flexibility and more options later down the line. This book will help you find a university place for September 2024.

Those applying for degrees in medicine, veterinary medicine and dentistry have an earlier application deadline (October 15, 2023) than the majority of applicants. This is the same date that Cambridge and Oxford universities also require applications to have been submitted. Relevant work experience is required for some degrees including medicine, as are aptitude and pre-assessment tests (detailed further in Chapter 2).

Use the dates below to find the key stages to a university place.

Key dates
February to July 2023
This is the time for chewing things over. What subject are you interested in studying? Where would you like to study it? The chapters of this book will help you whittle down your options with regards to choosing a subject and a university.

March 2023 onwards
Go to university Open Days. They are the best way of getting a feel for a university, its location, and what studying in a particular department or faculty would be like. Applicants need to pre-book places and should go to as many Open Days as they can, within reason. Plan carefully and make each one count. Virtual Open Days and events are also offered; they cut down the schlepping on trains and motorways and can fill the gaps where making another trip is not an option. For Open Day dates, consult each university's website – as detailed in Chapter 14.

July 2023
Registration starts for UCAS Apply, the online application system through which you will apply to universities. You will have a maximum of five choices when you complete your form.

September 2023
UCAS will begin to accept completed applications.

October 15, 2023
Deadline for applications to Oxford or Cambridge (you can only apply to one of them), and for applications to any university to study medicine, dentistry or veterinary medicine. Some courses require you to have completed a pre-application assessment test by this date.

January 15, 2024
Deadline for applications for all other universities and subjects (excluding a few art and design courses with a March 2023 deadline). This is the last date you can apply by, but it is better to get your application in beforehand; aim for the end of November 2023.

End of March 2024

Universities should have given you decisions on your applications by now if you submitted them by January 15, 2023.

April 2024 onwards

Apply for student loans to cover tuition fees and living costs.

Early May 2024

By this time, you should have responded to all university decisions. You must select a first choice, and if your first offer is conditional, a second choice, and reject all other offers.

Once you have accepted an offer, apply for university accommodation if you are going to need it. Universities have their own housing application deadlines – getting in early will often guarantee a space and may allow you first dibs on your choice of room.

First week of August 2024

Scottish examination results. If your results meet the offer from your first choice (or, failing that, your second choice), your place at university will be confirmed. If not, you can enter Clearing for Scottish universities to find a place on another course.

Second week of August 2024

A-level results announced. If your results meet the offer from your first choice (or, failing that, your second choice), your place at university will be confirmed. If not, you can enter Clearing. If you did better than expected and exceeded the conditions of your firm choice you can enter Adjustment, which gives you the chance to "trade up" and apply for a different course or university.

Mid to late September 2024

Arrive at university for Freshers' Week.

How This Book Can Help You

What and where to study are the fundamental decisions in making a successful university application.

How do I choose a course?
Most degrees last three or sometimes four years, some even longer, so you will need enthusiasm for, and some aptitude in, the subject. Also consider whether studying full-time or part-time will be best for you.

» The first half of Chapter 2 provides advice on choosing a subject area and selecting relevant courses within that subject.
» Chapter 12 provides details for 70 different subject areas. For each subject there is specific advice and a league table that provides our ranking of universities offering courses.

How will my choice of subject affect my employment prospects?
The course you choose will influence your job prospects after you graduate, so your initial subject decision will have an impact on your life long after you have finished your degree.

» The employment prospects and average starting salaries for the main subject groups are given in Chapter 3.
» The subject tables in Chapter 12 give the employment prospects for each university offering a course.
» Universities are working to increase the employability of their graduates. Examples are given in Chapter 3 and in the profiles in Chapter 14.

How do I choose a university?
While choosing your subject comes first, the place where you study also plays a major role. You will need to decide what type of university you wish to go to: campus, city or smaller town? How well does the university perform in league tables? How far is the university from home? Is it large or small? Is it specialist or general? Do you want to study abroad?

» Central to our *Guide* is the main *Times and Sunday Times* league table in Chapter 1. This ranks the universities by assessing their performance not just according to teaching quality and the student experience but also through seven other factors, including research quality, UCAS entry points, and graduate employment prospects.
» The second half of Chapter 2 provides advice on the factors to consider when choosing a university.
» Chapter 14, the largest chapter in the book, contains two pages on each university, giving a general overview of the institution as well as data on student numbers, contact details, accommodation provision, and the latest fees available. Note that fees and student support for 2023-24 will not be confirmed until August 2023, and you must check these before applying.
» For those considering Oxford or Cambridge, details of admission processes and profiles of all the undergraduate colleges can be found in Chapter 13.
» Chapter 9 gives advice about student life; focusing on alcohol, drugs, mental health and staying safe on campus.

» If you are considering studying abroad, Chapter 10 provides guidance and practical information.
» Specific advice for international students coming to study in the UK is given in Chapter 11.

How do I apply?
» Chapter 5 outlines the application procedure for university entry. It starts by advising you on how to complete the UCAS application, and then takes you through the process that we hope will lead to your university place for autumn 2024.

Can I afford it?
Note that most figures in Chapters 4 and 7 refer to 2023 and there will be changes for 2024, which you will need to check.
» Chapter 4 describes how the system of tuition fees and finance works. It looks at what you are likely to be charged, depending upon where in the UK you plan to study, and how much you can borrow. It also looks at other forms of financial support (including university scholarships and bursaries), and how to plan your budget.
» Chapter 7 provides advice on finding somewhere to live while you are at university. Sample accommodation charges for each university are given in Chapter 14.

How do I find out more?
The Times and Sunday Times Good University Guide website at **www.thetimes.co.uk/article/good-university-guide-in-full-tp6dzs7wn** will keep you up to date with developments throughout the year and contains further information and online tables (subscription required).

The UCAS website **www.ucas.com** offers a wealth of helpful advice and information, as do individual university websites. Statistical information can be found on the Discover Uni website **https://discoveruni.gov.uk/**

Introduction

With UCAS forecasting up to 1million university applicants in 2026 and the government introducing a shake-up of higher education funding from 2023, life continues to evolve apace at UK universities – even as the pandemic fades. Campuses had not long returned to business as usual when the Department for Education issued its response to Sir Philip Augar's independent review of post-19 education – the first major review into higher education ordered by the government in the six decades since 1963 – nearly three years after it was first published.

Central to the new plans is a desire to put the student finance system "on a more sustainable footing" and to make the higher education system "fairer for students and taxpayers", said the government. To achieve these ends, it has capped tuition fees and cut interest rates on loans, while also lowering the repayment thresholds for future graduates and extending repayment terms to 40 years. The Department for Education (DfE) is also seeking to limit student numbers as part of a clampdown on low-quality degrees and has put proposals to consultation for new minimum entry requirements for university to ensure pupils "aren't being pushed into higher education before they are ready".

Those applying for university place in 2022 faced a highly competitive year compared to recent ones – which saw unprecedented progression rates to university during Covid-19. Universities were more cautious in their offer-making for 2022, leading to a 54.3% overall offer rate at higher tariff institutions, down from 59.7% in 2021. But universities are shifting the dial on social inclusion and more students from the most disadvantaged backgrounds secured university places than ever before in 2022.

The growth in demand for places has not put off UK 18-year-olds, who represented 330,780 applicants in 2022 – an increase from 315,945 in 2021 (+4.7%) and even more of a leap up (+17.8%) from the 280,815 who applied in pre-pandemic 2019. The latest applications translated into 277,315 18-year-olds gaining a university place – the highest number ever to date. Demand among international students (not counting the EU) of all ages is also rising. In 2022, the number of accepted applicants from China was up 13.4% on 2021, as with new students from India (+43.7%) and Nigeria (+32.7%).

Demand for university places looks likely to keep climbing, given the current demographic trend in which the number of 18-year-olds in the UK's population is projected to increase by 2% to 3% almost every year throughout this decade. As competition hots up Clare Marchant,

UCAS' chief executive, advised in a blog for the Higher Education Policy Institute (HEPI) that students "place themselves in the strongest possible position by thinking ahead and putting together a Plan B or even a Plan C".

Interest in degree apprenticeships, which dovetail degrees with on-the-job experience, pay a salary and do not cost a penny in tuition fees, is growing. There was a 22.1% increase in the number of apprenticeship views on the UCAS website's Career Finder function compared to last year, showing more young people are looking for apprenticeship opportunities than ever before.

The government wants more of them and in September 2022 Multiverse – the education business run by Euan Blair, son of the former prime minister – announced it was the first apprenticeship provider to receive degree-awarding powers. This gives the company the ability to award its own degrees to apprentices that complete programmes. An initial cohort of 170 apprentices were enrolled on the programme at companies such as Rolls-Royce and MasterCard, and applications are open for 16-to-24-year-olds who are interested in the programme.

The shift towards fairer admissions to UK universities appears to be gathering pace. More applications were received and more young people admitted to universities from disadvantaged backgrounds in 2022 than in any previous year – as discussed in in Chapter 6, Where Students Come From. The application rate from 18-year-olds in the 20% of postcodes in England (Quintile 1) with the lowest progression to higher education stood at 28.8%, up from 27% in 2021 and more than 10 percentage points higher than in 2013. This compares to an application rate of 59.5% in the quintile of postcodes with the highest university participation: the gap between the two extremes at its narrowest ever.

Less encouragingly, another statistic, also published in September 2022, showed a 23% rise in the number of students withdrawing from higher education within a year of starting their higher education. Just shy of 40,000 students dropped out compared to around 32,000 the year before. Such an attrition rate is costly not only financially but also in wasted time and shattered ambitions.

Topped once again by Wrexham Glyndŵr in north Wales, our fifth annual social inclusion table ranks universities according to nine measures, dropout rates among them. The table reveals how successful (or not) UK universities are at delivering on their social role to attract and retain students with academic potential from all backgrounds. Today's applicants want to know about the composition of the student body they will be joining, and this table helps them in that quest.

Our chapter on Enjoying University Sport, which took a pandemic hiatus while sports facilities shuttered along with the rest of campuses, shines a light on the strength in depth of UK university sport – which enjoys some of the country's best facilities for sport and encourages participation just for fun or keeping fit as much as elite-level performance.

At Durham, our Sports University of the Year, it's the winning as well as the taking part that counts; by embracing all levels of skill Durham co-ordinates one of Britain's largest participation programmes with more than 75% of students engaged in sport and physical activity. The university has invested £47million in its indoor and outdoor sporting facilities over the past 10 years and has outstanding record of placing in the top three of the BUCS University Table since 2012.

Chapter 9 of our *Guide* looks at how students can find help and support when needed and what families can do to assist. Drinking, drug-taking and personal safety on campuses are front and centre, and the chapter aims to set a realistic tone. It offers helpful advice on how it is possible to give your child their autonomy while also checking in with them around the matters of drink, drugs, mental health and staying safe.

The price of tuition fees has not gone up for students from the UK and Ireland for now, but it has not gone down either – as had been proposed by the Augar review in 2019. But in

February 2020, research by the Institute of Fiscal Studies reconfirmed the salary premium, finding that a degree from a UK university increases a person's net earnings by at least £100,000 over their lifetime, after student loan repayments and taxes are factored in.

Some degrees do not offer good value for money though, and applicants need to find a sensible balance between following their dreams and getting into debt unwisely when choosing what and where to study. Investigate the findings in Chapter 3 of the new Graduate Outcomes survey, which shows what graduates are doing 15 months after finishing their degrees. Ideally, in the subjects you want to apply to study, you will see high proportions in high-skilled jobs and/or postgraduate study, and far fewer in jobs deemed low-skilled, or unemployed.

Most graduates do not regret going to university and carry fond memories of their undergraduate years with them through life – along with career advantages and intellectual enrichment. The right university cannot be pinpointed simply by a league table, but this *Guide* should provide all the information needed to draw up a shortlist for further investigation, which will help you make the right choice in the end.

Evolving higher education

In the 29 years that this book has been published, higher education has experienced numerous changes. Recommendations made in 2019 by the Augar review into post-18 education and funding have been slow to bear fruit as the government's attention has been focused elsewhere, but tuition fees – which it recommended reducing – remain in the news.

As recently as October 2021, officials from No 10, the Treasury, and the Department for Education were engaged in talks about a possible cut to fees but failed to reach an agreement in time for the chancellor's spending review that month. Loan repayment thresholds have also been the subject of debate, with ministers said to be considering cutting the repayment threshold down to £23,000 – in an effort to save the Treasury billions. At the time of going to press, adjustments to the existing threshold made in February 2022 are outlined in Chapter 4.

Britain's withdrawal from the European Union has brought significant change for students coming to the UK. As part of the Brexit divorce deal, students from EU countries, Iceland, Liechtenstein, Norway (EEA) and Switzerland are no longer eligible for "home" tuition fees of up to £9,250 in the UK. Nor can they continue to access tuition fee loans here. Instead, from the 2021-22 academic year, they have qualified for the higher rate of "international" tuition rates payable by those from the rest of the world. The UK has also left the Erasmus foreign exchange programme, an EU operation, and replaced it with the Turing Scheme – a national version that has funding confirmed until 2024-25.

The pattern of applications and enrolments has changed since the introduction of higher fees in 2012. Students are opting in larger numbers for subjects that they think will lead to well-paid jobs. While there has been a recovery in some arts and social science subjects, the trend towards the sciences and some vocational degrees is unmistakeable. Engineering and computer science degrees experienced significant upturns in the 2021 cycle, along with medicine and nursing. The decline in languages at degree level, meanwhile, is ongoing.

Most students take a degree at least partly to improve their career prospects, so some second-guessing of the employment market is inevitable. But most graduate jobs are not subject-specific, and even the keenest future forecasters are hard-pressed to predict employment hotspots four or five years ahead – which is when today's applicants will be looking for jobs.

Just as it may be unwise to second-guess employment prospects, the same goes for the competition for places in different subjects. Universities may close or reduce the intake to courses that have low numbers of applicants, while some of the more selective institutions may make more places available, especially to candidates who achieve good grades at A-level.

Using this *Guide*

The merger of *The Times and Sunday Times* university guides nine years ago began a new chapter in the ranking of higher education institutions in the UK. The two guides had 35 editions between them and, in their new form, provide the most comprehensive and authoritative assessments of undergraduate education at UK universities. Now in its second year in our main ranking, Hartpury University is the most recent addition to our league table and ministers are keen for new institutions to shake up the higher education system. Even those with university titles – the first criterion for inclusion in our table – take time to build up the body of data required to make meaningful comparisons.

Some famous names in UK higher education have never been ranked because they do not fit the parameters of a system that is intended mainly to guide full-time undergraduates. The Open University, for example, operates entirely through distance learning, while the London and Manchester Business Schools have no undergraduates. Birkbeck, University of London, which operates a broadly part-time course model, has dropped out of the table, though we still publish a profile of it in Chapter 14.

There are now 70 subject tables, and others will be added in due course because there is growing demand for information at this level. Successive surveys have found that students are more influenced by subject rankings than those for whole institutions.

A handful of changes to the basic methodology behind the tables has been introduced this year, outlined below, to best reflect the evolving higher education landscape since the separation of National Student Survey (NSS) scores. There is no longer a measure of service and facilities spend – this has been dropped from the ranking due to questions over the relevance of such data, and our concerns over the influence of actually quite small changes year on year on an institution's overall ranking.

This brings our academic ranking to encompass eight measures in total, down from nine previously. The graduate outcomes measure, meanwhile, has had its weighting increased from 1 to 1.5 in reflect to the importance of employability to applicants evaluating their options. The publication of the Research Excellence Framework (REF) 2021 results means we have updated our research scores, which were previously based on the REF 2014. We did not need to include an extra calculation regarding staff this time, as we did for the REF 2014, because the criteria for the new REF was changed so that all eligible staff were returned.

Recognising the impact of the pandemic, our ranking looks at the pre-pandemic 2019 degree outcomes and those from 2021, producing an average across the two years with a 2/3:1/3 weighting given to the pre-pandemic results. We have not used any 2020 outcomes this year.

The methodology for the new edition remains stable. The *Guide* has always put a premium on consistency in the way that it uses the statistics published by universities and presents the results. The overriding aim is to inform potential students and their parents and advisers, not to make judgements on the performance of universities. As such, it differs from the government's Teaching Excellence Framework (TEF), which uses some of the same statistics but makes allowance for the prior qualifications of students and uses an expert panel to place the results in context.

Our tables use the raw data produced by universities to reflect the undergraduate experience, whatever advantages or disadvantages those institutions might face. We also rank all 132 universities, while the TEF uses only three bands, leaving almost half of the institutions in our table on the same middle tier.

This year's tables

Oxford is No 1 in the main academic league table for the first time in 12 years, after a shake-up at the top of our main rankings. Its position is boosted by superb performances across all of our academic measures — including the lowest student-staff ratio of any institution (10.5:1) by a considerable margin. The university's league table ascent follows the global recognition of its groundbreaking work on the Covid-19 vaccine in partnership with AstraZeneca. Oxford was our University of the Year in 2021 as a result of its outstanding record during the crisis, and reached the shortlist in 2022.

St Andrew's settles for second place this year, having last year become the first university other than Oxford or Cambridge to top our (or any) domestic league table. It continues to enjoy levels of student satisfaction that most other academically elite universities can only marvel at.

Cambridge slips to No 3 after an eight-year reign in first place until 2021 – but the ancient university leads in 21 of our subject rankings — more than any other university. Cambridge also demands the highest entry standards: its last intake averaged 206 UCAS tariff points.

Improvements on almost every measure in our academic ranking make Bath our University of the Year. A steady march up our league table brings Bath to rank eighth overall this year — up from ninth for the past two editions and 11th before then. Strength across the board at the university includes placing fourth for satisfaction with the wider undergraduate experience in our analysis of outcomes from the latest National Student Survey and fifth for graduate prospects, with more than 90% of graduates in highly skilled jobs or further study within 15 months. Bath's course completion rate (96.2%) is the sixth best in the country.

After Cambridge's lead in 21 of our 70 subject rankings comes Oxford – which tops 11 of them. St Andrews, UCL and Glasgow each come top in five subject tables, while Warwick and Glasgow Caledonian lead in three and the London School of Economics (LSE), Imperial, Strathclyde,

Guide Award Winners

University of the Year	**University of Bath**
Runner-up	**University of Exeter**
Shortlisted	**University of Birmingham**
	University of Oxford
	University of Surrey
Scottish University of the Year	**University of St Andrews**
Welsh University of the Year	**Cardiff University**
Sports University of the Year	**Durham University**
University of the Year for Teaching Quality	**University of West London**
University of the Year for Student Experience	**University of West London**
University of the Year for Graduate Employment	**Imperial College London**
Modern University of the Year	**Nottingham Trent University**

Bath and Exeter each take the top spot in two tables. Seven other universities top one table each.

St Andrews is the leading Scottish university in our academic rankings – and wins our Scottish University of the Year title. The university continues to shake up the time-honoured order of our institutional table by outperforming third-place Cambridge once again. Its position is fuelled in part by remarkably high rates of student satisfaction, while St Andrews' entry standards are only one percentage point lower than the highest in the country at Cambridge. Queen's Belfast is Northern Ireland's top university by a clear margin. In Wales, Cardiff is our Welsh University of the Year for the second year in a row and is the best-performing institution in Wales in our academic rankings, climbing 10 places to 25th.

Impressive risers in our table include Falmouth, which has gained 45 places to =42nd, West London (up 34 places to 40th) and Teesside in =86th place – a 32-place rise. Going in the opposite direction, Chester has fallen 29 places to 97th and Staffordshire has declined by 30 places, to 106th.

Boasting the highest rates of student satisfaction in Britain, the University of West London (UWL) wins our University of the Year for Student Experience award — for the second time. In our analysis of the latest National Student Survey outcomes, UWL comes top for students' evaluation of both teaching quality and their wider undergraduate experience.

Ranked fifth in our main league table and last year's University of the Year, Imperial College London is our University of the Year for Graduate Employment for the second time in three years. The latest national Graduate Outcomes survey shows that 95.2% of graduates had moved on to high-skilled jobs or further study within 15 months, proving the talent pipeline to industry is unsurpassed from its courses specialising in science, medicine, engineering and business.

In sixth place overall, our Sports University of the Year Durham aims to be the university of choice for prospective students who are looking for a world-class degree and who want to develop their sporting journey. It co-ordinates one of Britain's largest participation programmes, with around 3,000 students representing it in the BUCS (British Universities and Colleges Sport) competitions in 137 teams. There is huge uptake of inter-college activities too, and students can participate in 18 sports across 700 teams on a weekly basis.

Nottingham Trent University (NTU), ranked at 42nd, wins our Modern University of the Year award. More undergraduates started at NTU in 2021 than at any other university. Students often find their experience impersonal in a large institution, yet NTU notches up a top-20 ranking for satisfaction with the overall undergraduate experience in our analysis of the latest NSS, published in summer 2022. For satisfaction with teaching quality, the university has overcome its pandemic blip, when it fell to joint 80th, to climb to 26th place.

Making the right choices

This *Guide* is intended as a starting point to finding the right course, a tool to help navigate the statistical minefield that applicants face as universities present their performance in the best possible light. There is advice on fees and financial questions, as well as all-important employment issues, along with the usual ranking of universities and 70 subject tables.

While some of the leading universities have expanded considerably in recent years, most will remain selective, particularly in popular subjects. Although the offer rate is promising, that does not mean that all students secure the university or course of their dreams. The demand for places is far from uniform, and even within the same university the level of competition will vary between subjects. The entry scores quoted in the subject tables in Chapter 12 offer a reliable guide to the relative levels of selectivity, but the figures are for entrants' actual qualifications. The standard offers made by departments will invariably be lower, and the grades those departments were prepared to accept were often lower still.

Making the right choice requires a mixture of realism and ambition. Most sixth-formers and college students have a fair idea of the grades they are capable of attaining, within a certain margin for error. Even with five course choices, there is no point in applying for a degree where the standard offer is so far from your predicted grades that rejection is virtually certain. If your results do turn out to be much better than predicted, there will be an opportunity through the Adjustment system, or simply through Clearing, to trade up to an alternative university.

Since the relaxation of recruitment restrictions, universities that once took pride in their absence from Clearing have continued to recruit after A-level results day. As a result, the use of insurance choices – the inclusion of at least one university with lower entrance standards than your main targets – has been declining. It is still a dangerous strategy, but there is now more chance of picking up a place at a leading university if you aimed too high with all your first-round choices. Some may even come to you if you sign up to the system that allows universities to approach unplaced candidates on Results Day if their grades are similar to those of other entrants.

The long view

School-leavers who will enter higher education in 2024 were not born when our first league table was published and most will never have heard of polytechnics, even if they attend a university that once carried that title. But it was the award of university status to the 34 polytechnics, over a quarter of a century ago, that was the inspiration for the first edition of *The Times Good University Guide*. The original poly, the Polytechnic of Central London, had become the University of Westminster. Bristol Polytechnic became the University of the West of England, and Leicester Polytechnic morphed into De Montfort University. The new *Guide* charted the lineage of the new universities and offered the first-ever comparison of institutional performance in UK higher education.

The university establishment did not welcome the initiative. The vice-chancellors described the table as "wrong in principle, flawed in execution and constructed upon data which are not uniform, are ill-defined and in places demonstrably false". The league table has changed considerably since then, and its results are taken rather more seriously.

While consistency has been a priority for the *Guide* throughout its 29 years, only five of the original 14 measures have survived. Some of the current components – notably the National Student Survey – did not exist in 1992, while others have been modified or dropped at the behest of the expert group of planning officers from different types of universities that meets annually to review the methodology and make recommendations for the future.

While ranking is hardly popular with academics, the relationship with universities has changed radically, and this *Guide* is quoted on numerous university websites. As Sir David Eastwood, now vice-chancellor of the University of Birmingham, said in launching an official report on university league tables that he commissioned as chief executive of the Higher Education Funding Council for England: "We deplore league tables one day and deploy them the next."

Most universities have had their ups and downs over the years, with the notable exceptions of Oxford and Cambridge. Both benefit from top research grades – a measure that carries an extra weighting in our table. They also have famously high entry standards, much the largest proportions of first and upper-second class degrees, and consistently good scores on every other measure. St Andrews, which also performs superbly across the board, has the edge over Oxbridge on student satisfaction – while Oxbridge has boycotted the NSS since 2016. Imperial College and University College London have seldom been out of the top five, with St Andrews joining them in recent years, while the LSE, Durham and Warwick have all been fixtures in the top 10.

There have been spectacular rises. As Thames Valley University in 2001, West London was bottom of our rankings, it is 40th this year. Lincoln is another former incumbent of the bottom spot (in 1999) when it was the University of Lincolnshire and Humberside. It is 53rd this year.

Since this book was first published, the number of universities has increased by a third and the full-time student population has rocketed. Individual institutions are almost unrecognisable from their 1993 forms. Nottingham, for example, had fewer than 10,000 students then, compared with more than 35,000 now. Manchester Metropolitan, the largest of the former polys, has experienced similar growth. Yet there are universities now which would have been too small and too specialist to qualify for the title in 1992. The diversity of UK higher education is celebrated as one of its greatest strengths, and the modern universities are neither encouraged nor anxious to compete with the older foundations on some of the measures in our table.

The coming years may bring more transformation in higher education, as the rising 18-year-old population increases the demand for higher education places over the next few years and universities are put under pressure by the government to justify the quality of their courses.

Recent experience reminds us what enduring institutions universities are, following the extraordinary period in which universities and students showed remarkable resilience in moving to an online model of teaching and learning. At the same time, closed campuses taught us just how highly students value in-person teaching and face-to-face contact time with academic staff and with each other. The ongoing increases in application rates among sixth-formers suggests that the appetite for UK higher education remains undimmed.

1 The University League Table

What makes a top university?

When tuition fees were first introduced in 1998, higher education became accountable for the investment it represented to students, their families and to taxpayers more widely. Information and statistics about universities and students came thick and fast as universities and the government adopted a commendably transparent approach to sharing information. Prior to this sharing of educational facts and figures, the somewhat nebulous notion of "reputation" was what largely counted as the means of judging a university's quality. The disclosure of data about higher education helps applicants to make informed decisions about what and where to study but navigating this abundance of publicly available information can be a complicated and at times confusing process.

The Times and Sunday Times University Guide weighs up university performance measures and combines them in a straightforward way that has armed generations of students with the knowledge and insights to make informed choices. The table in this chapter focuses on the fundamentals of undergraduate education and makes meaningful comparisons. Every element of the table has been chosen for the light it shines on the experience undergraduates encounter during their degrees, and their future prospects.

The information contained within our league table gives readers the chance to look under the bonnet of universities' performance. To get the most out of its content, it is worth reading through this introduction to our league table in order to gain an understanding of the measures used. There is no panel of "experts" involved in creating our league table: statistics do the talking instead. Critics may have reasons to discount any of the measures we use, but the package has struck a chord with readers. Our ranking has built a reputation as the most authoritative arbiter of changing fortunes in higher education.

Over 29 years of publication, our *Guide* has maintained consistency in its evaluations, confident that the measures used are the best currently available for the task. Some changes have been forced upon us though, naturally enough during the course of nearly three decades. When universities stopped assessing teaching quality by subject, our table lost its most heavily weighted measure. However, we now have the benefit of the National Student Survey (NSS), which allows us to reflect the student experience. More than two-thirds of final-year undergraduates give their views on the quality of their courses, a remarkable response rate that makes the results impossible to dismiss.

The student satisfaction measure is split in two. The "teaching quality" indicator reflects the average scores of the survey's sections on teaching, assessment and feedback, learning opportunities and academic support. The "student experience" indicator is drawn from the average of the sections on organisation and management, learning resources, the student voice and the learning community, as well as the final question on overall satisfaction. Teaching quality is favoured over student experience in our table and accounts for 67% of the overall student satisfaction score, with student experience making up the remaining 33%.

The basic information that applicants need in order to judge universities and their courses does not change, however. A university's entry standards, staffing levels, completion rates, degree classifications and graduate employment rates are all vital pieces of intelligence for anyone deciding where to study.

Research grades, while not directly involving undergraduates, bring with them considerable funds and enable a university to attract top academics.

The measures used are kept under review by a group of university administrators and statisticians, which meets annually. The raw data that go into the table in this chapter and the 70 subject tables in Chapter 12 are all in the public domain and are sent to universities for checking before any scores are calculated.

The various official bodies concerned with higher education do not publish league tables, and the Higher Education Statistics Agency (HESA), which supplies most of the figures used in our tables, does not endorse the way in which they are aggregated. But there are now numerous exercises, from the Teaching Excellence Framework to the annual "performance indicators" published by HESA on everything from completion rates to research output at each university, that invite comparisons.

Scrutiny of institutional league table positions is best carried out in conjunction with an examination of the relevant subject table – it is the course, after all, that will dominate your undergraduate years and influence your subsequent career.

How *The Times and Sunday Times* league table works

The table is presented in a format that displays the raw data, wherever possible. In building the table, scores for student satisfaction (combining the teaching quality and student experience scores), graduate outcomes and research quality were weighted by 1.5; all other measures were weighted by 1.

For entry standards, student/staff ratio, good honours and graduate prospects, the score was adjusted for subject mix. For example, it is accepted that engineering, law and medicine graduates will tend to have better graduate prospects than their peers from English, psychology and sociology courses. Comparing results in the main subject groupings helps to iron out differences attributable simply to the range of degrees on offer. This subject-mix adjustment means that it is not possible to replicate the scores in the table from the published indicators because the calculation requires access to the entire dataset.

The indicators were combined using a common statistical technique known as z-scores, to ensure that no indicator has a disproportionate effect on the overall total for each university, and the totals were transformed to a scale with 1,000 for the top score. The z-score technique makes it impossible to compare universities' total scores from one year to the next, although their relative positions in the table are comparable. Individual scores are dependent on the top performer: a university might drop from 60% of the top score to 58% but still have improved, depending on the relative performance of other universities.

Only where data are not available from HESA are figures sourced directly from universities. Where this is not possible, scores are generated according to a university's average performance on other indicators, apart from the measures for research quality, student/staff ratio and services and facilities spend, where no score is created.

The organisations providing the raw data for the tables are not involved in the process of aggregation, so are not responsible for any inferences or conclusions we have made. Every care has been taken to ensure the accuracy of the tables and accompanying information, but no responsibility can be taken for errors or omissions.

The *Times and The Sunday Times* league table uses eight important indicators of university activity, based on the most recent data available at the time of compilation:

» Teaching quality
» Student experience
» Research quality
» Entry standards

» Student/staff ratio
» Completion
» Good honours
» Graduate prospects

Teaching quality and student experience

The student satisfaction measure has been divided into two components which give final-year undergraduates' views of the quality of their courses. The National Student Survey (NSS) published in 2022 was the source of the data.

Where no data were available in the 2022 survey, the score from the 2021 survey was used. Where no data from the 2021 survey were available, the 2020 score was used.

» The National Student Survey covers eight aspects of a course, with an additional question gauging overall satisfaction. Students answer on a scale from 1 (bottom) to 5 (top) and the score in the table is the percentage of positive responses (4 and 5) in each section.
» The teaching quality indicator reflects the average scores of the first four sections, which contain 14 questions.
» The student experience indicator is drawn from the average scores of the remaining four sections, containing 12 questions, and the additional question on overall satisfaction.
» Teaching quality accounts for 67% of the overall score covering student satisfaction, with student experience making up the remaining 33%.
» The survey is based on the opinion of final-year undergraduates rather than directly assessing teaching quality. Most undergraduates have no experience of other universities, or different courses, to inform their judgements. Although all the questions relate to courses, rather than other aspects of the student experience, some types of university – notably medium-sized campus universities – tend to do better than others, while those in London, in particular, tend to do worse.

Research quality

This is a measure of the quality of the research undertaken in each university. The information was sourced from the 2021 Research Excellence Framework (REF), a peer-review exercise used to evaluate the quality of research in UK higher education institutions undertaken by the UK Higher Education funding bodies.

The overall quality of research is based on the 2021 REF. The output of the REF gave each institution a profile in the following categories: 4* world-leading; 3* internationally excellent; 2* internationally recognised; 1* nationally recognised and unclassified. The funding bodies have directed more funds to the very best research by applying weightings.

For the current edition of the *Guide*, we used the weightings adopted by UK Research and Innovation (UKRI) and Research England, published in 2020. A 4* output was weighted by a factor of 4, and 3* was weighted by a factor of 1. Outputs of 2* and 1* carry zero weight. The score was weighted to account for the number of staff in each unit of assessment. The score is presented as a percentage of the maximum possible score of 3. To achieve the maximum score, all staff would need to be at 4* world-leading level. There are no scores in this category for Buckingham (as a private university it fell outside of REF 2021).

Entry standards

This is the average score, using the UCAS tariff (see page 32), of new students under the age of 21 who took A and AS-Levels, Scottish Highers and Advanced Highers and other equivalent qualifications (eg, International Baccalaureate). It measures what new students achieved rather than the entry requirements suggested by the universities. The data comes from HESA for 2020-21. The original sources of data for this measure are data returns made by the universities to HESA.

» Using the UCAS tariff, each student's examination results were converted to a numerical score. HESA then calculated an average for all students at the university. The results have then been adjusted to take account of the subject mix at the university.

» A score of 144 represents three As at A-level. Although the vast majority of the top 40 universities in the table have average entry standards of at least 144, it does not mean that everyone achieved such results – let alone that this was the standard offer. Courses will not demand more than three subjects at A-level, and offers are pitched accordingly. You will need to reach the entry requirements set by the university, rather than these scores.

Graduate prospects

This measure is the percentage of full-time, UK-resident graduates undertaking further study or in a high-skilled job 15 months after graduation. The high-skilled employment data came from the new Graduate Outcomes survey, published by HESA in July 2022. It is based on 2019 and 2020 graduates interviewed up to September 2020 and September 2021 respectively. The results have been adjusted for subject mix.

Good honours

This measure is the percentage of graduates achieving a first or upper-second class degree. The results have been adjusted to take account of the subject mix at the university. The data comes from HESA for 2019-20 and 2020-21, averaged to offset any classification inflation due to the pandemic. The original sources of data for this measure are data returns made by the universities to HESA.

» Four-year first degrees, such as an MChem, are treated as equivalent to a first or upper-second.

» Scottish Ordinary degrees (awarded after three years of study) are excluded.

» Universities control degree classification, with some oversight from external examiners. There have been suggestions that, since universities have increased the numbers of good honours degrees they award, this measure may not be as objective as it should be. However, it remains the key measure of a student's success and employability.

Completion

This measure gives the percentage of students expected to complete their studies (or transfer to another institution) for each university. The data comes from the HESA performance indicators published in March 2022, and based on students entering in 2017–18 through to 2019-20.

» This measure is a projection, liable to statistical fluctuations.

Student/staff ratio

This is a measure of the average number of full-time equivalent students to each member of the academic staff, apart from those purely engaged in research. In this measure, a low value is better than a high value. The data comes from HESA for 2020–21. The original sources of data for this measure are data returns made by the universities themselves to HESA.

» The figures, as calculated by HESA, allow for variation in employment patterns at different universities. A low value means that there are a small number of students for each academic member of staff, but this does not, of course, ensure good teaching quality or contact time with academics.

» Student/staff ratios vary by subject; for example, the ratio is usually low for medicine. In building the table, the score is adjusted for the subject mix taught by each university.

» Adjustments are also made for students who are on industrial placements, either for a full year or for part of a year.

Rank	2021 rank		Teaching quality (%)	Student experience (%)	Research quality (%)	Entry standards (UCAS pts)	Graduate prospects (%)	Good honours (%)	Completion rate (%)	Student-staff ratio	Total	Page
1	2	Oxford	n/a	n/a	67	198	91.6	94.5	99	10.5	1000	492
2	1	St Andrews	84	80.5	53.8	204	86.9	92.6	95.9	11.8	992	520
3	3	Cambridge	n/a	n/a	69.7	206	92.6	93.5	99	11.6	991	362
4	5	London School of Economics	74.5	73.3	68	181	89.1	93.6	96.7	13.4	954	464
5	4	Imperial College London	74.9	77.2	73.9	197	95.2	92.4	97.9	11.7	939	432
6	6	Durham	74.9	70.8	55.9	183	87.3	92.6	97.2	13.7	880	390
7	7	University College London	73.8	73.8	66.8	178	86.4	91.4	94.8	11.1	878	560
8	9	Bath	76.7	79.7	53	170	90.9	90	96.2	15.4	868	332
9	8	Warwick	77	75.1	60.9	170	86.3	88	95.6	14.2	863	564
10	13	Edinburgh	68.6	67	61.5	188	84.6	91.5	94.3	11.5	827	398
11	10	Loughborough	75.7	79.2	52.5	153	85.4	85.8	93.4	13.8	814	468
12	11	Lancaster	77.6	76.6	57.4	146	82.6	82.9	94.1	14.1	805	442
13	21	Exeter	75.3	75.5	57.5	157	83.8	88.8	94.9	15.8	804	404
14	12	Glasgow	73.3	71.7	61.2	203	81.4	86.1	89.9	13.7	798	408
15	14	Bristol	71.2	69	66.2	165	84.7	91.2	95.9	14.1	790	354
16	16	Southampton	75.4	74.1	60.1	152	80.7	87.2	93.3	12.6	787	538
17	19	York	75.9	73.6	62.8	149	82	83.9	93.9	15.1	780	582
18	17	Strathclyde	76.7	75.1	53.1	202	83.8	84.6	91.1	19.1	779	544
19	20	Aberdeen	79.4	78.6	38.7	185	79.9	88.3	89.9	15	770	316
=20	25	Birmingham	71.3	70.4	61.9	154	84.2	88.3	95.4	14.9	748	340
=20	22	Sheffield	76.3	75	59.1	150	80.1	84.7	93.1	14.9	748	528
22	32	Surrey	78.6	79.2	53.3	138	84.4	81.1	90.4	16	742	550
23	15	Leeds	69	66.7	57	160	81.6	89	94	13.8	723	444
24	23	Manchester	69.5	66.3	64.4	162	83	84.8	93.9	14.3	714	470
25	=35	Cardiff	73	70.1	56.7	146	84.3	83.2	92.8	14.5	706	366

Rank	2021 rank		Teaching quality (%)	Student experience (%)	Research quality (%)	Entry standards (UCAS pts)	Graduate prospects (%)	Good honours (%)	Completion rate (%)	Student-staff ratio	Total	Page
26	18	King's College London	69.6	66.3	64.2	164	86.2	87.3	92.6	13.9	705	438
27	27	East Anglia	72.7	69.2	58	134	82.4	86.7	89.7	14.2	699	392
28	24	Queen's Belfast	73	71.3	52	148	84.5	85.5	92.3	15.9	693	506
29	26	Royal Holloway, London	74.1	72.7	53.6	129	73.8	84.2	92.7	16.2	691	518
=30	28	Nottingham	71.9	69.5	56.1	148	83.8	85.3	93.9	15.8	685	486
=30	34	Reading	75.1	74.5	51.1	124	77.4	83.6	92.3	16.6	685	510
32	=35	Dundee	74.5	70.1	51.1	178	82	79.7	89.4	14.9	681	388
=33	=30	Liverpool	71	69	55.6	141	78.8	81.8	92.5	13.8	665	456
=33	42	Newcastle	68.8	66.7	53.6	145	82.3	84.4	94.5	14.7	665	476
35	37	Leicester	73	72	53.6	129	75.3	81.2	91.4	13.7	659	452
36	40	Queen Mary, London	70.3	68.4	58.7	146	75.9	88.3	93	14.6	650	504
37	33	SOAS, London	68.5	62.7	51.9	145	74.6	84	84.9	14.6	636	532
=38	41	Stirling	76.2	72.8	43.8	169	73.7	76.9	85.9	18.6	635	542
=38	44	Ulster	78.2	75.7	47.8	128	75.6	80.6	88.2	20.3	635	558
40	74	West London	84.3	81.4	28.7	119	69	77.3	77.2	12.9	634	568
41	38	Aberystwyth	83.7	80.5	38.7	121	66	72.5	85.2	15.6	631	320
=42	87	Falmouth	79	72.9	48.8	125	60.6	77.6	n/a	14.8	630	406
=42	70	Nottingham Trent	78.1	76.1	41.9	121	71	72.1	88.9	15.3	630	488
=42	39	Swansea	74	70.4	47.5	131	78.1	80.3	89.9	16.2	630	554
=45	45	Aston	72.8	72.8	40.9	128	79.6	84.3	91.1	17	626	328
=45	64	Bangor	78.5	74.5	51.3	123	71	75.3	82.3	15.1	626	330
47	29	Harper Adams	76.8	75.9	19.5	123	71.6	73.2	92.2	13.8	616	418
48	46	Kent	71.9	69.2	52.9	125	74.2	81.1	89.7	17.7	615	436
49	=62	Northumbria	74.1	70.1	40.6	137	78.2	80	83.4	15.7	612	482
50	47	Sussex	71.6	69.6	52.9	136	70.6	78.4	92.3	17.3	609	552

Rank	2021 rank		Teaching quality (%)	Student experience (%)	Research quality (%)	Entry standards (UCAS pts)	Graduate prospects (%)	Good honours (%)	Completion rate (%)	Student-staff ratio	Total	Page
51	67	St Mary's, Twickenham	82.4	78.9	29.4	109	68.8	77	78.8	16	606	524
52	60	Glasgow Caledonian	75.1	72.2	38.5	168	78.6	82.5	86.4	22.9	603	410
53	49	Lincoln	75.8	73.5	38.4	120	70.2	77.6	88.8	16.1	599	454
54	43	Essex	73.3	72.5	50	114	72.6	79.7	87.6	16	598	402
55	51	Coventry	78.6	76.7	33.8	115	71	76.8	80.1	13.8	595	378
56	=52	Arts London	72.6	63	46	139	59.3	75.4	86.4	11.9	593	326
=57	=30	Heriot-Watt	66.5	66.7	48.7	172	79.3	81.9	86	18	592	422
=57	54	Oxford Brookes	72.5	70	32.8	117	74.6	79.1	90.8	14	592	494
59	57	Edinburgh Napier	77.3	74.4	32.9	150	77.7	81.3	82.7	22.1	590	400
60	71	Manchester Metropolitan	76.7	73.3	43.7	126	67.9	76.1	86.1	17.5	579	472
61	73	West of England	75.5	72.4	35.7	123	76.3	77	83.4	15.7	575	566
62	88	Portsmouth	77.2	73.2	39.1	112	73.7	76.3	84.9	16.8	574	500
63	69	Creative Arts	77.2	68.7	41.2	134	52.2	78.3	84.7	13.8	573	380
64	48	Keele	72.3	69.9	42	123	79.3	78.9	89.2	15.3	572	434
65	=62	Robert Gordon	81.2	76	20.8	156	77.6	72.9	85.2	20.8	569	512
66	50	Chichester	78	74.6	20.1	125	64.9	77.1	86.4	15.2	568	374
=67	=52	Hull	75.8	72.1	42.4	125	75.2	76	81.5	16.2	561	430
=67	66	Queen Margaret, Edinburgh	76.8	73.1	27.3	162	68.3	79.9	83.7	21.9	561	502
69	55	City, London	67.5	66.7	51.5	132	77.6	80.5	90.2	19.4	559	376
70	56	Norwich Arts	76.1	67.9	38.8	130	65.6	72.2	84.5	15.5	555	484
=71	=103	Leeds Arts	77.1	71.7	6	149	62.4	80.1	93.1	16.1	553	446
=71	93	Liverpool John Moores	75.2	74.1	32.8	139	71	75.4	83.8	18	553	460
73	75	Huddersfield	75.9	72.1	31.1	122	67.6	77.2	84.5	14.7	551	428
74	=58	Plymouth	75.3	72	38.6	127	77.7	76.5	85.3	17.3	547	496
75	82	Bishop Grosseteste	82.5	77	11.3	107	73.4	70.4	88.6	19.8	537	344

Rank	2021 rank		Teaching quality (%)	Student experience (%)	Research quality (%)	Entry standards (UCAS pts)	Graduate prospects (%)	Good honours (%)	Completion rate (%)	Student-staff ratio	Total	Page
76	=79	Arts Bournemouth	76.2	70.3	23	145	57.4	70.4	88.5	14.5	536	324
77	=103	Bath Spa	77.7	71.5	29.3	112	61.9	79.1	83.7	16.6	529	334
78	=58	Edge Hill	74	71.9	26.3	128	70.9	74	86.7	15.5	528	396
79	=83	York St John	80	75.1	19.6	110	66.6	76.5	85.1	18	527	584
=80	81	Liverpool Hope	78.5	73.4	22.3	114	64.8	74.3	82.9	16.3	524	458
=80	=101	Plymouth Marjon	81.6	77.3	17.4	119	68.8	75.8	80	19.2	524	498
=82	72	Sheffield Hallam	72.3	66.4	36	116	75.1	77.6	85.5	17.7	514	530
=82	78	St George's, London	65.6	60.9	48.8	144	91.7	80	93.7	13.1	514	522
84	=89	Greenwich	76.7	73.4	32.9	117	70.2	77.5	83.4	19.5	512	416
85	=89	Buckingham	75.5	71.3	n/a	117	79.9	69.1	85.7	n/a	509	358
86	118	Teesside	78.3	73.7	28	117	78.1	73	77.1	17.1	508	556
87	=106	Winchester	75.4	72.2	22	111	68.2	74.6	85.4	18.1	506	574
88	98	Salford	73.6	68.7	37.8	125	71.4	76.6	81.3	17.9	503	526
=89	=94	Abertay	78.7	73.2	24.6	148	70.5	78	76.3	24.2	501	318
=89	=106	Bournemouth	71.8	68.7	30.7	112	76.9	78.7	82.9	19.2	501	348
91	=96	Hertfordshire	75.6	71.8	39.2	106	72.4	70.6	83.4	16.5	499	424
92	=101	Kingston	75.4	72.1	34.6	118	70.3	72.5	82.5	17	498	440
93	=79	Cardiff Metropolitan	72.3	69.2	32	124	71.6	75.1	80	18.1	497	368
94	=83	Birmingham City	75.4	70.3	29	120	70.3	72.8	84	17.2	492	342
95	=89	Bradford	70.6	70.2	29.9	125	76.8	83	86.1	19.1	491	350
96	=94	Derby	78.8	74	21	118	68.9	68.4	80.1	15.8	490	386
97	68	Chester	74.4	65.2	21.1	120	72	74.1	83.2	15.1	489	372
=98	117	Brighton	71.4	64.8	41.4	111	73.6	72.2	83.9	17	487	352
=98	77	Sunderland	78.5	73.5	30.5	120	66.1	66.7	78.3	15.9	487	548
100	124	Leeds Trinity	78.2	76.2	15.1	107	65.5	79.7	78.3	21.5	486	450

Rank	2021 rank		Teaching quality (%)	Student experience (%)	Research quality (%)	Entry standards (UCAS pts)	Graduate prospects (%)	Good honours (%)	Completion rate (%)	Student-staff ratio	Total	Page
101	65	Roehampton	74.9	72.4	45.9	102	62.4	70.6	78.6	18.3	482	514
102	116	Royal Agricultural	75.8	78.7	24.2	114	67.6	66.9	90.4	21.5	481	516
103	99	South Wales	75.8	69.6	27.5	119	66.5	72.3	81.7	16.1	478	536
104	=83	Wales, Trinity St David	77.8	71.6	23.8	136	62.6	76.5	77.7	21.1	477	562
105	=112	Hartpury	82.2	76.9	15.8	121	66.2	62.5	n/a	23.6	475	420
106	76	Staffordshire	76	69.9	30	118	66.6	74.8	78.2	17.7	467	540
107	=108	Central Lancashire	74	68.9	30.4	125	72.9	73.3	74.8	16.2	463	370
108	61	Goldsmiths, London	63.8	54.7	45.5	127	65.5	83.6	78.6	13.9	462	414
109	115	Anglia Ruskin	76.8	71.4	30.2	110	67.4	76	79.3	19.4	457	322
=110	121	Brunel London	68.3	66.8	34	120	69	77.1	88.1	17.9	455	356
=110	86	Worcester	74.2	71.9	15.3	117	74.6	66.7	85.2	17.5	455	578
112	=96	Gloucestershire	72.4	68.6	21	118	67.4	72.2	81.1	17.2	454	412
113	=112	Leeds Beckett	74.9	70.8	26.7	107	69.7	75.2	79.9	21.7	452	448
114	=112	Solent	76.8	71.7	12.6	112	63.3	73.1	77.8	17.5	436	534
=115	123	Middlesex	73.5	70.2	30.4	107	72.7	72.6	76	17.1	432	474
=115	105	Suffolk	74.4	66.2	21.8	113	81	70.3	65.6	15	432	546
=115	129	Westminster	70	70	39.7	117	64.8	69.3	81.8	19.9	432	572
118	122	Newman, Birmingham	77.8	72.4	13.3	105	69.7	67.7	76.7	18	431	478
119	=119	Canterbury Christ Church	74.9	66.9	26.1	101	76.1	68.5	79.5	18.2	428	364
120	=110	Wrexham Glyndŵr	81.6	74.6	13.3	115	69	71.6	74	24.9	422	580
121	=119	Buckinghamshire New	81.1	75.9	17.6	111	66.5	57.9	72.3	15.4	417	360
=122	126	De Montfort	70.8	67.6	27.4	106	69.3	73.7	81.6	18.5	413	384
=122	=110	West of Scotland	74.9	67	19.2	139	70.7	74.2	78.3	23.5	413	570
124	=89	Bolton	80.8	76.8	10.6	117	64.9	66.1	76.3	16.4	404	346
125	=108	Northampton	74	69.3	13.8	107	70.2	69.6	81.5	17.7	402	480

Rank	2021 rank	Teaching quality (%)	Student experience (%)	Research quality (%)	Entry standards (UCAS pts)	Graduate prospects (%)	Good honours (%)	Completion rate (%)	Student-staff ratio	Total	Page
126	127 London South Bank	72.8	67.9	28.8	107	66.4	74.1	78.5	17.5	401	466
127	128 Wolverhampton	75.8	71.2	21.6	109	67.9	68.8	71.8	16.5	387	576
128	100 London Metropolitan	81.4	77.9	29.2	101	60.2	64.5	68.7	22.7	379	462
129	125 Cumbria	72.7	67.5	13.6	121	68.2	66.6	82.8	18.7	366	382
130	131 Ravensbourne, London	70	58.6	13.5	113	64	81.5	79.5	24.6	343	508
131	130 East London	73.6	69.6	22.8	101	64.3	72.1	77.3	26.2	334	394
132	132 Bedfordshire	76.4	71.5	30	107	68.5	64.8	56.2	27.4	308	336

2 Choosing What and Where to Study

Choice runs through education, as university applicants will know quite well by now. Those from the UK will already selected GCSEs and A-levels, or Higher and Advanced Higher subjects, from a vast array of options. Figuring out what to study and where to study it is the next decision, and it is a biggie. This is a milestone that will impact the rest of your life, to one extent or another, on many levels – from the intellectual and professional to the social and personal. Careers, scholarship and friendships are shaped during the undergraduate years. Many people meet their life partners at university, too. Such considerations are obviously mindblowing and light years into the dim and distant future for school-leavers filling out their UCAS forms. But they are worth bearing in mind, just the same.

Naturally, all considerations about what and where to study are under the microscope of student debt. The government forecasts that the average debt among students who started their course in 2021-22 will be £45,800 when they complete their course. Making informed but also aspirational decisions about a degree course is key to ensuring a wise choice that is likely to stand the test of time.

There are more than 35,000 undergraduate courses in Britain, as last totted up by UCAS in 2020. This *Guide* features 135 universities, and there are many colleges that applicants of certain specialisms will also be considering. Such breadth of choice may seem overwhelming, but there are plenty of tangible ways to whittle down your options.

Decision-making motivations range from the rational and logical to the inexplicable and emotive, a UCAS poll in 2020 found. A common thread, however, and one that chimes with widespread research, was that subject choice came first: 83% of students said they decided on their degree subject before thinking about the institution at which they would study it.

Enjoying a subject was the guiding principle for a resounding 99% of the students surveyed, but employability prospects are also increasingly taken into consideration – as they should be – with more than half of respondents reporting that high graduate employment rates had become more important to them since the pandemic.

The demand for places at university is continuing to climb and students are happy to be back on campuses and learning in person. Not even a global health pandemic stalled the upward trajectory of applications and enrolments to UK higher education institutions; the charms of university were in even sharper focus when compared with a world in which opportunities for travel and jobs were tightly limited. The popularity of going to university will be similarly undented by the rising cost of living, commentators suspect, although the financial pinch is likely to impact the quality of students' experiences in one way or another.

The new Graduate Outcomes survey shows what graduates of the subjects you are interested in are doing 15 months after finishing their degrees. Ideally, you will see high proportions in high-skilled jobs and/or postgraduate study, and far fewer in jobs deemed low-skilled, or unemployed. It is a useful tool for new applicants.

Some subjects and some universities carry more prestige than others. Such judgements are worth bearing in mind, as your future CV will be assessed according to them. This kind of thinking may not sit easily with everyone, but employers treat universities and subjects as yardsticks, not just the results gained on courses. Certain universities, however, may not occupy our upper rankings, but they might have particularly strong departments for individual subjects. Make the most of out of this Guide, and cross reference the subject-by-subject information in Chapter 12 with the university profiles and rankings in Chapter 14. The options are not endless, but they are many.

Be realistic in your choices. The course you apply to should be within your capabilities, although it will also need to keep you interested for three years-plus. A degree should broaden your options later in life, so be sensible about choosing one that can do that for you while keeping an eye on the career horizon. The technological advancements of the fourth industrial revolution are continually reshaping the world of work, and you want to be abreast of developments. Narrowing your focus at degree stage could limit what is open to you in five to 10 years' time. This Guide can inform you of what is possible, and what will make a wise choice.

Is higher education for you?

Being carried along with the flow is too easy. Maybe all your friends are going to university, or your parents expect it. If you apply for a course in your strongest A-level subject, things should work out OK and your career will look after itself, right? Or perhaps your driving motivation is to leave home in search of the UK's best music or clubbing scenes, or simply to put some sizeable portions of motorway between you and your parents. Considerations such as this are natural and will not necessarily lead to disaster. But now is the time to question whether university is the best way of fulfilling your ambitions. There are degree apprenticeships, or training schemes at big firms which could equally help you achieve what you want, minus the need to take out a student loan.

If studying for A-levels or equivalent qualifications has felt like torture, now may not be the time for you to go to university. Perhaps a job would be better, and possibly a return to education later in life would suit you more. Love of a subject is an excellent reason for taking a degree; it will help you focus your course search on those that reflect your passion. But if a degree is a means to a career for you, look carefully at employment rates for any courses you consider.

Setting your priorities

The majority of graduate jobs are not subject-specific; employers value the transferable skills that higher education confers. Rightly or wrongly, however, most employers are influenced by which university you went to, as mentioned above, so the choice of institution remains important.

Consider boosting your CV while studying by choosing a university that offers some sort of employment-related scheme. It could be work experience built into your degree, or a particularly active careers service.

Narrowing down the field

There is only a scramble for places on a relatively small proportion of courses that attract intense competition. Otherwise, there are plenty of places at good universities for candidates with sufficient qualifications. You just need to find the one that suits you best. For older applicants returning to education, relevant work experience and demonstrable interest in a subject may be enough to win a place.

Narrowing down your options

Too much choice is more of an issue. Narrow down your options by choosing a subject – or subject area – first, rather than a university. This can reduce the field considerably as not all universities offer all subjects. Having made this initial edit by subject, then factor in personal preferences such as location and type of university – campus or city? – and, by this point, you may already have the beginnings of a manageable list.

Next up is course content and what life is really like for students. Today's budding undergraduates are at an advantage in this regard. As well as having access to the informative and accurate contents of university prospectuses and websites, they can connect with current students online and do some digging. Most universities have an "Ask a Student" function, or similar, on their website, which will link you with a student ambassador for a live chat or call back. Another helpful source of information is **www.thestudentroom.com**, the country's largest online student community. You may already have used it while studying for your A-levels.

The peer-to-peer platform offers forums for students to discuss their options, ask for advice and build relationships. Current students on the courses and at the universities you are interested in may be happy to share their appraisals – although, bear in mind, that what they tell you may be biased in some direction or another. Cross-reference anything you have been told with factual sources of information such as ours, or the UCAS website.

The National Student Survey is an objective source of information which is available online, with a range of additional data about the main courses at each institution, at **www.officeforstudents.org.uk/advice-and-guidance/student-information-and-data**.

Visiting the university will give a truer picture yet; better still go to the department where you would be studying.

What to study?

As well as an interest that is sustainable for three-plus years in the subject you pick, you need to ensure you have the right qualifications to meet its entry requirements. Many economics degrees require mathemamtics A-level, for example, while most medical schools demand chemistry or biology. The UCAS website is a good starting point; it contains course profiles and entrance requirements (**www.ucas.com**), while universities' own sites offer more detailed information. The Russell Group of 24 leading universities' Informed Choices website is another go-to source of information regarding required subjects (**informedchoices.ac.uk**).

Your school subjects and the UCAS tariff

The official measure by which your results will be judged is the UCAS tariff, which gives a score for each grade of most UK qualifications considered relevant to university entrance, as well as for the International Baccalaureate (IB). The points system is shown on page 32. Two-thirds of offers are made in grades, rather than tariff points. This means universities may stipulate the grades they require in specific subjects, and determine which vocational qualifications are relevant to different degrees. In certain universities, some departments, but not others, will use the tariff to set offers. Course profiles on the UCAS website and/or universities' own sites should show whether offers are framed in terms of grades or tariff points. It is important to find out which, especially if you are relying on points from qualifications other than A-level or Scottish Highers.

Entry qualifications listed in the *Guide* relate not to the offers made by universities, but to the actual grades achieved by successful candidates who are under 21 on entry. For ease of comparison, a tariff score is included even where universities make their offers in grades.

'Soft' subjects

These are another big factor in what and where you study. The Russell Group scrapped its controversial list of preferred A-levels in 2019, after criticism that it contributed to a devaluation of creative and arts subjects. Previously however the group's Informed Choices website had a list of "facilitating subjects" comprising: maths and further maths, English, physics, biology, chemistry, geography, languages (classical and modern) and history, which are required by many degrees and welcomed by Russell Group universities generally.

The website advised sixth-formers to pick the majority of their A-levels from this list and to include at most one "soft" subject. Although these "soft subjects" were not listed specifically, a previous Informed Choices report named media studies, art and design, photography and business studies among the subjects that would normally be given this label. The current Informed Choices website offers more personalised guidance on A-level choices.

The facilitating subjects list may be gone, but its legacy is entrenched – which applicants to these universities should be very aware of when selecting their A-levels. It is better to keep more doors open than close any off at sixth form.

For most courses at most universities, there are no such restrictions, as long as your main subjects or qualifications are relevant to the degree you hope to take. Even so, the Russell Group lists are an indication of the subjects that admissions tutors may take more or less seriously, especially if you plan to apply to at least one leading university. Although only the London School of Economics has published a list of "non-preferred" subjects (see page 33), others may take a less formal approach but still apply similar weightings.

General studies is a separate matter, and some universities still do not regard it as a full A-level for entry purposes, while others – including some leading institutions – do.

Vocational qualifications

The Education Department downgraded many vocational qualifications in school league tables from 2014. This has added to the confusion surrounding the value placed on diplomas and other qualifications by universities. The engineering diploma has won near-universal approval from universities (for admission to engineering courses, and possibly some science degrees), but some of the other diplomas are in fields that are not on the curriculum of the most selective universities. Regardless of the points awarded under the tariff, it is essential to contact universities direct to ensure that a diploma or another vocational qualification will be an acceptable qualification for your chosen degree.

Admission tests

The growing numbers of applicants with high grades at A-level have encouraged the introduction of separate admission tests for some of the most oversubscribed courses. There are national tests in medicine and law that are used by some of the leading universities, while

UCAS tariff scores for main qualifications:

A-levels		AS levels	
Grade	**Points**	**Grade**	**Points**
A*	56	A	20
A	48	B	16
B	40	C	12
C	32	D	10
D	24	E	6
E	16		

Scottish Advanced higher		Scottish higher	
Grade	**Points**	**Grade**	**Points**
A	56	A	33
B	48	B	27
C	40	C	21
D	32	D	15

BTec Level 3			
National Diploma (post-2016)		**Extended Certificate**	
Grade	**Points**	**Grade**	**Points**
D*	28	D*	56
D	24	D	48
M	16	M	32
P	8	P	16

International Baccalaureate*			
Higher level		**Standard level**	
H7	56	S7	28
H6	48	S6	24
H5	32	S5	16
H4	24	S4	12
H3	12	S3	6

*The Extended Essay and Theory of Knowledge course are awarded A12, B10, C8, D6, E4
For Foundation Diploma, Extended Diploma and other BTec levels see UCAS website
For other qualifications see: ucas.com/ucas/ucas-tariff-points

Oxford and Cambridge have their own tests in a growing number of subjects. The details are listed on page 34. In all cases, the tests are used as an extra selection tool, not as a replacement for A-level or other general qualifications.

Making a choice

Your A-levels or Scottish Highers may have been straightforward to choose, but the range of subjects at university is vast. Even subjects you have studied at school may be quite different at degree level – some academic economists prefer their undergraduates not to have taken A-level economics because they approach the subject so differently. Other students are disappointed because they appear to be going over old ground when they continue with a subject that they enjoyed at school. Universities now publish quite detailed syllabuses, and applicants are advised to go through the fine print.

The greater difficulty comes in judging your suitability for the many subjects that are not on the school or college curriculum. Philosophy and psychology sound fascinating (and are), but you may have no idea what degrees in either subject entail – for example, the level of statistics that may be required. Forensic science may look exciting on television – more glamorous than plain chemistry – but it opens fewer doors, as the type of work portrayed in *Silent Witness* is very hard to find.

Academic or vocational?

There is frequent and often misleading debate about the differences between academic and vocational higher education. It is usually about the relative value of taking a degree, as opposed to a directly work-related qualification. But it also extends to higher education itself, with jibes about so-called "Mickey Mouse" degrees in areas that were not part of the higher education curriculum when most of the critics were students.

Such attitudes ignore the fact that medicine and law are both vocational subjects, as are architecture, engineering and education. They are not seen as any less academic than geography or sociology, but for some reason social work or nursing, let alone media studies and sports science, are often looked down upon. The test of a degree should be whether it is challenging and a good preparation for working life. Both general academic and vocational degrees can do this.

Nevertheless, it is clear that the prospect of much higher graduate debt is encouraging more students into job-related subjects. This is understandable and, if you are sure of your future career path, possibly also sensible. But much depends on what that career is – and whether you are ready to make such a long-term commitment. Some of the programmes that have attracted public ridicule, such as surf science or golf course management, may narrow graduates' options to a worrying extent, but often boast strong employment records.

As you would expect, many vocational courses are tailored to particular professions. If you choose one of these, make sure that the degree is recognised by the relevant professional body

---

"Traditional academic" and "non-preferred" subjects

The London School of Economics expects applicants to offer at least two of the traditional subjects listed below, while any of the non-preferred subjects listed should only be offered together with two traditional subjects.

Traditional subjects

- Ancient history
- Biology
- Classical civilisation
- Chemistry
- Computing
- Economics
- Electronics
- English (English language, English literature and English language and literature)
- Further mathematics
- Geography
- Government and politics
- History
- Languages: modern foreign, classic and community
- Law
- Mathematics
- Music
- Philosophy
- Physics
- Psychology
- Religious studies
- Sociology

Non-preferred subjects

- Any applied A-level
- Accounting*
- Art and design
- Business studies
- Citizenship studies
- Communication and culture
- Creative writing
- Design and technology
- Drama/theatre studies
- Film studies
- Health and social care
- Home economics
- Information and communication technology
- Leisure studies
- Media studies
- Music technology
- Physical education/sports studies
- Travel and tourism

*The LSE Department of Accounting considers accounting equally with other generally preferred subjects. Therefore, it will consider accounting alongside one other subject from the non-preferred list. However, the majority of departments continue to regard accounting as a non-preferred subject.
Critical thinking, general studies, global perspectives and research, knowledge and enquiry, project work and thinking skill are normally excluded subjects and will only be considered as a fourth A-level. They will not be accepted as part of a contextual offer.
Source: LSE

Admissions tests

Some of the most competitive courses now have additional entrance tests. The most significant tests are listed below. Note that registration for many of the tests is before 15 October and you will need to register for them as early as possible. All the tests have their own websites. Institutions requiring specific tests vary from year to year and you must check course website details carefully for test requirements. In addition over 50 universities also administer their own tests for certain courses. Details are given at: **www.ucas.com/undergraduate/applying-university/admissions-tests**

Law

Law National Admissions Test (LNAT): for entry to law courses at Bristol, Cambridge, Durham, Glasgow, King's College London, London School of Economics, Nottingham, Oxford, SOAS, University College London. Register from August; tests held from September to July.

Mathematics

Mathematics Admissions Test (MAT): for entry to mathematics at Imperial College London and mathematics and computer science at Oxford. Advised but not compulsory for applicants to mathematics at Warwick. The MAT is also taken into consideration by other universities, including Bath and Durham, for particular courses. Register by mid-September.

Sixth Term Examination Papers (STEP): for entry to mathematics at Cambridge, Warwick and Imperial College London (also occasionally requested by other universities). Check for registration and test dates at www.admissionstesting.org/for-test-takers/step/about-step

Test of Mathematics for University Admission (TMUA): results accepted by Bath, Cambridge, Cardiff, Durham, Nottingham, Lancaster, London School of Economics, Sheffield, Southampton, Warwick. Register by September 30. Test on October 18.

Medical subjects

BioMedical Admissions Test (BMAT): for entry to medicine at Brighton and Sussex Medical School, Cambridge, Imperial College London, Lancaster, Leeds (also for dentistry), Oxford (also for biomedical sciences) and University College London. Check **https://www.admissionstesting.org/for-test-takers/bmat/** for registration and test dates.

Graduate Medical School Admissions Test (GAMSAT): for graduate entry to medicine at Cardiff, East Anglia, Exeter, Liverpool, Nottingham, Plymouth (and dentistry), St George's, London, Swansea, Keele and St Andrews, Dundee, Sunderland, Ulster and Worcester. The GAMSAT test is offered in March and September.

Health Professions Admissions Test (HPAT-Ulster): for certain health profession courses at Ulster. The HPAT–Ireland test window will run from Friday, February 17 to Saturday, February 25, 2023.

University Clinical Aptitude Test (UCAT): for entry to medical and dental schools at Aberdeen, Anglia Ruskin, Aston, Birmingham, Bristol, Brunel, Cardiff, Chester, Dundee, East Anglia, Edge Hill, Edinburgh, Exeter, Glasgow, Hull York Medical School, Keele, Kent and Medway, King's College London, Leicester, Liverpool, Manchester, Newcastle, Nottingham, Plymouth, Queen Mary, University of London, Queen's University Belfast, Sheffield, Southampton, St Andrews, St George's, London, Sunderland, Surrey, Warwick and Worcester. Check **www.ucat.ac.uk/about-ucat/** for registration and test dates.

Cambridge University

Pre-interview or at-interview assessments take place for most subjects. Full details given on the Cambridge admissions website. See also STEP and BMAT above.

Please note Cambridge Assessment Admissions Testing is to withdraw from running a series of university admissions exams with effect from 2024-25. This includes BMAT (medicine), ENGAA (engineering), NSAA (natural sciences), and TMUA (mathematical skills) tests. For the academic year 2024-25 onwards, the seven UK medical schools that use BMAT tests as part of their admissions process (Brighton and Sussex, Imperial, Lancaster, UCL, Cambridge, Leeds and Oxford) will put alternative arrangements in place.

Oxford University

Pre-interview tests take place in many subjects that candidates are required to register for specifically by early October. Full details given on the Oxford admissions website. Tests usually at candidate's educational institution. See also LNAT, MAT and BMAT above.

(such as the Engineering Council or one of the institutes) or you may not be able to use the skills that you acquire. Most universities are only too keen to make such recognition clear in their prospectus; if no such guarantee is published, contact the university department running the course and seek assurances. In education, for example, by no means do all degrees qualify you to teach.

Even where a course has professional recognition, a further qualification may be required to practise. Both law and medicine, for example, demand additional training to become a fully qualified solicitor, barrister or doctor. Neither degree is an automatic passport to a job: only about half of all law graduates go into the profession. Both law and medicine also offer a postgraduate route into the profession for those who have taken other subjects as a first degree. Law conversion courses, though not cheap, are increasingly popular, and there are a growing number of graduate-entry medical degrees.

One way to ensure that a degree is job-related is to take a "sandwich" course, which involves up to a year in business or industry. Students often end up working for the organisation which provided the placement, while others gain valuable insights into a field of employment – even if only to discount it. The drawback with such courses is that, like the year abroad that is part of most language degrees, the period away from university inevitably disrupts living arrangements and friendship groups. But most of those who take this route find that the career benefits make this a worthwhile sacrifice. Growing numbers of traditional degrees now offer shorter periods of work experience.

Employers' organisations calculate that more than half of all graduate jobs are open to applicants from any subject, and recruiters for the most competitive graduate training schemes often prefer traditional academic subjects to apparently relevant vocational degrees. Newspapers, for example, may prefer a history graduate to one with a media studies degree; computing firms are said to take a disproportionate number of classicists.

A good degree classification and the right work experience are more important than the subject for most non-technical jobs. But it is hard to achieve a good result on a course that you do not enjoy, so scour prospectuses, and email or phone university departments, to ensure that you know what you are letting yourself in for. The responsiveness of universities to your approach – or not – will also give you an idea of how alert they are to ensuring that students know what they are letting themselves in for.

Most popular subject areas by applications 2021		Most popular subject areas by acceptances 2021	
1 Psychology (non-specific)	127,130	1 Law	27,970
2 Medicine	103,665	2 Psychology (non-specific)	23,500
3 Computer Science	97,005	3 Business Studies	20,510
4 Adult Nursing	94,670	4 Adult nursing	19,790
5 Language and Areas Studies	94,470	5 Design studies	18,420
6 Design Studies	93,470	6 Sport and Exercise Sciences	17,655
7 Sociology	91,460	7 Sociology	17,515
8 Sport and Exercise Sciences	81,980	8 Computer Science	17,010
9 Management Studies	73,705	9 Economics	14,200
10 Business Studies	73,515	10 Management Studies	11,600

Source: UCAS End of Cycle report 2022   Source: UCAS End of Cycle report 2022

Subject areas covered in this *Guide*

The list below gives each of the 70 subject areas that are covered in detail later in the book (in Chapter 12). For each subject area in that chapter, there is specific advice, a summary of employment prospects and a league table of universities that offered courses in 2020-21, ranked on the basis of an overall score calculated from research quality, entry standards, teaching quality, student experience and graduate employment prospects.

Accounting and Finance
Aeronautical and Manufacturing
  Engineering
Agriculture and Forestry
American Studies
Anatomy and Physiology
Animal Science
Anthropology
Archaeology and Forensic Science
Architecture
Art and Design
Bioengineering and Biomedical
  Engineering
Biological Sciences
Building
Business
Celtic Studies
Chemical Engineering
Chemistry
Civil Engineering
Classics
Communication and Media Studies
Computer Science
Creative Writing
Criminology
Dentistry
Drama, Dance and Cinematics
East and South Asian Studies
Economics
Education
Electrical and Electronic Engineering
English
Food Science
French
General Engineering
Geography and Environmental Sciences
Geology

German
History
History of Art
Hospitality, Leisure, Recreation and
  Tourism
Iberian Languages
Information Systems and Management
Italian
Land and Property Management
Law
Liberal Arts
Linguistics
Materials Technology
Mathematics
Mechanical Engineering
Medicine
Middle Eastern and African Studies
Music
Natural Sciences
Nursing
Pharmacology and Pharmacy
Philosophy
Physics and Astronomy
Physiotherapy
Politics
Psychology
Radiography
Russian
Social Policy
Social Work
Sociology
Sport Science
Subjects Allied to Medicine
Theology and Religious Studies
Town and Country Planning and
  Landscape
Veterinary Medicine

Studying more than one subject

If more than one subject appeals, you could consider Joint Honours – degrees that combine two subjects – or even Combined Honours, which will cover several related subjects. Such courses obviously allow you to extend the scope of your studies, but they should be approached with caution. Even if the number of credits suggests a similar workload to Single Honours, covering more than one subject inevitably involves extra reading and often more essays or project work. Applicants should also be sure to discuss their even-handed interest in both subjects in the personal statement of their UCAS form.

Many students choose a "dual" to add a vocational element to make themselves more employable – business studies with languages or engineering, for example, or media studies with English. Others want to take their studies in a particular direction, perhaps by combining history with politics, or statistics with maths. Some simply want to add a completely unrelated interest to their main subject, such as conservation biology and music production (offered at Liverpool Hope).

At most universities, however, it is not necessary to take a degree in more than one subject in order to broaden your studies. The spread of modular programmes ensures that you can take courses in related subjects without changing the basic structure of your degree. The number and scope of the combinations offered at many of the larger universities is extraordinary. Indeed, it has been criticised by academics who believe that "mix-and-match" degrees can leave a graduate without a rounded view of a subject. But if you are looking for breadth and variety, scrutinise university websites and prospectuses closely as part of the selection process.

What type of course?

Once you have a subject, you must decide on the level and type of course. Most readers of this *Guide* will be looking for full-time degree courses, but higher education is much broader than that. You may have neither the time or the money needed for a full-time commitment of three or four years at this point in life.

Part-time courses

Tens of thousands of people each year opt for a part-time course – usually while holding down a job – to continue learning and to improve their career prospects. The numbers studying this way have dropped considerably, but loans are available for students whose courses occupy between a quarter and three-quarters of the time expected on a full-time course. Repayments are on the same conditions as those for full-time courses, except that you will begin repaying after three years of study even if the course has not been completed by then. The downside is that universities have increased their fees in the knowledge that part-time students will be able to take out student loans to cover fees, and employers are now less inclined to fund their employees on such courses.

At Birkbeck, University of London, a compromise has been found with full-time courses taught in the evening. For courses classified as part-time, students pay fees in proportion to the number of credits they take.

Part-time study can be exhausting unless your employer gives you time off, but if you have the stamina for a course that will usually take twice as long as the full-time equivalent, this route should still make a degree more affordable. Part-time students tend to be highly committed to their subject, and many claim that the quality of the social life associated with their course makes up for the quantity of leisure time enjoyed by full-timers.

Distance learning

The pandemic showed that undergraduate teaching and learning is more possible to achieve remotely than many might have thought pre-Covid. If you are confident that you can manage without regular face-to-face contact with teachers and fellow students, distance learning is an option. Courses are delivered mainly or entirely online or through correspondence, although some programmes offer a certain amount of local tuition. The process might sound daunting and impersonal, but students of the Open University (OU), all of whom are educated in this way, are frequently among the most satisfied in the country, according to the results of the annual National Student Survey. Attending lectures or oversized seminars at a conventional university can be less personal than regular contact with your tutor at a distance – factors that mainstream universities have cottoned onto since being forced to pivot to remote teaching and learning in the pandemic.

This mode of study gives students ultimate flexibility to determine when and where they study. Distance learning is becoming increasingly popular for the delivery of professional courses, which are often needed to supplement degrees. The OU takes students of all ages, including school-leavers, not just mature students.

In addition, Massive Open Online Courses (MOOCs) are provided by many of the leading UK and American universities, usually free of charge. As yet, most such courses are the equivalent of a module in a degree course, rather than the entire qualification. Some are assessed formally but none is likely to be seen by employers as the equal of a conventional degree, no matter how prestigious the university offering the course. For those who are uncertain about committing to a degree, or who simply want to learn more about a subject without needing a high-status qualification, they are ideal.

A number of UK universities offer MOOCs through the Futurelearn platform, run by the Open University (**www.futurelearn.com**). But the beauty of MOOCs is that they can come from all over the world. Perhaps the best-known providers are Coursera (**www.coursera.org**), which originated at Stanford University, in California, and now involves a large number of American and international universities including Edinburgh, and edX (**www.edx.org**), which numbers Harvard among its members. MOOCs are also being used increasingly by sixth-formers to extend their subject knowledge and demonstrate their enthusiasm and capability to admissions tutors. They are certainly worth considering for inclusion in a personal statement and/or to spark discussion at an interview.

Foundation degrees

Even if you are set on a full-time course, you might not want to commit yourself for three or more years. Two-year vocational Foundation degrees have become a popular route into higher education in recent years. Many other students take longer-established two-year courses, such as Higher National Diplomas or other diplomas tailored to the needs of industry or parts of the health service. Those who do well on such courses usually have the option of converting their qualification into a full degree with further study, although many are satisfied without immediately staying on for the further two or more years that will be required to complete a BA or BSc.

Foundation courses

A growing number of short courses, usually lasting a year, are designed for students who do not have the necessary qualifications to start a degree in their chosen subject. Foundation courses in art and design have been common for many years and are the chosen preparation for a degree at leading departments, even for many students whose A-levels would win them a degree place elsewhere. Access courses perform the same function in a wider range of subjects for students without A-levels, or for those whose grades are either too low or in the wrong subjects to gain admission to a particular course. Entry requirements are modest, but students have to reach the same standard as regular entrants to progress to a degree.

Other short courses

A number of universities are experimenting with two-year degrees, encouraged by the government, squeezing more work into an extended academic year. The so-called "third semester" makes use of the summer vacation for extra teaching, so that mature students, in particular, can reduce the length of their career break. But only at the University of Buckingham, the UK's longest-established private university, is this the dominant pattern for degree courses. Other private institutions – notably BPP University – are following suit.

Earn while you learn

Degree apprenticeships are a serious alternative to university. They give students the best of both worlds by combining study at degree level with extended work experience at a named industrial or business partner. The government wants more degree apprenticeships and universities are expanding their offerings, which include accountancy, cybersecurity, law, finance, economic and social research, computing, nursing, healthcare sciences, data science, management and some branches of engineering. The average salary while learning is £18,000 but for some it is as high as £26,000. The hours are usually longer than for undergraduates and they have less holiday but degree apprentices graduate debt-free.

Clare Marchant, the chief executive of UCAS, has said that lingering snobbery among parents and teachers about degree apprenticeships must be tackled to boost take-up of the courses, while Michelle Donelan, in her role then as the universities minister, said in October 2021: "I want every university to be holding degree apprenticeships, not one or two."

The UCAS website has begun giving degree apprenticeships a bigger showing, suggesting to any users of its search function that they "search degree apprenticeships" too, whenever they tap in a degree they are looking for. Its Career Finder service helps students find jobs and apprenticeships. Applications for an apprenticeship are made directly to employers and, if successful, a student is then linked to a university to study part-time for the associated degree.

The proportion of 18-year-olds in England applying for degree apprenticeships increased from 17.7% 2020 to 18.3% in 2021, according to a survey by UCAS. The 2020 figure represents about 50,000 applicants and is probably an underestimate of the true number, as it counts only those who also applied to university.

Multiverse

Applicants can also make a direct application to the company. Weigh up the options on the government's "Find an Apprenticeship" page (**https://www.gov.uk/apply-apprenticeship**). Once you register, you can set up email and text alerts to inform you about new apprenticeship roles. You can also find a range of vacancies at **www.ratemyapprenticeship.co.uk**, which carries thousands of reviews.

Such apprenticeships take up to six years to complete and leave the graduate with a Bachelor's or even a Master's degree. Employers including Deloitte, PwC, BMW, Microsoft and the BBC are offering higher-level apprenticeships, although naturally not all are with household names such as these.

Yet more choice

No single guide can allow for personal preferences in choosing a course. You may want one of the many degrees that incorporate a year at a partner university abroad, or to try an exchange via the government's Turing Scheme, which has replaced Erasmus post-Brexit. Either might prove a valuable experience and add to your employability. Or you might prefer a January or February start to the traditional autumn start – there are plenty of opportunities for this, and not only at post-1992 universities.

In some subjects – particularly engineering and the sciences – the leading degrees may be Masters courses, taking four years rather than three (in England). In Scotland, most degree courses take four years and some at the older universities will confer a Masters qualification. Those who come with A-levels may apply to go straight into the second year. Relatively few students take this option, but it is easy to imagine more doing so in future at universities that charge students from other parts of the UK the full £9,250 for all years of the course.

Where to study

Several factors might influence your choice of university or college. Obviously, you need to have a reasonable chance of getting in, you may want reassurance about the university's reputation, and its location will probably be important to you as well. On top of that, most applicants have views about the type of institution they are looking for – big or small, old or new, urban or rural, specialist or comprehensive.

Campus universities tend to produce the highest levels of student satisfaction, but big city universities continue to attract sixth-formers in the largest numbers. You may surprise yourself by choosing somewhere that does not conform to your initial criteria but working through your preferences is another way of narrowing down your options.

Entry standards

Unless you are a mature student or have taken a gap year, your passport to your chosen university will probably be a conditional offer based on your predicted grades, previous exam performance, personal statement, and school or college reference.

Universities with highest and lowest offer rates

Highest		Lowest	
1 Aberystwyth University	97.6%	1 University of Oxford	19.1%
=2 Bishop Grosseteste University	95.1%	=2 University of Cambridge	21.6%
=2 Ravensbourne University London	95.1%	=2 London School of Economics	21.9%
4 University for the Creative Arts	92.4%	4 University of St Andrews	25.0%
5 University of Sussex	91.8%	5 Imperial College London	32.5%
6 Coventry University	91.3%	6 St George's, University of London	35.3%
7 University of Wolverhampton	90.8%	7 The University of Edinburgh	39.3%
8 York St John University	90.8%	8 University College London	42.8%
=9 University of Kent	90.2%	9 University of the Arts London	43.8%
=9 Cardiff Metropolitan University	90.2%	10 University of Strathclyde	44.9%
10 Nottingham Trent	90.1%		

UCAS: Applications 2021

Supply and demand dictate whether you will receive an offer, conditional or otherwise, see Chapter 5. Beyond the national picture, your chances will be affected both by the university and the subject you choose. A few universities (but not many) at the top of the league tables are heavily oversubscribed in every subject; others will have areas in which they excel but may make relatively modest demands for entry to other courses. Even in many of the leading universities, the number of applicants for each place in languages or engineering is still not high. Conversely, three As at A-level will not guarantee a place on one of the top English or law degrees, but there are enough universities running courses to ensure that three Cs will give you a chance somewhere.

Best paid graduates

(Median salary 15 months after graduating)

1	Imperial College London	£33,000
2	London School of Economics	£32,577
3	University College London	£30,450
=4	Cambridge	£30,000
=4	King's College London	£30,000
=4	Oxford	£30,000
7	St George's, London	£29,988
8	Bath	£29,200
9	Warwick	£29,060
=10	Bristol	£28,000
=10	Durham	£28,000
=10	Queen Mary, London	£28,000

HESA 2020-21 graduates

University websites and prospectuses and the UCAS website will give you the "standard offer" for each course, but in some cases, this is pitched deliberately low in order to leave admissions staff extra flexibility. The standard A-level offer for medicine, for example, may not demand A*s, but nearly all successful applicants will have one or more.

In Scotland, universities have started to publish two sets of standard offers: their normal range and another with lower grades for applicants from disadvantaged backgrounds. Contextual offers are a similar practice elsewhere in the UK and are increasingly widespread, using contextualised information about applicants' backgrounds to reduce the entry grades.

As already noted, the average entry scores in our tables give the actual points obtained by successful applicants – many of which are far above the offer made by the university, but which give an indication of the pecking order at entry. The subject tables (in Chapter 12) are, naturally, a better guide than the main table (in Chapter 1), where average entry scores are influenced by the range of subjects available at each university.

Location

The most obvious starting point is the country you study in. Most degrees in Scotland take four years, rather than the UK norm of three, which makes them more expensive, especially given the loss of the year's salary you might have been earning after graduation. Chapter 4 goes into the details of the system, but suffice to say that students from Scotland pay no fees, while those from the rest of the UK do. Nevertheless, Edinburgh and St Andrews remain particularly popular with English students, despite charging them £9,250 a year for the full four years of a degree starting in 2021.

Most popular universities by main scheme applications 2021

1	University of Manchester	88,330
2	University of Edinburgh	72,365
3	UCL (University College London)	68,085
4	King's College, London	67,390
5	University of Leeds	66,200
6	University of Bristol	58,185
7	University of Birmingham	56,850
8	University of Nottingham	55,375
9	Manchester Metropolitan University	55,230
10	Nottingham Trent University	47,685

Source: UCAS End of Cycle report 2021

The number of English students going to Scottish universities has increased almost every year since the fees went up, even though there would be no savings, perhaps because the institutions have tried harder to attract them. Fees – or the lack of them – are by no means the only influence on cross-border mobility: the number of Scots going to English universities rose sharply, despite the cost, probably because the number of places is capped in Scotland, but not any longer in England.

Close to home

Far from crossing national boundaries, however, students also choose to study near home, whether or not they continue to live with their family. This is understandable for Scots, who will save themselves tens of thousands of pounds by studying at their own fees-free universities. But there is also a gradual increase in the numbers choosing to study close to home either to cut living costs or for personal reasons, such as family circumstances, a girlfriend or boyfriend, continuing employment or religion. Some simply want to stick with what they know.

The trend for full-time students who do go away to study, is to choose a university within about two hours' travelling time. The assumption is that this is far enough to discourage parents from springing unannounced visits, but close enough to make the occasional trip home to get the washing done, have a decent meal and see friends. The leading universities recruit from all over the world, but most still have a regional core.

City universities

The most popular universities, in terms of total applications, are nearly all in big cities with other major centres of population within the two-hour travelling window. Students are drawn by the best nightclubs, top sporting events, high-quality shopping, cultural diversity and access to leading galleries, museums and theatres. Especially for those who live in cities already, city universities are a magnet. The big universities also, by definition, offer the widest range of subjects, although that does not mean that they necessarily have the specific course that is right for you. You might not actually go clubbing a lot or hit the shops that much, in spite of the inspiring marketing material that suggests you will, either because you cannot afford to, or because student life is more focused on the university than the city, or even because you are too busy studying.

Campus universities

City universities are the right choice for many young people, but it is worth bearing in mind that the National Student Survey shows that the highest satisfaction levels tend to be at smaller universities, often those with their own self-contained campuses. It seems that students identify more closely with institutions where there is a close-knit community and the social life is based around the students' union rather than the local nightclubs – at least in the first-year when more students tend to live in campus accommodation. There may also be a better prospect of regular contact with tutors and lecturers, who are likely to live on or near the campus.

Few UK universities are in genuinely rural locations, but some – particularly among the more recently promoted – are in relatively small towns. Several longer-established institutions in Scotland and Wales also share this type of setting, where the university dominates the town.

Importance of Open Days

By far the best way to be confident that any university is for you is to visit. The pattern of Open Days is likely to vary and many may remain virtual, post-pandemic, rather than physical events. Our profiles in Chapter 14 give each university's website for the latest information. Schools often restrict the number of open days that sixth-formers can attend in term-time, but some universities offer a weekend alternative. A full calendar of events is available at **www.opendays.com**.

Bear in mind, if you only attend one or two, that the event has to be badly mismanaged for a university not to seem an exciting place to someone who spends his or her days at school, or even college. Try to get a flavour of several institutions before you make your choice.

How many universities to pick?

When that time comes, of course, you will not be making one choice but five; four if you are applying for medicine, dentistry or veterinary science. (Full details of the application process are given in Chapter 5.) Tens of thousands of students each year eventually go to a university that did not start out as their first choice, either because they did not get the right offer or because they changed their mind along the way.

UCAS rules are such that applicants do not list universities in order of preference anyway – indeed, universities are not allowed to know where else you have applied. So do not pin all your hopes on one course; take just as much care choosing the other universities on your list.

The value of an 'insurance' choice

Until recently, nearly all applicants included at least one "insurance" choice on that list – a university or college where entry grades were significantly lower than at their preferred institutions. This practice has been in decline, presumably because candidates expecting high grades think they can pick up a lower offer either in Clearing or through UCAS Extra, the service that allows applicants rejected by their original choices to apply to courses that still have vacancies after the first round of offers. However, it is easy to miscalculate and leave yourself without a place that you want. You may not like the look of the options in Clearing, leaving yourself with an unwelcome and potentially expensive year off.

The lifting of recruitment restrictions in 2015 has increased competition between universities and seen more of the leading institutions taking part in Clearing. For those with good grades, this makes it less of a risk to apply only to highly selective universities. However, if you are at all uncertain about your grades, including an insurance choice remains a sensible course of action. Even if you are sure that you will match the standard offers of your chosen universities, there is no guarantee that they will make you an offer. Particularly for degrees demanding three As or more at A-level, there may simply be too many highly qualified applicants to offer places to all of them.

The main proviso for insurance choices, as with all others, is that you must be prepared to take up that place. If not, you might as well go for broke with courses with higher standard offers and take your chances in Clearing, or even retake exams if you drop grades. Thousands of applicants each year end up rejecting their only offer when they could have had a second, insurance, choice.

Reputation

The reputation of a university is something intangible, usually built up over a long period and sometimes outlasting reality. Before universities were subject to external assessment and the publication of copious statistics, reputation was rooted in the past. League tables are partly responsible for changing that, although employers are often still influenced by what they remember as the university pecking order when they were students.

The fragmentation of the British university system into groups of institutions is another factor: the Russell Group (**www.russellgroup.ac.uk**) represents 24 research-intensive universities, nearly all with medical schools; the million+ group (**www.millionplus.ac.uk**) contains many of the former polytechnics and newer universities; the University Alliance (**www.unialliance.ac.uk**) provides a home for 18 universities, both old and new, that did not fit into the other categories; while GuildHE (**www.guildhe.ac.uk**) represents specialist colleges and the newest universities. The Cathedrals Group (**www.cathedralsgroup.ac.uk**) is an affiliation of 16 church-based universities and colleges, some of which are also members of other groups.

Many of today's applicants will barely have heard of a polytechnic, let alone be able to identify which of today's universities had that heritage, but most will know which of two universities in the same city has the higher status. While that should matter far less than the quality of a course, it would be naïve to ignore institutional reputation entirely if that is going to carry weight with a future employer. Some big firms restrict their recruitment efforts to a small group of universities (see Chapter 3), and, however shortsighted that might be, it is something to bear in mind if a career in the City or a big law firm is your ambition.

Facilities

The quality of campus facilities is an important factor in choosing a university for most students. Only the course and the university's location tend to have a higher priority. Accommodation is the main selling point for those living away from home, but sports facilities, libraries (24-hour, ideally) and computing equipment also play an important part. Even upgraded campus nightclubs have become part of the facilities race that has followed the introduction of higher fees.

Many universities guarantee first-year students accommodation in halls of residence or university-owned flats. It is a good idea to know what happens after that. Are there enough places for second or third-year students who want them, and if not, what is the private market like? Rents for student houses vary quite widely across the country and there have been tensions because of a shortage of student accommodation in places, and sometimes with local residents in some cities. All universities offer specialist accommodation for disabled students – and are better at providing other facilities than most public institutions.

Special-interest clubs and recreational facilities, as well as political activity, tend to be based in the students' union – sometimes known as the guild of students. In some universities, the union is the focal point of social activity, while in others the attractions of the city seem to

Top 10 Universities for Quality of Teaching, feedback and support 2021 % satisfied with teaching quality		**Top 10 Universities for Overall Student Experience 2021**	
1 West London	84.3%	1 West London	81.4%
2 St Andrews	84.0%	=2 St Andrews	80.5%
3 Aberystwyth	83.7%	=2 Aberystwyth	80.5%
4 Bishop Grosseteste	82.5%	4 Bath	79.7%
=5 St Mary's, Twickenham	82.4%	=5 Loughborough	79.2%
=5 Hartpury	82.2%	=5 Surrey	79.2%
7 Plymouth Marjon	81.6%	7 St Mary's, Twickenham	78.9%
8 Wrexham Glyndŵr	81.6%	8 Royal Agricultural	78.7%
9 London Metropolitan	81.4%	9 Aberdeen	78.6%
10 Robert Gordon	81.2%	10 London Metropolitan	77.9%

Source: National Student Survey 2022   **Source:** National Student Survey 2022

overshadow the union to the point where facilities are underused. Students' union websites are included with the information found in the university profiles (Chapter 14).

University or college?

This *Guide* is primarily concerned with universities, the destination of choice for the vast majority of higher education students. But there are other options – and not just for those searching for lower fees. A number of specialist higher education colleges offer a similar, or sometimes superior, quality of course in their particular fields. The subject tables in Chapter 12 chart the successes of various colleges in art, agriculture, music and teacher training in particular. Some colleges of higher education are not so different from the newer universities and may acquire that status themselves in future years.

Further education colleges

The second group of colleges offering degrees are further education (FE) colleges. These are often large institutions with a wide range of courses, from A-levels to vocational subjects at different levels, up to degrees in some cases. Although their numbers of higher education students have been falling in recent years, the current fee structure presents them with an opportunity because they tend not to bear all the costs of a university campus. For that reason, too, they may not offer a broad student experience of the type that universities pride themselves on, but the best colleges respond well to the local labour market and offer small teaching groups and effective personal support.

FE colleges are a local resource and tend to attract mature students who cannot or do not want to travel to university. Many of their higher education students apply nowhere else. But, as competition for university places has increased, they also have become more of an option for school-leavers to continue their studies, as they always have been in Scotland.

Statistical comparisons of FE colleges, with their predominantly local, mature student populations, against universities, where undergraduates make up the main numbers, are not reliable. But it should be noted that the proportion of college graduates unemployed six months after graduation tends to be higher than at universities, and average graduate salaries lower. However, 14 further education colleges secured "gold" ratings in the first year of the government's Teaching Excellence Framework (TEF) – although more than twice as many found themselves in the lowest "bronze" category.

Both further and higher education colleges are audited by the Quality Assurance Agency and appear in the National Student Survey, as well as the TEF. In all three, their results usually show wide variation. Some demonstrate higher levels of satisfaction among their students than most universities, for example, while others are at the bottom of the scale.

Private universities and colleges

These were relatively insignificant in terms of size until recently, but the current fee regime may cause numbers at private universities and colleges to grow. Courses are mainly in business and law, and also in some other specialist fields (see pages 586-89).

By far the longest established – and the only one to meet the criteria for inclusion in our main table – is the University of Buckingham, which is profiled on pages 358-9. The best-known "newcomer" currently is BPP University, which became a full university in 2013 and offers degrees, as well as shorter courses, in both law and business subjects. Like Buckingham, BPP offers two-year degrees with short vacations to maximise teaching time – a model that other private providers are likely to follow.

Northeastern University London, formerly New College of the Humanities, graduated its first students in 2015, and offers a liberal arts-inspired curriculum. Having started out with fees of nearly £18,000 a year for all undergraduates, the college is now matching the "public sector" at £9,250 a year.

Two other private institutions have been awarded full university status. Regent's University, attractively positioned in London's Regent's Park, caters particularly for the international market with courses in business, arts and social science subjects priced at £20,500-£22,500 a year for 2023-24. However, about half of the students at the not-for-profit university, which offers British and American degrees, are from the UK or other parts of Europe.

The University of Law, as its name suggests, is more specialised. It has been operating as a college in London for more than 100 years and claims to be the world's leading professional law school. It offers law degrees, as well as professional courses, with fees for three-year degrees set at £9,250 in 2023-24 for UK students and £14,750 for the two-year version. The university has 15 UK campuses, in locations including London (where it has two), Nottingham, Birmingham, Bristol, Chester, Guildford, Manchester and Leeds, as well as at Exeter, East Anglia, Reading, and Liverpool universities.

There are also growing numbers of specialist colleges offering degrees, especially in the business sector. The London Institute of Banking & Finance (formerly ifs School of Finance), also dates back more than 100 years and now has university college status for its courses in finance and banking.

The Dyson Institute of Engineering and Technology, based at Malmesbury, in Wiltshire, welcomed its first 33 undergraduates in 2017 and began awarding its own degrees three years later. Funded entirely by Sir James Dyson, there are no fees, and students work at the nearby Dyson headquarters for 47 weeks a year. The New Model in Technology and Engineering, in Hereford, has received more than £20million in government funding and promises to give students a "head start on becoming a work-ready, world-conscious engineer".

There are two high-profile colleges specialising in football, and the London Interdisciplinary School was founded in 2017. Inevitably, they will take time to build up a track record, but there should be a market in the areas they offer.

Sources of information

With more than 130 universities to choose from, the Discover Uni and UCAS websites, as well as guides such as this one, are the obvious places to start your search for the right course. Discover Uni includes figures for average salaries at course level, as well as student satisfaction ratings and some information on contact hours, although this does not distinguish between lectures and seminars. The site does not make multiple comparisons easy to carry out, but it does contain a wealth of information for those who persevere. Once you have narrowed down the list of candidates, you will want to go through undergraduate prospectuses. All are available online and many universities still print hard copies, should you want a hefty book that includes details of every course to arrive in the post. Beware of generalised claims about the standing of the university, the quality of courses, friendly atmosphere and legendary social life. Stick to the factual information.

While the material that the universities publish about their own qualities is less than objective, much of what you will find on the internet may be completely unreliable, for different reasons. A simple search on the name of a university will turn up spurious comparisons of everything from the standard of lecturing to the attractiveness of the students. These can be seriously misleading and are usually based on anecdotal evidence, at best. Make sure that any information you consider comes from a reputable source and, if it conflicts with your impression, try to cross-check it with this *Guide* and the institution's own material.

Checklist

Choosing a subject and a place to study is a major decision. Make sure you can answer these questions:

Choosing a course

» Will my course enable my career and income goals?
» Do I want to study something I know from school, or something new?
» Are my qualifications right for the course?
» Will I enjoy my studies and stick with them?
» Will there be work experience opportunities?
» Will I cope with the demands made on myself?
» Is there good academic and wellbeing support?

Choosing a university

» Does my dream university offer the right course?
» Do I prefer a campus, city or smaller town setting?
» Is the student population predominantly male or female? Does it matter to me?
» Should I stay close to home to save money?
» How much will accommodation and study extras cost?
» What do students already there think of the university?
» I come from a state school, will I fit in?

Useful websites

The best starting point is the UCAS website (**www.ucas.com**), there is extensive information on courses, universities and the whole process of applying to university. UCAS has an official presence on Facebook (**www.facebook.com/ucasonline**) and Twitter (**@UCAS_online**) and now also has a series of video guides (**www.ucas.tv**) on the process of applying, UCAS resources and comments from other students.

For statistical information which allows limited comparison between universities (and for full details of the National Student Survey), visit: **www.discoveruni.gov.uk**

On appropriate A-level subject choice, visit **www.informedchoices.ac.uk**

Narrowing down course choices: **www.ukcoursefinder.com**

For a full calendar of university and college open days: **www.opendays.com**

Students with disabilities: Disability Rights UK: **www.disabilityrightsuk.org/how-we-can-help**

3 Assessing Graduate Job Prospects

Heart or head? This is the blunt dichotomy that degree selection can boil down to once career considerations are in the picture. Should you follow your heart and study a subject you love, regardless of where it might lead? Or should you choose a degree with a more secure career route? With financial concerns and the hopes and fears of parents on their shoulders, students have a tough decision to make. While university is not the only – or even a guaranteed – route into a fulfilling and rewarding career, many students who opt for higher education do so with thoughts of securing themselves professional work afterwards. Rather than a future that involves merely making ends meet, the hope is that a degree will help to secure a career that offers fulfilment, social standing and at least above-average pay.

The wisdom of Steve Jobs, founder of Apple, rings true for many: "The only way to do great work is to love what you do." Jobs' opinion chimes with advice from educational commentators who suggest that, other than needing a certain degree for a specific field of work, you should go for a subject that is likely to provide an enjoyable and fulfilling experience – which you will likely do best in. Experts also advise that applying to a degree you have no interest in just because it promises a high salary could cause frustration and failing to complete the course. Our *Guide* includes dropout rates, which run as high as one in four at some institutions.

But degrees do also need to represent a fair return on students' investment – a consideration that has been under scrutiny in the UK ever since the introduction of £9,000 tuition fees in 2012. With the average student debt hovering at around £48,500, on top of student loan reforms that are lowering repayment thresholds to £25,000, and extending terms to 40 years, choosing the wrong course is a costly miscalculation.

From the government's perspective, a degree should provide value for money to the taxpayer as well as to the student, partly because so many student loans will not be fully paid back – even under the new terms: if graduates either never earn above or slip below earning £27,295 (or £25,000 for new students in England from 2023) they do not need to make student loan repayments.

Graduate salaries are one way of evaluating whether a degree represents a good bet, although they are a crude tool and liable to vary depending on whether a university is located in an area of high or low employment, with high or low wages. *The Times and the Sunday Times*

Good University Guide league table rankings have never used salary data as a performance measure. Few would attempt to argue that trainee nurses and teachers, for example, should be put off going to university because the professions they are studying towards do not promise megabucks. We do, though, list median salaries for each subject group in this chapter's second table, and with the subject guides in Chapter 12, for reference.

Going to university is a very good investment for most students. According to the Institute of Fiscal Studies (IFS), male graduates can expect to be about £130,000 better off over their working lifetime than if they had not gone to university, after student loan repayments and extra taxes. For women, this figure is £100,000. According to the government, in 2020, young graduates typically earned £6,500 more per year than their non-graduate counterparts. The higher earnings of – and therefore taxes paid by – graduates also mean that sending about half of young people to university is a good deal overall for the taxpayer.

There are enormous variations in the difference a degree makes, however, as the IFS found in its 2020 research for the Department for Education. Only a tiny proportion, around 10%, are likely to rake in an extra £500,000 or more during their lifetime, with students of medicine and law among those in line for very high returns, while few creative arts students are likely to gain financially from their degree at all. Using the Longitudinal Education Outcomes (LEO) dataset, it found that a typical student can expect to gain about £70,000 from their degree, but that one in five students (or about 70,000 each year) is likely to end up financially worse off as a result of going to university.

The low salary returns from some arts and humanities degrees, combined with the government's focus on boosting science and technology, have led some universities to discontinue them or merge their teaching with other subjects.

Median earnings by degree subject five years after graduation (2013-14 graduates)

Medicine and Dentistry	£50,100	Allied Health Subjects	£27,800
Economics	£40,600	Health & Social Care	£27,400
Engineering	£36,800	Philosophy & Religious Studies	£27,400
Pharmacology, Toxicology & Pharmacy	£34,100	Biosciences	£26,700
Mathematical Sciences	£33,700	History & Archaeology	£26,400
Physics & Astronomy	£33,500	Celtic Studies	£26,200
Veterinary Science	£33,300	Sociology, Social Policy & Athropology	£25,600
Medical Sciences	£33,100	Sport and Exercise Science	£25,600
Architecture, Building & Planning	£32,800	General, Applied & Forensic Sciences	£25,500
Computing	£32,600	Combined & General Studies	£25,300
Chemistry	£30,700	Education & Teaching	£25,300
Politics	£30,400	English Studies	£24,900
Nursing & Midwifery	£29,600	Psychology	£24,900
Geography, Earth & Environmental Studies	£29,500	Media, Journalism & Communications	£24,500
Business & Management	£29,300	Agriculture, Food & Related Subjects	£23,100
Law	£28,600	Creative Arts & Design	£22,700
Languages & Area Studies	£28,500	Performing Arts	£22,000
Materials & Technology	£28,500		

Source: Department for Education, Graduate Outcomes, November 2022

Such a mismatch between students' investment and effort and their outcomes is naturally a cause for concern – and a driving force behind the relevance of university guides such as ours in helping applicants make well-informed choices. In its long-awaited response to the 2019 Philip Augar review of post-18 education and funding, the government is seeking to clamp down on low-quality degrees.

"There are still too many graduates who do not see the full benefit of going to university and in many cases this is because their degrees do not necessarily lead to well-paid employment," said culture secretary Michelle Donelan in February 2022, in her role then as higher and further education minister. Donelan also spoke of "continuing our focus on completion rates and courses leading to graduate jobs", in the same speech, and stated: "We think it is right that we have an open conversation with the public about whether we should to continue to allow pockets of poor-quality courses to grow uncontrollably." The Department for Education has since put forward proposals to include new minimum entry requirements for university, to ensure pupils "aren't being pushed into higher education before they are ready".

While no one can see into the future, applicants must attempt to evaluate the kind of career trajectory their potential degree could lead to. To spend money and time on university and then work in a job that could have been accessed without a degree adds up to a bad deal, however much you enjoyed the teaching, learning and broader all-round experience.

Changing times: from pandemic to cost of living crisis

UCAS's *Where Next?* analysis in 2021 revealed that more than 50% of university applicants reported that high graduate employment rates had become more important to them since the start of the pandemic. And the UK Labour Force Survey, run by the Office for National Statistics (ONS), showed that graduates remained at a career advantage over those without degrees. Coronavirus had a marked impact on the UK labour market in 2020, with unemployment increasing across the board, but graduates suffered less acutely than those without degrees.

Graduates are among the highest-skilled workers and play an important role in the economy, the ONS pointed out: they promote innovation and growth – crucial contributions in dealing with the challenges imposed by the pandemic. Graduates are also more occupationally and geographically mobile, which helps explain their employment in times of crisis. As well as specific skills related to their subject, graduates also have more general transferrable skills – such as writing, communication and critical thinking – that contribute to greater resilience in times of crisis. Demand for graduates remained high during the Covid pandemic, according to the Institute for Student Employers. In the spring of 2022, it said the number of graduate vacancies was 20% higher than before the pandemic in 2019.

Amid soaring energy bills, rising food prices and the threat of a recession, however, the graduates of 2022 faced further uncertainty in the jobs market. Research by careers platform Bright Network in autumn 2022 suggests they are hoping to secure higher pay rates. Students surveyed expected starting salaries to be over £30,000 – 25% more than the current national average starting salary – due to the rising cost of living. Students also expressed "genuine concerns around the economic climate, their careers and future working life".

What graduates are doing 15 months after leaving university by subject studied

	Subject	High-skilled job %	High-skilled job and studying %	Studying %	Lower-skilled job and studying %	Lower-skilled job %	Unemployed %	Total with positive outcome %
1	Medicine	92	5	3	0	0	0	100
2	Nursing	95	3	1	0	1	1	98
3	Dentistry	89	7	1	0	0	3	97
4	Radiography	91	4	2	0	2	2	97
5	Veterinary Medicine	95	1	1	0	2	1	97
6	Physiotherapy	91	3	1	0	2	2	96
7	Natural Sciences	59	5	25	0	6	5	89
8	Civil Engineering	75	4	8	0	7	5	87
9	Pharmacology & Pharmacy	71	6	10	0	6	7	87
10	General Engineering	77	2	7	0	8	5	87
11	Building	79	4	3	0	9	5	86
12	Chemical Engineering	71	3	11	0	9	6	85
13	Chemistry	57	3	24	1	10	5	84
14	Subjects Allied to Medicine	62	4	16	1	12	5	83
15	Physics & Astronomy	50	4	29	0	9	8	83
16	Electrical & Electronic Engineering	70	3	9	1	10	7	83
17	Economics	60	8	12	1	13	5	81
18	Mathematics	59	6	15	1	12	7	81
19	Celtic Studies	48	2	28	2	18	2	80
20	Materials Technology	55	3	20	0	13	7	79
21	Computer Science	71	3	6	0	12	9	79
22	Town & Country Planning & Landscape	64	4	10	1	18	3	79
23	Mechanical Engineering	65	3	10	1	14	7	79
24	Food Science	65	3	10	2	17	4	79
25	Bioengineering & biomedical engineering	56	2	20	0	12	10	78
26	Biological Sciences	46	4	27	1	17	6	77
27	Architecture	65	5	7	0	14	9	77
28	Geology	44	4	29	1	18	6	77
29	Anatomy & Physiology	44	4	28	1	18	6	77
30	Land & Property Management	66	6	4	0	18	7	76
31	Education	66	3	6	1	20	5	76
32	Russian	51	8	14	3	17	8	75
33	German	54	6	14	1	18	8	74
34	Italian	48	4	20	1	20	6	74
35	Middle Eastern & African Studies	58	7	8	1	20	7	73
36	Liberal Arts	54	3	13	2	22	5	72
37	Geography & Environmental Sciences	49	5	18	1	23	5	72
38	Aeronautical & Manufacturing Engineering	55	3	12	1	19	9	72
39	Iberian Languages	53	6	12	1	21	7	72
40	Social Work	62	4	5	1	23	5	72

What graduates are doing 15 months after leaving university by subject studied cont.

	Subject	High-skilled job %	High-skilled job and studying %	Studying %	Lower-skilled job and studying %	Lower-skilled job %	Unemployed %	Total with positive outcome %
41	Theology & Religious Studies	48	6	16	1	24	5	71
42	Information Systems & Management	63	3	5	0	17	12	71
43	French	52	4	13	2	24	5	71
44	Philosophy	44	5	20	1	23	7	70
45	Politics	48	5	15	2	23	6	70
46	Law	48	7	13	2	24	6	70
47	Anthropology	44	5	18	1	24	8	68
48	Classics & Ancient History	38	5	23	1	23	10	68
49	English	45	5	16	1	26	7	67
50	Business, Management & Marketing	55	4	6	1	26	7	66
51	History	40	4	19	2	28	7	65
52	Sport Science	45	6	13	2	31	4	65
53	Agriculture & Forestry	58	3	3	1	32	3	65
54	Music	50	5	8	2	29	6	64
55	Accounting & Finance	47	9	6	3	28	7	64
56	Archaeology & Forensic Science	43	3	16	1	30	7	63
57	History of Art, Architecture & Design	42	4	16	2	30	7	63
58	American Studies	38	5	17	2	31	6	63
59	Communication & Media Studies	53	3	5	1	30	8	62
60	Linguistics	42	4	15	0	33	6	61
61	Art & Design	54	2	4	1	31	9	60
62	East & South Asian Studies	41	4	12	3	28	12	60
63	Sociology	39	4	13	1	36	6	57
64	Psychology	34	5	15	3	37	6	57
65	Creative Writing	41	3	9	2	33	11	56
66	Social Policy	39	5	9	2	37	8	55
67	Drama, Dance & Cinematics	45	2	5	1	38	8	53
68	Hospitality, Leisure, Recreation & Tourism	44	2	5	2	40	7	53
69	Animal Science	35	2	14	1	42	6	52
70	Criminology	34	4	9	2	44	7	49

Note: This table is ranked on the proportion of graduates in high-skilled jobs after further study, and those combining low-skilled jobs with further study.
Source: HESA (Higher Education Statistics Agency) 2020-21

Graduate prospects in *Good University Guide* rankings

The measure we use to assess graduate prospects takes account of the rates of employment for graduates in the 70 subject areas in our *Guide* and distinguishes between types of work. The Graduate Outcomes (GO) survey is now in its third year, having replaced the Destination of Leavers from Higher Education (DLHE) survey. Both measure the same thing: what graduates do next, but the previous system gathered information six months after graduation,

What graduates are earning 15 months after graduation by subject studied

	Subject	High skilled work (median) £	Low and medium skilled £
1	Dentistry	39,000	—
2	Medicine	34,000	20,000
3	Pharmacology & Pharmacy	31,800	21,000
4	Veterinary Medicine	31,000	29,000
5	Natural Sciences	30,000	19,337
6	Chemical Engineering	30,000	22,000
7	General Engineering	29,070	23,456
8	Economics	30,000	22,750
9	Electrical & Electronic Engineering	28,560	24,000
9	Physics & Astronomy	28,000	20,000
9	Social Work	29,100	19,000
12	Aeronautical & Manufacturing Engineering	28,000	22,415
13	Mechanical Engineering	28,000	23,000
14	Materials Technology	28,000	21,000
15	Mathematics	28,000	21,000
16	Civil Engineering	27,500	21,000
=17	Building	27,000	22,500
=17	Computer Science	27,500	20,000
19	Bioengineering & biomedical engineering	27,000	20,500
=20	Chemistry	25,500	21,000
=20	Information Systems & Management	25,000	20,000
=20	Middle Eastern & African Studies	27,000	—
=20	Physiotherapy	25,000	—
=20	Politics	26,000	21,000
=20	Radiography	25,000	—
=20	Town & Country Planning & Landscape	25,000	21,000
=27	Nursing	24,907	20,400
=27	Subjects Allied to Medicine	24,907	18,813
29	Food Science	25,000	20,000
=30	Education	25,000	17,400
=30	Land & Property Management	25,000	20,700
32	German	25,000	20,400
=33	Agriculture & Forestry	25,000	21,000
=33	Anatomy & Physiology	25,000	19,000
=33	Business, Management & Marketing	25,000	21,000
=33	Celtic Studies	25,000	13,000
=33	French	25,000	20,500
=33	Geography & Environmental Sciences	25,000	20,000
=33	Geology	25,000	20,000
=33	Iberian Languages	25,000	20,000
=33	Italian	25,000	—

What graduates are earning 15 months after graduation by subject studied

cont.

Subject	High skilled work (median) £	Low and medium skilled £
=33 Philosophy	25,000	19,909
=33 Russian	25,714	22,000
=33 Theology & Religious Studies	25,000	18,250
45 Liberal Arts	25,000	19,600
=46 Accounting & Finance	25,000	21,000
=46 Biological Sciences	24,500	19,600
=48 Anthropology	24,500	21,000
=48 East & South Asian Studies	25,714	20,500
=48 History	25,000	20,000
=48 Linguistics	25,000	19,000
52 Social Policy	24,100	20,000
=53 Architecture	22,000	19,500
=53 Classics & Ancient History	25,000	20,000
=53 English	23,650	19,000
=53 History of Art, Architecture & Design	23,000	20,000
57 Sociology	24,000	19,357
=58 American Studies	23,000	19,000
=58 Archaeology & Forensic Science	21,800	19,000
=58 Criminology	23,000	19,550
=58 Hospitality, Leisure, Recreation & Tourism	22,500	20,000
=58 Law	22,000	20,000
=58 Psychology	23,000	18,900
=58 Sport Science	23,215	18,500
=65 Animal Science	21,500	18,500
=65 Art & Design	22,000	19,000
=65 Communication & Media Studies	21,500	20,000
=65 Drama, Dance & Cinematics	22,000	19,000
=65 Music	22,000	18,345
70 Creative Writing	21,000	18,000

Note: This table is ranked by the median salary of those in highly-skilled employment in each subject area. Where high-skilled salaries are equal, medium-skilled salaries are used as a separator.

Source: HESA (Higher Education Statistics Agency), Graduate Outcomes Survey, published July 2022
Covers graduates in employment and self-employment/freelance work, first degree UK-domiciled students only

whereas GO conducts its survey 15 months after graduates have finished their degrees. The longer timeframe better reflects changes in work patterns, with many graduates doing internships, travelling or sampling the jobs market before plumping for a career path.

The GO survey has caused our graduate prospects measure to evolve. So, we now look at the proportion of graduates in high-skilled (instead of graduate-level) jobs or postgraduate study. This *Guide* uses a definition of a high-skilled job from the Higher Education Statistics Agency

(HESA), which conducts the GO survey. Universities that got the best graduate prospects scores in the previous measure have been largely unaffected by the new measure and continued to perform strongly, while for some universities very different results emerged.

The latest graduate labour market statistics showed that working-age graduates and postgraduates continue to have higher employment rates than non-graduates. The employment rates for working-age graduates and postgraduates increased in 2021 while it fell for working-age non-graduates, representing the first time that the gap has widened between graduates and non-graduates since 2013.

In 2021, the employment rate for working-age graduates (those aged 16-64) was 86.7%, an increase of 0.4 percentage points on 2020 (86.3%). For working-age postgraduates the employment rate was 88.2%, an increase of 0.1% on 2020 (88.1%). For working-age non-graduates the employment rate was 70.2%, a decrease of 0.9% on 2020 (71.1%). In 2021, the median salary for working-age graduates was £36,000. This was £10,000 more than working-age non-graduates (£26,000) but £6,000 less than working-age postgraduates (£42,000).

Future-proof degrees?

Everyone knows that there have been changes to the world of work in the last few decades, however reminding young people that the jobs they will do have not been invented yet can be unhelpful, dispiriting and confusing. As we saw during the pandemic, applications to study nursing and medicine reached new heights, with applicants driven not only by the desire to help others in front line roles, but also attracted by the security of such jobs – especially as furlough and job losses created disruption in many other fields.

Advances in robotics and artificial intelligence will mean some jobs are on the way out, but roles needed to develop new technologies and new solutions are expanding. The stuff that makes us different from machines, such as emotional intelligence, analytical skills and caring, will also be vital in the future jobs market, as will creativity and resilience. A rounded university education with experience both in and out of the classroom or laboratory will help to hone such "soft" skills. As for resilience, current and incoming students have been building their bounce-back-ability through the many adaptations they have had to make to what used to be normal life, such as adjusting to blended online learning, examination changes, vaccines and social distancing.

Parents' well-meant career advice is often 20 or 30 years out of date. Careers experts recommend finding something you care about, and something you are good at, and linking the two to find a job that will be rewarding. Some suggest looking at the United Nations' Sustainable Development Goals (SDGs) and aligning careers to them: improving health and education, reducing inequality, spurring economic growth and conserving the environment – these are problems whose solutions are long-term, and their higher purpose chimes with the interests of the current generation of students. You could work as an expert in these fields, or use other professional skills within the context of these SDGs.

By keeping your eye on the horizon to see what trends and changes are coming, you stand a chance of picking a future-proof field of work. Automation is changing professions, not wiping them out entirely.

Graduate employment and underemployment

Competition for graduate jobs, with their salary premium over a working lifetime, remains stiff. The Office of National Statistics (ONS)'s Annual Population Survey estimates that there were over 15million people with degree or equivalent qualifications working in the UK at the end of

2020, and that 43% of the UK working age population (aged 16–64) had a degree or equivalent. The high proportion of graduates in the overall population means that they may now take longer than their predecessors to find the right career opening. Employers' ideas of which jobs require a degree, and of the roles for which they prefer graduates change over time. Nurses have not always been required to take a degree, but the job now needs skills that were not part of the profession 20 years ago. The same is true of many occupations. Even in jobs where it may be possible to do the work involved without a degree, having taken one makes it easier to get hired in the first place.

Surveys have found that a sizeable proportion of graduates consider themselves working in a job that does not require a degree – an experience known as being underemployed. Scoping out a job via internships rather than going for whatever is immediately available for the highest salary can be a wise move.

The graduate labour market

The contents of this *Guide* – particularly in the subject tables – should help to create a nuanced picture. A close examination of individual universities' employment rates in your subject – possibly supplemented by the salary figures on the Discover Uni website – will tell you whether national trends apply to your chosen course (**https://discoveruni.gov.uk**).

Even without the health pandemic and Brexit, for the boom years of graduate employment to return, there will have to be stronger recruitment by small and medium-sized companies, as well as the big battalions. The number of self-employed graduates will increase, in line with universities reporting growing demand for their business start-up and incubator services. If you are considering the graduate entrepreneur route, explore what your chosen university offers, because business hub services vary considerably in scale and sophistication.

Subject choice and career opportunities

For those thinking of embarking on higher education in 2023, the signs are still positive. But in any year, some universities and some subjects produce better returns than others. The tables on the pages that follow give a more detailed picture of the differences between subjects at a national level, while the rankings in Chapters 1 and 12 include figures for each university and subject area. There are a few striking changes, but mainly among subjects with relatively small and fluctuating numbers of graduates.

In the employment table, subjects are ranked according to the proportion employed in jobs categorised by HESA as high-skilled, and include those undertaking further study, whether or not combined with a high-skilled job. The level of detail we provide about types of job is illuminating; some similar tables do not make a distinction between different sorts of work, which can mislead applicants into thinking all universities and subjects offer uniformly rosy employment prospects.

The definitions of both a high-skilled and a graduate job are controversial. But HESA relies on the Standard Occupational Classification, a complex series of definitions drawn up by the ONS. New universities, in particular, often claim that the whole concept of a graduate job immediately after graduation fails to reflect reality for their alumni. In any case, a degree is about enhancing your whole career, not just your first job out of college.

That said, the tables in this chapter will help you assess whether your course is likely to pay off in career terms, at least to start with. They show both the amount you might expect to earn with a degree in a specific subject, and the odds of being in work. They reflect the experience 15 months after graduation of those who completed their degrees in 2018, so the picture may have improved by the time you leave university. The pattern of success rates for specific subjects and institutions, however, are unlikely to have changed radically.

It is worth considering that at age 25 the average male graduate earns 5% more per year than the average female graduate, even though women are more likely to get first-class or upper second degrees. By the age of 30 – before most graduates start having children – the gender pay gap in annual earnings has extended to 25%. Without maternity leave to explain such a pay gulf, analysts have suggested it may be down to women choosing degrees that are less likely to translate into as high-paying careers as their male counterparts.

The table of employment statistics from the new GO survey reveals some unexpected results. For example, only 66% of business, management and marketing graduates are working in high-skilled jobs or doing further study, though this is slightly more than the 64% of accounting and finance graduates who achieved similar positive outcomes. The Celtic studies, town and country planners, economists and food scientists fare a lot better. All seven branches of engineering are in the top 20 subjects for starting salaries, and six out of seven of them are in the top 25 for graduate outcomes.

The employment table also shows that graduates in some subjects, especially sciences such as physics and astronomy, biological sciences, chemistry and geology, are more likely to undertake further study than in others, such as those in art and design or hospitality. A range of professions now regard a Masters degree as a basic entry-level qualification. Those going into subjects such as art and design appreciate that these, too, have their own career peculiarities. Periods of freelance or casual work are common at the start of a career and may become an enduring choice. Less surprisingly, doctors and dentists are virtually guaranteed a job, as are nurses.

The second table, on pages 53-4, gives average earnings of those who graduated in 2020, recorded 15 months after leaving university. It contains interesting, and in some cases surprising, information about early career pay levels. Few would have placed social work in the top 10 for graduate pay. Nursing returned to the top 30, having dropped to 41st place in our previous edition.

It is important, of course, to consider the differences between starting salaries and the long-term prospects of different jobs. Over time, the accountants may well end up with bigger rewards, despite being £1,407 a year worse off than the nurses in our early-career snapshot. In any case, it is important to realise that once you ignore the higher incomes available to medics and other elite professionals, early graduate incomes vary less than you might think from subject to subject.

Seven subjects (chemistry; information systems and management; Middle Eastern and African studies; physiotherapy; politics; radiography; and town and country planning and landscape) tie at £25,000 in our salary ranking. A further 12 tie at £24,000 (German; agriculture and forestry; anatomy and physiology; business management and marketing; Celtic studies; geography and environmental sciences; geology; Iberian languages; Italian; philosophy; Russian; and theology and religious studies). There is so little between them, in fact, that where high-skilled salaries are equal, medium-skilled salaries are used as a separator. That's why you should consider the lifetime earnings you might derive from these subjects, and your own interests and inclinations, at least as much as this snapshot.

Enhancing your employability

Graduate employability has become the holy grail of degree education since higher fees were introduced in most of the UK. Virtually every university has an initiative to enhance their graduates' prospects. Many have incorporated specially designed employability modules into degree courses; some are certificating extracurricular activities to improve their graduates' CVs;

and many more are stepping up their efforts to provide work experience to complement degrees. Opinion is divided on the value of such schemes.

Some of the biggest employers restrict their recruitment activities to a small number of universities, believing that these institutions attract the brightest minds and that trawling more widely is not cost-effective. The High Fliers survey reported that the 10 universities most targeted by the largest number of top graduate employers in 2021-22 were Manchester, Nottingham, Bristol, Birmingham, Leeds, Warwick, Cambridge, Sheffield, Edinburgh and Oxford.

Some top law firms and others in the City of London have introduced institution-blind applications, but big employers' links with their favourite recruiting grounds are likely to continue. Widening the pool of universities from which they set out to recruit is costly, and can seem unnecessary if employers are getting the people they think they need. They will expect outstanding candidates who went to other universities to come to them, either on graduation or later in their careers. But most graduates do not work in the City, and most students do not go to universities at the top of the league tables.

University schemes

If a university offers extra help towards employment, consider whether its scheme is likely to work for you. Some are too new to have shown results in the labour market yet, but they may have been endorsed by big employers or introduced at an institution whose graduates already have a record of success in the jobs market. They might involve classes in CV writing, interview skills, personal finance, entrepreneurship and negotiation skills, among many other topics. There can be guest lectures and demonstrations, or mock interviews, by real employers, to assess students' strengths and weaknesses. In time, these extras may turn into mandatory parts of a degree, complete with course credits.

The value of work experience

The majority of graduate jobs are open to applicants from any discipline. For these general positions, employers tend to be more impressed by a good degree from what they consider a prestigious university than by an apparently relevant qualification. Here numeracy, literacy and communication – the skills needed to function effectively in any organisation – are vitally important.

Specialist jobs, for example in engineering or design, are a different matter. Employers may be much more knowledgeable about the quality of individual courses, and less influenced by a university's overall position in league tables, when the job relies directly on knowledge and skills acquired as a student. That goes for medicine and architecture as well as computer games design or environmental management.

In almost all fields of employment, however, work experience has become increasingly valuable. Results of the High Fliers survey show that work experience schemes have become an integral part of recruiting new graduates. Students who apply for work experience in their first or second year at university go through similar selection processes to graduates, which works as a kind of pre-vetting for a job after graduation. The number of paid placements has risen sharply.

Although employers continued to engage young people for virtual internships to an extent during the pandemic, employers cut opportunities by 40%, research by the Institute of Student Employers (ISE) found. But in 2022, 71% of ISE employers were offering work experience, compared to 60% in 2021. Many work experience programmes continue to be hybrid, however; of ISE members, 37% reported that placement schemes will be face-to-face, 4% online, and 33% hybrid.

Sandwich degrees, which include extended programmes of up to a year at work, have always boosted employment prospects. Graduates – often engineers – frequently end up working where they undertook their placement. And while a sandwich year will make your course take longer, it will not cost a full year's-worth of tuition fees.

Many conventional degrees now include shorter placements that should offer some advantages in the labour market. Most big graduate employers offer some provision of this nature, although access to it can be competitive.

A growing number of employers are also offering degree apprenticeships, in partnership with a wide range of universities. Even Cambridge has some at postgraduate level and is developing more. They generally take longer than a traditional degree, but there are no tuition fees, apprentices are paid a salary, and there is usually a guaranteed job at the end. Gillian Keegan, the new Secretary of State for Education (at the time of writing), is the first degree-level apprentice to enter parliament and an advocate for this route.

If you opt for a traditional degree without a work placement, consider arranging your own part-time or temporary employment. The majority of full-time students now take jobs during term time, as well as in vacations, to make ends meet. But such jobs can boost your CV as well as your bank balance. Inevitably, the more prosperous cities are likely to offer more employment opportunities than rural areas or conurbations that have been hard hit by recession.

Consider part-time degrees

Another option is part-time study. Although enrolments have fallen sharply both before and since the big 2012 increases in fees, there are now loans available for most part-time courses. Employers may be willing to share the cost of taking a degree or another relevant qualification, and the chance to earn a wage while studying has obvious attractions. Bear in mind that most part-time courses take twice as long to complete as the full-time equivalent. If your earning power is linked to the qualification, it will take that much longer for you to enjoy the benefits.

Plan early for your career

Whatever type of course you choose, it is sensible to start thinking about your future career early in your time at university. There has been a growing tendency in recent years for students to convince themselves that there would be plenty of time to apply for jobs after graduation. In the current employment market, all but the most obviously brilliant graduates need to offer more than just a degree, whether it be work experience, leadership qualities demonstrated through clubs and societies, or commitment to voluntary activities. Many students finish a degree without knowing what they want to do, but a blank CV will not impress a prospective employer.

Sometimes a side hustle can work out well for your CV as well as your bank balance; big brands use student ambassadors to help spread the word about their latest projects, providing the opportunity to develop your skills in marketing, social media strategy and content creation, while also earning money.

Useful websites

Prospects, the UK's official graduate careers website: **www.prospects.ac.uk**
For career advice, internships and student and graduate jobs: **www.milkround.com**
For graduate employment (and other) statistics: **www.discoveruni.gov.uk**
High Fliers research: **www.highfliers.co.uk**

4   The Bottom Line: Tuition Fees and Finance

Students starting their degrees in September 2023 will be the first to sign on the dotted line for the new-style student loan. Sweeping changes to the system in England were announced by the government on February 24, 2022. The reforms include lowering the student loan repayment threshold to £25,000 a year (from £27,295) and increasing the length of time over which graduates repay their loans by 10 years (from 30 years to 40 years). The student loan interest rate is also being cut to the Retail Price Index (RPI) rate of inflation (from RPI +3%) for students starting courses from 2023-24. Tuition fees, meanwhile, are being frozen at £9,250 for another two years.

The measures are part of the government's long-awaited response to the 2019 independent review of the higher education system by banker Sir Philip Augar. First-time students are not the only ones impacted by the new financial regime, however. Under its rules, students who have started university in England and Wales since 2012 (those on Plan 2 loans) will see their repayment threshold frozen only until 2025. Which means these students are affected nearly as much by changes in repayment thresholds as students from the 2023 cohort onwards – but without the benefit of lower interest rates.

Ministers have said that the new system will be fairer to the taxpayer by reducing the subsidy for university degrees. "We are freezing tuition fees and slashing interest rates for new student loan borrowers, making sure that under these terms no one will pay back more than they have borrowed in real terms," stated culture secretary Michelle Donelan, when she was minister for further and higher education until July 2022.

Experts who have totted up the numbers say, however, it will disproportionately benefit students from wealthy families. Under the old system student loans are repaid until they are cleared, or for up to 30 years after university. By raising the repayment period to 40 years, more graduates earning low or mid-range salaries will keep paying for many more years, thus increasing their repayments by thousands of pounds. Some will still be making payments beyond their 60th birthday. Those who earn the highest salaries who would clear their loan within 30 years will not be impacted, which – combined with the lower interest rate under the new system – means the highest-earning graduates will repay "around £20,000 less", the Institute for Fiscal Studies (IFS) has forecast.

Its feathers ruffled by such reporting, the government's Education Hub blog is at pains to clarify that: "Anyone earning under £25k won't repay anything." It also clarifies that "New borrowers starting in the 23-24 academic year are expected to borrow an average of £39,300, in 21-22 prices. Under our proposals we forecast that the average borrower will repay £25,300 in 2021-22 prices over the course of their loan. This compares to £19,500 under the current [pre-2023] system."

As figures fly between thinktank economists and government officials, founder of the Money Saving Expert website and former head of the Independent Taskforce on Student Finance Information, Martin Lewis, asserts: "The plans will see most university leavers pay far more for their degrees over their lifetime than they do now. It effectively completes the transformation of student 'loans' for most, into a working-lifelong graduate tax."

Summary of the changes

	Repay	Maximum term	Interest added	Impact
England 2022 starter	9% over £27,295. **New:** frozen until 2025. On £30,000 income, you repay £243 per year	30 years (from April after leaving)	Up to RPI +3%	State pays 44p per £1. Only 23% likely to clear in full
England 2023 starter	9% over £25,000 (frozen until 2026-27). On £30,000 income, you repay £450 per year	40 years (from April after leaving)	RPI (so no 'real' cost)	State pays 19p per £1. 52% likely to clear in full

Source: moneysavingexpert.com

For new undergraduates, the changes are likely to feel at least a tad unjust, especially given that the MPs responsible for coming up with them largely got their higher education for free. But the government said it was tackling the problem of unpaid student loans "head-on, rather than passing the problem on to future generations". As to whether the decreasing rate of government subsidy will affect prospective students' choices remains to be seen.

Tuition fees history

Up until 1998, tuition at UK universities was free. The £1,000 annual fees introduced that year represented a seismic shift in higher education at the time, and in British society more widely. These fees were paid upfront by students at the start of the academic year. In 2006, fees were raised to £3,000 and a new system of variable deferred fees and tuition fees loans was introduced. From then on, fees rose gradually by inflation until 2012 when tuition fees were raised to £9,000 per year – a move met by protest marches, campus occupations and students voting with their feet as evidenced by a downturn in applications to university. Student finance reformed at the same time to include raising the repayment threshold to £21,000 and introducing a variable tiered rate of interest on student loans.

Fees up to £9,250 were first introduced in 2017-18 and have not gone up since. Application and enrolment numbers have regained the ground they lost in the immediate years after 2012, students appearing to have become resigned to the regime.

There are some exceptions to these upper limits; private providers are not subject to fee caps, and the maximum fee for accelerated degree courses in England is £11,100. However, a fee loan will only be made available up to £9,250 and any shortfall must be met by the student.

Most students pay the maximum fees, but tuition costs vary more widely than the upper limits suggest, with bursaries and fee waivers bringing down the price for students from low-income households, while merit-based scholarships – which are sometimes, but not always linked to household incomes – are similarly valuable to those in receipt of them.

Some universities have substantial endowments to fund their bursaries and scholarships programmes, such as the prestigious London School of Economics and Political Science, which in recent years has awarded around £4million annually in scholarships and financial support to its undergraduates.

About half of full-time students qualify for some form of financial assistance at the University of West London. Provision includes 400 undergraduate bursaries of £500 per year of study to students from low-income households. Path to Success scholarships for those taking a four-year degree with a foundation year are worth £2,000, paid in instalments and on condition of progression criteria. Aspire cards provide £200 funds for use in the online student shop (£100 for part-time students), and core textbooks.

This *Guide* quotes the higher headline fees, but even these will vary according to whether you are from the UK or overseas, studying full-time or part-time, and whether you are taking a foundation degree or an honours programme. For 2022-23, international medical students at Imperial College London are paying £46,650 per year in tuition fees (a figure that has risen with inflation to £50,400 for 2023-24 entry). Not far away at Kingston University, UK students on the early-years foundation course are being charged £6,300 per year.

EU students who started studying in the UK before Brexit qualified for "home fees" of £9,250 per year, which those already on courses before the transition period ended on December 3, 2020, still pay. However, any who have joined since are classed as international students – with higher fees to match.

Here we focus on full-time honours degrees for British undergraduates, and the EU students who escaped the higher international fees: these students make up the biggest group on any UK campus.

An important fact easy to overlook is that some universities guarantee fees will be fixed at the first-year rate for the whole of your course, while others make no such promise. Applicants are advised to check the fees pages of individual universities closely.

It is also worth noting that during work placements or years abroad fees cannot exceed £1,850 (20% of the full-year fee) for work placements and £1,385 for a year abroad and are often less. So, the costs incurred by extending an undergraduate degree to four years by adding a year abroad or in industry are mainly purely living related.

Fees and loans

Marginal fluctuations in fee levels and bursary provision between universities tend not to be the basis upon which applicants make their degree choices, however. Numbers from the poorest socioeconomic groups are at record levels, although they remain severely underrepresented compared with more affluent groups.

Most readers of *The Times and Sunday Times Good University Guide* will be choosing full-time undergraduate or foundation degree courses. The fees for 2023 entry are listed alongside each university's profile in Chapter 14 wherever available. Details of English universities' bursaries and scholarships are on the website of the Office for Students (OfS) in the pages on access and participation plans. Universities have their own fees and funding web pages as well, which are good places to source up-to-date information regarding financial help.

Institutions in Scotland, Wales and Northern Ireland continue to have lower charges for their own residents but charge varying amounts to students from other parts of the UK. Only those living in Scotland and studying at Scottish universities will escape all fees, although there are reduced fees for those normally living in Wales and Northern Ireland.

The number of bursaries and scholarships offered to reduce the burden on new students has been falling since OFFA, the former Office for Fair Access, suggested that such initiatives do little to attract students from low-income households. Following this logic, the government turned the grants paid to the poorest students into loans, although it is restoring some maintenance grants, for example for nurses.

Alternative options

Some further education colleges offer substantial savings on the cost of a degree, or of a foundation degree, but they tend to have very local appeal, and their subject range tends to be largely vocational. The private sector may grow in popularity, following the success of two-year degrees at the University of Buckingham and BPP University in particular. Regent's University, one of the latest to be awarded that title, charged £18,500 or £21,500 (depending on the subject) in 2022-23 for all students, irrespective of their place of origin. Their website has not yet indicated any fees rises for 2023-24. Northeastern University London (formerly New College of the Humanities), also in London, now charges the standard £9,250, having originally come in at twice the price. For 2023-24, the international fee is from £21,000 to £25,000 (subject depending).

Impact on subject and university choice

Even among full-time degrees, the pattern of applications and enrolments has varied considerably since the introduction of higher fees. Back in 2018, the big losers among academic disciplines included technology subjects, languages and literature. Winners included medicine and, perhaps unexpectedly, the social sciences. Nursing and medicine experienced application booms in 2020 as a result of the health pandemic's spotlight on frontline health workers. The career security offered by these subjects is also of value to students.

In general terms, over the eight years since higher fees were introduced, science and business subjects have done better than the arts, as students have made their own assumptions about future career prospects. IT, engineering, physical sciences and law are ahead of 2010 application numbers and languages and linguistics are down. In the 2021 admissions cycle, subjects allied to medicine had the most enrolments.

Universities vary the courses they offer, in response to the perceived demand from students, much more frequently than they used to. A drop in applications may mean less competition for places, or it may lead universities to close courses, possibly intensifying the race for entry. The only reliable forecast is that competition for places on the most popular courses will remain stiff, just as it has been since before students paid any fees.

Two-year degrees are so far mainly the domain of the private universities. The University of Law, for example, already does degrees in this way. It charged £11,100 per year in 2022-23, a saving of £5,550 on a three-year course, which the same institution also offers at the standard £9,250, alongside less expensive online options. This option will remain at £9,250 a year for 2023-24 but the two-year course fee will increase to £14,750 per annum. A two-year course gets you into the workforce faster and reduces spending on living costs. However, this approach also cuts out much chance of holiday earnings and of sandwich courses or placements, where students can often get paid and gain work experience.

Degree apprenticeships

The option of studying for a degree with no fees at all, by taking a degree apprenticeship sponsored by an employer, is growing. Multiverse – the apprenticeship provider run by Euan Blair (son of Tony, the former Labour prime minister) – is becoming the first apprenticeship provider to be approved to directly award its own degrees, the Office for Students announced in September 2022. The initial subject focus will be on data science and technology.

Many other degree apprenticeships are in professional areas, such as childcare, accounting, policing and social work, but there are others in the sciences, business subjects, some social sciences and IT. On the whole, students spend the majority of their time at work with their sponsoring employer – and receiving a wage, rather than having to access loans - with varying periods at university.

The degree versus degree apprenticeship debate is fairly even-handed. Financially, degree apprenticeships – which are known as graduate apprenticeships in Scotland – are a no-brainer; you do not pay tuition fees, plus you will get a salary for a job that is building experience for your future career, rather than a typical part-time role just to boost your current account. Those who last the course of up to five years will be met with immediate employment, and many employers pay those who complete the qualification more than traditional graduates because they will have been with them for longer and be more valuable in the short term.

However, some feel that the apprenticeship route is too new for the long-term prospects to be certain, as is whether the qualification will have the same currency and be as portable as a traditional degree in mid-career. And even though barriers between vocational and academic education are being broken down, only a few thousand young people started higher level apprenticeships in 2021.

Getting the best deal

Student support packages mean applicants can shop around, particularly if their family income is low. But the best deal, even in purely financial terms, is one that leads to a rewarding career. By all means compare the full packages offered by individual universities but consider too whether marginal differences of a few hundred pounds in headline fees, repaid over 30 or 40 years, matter as much as the quality of the course and the likely advantages it will confer in the employment market. Scottish students can save themselves £27,750 by opting to study in their home country. That is a very different matter to the much smaller saving that is available to students in England. So, it is all a matter of judgement.

The financial relief offered by means-tested bursaries may be impossible to ignore for those who qualify for them. No one has to pay tuition fees while they are a student, but you still have to find thousands of pounds in living costs to take a full-time degree. In some cases, bursaries may make the difference between being able to afford higher education and having to pass up a potentially life-changing opportunity. Some are worth up to £3,000 a year, although most are less generous than this, often because large numbers of students qualify for an award.

Some scholarships are even more valuable, and are awarded for sporting and musical prowess, as well as academic achievement. Most scholarships are not means-tested, but a few are open only to students who are both high performers academically and from low-income families.

International students

For more information on international tuition fees, please refer to Chapter 11, Coming to the UK to Study.

Financing your studies

The need for enough money to live on at university and the likelihood that for the majority of students, some debt will be involved, remain constants in higher education – whatever changes in fees may be dictated by government policies.

Most students take out both tuition fee and maintenance loans to cover the cost of studying and living. These are technically two types of funding, but the total amount borrowed is known as their Student Loan. It now costs almost £30,000 to pay for university tuition, and that is before including rent, bills, food and some fun nights out. But try not to focus on the headline figures. Yes, there is going to be a debt and it is likely to be considerable, but student loan debts are not quite like other sorts of commercial borrowing – such as on credit cards or via a mortgage. As discussed earlier in this chapter, some commentators argue they work out more like a graduate tax.

Each UK country has its own student finance system. The following sections of this chapter relate to the loans and costs incurred by students from England, while the broader content relates to students across the UK. The facts and figures for those from Northern Ireland, Wales and Scotland are detailed separately later in the chapter.

Tuition fee loans

Full-time students can borrow up to the full amount of £9,250 needed to cover tuition fees wherever they study in the UK. Those studying an accelerated degree course could get up to £11,100. This loan is not dependent upon household income. New part-time students can apply for loans of up to £6,935 for tuition fees in an academic year.

Maintenance Loan entitlement, England 2022–23

Household income	Living at home	Living away from home but not in London	Living away from home and studying in London
£25,000	£8,171	£9,706	£12,667
£30,000	£7,484	£9,012	£11,961
£35,000	£6,796	£8,318	£11,255
£40,000	£6,108	£7,623	£10,549
£45,000	£5,420	£6,929	£9,843
£50,000	£4,733	£6,234	£9,136
£55,000	£4,045	£5,540	£8,430
£58,220	£3,602	£5,093	£7,975
£60,000	£3,597	£4,845	£7,724
£62,286	£3,597	£4,528	£7,401
£65,000	£3,597	£4,524	£7,018
£70,000	£3,597	£4,524	£6,312
£70,004+	£3,597	£4,524	£6,311

Source: Student Finance England

Students never get their hands on the tuition fee loans cash; the money is paid straight to the university. This way there is no risk of blowing the lot on something other than funding studies or running late with payments.

Maintenance loans

These are designed to help full-time home students pay for their living expenses – rent, food, travel, bills, going out, clothes, gym fees and so on. Maintenance loans are partly means-tested and the amount that can be borrowed depends on family income, whether the university is in London or elsewhere in the UK, and whether students live at home with their family or independently.

Maximum loan amounts in 2022-23:

» £8,171 for students living at their family home during term time.
» £9,706 for students living away from home outside London.
» £12,667 for students living away from home in London.
» £11,116 for students living and studying abroad for at least one term as part of their UK course.

In general, students must be under 60 on the first day of the first academic year of their course. However, in England over-60s can access a lower means-tested loan for living costs, of up to £ 4,106.

Maintenance loans are paid straight into students' bank accounts in three instalments throughout the year. Budgeting to make each loan last until the next instalment is down to students. The final Maintenance loan payment is a bit smaller than in the years before, because student life ends in June/July of that year, and with it the entitlement to a student loan.

For most 18-year-old freshers, the sight of their current account being hit with probably its biggest single cash injection ever may bring a rush of blood to the head. More sobering, however, may be the surprise that the interest clock starts ticking on the loan from the day of the initial payment, usually the first day of the first term. It keeps ticking until the April after students finish their course, which is when repayment may or may not begin. For part-time students earning over the threshold, repayment starts four years after starting to receive the loan, even if they are furthering their studies then rather than working.

Before the latest reforms, the most recent significant change to the student finance system, in 2016-17, was the abolition of grants – which do not require repayment – in England for students from low-income families, and their replacement by increased maintenance loans. As with the introduction of tuition fees, there has been no immediate impact on students. Repayments are in line with those for tuition fee loans. But critics have said many low and middle-income students could be put off university by having to accrue more debt, and in 2020 the government reintroduced maintenance grants for nurses, as detailed below.

NHS bursaries

Eligible full-time NHS students can apply for a bursary from the NHS, plus a £1,000 grant from the NHS and a reduced Maintenance loan from Student Finance England. For those eligible for an NHS bursary, the NHS pays their standard tuition fees directly to their university.

The student nursing bursary returned in September 2020, having been scrapped in 2015. Under the funding arrangements, all nursing students qualify for at least £5,000 a year maintenance grant – which is commonly known as the bursary. Those who plan on working in a branch of nursing suffering from severe shortages can also access a further £1,000. Beyond this, another £2,000 is accessible in childcare allowances. Only part of the bursary is means-tested, and some student nurses may be eligible to more bursary funding subject to the means-testing.

Student nurses do not have to repay the maintenance grants, as they are not loans. And having the bursary doesn't impact student nurse's access to a full student loan through the Student Loans Company.

Interest rates

Student loan interest rates are based on the RPI, the rate at which prices rise. Under the outgoing system, while studying and until the April following graduation, students are charged RPI + 3% (although those taking out student loans from 2023 will be charged RPI only). From that point, interest accrues on a sliding scale of RPI plus up to 3% until they reach a salary of £47,835, after which it remains at RPI plus 3% however much they earn. As an idea of what to expect on the sliding scale, those earning a midway salary of £37,205 will accrue interest of RPI + 1.5%.

The interest rate changes every September, based on the RPI rate of inflation in the year to the previous March. However, the interest rate has been capped until August 31, 2023, due to inflation. Interest rates on Plan 2 loans will not go above 7.3% while the cap is in place

The interest rate changes every September, based on the RPI rate of inflation in the year to the previous March. The RPI rate was 2.6% in March 2020, so in 2021 student loan interest was charged at 2.6% to 5.6%, depending on whether the student was still studying and how much they were earning. If students lose touch with the Student Loans Company, RPI plus 3% is automatically applied to their debt.

The disappearing debt

After 30 years in England, or 40 under the new scheme (this varies a little elsewhere in the UK – please see further down this chapter), the debt is written off. Because the repayments seem modest for anyone with a qualifying income, and because of the 30-year rule, student debt is a lot more forgiving than a mortgage or a credit card, where the bills keep on coming even if you are out of work. The Student Loans Company is probably the only lender in Britain that hands out tens of thousands of pounds without a credit check.

Repaying the student loan

Student loan debt works very differently from other types of borrowing. If you take a personal loan or a mortgage, for example, what you repay is based on how much is borrowed, the interest rate and the loan term. With student loan repayments what you repay is based solely on what you earn. At the time of writing, graduates start repaying the debt once they earn more than £27,295. Once they hit the threshold they then pay 9% of anything they earn above this level. So if you earn £30,000, you repay £243.45 a year. A graduate keeps repaying their loan until they have cleared it, or for 30 years from the April after they graduate. If they have not cleared it by then, the outstanding debt is written off.

In other words, the interest added is not the interest paid. That depends on future earnings. Some graduates will not repay any interest and some will not earn enough to repay all of it. Contrary to the majority of debts, which are better to clear as early as possible, students should not start repaying student loans before the April after leaving university, as this can result in overpaying – which tens of thousands of students have done in the past, and can now reclaim.

The Student Loans Company website has information to guide prospective students through these arrangements and also gives examples of levels of repayment (**www.studentloanrepayment.co.uk**).

Affording to live

Making ends meet is a constant university challenge, and students have always proved resourceful. Analysis by the National Union of Students confirmed what students already knew, that the maintenance loan does not provide enough money to cover the real cost of living. For students from England, the maximum maintenance loan increased by just 2.3% in 2022-23, despite inflation far surpassing that. Typically, the No 1 one source of topping up the coffers is parents, whose financial assistance is implied, if not explicit, in the government's approach to student funding. Part-time jobs, savings and bursaries and scholarships also contribute to the student purse. For more information see Chapter 7.

The Student Money Survey 2022 from **www.savethestudent.org** found that average undergraduate spending was £924 per month, with rent the biggest outlay at an average of £418 per month. The impact of the rising cost of living on students is evident in the survey results, which revealed that 82% of students worried about not being able to make ends meet (up from 71% for the same question in the previous year's survey) and that 52% (up from 36%) had considered dropping out for that reason. One in 10 of the students surveyed had used a food bank in the past year.

The annual NatWest Student Living Index for 2022 reported that student loans now account for almost half (49%) of students' monthly income. This has edged down from 2021, with parental support and personal income playing a bigger role. However, fewer than one in five students cover their rent with personal income. Parents and family account for 44%. Average monthly term-time income has climbed 65% this year.

The index confirmed that for students across the UK, rent remains the biggest monthly spend, followed by supermarket shopping, household bills, clothes, car running costs and booze-free going out to gigs, theatres and cinemas, while alcohol comes in at sixth places. With lockdown restrictions lifted, student spending on going out has surged, reaching a monthly average of £44.70.

Newcastle tops the chart, with Southampton at the bottom. The remainder of students' money is spent on takeaways, travel and activities with a small amount going to charity and an average of £26.25 per month invested in cryptocurrency.

Value for money

Most surveys suggest that on average, a degree still offers a worthwhile return on the financial investment involved in going to university. Future salary expectations are better for graduates than those without degrees, even taking into consideration the wages that might otherwise have been earned while studying instead. Our Subject-by-Subject Guide in Chapter 12 delves deeper into graduate outcomes and salaries.

Budgeting

Help is at hand to avoid the financial abandon of splurging huge portions of a student loan in the first month. University websites, UCAS at **www.ucas.com/finance/managing-money/ student-budgeting-tips** and many others offer guidance on preparing a budget. List all likely income (loans, bursaries, part-time work, savings, parental support) and compare this with expected outgoings. It pays to be realistic, rather than too optimistic, about both sides of the equation. With care, it should be possible to end up either only slightly in the red, or preferably far enough in the black to be able to afford some of the things you like.

Aldi, Lidl and other budget supermarkets are godsends when it comes to stretching the budget, even if shopping at one means needing to get a taxi home – share with a housemate and split the cost, there will still be significant savings on the prices at the nearby Tesco Metro or Sainsbury's Local. No one is condoning binge drinking, but with "pre-drinks" before a night out popular, great savings can be made by stocking up on the budget versions of well-known drinks and snacks. Shopping online, while not offered by the budget supermarkets, can also be cost effective if you stick to own brand products, as the temptation of popping extra items into the trolley at will is removed and any delivery fee can be shared with housemates. Some parents like to send supermarket deliveries to their student.

Cookery how-tos on YouTube, TikTok, Instagram et al have brought meal prep guidelines to smartphones, so there is no excuse not to learn at least a few basics. Sharing a meal with housemates is great for bonding, while leftovers in Tupperware are a weapon in the fight against splurging more than is affordable on daily café lunches. The same goes for a carry-cup for hot drinks.

More than two-thirds of 18-24-year-olds reported they received no financial education at school, according to a report by the National Association of Student Money Advisors (NASMA). Keeping track of finances is not every student's idea of a good time but it is certain to provide greater freedom for enjoying university life. Most graduates will have to grapple with

---

Funding timetable

It is vital that you sort out your funding arrangements before you start university. Each funding agency has its own arrangements, and it is very important that you find out the exact details from them. The timings below give general indications of key dates.

March/April

» Online and paper application forms become available from funding agencies.
» You must contact the appropriate funding agency to make an application. This will be the funding agency for the region of the UK that you live in, even if you are planning to study elsewhere in the UK.
» Complete application form as soon as possible. At this stage, select the university offer that will be your first choice.
» Check details of bursaries and scholarships available from your selected universities.

May/June

» Funding agencies will give you details of the financial support they can offer.
» Last date for making an application to ensure funding is ready for you at the start of term (exact date varies significantly between agencies).

August

» Tell your funding agency if the university or course you have been accepted for is different from that originally given them.

September

» Take letter confirming funding to your university for registration.
» After registration, the first part of funds will be released to you.

spreadsheets during their working life, and they make balancing the student budget simpler. Nobody enjoys a "card refused" message popping up on their Applepay display.

Make full use of student travel cards and shopping discounts, and shop around for the best calls and data deals on mobile phones. The 2022 NatWest Student Living Index put average monthly mobile phone spending at £20.56, while groceries and household items came in at £76.29 a month, £43.34 went on alcohol and £35.92 on books and other course-related material.

Study costs

The average student spent about £1,000 a year on costs associated with course work and studying, a survey by the NUS estimated – mainly on books and equipment. Some courses require much higher course spends than others, and extra financial support may be available for certain – but not all – things. Take out library text books or buy them second-hand from students who don't need them anymore to avoid racking up huge book shop bills incurred by a long reading list.

Overdrafts and credit cards

These are the more expensive forms of debt, and best avoided if at all possible. Many banks offer free overdraft facilities for students but going over the limit without prior arrangement can result in high charges. Credit cards can be useful if managed properly, ideally by setting up a direct debit to pay off the full balance every month, thus avoiding paying any interest. To pay only the minimum charge each month can end up costing a small fortune over a long period. Those inclined to spend impulsively without keeping track of spending are probably better off without a credit card and should stick with a debit card.

Insurance

Most students arrive at university with laptops and other goodies such as games consoles, sports equipment, musical instruments, mobile phones and bikes that are tempting to thieves. It is estimated that around a third of students fall victim to crime at some point during university. A reasonable amount of cover for these items should be found by shopping around, without it costing you an arm and a leg. It may also be possible to add this cover cheaply to parents' domestic contents policy (probably at their expense). See page 110.

Living in one country, studying in another

As each of the countries of the UK develops its own distinctive system of student finance, the effects on students leaving home in one UK nation to go and study in another have become knottier. UK students who cross borders to study, pay the tuition fees of their chosen university and are eligible for a fee loan, and maybe a partial grant, to cover them. They are also entitled to apply for the scholarships or bursaries on offer from that institution. Any maintenance loan or grant will still come from the awarding body of their home country. If you are in this position, you must check with the authorities in your home country about the funding you are eligible for. You should also contact your own government about support on offer if you are from the Channel Islands or the Isle of Man.

Following Britain's departure from the European Union, EU students from are charged the same tuition fees as those paid by international students from further afield. International students may be considered for some scholarships and bursaries by individual institutions.

Applying for support

English students should apply for grants and loans through Student Finance England, Welsh students through Student Finance Wales, Scottish students through the Student Awards Agency for Scotland, and those in Northern Ireland through Student Finance NI or their Education and Library Board.

Applications should be made as soon as the offer of a place at university has been received. Don't expect things to happen automatically. For instance, students have to tell the Student Loans Company to pay the tuition fees they owe to the university.

University scholarships and bursaries

Shop around for university bursaries, scholarships and other sponsorship packages, and seek other forms of supplementary support. There may be fee reductions for groups, including local students, which are usually detailed on university websites. There is funding for students with disabilities or family responsibilities; or for those taking subjects such as social work or medicine, with wide public benefit, as well as a range of charities with their own criteria.

The Scholarship Hub, a database of scholarships, suspects UK students could be missing out on funding worth over £150million a year as organisations offering scholarships often struggle to get enough applications. The database is free, but it requires a subscription to access advice about how to apply and to use enhanced search tools.

Most bursaries are means-tested, while scholarships are via open competition. Some universities offer eligible students the choice of accommodation discounts, fee waivers or cash. Most also have hardship funds for those who find themselves in financial difficulties. Many charities for specific industries or professions have a remit to support education, and many have bursaries for anyone studying a related subject. The Directory of Grant-Making Trusts lists bodies that make one-off or regular awards to all kinds of causes, often including deserving students. Only available in hard copy, a library visit may be required to see it for free.

Take note of the application procedures for scholarships and bursaries. They vary between institutions, and even from course to course within institutions. Specific awards may have specific application deadlines. In some cases, the university will work out for you whether you are entitled to an award by referring to your funding agency's financial assessment. If your personal circumstances change part-way through a course, entitlement to a scholarship or bursary may be reviewed.

Advice on scholarships and bursaries is usually included in a university's website or prospectus and many institutions also maintain a helpline. Is the bursary or scholarship automatic or conditional? When will you find out whether your application has been successful? For some awards, this won't be until after exam results.

Students with disabilities

Extra financial help is available to disabled students, whether studying full-time or part-time, through Disabled Students' Allowances, which are paid in addition to the standard student finance package. They are available for help with education-related conditions such as dyslexia, and for other physical and mental disabilities. They do not depend on income and do not have to be repaid. The cash is available for extra travel costs, equipment and to pay helpers. For 2022-23, the maximum amount available for eligible students in England for support – including a non-medical helper, extra travel, or specialist equipment – is £25,575 a year.

The NHS Business Services Authority has a Student Services Arm which runs the NHS Learning Support Fund, worth investigating by those planning to study health or social work.

Further sources of income

There are various types of support available for students in particular circumstances, other than the main loans, grants and bursaries.

» Undergraduates in financial difficulties can apply for help from their university's student hardship fund. These provide support for anything from day-to-day study and living costs to unexpected or exceptional expenses. The university decides which students need help and how much to award them. These funds often target older or disadvantaged students, and finalists in danger of dropping out. The sums range up to a few thousand pounds, are not repayable and do not count against other income.

» Students with children can apply for a Childcare Grant. For 2022-23, this was up to £183.75 a week for a first child and up to £ 315.03 for two or more children. There was also a Parents' Learning Allowance of up to £1,863 a year in 2022-23 for help with course-related costs.

» Students with a partner, or another adult family member who is financially dependent on them, can apply for an Adult Dependants' Grant of up to £3,263 a year for 2022-23.

Part-time work

A part-time term-time job is a fact of life for almost half of students. The challenge is to not let the part-time job get in the way of studying. A survey by the NUS found that 59% of students who worked felt it had an impact on their studies, with 38% missing lectures and over a fifth failing to submit coursework because of their part-time jobs.

Student employment agencies, found on many university campuses, match employers with students seeking work, sometimes offering jobs within the university itself. They also ensure both minimum wages and the maximum number of hours worked in term time, typically 15 hours a week. Students sometimes make money from freelance work and student businesses, but most take casual work in shops, restaurants, bars and call centres. Most students get a job during the holidays, including those who don't have one in the term.

How the £9,250 fee system works

What follows is a summary of the position for British students in late 2022. While there are substantial differences between the four countries of the UK, there is one important piece of common ground. Upfront payment of fees is not compulsory, and students can take out a fee loan from the Student Loans Company to cover them. This is repayable in instalments after graduation when earnings reach £27,295 for English students (£25,000 in future), a threshold set by the government.

The most you can borrow to pay fees is £9,250, with lower sums for private colleges (up to £6,165) and part-time study, where the cap is £6,935 at public institutions and £4,625 at private ones. There are different levels of fees and support for UK students who are not from England. New students enrolling at UK universities from all international countries, including those in the EU, will pay the same international rate, which is usually much higher than the home rate. EU students already registered on courses before December 31, 2020, qualify for the home rate of fees for the remainder of their course. The latest information on individual universities' fees at the time of going to press is listed alongside their profiles in Chapter 14.

With changes, large or small, becoming almost an annual occurrence, it is essential to consult the websites of the relevant government agencies.

Tuition fees by region for courses starting in 2023

Student's home region	Studying in England	Studying in Scotland	Studying in Wales**	Studying in Northern Ireland
England	Up to £9,250	Up to £9,250*	Up to £9,000	Up to £9,250
Scotland	Up to £9,250	No fee	Up to £9,000	Up to £9,250
Wales*	Up to £9,250	Up to £9,250	Up to £9,000	Up to £9,250
Northern Ireland	Up to £9,250	Up to £9,250	Up to £9,000	Up to £4,630
EU and other international**	Variable	Variable	Variable	Variable

*Students who live in Wales will be entitled to tuition fees and means-tested maintenance grants.

**This will not apply to Irish nationals living in the UK and Ireland whose right to study and to access benefits and services will be preserved on a reciprocal basis for UK and Irish nationals under the Common Travel Area arrangement.
Note that honours degrees in Scotland take four years and some universities charge £9,250 for each year.

Fees correct at time of going to press.

Source: UCAS

Fees in England

In England, the maximum tuition fee for full-time undergraduates from the UK or anywhere in the European Union will be £9,250 a year in 2022-23. As we have seen, most courses will demand fees of £9,250 or close to it.

In many public universities, the lowest fees will be for foundation degrees and Higher National Diplomas. Although some universities have chosen to charge the full £9,250 a year for all courses, these two-year courses will remain a cost-effective stepping stone to a full degree, or a qualification in their own right, at many universities and further education colleges. Those universities that offer extended work placements or a year abroad as part of a degree course, will charge much less than the normal fee for this "year out". The maximum cost for a placement year is 20% of the tuition fee (£1,850), and for a full year abroad, 15%. If you spend only part of the year abroad, you will probably have to pay the whole £9,250.

Fees in Scotland

At Scottish universities and colleges, students from Scotland pay no fees directly. The universities' vice-chancellors and principals have appealed for charges to be introduced at some level to save their institutions from falling behind their English rivals in financial terms, but Alex Salmond, when he was Scotland's First Minister, famously declared that the "rocks will melt in the sun" before this happens.

Students whose home is in Scotland and who are studying at a Scottish university apply to the Student Awards Agency for Scotland (SAAS) to have their fees paid for them. Note, too, that three-year degrees are rare in Scotland, so most students can expect to pay four years of living costs.

Students from England, Wales and Northern Ireland studying in Scotland will pay fees at something like the scale that applies in England and will have access to finance at similar levels to those available for study in England. It is worth noting, however, that some courses offer considerable savings, such as Robert Gordon University in Aberdeen, for example, has a fee of £6,000 per year for some four-year courses, including a BA in Accounting and Finance.

The majority of Scottish universities offer a "free" fourth year to bring their total fees into line with English universities, but Edinburgh and St Andrews are charging £9,250 in all four years of their degree courses.

Scottish maintenance bursaries and loans 2022–23

Young student (under 25 at start of course)				Independent student (25+)			
Income	Loan	Bursary	Total	Income	Loan	Bursary	Total
Up to £20,999	£6,100	£2,000	£8,100	Up to £20,999	£7,100	£1,000	£8,100
£21,000–£23,999	£6,100	£1,125	£7,225	£21,000–£23,999	£7,100	–	£7,100
£24,000–£33,999	£6,100	£500	£6,600	£24,000–£33,999	£7,100	–	£7,100
Over £34,000	£5,100	–	£5,100	Over £34,000	£4,750	–	£4,750

UK paramedic, nursing and midwifery students studying in Scotland are eligible for bursaries of £10,000 for the first three years and £7,500 for the fourth year of a course, but only if they intend to stay and work in Scotland after qualifying. There is a separate dental bursary scheme.

Source: Students Awards Agency Scotland

Student loans and grants for Scottish students

Scottish students pay no tuition fees at their own universities and can apply for up to £9,250 per year as a loan for fees elsewhere in the UK. They must reapply for this loan each year.

Unlike the other UK countries, Scotland uses a band system to calculate the combination of bursary and loan, rather than precise household income. So, in 2022-23, students from a family with an income below £20,999 could get a £2,000 Young Students' Bursary (YSB) as well as a loan of £6,100 – making £8,100. For incomes from £21,000 to £23,999, the bursary is £1,125 and the loan remains the same, and for those earning £24,000 to £33,999, the bursary is only £500, making a total of £6,600. Above £34,000, no bursary is available and the maximum loan falls to £5,100.

These figures remain the same regardless of whether students live at home or where they are studying in the UK. Higher loans but more limited bursaries are available for "independent" students – those who are married, mature (25 or over) or without family support. Maintenance support loans in Scotland are not available to students aged over 55, and students must be under 60 to enrol on the first day of their course.

Scotland's SAAS agency already has the repayment threshold set at £25,000. Interest is linked to the Retail Price Index, as in Northern Ireland. Repayments continue until the loan is paid off, with any outstanding amount being cancelled after 35 years.

As elsewhere in the UK, there are special funds for people with disabilities and other special needs, and for those with children or adult dependants. No tuition fee loans are required by Scottish students studying in Scotland, but such loans are available for Scottish students studying elsewhere in the UK.

Fees in Wales

All Welsh universities apply £9,000 tuition fees. Students who live in Wales will be able to apply for a tuition fee loan as well as a tuition fee grant, wherever they study. You can get a combined loan and grant for up to £9,000 if you study in Wales, or £9,250 for Scotland, England or Northern Ireland, but only a loan, of up to £6,165, for study in a private institution

Student loans and grants for Welsh students

For 2022-23, the maximum maintenance award is £9,095 for students living at home, £10,710 for those living away from home and outside London, and £13,375 for those living in London. These sums are mainly an outright grant to those from low-income households. So, if total household income is £18,370 or less, £8,100 of the total £10,710 maintenance award is a grant (and therefore does not need to be repaid) and only £2,610 a loan. But if income is over £59,200, then £9,710 is repayable and only £1,000 is a grant. The same logic applies to other levels of support, while part-time students can get a variable loan or grant that depends upon income and the intensity of their course.

Tuition fee loans are available to cover the whole £9,000 of tuition fees in Wales, or £9,250 for Welsh students in Scotland, England or Northern Ireland (£6,165 for a private provider). Those studying part-time in Wales (or at the Open University) can apply for a loan of up to £2,625. Elsewhere in the UK they can apply for up to £6,935, or for courses at private institutions, £4,625.

Welsh Education Minister Jeremy Miles announced in October 2022 that Wales will continue under the current graduate repayment system for a further year in 2023-24. That means that new borrowers will continue to use the £27,295 repayment threshold and 30-year repayment period. Interest repayments are at RPI up to RPI+3%, as per the pre-2022 system in England. In addition, students in Wales are also able to apply for Welsh government support for parents of young children, for adult learners, for those with adult dependants and for those with disabilities. This support can cover carer costs as well as equipment and general expenditure.

Fees in Northern Ireland

The two universities of Northern Ireland are charging local students £4,630 a year for 2022-23. For students from elsewhere in the UK, the fee is £9,250 for Queen's Belfast and for the University of Ulster.

Student loans and grants for Northern Ireland students

Maintenance grants of up to £3,475 are available to students, the exact amount dependent on household incomes. The maximum loan is reduced by the size of any grant received. Loan repayments of 9% of salary start once income reaches £20,195, a lower threshold than in England, Scotland or Wales, and interest is calculated on the Retail Price Index or 1% above base rate, whichever is lower. The loan will be cancelled after 25 years, quicker than elsewhere in the UK.

There are also special funds for people with disabilities and other special needs, and for those with children or adult dependants. Students studying in the Republic of Ireland can also borrow up to €3,000 a year to pay their Irish tuition contribution and may be able to get a bursary to study there. Tuition fee loans are available for the full amount of tuition fees, regardless of where you study in the UK.

Useful websites

The "fees and funding" pages on university websites provide the most up-to-date information on costs of individual courses – especially for rates paid by international students, which vary. Universities also publish details of the financial help available, and how to apply.

It is essential to consult the latest information provided by government agencies. The following websites will outline any major developments.

England: **www.gov.uk/student-finance**
Wales: **www.studentfinancewales.co.uk**
Scotland: **www.saas.gov.uk**
Northern Ireland: **www.studentfinanceni.co.uk**
Office for Students: **www.officeforstudents.org.uk**

For the basics of fees, loans, grants and other allowances: **www.gov.uk/student-finance**
UCAS provides helpful advice: **www.ucas.com/money**
Office for Students: **www.officeforstudents.org.uk**
All UK student loans are administered by the Student Loans Company:
www.gov.uk/government/organisations/student-loans-company
HMRC information on the tax position of students: **www.gov.uk/student-jobs-paying-tax**
For finding out about availability of scholarships: **www.thescholarshiphub.org.uk** (requires subscription fee). Or go direct to university websites, where their scholarship and bursary provision will be detailed.

5 Making Your Application

The UK's predicted grades admissions system is here to stay, as plans to make students apply to universities after receiving their exam results have been shelved by the government. A rarity in the education sector globally, and unique to the UK among developed countries, the predicted grades admissions system was on the cusp of reform at the time of our *Guide*'s previous edition, described as "readyish" to go by government advisors. But the Department for Education confirmed in February 2022 that, following a four-month consultation held in 2021, it found there was "some support for post-qualifications admissions, but this is not strong enough to indicate that this is the right time for such a major upheaval".

Moving to a post-qualifications model (PQA) is reportedly not hugely popular with universities, whose time to support students through the applications process would be squeezed – a constraint they predicted would hit those from socially disadvantaged backgrounds hardest. But research by educational charity the Sutton Trust in 2020 found that 66% of students felt a post-qualification approach would be fairer than predicted grades.

Clare Marchant, chief executive of UCAS (the University and Colleges Admissions System), says it is already committed to a "well-developed ongoing programme of reform that has student choice, transparency, and fair access at its heart.

"Being able to support all students, help them make well-informed decisions about their futures and give them more flexibility as they apply was never dependent on post-qualification admissions," Marchant says, adding that the UCAS Clearing Plus system, used by more than 15,000 UK students, means there is "already…an element of post-qualification admissions in the system that is working well".

UCAS was formed in 1992 through the merger of the former university admissions system UCCA and the former polytechnics admissions system PCAS. UCAS makes the process of applying to university as straightforward as possible. Everything happens online and UCAS provides clear instructions, tips and suggestions of how best to navigate each section along the way.

Be prepared for the UCAS website to oust Instagram from your browser's top spot, at least in the run-up to submitting your application, and for its various stages to be part of your life until a university place has been secured. The UCAS hub is your one-stop-shop for everything from details of more than 35,000 courses, open days and key dates, to top tips based on where you are in the application process, handy to-do lists and reminders to keep you on track. It also offers personalised careers information and advice and includes tools such as a personal statement builder, tariff calculator and apprenticeship finder.

Your grades will be the most important factor in winning a place at university, but what goes on the application form is more important than many students realise. There is a knack to making the kind of application that will stand out to admissions tutors, and which will convey your knowledge of and enthusiasm for your chosen subject, preferably with supporting evidence from your school or college.

It pays to keep your eye on the ball at this stage on the journey to university. Under the current system, applicants must decide on up to five choices months before they take their final exams, you do not have to use all five of them but doing so gives you the best chance of success.

The application process

Almost all applications for full-time higher education courses go through UCAS, including those to the conservatoires, which come with separate guidance and processes on the UCAS website.

Applications for degree apprenticeships are exceptions to the rule, however, and should be made to employers rather than universities. Deadlines differ between employers. You can apply for as many apprenticeships as you want, on top of your university applications. Many recruit through the **www.gov.uk/apply-apprenticeship** website, which also has links to vacancy information, as does UCAS at **https://careerfinder.ucas.com/**.

Some universities that have not filled all their places on conventional degrees, even during Clearing, will accept direct applications up to and sometimes after the start of the academic year, but UCAS is both the official route and the only way into the most popular courses.

Registering with Apply

Applications kick off by registering with Apply. School and college students will be given a "buzzword" by their tutor or careers adviser – you need this in order to login to register. It links your application to the school or college so that the application can be sent electronically to your referee (usually one of your teachers) for your reference to be attached. If you are no longer at a school or college, you do not need a buzzword, but you will need details of your referee. Apply is available 24 hours a day, and, when the time comes, information on the progress of your application may arrive at any time. More information is given on the UCAS website.

Clicking on "Apply" begins the process for providing your personal details and generating a username and password, as well as reminding you of basic points, such as amending your details in case of a change of address. You can register separate term-time and holiday addresses – a useful option for boarders, who could find offers and, particularly, the confirmation of a place,

---

The main screens to be completed in UCAS Apply

» Personal and contact details, and some additional non-educational details for UK applicants.

» Student finance arrangements (UK applicants only), and up to five course choices.

» Details of your education so far, including examination results and those still to be taken.

» Your employment history, listing any paid or voluntary work you have done.

» Your personal statement.

» A reference from one of your teachers.

» View all details to make sure they are correct and reflect your preferences.

» Pay for the application. For the 2023-24 UCAS round it costs £27, or £22.50 if you're applying for just one course.

going to their school when they are miles away at home. Remember to keep a note of your username and password in a safe place.

Throughout the process, you will be in sole control of communications with UCAS and your chosen universities. Only if you nominate a representative and give them your unique nine-digit application number (sent automatically by UCAS when your application is submitted), can a parent or anyone else give or receive information on your behalf, perhaps because you are ill or out of the country.

Video guides on the application process are available on the UCAS website. Once you are registered, you can start to complete the Apply screens. The sections that follow cover the main screens.

Personal details

This information is taken from your initial registration, and you will be asked for additional information, for example, on ethnic origin and national identity, to monitor equal opportunities in the application process. UK students will also be asked to complete a student finance section designed to speed up any loan application you might make.

UCAS has introduced seven new questions for the 2023 entry cycle, as part of its commitment to widening participation. They allow student to self-declare important information about their circumstances, so they can be connected to the right support for their needs. The new questions cover:

» Students estranged from their parents
» Students with caring responsibilities
» Students with parenting responsibilities
» Refugees, asylum seekers and those with limited leave to remain in the UK
» Students from UK Armed Forces families
» UK Armed Forces veterans and Service leavers
» A self-declared free school meals question

Choices

In most subjects, you will be able to apply to a maximum of five universities and/or colleges. The exceptions are medicine, dentistry and veterinary science, where the maximum is four, but you can use your fifth choice as a back-up to apply for a different subject.

The other important restriction concerns Oxford or Cambridge, because you can only apply to one or the other; you cannot apply to both universities in the same year, nor can you apply for more than one course there. For both universities you may need to take a written test and submit examples of your work, depending on the course selected. In addition, for Cambridge, many subjects will demand a pre-interview assessment once the university has received your application from UCAS, while the rest will set written tests to be taken at interview.

The deadline for Oxbridge applications – and for all medicine, dentistry and veterinary science courses – is October 15. For all other applications the deadline is January 15 (or March 24 for some specified art and design courses). The other exceptions to this rule are the relatively small but growing number of courses that start in January or February. If you are considering one of these, contact the university concerned for application deadlines.

Most applicants use all five choices. But if you do choose fewer than five courses, you can still add another to your form up to June 30, as long as you have not accepted or declined any offers. Nor do you have to choose five different universities if more than one course at the same institution attracts you – if you are keen on one institution in particular, applying for one course with lower entrance requirements than the other is a good way of hedging your bets. Universities are not allowed to see where else you have applied, or whether you have chosen the same subject elsewhere. But they will be aware of multiple applications within their own institution. Remember that it is more difficult to write a convincing personal statement if it has to cover two subjects.

For each course you select, you will need to put the UCAS code on the form – and you should check carefully that you have the correct code and understand any special requirements that may be detailed on the UCAS description of the course. It does not matter in what order you enter your choices as all are treated equally. You will also need to indicate whether you are applying for a deferred entry (for example, if you are taking a gap year – see page 88).

Education

This is where you provide details of the schools and colleges you have attended, and the qualifications you have obtained or are preparing for. The UCAS website gives plenty of advice on the ways in which you should enter this information, to ensure that all your relevant qualifications are included with their grades. While UCAS does not need to see qualification certificates, it can double-check results with the examination boards to ensure that no one has exaggerated their results.

In the Employment section that follows, add details of any paid jobs you have had (unpaid or voluntary work should be mentioned in your personal statement).

Personal statement

It is never too early to get cracking on your personal statement, as you will need it finished and in pristine form before making applications. Plan, write and check this statement with consideration and care – but do not agonise over the first line, this is best left to the end once the rest of the content has been included and distilled.

Your personal statement is key to standing out from the crowd. It is the only part of the application process where you get to tell the universities why they should pick you. A part-time job, volunteering and other extracurricular activities can be useful ways of demonstrating that you have the skills and experience for university study. These could involve anything from learning survival skills during the Duke of Edinburgh's Award scheme to taking part in music or sports activities, or helping at a charity.

Don't just list your skills – be they communication and leadership or the ability to work in a team and manage time well – try to provide examples of when you have demonstrated them. Admissions tutors want to see evidence of your interest in and commitment to your chosen subject. Avoid using the word "passion" – let it jump off the page. If you enjoy reading, which many people do, say which authors or books inspire you, and why. Again, ensure your account is based on lived experiences, not what you think the UCAS admissions tutor would want you to say. Your UCAS form also has your teacher's reference and your statement should be in line with their summary of your abilities and interests.

While stopping short of exaggerating or out-and-out lying, this is an opportunity to promote yourself; if that makes you cringe and clam up, ask for help from your parents, friends and teachers.

The personal statement is not the place to discuss exam grades – qualifications are covered elsewhere on your UCAS form. Academic staff in charge of admissions look for potential beyond the high grades that increasing numbers of candidates bring. To stand out, do your homework on your chosen degree, show an interest in the subject by listening to podcasts, following lecturers on Twitter, reading articles. Highlight the experiences you've gained that are related to the syllabus you are applying to – clubs, lectures, visits, vlogs you have created, blogs you have written, work experience and wider reading around the subject.

Practical work experience or volunteering in medical or caring settings should be included by those applying to study medicine – but don't just list what you've done, reflect on what these experiences taught you about working as a doctor and how you are suited to the training and profession. The same approach goes for other vocational degrees; explain how you see yourself using the qualification. Work experience in any setting requires a similar approach; merely namechecking a prestigious company you have been lucky enough to get a placement at will not impress admissions tutors – tell them what you learnt from the organisation and how it relates to the degree you are applying to study.

Take advice from teachers and, if there is still time before you make your application, look for some subject-related activities that will help round out your statement.

Mention the accomplishments which suggest you will turn out to be a productive member of the university and, eventually, a successful graduate. Leading activities outside your school or college are ideal, or other responsibilities you have taken on. Show the admissions tutors that you can take initiative and be self-disciplined, since higher education involves much more independent study than sixth-formers are used to.

Think hard about why you want to study your chosen subject – especially if it is one you have not taken at school or college – and align your interests and skills with the course. Showing commitment to the full course is important, so admissions officers are convinced you will get good results for its duration. Some applicants' five choices will cover more than one subject, and in this situation try to make more general comments about your academic strengths and enthusiasms and avoid focusing on just one of the courses.

If you are an international (EU and non-EU) student you should also include why you want to study in the UK, detail your English language skills, and any English courses or tests you've taken and why you want to be an international student, rather than study in your own country. Mature students can talk about any alternative entry requirements you've used – such as an access course – that show skills and knowledge gained through previous experiences.

Take advantage of the help offered by your school or college. Your teachers see personal statements every year and will have a feel for ones that have gone down well for former students.

UCAS tips on how to write your personal statement

Start by listing the key things you want an admissions tutor to know about you on a separate document. Don't worry at this stage about your wording being perfect. It's more about including all the reasons you should be offered a place. There is no actual formula to follow with a personal statement; what really matters is that it is true to you.

» Study the course description to assess what the universities are looking for in successful candidates; it will help you detail the skills and qualities you can bring to the subject.

» Be cautious about using humour, quotes or anything quirky. What can be said in person with a smile can fall flat, or be perceived as immature or unsuitable, in a remote in-tray.

» Be keen, and keep it simple. Admissions tutors have mountains of documents to plough through: a relevant, concise statement is likely to be memorable.

» Check the character and line limit – you have 4,000 characters and 47 lines. That's about two sides of A4.

» Proofread aloud, and ask family, advisers, and teachers to check. Redraft, if you need to. Then make sure the spelling, punctuation, and grammar are correct.

» Copy and paste your statement into your online application. Save it regularly, the site times out after 35 minutes of inactivity.

Timetable for applications for university admission in 2023-24

At the time of writing UCAS had not confirmed the exact dates for the application schedule. Please check the UCAS website for the most recent information.

2023

January onwards	Find out about courses and universities. Check schedule of open days.
February onwards	Attend open days.
early July	Registration starts for UCAS Apply.
mid September	UCAS starts receiving applications.
October 15	Final day for applications to Oxford and Cambridge, and for most courses in medicine, dentistry and veterinary science.

2024

January 15	Final day for all other applications from UK and EU students.
January 16–end June	New applications continue to be accepted by UCAS, but only considered by universities if the relevant courses have vacancies.
late February	Start of applications through UCAS Extra.
March 24	Final day for applications to art and design courses that specify this date.
end March	Universities should have sent decisions on all applications received by January 15.
early May	Final time by which applicants have to decide on their choices if all decisions received by end March (exact date for each applicant will be confirmed by UCAS). **If you do not reply to UCAS, they will decline your offers.** UCAS must have received all decisions from universities if you applied by January 15.
early June	Final time by which applicants have to decide on their choices if all decisions received by early May.
start of July	Any new application received from this time held until Clearing starts. End of applications through UCAS Extra.
early July	International Baccalaureate results published.
early August	SQA results published. Scottish Clearing starts. (to be confirmed)
mid August	A-level results published. Full Clearing and Adjustment starts. (to be confirmed)
end August	Adjustment closes. Last time for you to meet any offer conditions, after which university might not accept you.
late October	End of period for adding Clearing choices and last point at which a university can accept you through Clearing.

UCAS provides a checklist of themes to cover and websites such as **www.studential.com** and **www.thestudentroom.co.uk** provide tips as well. By this point in your academic career, the perils of cut-and-paste plagiarism are probably clear to you. Do not be fooled into thinking you can lift content from one of the personal statement help websites. UCAS and universities have software that spots plagiarism and have caught out plenty of applicants over the years.

It may be tempting to shoehorn in as much information as the space will allow, but err on the side of reserve. Admissions officers will have piles of these to read and giving them a thoughtfully edited statement is likely to be looked upon kindly. Compose your statement on Word or similar and avoid kicking off with a dreary cliché. Equally, though, do not start with an overly florid introduction – the best personal statements get to the point quickly. Let someone you trust proofread your statement before you paste a copy into Apply and press send; a second pair of eyes is hugely beneficial to the personal statement.

References

Hand-in-hand with your personal statement goes the reference from your school, college or, in the case of mature students, someone who knows you well, but is not a friend or family member. Since 2014, even referees who are not your teachers have been encouraged to predict your grades, although they are allowed to opt out of this process. Whatever the source, the reference has to be independent – you are specifically forbidden to change any part of it if you send off your own application – but that does not mean you should not try to influence what it contains.

Most schools and colleges conduct informal interviews before compiling a reference, but it does no harm to draw up a list of the achievements that you would like to see included, and ensure your referee knows what subject you are applying for. Referees cannot know every detail of a candidate's interests and most welcome an aide-memoire.

The UCAS guidelines skirt around the candidate's right to see his or her reference, but it does exist. Schools' practices vary, but most now show the applicant the completed reference. Where this is not the case, the candidate can ask UCAS customer service to send a copy of their application as a subject access request, which includes the reference. Better, if you can, to see it before it goes off, in case there are factual inaccuracies that can be corrected.

Timing

The general deadline for applications through UCAS is January 15, but even those received up to June 30 will be considered if the relevant courses still have vacancies. After that, you will be limited to Clearing, or an application for the following year. If your form arrives with the deadline looming, you may appear less organised than others; and your application may be one of a large batch that receives a more cursory first reading. Under UCAS rules, last-minute applicants should not be at a disadvantage, but why take the risk?

The best advice is to get your application in early: before Christmas, or earlier if possible. Applications are accepted from mid-September onwards, so the autumn half-term is a sensible target date for completing the process. Universities tend to start considering applications as soon as they arrive, so some early applicants will already be holding offers from universities. Other universities will not start making offers until after all applications are in, so offers will be sent out after January 15.

Next steps

Once your application has been processed by UCAS, you will receive an email confirming that it has been sent to your chosen universities and summarising what will happen next. The email will also confirm your personal ID, which you can use to access "Track", the online system that allows you to follow the progress of your application. Check all the details carefully: you have 14 days to contact UCAS to correct any errors.

After that, it is just a matter of waiting for universities to make their decisions, which can take days, weeks or even months. Some obviously see an advantage in being the first to make an offer – it is a memorable moment to be reassured that at least one of your chosen institutions wants you. Others take much longer, perhaps because they have so many good applications to consider, or maybe because they are waiting to see which of their applicants withdraw when Oxford and Cambridge make their offers. Universities are asked to make all their decisions by the end of March, and most have done so long before that.

Interviews

Unless you are applying for a professional training degree in health or education that brings you into direct contact with the public, the chances are you will not have a selection interview. For prospective medics, vets, dentists or teachers, a face-to-face assessment of your suitability will be crucial to your chances of success. Likewise in the performing arts, the interview may be as important as your exam grades. Cambridge still interviews most applicants in all subjects and Oxford interviews about 40% to 45% of applicants, see Chapter 13, while a few of the other top universities also see a significant proportion. But the expansion of higher education has made it impractical to interview everyone, and many admissions experts are sceptical about interviews.

What has become more common, however, is the "sales" interview, where the university is really selling itself to the candidate. There may still be testing questions, but the admissions staff have already made their minds up and are actually trying to persuade you to accept an offer. Indeed, you will probably be given a clear indication at the end of the interview that an offer is on its way. The technique seems to work, perhaps because you have invested time and nervous energy in a sometimes lengthy trip, as well as acquiring a more detailed impression of both the department and the university.

The difficulty can come in spotting which type of interview is which. The "genuine" ones require extensive preparation, revisiting your personal statement and reading beyond the exam syllabus. Impressions count for a lot, so dress smartly – even if your interview is being held via video call – and make sure that you are on time. Have a question of your own ready, as well as being prepared to give answers.

While you would not want to appear ignorant at a sales interview, lengthy preparation might be a waste of valuable time during a period of revision. Naturally, you should err on the side of caution, but if your predicted grades are well above the standard offer and the subject is not one that normally requires an interview, it is likely that the invitation is a sales pitch. It is still worth going, unless you have changed your mind about the application.

Offers

When your chosen universities respond to your application, there will be one of three answers:
» Unconditional Offer (U): This used to be a possibility only if you applied after satisfying the entrance requirements – usually if you were applying as a mature student, while on a gap year, after resitting exams or, in Scotland, after completing Highers. However, a number of universities competing for bright students now make unconditional offers to those who are predicted high grades – just how high will depend on the university. If you are fortunate (and able) enough to receive one, do not assume that grades are no longer important because they may be taken into consideration when you apply for jobs as a graduate.

» Conditional Offer (C): The vast majority of students will still receive conditional offers, where each university offers a place subject to you achieving set grades or points on the UCAS tariff.
» Rejection (R): You do not have the right qualifications or have lost out to stronger competition.

English universities were banned from making "conditional unconditional" offers during the pandemic until September 2021. This type of offer – which only becomes unconditional once an applicant accepts it as their firm choice – was the focus of controversy pre-Covid, with more than 20 universities that were making the highest proportions of conditional unconditional offers named and shamed by the education secretary of the time, who argued that it was unethical to restrict such offers to those who made the university their first choice.

Universities UK (UUK), which represents the sector, published its code of fair admissions in 2022, setting out how processes must support "student choice". The code says that universities should not make conditional unconditional offers, or offers with significantly lower grade requirements based on applicants making their institution a firm choice. Conditional unconditional offer-making has since fallen from a high of 15.7% of all offers made in 2020 to 3.3% in 2021.

Any remaining unconditional offers might tempt a candidate to lower his or her sights and accept a place that would not have been their first choice otherwise. As long as this is not the case, however, there is no reason to spurn such an offer if it comes, as long as you do not take your foot off the pedal in the run-up to exams.

If you have chosen wisely, you should have more than one offer to choose from, so you will be required to pick your favourite as your firm acceptance – known as UF if it was an unconditional offer and CF if it was conditional. Candidates with conditional offers can also accept a second offer, with lower grades, as an insurance choice (CI). You must then decline any other offers that you have.

You do not have to make an insurance choice – indeed, you may decline all your offers if you have changed your mind about your career path or regret your course decisions. But most people prefer the security of a back-up route into higher education if their grades fall short. Some 27,825 took up their insurance choice in 2020 – around 6% of the total number of the admission cycle's acceptances and a decline of 11% compared with 2019's insurance choice acceptances. You must be sure that your firm acceptance is definitely your first choice because you will be allocated a place automatically if you meet the university's conditions. You cannot change your mind at this stage because UCAS rules will not then allow a switch to your insurance choice.

The only way round those rules, unless your results are better than your highest offer (see Adjustment, below), is through direct contact with the universities concerned. Your firm acceptance institution has to be prepared to release you so that your new choice can award you a place in Clearing. Neither is under any obligation to do so but, in practice, it is rare for a university to insist that a student joins against his or her wishes.

UCAS Extra

If things do go wrong and you receive five rejections, that need not be the end of your higher education ambitions. From late February until early July, you have another chance through UCAS Extra, a listing of courses that still have vacancies after the initial round of offers. Extra is sometimes dismissed (wrongly) as a repository of second-rate courses. In fact, even in the boom years for applications, most Russell Group universities still have courses listed in a wide variety of subjects.

You will be notified if you are eligible for Extra and can then select courses marked as available on the UCAS website. You will be able to submit a new personal statement for Extra. Applications are made, one at a time, through UCAS Track. If you do not receive an offer, or you choose to decline one, you can continue applying for other courses. About half of those applying through Extra normally find a place. The numbers using Extra in 2020 declined for the fourth consecutive year to 4,450, but it remains a valuable route for those who need it. Why wait for the uncertainty of Clearing if there are places available on a course that you want?

Results Day

Rule No 1 on results day is to be at home, or at least within easy communication – this is not the day to rely on intermittent wi-fi reception in a far-flung location. Not that you need to be at home to wait for the post or look for your name on a sixth-form noticeboard; Track has removed the agony of opening the envelope or scanning a results list. On the morning of A-level results day, the system informs those who have already won a place on their chosen course.

If you get the grades stipulated in your conditional offer, the process should work smoothly, and you can begin celebrating. Track will let you know as soon as your place is confirmed, and the paperwork will arrive in a day or two. You can phone the university to double check, but it should not be necessary.

If the results are not what you hoped – and particularly if you just miss your grades – you need to be on the phone and taking advice from your school or college. In a year when results are better than expected, some universities will stick to the letter of their offers, perhaps refusing to accept your AAC grades when they had demanded ABB. Growing numbers will forgive a dropped grade to take a candidate who is regarded as promising, rather than go into Clearing to recruit an unknown quantity. Admissions staff may be persuadable – particularly if there are extenuating personal circumstances. Try to get a teacher to support your case and be persistent. Showing commitment is a good thing.

If your results are lower than predicted, one option is to ask for papers to be re-marked, as growing numbers do each year. The school may ask for a whole batch to be re-marked, and you should ensure that your chosen universities know this. If your grades improve as a result, the university will review its decision, but, if by then it has filled all its places, you may have to wait until next year to start.

If you took Scottish Highers, you will have had your results for more than a week by the time the A-level grades are published. If you missed your grades, there is no need to wait for A-levels before you begin approaching universities. Admissions staff at English universities may not wish to commit themselves before they see results from south of the border, but Scottish universities will be filling places immediately.

Adjustment

If your grades are better than those demanded by your first-choice university, there is an opportunity to "trade up". The adjustment period runs from when you receive your results until August 31, and you can only use it for five 24-hour periods during that period, so there is no time to waste.

First, go into the Track system and click on "Register for Adjustment" and then contact your preferred institutions to find another place. If none is available, or you decide not to move, your initial offer will remain open.

The number of students switching universities in this way has not increased as much as many observers expected, perhaps because Clearing has become much more flexible. Indeed, following several big drops, numbers declined by 56% in 2020, but there were still 260 successful candidates.

The process has become an established part of the system and, without the previous restrictions on the number of students they could recruit, many leading universities see it as a good source of talented undergraduates. UCAS does not publish a breakdown of which universities take part, but it is known that many students successfully go back to institutions that had rejected them at the initial application stage. Even if you are eligible for Adjustment, you may decide to stick with the offer you have, but it is worth at least exploring your options.

Clearing

If results morning did not elicit a "yay, I got in!" moment, put plan B into action and find a university place through Clearing. There will be plenty of options at a good range of universities. In 2021, more than 56,000 students secured their university places through UCAS Clearing, with around 15,000 using the service without having applied to university earlier in the year. Students can also use clearing to change their mind and UCAS analysis revealed 14,760 of UK 18-year-olds used this route to switch courses in the 2022 admissions cycle. Of those students, 11,800 (80%) secured a new place at an equivalent or higher tariff university.

Contrary to popular belief Clearing does not open for the first time on A-level results day, it begins on July 5, International Baccalaureate results day, and runs until October 19. The busiest day, however, will be August 18, when A-level students find out their grades. As long as you are not holding any offers and you have not withdrawn your application, you are eligible automatically. You will be sent a Clearing number via Track to quote to universities.

With recruitment restrictions lifted, universities that used to regard their absence from Clearing as a point of pride are appearing in the Clearing vacancy lists, and candidates will see options at the coveted research-led institutions included. Certain courses have more availability than others though, and more universities are seeking to expand particularly in arts, social sciences and business subjects. Some subjects, such as medicine and dentistry, do not show up in Clearing as they are so oversubscribed. Only a handful of universities do not take part these days, including Oxford, Cambridge, Imperial, the London School of Economics, and St Andrews.

The most popular courses may fill up quickly, but many remain open up to and beyond the start of the academic year. And, at least at the start of the process, the range of courses with vacancies is much wider than in Extra.

There are now two ways of entering Clearing: the traditional method of ringing universities that still have vacancies, or by signing up for the service in which up to five universities approach candidates with suitable grades for one of their courses. The latter, newer way of entering begins with an email from UCAS issuing a code word that universities will use when they make contact with applicants on Results Day or later. UCAS advises students to approach universities themselves in any case, but the new system may take some of the anxiety out of Clearing.

On the basis of making your own approaches, the first step is to trawl through the lists on the UCAS website, and elsewhere, before ringing the university offering the course that appeals most, and where you have a realistic chance of a place – do not waste time on courses where the standard offer is far above your grades. Universities have all hands on deck running Clearing hotlines and are adept at dealing with lots of calls in a short period, but even so you can spend a long time trying the phone while the most desirable places are beginning to disappear.

If you can't get through, send an email setting out your grades and the course that interests you, but keep trying by phone, too. Schools and colleges open on Results Day, and teachers should be willing to help with these calls, especially if you are in a panic. A good way of managing the calls is to let the teacher ring, get through to the university and then pass the phone to the applicant. At the end of calls do a round-up of next steps, as in the melee it is possible to misunderstand or forget things, such as requests for more information or follow-up forms to be filled out.

Wise students will not to have waited for Results Day to draw up a list of possible Clearing targets. They will have had their list researched and ready to deploy if the time comes in advance. Many universities publish lists of courses that are likely to be in Clearing on their websites from the start of August. Reconsider some of the courses you mulled over when making your original application, or others at your chosen universities that had lower entrance requirements. But beware of switching to another subject simply because you have the right grades – you still have to sustain your interest and be capable of succeeding over three or more years. Many of the students who drop out of degrees are those who chose the wrong course in a rush during Clearing.

In short, start your search immediately if you find yourself in Clearing, and act decisively, but do not panic. You can make as many approaches as you like, until you are accepted on the course of your choice. Remember that if you changed your personal statement for applications in Extra, this will be the one that goes to any universities that you approach in Clearing, so it may be difficult to return to the subjects in your original application.

Most of the available vacancies will appear in Clearing lists, but some of the universities towards the top of the league tables may have a limited number of openings that they choose not to advertise – either for reasons of status or because they do not want the administrative burden of fielding large numbers of calls to fill a handful of places. If there is a course that you find particularly attractive – especially if you have good grades and are applying late – it may be worth making a speculative call. You may be on the spot at just the right moment.

What are the alternatives?

If your results are lower than expected and there is nothing you want in Clearing, there are several things you can do. The first is to re-sit one or more subjects. The modular nature of most courses means that you will have a clear idea of what you need to do to get better grades. You can go back to school or college or try a "crammer". Although some colleges have a good success rate with re-takes, you have to be highly focused and realistic about the likely improvements. And some of the most competitive courses, such as medicine, may demand higher grades for a second application.

Other options are to get a job and study part-time, or to take a break from studying and return later in your career. You may have considered an apprenticeship before applying to university; the number and variety are growing all the time, so it may be worth another look. The UCAS Progress service provides information on apprenticeship opportunities post-16 and has a search tool for higher and degree apprenticeship vacancies.

The part-time route can be arduous – many young people find a job enough to handle without the extra burden of academic work. But others find it just the combination they need for a fulfilling life. It all depends on your job, your social life and your commitment to the subject you will study. Many universities now have a majority of mature students, so you need not be out of place if this is your chosen route.

Taking a gap year

The other popular option is to take a gap year. In most years, about 7% of applicants defer their entry until the following year while they travel or do voluntary or paid work. But in 2021 the overall number of students postponing their starts rose by 12% to 28,880 – the highest figure in a decade, most of them school-leavers. A whole industry has grown up around tailor-made activities, many in Asia, Africa or Latin America. Some have been criticised for doing more for the organisers than the underprivileged communities that they purport to assist, but there are programmes that are useful and character-building, as well as safe. Most of the overseas programmes are not cheap, but raising the money can be part of the experience.

Various organisations can help you find voluntary work. Some examples include vInspired (**www.vinspired.com**) and Plan my Gap Year (**www.planmygapyear.co.uk**). Voluntary Service Overseas (**www.vsointernational.org**) works mainly with older volunteers but has an offshoot, run with five other volunteering organisations, International Citizen Service (**www.volunteerics.org**), that places 18–25-year-olds around the world.

The alternative is to stay closer to home and make your contribution through organisations like Volunteering Matters (**http://volunteeringmatters.org.uk**) or to take a job that will make higher education more affordable when the time comes. Work placements can be casual or structured, such as the Year in Industry Scheme (**www.etrust.org.uk**). Sponsorship is also available, mainly to those wishing to study science, engineering or business. Buyer beware: we cannot vouch for any of these and you need to be clear whether the aim is to make money or to plump up your CV. If it is the second, you may end up spending money, not saving it.

Many admissions staff are happy to facilitate gap years because they think it makes for more mature, rounded students. The longer-term benefits may also be an advantage in the graduate employment market. Both university admissions officers and employers look for evidence that candidates have more about them than academic ability. The experience you gain on a gap year can help you develop many of the attributes they are looking for, such as interpersonal, organisational and teamwork skills, leadership, creativity, experience of new cultures or work environments, and enterprise.

There are subjects – maths in particular – that discourage a break because it takes too long to pick up study skills where you left off. From the student's point of view, you should also bear in mind that a gap year postpones the moment at which you embark on a career. This may be important if your course is a long one, such as medicine or architecture.

If you are considering a gap year, it makes sense to apply for a deferred place, rather than waiting for your results before applying. The application form has a section for deferments. That allows you to sort out your immediate future before you start travelling or working and leaves you the option of changing your mind if circumstances change.

Useful websites

The essential website for making an application is, of course, that of UCAS:
www.ucas.com/undergraduate/applying-to-university
For applications to music conservatoires: **www.ucas.com/conservatoires**
For advice on your personal statement:
www.ucas.com/ucas/16-18-choices/search-and-apply/writing-ucas-progress-personal-statement

Gap years
For links to volunteering opportunities in the UK: **www.do-it.org**
For links to many gap year organisations: **www.yearoutgroup.org**

6 Where Students Come From

Towards fairer admissions

More applications were received and more young people admitted to universities from disadvantaged backgrounds in 2022 than in any previous year. The application rate from 18-year-olds in the 20% of postcodes in England (Quintile 1) with the lowest progression to higher education stood at 28.8%, up from 27% in 2021 and more than 10 percentage points higher than in 2013. This compares to an application rate of 59.5% in the quintile of postcodes with the highest university participation, the gap between the two extremes at its narrowest ever.

The numbers translated into 31,890 students entering university last autumn from Quintile 1, up from 30,280 in 2021 and 26,000 in 2019, 5% and 23% higher respectively. In Scotland, the application rate in the 20% of postcodes with the highest levels of deprivation stood at 21.3%. So far, so fair.

A less encouraging statistic also published in September 2022 showed a 23% rise in the number of students withdrawing from higher education within a year of starting. Just shy of 40,000 students dropped out compared to around 32,000 the year before, according to Student Loans Company data. This attrition rate – costly not just in terms of wasted money, but also wasted time and shattered ambitions – should come as no great surprise, given the cohort who began their studies in September 2021 had largely chosen universities without visiting them, had not taken any A-level examinations, and had suffered more than any other school exit cohort from the effects of the pandemic.

However, in the context of achieving fairer admissions to university, of greater concern and an ongoing challenge will be the likelihood that among those 40,000 withdrawals are likely to be a disproportionate number of students drawn from disadvantaged backgrounds – those hit hardest also by the impacts of the cost of living crisis.

And there is more trouble coming down the track. The Covid pandemic, which hit in March 2020, has disproportionately affected the education of the socially disadvantaged and the education system, from primary schools to universities, will be wrestling with the consequences of that for the next decade or more. The first Standard Assessment Tests (SATs) to be taken in three years showed the widest disadvantage gap since 2012, according to Department for Education figures published in September 2022.

The gap summarises the attainment gap between disadvantaged and all other pupils. Having shrunk year on year from 3.23 in 2012 to 2.91 in 2019, it rose to 3.21 in 2022. National analyses of GCSEs/A-levels and other public examinations taken in summer 2022 are also expected to show that, while the achievements of most children bore some resemblance to the results achieved pre-pandemic in 2019, the attainment gap between children from disadvantaged backgrounds and their more advantaged peers has widened considerably.

For universities (particularly the highly selective ones) that are under pressure to diversify their intakes, these trends are worrying, putting a huge stress on the contextual offers system and other initiatives to work efficiently in identifying the students likely to thrive who might not have the quality of results at first sight to prove that.

John Blake, the new director for Fair Access and Participation at the Office for Students, warned in September 2022 that in a "nation recovering from the coronavirus pandemic, the greatest disruption of our society since the Second World War, and now also dealing with the impacts of global crises on inflation and the cost of living, [there is] the very real risk that the cumulative effect of all those impacts may cost us, as a society, decades of progress on social mobility."

In outlining plans for a new "equality of opportunity risk register" for universities to sign up to, Blake put universities on notice: "We will hold universities and colleges accountable for undertaking and evaluating the interventions they have committed to, ensuring that they are taking action to tackle risks to equality of opportunity." Pandemic or no, universities will be expected to maintain the progress of recent years towards a fairer admissions process.

The table

Five editions on from its introduction, therefore, our social inclusion ranking is more pertinent than ever. As well as providing a benchmark by which to measure change going forward, it also shines a light on admissions from some of the underrepresented groups on campuses and their subsequent prospects and performance. Today's applicants want to know about the composition of the student body they will be joining, and the tables on pages 98-101 help them in that quest.

We have two social inclusion rankings; one for England and Wales, with Scottish institutions ranked separately on account of a different measure of social deprivation – the Scottish Index of Multiple Deprivation (SIMD) – which captures better the position in the 15 Scottish universities than the POLAR4 (Participation of Local Areas) measure used for England and Wales.

SIMD and POLAR4 are not directly comparable: one measures deprivation across several criteria, the other participation in higher education only. The two universities in Northern Ireland, Queen's Belfast and Ulster, are excluded from the ranking owing to differences in the country's school system which has a high proportion of selective grammar schools, making comparisons with the rest of the UK on social mix invalid via the methodology adopted in this guide.

We have once again resisted the suggestion to include some or all the measures contained within the social inclusion tables as part of our wider academic ranking. There is good reason for this: a university with a poor record for social inclusion may still have an excellent record for teaching and research. It might be a very good university with an outstanding global and national reputation, but with a socially narrow recruitment profile. By using the two multi-indicator, multi-institution tables that we publish together (alongside the relevant subject table) prospective students can identify the universities which are the best fit for them academically and where they might feel most at home socially.

The full list of equally-weighted indicators used in *The Times* and *The Sunday Times* social inclusion ranking for England and Wales is:

- » recruitment from non-selective state schools
- » recruitment from all ethnic minorities
- » a measurement of the black achievement gap
- » recruitment from deprived areas (using POLAR4)
- » a measurement of the deprived areas dropout gap
- » recruitment of white, working-class males
- » recruitment of first-generation students
- » recruitment of mature students (those 21 or older on admission)
- » recruitment of disabled students

For Scottish institutions, there is no measure of the deprived areas dropout gap and the deprived areas measure is based on SIMD, rather than POLAR4, as outlined above.

With the exception of the admissions data for non-selective state schools, all the other indicators are in the public domain. The uniqueness of this social inclusion ranking is in combining these several strands of data together to build an overall picture of the social mix at each institution, and to measure university performance in two key areas: black achievement, and whether students from the most deprived areas fail to complete their courses than those recruited from more advantaged districts.

The table is presented in a format that displays the raw data in all instances. No adjustment is made for university location, so a university with a strong, local recruitment pattern in an area of low ethnic minority population is unlikely do well on the measure covering the ethnicity of the intake. This was most notably the case with Wrexham Glyndŵr, which is for the fifth successive year the most socially inclusive university in the UK according to our ranking but had just 6.1% of its 2021 intake drawn from ethnic minorities.

However, by combining the indicators using a common statistical technique known as z-scoring, we have ensured no single indicator has a disproportionate effect on the overall total for each university. The totals for each university were transformed to a scale with 1,000 for the top score and the performance of all universities measured relative to that of the university ranked No 1.

Just as with our academic ranking, the organisations providing the raw data for the table are not involved in the process of aggregation, and are not responsible for any conclusion or inferences we have made. Every care has been taken to ensure the accuracy of the table and accompanying analysis, but no responsibility can be taken for errors or omissions.

The indicators used and what can be learned from them are outlined in turn below.

Non-selective state school admissions

For many years, the Higher Education Statistics Agency (HESA) has published as part of its annual performance indicators, the proportion of students admitted to universities from all state schools. Among the entrants included in this proportion are those attending the 163 state grammars in England and the voluntary grammars in Northern Ireland. However, state school admissions to all universities stripped of the academically-selective grammar school sector are not published elsewhere. Removing the grammar school sector from the equation reveals the proportion of students admitted to each university in 2020-21 from the largely non-selective state secondary schools (comprehensives and most academies) attended by around 80% of university applicants.

This is the indicator that has seen greatest change over the four editions of the social inclusion ranking. There are now just three universities – two fewer than last year – where fewer than half the students admitted came from comprehensives and academies: Imperial College London (45.5%, up 3.1 percentage points on last year), Cambridge (48.5%, up 0.7 percentage points) and Durham (49.1%, up 0.1 percentage points). At the other end of the non-selective state school admissions ranking, Teesside, Bolton and Newman University, Birmingham, all admitted 99% of their students from this educational background, closely followed by West of Scotland (98.7%), and Wrexham Glyndŵr and Bedfordshire (both 98.5%).

Over the five editions of this ranking, the number of universities where less than half the students are recruited from non-selective state schools has halved, and Oxford has removed itself from that cohort completely for the first time this year, with 52.2% of students drawn from comprehensives and academies in 2020-21. This figure is up 6.6 percentage points since last year, 9.7 percentage points over two years, and 12.8 percentage points from our first ranking in 2018 – a sharply accelerating rate of change. Cambridge, which admitted 40.1% of its students from non-selective state schools in our 2018 table, has increased the proportion by a still significant 8.4 percentage points over the intervening period, but now lags behind its principal domestic rival. The rate of change in the school backgrounds of entrants to Oxbridge is vastly outstripping most of its highly-selective rivals – and arguably directly impacting upon them.

While it is true that some of the displaced students educated in independent schools are looking to America, the prohibitive cost means other UK universities are seeing a significant upturn in recruitment of privately educated students. So, as the proportion of privately educated students at Oxford has fallen 6.5 percentage points in background data for this year's social inclusion ranking from 37.8% to 31.3% of the intake (and at Cambridge it is down to 30%), the proportion of privately educated students admitted to Durham has gone up 1.9 percentage points from 36.5% to 38.4%, while at St Andrews the proportion is up from 36.2% to 36.9%. Exeter has seen the proportion rise from 30.6% in our 2018 ranking to 34.5% now. For the first time, neither Oxford nor Cambridge feature in the top five UK university destinations for the privately educated.

When Dorothy Byrne, president of Murray Edwards College, Cambridge, said in September 2022 that the proportion of state-educated students admitted to Cambridge should match their distribution in UK schools (where the state/independent split is 93%/7%, aged 11-16), it was catnip to those who felt privately educated applicants were suddenly getting a rum deal at our two oldest universities. Her comments are nowhere near to the reality at Oxbridge (even with the recent changes), but our latest data appears to back up the wider trend towards admitting more students from the non-selective state sector at our most selective universities.

Just 17 universities (five fewer than last year) now take less than 70% of their students from non-selective state schools; 12 of the 17 are members of the highly selective research-led Russell Group. The vast majority of universities (98 in all, three more than last year) admit more than 80% of their students from this demographic.

Ethnic minority admissions

Data gathered from the 2021 admissions cycle by UCAS shows the proportion of entrants to each university drawn from black, Asian, mixed and other ethnic minorities.

Eight London universities feature in the top 10, all with at least 67.8% of their students drawn from ethnic minorities – ranking behind Bradford, our University of the Year for Social Inclusion in 2019, which recruited 86.3% of its students from ethnic minorities, and Aston (85.6%). The most ethnically diverse London universities are SOAS (81.7%), City, University of London (81.3%), Queen Mary (77%), Brunel London (76.7%) and St George's (76.5%). Queen Mary, London is by some distance the most ethnically diverse of the Russell Group student communities and continues to lead the way in the social inclusion ranking overall among the 24-member group.

The least ethnically diverse university is the Royal Agricultural University, based in Cirencester, Gloucestershire, where 1.4% of the intake was drawn from ethnic minorities in 2021, followed by Highlands and Islands (3.3%), Bishop Grosseteste (3.7%) and Harper Adams (4.1%). Two of the bottom four on this measure are institutions offering largely land-based courses, traditionally attracting low ethnic minority participation. All four universities are in areas of the country with relatively small ethnic minority populations.

Black achievement gap

One of the two university output measures in the social inclusion ranking, the data here is among the most arresting in the survey. We were unable to create a reliable measure of the black achievement gap in 11 universities – Abertay, Aberystwyth, Bishop Grosseteste, Harper Adams, Hartpury, Highlands and Islands, Norwich Arts, Plymouth Marjon, Queen Margaret, Royal Agricultural and Stirling – because there were simply too few black graduates for effective analysis over the two-year period 2019-21.

Where we could compare the proportions of white and black students gaining first-class or 2:1 degrees, the negative gap in achievement between the groups was at least 20 percentage points in 45 institutions. While this represents a significant improvement over last year, when 60 universities saw a greater than 20 percentage point discrepancy, we need more data before we can be confident of a trend rather than a quirk arising from the relatively small numbers of students involved in the measure of black achievement in all institutions.

The gap was commendably narrow (less than 10 percentage points) in 17 institutions, four more than last year. In none of them did black students achieve as well – or better even – than their white counterparts (although Glasgow came close).

The universities with the widest negative percentage point gap for black achievement (showing low attainment by black students) were Buckingham (-39.9%), Canterbury Christ Church (-37.5%), Glasgow Caledonian (-36.8%), Solent (-35.7%), and York St John (-35.5%). Buckingham, Canterbury Christ Church and York St John were in last year's bottom five also.

The universities where black students performed the best in relation to their white counterparts were Glasgow (-0.1%), University College London (-2.1%), Imperial College London (-2.5%), the London School of Economics (LSE, -3.2%) and Essex (-3.9%). Four of the top five places here are taken by Russell Group institutions, so often lagging in other areas of the social inclusion ranking, offering evidence that while the numbers ticking a social inclusion box in our highly-selective universities might be lower, once admitted their levels of achievement are hard to tell apart from those drawn from more traditional university-going backgrounds.

White working-class males

There have been countless reports in recent years about the educational underachievement of this group of children. It begins in primary school, accelerates in secondary school, and reaches its logical conclusion with significant underrepresentation at university. As with other measures in our social inclusion ranking, it is not fair to expect universities to correct the systemic failings of the wider education system.

Nevertheless, some universities offer significantly more opportunities to this often excluded social group. Those doing most are Sheffield Hallam and Plymouth Marjon (both 11.9% of entrants in 2021), Highlands and Islands (11.7%), Abertay (11.2%), Staffordshire and Liverpool John Moores (both 10.8%), Liverpool Hope (10.2%) and Teesside, our University of the Year for Social Inclusion for 2022 (10%), see their individual profiles, Chapter 14. These are the only universities where white working-class boys make up over one in 10 or more of the student population.

At the opposite end of the spectrum, at these five institutions white male students with a working-class background make up between 1 in 111 and 1 in 59 of students on campus: Buckingham (0.9% and the university with the lowest proportion for the second successive year), St George's London (1.5%), University College London (1.6%) and Suffolk and Cambridge (both 1.7%). While more common than unicorns, white working-class men are a rare sighting here and at the 43 universities where they make up fewer than one in 25 of the student population. This group's access to higher education continues to be one of the more pressing areas in need of action.

Deprived areas

This data is drawn from 2020-21 and looks at the home postcode of all university recruits, putting them into one of five pots, according to the level of participation in higher education.

For England and Wales, this indicator records the proportion of students recruited from Quintile 1 (of POLAR4 data) – the 20% of areas that have the lowest participation rates in higher education. In Scotland, this indicator records the proportion of students recruited from postcodes which fall into the bottom 20% of postcodes with the highest levels of deprivation measured to the Scottish Index of Multiple Deprivation (SIMD20).

Like all indicators, this one has limitations, chief among which is that London overall has high participation rates in higher education relative to the rest of the UK, so very few London-based university entrants fall into Quintile 1 (Q1), meaning that London universities score relatively poorly across the board on this measure, even if they have a socially diverse intake of students. (The strength of performance of many London institutions in other indicators – for example, high recruitment from ethnic minorities and a narrow black achievement gap – confirms this to be the case.)

Teesside (31.1%) and Sunderland (29.9%), which held the title of our University of the Year for Social Inclusion in 2021, record the highest proportions of students recruited from Q1. Both institutions recruit heavily within their immediate surrounds, the northeast being the English region with the lowest participation rate in higher education. Hull (28.8%) is ranked third on this measure. Wrexham Glyndŵr and Bishop Grosseteste (both 28.2%) are also in the top five for Q1 recruitment.

At the other end of the scale, London universities account for four of the five institutions with the lowest recruitment from Q1, headed by SOAS (2%) and followed by Royal Agricultural (2.8%), City, University of London (2.9%), Queen Mary, London (3%) and St George's, London (3.3%). Oxford, in particular, shows a sharp improvement on this measure with the proportion of Q1 students rising from 4.2% in our previous ranking to 6.4% this year, an increase of 52% albeit on a low base.

In Scotland, the highest rates of recruitment of students falling into SIMD20 are to be found at West of Scotland (29.9%) and Glasgow Caledonian (23%), while the two Aberdeen universities, Robert Gordon (6.1%) and Aberdeen (7.9%), have the lowest rates. Both Edinburgh (9.1%) and St Andrews (10.2%) see their proportions of SIMD20 students fall back in this year's ranking from 10.8% and 11% respectively.

Deprived areas dropout gap

This indicator is used in the England and Wales social inclusion ranking only – and there is a strong correlation between performing well on this measure and a high ranking for social inclusion overall. Drawing upon the same POLAR4 data as above, it measures student outcomes from each of the five social quintiles. The proportion of students dropping out who were recruited from Q1 (the one-fifth of postcodes where university participation is the lowest) is compared to the proportion dropping out who were recruited from Quintiles 2, 3, 4 and 5 (Q2-5). A negative score in this section of the ranking indicates a higher proportion of students is dropping out from Q1 than those recruited from areas where more children go to university. Already underrepresented in the student population overall, this measure identifies those universities where Q1 students who do get in are more likely to fail to see their courses through.

The universities with the biggest negative percentage point gap for deprived area dropouts – where a bigger proportion of students from the most deprived areas fail to complete their courses than among the rest of the student population – are Liverpool Hope (-9%), Chichester (-7%), Cumbria and Falmouth (both -6%), and York St John (-5.7%). This is especially concerning for Liverpool Hope and Chichester, which are among the 20 universities to admit most students from Q1. Weakness on this measure is reflected in the overall social inclusion ranking for these five universities, which lie between 47th (Cumbria) and 94th (Falmouth) overall.

As Chris Millward, Professor of Practice in Education Policy at the University of Birmingham, observed in a blog for the Higher Education Policy Institute in November 2021: "The promotion of equality of opportunity is only meaningful if it improves outcomes: there is no point to it otherwise, let alone spending more than half a billion pounds on it each year as we do in English higher education today."

The universities performing most strongly in this aspect of widening participation, where a smaller proportion of students from Q1 drop out compared to the rest of the student population as whole, are Suffolk (+7%), Ravensbourne and Bedfordshire (both +6%), Goldsmiths, London (+5.9%) and West London (+4%) – all of them ranked in the top 30 of the social inclusion ranking overall.

First generation students

This measure records the proportion of students recruited from homes where neither parent attended university. This indicator is considered one of the most informative in assessing the overall inclusiveness of university recruitment strategies. Once again, performance varies considerably from those where 60% or more of their students identify as first generation – Newman (72.2%), Wolverhampton (69.5%), Bradford (67.4%), Sunderland (61.9%), Staffordshire (60.9%) and Bishop Grosseteste (60.7%) – to those where fewer than a quarter of students come from homes where parents did not go to university – Cambridge and Oxford (both 16.3%), St Andrews (18.1%), Edinburgh (19.5%), Durham (23.4%), Bath (23.7%) and Bristol (24.3%).

Among the universities admitting fewest first-generation students this year, only Edinburgh and Bath were admitting fewer than recorded in last year's social inclusion ranking. So, here again slow progress is being made. Of course, as more and more students attend university and, in turn, become parents themselves, the proportions of first-generation students will eventually go down across the board.

Mature students

Mature students are returners to education and often win places with "life" qualifications, rather than A-levels. This immediately makes the group more diverse than the young entrants, who come mostly straight from school or via a gap year.

The age of the student population can have a major impact on the social scene on campus. Older students, particularly those with partners (and even children!) are less likely to be found clubbing or propping up the bar late into the evening. Universities with a very small number proportion of mature undergraduates – the LSE (1.4%), Loughborough (1.8%), Oxford (2.5%), Bath (2.7%) and Durham (3.1%) – are likely to have a livelier campus social life than Suffolk (86.6% mature admissions), London Metropolitan (78.4%), Buckinghamshire New (74.9%), Bolton (74.8%) and Trinity St David (73.6%).

Disabled students

This indicator measures the proportion of all students in higher education in receipt of Disability Support Allowance (DSA). It is part of the bigger HESA dataset on widening participation, published in February 2022 and is based on data from the 2020-21 academic year.

As with the other indicators, there is a significant difference between the universities at the top – Wrexham Glyndŵr where HESA records 19.8% of students as being in receipt of DSA, Harper Adams (17.7%) and Arts London (17.3%) – and those at the bottom – West of Scotland (1.1%), Glasgow Caledonian and Aston (both 2.2%).

The overall picture

Social inclusion in British universities is evolving and considered a priority in all institutions. However, because of the different starting points for each university, the picture on the ground varies considerably from place to place. Oxford and Cambridge are moving at pace on a number of our measures, but they are not shifting in our ranking. Indeed, Cambridge is further adrift at the foot of the table than ever. This is because our ranking reflects relative performance and the whole university sector is making strides in improving social diversity on campus. This is a good thing and the widening use of contextual offers gives this process a chance of continuing despite the challenges presented by the pandemic which have impacted the academic achievement of the disadvantaged disproportionately.

So, what do this year's social inclusion rankings tell you? It is not possible to appear near the top of them if an institution is only achieving well on one or two of the measures of social inclusion that *The Times* and *The Sunday Times* have chosen. Success in the tables comes from broadly-based achievement in recruiting from areas of society least represented in higher education, and then seeing those students progress with their degrees and achieve well. Appearing near the foot of the tables does not mean social diversity is a non-consideration, simply that the numbers recruited from underrepresented groups are vastly lower compared to institutions ranked higher.

A different set of metrics looking at the same subject matter might produce a very different looking table, which is why it is necessary to understand what is being measured here. Based on the measures we have chosen the top three in the academic rankings – Oxford, St Andrews and Cambridge – appear at the bottom (or second bottom in Scotland in St Andrews' case) of our social inclusion rankings. Wrexham Glyndŵr, placed 120th in our academic ranking of 132 institutions, is top in England and Wales for social inclusion. Fifteen of the bottom 20 universities for social inclusion in England and Wales (and two of the bottom three in Scotland) are highly selective Russell Group universities.

Used in conjunction, our academic and social inclusion rankings provide an intriguing insight to likely academic and professional success, the quality of the student experience, and the social, ethnic and educational mix of students likely to be found in the university lecture theatres and the after-hours clubs and bars. But whatever the student recruitment profile of the university you are considering, don't decide where to apply on that basis alone. If applicants from non-traditional backgrounds don't apply to those ranked lower for social inclusion, then it only makes it easier for the status quo to prevail.

Social Inclusion Ranking for England and Wales

Rank	Last year's rank	Institution	State educated (non-grammar) (%)	Ethnic minorities (%)	Black achievement gap (%)	White working-class males (%)	Low participation areas (%)	Low participation areas dropout gap (%)	First generation students (%)	Disabled (%)	Mature (%)	Total
1	1	Wrexham Glyndŵr	98.5	6.1	-19.4	6.3	28.2	n/a	59.6	19.8	69.5	1000
2	3	Plymouth Marjon	95.4	6.8	n/a	11.9	16.1	1	56.4	16.1	34.3	917
3	4	Teesside	99	14.7	-14.6	10.0	31.1	-2.6	57.3	10.5	47.9	892
4	2	Bishop Grosseteste	94.5	3.7	n/a	5.8	28.2	1	60.7	15.9	32.9	891
5	=12	Bradford	95	86.3	-9.5	1.9	10.0	-1.7	67.4	10.5	28.7	794
6	9	Sunderland	96.1	16.7	-26.3	7.5	29.9	-2.2	61.9	5.7	68.6	790
7	5	Bolton	99	29.4	-23.2	4.2	17.5	1	57.5	8.7	74.8	788
8	15	Wolverhampton	97.4	52.0	-18.1	4.4	21.2	-4.3	69.5	8.1	48.1	784
9	6	Staffordshire	96.3	16.5	-32.8	10.8	24.6	-1.9	60.9	10.1	39.1	781
10	=12	Newman	99	45.4	-31.9	3.8	21.4	-3	72.2	12.6	43.4	778
11	7	Suffolk	97	18.6	-27.5	1.7	20.1	7	57.8	4.3	86.6	770
12	14	East London	96.9	66.1	-15.9	3.0	6.4	2.7	56.7	7.2	57.1	767
13	=10	West London	94.7	52.6	-20.5	2.5	7.4	4	55.7	8.2	70.4	764
14	8	Wales Trinity St David	97.8	5.2	-13.8	4.1	12.5	n/a	49.7	12	73.6	757
15	24	Sheffield Hallam	95.8	21.2	-25.3	11.9	24.4	-3.1	52.1	9.2	23.3	753
16	19	Hull	93.9	13.6	-16.7	8.5	28.8	-3.4	53.0	7.7	32.6	745
=17	26	Buckinghamshire New	94.3	30.7	-8.3	6.9	11.6	0.5	47.8	2.7	74.9	743
=17	20	Huddersfield	95	46.3	-12.4	5.8	16.1	-0.2	57.2	7.2	23.4	743
19	16	Derby	96.1	27.1	-26.7	6.3	24.7	-1.6	53.7	10.4	38.7	741
20	21	Ravensbourne, London	93.7	49.6	-18.1	6.6	6.0	6	47.8	9.3	18.7	740
21	27	Middlesex	97.8	73.5	-10.0	2.5	4.5	1.9	57.1	5.2	46.2	736
22	=22	Greenwich	94	55.3	-18.4	5.5	7.4	3	57.3	6.3	34.9	728
23	30	Roehampton	97	64.8	-18.4	5.6	4.4	2.9	52.0	7	36.4	727
=24	17	Anglia Ruskin	93	31.5	-21.5	5.1	16.3	-0.3	53.5	5.4	71.9	715
=24	31	Chester	94.5	7.2	-14.6	7.9	20.0	-2.9	54.3	8.2	38.1	715
=26	=10	Bedfordshire	98.5	56.1	-31.8	2.1	7.6	6	58.8	4.1	71.3	712
=26	28	Goldsmiths, London	87.7	51.5	-15.0	4.3	5.0	5.9	45.9	9.3	28.4	712
28	18	London South Bank	96	67.8	-20.1	3.1	5.6	3.5	52.8	6.3	41.8	702
29	25	Cardiff Metropolitan	94.2	12.9	-15.4	8.1	16.0	n/a	45.7	9.9	21.7	692
30	=54	Essex	92.6	44.4	-3.9	5.4	14.7	-1.6	46.9	5.3	26.7	689
31	=33	Gloucestershire	92.8	8.1	-16.7	7.6	13.1	-0.1	47.2	10	35.2	688
32	41	Creative Arts	92.9	25.3	-12.4	5.1	12.4	0	48.0	8.5	38.4	686
=33	35	Northampton	97.5	41.3	-21.6	4.4	16.7	0.3	51.8	5.8	36.8	678
=33	42	South Wales	95.9	10.4	-25.5	6.8	22.6	n/a	42.9	8.8	42.8	678
35	37	De Montfort	96	53.4	-25.8	4.3	16.1	-0.9	49.8	11	19.3	677

36	=33	Birmingham City	96.6	59.3	-20.3	3.3	16.0	-1.2	56.2	6.7	24.2	674
37	29	London Metropolitan	96.8	56.4	-22.6	2.1	7.1	1	53.5	3.6	78.4	673
38	65	Lincoln	93.3	11.1	-20.7	9.3	19.8	-3.2	51.8	9.9	12.2	672
39	40	Keele	83.8	35.2	-12.4	5.5	18.6	-0.3	43.7	8.7	17.5	665
=40	=22	Leeds Trinity	97.6	23.1	-20.1	3.1	19.1	-4	59.8	3.8	69.8	657
=40	38	Portsmouth	91.4	31.7	-19.4	7.6	17.0	-1	45.6	8.1	15.6	657
42	32	Solent	96.2	17.3	-35.7	9.3	20.2	-0.8	48.1	6.2	44.2	656
=43	=51	Canterbury Christ Church	91.9	28.0	-37.5	6.7	19.3	-3.3	56.7	7.2	64.0	654
=43	=44	Central Lancashire	97	34.6	-27.5	6.7	14.2	-3.6	51.9	9	40.2	654
=45	53	Hertfordshire	96.3	58.4	-16.4	3.6	7.0	1.7	51.7	5.4	24.9	652
=45	49	Worcester	97	12.2	-22.6	6.0	14.4	-5	51.1	12.5	40.8	652
47	=44	Cumbria	95.3	12.7	-17.6	4.1	16.3	-6	55.2	8.5	64.9	650
48	46	Winchester	93.3	9.4	-23.4	6.6	14.2	-0.8	49.1	12	20.6	647
49	60	Plymouth	86.4	15.0	-17.3	7.5	15.2	-3.1	45.1	10.7	32.5	646
50	36	Aberystwyth	91	6.5	n/a	9.7	12.1	n/a	37.1	11.8	15.7	643
=51	39	Norwich Arts	93.7	11.1	n/a	8.3	16.9	-5	44.7	12.6	11.6	639
=51	64	Leeds Arts	92.9	9.5	-10.2	4.2	15.4	0	41.6	11.7	10.7	639
53	50	Arts London	88.7	31.2	-20.5	4.2	7.5	-0.3	37.6	17.3	18.5	636
54	48	Brunel London	93.2	76.7	-16.8	3.6	3.5	1.9	50.8	5.9	12.5	635
55	63	Westminster	94.7	73.1	-20.6	3.3	5.2	0.2	55.8	5.6	19.5	626
=56	56	Coventry	94.4	62.3	-18.4	4.0	13.1	-0.8	46.8	4.5	22.1	620
=56	=54	Salford	96.1	34.4	-21.9	6.2	15.7	-2	46.5	5.7	28.8	620
=58	=51	Bangor	94	8.8	-27.4	7.5	13.0	n/a	44.3	10.1	33.6	616
=58	47	Queen Mary, London	82.9	77.0	-5.5	2.5	3.0	1.9	46.1	5.8	9.0	616
60	59	Kingston	95.5	65.1	-18.6	3.1	5.4	-2.4	51.5	7.9	27.4	615
61	=74	Brighton	90.1	22.3	-18	6.9	14.2	-5.3	45.4	9.9	29.2	609
62	68	St Mary's, Twickenham	92.9	32.7	-15.5	6.4	5.4	-4	45.6	10.4	26.6	607
63	43	Edge Hill	96.7	8.3	-27.4	7.4	20.0	-3.4	51.8	6.8	22.7	597
64	=76	SOAS, London	86.1	81.7	-10.7	1.8	2.0	n/a	47.2	8.3	13.7	592
65	=57	Liverpool John Moores	89.7	13.0	-26.4	10.8	17.8	-4.2	51.2	5.2	19.1	591
=66	67	Bournemouth	91	15.4	-26.8	7.6	12.6	-1.1	48.0	8.2	20.8	589
=66	=70	Leeds Beckett	92.4	21.3	-20.2	7.7	18.8	-4.1	42.1	7.3	16.0	589
68	82	Hartpury	90.9	6.8	n/a	7.2	14.0	-4	45.3	10.4	17.9	587
69	62	Liverpool Hope	91.2	11.9	-29.5	10.2	21.6	-9	49.5	10	21.4	586
70	66	West of England	92.1	19.5	-30.6	6.8	15.2	-1.5	41.8	9.4	27.7	584
71	72	City, London	88.7	81.3	-13.4	1.8	2.9	n/a	58.5	3.9	12.8	574
72	=57	Aston	87.8	85.6	-14.2	1.9	11.6	-1.6	53.6	2.2	4.7	573
73	61	Northumbria	88.6	11.1	-31.0	8.2	18.4	-2.2	50.6	6.3	19.7	567
74	70	Manchester Metropolitan	93	39.0	-17.2	5.1	14.7	-3.9	50.0	4.6	14.1	566
75	79	Sheffield	77.3	22.0	-6.9	5.0	10.3	-1.4	32.6	10.8	10.3	557
76	73	Leicester	82.3	58.2	-15.2	3.2	9.8	0.6	39.4	6.3	9.0	556
77	=76	Swansea	92.1	18.8	-15.7	7.0	12.4	n/a	37.0	5.2	20.5	555
78	80	Kent	79.8	45.8	-15.7	5.2	11.5	-2.2	46.6	6	9.7	552
79	78	Harper Adams	77.2	4.1	n/a	4.8	8.3	n/a	35.3	17.7	15.1	550
80	85	King's College London	70.6	66.4	-5.6	1.9	4.6	-0.5	38.8	6.9	17.2	539
81	91	Surrey	79.9	37.1	-11	4.0	7.9	-1.3	40.8	6.8	16.9	535
82	83	Royal Holloway, London	80.3	52.9	-16.8	3.4	4.6	1.2	40.3	8.3	4.7	534

Social Inclusion Ranking for England and Wales cont

Rank	Last year's rank	Institution	State educated (non-grammar) (%)	Ethnic minorities (%)	Black achievement gap (%)	White working-class males (%)	Low participation areas (%)	Low participation areas dropout gap (%)	First generation students (%)	Disabled (%)	Mature (%)	Total
83	84	East Anglia	83.2	23.0	-13.8	6.3	12.8	-3.4	39.6	6.7	14.2	533
84	88	York St John	96.7	6.8	-35.5	7.5	17.0	-5.7	47.2	8.8	22.1	521
=85	=74	Bath Spa	93.7	8.6	-30.0	5.3	15.4	-5.6	41.7	12.8	17.7	520
=85	69	St George's, London	73.9	76.5	-14.1	1.5	3.3	n/a	35.5	7.5	35.1	520
87	86	Sussex	81.6	28.2	-17.4	4.5	8.9	-2.9	38.4	9.6	12.6	507
88	87	Nottingham Trent	87.2	28.8	-27.3	5.5	14.7	-2.8	41.5	7.3	10.5	505
89	81	Chichester	93.6	6.8	-34.1	6.5	19.1	-7	46.8	9.4	22.0	504
90	92	Reading	76.4	33.1	-9.3	3.3	6.9	-1.3	35.9	7.8	10.1	494
91	90	Manchester	72.3	33.3	-14	3.1	8.8	-0.2	32.8	8.5	7.7	478
92	94	Arts Bournemouh	91.9	12.2	-28.5	4.0	9.0	-1	38.8	9	11.5	466
93	89	Lancaster	78.3	19.6	-18.8	5.4	8.0	-0.4	34.7	7.3	3.9	462
94	93	Falmouth	92	7.6	-32.5	7.3	10.3	-6	33.8	11.4	19.1	459
95	=95	York	73.9	15.7	-17.8	5.3	9.8	-2	31.6	8.2	7.4	442
96	97	Southampton	72.1	24.2	-17.3	4.5	8.1	-0.6	33.1	6.2	9.6	436
97	99	Warwick	63.4	43.1	-6.5	3.2	5.7	-3.3	31.7	6.6	7.8	422
98	100	University College London	51.7	58.2	-2.1	1.6	4.3	0.6	27.4	4.8	6.5	415
99	102	Leeds	71.8	21.9	-15.1	3.9	8.9	-3.1	33.8	6.5	6.8	405
=100	103	Birmingham	70.6	34.1	-14.5	2.5	8.4	-1.6	32.6	5.8	4.5	404
=100	104	Liverpool	74.8	16.4	-19.2	4.6	9.1	-4.5	39.2	6.7	8.7	404
102	101	Cardiff	77.3	19.0	-16.5	4.0	9.1		31.6	5.6	11.7	402
103	=95	Loughborough	66.6	24.8	-15.1	5.1	6.5	-3.6	32.3	8.1	1.8	399
104	98	Oxford Brookes	65.6	17.1	-23.6	3.7	6.9	-2.5	35.8	9	17.9	391
105	105	London School of Economics	51.4	62.6	-3.2	1.8	7.0	n/a	32.1	4.7	1.4	390
106	108	Nottingham	64.3	30.4	-18.2	3.1	8.3	-2.5	30.4	6.2	6.0	360
107	106	Newcastle	66	13.5	-13.5	4.6	8.8	-4.1	32.4	4.7	5.3	351
108	109	Exeter	53.6	10.6	-9.5	3.4	5.7	-1.5	26.3	8	6.7	350
109	110	Durham	49.1	13.7	-7.3	3.3	7.6	0.4	23.4	5.8	3.1	345
110	113	Royal Agricultural	55.9	1.4	n/a	3.6	2.8	n/a	36.7	10.8	30.1	343
111	111	Buckingham	87.5	42.0	-39.9	0.9	8.5	n/a	31.1	4.9	36.7	340
112	107	Bath	56.2	17.9	-10.8	3.6	5.3	-0.8	23.7	6.2	2.7	336
113	114	Bristol	60.3	20.1	-8.9	2.9	6.9	-3.9	24.3	5.8	6.4	321
114	112	Imperial College London	45.5	61.6	-2.5	1.9	4.5	n/a	25.7	2.4	7.6	319
115	115	Oxford	52.2	23.7	-10.4	2.0	6.4	n/a	16.3	9.3	2.5	289
116	116	Cambridge	48.5	29.1	-7.2	1.7	5.0	n/a	16.3	4.3	4.0	226

Social Inclusion Ranking for Scotland

Rank	Last year's rank	Institution	State educated (non-grammar) (%)	Ethnic minorities (%)	Black achievement gap (%)	White working-class males (%)	Deprived areas (%)	First generation students (%)	Disabled (%)	Mature (%)	Total
1	1	Abertay	94.8	8.7	n/a	11.2	16.8	46.5	5.8	40.5	1000
2	2	West of Scotland	98.7	10.7	-30.5	7.1	29.9	48.3	1.1	59.6	945
3	4	Queen Margaret, Edinburgh	95.3	7.0	n/a	5.5	13.1	41.7	11.3	43.4	898
4	5	Glasgow Caledonian	96.4	14.5	-36.8	8.4	23.0	43.1	2.2	41.2	863
5	3	Edinburgh Napier	92.8	10.2	-14.9	7.1	12.5	39.6	6	40.0	824
6	9	Dundee	84.7	12.2	-7.0	5.5	16.4	41.4	5.3	31.2	823
7	7	Highlands and Islands	98.0	3.3	n/a	11.7	8.6	42.5	3.3	57.6	819
8	10	Strathclyde	90.4	13.9	-18.4	6.7	21.6	37.4	2.9	18.7	772
9	6	Stirling	90.3	5.9	n/a	6.7	13.4	38.5	8.6	30.4	745
10	8	Heriot-Watt	85.3	13.2	-18.5	7.7	13.4	33.1	5.4	23.4	732
11	11	Aberdeen	81.1	14.2	-11.1	7.5	7.9	30.7	6.1	15.8	691
12	12	Robert Gordon	94.9	10.1	-32.8	7.0	6.1	34.9	4.2	38.5	607
13	13	Glasgow	78.3	12.3	-0.1	4.6	14.8	25.6	3.1	13.9	591
14	14	St Andrews	56.5	15.8	-15.2	3.5	10.2	18.1	6.2	3.8	400
15	15	Edinburgh	57.8	12.8	-11.4	2.8	9.1	19.5	5.7	8.1	363

7 Finding Somewhere to Live

Shocked to discover that their parents' house rules are actually quite sensible, student house-sharers cite leaving the dirty dishes out as the No 1 niggle with their kitchen co-users. And upon flying the nest after 18 years of living in miraculously sanitary environs, students find house-sharers' reluctance to help with cleaning in general the second-worst trait, results of the Student Accommodation Survey 2022 revealed. Making too much noise is the third most annoying habit while leaving hair in plug holes and failure to change the toilet roll also fall under the toxic housemate banner. See table, page 111.

So far, so predictably infuriating for most freshers. Starting university is, for most, the first taste of independent living, and setting up home with other new students takes some acclimatising. But the rising cost of living is squeezing students' domestic contentment on another level. According to a survey by the Office for National Statistics, whose results were published in November 2022, almost two-thirds (62%) of students had already cut back on food shopping, nearly two in five (38%) had reduced their use of gas and electricity to keep costs down, and more than half (52%) had relied on savings to get by. More than three-quarters (77%) said they were worried the crisis would affect how well they did in their degree. Four in 10 (40%) said they were studying more at home to save on costs rather than going to campus, and one in five (21%) were attending lectures remotely where possible.

The added pressure on the student purse highlights the need for safe, comfortable and affordable accommodation – which has always been key to helping students settle happily into all that university life has to offer. Aside from tuition fees, accommodation represents students' biggest financial outlay. According to the latest figures published by student housing charity Unipol and the National Union for Students (NUS) in their 2021 *Accommodation Costs Survey*, the average annual cost for a room in purpose-built accommodation in the UK now stands at £7,374 outside London, and £9,488 in the capital. This worked out at an average weekly rent of £166 in the 2021-22 letting year. These rents almost always include all utilities and the internet.

University-owned halls are only marginally cheaper, at £13 less per week on average than those in the private sector. The Unipol/NUS survey reveals a steep upward curve in housing costs: rents have risen by 16% since its 2018-19 edition and have soared by 61% since the 2011-12 survey.

In its 2022 report Save the Student, the student money website put average rents across all types of housing slightly lower than Unipol/NUS, at £418 per month (£3 less than in its 2021 report, but still part of a long-term upward trend). With energy costs spiralling, students and their families have been negotiating hard with landlords to ensure bills are included in rent – if they are not automatically. In a separate piece of research Save The Student found that of students who did not have energy bills included in their rent, four in five were worried about increasing costs, three in five had already seen their energy bills go up and three-quarters said they've had to cut back on heating due to how much the bills cost.

Even before the cost of living crisis students – and their families – have had to dig deep to cover accommodation costs. Rent consumes almost all of a full maintenance loan, but the average student receives less than the full whack, getting just £485 per month from their allocation. Going by the Unipol/NUS figures, 88% of a full maintenance grant gets eaten by rent in London, leaving students just £38 per week to spend on anything else. Outside of London, accommodation costs account for 72% of the maximum loan, leaving students with £69.52 to spend on other living costs.

Plugging the financial hole falls most commonly to parents, who on average stump up £149.80 a month per month for their student's accommodation, according to Save the Student.

What do students get in return for all this financial outlay? The chances are that for most parents their child's university digs will bear little resemblance to the standard of room they lived in when studying. Student accommodation has evolved enormously over the years. Private providers now dominate the market and represented 70% of the bed spaces surveyed in the new Unipol/NUS report. And as ambitious refurbishments modernise campuses up and down the country, en-suite and studio rooms are replacing cheaper, older stock in university-owned halls, too.

In the news

With demand for halls greater than supply, rents rising, and billions of pounds committed to residences each year, private student housing has become one of the property market's biggest growth areas. Some developments have fallen short of completion deadlines in recent years however, leaving students having to be re-housed at the last minute.

But it was housing shortages in some student cities that made the headlines at the start of the 2022 autumn term. In Durham, anxious students waited outside estate agents' offices through the

Term-time accommodation of full-time and sandwich students 2020–21

Provider maintained property	335,300	17%
Private-sector halls	171,280	8%
Parental/guardian home	456,870	23%
Own residence	391,150	19%
Other rented accommodation	576,620	28%
Other	79,690	4%
Not in attendance at the provider	17,870	1%
Not known	74,510	
Total	2,103,290	

Source: HESA 2021 (adapted)

Top Tenancy Problems for Students

1	Lack of water/heating	30%
2	Damp	26%
3	Disruptive building work	17%
4	Rodents and pests	15%
5	Inappropriate/unannounced landlord visits	13%
=6	Break-ins or burglaries	7%
=6	Smoke or carbon monoxide alarms not working	7%
=6	Dangerous living conditions	7%
9	Other	5%
10	Bed bugs	4%

Source: National Student Accommodation Survey 2022
Based on 1,200 responses

night. The lack of student houses available meant that by 7.30am there were flocks of applicants waiting when they opened at 8am. The chaos saw students signing housing contracts against the windows of nearby shops, and many had not even viewed the property that they had signed for.

In Manchester, a vast shortage of stock in the most popular areas with students has meant that have had to broaden their search and commute further distances. John-Paul Case, head of metropolitan lettings at Savills in Manchester, told the *Manchester Evening News* in early September 2022: "It's really a case of you snooze, you lose – and we can expect competitive bidding to heighten the closer we get to the new academic year starting, continuing to push rents up."

Housing shortages in Bristol, where University of the West of England students were offered accommodation in Newport, nearly an hour from the main campus, and Glasgow, where students were told in 2022 not to enroll on courses or travel to the city without first securing accommodation, also made the news. But Martin Blakey, the Chief Executive of Unipol wrote in a blog for HEPI (the Higher Education Policy Institute) that the issue is more widespread than has been reported: "Brighton and York also have shortages and others are now getting, at best, very tight supply. These include Bradford (after a decade of a significant surplus), Leeds, Liverpool, London and Newcastle."

There is a combination of factors at play that has led to these accommodation shortages. The rapid growth of private sector halls of residence meant many universities were able to buy in beds at very short notice if their intake overshot their own supply of rooms. But, following the financial burden of reimbursing students for unused accommodation during the pandemic, private sector housing providers have been marketing their rooms earlier, letting directly, and letting more of their stock to returning students – rather than just first-years.

At the same time, there is a decline in the number of "on-street" bed spaces as private landlords move out of the student sector – which proved unstable during Covid-19 and are now more challenging to rent with bills included, due to the meteoric increases in energy costs. Instead, landlords are showing a preference for renting to the more reliable young professionals market. Fewer "on-street" housing is, in turn, sending more returning students to private halls of residence. The rapid growth of these accommodation blocks has also slowed down, just at a time when demand is on the up.

Feeling insecure about housing is far from ideal when students are hoping for a smooth transition from home to university, and the friendship groups known to blossom among housemates. Having to commute further to study is a drain on time, and living in non-student areas limits the potential for part-time work and can be isolating.

With universities slow to react and no immediate solution in sight, new students are advised to plan their accommodation as early as they can, and to know their rights. The NUS says: "A nationwide housing shortage is pushing students into ever more desperate situations, and rogue landlords might exploit inexperienced students who have never rented before by acting illegally. The NUS believes that every student has the right to affordable and secure housing." Advice and support on all things housing is listed at **www.nus.org.uk/student-renters-rights-hub**.

Responding to accommodation shortages north of the border, NUS Scotland president Ellie Gomersall commented in *The National* newspaper in August 2022: "There are students across Scotland right now struggling to get accommodation for the year ahead, facing a choice between sofa-surfing or paying sky-high rents … Last week we saw another record number of students from the most deprived communities accepted to university but if we don't get a grip on our broken student housing system, we're just setting students up to fail." NUS Scotland has called for a student housing strategy, coupled with rent controls and a student housing guarantee.

Student life unlocked

Campuses and high streets have returned to business as usual and the unsettling experience for students of being confined to their rooms for virtual learning is now thankfully consigned to (very recent) history. Online teaching to some extent or another has become part of higher education, however, which means student accommodation is a place of work as well as place to live – so, ensuring good learning conditions along with the living environment is a must.

Halls of residence

First-years are guaranteed a space in halls by many universities, but spaces are usually limited so it pays to meet application deadlines – especially given the current shortages in some locations. Applying early might help you get first pick of the different types of room available, too. Any rooms left over are allocated to postgraduates, international students in any year of study and some returning, non-first-year students. Institutions that recruit significant numbers in Clearing have rooms available late in the admissions cycle. Some universities reserve a small proportion of accommodation for students with families.

While halls are generally the preferred option for freshers, they are also the priciest – not only in private developments but in many cases in university-owned accommodation, too, making affordability a sticking point – as discussed earlier. Some private blocks come with high-spec interiors and swanky extras including gyms. Most developments are in big complexes, but there are also niche providers such as Student Cribs, which converts properties to a more luxurious standard than usual digs. The firm now operates in 25 cities.

Unite Students is one of the country's biggest providers and has 74,000 beds across 172 properties in 25 towns and cities nationwide. UPP has over 36,000 residential places in operation or under construction in complexes built for 15 universities, usually on campus, and where rents are negotiated with the university, often in consultation with the students' union.

The 2021 *National Student Accommodation Survey* found that 15% of students were living in private halls, up from 8% four years ago, but university accommodation still accounts for a much higher 34% of students, while 39% have a private landlord, 10% live with their parents, and 1% own their home.

In the Global Student Living (UK and Ireland) 2022 awards, Fresh – which has accommodation in 32 locations – won the top provider gong, while Student Living at the University of Derby won the best student living prize. Prime Student Living earned the best value for money award. The company operates in six student cities where it offers washer dryers and dishwashers, games rooms and gyms included in the rent. Queen Margaret University, London was named the best for customer service.

Price and location are likely to be more important to students than who owns the property, but when it comes to student accommodation: *caveat emptor*! Standards can be variable, prices may leave little to live on, and horror stories recounted in surveys by Save the Student mention heating and hot water issues, damp, smoke or carbon monoxide alarms that do not work, rodents and pests, and inappropriate visits from landlords.

Living at home

If students live within commuting distance of a good university, the option of dodging hefty rent and household bills is tempting. This may be a permanent shift, given the rising costs of student housing and of living more broadly, with coupled the willingness of many young people, student or not, to live with their parents well into their twenties.

Stay-at-home students tend to have longer commutes to campus than those in their own digs, the extra journey time a worthwhile compromise. Not only school-leavers live at home; the proportion includes mature students, many of whom live in their own homes rather than with their parents. The trend is four times more common at post-1992 universities than at older universities, reflecting the larger numbers of mature students with family responsibilities at the newer universities and a generally younger and more affluent student population at the older ones.

Before opting to stay at home solely on the basis that it makes financial sense, it is important to consider the relationship with your parents and the availability of quiet space in which to study. You will still be entitled to a maintenance loan, although for 2022-23 it is a maximum of £8,171 in England, rather than £9,706 if you were living away from home outside London, or £12,667 in London. There is no higher rate for anyone living at home in London, which seems unreasonable given the high cost of transport and other essentials in the capital.

The downside is that you may miss out on a lot of the student experience, especially the social scene and the opportunity to make new friends. Research has found that students who live at home are less likely than others to say they are learning a lot at university, and a survey by the Student Engagement Partnership suggests that they find life unexpectedly "tiring, expensive and stressful". Issues affecting their quality of life include travel, security and the lack of their own space. But remember that you can always move on later. Many initially home-based students do so in their second year.

Living away from home

Most of those who can afford it still see moving away to study as an integral rite of passage. There is no other option for those whose chosen course is at a university further than commuting distance. Others look forward to broadening their experiences in a new, unexplored location.

For the fortunate majority, the search for accommodation will be over quickly because the university can offer a place in one of its halls of residence or self-catering flats. But for others, there will be an anxious search for a room in a strange city. Most universities will help with this if they cannot offer accommodation of their own.

The practicalities of living independently loom large for students who go away to university. The location and the type of accommodation may even influence your choice of university, since there are big differences across the sector and the country.

How much will it cost?

Rents vary so much across the UK that national averages can bear little resemblance to what you end up paying. The 2022 NatWest Student Living Index found a range from £200 a month in Edinburgh and £396 in Newcastle to £505.50 in London and £556.60 in Manchester – the dearest and higher than the capital.

Such figures conceal a wide range of actual rents, particularly in London. This was always the case but has become even more obvious with the rapid growth of a luxury market at the same time as many students are willing to accept sub-standard accommodation to keep costs down.

A series of recent reports suggest that the need for good wi-fi has overtaken reasonable rents as students' top priority in choosing accommodation. A survey by **mystudenthalls.com** found that a big, bright room, good wi-fi, friendly people, a clean kitchen and a good gym are the top things students say they value in a place to live. The same website has lists some of the most Instagrammable student accommodation, among them The Stay Club Colindale, London, with its neon graphic art, and the £45million Finnieston complex in Glasgow, made up of true club suites (studios) and bedrooms in shared apartments – where a giant slide takes residents from the first to the ground floor.

Fabulous though such digs sound, being able to afford them must be a priority. Many students will not receive the full maintenance loan, due its means-testing against household income. Cash is needed upfront for deposits, and/or a guarantee, probably from your parents, that the rent will be paid. Most universities with a range of accommodation find that their most expensive rooms fill up first, and that students appear to have higher expectations than they used to.

Another consideration is that both living costs and potential earnings should be factored into calculations when deciding where to live. Taking account of both income and outgoings, the 2022 NatWest index shows Edinburgh, Glasgow, Leeds and Canterbury to have replaced London as the regions with the highest student cost of living, while Cardiff offers the best value for money, followed by Cambridge, Southampton and Sheffield.

The choices you have

» University hall of residence, with individual study bedrooms and a full catering service. Many will have en-suite accommodation.
» University halls, flats or houses where you provide your own food.
» Private, purpose-built student accommodation.
» Rented houses or flats, shared with fellow students.
» Living at home.
» Living as a lodger in a private house.

Making your choice

Choosing somewhere cheap is a false economy if it ends up making you feel depressed and isolated. Most students who drop out of university do so in the first few months, when homesickness and loneliness can be felt most acutely.

Being warm and well-fed is likely to have a positive effect on your studies. University halls offer a convenient, safe and reliable standard of accommodation, along with a supportive community environment. The sheer number of students – especially first-years – in halls makes this form of accommodation an easy way of meeting people from a wide range of courses and making friends. If meals are included, this extra adds further peace of mind both for students and their parents. But only a tiny proportion of places are catered.

Wherever you choose to live, there are some general points you will need to consider, such as how safe the neighbourhood seems to be, and how long it might take you to travel to and from classes. A survey of travel time between term-time accommodation and university found that most students in London can expect a commute of at least 30 minutes and often over an hour, while students living in Wales are usually much less than 30 minutes away from their university.

In Chapter 14, we provide details of what accommodation each university offers, covering the number of places, the costs, and their policy towards first-year students.

New student accommodation

At the top end of the market, private firms usually lead the way, at least in the bigger student cities. Companies such as UPP and Unite Students offer some of the most luxurious student accommodation the UK has seen, either in partnership with universities or in their own right.

Rooms in these complexes are nearly always en-suite and with internet access, and may include other facilities such as your own phone line and satellite TV. Shared kitchens are top-quality and fitted out with the latest equipment. This kind of accommodation naturally comes at a higher price but offers the advantages of flexibility both in living arrangements and through a range of payment options.

University halls of residence

Many new or recently refurbished university-owned halls offer a standard of accommodation that is not far short of the privately-built residences. This is partly because rooms in these halls can be offered to conference delegates during vacations. You will probably find that they are in great demand and you may have to get your name down quickly to secure one of the fancier rooms. That said, you can often get a guarantee of accommodation if you give a firm acceptance of an offered place by a certain date in the summer.

If you have gained your place through Clearing, this option may not exist, although rooms in private halls might still be on offer at this stage. The delays experienced in development completions in recent years underline the importance of ensuring, as far as possible, that any newbuilds are on time and have the seal of approval.

Cladding is a particular concern and not one that is easily assuaged. An incident in Bolton raised safety concerns as fire ripped through a relatively new hall of residence with cladding, though it appeared to have met building regulations and not be the type used on Grenfell Tower. Students were evacuated and two were treated by paramedics, but fortunately none came to serious harm.

While a few halls are single-sex most are mixed, and often house over 500 students. In student villages, the numbers are now counted in thousands and are great environments for making friends and becoming part of the social scene.

One possible downside is that big student housing developments can also be noisy places where it can be difficult at times to get down to some work. Surveys of students have revealed that for those who found noise a problem, peace and quiet was a higher priority than access to public transport or good nightlife. Many university libraries, especially new ones, are now open 24 hours a day.

Self-catering

Very few universities offer catered halls of residence and self-catering is the norm. Invest in sturdy crockery and basic utensils – the sort of kit that will survive novice cookery skills and shared kitchens. To avoid reliance on instant noodles and takeaways it is wise to master at least a few culinary basics – pasta bakes are hard to get wrong and affordable to whip up. Sharing meals with housemates can be a sociable way of settling in.

Catering in university accommodation

Many universities have responded to a general increase in demand from students for a more independent lifestyle by providing more flexible catering facilities. A range of eateries, from fast food outlets to more traditional refectories, can usually be found on campus or in student villages. Students in university accommodation may be offered pay-as-you-eat deals as an alternative to full-board packages.

What to do after the first year?

After your first year of living in university residences you may well wish, and will probably be expected, to move out to other accommodation. The main exceptions are the collegiate universities, particularly Oxford and Cambridge, but also others. Students from outside the EU are also often guaranteed accommodation.

At a growing number of universities, where there is a sufficiently large stock of residential accommodation, it is not uncommon for students to move back into halls for their final year. The autumn and winter months are the most common times to view properties for those planning to move.

Practical details

Whether or not you have decided to start out in university accommodation, you will probably be expected to sign an agreement to cover your rent. Contract lengths vary. They can be for around 40 weeks, which includes the Christmas and Easter holiday periods, or for just the length of the three university terms. These term-time contracts are common when a university uses its rooms for conferences during vacations. Check whether the university has secure storage space for you to leave your belongings. Otherwise, you will have to make arrangements to take everything home or store belongings privately between terms.

International students may be offered special arrangements by which they can stay in halls during the short vacation periods. Organisations like **www.hostuk.org** can arrange for international students to stay in a UK family home at holiday times such as Christmas.

Parental purchases

One option for affluent families is to buy a house or flat and take in student lodgers. This might not be the safe financial bet it once appeared, but it is still tempting for many parents. Estate agents Knight Frank have had a student division since 2007. Those who are considering this route tend to do so from their first year of study to maximise the return on their investment.

Being a lodger or staying in a hostel

A small number of students live as a lodger in a family home, an option most frequently taken up by international students. Students with certain religious affiliations or from a particular country may wish to consider living in a hostel run by a charity catering for a specific group. Most of these are in London. There are also specialist commercial providers such as Mansion Student India, which runs housing for Indian students in the UK (**https://www.mansionstudent.co.uk/internationals/**).

Renting from the private sector

Forty per cent of students live in privately rented flats or houses, according to Save the Student's 2022 survey. Every university city or town has historically been awash with such accommodation. Indeed, this type of accommodation has grown to the point where so-called "student ghettoes," in which local residents feel outnumbered, have become a hot political issue in some cities. Into this traditional market for rented flats and houses have come the new private-sector complexes and residences, adding to the options.

While there are always exceptions, a much more professional attitude and approach to managing rented accommodation has emerged among smaller providers, thanks to a combination of greater regulation and increasing competition. Nevertheless, it is wise to take certain precautions when seeking out private residences.

How to start looking for rented property

Start this process as soon as you have accepted a place. Contact your university's accommodation service and ask for its list of approved rented properties. Some have a Student

Accommodation Accreditation Scheme, run in collaboration with the local council. To get onto an approved list under such schemes, landlords must show they are adhering to basic standards of safety and security, such as having an up-to-date gas and electric safety certificate.

University accommodation officers should also be able to advise you on any hidden charges. For instance, you may be asked to pay a booking or reservation fee, and there are sometimes fees for references or for drawing up a tenancy agreement. The practice of charging a "joining fee", however, has been outlawed.

Speak to older students with first-hand experience. Most universities have a clickable "Chat to a Student" icon on their website, and the online community of students nationwide is another helpful source for getting your ear to the ground (www.thestudentroom.com). Certain areas of town may be notorious among and you can try to avoid them. What I Wish I Knew About University, a Facebook group featuring over 34,000 members, is a helpful source of peer-to-peer advice. Think Mumsnet, but for student-age children.

Making a choice

Once you have made an initial choice of the area you would like to live in and the size of property you are looking for, the next stage is to look at possible places. If you plan to share, it is important that you all have a look at the property. If you will be living by yourself, take a friend with you when you go to view a property, since he or she can help you avoid any irrational or rushed on-the-spot decisions. Don't let yourself be pushed into signing on the dotted line there and then. Take time to visit and consider options, as well as checking out the local facilities, transport and the general environment at various times of the day and on different days of the week.

If you are living in private rented accommodation, it is likely that at least some of your neighbours will not be students. Local people often welcome students, but resentment can build up, particularly in areas of towns and cities that are dominated by student housing. It is important to respect your neighbours' rights, and not to behave in an antisocial manner.

Security in Student Housing

» Make sure that your rental property has five-lever mortise locks as well as standard catch locks on the front and back doors. Without these, contents insurance may be invalid. And use them when you go out. Ask if the locks have been changed and, if not, if previous tenants have returned all keys.
» Check that furniture and furnishings provided comply with basic fire resistance standards, that there are working smoke alarms, and that you see up-to-date gas and electricity certificates.
» Be careful about letting anyone in behind you into the house or your halls of residence. People often leave their flat or bedroom doors unlocked. It's best to ask those seeking entry to buzz whomever they're visiting instead.
» Invest in a light-timer for when you're out and don't advertise your departure on social media.
» It might seem slightly over the top, but tuck away your laptop, electronics and any jewellery when you go out. Take valuables home if you're vacating your rooms for any length of time.
» If you prefer your desk at a window, make sure you move costly equipment out of sight when not in use.
» Hide packaging for your laptop, mobile and any other pricey purchases. Just dumping the box next to the bins is tantamount to advertising 'Expensive new gadgets here'.
» Call the taxi from down the street. That way, no one knows which house you've just left empty.
» Not getting contents insurance is a false economy. You may be able to add items to your parents' home insurance.
» Register valuables on the UK National Property Register at www.immobilise.com. And use a good bike lock.

Source: www.savethestudent.org and NUS (adapted)

Preparing for sharing

How well you cope with some of the downsides of sharing will be partly down to the kind of person you are and where you are on the spectrum between laidback and highly strung. But it will help a lot if you are co-habiting with people whose outlook on day-to-day living is not too far out of line with your own

Some students sign for their second-year houses as early as November. While it is good to be ahead of the rush, you may not yet have met your best friends at this stage. If you have not selected your own group of friends, universities and landlords can help by taking personal preferences and lifestyle into account when grouping tenants together. Potential issues to consider include whether any of the housemates smoke or own drums or DJ decks. It will also be important to sort out broadband arrangements that will work for everyone. It is a good idea to agree a rota for everyone to share in the household cleaning chores from the start. Otherwise, it is almost certain that you will live in a state of unhygienic squalor, or that one or two individuals will be left to clear up everyone else's mess.

Top 10 most annoying housemate problems

1	Leaving dirty dishes out	51%
2	Not helping with cleaning	44%
3	Being too loud	37%
4	Leaving food to rot	35%
5	Leaving lights/appliances on	33%
6	Not removing hair from plugholes	24%
7	Stealing food	22%
=8	Not changing the toilet roll	20%
=8	Leaving windows open	20%
10	Taking long showers	15%

Source: National Student Accommodation Survey 2021
Based on more than 1,200 responses

The practical details about renting

It is a good idea to ask whether your house is covered by an accreditation scheme or code of standards. Such codes provide a clear outline of what constitutes good practice as well as the responsibilities of both landlords and tenants. Adhering to schemes like the National Code of Standards for Larger Student Developments compiled by the Accreditation Network UK may well become a requirement for larger properties, including those managed by universities (**www.anuk.org.uk**).

At the very least, make sure that if you are renting from a private landlord, you have his or her telephone number and home address. Some can be remarkably difficult to contact when repairs are needed or when deposits are due to be returned.

Multiple occupation

If you are renting a private house, it may be subject to the Housing Act 2004 in England and Wales (similar legislation applies in Scotland and Northern Ireland). Licenses are compulsory for all private houses in multiple occupation (HMOs) with three or more storeys and that house five or more unrelated residents. The provisions of the Act also allow local authorities to designate whole areas in which HMOs of all sizes must be licensed. This means that a house must be licensed, well-managed and must meet various health and safety standards, and its owner subject to various financial regulations. There is more on this at **www.gov.uk** under Private Renting (**https://www.gov.uk/private-renting**).

Tenancy agreements

Whatever kind of accommodation you go for, you must be sure to have all the paperwork in order and be clear about what you are signing up to. If you are taking up residence in a shared house, flat or bedsit, the first document you will have to grapple with is a tenancy agreement or lease offering you an "assured shorthold tenancy". Since this is a binding legal document, you should be prepared to go through every clause with a fine-tooth comb. Remember that it is much more difficult to make changes or overcome problems arising from unfair agreements once you are a tenant than before you become one.

You would be well advised to seek help in the likely event of your not fully understanding some of the clauses. Your university accommodation office or students' union is a good place to start. A Citizens Advice Bureau or Law Advice Centre should also be able to offer you free advice.

In particular, watch out for clauses that may make you jointly responsible for the actions of others. If you name a parent as a guarantor to cover any costs not paid by you, they may also be liable for charges levied on all tenants for damage that was not your fault. A rent review clause could allow your landlord to increase the rent at will, whereas without such a clause, they are restricted to one rent rise a year. Make sure you keep a copy of all documents and get a receipt (and keep it somewhere safe) for anything you have had to pay for that is the landlord's responsibility.

Contracts with private landlords tend to be longer than for university accommodation. They will frequently commit you to paying rent for 52 weeks of the year. Leaving aside the cost, there are probably more advantages than disadvantages to this kind of arrangement. It means you don't have to move out during vacations. You can store your belongings in your room when you go away (but don't leave anything valuable behind if you can help it). You may be able to negotiate a rent discount for periods when you are not staying in the property. The other advantage, particularly important for cash-strapped students, is that you have a base from which to find work and hold down a job during the vacations.

Deposits

On top of the agreed rent, you will need to provide a deposit or bond to cover any breakages or damage. This will probably set you back the equivalent of another month's rent. The deposit should be returned, minus any deductions, at the end of the contract. However, be warned that disputes over the return of deposits are common, with the question of what constitutes reasonable wear and tear often the subject of disagreements between landlord and tenant.

To protect students from unscrupulous landlords, the 2004 Housing Act introduced a National Tenancy Deposit Scheme under which deposits are held by an independent body. There are details at **citizensadvice.org.uk**. You may also be asked to find guarantors for your rent payments – in practice, usually your parents.

Inventories and other paperwork

You should get an inventory and schedule of condition of everything in the property. This is another document that you should check carefully and make sure that everything listed is as described. Write on the document anything that is different. The NUS suggests taking photographs of rooms and equipment when you first move in (setting the correct date on your camera), to provide you with additional proof. If you are not offered an inventory, then make one of your own. You should have someone else witness and sign this, send it to your landlord, and keep your own copy. Keeping in contact with your landlord and developing a good relationship with him or her will also do you no harm.

You should ask your landlord for a recent gas safety certificate issued by a qualified Gas Safe Register engineer, a fire safety certificate covering the furnishings, and a record of current gas and electricity meter readings.

Take your own readings of meters when you move in, too. This also applies to water meters if you are expected to pay water rates (although this isn't usually the case). The NUS issues its own advice on how to keep down energy bills, at **http://studentswitchoff.org/save-energy-rented-accommodation**. The union says that the average student in private rented accommodation spends £500 a year on energy, so you can save money and cut down carbon emissions.

Finally, students are not liable for council tax. If you are sharing a house only with other full-time students, then you will not have to pay it. However, you may be liable to pay a proportion of the council tax bill if you are sharing with anyone who is not a full-time student. You may need to get a council tax exemption certificate from your university as evidence that you are not liable for it.

Safety and security

Once you have arrived and settled in, remember to take care of your own safety and the security of your possessions. You are particularly vulnerable as a fresher, when you are still getting used to your new-found independence. This may help explain why so many students are burgled or robbed in the first six weeks of the academic year. Take care with valuable portable items such as mobile phones, tablets and laptops, all of which are desirably saleable items for thieves. Ensure you don't have them obviously on display when you are out and about and that you have insurance cover. If your mobile phone is stolen, call your network or 08701 123 123 to immobilise it. Students' unions, universities and the police will provide plenty of practical guidance when you arrive.

Useful websites

For advice on a range of housing issues, visit: **www.nus.org.uk/more/faqs/housing-and-rent**

The Shelter website has separate sections covering different housing regulations in England, Wales, Scotland and Northern Ireland: **www.shelter.org.uk**

As examples of providers of private hall accommodation, visit:
www.upp-ltd.com   **http://thestudenthousingcompany.com**
http://www.unitestudents.com/   **www.student-cribs.com**

A number of sites will help you find accommodation and/or potential housemates, including:
www.accommodationforstudents.com   **www.studentpad.co.uk**
www.uniplaces.com   **www.studentcrowd.com**
www.sturents.com   **http://student.spareroom.co.uk**

Accreditation Network UK is at: **https://www.anuk.org.uk**

www.hostuk.org helps international students meet British people and families in their homes

8 Enjoying University Sport

It's the winning as well as the taking part that counts when it comes to sport at the University of Durham. Embracing all levels of skill, Durham co-ordinates one of Britain's largest participation programmes with more than 75% of students engaged in sport and physical activity. Around 3,000 of them represent the university in BUCS (British Universities and Colleges Sport) competitions in 137 teams, cementing Durham's outstanding record of placing in the top three of the BUCS University Table since 2012. There is huge uptake of inter-college activities too, and students can participate in 18 sports across 700 teams on a weekly basis. A further 2,500 students use the college gyms across campus and 10,000 community users access university sports facilities each year, working directly with student clubs and volunteers.

Winner of the *Times* and the *Sunday Times* Sports University of the Year 2023 award (a title it first held in 2015), Durham has invested £47million in its indoor and outdoor sporting facilities over the past 10 years. Based at the university's Sports and Wellbeing Park and Racecourse – both centrally located on campus – provision includes rubber crumb and grass pitches, tennis courts, boathouses (used mostly by the colleges) and cricket pitches, while indoor facilities range from a sports hall that can accommodate 1,600 spectators to a cricket centre, two strength and conditioning hubs, and an indoor rowing tank, as well as a hydrotherapy pool and cryotherapy chamber.

On top of the extensive facilities, Durham attracts elite student athletes by awarding 12 vice-chancellor sport scholarships annually, worth £2,000 for each year of the scholar's undergraduate career. For those competing just below national level, a further 36 Palatinate scholarships are offered, their value ranging from £500 to £2,000.

"Our sporting philosophy is to provide opportunities for exceptional people to do exceptional things," says Mark Brian, head of sport and physical activity at Durham. The university is a British Rowing Performance Centre, England and Wales Cricket Board Centre of Excellence, holds British Fencing Centre status, Lawn Tennis Association University Performance Centre status, and is also a funded Rugby Football Union centre. As well as the BUCS competitions, Durham teams also compete in the England Hockey National Leagues, the British Basketball League, the FA Women's Championship and the England Volleyball Super League. It is a TASS (Talented Athlete Scholarship Scheme) hub and has UK Anti-Doping certification.

All of which makes Brian's assertion that "few universities so successfully and consistently combine sporting and academic excellence" hard to contest. In our academic league table, Durham takes sixth place in this year's elite top 10, as it did in our previous edition. "We would like to be seen as the university of choice for those prospective students who are looking for a world-class degree and who want to continue their sporting journey to pick Durham," says Brian. "Sport at Durham is built on teamwork: we grow leaders, and we are stronger because of our partnerships.

"Sport is for everyone. We help our students try new things, to uncover their talents, to make a difference to those around them, to be fit and healthy and be the best that they can be."

For most applicants, the sports facilities are not what is going to seal the deal on their university choice, but sporting opportunities are on the radar of many. Students expect gyms and other facilities that are on a par with their local clubs — and generally now they get them. Clued-up universities are aware they have to work harder to meet the expectations of fee-paying students who want to play sport, work out and try new activities. They have boosted provision to meet this demand on such a scale that, nationally, UK university sports facilities are said to be worth astonishing £20bn.

The benefits of university sport are not limited to the outcomes on the field, pitch or court, as Brian explains: "Not only does it help to keep our students active and healthy, but it also provides social opportunities and a sense of belonging that can be particularly important in the early days when settling in at university."

Research for BUCS suggests that at least 1.7million students take part in regular physical activity, from gym sessions to competitive individual or team sports. There are good reasons, beyond fitness, for doing so, according to BUCS reports. Those who are physically active expect higher grades and are more confident of securing a graduate job than less active students. There are 54 sports listed on the BUCS website, from American football to windsurfing.

Strength in depth across the UK

If Loughborough University were a country, it would have outperformed Sweden, Switzerland and Belgium at the Tokyo 2020 Olympics. A stellar team of current and past students, together with others who trained at the university's world-class sports facilities, won 14 medals – including three golds. Among those to podium was the swimmer Adam Peaty, who won two gold medals in the men's 100m breaststroke and the mixed 4 x 100m medley relay, and the triathlete Alex Yee, who won gold and silver in the individual and mixed relay.

Ever competitive, Loughborough claims its campus represents the best square mile of sports facilities in the world, let alone the British higher education sector. Its student athletes across sporting disciplines have topped the British Universities and Colleges Sport (BUCS) points table for inter-university competition almost throughout the league's 40-year history.

Loughborough, our *Times* and *Sunday Times* Sports University of the Year last year, has won the title three times (more often than any other university) in recognition of its unparalleled elite success, extraordinary sports facilities and an atmosphere that encourages widespread participation among students.

In the past 15 years, Loughborough has invested £60million in sporting facilities on its 440-acre campus on the edge of the Leicestershire market town. New resources include two world-class gyms, a High Performance Athletics Centre, the Paula Radcliffe Athletics Track, the National Cricket Performance Centre, its Netball Centre that hosts England Netball, and a huge range of pitches — plus the £6million pool where Peaty has been training since 2017. It is also a British Swimming National Centre and British Triathlon Performance Centre. All this is backed up by technical facilities such as a human performance laboratory, technical analysis suite, nutritional analysis room and sports medicine service.

British Universities and Colleges Sports (BUCS) league table positions Top 50

University	2021-22	2020-21	*2018-19	University	2021-22	2020-21	*2018-19
Nottingham	1	1	2	Northumbria	26	13	10
Durham	2	3	3	Cambridge	27	25	20
Loughborough	3	2	1	Stirling	28	10	11
Exeter	4	5	5	Essex	29	32	34
Edinburgh	5	4	4	Cardiff Metropolitan	30	21	16
Bath	6	6	6	Surrey	31	31	30
Nottingham Trent	7	11	13	York	32	37	42
Bristol	8	8	8	Bournemouth	33	33	23
Birmingham	9	7	7	East Anglia	34	45	38
Newcastle	10	9	9	Oxford Brookes	35	35	37
Cardiff	11	12	14	Portsmouth	36	39	51
Liverpool	12	19	21	Sheffield Hallam	37	34	29
Oxford	13	20	12	Strathclyde	38	29	32
Imperial College London	14	17	25	West of England	39	36	40
Leeds	15	16	19	Aberdeen	40	44	41
Warwick	16	26	24	Brunel	41	41	36
King's College London	17	30	33	Kent	42	=50	50
University College London	18	15	28	Lancaster	43	40	44
St Andrews	19	18	26	Manchester Metropolitan	44	38	35
Leeds Beckett	=20	22	15	Dundee	45	46	58
Manchester	=20	23	22	Leicester	46	42	39
Sheffield	22	24	17	Reading	47	43	48
Swansea	23	14	18	Heriot-Watt	48	-	60
Southampton	24	28	31	Sussex	49	=47	61
Glasgow	25	27	27	Derby	50	=50	49

Source: BUCS 2022
Compiled from results in league, cup and individual competitions across a range of sports.
Nottingham scored 3,759 to top the table. Leeds Beckett and Manchester in =20th place scored 1,401.
*There was no league table in 2019-20 because of the pandemic

Students at the University of Nottingham have access to £40million sports facilities used by elite athletes, and under a "sport for all" banner the university's ambition is to engage, inspire and excel. Two-times winner of our Sports University of the Year award, Nottingham has never finished outside the BUCS league's top 10 – and is the reigning champion for 2021-22.

Building on its strong sporting tradition, in 2016 Nottingham raised the money to develop a sports village with the help of Nottingham alumnus and Carphone Warehouse founder, David Ross. The wide range of facilities at the David Ross Sports Village includes a high-performance athletics zone, dedicated martial arts studio and all-glass squash court. There is a sports injury clinic in the complex – as well as a Finnish sauna, steam room, arctic ice fountain and ice-cold bucket shower. About 25,000 of the university's 36,000 students engage with sporting programmes at some level – from using one of the 200 stations at the gym now and again to winning one of 200 sports scholarships and competing at the Olympics.

At the University of Birmingham, a £55million sports centre includes the only 50m pool in the region – to add to its already impressive facilities, while Solent has a recently-opened £28million sports development. Bath was the first UK university to offer sporting scholarships to student athletes in 1976 and now provides more than 50 each year. Its £35million Sports Training Village hosts 1.6million visits each year, by everyone from high-performance athletes and the public to students and staff, including 43 community sports clubs. Bath has a £1.6million London 2012 legacy swimming pool, which is used by 310,000 people a year, and the Team Bath gym is gaining a £3.5million extension.

Such facilities attract elite performers and are often used for high-level teaching, but they are also available for day-to-day use by undergraduates. Comparing such facilities is not easy, but most universities display them prominently on their websites and offer taster sessions on open days. There are brief descriptions of the bigger developments in the university profiles in Chapter 14.

Sporting opportunities

Some specialist facilities may be reserved at times for elite performers, but all universities are conscious of the need for wider access. Many institutions still encourage departments not to schedule lectures and seminars on Wednesday afternoons, to give students free time for sport. There are student-run clubs for all the major sports and – particularly at the larger universities – a host of minor ones. In addition, there are high-quality gyms, with staff on hand to devise personalised training regimes and to run popular activities such as Zumba and Pilates. The cost varies widely between universities, and membership fees can represent a large amount to lay out at the start of the year, but most provide good value if you are going to be a regular user.

Sport for all

At most universities, attention is mainly focused on "sport for all". Beginners are welcomed and coaching provided in a range of sports, from ultimate frisbee to tai-chi, that would be difficult to match outside the higher education system. Check on university websites to see whether your usual sport is available, but do not be surprised if you come across a new favourite when you have the opportunity to try out something different. Many universities have programmes designed to encourage students to take up a new sport, with expert coaching provided.

All universities are conscious of the need to provide for a spread of ability – and disability. University teams demand a hefty commitment in terms of training and practice sessions – often several times a week – and in many sports standards are high. University teams often compete in local and national leagues.

For those who are looking for competition at a lower level, or whose interests are primarily social, there are thriving internal, or intramural, leagues. These provide opportunities for groups from halls of residence or faculties, or even a group of friends, to form a team and participate on a regular basis.

Some universities have cut back sports budgets, but representative sport continues to grow. There are home nations competitions at international level in some sports and in London over 30 institutions take part in the London Universities Sport League. This now involves almost 450 teams – male, female and mixed – competing at a variety of levels in 15 different sports

First-year sport

Halls of residence sport is a great way of meeting like-minded people from your accommodation and over the course of the years, friendly rivalries often develop with other halls or flats.

Generally, there will be teams for football (five-a-side and 11-a-side), hockey, netball, cricket, tennis, squash, badminton and even golf.

Other opportunities

You may even end up wanting to coach, umpire or referee – another area in which higher education has much to offer. Many university clubs and sports unions provide subsidised courses for students to gain qualifications. Or you might want to try your hand at some sports administration, with an eye to your career. In most universities there is a sports (or athletic) union, with autonomy from the main students' union, which organises matches and looks after the wider interests of those who play.

Universities that excel

Winners of the *Sunday Times* Sports University of the Year award, launched in 2014, represent some – but not all – of the UK's leading sporting universities.

2023 Durham	2018 Bath
2022 Loughborough	2017 Loughborough
2021 Nottingham	2016 Exeter
2020 Stirling	2015 Durham
2019 Nottingham	2014 Loughborough

Leeds Beckett, Brunel, Cardiff Metropolitan and St Mary's Twickenham are some of the other institutions with excellent sports pedigrees.

The Boat Race between Oxford and Cambridge universities and the Varsity Match (in rugby union) are the only UK university sporting events with a big popular following – although there are varsity matches in many university cities that have become big occasions for students. Be aware, though, that success in school sport is not a passport to an Oxbridge place; such special consideration for sporty undergraduates is long gone.

Representative sport

There were more than 120 BUCS athletes representing Team GB and other countries in the Tokyo Olympics. If BUCS was a country, based on the number of its athletes who won medals, it would have placed seventh in the Olympic medal table and ninth in the Paralympic table, with 88 medals in total.

BUCS is the national organisation for higher education sport in the UK, providing a comprehensive, multi-sport competition structure and managing the development of services and facilities for participatory, grass-roots sport and healthy campuses, through to high-performance elite athletes.

BUCS (**www.bucs.org.uk**) runs championships, leagues and/or individual competitions in almost all of the 54 sports it lists. It ranks participating institutions based on the points earned in the competitive programme, although the pandemic has disrupted this for the past two years. In the 2021-22 season (excluding BUCS cricket), 4,914 teams from 140-plus universities competed in more than 26,296 BUCS matches, 21,245 league fixtures and 4,470 knockout fixtures. There is also international competition in a number of sports, and the World Student Games have become a big occasion in the international sporting calendar.

How much?

Students who are used to free (if inferior) facilities at school often get a nasty surprise when they find that they are expected to pay to join the Athletic Union and then pay again to use the gym or play football. Because most university sport is subsidised, the charges are reasonable compared to commercial facilities, but the best deal may require a considerable outlay at the start. Some universities include sports facility membership as part of the £9,250 fee, but most offer a variety of peak and off-peak membership packages.

Outdoor sports are usually charged by the hour, although clubs will also charge a membership fee. You may be required to pay up to £90 for membership of the Athletic Union, although most universities also offer pay-as-you-play options. Fees for intramural sport are seldom substantial; teams will usually pay a fee for the season, while courts for racket sports tend to be marginally cheaper per session than in other clubs.

How far away?

The other common complaint by students is that the playing fields are too far from the campus – understandable in the case of city-centre universities, but still aggravating if you have to arrange your own transport. This is where campus universities have a clear advantage. For the rest, there has to be some trade-off between the quality of outdoor facilities and the distance you have to travel to use them.

Sport as a degree subject

Over 15,600 students started sports science courses in 2021, making it one of the most popular degree choices. A separate ranking for the subject is on page 272. Many degrees in the sports area focus on management, with careers in the leisure industry in mind.

Sports scholarships

Sports scholarships are for elite performers, regardless of what they are studying – indeed, they exist at universities with barely any degrees in the area. Imported from the USA, scholarships now exist in an array of sports. Their value varies considerably – sometimes according to individual prowess. Many offer benefits in the form of coaching, equipment or access to facilities.

The government-funded Talented Athlete Scholarship Scheme (TASS) is worth up to £3,500 per year for students at English universities who have achieved national recognition at under-18 level and are eligible to represent England in one of 38 different sports. Sixty-six medals were won by TASS athletes at the Tokyo Olympic and Paralympic Games. The Scottish equivalent, Winning Students Scotland, awards scholarships worth up to £6,000 a year.

Part-time work

University sports centres are an excellent source of term-time (and out-of-term) employment. You may also be trained in first aid, fire safety, customer care and risk assessment – all useful skills for future employment. The experience could help secure a job in commercial or local authority facilities – and even for roles such as stewarding at football grounds and music venues. Most universities also have a sabbatical post in the Athletic Union or similar body, a paid position with responsibility for organising university sport and representing the sporting community within the university.

9 Staying Safe and Seeking Help on Campus

Cramming the car boot with duvets and crockery and setting off across Britain's motorways, parents and carers are full of hope that university will be a brilliant experience for their budding undergraduate, one that will help them grow into a well-rounded, self-sufficient adult. Drop-off at halls is a moment for jubilation, tearful farewells, and excited ambitions for the future. But whether you are a "sling-and-fling parent" who can't wait to roar off to celebrate having a quieter house, a twice-daily Skyper, or a first-night settling-in sleepover parent, everyone worries about how their fresher is going to get on.

With such a lot of change – and an unprecedented loosening of the apron strings – concern for the welfare of your first-year is natural. Few school leavers will be used to the autonomy around alcohol, drugs and relationships that university life brings. And for students of all ages, after the build-up of getting into their chosen course and university some may feel anxious at the prospect of degree-level academia, or suffer a confidence wobble among others who are at least as clever and hardworking as they are. Or perhaps finding their feet socially is the challenge.

On top of these usual pressures, the current generation of students has had to deal with Covid-19's impact. Research by Student Minds revealed that 52% of students feel isolated and 64% say their mental wellbeing has been affected by the pandemic. "There are lots of studies showing that students are being stressed from multiple directions – including the rising cost of living, alongside all of the global issues; we've got a generation of students that are really concerned about climate change and about global political issues and conflicts," notes Professor Nic Beech, chair of a Universities UK taskforce on student drug use and vice-chancellor of Middlesex University. "And they are trying to find their way in life. There is pressure on them to perform, to succeed, to not let their families down," he adds.

The extent to which universities are "in loco parentis" is an issue of discussion within the higher education sector. The age of majority was lowered to 18 from 21 back in 1970, meaning that universities could do away with rules around hall of residence curfews, restrictions on guests and dress codes. Such constraints would seem ridiculous now. Universities are also too big to keep tabs on all students all of the time.

But universities do provide support and guidance to students on issues of alcohol, drugs, sexual consent and respect, though provision is distinctly variable. For two years now we have used our annual survey to ask the universities in our Guide what compulsory modules they run covering alcohol use, drug-taking, social tolerance and sexual consent. Their responses reveal that few make it a requirement for students to attend sessions in all four categories, although courses covering drugs and alcohol and mandatory sessions on sexual consent are increasingly becoming part of the university landscape. Guidance and support in all four measures is almost always on hand, however, for students who seek it out themselves or who sign-up to courses or training offered by the university and/or its students' union.

Parental worrying is normal but it is possible to give your child independence while also checking in with them around the major issues: drinking, taking drugs, sex and staying safe – both physically and mentally – on campus

The first round

Much of the university social scene revolves around campus or college bars, and Freshers' Week traditionally has a packed itinerary of club nights and boozy social mixer events. This extends to accommodation, with pre-drinks a cheap alternative to paying bar prices. Students often aim to get sozzled enough before they go out to ensure an inexpensive night once they do. In an *Alcohol Impact* survey carried out by the NUS (National Union of Students) in 2018–19, more than half of the 793 respondents said they regularly drank at home or a friend's house before a night out, and 29% stated they deliberately got drunk at pre-drinks.

Sobering thoughts

The long-term health conditions caused by regular over-consumption of alcohol are unlikely to be at the forefront of the minds of freshly independent 18-year-olds as they knock back another Jägerbomb, but the impact that the culture of student drinking can have on their social circle and academic progress may hit home. Teetotal students can feel isolated, while those drinking to excess can find themselves missing deadlines, involved in antisocial behaviour or letting their guard down around personal safety. Universities and student organisations have woken up to these issues.

Last orders

The NUS runs the *Alcohol Impact* programme, which partners with universities to reduce harm. Originally set up to tackle drunk, antisocial behaviour, the programme had the knock-on effect of increasing student wellbeing, while making campus a more inclusive place for non-drinkers. It recommends 50 different actions to reduce harm around drinking, from training bar staff to help intoxicated students, to working with the local community to ensure students get home safely from a night out. So far, 31 universities have participated, and you can find out more at **https://www.drugandalcoholimpact.uk/**.

For non-drinkers, there may well be an active sober social scene on campus. In the 2018–19 NUS *Alcohol Impact Report*, 40% of respondents said they got drunk less than once a week. There are an increasing number of dry societies and booze-free social events at universities

Offering sober-minded advice

Preaching sobriety to students tends not to be the most effective approach. The team behind the NUS *Alcohol Impact* survey advise fostering an open chat about alcohol over-consumption. A good way to get the conversation going is by explaining how to take care of someone else who has drunk to excess.

A harm reduction approach is even more important when hall parties take over. Pack an alcohol measure with your student's kitchen equipment (some universities give them out to encourage drinking responsibly). Cringe though some might when storing their drinks measure in a communal kitchen cupboard, it might just work. And if having a measure does not result in your child fastidiously keeping a drinks diary, it could at least make them think before sloshing down another huge glug.

Finally, trust them. The *Alcohol Impact* survey revealed 80% of respondents agreed that drinking too much can spoil a good night. Parents who are worried about their child's drinking can find useful resources at **DrinkAware.co.uk**.

Chasing the high

There are lots of assumptions about students' inclinations for taking drugs, but "essentially there's very little written about student drug use", says Beech. The Dame Carol Black independent review of drug use for the government provided some pointers in 2020, however. "It looked at the whole population – not just students – and showed that for the age range of the majority of students there had been a big increase, particularly in powder cocaine use – which has gone up 25% in the past decade. Are students immune to that? We have to doubt that; they are part of society, not separate to it," notes Beech.

Taking the Hit, another NUS study (published 2018), surveyed 2,081 students at 151 institutions. It found that 39% said they currently used drugs, and 17% had used them in the past. Cannabis was the most popular, used at some point by 94% of respondents. It was closely followed by "club drug" Ecstasy/MDMA, with cocaine and nitrous oxide also making the list.

"Study drugs" are also favourites, purportedly taken by students to improve concentration and keep them writing essays into the early hours. Substances such as Ritalin and Modafinil were taken by one in 10 of the respondents, utilising prescription-only medicines usually procured via other methods to keep them focused during deadlines.

Just say no?

A solely punitive approach to drug use isolates students rather than aiding them. Four in ten of the respondents to *Taking the Hit* said they wouldn't feel comfortable disclosing their drug use to their university for fear of punishment. "The trouble is that as soon as people feel isolated their wellbeing goes down, they are hesitant to socialise and that puts them more into the position where drugs and alcohol are likely to be the sort of thing that they go to," notes Beech. Through its work the student drug use taskforce is "about trying to help people make better choices, feel supported, and not isolated," he explains. "It's about student success and student wellbeing."

The taskforce is the UK's first on student drug use and Universities UK is working in partnership with Unite Students, Guild HE and Independent HE to set out a common approach to reduce harms from drug use and better tackle supply. Its remit encompasses a survey of about 5,000 students and it is working with the police around supply and looking into policy and practice on drug use for universities. The findings are due to be published in a report in March 2023.

"In a sense the core message to students is: we're with you, we care about you and we need to … listen to you if you've got issues like this, or if you're worried about others around you – because students who don't take drugs are actually really affected by it as well," says Beech, the Universities UK student drug use taskforce chair.

Similarly, the NUS' *Drug and Alcohol Impact* scheme aims to refocus the conversation on drugs towards reducing harm, and building healthier, safer, more productive student communities.

Students for Sensible Drug Policy (SSDP) is an international grassroots organisation, advocating a change in drug policy on campuses and an "end to the war on drugs" and acknowledgement of the many reasons behind drug use, including mental health management and peer pressure. The goal is to empower students to make informed decisions, stating that pastoral and medical needs will always be prioritised over disciplinary proceedings.

This is not to say that drugs will soon be permissible on campuses. Of the 151 institutions surveyed in the *Taking the Hit* report, more than half took a firmer line than the law, penalising students for technically legal drug use. Accommodation contracts often have an outright ban on drugs, threatening eviction.

What can parents do?

Open dialogue equips your child with harm reduction knowledge. By discussing the effects of certain drugs, and what to do if someone has a bad reaction or overdoses, students will garner information that could end up saving a life. To facilitate such a potentially thorny chat, the NUS *Alcohol and Drugs Impact* scheme recommends taking a bystander approach. By saying "your friends may take drugs, these are the risks they are undertaking" you make sure that they get the information for themselves while not directly tackling them on it. This may help young people to understand the risks in a non-judgmental, safe space.

University drug policies vary, so read the fine print. Websites such as **talktofrank.com** and **Volteface.me** provide information on the effects that different substances can have and advice on how to talk to young people about drugs.

Consent

Sexual assault and violence on UK campuses is a very real problem, as highlighted in 2020 by the website **everyonesinvited.uk**, which reported survivors' testimonies of sexual abuse in 93 institutions profiled in the *Good University Guide*. Through freedom of information requests, Eva Tutchell and John Edmonds, authors of *Unsafe Spaces: Ending Sexual Abuse in Universities*, estimate there are between 50,000 and 100,000 sexual assaults at British universities every year.

"The first thing that amazed us was that universities, research-based organisations, have made no real attempt to collect authoritative information about sexual assaults on campuses," Edmonds says. "If you haven't got the evidence, the specialist knowledge, how do you put together a programme that is likely to work? They rely on reports made by students and by junior staff, but everybody knows that these sexual assaults are massively underreported."

In a nationwide study, campaign group Revolt Sexual Assault and student website The Student Room polled 4,500 students from 135 universities in 2018. About 70% of women respondents said they experienced sexual violence at university; among males the figure was 26%; for non-binary 61% and for disabled respondents 73%. Just 6% reported it to the university. Reasons for this can include students not feeling they'll be heard or protected.

The NUS thinks that universities need to look at their reporting systems. Edmonds and Tutchell believe that universities hope to avoid legal cases, protect their reputation and "keep everybody quiet". A report by the BBC in 2019 showed that universities had spent £87million in 2017–18 on non-disclosure agreements to stop bullying, discrimination and sexual misconduct allegations being made public.

Sex and relationships among students

Are any universities getting it right? Edmonds and Tutchell conclude that there are a few who "haven't always got it right, but are taking it seriously". They include: Aberdeen; Cambridge; Goldsmiths; Imperial College London; Lancaster, the London School of Economics; Oxford; and Sussex. Findings of a poll of student's personal lives by the Higher Education Policy Institute (HEPI) for its report *Sex and Relationships Among Students*, published in 2021, revealed that more than half of students think it should be compulsory to pass a sexual consent assessment before entering higher education (26% "strongly agree" and 32% "slightly agree").

Most students (59%) reported that they were "very confident" about "what constitutes sexual consent" but only half as many (30%) said they were "very confident" about how to navigate sexual consent after alcohol has been consumed. Two-thirds of students said they knew how to challenge inappropriate sexual behaviour (with 23% saying they feel "very confident" in doing so and 43% "fairly confident").

In the news

Unfortunately, it often takes scandal and media pressure to instigate change. St Andrews was under the spotlight in 2020 after dozens of allegations of sexual assault, several against an American-style fraternity at the university. A freedom of information request found that 42 reports of sexual assault and harassment had been made in the five years to 2020. Responding, the university hired a sexual violence support worker to support survivors.

Fiona Drouet's daughter, Emily, was subjected by her boyfriend, Angus Milligan, to a campaign of physical and emotional abuse at Aberdeen University, which ended in her taking her own life. Today, Drouet is the chief executive of the charity Emily Test, which campaigns for better protection for students.

The organisation is asking universities to commit to a Gender-Based Violence charter, where they must examine their current systems and policies to see if they pass the "Emily test" – whether they could have saved Emily's life. The charity has drafted a list of minimum standards that include educating and empowering staff and students, and easily accessible and compassionate help for victims and survivors. "It won't stop assaults and rape on campus, but it will tackle the issue of a generation that do not understand consent, sexual assault or rape," Drouet says.

Reframing the birds and the bees

Mandy Saligari, a therapist who specialises in treating teenagers and young adults, says that understanding the intricacies of consent is the key to helping your child protect themselves and others. "So, start off by saying, 'I know you are going to roll your eyes, but I need you to listen because this is important'. Do not get put off by your child saying, 'Oh, no!' – you have the right to fulfil your parental duty.

"Teenagers need to understand that there is no 'point of no return'. At any stage, either party can stop and say, 'I do not want to do this'. You are not a prick-tease if you go three-quarters of the way and then say you don't want to continue. And if you are a boy and you hear 'No', stop straight away. Tell your teenager they should not be afraid to assert their sexual boundaries."

The uncomfortable truth is that most people who experience sexual violence, experience it from someone close or known to them, or perhaps someone who doesn't actually understand what consent is.

In retrospect, following Emily's suicide, Drouet thinks that she was a naive parent. She'd tell her daughter to mind her drink wasn't spiked and not be out alone, but never discussed coercion or abuse.

"I never said: 'this is what you should do if you find yourself in a relationship where you feel you're not free to do the things that you want to do, you're being put down all the time, you're being blackmailed or asked to do things sexually that you're not comfortable with'," she said.

Another thing to do as a parent is to make sure your child feels able to talk to you without judgment or blame. According to Edmonds, until you start talking to victims, you don't realise "how little you know – the hurt, the secrecy, the guilt, the whole gamut is just awful."

"So, if the worst should happen, think before you react," Drouet says. "Remember that no one asks to be abused. We need to educate ourselves as parents. It's never the victim's fault."

Sex education in schools rarely covers issues of consent, so equip your child with practical information about support services on offer. Finally, if your child is sexually active, make sure they know how to access contraceptive services and sign up to a GP as soon as possible.

Troubled minds

The kids are not always all right, so friends and family are correct to be vigilant. Jenny Smith, policy manager at Student Minds, is particularly concerned for new students. "The start of a new academic year is a key pressure point. Students may be worried about their academic capability, establishing new friendships, or making ends meet financially."

The onset of mental health conditions often overlaps with the age when most students go to university. Research shows that both the number of suicides and those dropping out were increasing before the pandemic, and in 2019 mental health conditions were the second most declared disability, following a 20% increase.

Depression rates across the general public have doubled, according to the Office for National Statistics (ONS). John de Pury, mental health policy lead for Universities UK, believes that financially disadvantaged; black, Asian and ethnic minority; disabled; and LGBTQ students are most acutely at risk.

Tackling the load

An ONS study, published in October 2021 found that 37% of students were showing signs of moderate to severe depression and 39% had some form of anxiety. The Office for Students (OfS) announced in 2022 that it would be distributing £15million to higher education providers in the 2022–23 academic year to fund student mental health support. It is meant to enable universities and colleges to develop effective joint working between their student support services and local NHS mental health services. As well as creating more joined-up care for students, the funding should help universities meet increasing demand for mental health services. University provision is diversifying, with the pandemic hastening a trend towards web-based counselling and therapy apps, while more traditional in-person appointments are still part of most offerings.

The first league table of university mental health rankings was published in 2002 by the charity HUMEN. Accessible at **www.wearehumen.org/uni/** the list is based on a one-year study of more than 7,200 students sharing their levels of satisfaction and engagement with universities' mental health provision, combined with data on mental health budgets and staff training. Reading, Oxford and Central Lancashire lead the rankings, in that order.

How can parents help?

The role of a parent or guardian has never been more important. Family and friends are often the first to know when students are unwell. If your prospective student is worried about the future, tell them that they are not alone. Suggest that, while there are many things that are out of our control, they can always reach out to you with their concerns and other people at university. Research what support is available to your child and spend time brainstorming helpful strategies together.

Student Minds has launched Student Space, offering free wellbeing resources and support via phone, text, webchat or email to all university students in England and Wales. For parents and carers worried about their child's mental health, the Parents' Helpline at Young Minds offers free, confidential advice. For other resources and information visit the Student Minds parents' FAQ page at **www.studentminds.org.uk/supportforparents.html**.

Digital personas

Even with the re-opening of campuses, this generation of students is facing the most online-based experience to date. In the past decade, higher education has increasingly seen coursework set, essays handed in and gradings taking place digitally. Lectures are recorded and uploaded onto student interfaces.

Along with online learning, students should be aware of the impact their online persona has. Posting on social media and messaging online are not private affairs, and many students have been exposed in supposedly confidential group chats, or by statuses on a private profile. Once posted online – be it a compromising photo, crass opinion or cruel "banter" – then it is there to stay. Digital footprints follow you, whether you like it or not.

Students at Durham rightly fell foul of this in September 2020, when a group chat containing multiple misogynistic, racist and discriminatory views was leaked. One student had his offer withdrawn. In a similar online exposure, 11 students at Warwick were suspended for making rape jokes, racist statements and anti-Semitic slurs in an online conversation.

Remind your child that things they post today may be seen not only by their university but by future employers. Caution them not to post anything they wouldn't be comfortable having read back to them in an interview, or in front of a lecture hall of peers.

Universities have social media guidelines for students and your child will be seen as a representative of the university, whether posting on a private page or not. Clue them up on this before they go and remind them that nothing is truly private.

Keeping an eye online

Try not to fall into helicopter parenting. Your child is unlikely to accept you as a friend on social media sites or share everything with you. If you give them space, they are more likely to willingly talk to you when they want to. Encourage privacy settings so their posts can't be shared beyond the intended audience.

If you're concerned that they might be feeling isolated, stay in touch. The key is open dialogue and reserving your own judgment. Developing this relationship before your child goes to university will reap dividends as they navigate their time away.

Useful websites

For alcohol information: **http://www.alcoholimpact.nus.org.uk/   www.drinkaware.co.uk**
For information about drugs: **www.talktofrank.com   www.ssdp.org**
For information around consent: **www.nusconnect.org.uk   www.revoltsexualassault.com**
For information about mental health services the first point of reference should be a university's student support services.
For more general information: **www.studentminds.org.uk   www.youngminds.org.uk**

10 Going Abroad to University

For students who want to broaden their horizons, going abroad to study delivers on multiple levels. Embarking on university life thousands of miles from home means experiencing new cultures first-hand and growing in independence on a global scale. Jet-set students can hone their language skills and benefit from a fresh take on education. Traits they develop while studying overseas – such as flexibility and cultural mobility – are likely to help them stand out in the careers market.

There is remarkably little official scrutiny of how many students leave the UK, let alone where they go. But according to Unesco, which monitors the global flow of students in higher education, the numbers of UK students going abroad as part of a UK degree has reached more than 40,000. This is a drop in the ocean compared to our international peers, however: France has nearly 109,000 studying abroad and the number of German students overseas was close to 124,000 at Unesco's last count. Nepal, which has half the UK's population, has many more students overseas than the UK.

The high quality of UK universities is chief among the explanations for home students preferring to stay put. British universities are second only to those in the US in all international rankings and at present they offer enough places to meet demand. Our collectively poor language skills also limit the British taste for foreign study – unlike in most other countries where young people tend to be proficient in at least one second language by their late teens. On top of language barriers, studying in EU countries has become more complicated and expensive since Brexit.

Cost is another big factor deterring Brits from going abroad to study. Predictions that price would become less of an issue once UK degrees charged £9,000-a-year from 2012 have been slow to translate into a long-term overseas study stampede. Even taking into account grants, loans and scholarships, access to studying at university abroad is limited to those with the finances to make it happen.

The American dream

For those who do opt to study abroad there is one destination in a league of its own: America. Almost twice the number of UK students went to the US than went to Germany, the country that hosted the second-largest cohort, Unesco's latest data shows. Sharing a common language is a big plus for Brits in the US, as is the liberal arts curriculum Stateside, which allows students to apply to university without specifying a subject and spend the first two years of a four-year Bachelor's degree studying a wide range of classes before majoring in a specific field.

The Fulbright Commission, which promotes US-UK educational exchanges, estimates that most years there are between 11,000 and 11,500 British students studying at US universities at all levels – undergraduate, postgraduate and study abroad programmes. Although the pandemic's lockdowns and travel bans reduced the numbers in 2020-21, they were up to 10,292 in 2021-22 (a 28.2% increase on the year before). Rowena Boddington, advising and marketing director at the Fulbright Commission, thinks this number will continue to climb over the next couple of years.

Private privilege

The popularity of American higher education among UK students is on the rise especially in private schools – many of which have dedicated staff to assist in US university applications, and where sixth-formers' US destination successes are flagged on a par with their Oxbridge numbers. Some experts fear a "brain drain" of talented British students to American universities, as Oxford and Cambridge reduce the numbers of offers they make to private school pupils.

Eton College states on its website that more than 15% of school-leavers apply to US universities. A total of 36 Eton students started at American universities in 2021 – including Yale, Princeton and Harvard – nearly as many as the school sent to Oxbridge. At King's College Wimbledon, 26 applied to American universities in 2021 — about one in eight of the year group. At St Paul's School in southwest London, 30 students accepted offers from American universities in 2021, up from 22 in 2015. The Ivy League has joined Oxbridge as a battleground for private school pupils and their ambitious parents, it would seem.

In its 2022 census, the Independent Schools Council noted that 5% of pupils from ISC schools entering higher education chose to attend an overseas university. It also found that universities in the USA were the most popular, attracting 47% of this set of pupils.

David Hawkins, founder of The University Guys – which helps students make successful applications to international universities – has noticed an upturn in interest in US universities lately, with students attracted by three main factors: "The standard of the facilities; the much-increased teaching and contact hours; and the ability for a broader university experience – more subjects, the campus experience, sports/music/drama," he explains.

Top 10 destinations for UK students studying abroad		Best Student Cities in the World	
1 United States	9,646	1 London	United Kingdom
2 Germany	4,999	=2 Munich	Germany
3 Bulgaria	2,702	=2 Seoul	South Korea
4 Australia	2,575	4 Zurich	Switzerland
5 Ireland	1,634	5 Melbourne	Australia
6 Canada	1,389	6 Berlin	Germany
7 Spain	1,126	7 Tokyo	Japan
8 France	1,071	8 Paris	France
9 Austria	907	9 Sydney	Australia
10 Denmark	888	10 Edinburgh	United Kingdom
Source: Unesco 2021		Source: QS 2023	

Such privilege should not be the preserve of private school students only, believes the Sutton Trust educational charity and champion of social mobility – which delivers a US programme in conjunction with the Fulbright Commission. The scheme is directed at low-income, first-generation students in Year 12 at British state schools. Since its 2012 launch the programme has sent more than 500 state-educated school-leavers to over 75 American universities – including to highly selective institutions Harvard, in Cambridge Massachusetts; Stanford in California; and Duke in North Carolina.

The big-name universities – and global ranking big hitters – attract a lot of interest from UK students. But it's worth considering what the Ivy League is and what it isn't, advises Boddington.

"Some people think it's the equivalent of the Russell Group – it's not. The Ivy League is only universities in the northeast corner of the US, and it is a sports league. They are within driving distance of each other, they play football against each other. But there are lots of other selective schools that are not in the Ivy League – Stanford (in California), MIT (Massachusetts Institute of Technology), etc."

"Ivy Plus" is the term that encompasses both the Ivy League and a handful of similarly prestigious universities with lively traditions, large endowments and renowned alumni – such as Stanford, MIT, the University of Chicago, and Duke. Some lists also count Northwestern in Illinois; Johns Hopkins in Baltimore; and Caltech in Pasadena, California; as Ivy Plus.

Boddington encourages applicants "to recognise that there's more than six or seven universities in the US. I see students who are willing to be open-minded and explore what's out there be particularly successful in winning places."

In its 2022 census, the ISC showed that the top destinations in North America (including Canada) for ISC school pupils were – in descending order – the University of Toronto; New York University; the University of Chicago; McGill University, Montreal; the University of California, Berkeley; Boston University; and Columbia University, New York City.

Half the global top 10 universities in the QS ranking are in America, but Hawkins, points out a fact that UK families often overlook: "America also has colleges that only do undergraduate degrees, like Amherst (in Massachusetts), and Pomona (in California). Some of them are more selective than the Ivy League but they aren't in the rankings because they don't have academic research and postgraduate degrees."

Coming to America?

Applying to US universities is completely different to applying to UK institutions, and is based on fundamentally different concepts, as Hawkins explains.

"The biggest issue is going to be that what you are actually applying for is different. In the UK, you apply to study a subject. In the US, you apply to join a community. The bigger question that a university has to answer when selecting a student is 'do you fit here?', not 'are you good at what you want to study'. Because of this, US applications require huge amounts more information about each student, and students have to answer many more questions."

There are also questions that applicants to US universities should ask that they might not ask about a UK university, such as: what is the culture of this institution? America's polarised states offer varying experiences.

"Going to university in Georgia is going to feel different to going to a university in Massachusetts. Going to a university with a Catholic tradition, like Boston College or Notre Dame (in Indiana), is going to feel very different to going to a very urban, secular university like Northeastern (also in Boston) or NYU (New York).

"The Canadian universities McGill, British Columbia and Toronto are great but they're huge – they educate about as many undergraduates as the top 20 in America put together," notes Hawkins. Universities have their quirks, too – did you know that you have to pass a swimming test to get a degree from Columbia in New York?

"Applying to Columbia and applying to Brown (in Rhode Island) is like trying to do a UCAS application for physics and fine art – they are two completely different experiences, and people here tend not to know that," Hawkins adds.

The University Guys has two big messages to everyone considering applying to the US: "Start early and work harder," says Hawkins. Year 12 is when students should really ramp up their application efforts. Founded in 2019, The University Guys helps families navigate the process and make sense of the stuff that gets lost in translation as it crosses the pond – it is one of a growing number of such providers (**www.theuniversityguys.com**).

The Fulbright Commission offers free online guides on applying to US universities, an advice phone line and organises USA College Day each September, Europe's largest US university college fair (**www.fulbright.org.uk/going-to-the-usa/undergraduate; www.fulbright.org.uk/events/usa-college-day-2023**).

The bottom dollar

There's no avoiding the fact that university in the US can be very expensive. "Families I meet with are often very aware of this fact, and are keen to know what options there might be to reduce (or even completely wipe out) costs," says Hawkins.

Tuition fees vary; there are so many universities in the US, some with much lower fees and some with mind-bogglingly high prices. At Harvard, for example, in 2022-23, the total cost per year for a student – including tuition, fees, room and board, books, travel, and personal expenses comes to between $80,263 and $84, 413 (approximately £66,590 to £70,026).

According to the College Board, for tuition alone in 2022-23 the average published annual fees are $28,240, per year (£23,414) at public universities for out-of-state students and $39,400, (£32,667) at private universities. However, not everyone pays these sticker prices – scholarships and grants can significantly reduce fees – but only for those who qualify. Unfortunately, the British student loan cannot be taken to the US so it is down to families to find the funding.

American universities extend the same financial aid to international students as they do to home undergraduates, which comes either as a sport scholarship, merit scholarship or as needs-based help. The most common awards are in sport scholarships, says Hawkins. "US college sport is big business. The scholarship is a coach of a team using some of his or her budget to recruit students. So, if you are a very talented hockey player and the coach at Duke wants you, the coach at Duke is using his or her budget to fund you through university. The whole thing is about getting a coach to want you."

Merit scholarships can be in a wide range of talents such as volunteering or music, and different universities offer different awards. Needs-based aid is a means-tested form of funding, "So you could have two students going to Harvard, one of them could be paying $80,000 or so a year, the other one could be paying nothing. And that determination is entirely based on the family's financial circumstances," explains Hawkins.

Middle-class dreams of packing your teen off to a prestigious US university on a massive scholarship should be reined in, however. "Some of the top US universities only offer need-based aid, the Ivy League among them. So if the only money available is need-based, and you come from a relatively well-off family, you are unlikely to find that the route to a free US education lies in the Ivies," advises Hawkins.

Working in the USA

Student visas end when students have finished studying, and if they don't have a US visa or citizenship then they need to return to their home country. But an Optional Practical Training (OPT) visa is offered to graduates. They can apply as they finish their studies. "It means that they don't have to have an employer who is willing to sponsor a work visa for them," explains Boddington. In practical terms it extends the student visa into this OPT period.

"The idea is that a graduate can get a job in a field related to their major and get practical experience before returning home. For students in STEM (science, technology, engineering, mathematics) fields, an OPT visa can be for up to three years and for students in non-STEM fields it lasts for up to one year." Meanwhile students who return to Britain to apply for jobs have gained international experience and cross-cultural competency that makes them stand out.

Europe

British students already living in an EU country before the clock struck midnight on December 31, 2020, have continued to have the same educational rights as that country's nationals. UK citizens studying – or planning to study – in Ireland continue to be covered by the Common Travel Area arrangements, which guarantees "home" fees, lower than those charged to international students, for the future. The beneficial financial arrangements with Ireland, along with the university's academic clout, helps explain the ongoing popularity of Trinity College Dublin – which ranks eighth among the top destinations of ISC pupils attending non-UK universities.

It is up to individual EU member states to determine their approach to tuition fees for UK nationals, post-Brexit. Some countries, such as Germany – the second most popular destination for UK students studying abroad – have always charged the same fees to students from anywhere else in the world, not just the EU, and have continued to do so post-Brexit. In other countries, such as Denmark, British citizens without permanent residency are now liable to pay university tuition fees.

The Netherlands, which regularly promotes its universities to UK students and offers more undergraduate degrees taught in English than many other countries, withdrew funding and fee benefits post-Brexit for UK students, who now pay international fees which range from around £5,500 a year to £13,500 for most courses, and more than £30,000 per annum for medicine. Dutch tuition fee loans, available for the full amount to EU students who are resident in the Netherlands throughout their studies, have stopped for UK students. Unsurprisingly, there has been a sharp decline in the number of UK students enrolling at Dutch universities – including a 25% drop between 2020-21 and 2021-22 – according to data from Nuffic, the Dutch international education agency.

Since Brexit, UK students have had to wrangle with immigration regulations in the EU. UK nationals are only able to stay in an EU country for 90 out of every 180 days without a visa.

There are more than 10,000 UK students at Continental European universities and colleges, according to Unesco. But a minority are undergraduates. More courses are taught in English at postgraduate level.

Nearly all first degrees in France are taught in the mother tongue, though the number taught in English has risen to 125 programmes, as listed on the Campus France website (**www.campusfrance.org/en**) at the Licence (Bachelor's equivalent) level.

Germany attracts large numbers of international students and the DAAD website (**www.daad.de/en**) lists 317 undergraduate programmes taught wholly or mainly in English. Many are at the 20 private German universities, however, like Jacobs University in Bremen, which charges €20,000 (approximately £17,000) in tuition fees a year. The public sector has abolished tuition fees, but you need to hunt down the courses as they are relatively scarce.

Most Continental courses are longer than their UK equivalents, adding to the cost and to lost earnings from extra time at university. Travel costs will be more, too. The cost of living varies, from lower than the UK in southern Europe, to higher in Scandinavia.

The shorter-term schemes offered by the new national exchange scheme detailed below or arranged by UK universities with partners across the world, represent much less of a commitment academically, emotionally and financially than taking your whole degree abroad.

Exchange students

Named after the mathematician Alan Turing, the UK's new Turing scheme has replaced Erasmus, the EU student exchange programme that the UK decided to withdraw from after Brexit. Backed by £110million government funding, the Turing scheme provides grants for students in study and work placements across the world. It provided funding for more than 41,000 students in study and work placements across the world during the 2021-22 academic year and the government has confirmed financial support for the scheme to 2024-25.

Under the Turing scheme, schools, colleges and higher education providers apply for funding for exchange projects on behalf of their students. If successful, they are then able to provide their students with funding to support study and work placements abroad. Funding amounts vary, depending on where students are going and for how long. For example, a student going to Spain for a placement lasting between four and eight weeks could be eligible for £120 per week. For placements lasting over eight weeks, they could be eligible for £335 per month. There is a more generous rate for disadvantaged students, plus help with travel costs.

The new programme has a global reach and provides placements across the world. UK students did not have to pay tuition fees when studying abroad under Erasmus because the reciprocal scheme allowed EU students to come and study in the UK as well. The Turing scheme does not pay tuition fees for UK students studying abroad or for students from other countries studying in the UK. Instead, universities are expected to waive tuition fees for the placement.

As part of an arrangement with the Irish government, students at universities in Northern Ireland, however, can still participate in Erasmus+ as well as the Turing scheme.

Students in Wales have access to the newly launched International Learning Exchange programme in place of Erasmus+. The scheme is running from 2022–26, supported by an investment of £65million from the Welsh government.

Advantages of studying abroad

Schools, universities and students themselves are enthusiastic about studying abroad. It is exciting, offers new challenges and introduces young people to a global working environment. A study stint abroad on a CV shows employers that the applicant has a maturity and breadth of experience that stands out from other candidates.

British universities overseas

It is possible to have your academic cake and eat it, by attending a British university in another country. Nottingham University, for example, has campuses in China and Malaysia; Middlesex can offer Dubai or Mauritius, where students registered in the UK can take part or all of their degrees. Other universities, such as Liverpool, also offer an international experience (in China, in Liverpool's case) and degrees from both universities.

A new UK University Overseas Campuses Network launched in 2021, founded and co-chaired by the University of Nottingham and Newcastle University, with support from Universities UK International. Bringing together an initial membership of 17 UK universities with 27 campuses located in 17 countries across the world, the network represents institutions providing a British education to more than 60,000 students and employing upwards of 5,000 staff.

Upon its launch Vivienne Stern, director of Universities UK International, said: "UK overseas campuses are a success story. Over 30 UK universities have a physical presence overseas, hosting a growing number of students and local staff from a wide diversity of backgrounds."

Postgraduate options

In most cases, however, an overseas study experience means a foreign university. Postgraduate degrees used to be the preferred qualification to pursue abroad, and it is worth considering spending your undergraduate years in the UK before going abroad for more advanced study.

Where do students go to?

After America (9,646 UK students) and Germany (4,999), the latest figures from Unesco place Bulgaria (2,702), Australia (2,575), Ireland (1,634) and Canada (1,389) after it, see table on page 128. A few British students find their way to unexpected locations, like the Republic of Moldova or Indonesia, but usually for family reasons or to study the language.

Bear in mind that studying abroad can be the start of a much lengthier relocation, visa regulations allowing. University is where lots of people meet their spouses and set sail in their careers. Is the other side of the Atlantic, or the world, where you see yourself potentially settling down?

Which countries are best?

A memorable and valuable all-round experience is up there with the need for a good course when searching for a university overseas. Location is a big deal for most students – the country and the city – as is the reputation of the institution. QS publishes an annual ranking of student cities, using the opinions of current students to rate university locations on factors including affordability and desirability. London topped the ranking in 2023, followed by Munich, Seoul and Zurich. See table page 128.

Many Asian countries, such as Japan, are looking to recruit more foreign students. The high cost of living and unfamiliar language in Japan may seem hard to crack, but support for international students and courses taught in English are on the rise. As with any non-English speaking country, though, even if you are taught in English, you still need enough of the local language to get by in shops, on transport and to make friends.

China is worth considering, if you can get used to the dormitory accommodation that is the norm at most universities. The country's leading institutions are climbing the world rankings and improving their facilities, and the potential headstart in business offered by studying in China is hard to ignore. Hong Kong, which has several world-ranked universities and feels familiar for Britons, is a popular alternative to mainland Chinese universities, although the security situation has to be kept under review.

Global rankings: which university is best?

Going abroad to study is a big and expensive decision, and you want to get it right. A university that is taken seriously around the world should be your ambition.

Top Universities in the World

Rank	(Last year)	Institution	Country
2022	**2021**		
=1	1	Harvard University	USA
=1	2	Stanford University	USA
=3	5	University of Cambridge	UK
=3	=3	Massachusetts Institute of Technology (MIT)	USA
5	=3	University of Oxford	UK
=6	6	California Institute of Technology (Caltech)	USA
=6	8	Princeton University	USA
8	7	University of Chicago	USA
9	9	Yale University	USA
10	=13	Imperial College London	UK
=11	=13	ETH Zurich – Swiss Federal Institute of Technology	Switzerland
=11	15	University of California, Berkeley (UCB)	USA
13	10	Columbia University	USA
14	11	University of Pennsylvania	USA
15	12	University College London	UK
=16	17	Cornell University	USA
=16	16	Johns Hopkins University	USA
18	18	Tsinghua University	China
19	22	Peking University	China
20	19	University of Toronto	Canada
21	20	University of Michigan-Ann Arbor	USA
22	21	University of California, Los Angeles (UCLA)	USA
23	24	The University of Edinburgh	UK
24	23	The University of Tokyo	Japan
=25	25	Northwestern University	USA
=25	26	New York University (NYU)	USA
27	28	The University of Melbourne	Australia
28	=29	National University of Singapore (NUS)	Singapore
=29	=29	Duke University	USA
=29	27	University of California, San Diego (UCSD)	USA
31	33	Université Paris Sciences et Lettres	France
=32	31	The University of Manchester	UK
=32	32	King's College London	UK
34	36	University of Washington	USA
35	34	University of British Columbia	Canada
36	39	Technical University of Munich	Germany
37	38	Nanyang Technological University, Singapore (NTU)	Singapore
=38	35	Kyoto University	Japan
=38	50	Zhejiang University	China
40	43	The University of Hong Kong	Hong Kong
41	40	Ludwig-Maximilians-Universität München	Germany

=42	**37** McGill University	Canada
=42	**42** The University of Queensland	Australia
=44	**49** Fudan University	China
=44	**60** Shanghai Jiao Tong University	China
46	**48** The University of Sydney	Australia
47	**41** École Polytechnique Fédérale de Lausanne (EPFL)	Switzerland
48	**45** The Australian National University	Australia
49	**=61** Monash University	Australia
50	**46** Ruprecht-Karls-Universität Heidelberg	Germany
51	**=53** The University of New South Wales (UNSW Sydney)	Australia
52	**=53** Carnegie Mellon University	USA
53	**57** University of Illinois at Urbana-Champaign	USA
54	**59** Seoul National University	South Korea
55	**58** The Chinese University of Hong Kong (CUHK)	Hong Kong
56	**51** Washington University in St Louis	USA
57	**44** University of Texas at Austin	USA
58	**56** Karolinska Institute, Stockholm	Sweden
59	**=61** Sorbonne University	France
60	**52** The London School of Economics and Political Science (LSE)	UK
61	**47** University of Wisconsin-Madison	USA
=62	**65** The Hong Kong University of Science and Technology	Hong Kong
=62	**55** University of North Carolina at Chapel Hill	USA
64	**67** Université Paris-Saclay	France
65	**=63** KU Leuven	Belgium
66	**=75** University of Bristol	UK
=67	**69** University of Amsterdam	Netherlands
=67	**=71** University of Southern California	USA
=69	**70** University of California, San Francisco	USA
=69	**68** Utrecht University	Netherlands
=71	**66** University of Copenhagen	Denmark
=71	**73** University of California, Santa Barbara	USA
73	**=71** Brown University	USA
74	**=63** University of Zurich	Switzerland
75	**77** Georgia Institute of Technology	USA
76	**84** University of Science and Technology of China	China
77	**=75** Delft University of Technology	Netherlands
78	**80** KAIST – Korea Advanced Institute of Science & Technology	South Korea
79	**82** University of Groningen	Netherlands
80	**=86** Institut Polytechnique de Paris	France
81	**=98** The Hong Kong Polytechnic University	Hong Kong
=82	**81** Rockefeller University	USA
=82	**74** University of Minnesota, Twin Cities	USA
=84	Yonsei University	South Korea
=84	**=86** University of Maryland, College Park	USA
86	**83** University of Colorado at Boulder	USA
=87	**=88** City University of Hong Kong	Hong Kong

Top Universities in the World cont.

=87	85	The University of Texas Southwestern Medical Center at Dallas	USA
=89	=91	Tokyo Institute of Technology (Tokyo Tech)	Japan
=89		University of California, Irvine	USA
91	=88	Wageningen University	Netherlands
92	=96	Vanderbilt University	USA
=93	93	University of Glasgow	UK
=93	94	University of Geneva	Switzerland
95	=98	University of California Davis	USA
=96	78	The University of Warwick	UK
=96		University of Bonn	Germany
98		Erasmus University Rotterdam	Netherlands
=99		Universidad de Buenos Aires (UBA)	Brazil
=99	95	University of Oslo	Norway

Averaged from positions in the QS World University Ranking (QS); the Academic Ranking of World Universities (ARWU – Shanghai ranking); and *Times Higher Education* (THE) for 2022

Contact the National Recognition Centre for the UK (**www.enic.org.uk**), which examines the compatibility and acceptability of qualifications from around the world, or ask the UK professional body in question – an engineering institution, law society or dental council, for instance – about the qualification you are interested in.

Will my degree be recognised?

Even in the era of globalisation, you need to bear in mind that not all degrees are equal. Unlike the MBA, which has an international system for accrediting courses and a global admissions standard, many professional courses need a qualification recognised by the relevant professional body. It is understandable that to practise law in England, you need to have studied the English legal system. For other subjects, the issues are more about the quality and content of courses outside UK control.

At the moment, there are three main systems for ranking universities internationally. One is run by QS (Quacquarelli Symonds), an educational research company in London (**www.topuniversities.com**). Another is by Shanghai Ranking Consultancy, a company set up by Shanghai Jiao Tong University, in China, and is called the Academic Ranking of World Universities (ARWU) (**www.shanghairanking.com**). The third is produced by *Times Higher Education* (**www.timeshighereducation.com/world-university-rankings**), a weekly magazine with no connection to *The Times* newspaper, which published the QS version until 2010.

The QS system uses measures including academic opinion, employer opinion, international orientation, research impact and staff/student ratio to create its listing, while the ARWU takes account of Nobel Prizes and highly-cited papers, which are more related to excellence in scientific research. *Times Higher Education* added a number of measures to the QS model, including research income and a controversial global survey of teaching quality.

Naturally, the different methodologies produce some contrasting results – as evidenced by the three main rankings each having a different university at the top. The table on these pages is a composite of the three main rankings, which places Harvard at the top and includes four UK universities in the top 15. See page 134.

In practice, if you go to a university that features strongly in any of the tables, you will be at a place that is well-regarded around the world. Even the 200th university on any of these rankings is an elite institution in a world with way more than 5,000 universities.

The main international rankings focus largely on research and tend to favour universities which are good at science and medicine. This is why places that centre on the humanities and the social sciences, such as the London School of Economics, can appear in deceptively modest positions. It is also worth bearing in mind that the rankings look at universities as a whole and offer limited information on specific subjects. QS first published global rankings in 26 subjects in 2011 and has increased its output now to 51 subjects.

Other options for overseas studies

A language degree will typically involve a year abroad, and a look at the UCAS website will show many options for studying another subject alongside your language of choice.

Many degrees offer a year abroad, either studying or in a work placement, even to those who are not taking a language. Shorter credit-bearing courses with partner institutions overseas are another option offered by UK universities. The best approach is to decide what you want to study and then see if there is a UK university that offers it as a joint degree or with a placement abroad. Do a background check on all the universities involved to ensure they are well-regarded, which is where the websites of global rankings will come in handy.

Useful websites

Prospects: studying abroad: **www.prospects.ac.uk/postgraduate-study/study-abroad**
Association of Commonwealth Universities: **www.acu.ac.uk**
Campus France: **www.campusfrance.org/en**
College Board (USA): **www.collegeboard.org**
DAAD (for Germany): **www.daad.de/en**
Study in Holland: **www.studyinholland.co.uk**
Education Ireland: **www.educationinireland.com/en**
Erasmus Programme (EU): **www.erasmusplus.org.uk**
Finaid (USA): **www.finaid.org**
Fulbright Commission: **www.fulbright.org.uk**
Study in Australia: **www.studyinaustralia.gov.au**
Study in Canada: **www.studyincanada.com**

11 Coming to the UK to Study

One in 10 international students had decided by the age of 11 to study abroad and half are following in the footsteps of a parent, a report published in 2022 by UCAS revealed. In the same study, the Universities and Colleges Admissions Service forecast that the volume of international undergraduate applicants to UK universities will increase by 46% from around 144,000 last autumn to 208,500 by 2026. With borders reopening, the report gathered insights from 1,300 students planning to study internationally and showed there is renewed interest in living in the UK, with the NHS and English language a particular draw.

Almost nine out of 10 students (88%) said they viewed the UK as a positive, or very positive, place to study and 77% were applying to UK universities because of its strong academic reputation. At the end of the 2021 admissions cycle UCAS registered a 12% increase in applications from international students (to 111,255), with 54,030 accepted (up 2%).

The figures highlight the underlying strength of UK universities, which has caused demand to hold up among international students – even as the withdrawal of home fee status for EU students has prompted those from the Continent to vote with their feet. In the 2021 admissions round there were 31,670 applicants from within the EU (down 40% year-on-year), with 16,025 accepted (down 50%).

The UK higher education sector has a reputation for being welcoming, diverse and offering easy access to international students. When the pandemic hit and travel restrictions ensued, universities including Imperial College London, Exeter and Bristol chartered flights to bring students over in time for the start of term. Indeed, study is a major reason that people move to the UK – the Migration Observatory at the University of Oxford found. Figures from Unesco show the UK to have been the second most popular destination in the world for international students throughout the years, behind only the USA.

Having fewer EU students on campuses represents a sore loss of some of that prized cultural diversity, and the change in fee status is a blow to the social and academic mobility offered by the formerly excellent value higher education available to students from EU countries. When the UK was in the EU, students from other member countries only had to pay up to £9,250 per year, the same as British nationals. Since August 2021, tuition fees for all international students have been set by the universities, and costs vary – with some leading universities charging a premium.

The range charged by each university is listed with its dedicated university profile in Chapter 14 of our *Guide*. Most fall broadly between around £11,000 and £25,000, with classroom-based subjects such as the humanities at the cheaper end. Subjects such as the engineering disciplines can cost over £35,000 while medical and veterinary degrees can sometimes reach up to around £64,000. The upturn in recruitment of fee-paying international students consequently helps universities to balance the books, especially in light of calls from some vice-chancellors to raise income by increasing domestic tuition fees.

Online learning may help re-engage price-sensitive students from the EU. There are plans to entice EU students with awards via the GREAT Scholarships system for students from around the world, which the British Council has been lobbying the cabinet to extend with an EU scheme. At the last count, Italian and French students remained the two largest cohorts from the EU in the UK, with 14,605 and 14,090 students respectively studying in 2020–21.

Chinese students make up the UK's largest cohort of international students, representing more than a third of non-EU overseas students in 2021 – by far the highest proportion from a single country. India, Hong Kong and Malaysia follow in second, third and fourth places, and among EU countries Romania, Poland and Spain sent the most students, in that order.

The top countries for sending international students to the UK

EU countries (top 20)		%	Non-EU countries (top 20)		%
Romania	11,032	0.1	China	55,538	0.3
Poland	8,898	0.1	India	16,777	0.1
Spain	8,835	0.1	Hong Kong (Special Administrative	12,803	0.1
France	8,771	0.1	Region of China) [Hong Kong]		
Italy	7,841	0.1	Malaysia	8,815	0.0
Portugal	6,584	0.1	United States	7,956	0.0
Cyprus (European Union)	6,221	0.1	Singapore	5,214	0.0
Germany	5,596	0.1	Nigeria	5,183	0.0
Greece	5,488	0.1	Kuwait	4,763	0.0
Bulgaria	4,985	0.0	United Arab Emirates	4,707	0.0
Ireland	4,860	0.0	Pakistan	4,111	0.0
Lithuania	3,733	0.0	Canada	3,484	0.0
Czech Republic	2,324	0.0	Korea (South) [Korea, Republic of]	2,998	0.0
Hungary	2,112	0.0	Saudi Arabia	2,994	0.0
Sweden	1,999	0.0	Switzerland	2,681	0.0
Belgium	1,952	0.0	Norway	2,575	0.0
Slovakia	1,672	0.0	Qatar	2,104	0.0
Netherlands	1,627	0.0	Thailand	2,060	0.0
Finland	1,370	0.0	Russia [Russian Federation]	1,946	0.0
Latvia	1,230	0.0	Turkey	1,825	0.0
			Egypt	1,799	0.0
Total (all non-UK EU)	**102,870**		**Total (all non-EU)**	**183,120**	

Note: First degree non-UK students

The relationship between the UK and its international students is reciprocal, as highlighted by research conducted by educational thinktank the Higher Education Policy Institute (HEPI) in conjunction with Universities UK International. The analysis calculated that international students contribute more than £25.9bn to the UK's economy, with every part of the UK financially better off – on average by £390 per person – because of them. Nick Hillman, director of HEPI, says: "This report confirms higher education is one of the UK's greatest export earners. The benefits reach every part of the UK, from Land's End to John O'Groats. But international students do not just bring financial benefits. They also bring educational benefits by making our campuses more diverse and exciting places to be."

However, in the latter half of 2022 reports circulated that the government is considering clamping down on the number of foreign students travelling to the UK to study, after official figures published by the Office for National Statistics (ONS) showed net immigration to Britain rose by record levels in the year before. Of significance to the higher education sector is that almost 40% of the 704,000 non-EU nationals who came to the UK in the year to June 2022 arrived on study visas. New restrictions on international students bringing family members seem likely (at the time of writing), after the number of dependents almost tripled in a year.

Those who win places at leading universities may be better placed should restrictions be implemented, however, as the government seeks to penalise universities with high dropout rates and low graduate earnings. A spokesman for the Prime Minister, Rishi Sunak, said that "looking at the figures and considering all options to make sure the immigration system is delivering does include looking at the issue of student dependents and low-quality degrees." Home secretary Suella Braverman has also called the quality of degrees taken by international students into question, adding: "I think it's legitimate to question whether that is going to serve our economic objectives, and taking a more discerning, smart approach to the number of student visas."

Any curbs on international student numbers would be a reversal after the 2019 International Education Strategy, which set a target of 600,000 foreign students by 2030 to boost the value of Britain's education exports to £35bn per year. The target was met in 2020-21, and celebrated by the government when Sunak was chancellor.

"The fact that our universities attract students from around the world is an asset for the UK," commented Dr Tim Bradshaw, chief executive of the Russell Group. "Proposals that limit or restrict that asset would be a mistake, damaging local economies and contradicting the government's own International Education Strategy. It also sends the wrong signal about the UK on the global stage. Worse, it is free marketing for our competitors in Australia, Canada and the US."

Why study in the UK?

There is much to recommend a degree in Britain. Global surveys have shown that British universities are seen to offer high quality in a relatively safe environment, with the added bonus of students being immersed in the English language. Degree courses here, both undergraduate and postgraduate, are shorter than the average length worldwide, which helps balance our relatively high living costs. The fall in the value of the pound recently has added to the country's appeal.

In terms of academic standing, the QS World University Rankings 2023 include 89 UK universities. Four of them are in the global top 10, with a further 13 in the global top 100. *Times Higher Education's* World University Rankings 2022 have Oxford in first place globally and include 28 British universities in the top 200.

As well as the strong reputation of UK degrees and the opportunity to be taught in and soak up the English language, research shows that most international graduates are well-rewarded when they return home. A government-commissioned report showed that graduates of UK universities earn much higher salaries than those who studied in their own country. The starting salaries of UK graduates in China and India were more than twice as high as those for graduates educated at home, while even those returning to the USA saw a salary premium of more than 10%.

Students who take the plunge to travel abroad to study are likely to be bright and highly motivated, so some uplift in such students' outcomes is to be expected. Unless they have government scholarships, most international students have to be from relatively wealthy backgrounds to afford the fees and other expenses involved. But the scale of increase demonstrated in the report suggests that a UK degree remains a good investment. Three years after graduation, 95% of the international graduates surveyed were in work or further study. More than 90% had been satisfied with their learning experience and almost as many would recommend their university to others.

A popular choice

Nearly all UK universities are cosmopolitan and in many you can expect to have fellow students from more than 100 countries. Almost one student in five is from outside the UK – 6% from the EU and 14% from the rest of the world. More full-time postgraduates – the fastest-growing group – come from outside the UK than within it.

The universities most favoured by EU and non-EU students

Institution (top 20)	EU students	Institution (top 20)	Non-EU students
University College London	3,370	University College London	8,377
Coventry University	3,368	The University of Manchester	7,327
King's College London	3,158	Coventry University	6,184
University of Bedfordshire	2,568	The University of Edinburgh	5,740
The University of Manchester	2,373	University of the Arts, London	5,303
The University of Edinburgh	2,317	King's College London	5,296
University of the Arts, London	2,279	The University of Liverpool	4,404
The University of Warwick	2,201	The University of Birmingham	3,945
Anglia Ruskin University	2,127	Imperial College of Science, Technology and Medicine	3,888
The University of West London	2,082	The University of Leeds	3,811
The University of Glasgow	1,921	The University of Sheffield	3,744
De Montfort University	1,863	University of Nottingham	3,437
The University of Essex	1,850	The University of Warwick	3,345
The University of Aberdeen	1,843	University of Durham	3,208
Imperial College of Science, Technology and Medicine	1,670	The University of Bristol	3,007
The University of Westminster	1,661	The University of Exeter	2,927
The University of Greenwich	1,655	The University of St Andrews	2,816
Middlesex University	1,522	The University of Sussex	2,710
Solent University	1,479	The University of Glasgow	2,494
The University of Lancaster	1,420	The University of Lancaster	2,419

Note: First degree non-UK students

More than 90% of international students declare themselves satisfied with their experience of UK universities in surveys by i-graduate, the student polling organisation, although they are less enthusiastic in the National Student Survey and more likely than UK students to make official complaints. Nevertheless, satisfaction increased by eight percentage points in four years, according to i-graduate. International students are particularly complimentary about students' unions, multiculturalism, teaching standards and places of worship. Their main concerns tend to be financial, partly because of a lack of employment opportunities. However, since summer 2021, international students who have successfully completed an undergraduate or master's degree have been able to benefit from two years' work experience in the UK upon graduation, through the new Graduate Route. Students who complete their PhD will be able to stay for three years.

The number of students taking UK degrees through a local institution, distance learning or a full branch campus of a UK university was already growing even before the health pandemic heralded widespread blended online learning. The numbers grew by 70% in a decade and are likely to rise further as a result of the post-Brexit fee changes. Over 30 UK universities have a physical presence overseas and the success of these international hubs has led to the formation of a new UK University Overseas Campuses Network, representing institutions providing a British education to more than 60,000 students and employing upwards of 5,000 staff. Most branch campuses are in Asia or the Middle East. Coventry – which was the most popular UK university with EU students in 2020 – has set up in Poland.

Where to study in the UK

The vast majority of the UK's universities and other higher education institutions are in England. Of the 135 universities profiled in this *Guide*, 107 are in England, 15 in Scotland, eight in Wales and two in Northern Ireland. Fee limits in higher education for UK and EU students are determined separately in each administrative area. Historically this brought some benefits for EU students, such as those who chose to study in Scotland where they paid no tuition fees. Under the new regulations however, all undergraduates from outside the UK are charged the international rate of fees.

Within the UK, the cost of living varies by geographical area. London is home to University College London, the most popular university with non-EU students in 2021, even though it is the most expensive city. Incoming students should find out as much as they can about what living in Britain is like. Further advice and information is available through the British Council at its offices worldwide, at more than 60 university exhibitions that it holds around the world every year, or at its Education UK website: **https://study-uk.britishcouncil.org**. Also useful is the information provided by the UK Council for International Student Affairs (UKCISA) at **www.ukcisa.org.uk**.

Universities in all parts of the UK have a reputation for high-quality teaching and research, as evidenced in global rankings such as those shown on pages 134-6. They maintain this standing by investing heavily in the best academic staff, buildings and equipment, and by taking part in rigorous quality assurance monitoring. The Office for Students is the chief regulatory body for higher education in England, overseeing organisations such as the Quality Assurance Agency for Higher Education (QAA), which remains the arbiter of standards. Professional bodies also play an important role in relevant subjects.

Although many people from outside the UK associate British universities with Oxford and Cambridge, the reality at most higher education institutions is quite different. Some universities do still maintain ancient traditions, but most are modern institutions that place at least as much emphasis on teaching as on research and offer many vocational programmes, often with close links to business, industry and the professions. The table on page 141 shows the universities that are most popular with international students at undergraduate level. Although some are among the most famous names in higher education, others achieved university status only in the past 30 years.

What subjects to study?

Strongly vocational courses are favoured by international students. Many of these in professional areas such as architecture, dentistry or medicine take one or two years longer to complete than most other degree courses. Traditional first degrees are mostly awarded at Bachelor level (BA, BEng, BSc, etc.) and last three to four years. There are also some "enhanced" first degrees (MEng, MChem, etc) that take four years to complete. The relatively new Foundation degree programmes are almost all vocational and take two years to complete as a full-time course, with an option to study for a further year to gain a full degree. The table below shows the most popular subjects studied by international students. You need to consider the details of the degree you wish to study and ensure that you have looked at the ranking of that university in our main league table in Chapter 1 and in the subject tables in Chapter 12.

The most popular subjects for international students

Subject Group	EU students	Non-EU students	Total students	% of all international students
Business, Management & Marketing	17,271	33,001	50,272	17.6
Computer Science	8,228	11,800	20,028	7.0
Accounting & Finance	2,346	15,275	17,622	6.2
Law	4,241	10,952	15,192	5.3
Art & Design	5,324	8,230	13,554	4.7
Biological Sciences	5,910	6,471	12,381	4.3
Economics	2,860	8,753	11,613	4.1
Psychology	5,087	4,811	9,899	3.5
Mathematics	2,046	6,455	8,501	3.0
Politics	3,875	4,303	8,179	2.9
Electrical & Electronic Engineering	1,344	6,321	7,665	2.7
Drama, Dance & Cinematics	4,341	3,088	7,429	2.6
Mechanical Engineering	1,745	5,308	7,053	2.5
Communication & Media Studies	2,717	3,888	6,605	2.3
Medicine	1,602	4,706	6,309	2.2
Hospitality, Leisure, Recreation & Tourism	2,576	2,391	4,967	1.7
Aeronautical & Manufacturing Engineering	1,676	3,138	4,814	1.7
Architecture	1,645	3,023	4,668	1.6
Civil Engineering	756	3,542	4,298	1.5
Physics & Astronomy	1,723	1,934	3,658	1.3
Total	**102,870**	**183,120**	**285,990**	

Note: First degree non-UK students
Note: 'Other' excluded from subject rank but numbers are included in totals, which are also used to calculate the %s

English language proficiency

The universities maintain high standards partly by setting demanding entry requirements, including proficiency in English. For international students, this usually includes a score of at least 5.5 in the International English Language Testing System (IELTS). Under visa regulations introduced in 2011, universities are able to vouch for a student's ability in English. This proficiency will need to be equivalent to an "upper intermediate" level (level B2) of the CEFR (Common European Framework of Reference for Languages) for studying at an undergraduate level (roughly equivalent to an overall score of 5.5 in IELTS).

There are many private and publicly funded colleges throughout the UK that run courses designed to bring the English language skills of prospective higher education students up to the required standard. However, not all of these are government approved. Some private organisations such as INTO (**www.intostudy.com**) have joined with universities to create centres running programmes preparing international students for degree-level study. The British Council also runs English language courses.

Tougher student visa regulations were introduced in 2012 and have since been refined. Although under the current system, universities' international students should not be denied entry to the UK, as long as they are proficient in English and are found to have followed other immigration rules, some lower-level preparatory courses taken by international students have been affected. It is, therefore, doubly important to consult the official UK government list of approved institutions (web address given at the end of this chapter) before applying.

How to apply

The information below is best read in conjunction with that provided in Chapter 5, which deals with the application process in some detail.

Some international students apply directly to a UK university for a place on a course, and others make their applications via an agent in their home country. But most applying for a full-time, first-degree course do so through the Universities and Colleges Admissions Service (UCAS). If you take this route, you will need to fill in an online UCAS application form at home, at school or perhaps at your nearest British Council office. There is plenty of advice on the UCAS website about the process.

Whichever way you apply, the deadlines for getting your application in are the same. Under the regulations at the time this *Guide* went to press, for those applying from within an EU country, application forms for most courses starting in 2023 must be received at UCAS by January 15, 2023. Note that some art and design courses have a later deadline of March 24. Applications for Oxford and Cambridge and for all courses in medicine, dentistry and veterinary science have to be received at UCAS by October 15 each year.

If you are applying from a non-EU country to study in 2023, you can submit your application to UCAS at any time starting from September 1, 2022 to June 30, 2023. Most people will apply well before the June 30 deadline.

Entry and employment regulations

Visa regulations have been the subject of continuing controversy in the UK and are often hotly contested by universities. Recent governments have been criticised for increasing visa fees, doubling the cost of visa extensions, and ending the right to appeal against refusal of a visa.

The current points system for entry – known as Tier 4 – came into effect in 2009. Under this scheme, prospective students can check whether they are eligible for entry against published criteria, and so assess their points score. Universities are also required to provide a Confirmation of Acceptance for Studies (CAS) to their international student entrants, who must have secured an unconditional offer, and the institution must appear as a "Tier 4 Sponsor" on the Home Office's Register of Sponsors. Prospective students have to demonstrate that, as well as the necessary qualifications, they have English language proficiency and enough money for the first year of their specified course. This includes the full fees for the first year and, currently, living costs of £1,334 a month, up to a maximum of nine months, if studying in London (£1,023 a month in the rest of the UK). Under the current visa requirements, details of financial support are checked in more detail than before.

All students wishing to enter the UK to study are required to obtain entry clearance before arrival. The only exceptions are British nationals living overseas, British Overseas Territories citizens, British protected persons, British subjects, and non-visa national short-term students who may enter under a new Student Visitor route. All overseas students must now obtain a Tier 4 student visa, including those from EU countries, Iceland, Liechtenstein, Norway and Switzerland. Fees are £348, plus an annual healthcare surcharge. As part of the application process, biometric data will be requested and this will be used to issue you with a Biometric Residence Permit (BRP). You will need a BRP to open a UK bank account, rent accommodation or establish your eligibility for benefits and services or to work part-time, for example. The details of the regulations are continually reviewed by the Home Office. You can find more at **www.gov.uk/tier-4-general-visa**.

Irish nationals have the right to live and work in the UK, under the UK-Ireland Common Travel Area arrangements. Irish students will not need to apply for a student visa or the graduate immigration route.

Bringing your family

Since 2010, international students on courses of six months or less have been forbidden to bring a partner or children into the UK, and the latest reforms extend this prohibition to all undergraduates except those who are government sponsored. Postgraduates studying for 12 months or longer will still be able to bring dependents to the UK.

The family members you are allowed to bring with you are your husband or wife, civil partner (a same-sex relationship that has been formally registered in the UK or your home country) or long-term partner and dependent children. In light of recently mooted plans to curb the numbers of family members international students may bring with them to the UK it is important to check the latest information at **www.ukcisa.org.uk**.

Support from British universities

Support for international students is more comprehensive than in many countries and begins long before you arrive in the UK. Many universities have advisers in other countries. Some will put you in touch with current students or graduates who can give you a first-hand account of what life is like at a particular university. Pre-departure receptions for students and their families, as well as meet-and-greet arrangements for newly-arrived students, are common. You can also expect an orientation and induction programme in your first week, and many universities now have "buddying" systems where current students are assigned to help new arrivals. Each university also has a students' union that organises social, cultural and sporting events and clubs. Both the university and the students' union are likely to have full-time staff whose job it is to look after the welfare of students from overseas.

International students with pre-settled/settled status under the EU Settlement Scheme and studying in the UK for six months or more have free access the National Health Service (NHS). They also benefit from subsidised dental and optical care under NHS rules, plus access to a professional counselling service and a university careers service. Non-EU students will have had to pay a healthcare surcharge to benefit from this.

Those international students coming into the UK on a student visa or any other visa which included paying the Immigration Health Surcharge as part of their visa application are then also entitled to free access to the NHS and can register with a GP as a permanent patient.

At university, you will naturally encounter people from a wide range of cultures and walks of life. Getting involved in student societies, sport, voluntary work, and any of the wide range of social activities on offer will help you gain first-hand experience of British culture, and, if you need it, will help improve your command of the English language.

Useful websites

The British Council, with its dedicated Study UK site designed for those wishing to find out more about studying in the UKK:
https://study-uk.britishcouncil.org/

The UK Council for International Student Affairs (UKCISA) provides a wide range of information on all aspects of studying in the UK:
www.ukcisa.org.uk

UCAS, for full details of undergraduate courses available and an explanation of the application process:
www.ucas.com/undergraduate/applying-university/ucas-undergraduate-international-and-eu-students

For the latest information on entry and visa requirements:
www.gov.uk/tier-4-general-visa

Register of sponsors for Tier 4 educational establishments:
www.gov.uk/government/publications/register-of-licensed-sponsors-students

For a general guide to Britain, available in many languages:
www.visitbritain.com

12 Subject by Subject Guide

Perhaps surprisingly, the best course in the subject you want to study might not be at the university with the highest league table position or the oldest foundation. Some fairly modest universities are specialists in niche areas – as evidenced by their research outputs, graduate career successes and feedback from current students. Or, it could turn out that the best course happens to be offered at a top-end, ancient university that you had not considered before.

Or maybe the subject you loved at A-level is taught quite differently at degree level and would turn out an uninspiring choice for a three-year undergraduate commitment. Employment prospects are another factor; they might be dire for the subject you love – but some digging down can elicit the individual institutions that buck that trend, thus bringing the best of both worlds within sight.

The wealth of publicly available statistics means applicants can be well-equipped to make a thorough assessment of whether a certain subject – or course in that subject at a particular university – is going to give them what they are looking for. Research shows that applicants are wise to how important subject rankings are; the majority take more notice of subject tables than of institutional rankings – though it is the latter that tend to grab the headlines.

This chapter offers pointers to the leading universities in a wide range of subjects. Many, such as psychology and mechanical engineering, have their own table. Others are grouped together in broader categories, such as "subjects allied to medicine". If you see a dash (–) this denotes a score is not available because the number of students is too small for the outcome to be statistically reliable. Please also be aware that it is possible not all institutions listed in a particular area will be running courses in 2023-24, as university curriculums vary frequently.

The subject tables include scores from the National Student Survey (NSS). These distil the views of final-year undergraduates on various aspects of their course, with the results presented in two columns. "Teaching Quality" reflects the average scores in the sections of the survey focusing on teaching, assessment and feedback, learning opportunities and academic support. "Student Experience" is derived from the average of the NSS sections covering organisation and management, learning resources, student voice and learning community, as well as the survey's final question: overall satisfaction.

The three other measures used in our tables are research quality, students' entry qualifications and graduate employment outcomes. The Education table uses a fifth indicator, Ofsted grades, a measure of the quality of teaching based on Ofsted inspections of teacher training courses. None of the measures is weighted. A full explanation of the measures is given on the next page.

Cambridge is again the most successful university among our subject rankings. It tops 21 of the 70 tables; Oxford heads 10; St Andrews, UCL and Glasgow each come top in five subject tables; Warwick, Glasgow Caledonian and the LSE lead in three; and Imperial, Strathclyde, Bath and Exeter each take the top spot in two tables. Seven other universities top one table each.

Research quality

This information is sourced from the 2021 Research Excellence Framework (REF), a peer review exercise used to evaluate the quality of research of UK higher education institutions, undertaken by the Higher Education Funding Bodies. The output of the REF gave each institution a profile in the following categories: 4* world-leading; 3* internationally excellent; 2* internationally recognised; 1* nationally recognised and unclassified. The funding bodies have directed more funds to the very best research by applying weightings. For the 2024 edition of our *Guide*, we used the weightings adopted by UK Research and Innovation (UKRI) and Research England, published in 2020. A 4* output was weighted by a factor of 4, and 3* was weighted by a factor of 1. Outputs of 2* and 1* carry zero weight.

The score was weighted to account for the number of staff in each unit of assessment. The score is presented as a percentage of the maximum possible score of 3. To achieve the maximum score, all staff would need to be at 4* world-leading level. There are no scores in this category for Buckingham (as a private university it fell outside of the REF 2021).

Entry standards

This is the average UCAS tariff score for new students under the age of 21, based on A- and AS-levels and Scottish Highers and Advanced Highers, and other equivalent qualifications (including the International Baccalaureate), taken from HESA data for 2020–21. Each student's examination grades were converted to a numerical score using the UCAS tariff. The points used in the tariff appear on page 32.

Teaching Quality and Student Experience

The student satisfaction measure is divided into two components, taken from the National Student Survey (NSS) results published in 2022. Unlike in previous years, we did not use 2021's scores as a replacement where data was missing as the years are not considered comparable due to COVID. Where NSS data was not available, the latest available scores for Teaching Quality and Student Experience were adjusted by the percentage point change in each subject between that year and 2022. This applies mainly to Oxford and Cambridge, which last met the threshold as entire universities in 2016 due to their boycott of the NSS. Other institutions with missing scores will receive a replacement score based on their other metrics. The adjusted scores were used for z-scoring only, and do not appear in the final table.

The NSS covers eight aspects of a course, with an additional question gauging overall satisfaction. Students answer on a scale from 1 (bottom) to 5 (top) and the score in the table is calculated from the percentage of positive responses (4 and 5) in each section. The Teaching Quality indicator reflects the average scores for the first four sections of the survey. The Student Experience indicator is drawn from the average scores of the remaining sections and the overall satisfaction question. Teaching Quality is favoured over Student Experience and accounts for 67% of the overall student satisfaction score, with Student Experience making up the remaining 33%.

Graduate prospects

This is the percentage of graduates in high-skilled jobs or undertaking graduate-level study 15 months after graduation, recorded in the Graduate Outcomes survey published in June 2022 and based on 2020 graduates.

A low score on this measure does not necessarily indicate unemployment – some graduates may have taken jobs that are not categorised as professional work. The averages for each subject are given at the foot of each subject table in this chapter and in two tables in Chapter 3, see pages 51-4.

Note that in the tables that follow, when a figure is followed by a *, it refers to data from a previous year.

The subjects listed below are covered in the tables in this chapter:

Accounting and Finance
Aeronautical and Manufacturing Engineering
Agriculture and Forestry
American Studies
Anatomy and Physiology
Animal Science
Anthropology
Archaeology and Forensic Science
Architecture
Art and Design
Bioengineering and Biomedical Engineering
Biological Sciences
Building
Business, Management and Marketing
Celtic Studies
Chemical Engineering
Chemistry
Civil Engineering
Classics and Ancient History
Communication and Media Studies
Computer Science
Creative Writing
Criminology
Dentistry

Drama, Dance, Cinematics and Photography
East and South Asian Studies
Economics
Education
Electrical and Electronic Engineering
English
Food Science
French
General Engineering
Geography and Environmental Sciences
Geology
German
History
History of Art, Architecture and Design
Hospitality, Leisure, Recreation and Tourism
Iberian Languages
Information Systems and Management
Italian
Land and Property Management
Law
Liberal Arts
Linguistics

Materials Technology
Mathematics
Mechanical Engineering
Medicine
Middle Eastern and African Studies
Music
Natural Sciences
Nursing
Pharmacology and Pharmacy
Philosophy
Physics and Astronomy
Physiotherapy
Politics
Psychology
Radiography
Russian and East European Languages
Social Policy
Social Work
Sociology
Sports Science
Subjects Allied to Medicine
Theology and Religious Studies
Town and Country Planning and Landscape
Veterinary Medicine

Accounting and Finance

The London School of Economics takes first place in our Accounting and Finance table this year. It has outdone all 98 other universities for the quality of its research in the recent Research Excellence Framework 2021 exercise and also claims the fourth-best graduate prospects, and its student satisfaction ranking falls within the top 20 for both teaching quality and the wider experience. Strathclyde, the table's former leader, is in second place, while Glasgow, which ties at =7 with Exeter and Manchester, has the highest entry standards. Warwick and Bath rank third and fourth respectively – just as they did in our previous edition.

For graduate prospects Queen's Belfast is out in front, with 94% of graduates in high-skilled work or further study 15 months on from their degrees. More than 90% of graduates from Bath and Leeds had also achieved these career outcomes when surveyed. But perhaps surprisingly, accounting and finance do not set our graduate prospects measure alight: they rank 55th out of 70 subject areas – down from 61st last year and 43rd the year before. Forty-seven per cent of graduates were working in high-skilled jobs when surveyed 15 months on from their degrees, while 9% were continuing their studies and 6% were combining both. Nearly three in 10 (28%) were working in jobs classified as "low-skilled". For salaries they place a little higher at 46th, with graduates starting out on £25,000 – on average.

Often taken together, accounting and finance share a focus on matters monetary, business and management. Each subject also has its differentiating features, however; accounting is the more defined topic that looks specifically at how money flows in and out of a company, while finance is broader – encompassing long-term management of assets, liabilities and growth.

Maths A-level is useful but not an essential requirement, except by a few leading universities. Business, economics and statistics are among the other A-levels that universities look for. Entry standards vary considerably by institution. Accounting and finance students arrived at Buckinghamshire last year with an average of 80 UCAS points, the lowest tariff score out of all 99 universities listed – although, conversely, it ranks in the top 10 for student satisfaction with both teaching quality and the wider experience. At the other end of the scale students at Glasgow achieved entry grades equating to 219 UCAS points. Twenty-eight universities averaged over 144 UCAS points (equivalent to three As at A-level), and 17 averaged under 100 points.

Accounting and Finance	Teaching quality %	Student experience %	Research quality %	Entry standards (UCAS points)	Graduate prospects %	Overall score
1 London School of Economics	80.7	82.2	69.0	176	89.9	100
2 Strathclyde	80.9	80.6	52.5	213	82.1	99.1
3 Warwick	84.4	85.6	65.2	159	87.3	98.8
4 Bath	80.2	84.2	65.2	151	92.9	97.9
5 Leeds	77.7	78.8	62.3	168	91.3	97.4
6 Durham	83.2	83.9	55.8	151	87.9	96.2
=7 Exeter	80.2	82.6	63.5	145	88.3	96.1
=7 Glasgow	69.5	71.5	57.2	219	80.6	96.1
=7 Manchester	77.1	79.5	66.2	165	83.0	96.1
10 King's College London	78.5	85.4	63.0	157	—	95.6
11 University College London	74.8	81.5	62.3	172	—	95.4

=12	City	76.6	78.5	67.2	151	79.9	94.3
=12	Edinburgh	68.8	73.3	59.0	185	84.6	94.3
14	Liverpool	83.3	85.1	58.0	143	70.1	92.8
15	Queen's Belfast	75.0	77.3	40.5	152	94.0	92.4
=16	Lancaster	78.4	80.3	59.2	130	80.4	92
=16	Southampton	80.7	83.3	52.0	147	74.2	92
18	Aberdeen	77.9	76.8	32.2	181	81.0	91.8
19	Birmingham	78.1	77.0	55.2	147	76.3	91.6
20	Loughborough	71.9	80.5	49.2	147	85.2	91.3
21	Ulster	83.2	81.0	45.8	123	82.2	90.9
22	East Anglia	76.7	78.3	57.8	127	80.0	90.7
23	Surrey	76.0	78.1	54.8	127	77.6	89.7
24	Reading	78.5	81.6	46.2	124	79.0	89.3
25	Glasgow Caledonian	80.1	79.2	25.8	180	67.7	89
26	Newcastle	73.1	73.8	40.5	143	80.1	88
=27	Bristol	66.0	68.9	46.0	158	79.3	87.7
=27	Robert Gordon	87.9	86.6	19.0	171	55.5	87.7
=27	Sheffield	74.4	79.0	48.8	130	72.4	87.7
=30	Aston	73.7	75.8	43.5	128	79.7	87.6
=30	Dundee	72.6	74.4	28.5	185	68.5	87.6
=32	Bangor	91.6	89.3	32.2	110	63.6	87.2
=32	Swansea	78.3	79.2	38.8	129	73.2	87.2
34	Stirling	71.2	73.8	38.2	177	63.1	87
=35	Cardiff	60.6	60.5	56.0	144	85.5	86.9
=35	Heriot-Watt	63.8	63.6	38.2	176	79.1	86.9
=37	Nottingham	64.1	65.0	46.8	145	82.8	86.4
=37	Queen Mary, London	69.7	71.2	53.2	150	63.6	86.4
39	Sussex	74.5	76.8	50.7	132	63.9	86.3
40	Royal Holloway, London	78.6	78.9	43.0	117	65.3	85.4
41	Liverpool John Moores	85.8	81.3	21.0	126	65.2	84.8
42	Nottingham Trent	81.4	81.7	34.2	115	63.4	84.5
43	Northumbria	78.1	80.2	28.2	132	64.7	84.4
44	Portsmouth	82.3	79.8	37.8	102	62.2	83.7
45	Leicester	66.6	67.7	45.8	121	73.1	83.3
46	Worcester	89.6	85.0	12.5	107	—	83
47	Aberystwyth	85.6	88.6	22.8	107	57.4	82.8
=48	Edinburgh Napier	74.8	71.6	20.0	161	58.9	82.7
=48	Plymouth	78.1	81.4	28.7	107	66.4	82.7
50	Kent	70.5	67.9	37.2	122	70.0	82.5
51	Oxford Brookes	74.1	74.5	26.0	118	71.5	82.4
52	Edge Hill	84.9	81.8	21.0	121	51.9	81.8
53	Manchester Metropolitan	75.8	75.3	42.8	119	50.7	81.7
54	Chester	78.8	73.8	25.2	116	63.0	81.6
55	Greenwich	79.8	80.4	33.2	110	53.3	81.5
=56	Essex	70.8	73.9	39.8	107	64.7	81.3
=56	Lincoln	75.9	76.6	25.0	107	67.9	81.3

Accounting and Finance cont.

	Teaching quality %	Student experience %	Research quality %	Entry standards (UCAS points)	Graduate prospects %	Overall score
=58 Coventry	79.4	80.6	33.2	102	56.1	81.2
=58 Staffordshire	72.6	73.1	38.8	—	57.8	81.2
60 Kingston	80.3	80.8	24.0	101	58.9	80.5
=61 Roehampton	76.6	79.9	32.8	92	—	80.4
=61 West London	94.1	93.3	—	108	48.3	80.4
63 West of England	73.2	77.1	27.3	108	63.9	80.3
64 South Wales	82.5	83.6	9.0	113	57.9	79.9
65 Hull	74.5	68.7	29.5	115	58.3	79.6
=66 Anglia Ruskin	75.8	77.7	45.8	89	48.2	79.4
=66 Keele	71.6	71.1	24.8	108	67.0	79.4
68 Central Lancashire	74.4	74.0	28.2	124	50.0	79.2
69 Brighton	69.9	63.2	28.5	97	74.5	79.1
=70 Bournemouth	73.5	73.6	23.0	97	66.0	78.8
=70 Middlesex	72.2	72.2	46.2	98	48.8	78.8
=72 West of Scotland	77.4	74.0	10.5	137	51.8	78.7
=72 Winchester	69.8	80.1	22.2	103	63.6	78.7
74 Wolverhampton	87.0	85.6	20.2	87	46.3	78.6
75 De Montfort	77.1	77.0	19.0	95	60.9	78.3
=76 Brunel	70.9	70.8	30.2	117	51.8	78.1
=76 Cardiff Metropolitan	75.8	71.8	14.0	102	65.0	78.1
78 Westminster	63.5	68.4	37.5	118	56.3	78
79 Hertfordshire	75.1	72.9	29.0	98	52.7	77.7
80 Huddersfield	72.1	71.7	23.2	114	52.1	77.2
=81 London Metropolitan	78.8	79.8	22.0	87	50.6	77
=81 Sheffield Hallam	70.3	69.1	23.5	110	57.3	77
83 Derby	81.3	80.5	18.0	103	41.6	76.7
84 Leeds Beckett	76.4	76.7	8.2	96	60.7	76.5
85 York St John	76.2	76.0	9.8	102	—	76.1
86 Bedfordshire	74.2	70.8	22.0	101	50.9*	76
87 East London	86.3	85.3	11.0	81	41.7	75.6
88 Sunderland	80.0	79.2	—	103	51.3	75.3
89 Salford	67.6	66.7	24.8	114	47.5	74.8
90 London South Bank	76.0	75.5	21.5	98	39.0	74.5
91 Teesside	69.3	71.5	—	101	65.8	74.3
92 Canterbury Christ Church	72.0	67.0	13.2	86	59.2	73.9
93 Birmingham City	70.8	69.7	11.2	107	49.2	73.6
94 Bradford	57.1	62.6	38.2	112	45.6	73.3
95 Solent, Southampton	78.2	74.8	—	88	50.0	72.8
96 SOAS, London	49.3	44.8	44.2	127	—	72.2
97 Northampton	74.3	75.1	1.2	95	43.2	71.4
98 Gloucestershire	61.2	64.1	8.8	99	—	68.8
99 Buckinghamshire New	70.9	66.9	—	80	44.7*	68.4

Employed in high-skilled job	47%	Employed in lower-skilled job	28%
Employed in high-skilled job and studying	9%	Employed in lower-skilled job and studying	3%
Studying	6%	Unemployed	7%
High skilled work (median) salary	£25,000	Low/medium skilled salary	£21,000

Aeronautical and Manufacturing Engineering

The courses under this category focus predominantly on aeronautical or manufacturing engineering (often called production engineering), but the table also includes some degrees with the mechanical title. Degree apprenticeships may appeal in this area, with earn-while-you-learn routes offered at leading firms such as Rolls-Royce, though they do not feature in this table.

Categorised by UCAS as aeronautical and aerospace engineering, both applications and enrolments rose for the eighth successive year in 2021, when 3,895 undergraduates started courses. Production and manufacturing engineering disciplines attracted a further 2,055 students. Entry standards can be stiff: 10 of our table's 43 universities averaged over 150 UCAS points in 2021's admissions round and two, Imperial and Glasgow, averaged over 200 points.

Imperial tops the table for the second year running, its position boosted by having the top research rating in the subjects as well as the highest entry standards in 2021, at 211 UCAS points. It also achieved a top five result for student satisfaction with the wider experience – often a weak point for research-led universities. Almost all (98.1%) of Cambridge graduates were in high-skilled work or further study 15 months after their degrees – which puts Cambridge in front for graduate prospects. It is second for its strength in research and occupies the same position in the table overall. Having occupied second place in our previous edition's table, Bristol sits third this year.

The older institutions dominate the upper end of the table, with Teesside in 21st place the highest-ranked post-1992 university, followed by Bolton in 24th. These two universities perform especially strongly for rates of student satisfaction, placing in the top three for both teaching quality and the wider experience. But Sheffield comes out top for the student experience alone.

Most courses require maths and physics, and other desirable subjects include IT or computing, further maths, and design technology. Starting salaries of £28,000 rank the subjects 12th and 72% of graduates were in high-skilled jobs or further study when last surveyed. However, with 19% of graduates in work deemed low-skilled, and 9% unemployed, the subjects only place 38th overall in our graduate prospects measure.

Aeronautical and Manufacturing Engineering	Teaching quality %	Student experience %	Research quality %	Entry standards (UCAS points)	Graduate prospects %	Overall score
1 Imperial College	70.8	81.2	81.0	211	89.8	100
2 Cambridge	—	—	77.2	—	98.1	97.2
3 Bristol	80.6	80.9	68.0	185	85.0	97
4 Sheffield	82.3	86.0	66.8	153	84.7	94.6
5 Southampton	72.8	75.5	70.0	174	87.8	94.4
6 Bath	75.1	77.0	49.5	182	91.4	93.6
7 Heriot-Watt	75.0	70.3	55.5	183	—	92.7
=8 Leeds	71.7	71.2	64.8	172	75.1	90.1
=8 Surrey	75.6	79.1	55.2	141	87.2	90.1
10 Ulster	84.2	82.0	49.8	123	87.3	89.9

		Teaching quality %	Student experience %	Research quality %	Entry standards (UCAS points)	Graduate prospects %	Overall score
11	Nottingham	70.3	69.1	59.0	149	90.0	89.6
12	Strathclyde	72.9	68.7	52.8	—	87.8	89.1
13	Glasgow	61.0	62.3	61.5	203	73.5	88.7
14	Loughborough	69.9	75.6	46.5	155	85.9	88.2
15	Queen Mary, London	62.3	69.9	66.0	142	79.3	85.9
16	Swansea	72.8	75.7	48.8	130	77.4	84.9
17	Liverpool	65.5	68.7	57.0	140	76.9	84.5
18	Queen's Belfast	64.7	61.0	51.0	142	83.3	84.2
19	Manchester	60.5	62.9	63.0	159	69.5	83.8
20	Aston	76.9	77.8	35.2	119	79.2	83.6
21	Teesside	85.9	82.8	18.8	127	73.1	83.3
22	Leicester	75.1	77.4	39.8	133	66.1	82.3
23	Sussex	74.0	74.2	29.5	132	74.5	81.9
24	Bolton	84.9	85.3	22.0	106	—	81.8
25	West of England	69.5	70.2	30.8	125	81.0	81.3
26	Coventry	77.9	80.5	23.5	128	67.7	80.8
27	West of Scotland	80.4	77.1	16.5	137	58.3*	78.9
28	Huddersfield	67.0	67.6	32.5	126	—	78.2
29	Brunel	63.2	65.0	33.0	128	71.5	77.8
30	Derby	77.3	74.4	14.0	115	—	77.4
31	Brighton	73.5	75.5	36.5	98	62.4	77.2
32	Salford	63.5	67.7	33.2	125	65.7	76.7
33	Birmingham City	71.1	68.7	17.5	115	—	75.3
34	Staffordshire	76.2	70.6	25.5	111	51.4	74.7
=35	Central Lancashire	62.6	60.6	23.0	124	66.7	74.5
=35	South Wales	73.6	71.0	26.8	122	47.8	74.5
37	De Montfort University	67.2	76.1	21.8	102	—	74.4
38	Hertfordshire	68.7	69.2	33.0	103	57.1	74.3
39	Sheffield Hallam	57.5	56.4	30.0	114	70.5	73.6
40	Portsmouth	74.1	67.5	21.0	100	53.8	72.6
41	City	50.2	55.3	32.5	111	72.0	72.2
42	Wolverhampton	59.8	49.4	18.2	102	69.2	70.3
43	Kingston	62.4	62.0	17.2	106	45.9	67.6

Employed in high-skilled job	55%	Employed in lower-skilled job	19%
Employed in high-skilled job and studying	3%	Employed in lower-skilled job and studying	1%
Studying	12%	Unemployed	9%
High skilled work (median) salary	£28,000	Low/medium skilled salary	£22,415

Agriculture and Forestry

Queen's Belfast holds on to the lead it took last year in our Agriculture and Forestry table. The Northern Ireland university has the top score for research – based on the results of the new

2021 Research Excellence Framework as well as the highest entry standards. For student satisfaction, Reading leads on both the measure of teaching quality and of the wider undergraduate experience. Nottingham, which topped the table two years ago, settles for third place this year. In fifth place, Harper Adams outdoes the other specialist institution in the table, Royal Agricultural.

Following a small surge in the numbers starting degrees in agriculture in 2020, they fell back to just below the 2,000 mark in 2021. Forestry and arboriculture degrees attract much smaller numbers, with just 90 new undergraduates beginning degrees in the 2021 admissions cycle.

The two subjects place 53rd out the 70 subjects in our graduate prospects ranking, with 65% of graduates place in high-skilled jobs or further study 15 months after completing their degrees. Of these 70.2% of Harper Adams graduates had secured these outcomes, followed by Newcastle (69%) and Nottingham (67.1%). Average starting salaries of £25,000 compare more favourably, ranking comfortably among the upper half of subjects in 33rd place.

Agriculture and Forestry	Teaching quality %	Student experience %	Research quality %	Entry standards (UCAS points)	Graduate prospects %	Overall score
1 Queen's Belfast	76.0	70.1	69.2	149	63.8	100
2 Aberystwyth	79.0	75.6	48.8	141	62.1	97.5
3 Nottingham	76.0	69.3	52.0	132	67.1*	96.4
4 Reading	84.5	84.7	42.5	128	53.1	94.7
5 Newcastle	70.8	71.2	42.8	130	69	94.6
6 Harper Adams	78.2	79.4	19.5	125	70.2	94.4
7 Royal Agricultural University	73.7	79.3	24.2	114	58.2	88.8

Employed in high-skilled job	58%	Employed in lower-skilled job	32%
Employed in high-skilled job and studying	3%	Employed in lower-skilled job and studying	1%
Studying	3%	Unemployed	3%
High skilled work (median) salary	£25,000	Low/medium skilled salary	£21,000

American Studies

Most American Studies degrees concentrate on the culture, literature, history and politics of America and Canada, and students are often offered the opportunity of spending a year at a university in one of the two countries as part of a four-year course. The leading universities look for English language, English literature and history A-levels, while politics is also considered useful. Entry standards in 2021 were highest at University College London (UCL), where entrants averaged 175 UCAS tariff points, while no universities averaged under the 116 points at Manchester Metropolitan.

The high entry standards and rates of student satisfaction that rank in the top three have boosted UCL into first place, ousting last year's winner Sussex from the top of our table this year. Results of the new 2021 Research Excellence Framework place Birmingham in the lead, ahead of Manchester. But for the second year running in the most recent National Student Survey, American studies students at Hull reported the highest levels of satisfaction with teaching quality by a clear margin, as with the wider undergraduate experience.

Placing 58th out of 70 subject areas, American studies has gained a little ground in our graduate prospects measure this year. Fifteen months after finishing their degrees, 38% of graduates were in high-skilled jobs and a further 22% were either engaged in postgraduate study, or combining studies with a professional job. Conversely, 31% of graduates were in jobs deemed low-skilled, but only 6% were unemployed – half the proportion that was in the previous Graduate Outcomes survey. For starting salaries, American studies places the subject 58th out of 70 areas, with graduates attracting average starting salaries of £23,000.

Applications and enrolments declined in 2021, but the subject remains offered by 50 higher education providers on the UCAS website, often in combination with another.

American Studies	Teaching quality %	Student experience %	Research quality %	Entry standards (UCAS points)	Graduate prospects %	Overall score
1 University College London	81.3	76.3	65.7	175	—	100
2 Sussex	79.5	71.0	65.1	137	70.8	94.5
3 Hull	90.9	86.7	55.5	131	68.0	93.6
4 Birmingham	69.5	64.3	68.8	—	67.0	92
5 Nottingham	64.9	58.1	63.7	132	71.9	90.6
6 Manchester Metropolitan	83.0	72.2	61.8	116	—	90.3
7 East Anglia	75.0	68.7	63.0	125	66.0	90
8 Manchester	67.4	64.0	66.5	141	61.5	89.3
9 Swansea	76.9	64.6	45.2	120	67.2	85.3
10 Portsmouth	75.3	71.1	51.7	—	55.7*	82.5

Employed in high-skilled job	38%	Employed in lower-skilled job		31%
Employed in high-skilled job and studying	5%	Employed in lower-skilled job and studying		2%
Studying	17%	Unemployed		6%
High skilled work (median) salary	£23,000	Low/medium skilled salary		£19,000

Anatomy and Physiology

Very few courses included in this table actually have the title of anatomy or physiology. Far more common are degrees titled biomedical science. A two-science minimum at A-level usually means biology and chemistry, although physics is also an option. The leading universities look for maths, too. The subject area is growing in popularity and attracted 9,640 new undergraduates in 2021.

Graduate prospects are promising; anatomy and physiology rank 29th out of 70 subject areas, with 44% of graduates in high-skilled employment, 4% engaged in further study and 28% combining the two. Average starting salaries of £25,000 place the subjects above midway too, at 33rd place.

Boasting the highest rates of student satisfaction with both teaching quality and the wider experience, as well as the highest entry standards in 2021, Aberdeen tops our Anatomy and Physiology table. It finished in third place in our previous edition, behind Oxford and Cambridge which tied at No 1, but each university only had REF data for the subjects this year so could not be included.

The older institutions occupy the table's top 10, but it is the graduates of modern university Huddersfield that have the edge in the jobs market, according to the latest data, which showed more than nine out of 10 (92%) were in high-skilled work or/and further study 15 months on from their degrees. Swansea and the University of the West of England are only a hair's breadth behind Huddersfield on this measure. Outcomes of the new Research Excellence Framework 2021 put Dundee top for research quality.

Anatomy and Physiology

		Teaching quality %	Student experience %	Research quality %	Entry standards (UCAS points)	Graduate prospects %	Overall score
1	Aberdeen	87.8	90.9	33.2	217	88.5	100
2	Glasgow	80.7	81.5	55.8	213	76.0	97.4
3	Edinburgh	72.0	71.5	69.2	179	83.8	96.1
=4	Loughborough	75.3	80.4	66.8	159	—	96
=4	University College London	84.0	81.2	64.0	—	76.4	96
6	Dundee	75.8	69.6	78.0	181	73.3	95.5
=7	Bristol	74.9	73.3	57.4	158	86.4	94.1
=7	Swansea	67.2	67.2	66.8	150	91.7	94.1
9	Bangor	80.3	68.3	59.8	122	83.3	91.8
=10	Nottingham	79.3	80.0	54.0	129	80.3	91.5
=10	Queen's Belfast	66.4	60.3	69.2	156	82.1	91.5
12	West of England	72.8	73.7	42.8	118	91.5	89.8
13	Plymouth	74.5	76.1	38.5	—	84.1	89.5
14	Leeds	72.0	71.5	52.0	150	76.7	89.2
15	Huddersfield	74.5	79.1	22.5	133	92.0	88.6
16	Manchester Metropolitan	75.7	68.9	51.2	139	75.6	88.5
=17	Portsmouth	81.2	78.1	57.5	—	62.5	88.2
=17	St George's, London	76.4	68.4	50.2	130	—	88.2
19	Reading	72.5	75.3	37.5	—	79.1*	86.7
20	Leicester	64.5	60.3	53.5	127	81.8	86.2
21	Coventry	84.5	83.7	24.8	115	75.3	85.9
22	Liverpool	70.3	73.8	46.8	145	68.7	85.5
23	Ulster	72.6	73.5	53.5	125	67.7	85.4
24	Essex	76.3	78.5	42.5	101	—	85
25	Newcastle	61.2	63.1	58.8	152	67.7*	84.5
26	Westminster	76.4	74.1	36.8	111	—	84.2
27	King's College London	65.7	63.5	50.0	—	71.4	82.9

Employed in high-skilled job	44%	Employed in lower-skilled job	18%
Employed in high-skilled job and studying	4%	Employed in lower-skilled job and studying	1%
Studying	28%	Unemployed	6%
High skilled work (median) salary	£25,000	Low/medium skilled salary	£19,000

Animal Science

Our Animal Science table was first launched eight years ago to reflect the growing interest in the subjects. Such popularity is continuing to gather pace, as evidenced by the 10% rise in applications in 2021, year on year. The number of new students enrolling on courses has stayed stable, ranging from 2,425 to 2,470 over the past three years.

Our table has gained another two universities this year, on top of the 13 that joined in our previous edition. Extracted from the agriculture category, degrees range from animal behaviour to equine science and veterinary nursing. Most degrees will ask for biology and probably chemistry.

Glasgow, which last topped the table two years ago, returns to No 1. It has the highest entry standards by some distance, with new entrants averaging 204 UCAS points. Surrey, in fourth place overall, averaged the second-highest tariff of 155 points.

Nottingham Trent, winner of our Modern University of the Year award, outdoes all others for student satisfaction with teaching quality and is second only to Royal Agricultural for satisfaction with the wider experience. The Royal Veterinary College, in 15th place overall, leads the four specialist institutions in the table, closely followed by Hartpury in 16th.

Queen's Belfast joins the top 10 of the table, which otherwise features the same universities as it did in our previous edition, but ordered differently.

High starting salaries are not the main attraction for animal science students. The subjects place fifth from bottom in our salaries ranking, with average annual wages of £21,500 for graduates. Career prospects more broadly fare even more poorly compared with other subject areas, ranking 69th out of 70. Only 35% of graduates were in high-skilled jobs when surveyed 15 months after their degrees, while 2% were furthering their studies and 14% were juggling both. Meanwhile, 42% were working in jobs classified as "low-skilled" but only 6% were unemployed.

Some universities buck the overall employment trend for the subjects, most noticeably Middlesex – where 100 per cent of graduates had secured the top outcomes 15 months on from their courses, followed by those at Surrey (96.6%). But at the other end of the scale only 34.7% of Plymouth graduates had secured such career outcomes 15 months after finishing their degrees.

Animal Science	Teaching quality %	Student experience %	Research quality %	Entry standards (UCAS points)	Graduate prospects %	Overall score
1 Glasgow	80.4	75.8	64.8	204	61.5	100
2 Bristol	81.8	81.0	60.2	148	78.1	94.8
3 Manchester	69.4	60.5	69.5	154	73.6	91.3
4 Surrey	77.9	70.1	—	155	96.6*	88.7
5 Liverpool	66.2	64.8	68.2	143	66.7	87.9
6 Sussex	79.2	72.2	49.8	135	65	87.7
7 Royal Holloway, London	76.2	76.8	43.5	136	—	86.3
8 Queen's Belfast	61.5	65.6	69.2	134	69.2	86
9 Cardiff	70.9	68.5	53.5	—	62.5*	84.9
10 Nottingham	73.7	74.3	52.0	133	54.7	84.7
11 Aberystwyth	80.7	79.9	48.8	121	50.8	84.1
12 Newcastle	71.3	76.2	58.8	135	46.3	84
13 Plymouth	77.9	79.2	58.2	134	34.7	83.7
14 Bangor	72.6	68.7	67.5	118	50.3	83
15 Royal Veterinary College	78.3	66.9	—	131	79	81.8
16 Hartpury	81.6	75.2	15.8	119	60.9	80.7
17 Lincoln	83.4	80.0	—	130	58.1	80.4
18 Liverpool John Moores	72.0	69.6	28.7	142	45.3	80.2
=19 Harper Adams	75.5	71.0	—	124	73.2	79.5
=19 Oxford Brookes	70.7	78.8	39.5	127	42.2	79.5
21 Nottingham Trent	85.5	83.2	—	130	44.7	78.9
22 Middlesex	56.4	46.1	—	128	100	77.7
23 Royal Agricultural University	77.3	84.2	—	117	50	76

	Teaching quality %	Student experience %	Research quality %	Entry standards (UCAS points)	Graduate prospects %	Overall score
24 Derby	78.8	78.0	—	119	48.3	75.8
25 Edinburgh Napier	51.0	38.7	—	146	83	75.4
26 Greenwich	69.4	71.1	—	123	55.6	74.6
27 Cumbria	79.8	74.9	—	120	38.6	74.1
28 Canterbury Christ Church University	81.5	73.7	9.5	92	—	72.5
29 Chester	67.5	59.9	6.2	125	41.8	71.8
30 Roehampton	76.3	67.8	—	101	46.4	71.2
31 Anglia Ruskin	64.4	51.8	17.8	102	54.7	70.9

Employed in high-skilled job	35%	Employed in lower-skilled job	42%
Employed in high-skilled job and studying	2%	Employed in lower-skilled job and studying	1%
Studying	14%	Unemployed	6%
High skilled work (median) salary	£21,500	Low/medium skilled salary	£18,500

Anthropology

London School of Economics takes the lead in our Anthropology table this year, following a resounding success in the latest Research Excellence Framework 2021 – in which work by LSE academics came out top in our analysis. East Anglia, in ninth place overall, did almost as well as LSE in the 2021 REF, and places second for research quality.

The study of humans and human society, from the physical evolution of the human body and brain, to the political, cultural and linguistic practices of modern societies, anthropology has tended to be the preserve of old universities. Cambridge, the former No 1, ties in second place this year with Oxford, while SOAS has moved up 11 places to sit fourth. Liverpool John Moores is the highest-ranked modern university, in 16th place, and has the second-best rates of student satisfaction with the wider experience – outdone only by Brunel on this measure. St Andrews leads on student satisfaction with teaching quality.

Oxford averaged the highest entry standards among its 2021 cohort of new students, at 201 UCAS points, while nearly half (11 universities) of the table averaged over 150 points (where 144 UCAS points is equivalent to AAA at A-level). Employment prospects for anthropology graduates remain rooted to the lower portion of our table however, in which the subject sits 47th this year.

When last surveyed 15 months after finishing their degrees, 44% of graduates were in professional jobs, 5% were furthering their studies and 18% were combining both. Just under a quarter (24%) were working in jobs deemed low-skilled while 8% were unemployed. Queen's Belfast does better than the rest however, with the latest data showing more than seven in 10 of its anthropology graduates securing high-skilled work or postgraduate study 15 months on. For median starting salaries, anthropology occupies almost the same position (48th out of 70 subject areas), with £24,500 annual earnings overall.

Anthropology	Teaching quality %	Student experience %	Research quality %	Entry standards (UCAS points)	Graduate prospects %	Overall score
1 London School of Economics	78.8	78.1	73.2	171	84.4	100
=2 Cambridge	—	—	40.8	198	89.9	94.9
=2 Oxford	76.3	68.7	54.2	201	—	94.9
4 SOAS, London	79.3	75.7	61.8	150	78.4	94.4

Anthropology cont.

		Teaching quality %	Student experience %	Research quality %	Entry standards (UCAS points)	Graduate prospects %	Overall score
5	University College London	82.0	74.8	52.2	168	78	94.3
6	Aberdeen	84.0	79.3	42.2	182	74.5	93.4
7	St Andrews	83.2	75.7	49.2	187	66.7*	92.8
8	Manchester	82.8	75.3	61.3	151	67.9	92.6
9	East Anglia	71.5	70.1	70.8	130	76.2	91.6
10	Bristol	77.2	68.5	58.8	143	74.9	91.1
11	Durham	73.7	65.2	54.8	165	72.7	90.2
12	Sussex	78.7	73.3	53.8	138	68.3	88.9
13	Birmingham	69.5	60.2	67.0	139	—	88.5
14	Edinburgh	69.1	60.3	51.7	169	72.1	88.2
15	Portsmouth	79.9	70.4	51.7	—	56.5*	85.5
16	Liverpool John Moores	78.3	82.1	28.7	138	70.4	84.8
17	Queen's Belfast	72.2	65.3	41.5	135	70.8*	84.3
=18	Exeter	75.1	70.9	46.8	152	55.8	84.1
=18	Kent	72.8	64.0	51.2	123	65.8	84.1
20	Plymouth	74.4	71.5	47.1	107	—	82.7
21	Bournemouth	71.2	67.8	50.5	108	64	82.2
22	Brunel	80.5	82.3	34.8	106	57.1	80.9
23	Oxford Brookes	69.7	69.9	34.8	107	68.4	79.8
24	Goldsmiths, London	58.2	41.6	51.5	120	56	75.6

Employed in high-skilled job	44%	Employed in lower-skilled job	24%
Employed in high-skilled job and studying	5%	Employed in lower-skilled job and studying	1%
Studying	18%	Unemployed	8%
High skilled work (median) salary	£24,500	Low/medium skilled salary	£21,000

Archaeology and Forensic Science

Reconfirming its established lead in our Archaeology and Forensic Science table, Cambridge attracts the highest entry standards – an average of 191 UCAS points among 2021's entrants – and tops our employability ranking, with almost nine in 10 graduates working in high-skilled jobs and/or engaged in postgraduate study 15 months after their degrees. Much improved results in the new 2021 Research Excellence Framework, compared with the previous exercise in 2014, has trigged an eight-place rise into second place for Durham this year. But Reading outdoes all others in the table for research and ties in eighth place overall. With entry standards just one UCAS tariff point lower than those at Cambridge, Oxford sits third.

Seventh-ranked Sheffield had the most satisfied students in the subjects when the National Student Survey (NSS) took its 2021 census, and places top for both of our NSS-derived measures: teaching quality and the wider undergraduate experience. Coventry is runner-up for student satisfaction, again across both metrics included in the table.

With graduate starting salaries of £21,800, archaeology and forensic science places in the bottom 15 of the 70 subject areas in our ranking. For employability they do slightly better, at 56th, with 43% of graduates working in high-skilled jobs when surveyed 15 months on from their degrees, 3% engaged in postgraduate study and 16% combining further study with professional-level work. Three in 10 graduates were employed in jobs deemed "low-skilled" however.

While most archaeology courses have no subject requirements, the leading universities will usually require a science subject. Geography and history are also relevant A-levels. Courses in subjects classified by UCAS as forensic and archaeological sciences attracted nearly 11,000 applications in 2021 (up by around 8% on the year before) and welcomed 2,635 new undergraduates.

Archaeology and Forensic Science	Teaching quality %	Student experience %	Research quality %	Entry standards (UCAS points)	Graduate prospects %	Overall score
1 Cambridge	—	—	71.0	191	87.3*	100
2 Durham	86.4	78.9	70.2	157	84.7	98.4
3 Oxford	—	—	61.8	190	—	97.3
4 Edinburgh	80.0	70.3	59.1	190	—	96.8
5 York	83.2	77.4	63.0	133	80.8	93
6 Southampton	83.8	83.0	69.8	131	74.3	92.8
7 Sheffield	94.4	91.8	34.0	—	74.3	92
=8 Exeter	83.0	74.7	58.8	148	73.9	91.9
=8 Reading	87.4	88.7	76.5	117	68.1	91.9
10 Newcastle	86.6	80.2	47.8	124	80.3	90.6
11 Glasgow Caledonian	74.8	69.6	61.0	158	67.6	89.4
12 University College London	75.7	76.1	55.8	152	67.4	88.8
13 Birmingham	78.2	74.1	54.2	139	—	88.6
14 Cardiff	76.5	70.1	58.0	123	78.1	88.3
15 Queen's Belfast	82.8	77.2	51.2	128	—	88.1
16 Dundee	81.1	75.4	50.2	—	69.4*	87.6
17 Liverpool	82.0	75.5	43.5	134	69.5	86.8
18 Northumbria	72.3	71.9	53.5	135	—	85.9
=19 Leicester	74.1	69.1	70.0	118	65.1	85.6
=19 Robert Gordon	77.7	77.6	—	155	83.9	85.6
21 Nottingham	74.7	64.0	51.5	132	70.2	85.3
22 Bradford	74.0	75.6	38.2	113	81.6	85.2
23 Kent	83.4	79.8	—	135	78.8	83.6
24 Staffordshire	84.0	77.3	31.0	117	68.2	83.5
=25 Central Lancashire	86.9	86.6	32.8	122	55.9	82.7
=25 Huddersfield	82.0	81.2	24.0	126	—	82.7
27 West of Scotland	73.1	68.4	28.7	139	67.7*	82.2
=28 Liverpool John Moores	69.0	70.4	28.7	146	65.4	81.7
=28 Teesside	85.1	81.8	18.8	124	62.9	81.7
30 Nottingham Trent	75.8	78.5	—	133	76	80.9
31 Chester	78.0	64.7	22.5	106	76.8	80.7
32 Keele	75.7	73.2	48.0	132	49.4	80.6
33 Anglia Ruskin	84.2	81.3	33.8	108	56	80.2
34 Lincoln	76.6	75.3	27.8	118	57.1	78.5
35 Coventry	89.7	88.8	—	110	59.9	78.4

		Teaching quality %	Student experience %	Research quality %	Entry standards (UCAS points)	Graduate prospects %	Overall score
36	Bournemouth	66.0	67.3	50.5	111	55.8	77.8
37	Winchester	83.5	78.1	16.0	102	59.9	77.4
38	Wolverhampton	83.1	78.1	—	103	66.7	76.8
39	Kingston	70.8	62.8	38.5	101	—	76.4
40	West London	76.5	76.9	—	118	64	76.3
41	West of England	67.9	65.5	—	128	68.3	75.5
42	De Montfort	73.2	75.6	—	107	67.1	75.1
=43	Canterbury Christ Church	71.8	64.9	17.8	88	69.2	74.7
=43	Hull	48.1	48.8	55.5	124	—	74.7
45	Derby	59.1	57.7	—	117	68.4	71.7
46	London South Bank	81.0	78.7	—	95	46.9	70.6
47	South Wales	71.6	64.3	—	112	51.3	70.1

Employed in high-skilled job	43%	Employed in lower-skilled job	30%
Employed in high-skilled job and studying	3%	Employed in lower-skilled job and studying	1%
Studying	16%	Unemployed	7%
High skilled work (median) salary	£21,800	Low/medium skilled salary	£19,000

Architecture

There are usually no essential subjects required to study architecture, although the leading universities will look for a mixture of art and science, and a portfolio is essential. Entry standards in 2021 ranged from the 99 UCAS tariff points averaged by entrants to Ravensbourne, Wolverhampton and East London, up to the 205 points averaged at Cambridge.

Early career trajectories are positive; almost two-thirds (65%) of graduates were in professional jobs 15 months after their degrees according to the latest data, which combined with 14% in postgraduate study and/or a professional-grade job ranks the subject 27th out of 70 areas. Emerging architects are not put off by the modest starting salaries of £22,000 as those in the industry know this soon changes. It takes most architects seven years to fully qualify, of which a degree is the first step. Such a timeframe asks a lot of students' dedication to the profession and of their financial wherewithal to support themselves. Course materials add to costs.

Cambridge has toppled Bath from the No 1 spot in our Architecture table this year, boosted by the best outcomes in the new 2021 Research Excellence Framework, as well as by the highest entry standards. Bath sits in fifth place this year while Loughborough is runner-up once again, its position maintained by the second-best research quality rating and top-10 rates of student satisfaction with both teaching quality and the wider experience.

Ulster tops both measures of student satisfaction: teaching quality and the wider experience, while Liverpool and the West of England follow it for the broad undergraduate experience and East London and Cardiff Metropolitan sit second and third respectively for teaching quality. At the other end of the scale, architecture students at Brighton and Lincoln were the least satisfied when responding to the most recent National Student Survey.

Architecture

	Teaching quality %	Student experience %	Research quality %	Entry standards (UCAS points)	Graduate prospects %	Overall score
1 Cambridge	—	—	74.8	205	89.5	100
2 Loughborough	84.2	78.4	72.0	161	96.0*	99.4
3 Cardiff	81.0	74.5	67.5	171	92.5	97.6
4 Sheffield	76.7	78.1	71.8	168	90.7	97
5 Bath	82.6	81.4	49.5	196	86.2	96.7
6 Edinburgh	78.2	72.2	59.0	187	85.2	95.2
7 Strathclyde	71.8	59.1	50.2	202	91.1	93.5
8 Ulster	90.9	84.6	54.2	128	85.0	93.4
9 Nottingham	76.2	73.0	59.0	156	87.6	92.6
10 Manchester School of Architecture	77.5	77.1	53.2	166	81.3	91.9
11 Liverpool	85.8	83.2	55.2	149	73.1	91.5
12 West of England	83.5	83.1	40.8	148	82.1	90.5
13 University College London	74.0	63.3	61.0	173	76.6	90.4
14 Newcastle	72.7	72.0	56.0	166	73.2	88.8
15 Kingston	82.4	74.1	63.0	126	69.1	88
16 Queen's Belfast	73.5	73.3	36.5	144	90.0	87.8
17 Plymouth	79.4	74.1	49.0	112	85.7	87.6
18 Kent	71.2	68.8	61.0	134	79.3	87.5
19 Coventry	78.9	78.3	54.2	114	78.0	87.2
=20 Robert Gordon	85.2	81.7	14.0	161	78.4	86.8
=20 University for the Creative Arts	84.3	80.6	41.2	131	72.4	86.8
22 Liverpool John Moores	74.0	69.7	38.2	147	82.5	86.5
23 Nottingham Trent	77.3	75.4	38.0	117	86.7	86
24 Reading	71.0	63.2	53.5	129	80.0	85.3
=25 Birmingham City	83.7	80.4	34.8	135	67.3	84.8
=25 Salford	76.7	77.4	43.5	124	74.0	84.8
27 Oxford Brookes	77.1	72.7	33.2	135	75.8	84.1
28 University of the Arts London	66.7	59.6	46.0	149	77.8	84
=29 Sheffield Hallam	75.3	69.8	43.2	116	76.4	83.4
=29 Westminster	78.9	77.8	38.2	128	67.5	83.4
31 Northumbria	73.3	73.0	25.0	139	79.2	83.1
32 Leeds Beckett	76.0	66.8	24.5	103	91.7	82.6
33 Edinburgh Napier	63.1	65.2	38.0	130	84.0	82.3
34 Portsmouth	70.2	66.3	41.8	110	79.8	81.9
=35 Arts University, Bournemouth	76.7	64.9	23.0	119	80.0	81.1
=35 Dundee	69.3	61.5	—	179	82.2	81.1
37 Huddersfield	71.2	70.1	36.5	126	67.4	80.3
38 Cardiff Metropolitan	86.8	81.9	—	104	76.0*	79.4
39 De Montfort	65.0	64.8	40.5	106	76.5	79.2
40 Hertfordshire	72.3	74.8	24.2	102	72.0	78.1
41 Anglia Ruskin	77.6	67.2	23.8	106	—	77.8
=42 Derby	76.8	76.8	—	109	78.6	77.5

Architecture cont.

	Teaching quality %	Student experience %	Research quality %	Entry standards (UCAS points)	Graduate prospects %	Overall score
=42 Greenwich	71.9	63.6	30.0	124	62.5	77.5
44 East London	87.9	81.7	25.0	99	47.9	76.9
45 London South Bank	82.0	72.6	35.0	114	44.0	76.6
46 Wolverhampton	74.8	71.4	20.0	99	—	76
47 Central Lancashire	81.4	77.8	—	121	60.9	75.8
48 Lincoln	57.9	51.5	12.2	114	86.1	74.5
49 Brighton	54.8	52.9	53.0	110	58.5	73.9
50 London Metropolitan	78.4	70.2	—	118	56.5	73
51 Ravensbourne	68.4	60.5	—	99	63.6	69.6

Employed in high-skilled job	65%	Employed in lower-skilled job		14%
Employed in high-skilled job and studying	5%	Employed in lower-skilled job and studying		0%
Studying	7%	Unemployed		9%
High skilled work (median) salary	£22,000	Low/medium skilled salary		£19,500

Art and Design

Oxford remains at the top of the Art and Design table for the second year running, its ranking boosted by results of the latest Research Excellence Framework 2021 which put it comfortably in front of all 81 other universities in the table. Behind Oxford on research quality is Westminster, which ties in 14th place overall. Oxford also attracted by far the highest entry standards in 2021, with entrants averaging an eye-watering 241 UCAS points – among the highest tariff scores of any subject table in our *Guide*. Newcastle (which topped the table two years ago) and Glasgow also averaged over 200 UCAS points. At the other end of the scale only three universities (Canterbury Christ Church, Bedfordshire and East London) have entry standards below 100 tariff points, on average.

In fifth place, Kingston is the highest-ranked modern university while Falmouth, at 32nd, places the highest of the six specialist institutions, followed by Arts London in joint 35th. Even though the majority of art and design courses are at post-1992 universities and/or the specialist arts institutions, the older universities dominate the top-10 of our table, due largely to their higher entry standards – although most artists would argue that entry grades are less significant than in other subjects.

Several renowned art schools are now part of the Russell Group and other high-tariff universities: such as the Ruskin School of Art (Oxford), Slade School of Fine Art (University College London) and the Duncan Jordanstone College of Art and Design (Dundee). Fine art has long been a strength at Newcastle, a former leader of this table, which settles for seventh place this year. Selection rests primarily on the quality of candidates' portfolios and many undergraduates enter via a one-year Art Foundation course. Even the research-led Russell Group of universities do not require any essential A-levels, although they do advise that art and design subjects are preferred.

The highest rates of student satisfaction with both teaching quality and the wider experience are at 56th-ranked Suffolk, our analysis of the latest National Student Survey found. Modern universities have the edge over their older peers for satisfaction rates, with Canterbury Christ Church, Staffordshire, Robert Gordon and Buckinghamshire New all featuring in the upper reaches of these measures.

Art and design are among the biggest recruiters in higher education, with more than 119,200 applications in 2021 and nearly 23,600 new students starting courses. Design studies is much the largest area while fine art – though it accounts for a far smaller proportion of students – still attracted over 4,000 new starters in 2021.

The subjects always feature in the lower reaches of employment tables and sit 61st out of 70 subject areas this year, with six out of 10 graduates in high-skilled work or/and further study 15 months on. But the trend for graduates not going straight into high-skilled jobs tends not to be a surprise to artists and designers, who accept they may have a period in low-paid self-employment early in their career. Some universities buck the trend however, such as joint 54th-ranked Brunel and sixth-place Bangor, which come first and second for graduate prospects, each with over 82% of graduates already in professional jobs or further study 15 months after their degrees.

Art and Design	Teaching quality %	Student experience %	Research quality %	Entry standards (UCAS points)	Graduate prospects %	Overall score
1 Oxford	—	—	88.8	241	—	100
2 Loughborough	83.6	80.7	51.7	175	77.7	94
3 Glasgow	68.7	74.3	68.8	204	—	93
4 Lancaster	81.1	78.5	59.5	156	71.0	90.6
5 Kingston	82.3	74.1	63.0	173	61.1	89.7
6 Bangor	84.9	75.9	40.2	127	82.5	89.3
7 Newcastle	80.1	74.2	61.0	207	49.1	88.5
8 Reading	81.3	75.2	51.8	131	72.2	87.4
9 Edinburgh	73.2	65.4	54.0	174	66.7	87.3
10 Leeds	67.6	63.1	54.8	163	73.5	86.9
11 Dundee	72.0	64.6	57.2	177	62.7	86.5
12 Glasgow Caledonian	81.9	78.7	13.8	174	71.0	86.3
13 Nottingham Trent	78.0	74.5	53.0	141	67.0	86.2
=14 Goldsmiths, London	73.1	64.5	57.5	177	60.3	86.1
=14 Staffordshire	88.7	84.0	53.5	130	58.2	86.1
=14 Westminster	73.3	68.3	75.5	142	61.3	86.1
17 Sheffield Hallam	85.7	81.1	57.0	119	63.0	86
=18 Bournemouth	78.6	77.6	38.5	107	81.4	85.7
=18 Manchester	80.6	80.1	63.0	150	53.7	85.7
20 Coventry	79.4	75.2	54.2	127	67.5	85.6
21 Teesside	83.3	81.0	49.2	118	66.9	85.4
22 Manchester Metropolitan	81.2	74.2	51.7	153	58.2	85.3
23 Lincoln	83.7	78.7	43.8	127	66.0	85.1
=24 Canterbury Christ Church	95.7	90.1	38.0	98	64.4*	85
=24 Northumbria	76.6	68.1	45.8	147	67.7	85
=24 West of England	85.3	78.7	36.0	151	60.8	85
27 Southampton	78.6	70.4	56.5	150	57.1	84.4
28 Edinburgh Napier	75.7	73.6	23.5	175	64.6	84
29 Liverpool John Moores	75.8	69.8	38.2	176	58.0	83.8
30 University College London	53.5	39.2	64.7	192	65.2*	83.1
31 Portsmouth	83.6	76.8	41.8	118	63.4	83
32 Falmouth	78.4	72.0	48.8	140	57.6	82.7

Art and Design cont.

		Teaching quality %	Student experience %	Research quality %	Entry standards (UCAS points)	Graduate prospects %	Overall score
33	Aberystwyth	86.3	72.9	41.0	133	55.2	82.2
34	Robert Gordon	92.2	83.4	13.8	168	48.8	82.1
=35	University of the Arts London	73.4	63.6	46.0	147	60.4	81.9
=35	Ulster	74.6	63.5	54.5	125	62.6	81.9
=35	South Wales	88.0	78.2	35.8	122	57.1	81.9
=38	Brighton	69.7	59.0	53.0	140	63.5	81.8
=38	Oxford Brookes	82.3	78.0	25.5	137	61.4	81.8
=40	Huddersfield	83.8	78.9	30.8	129	59.5	81.7
=40	Wales Trinity St David	81.6	68.0	20.8	152	62.8	81.7
42	Cardiff Metropolitan	71.0	64.4	56.2	130	61.5	81.6
43	Norwich University of the Arts	77.5	70.4	38.8	134	61.3	81.5
44	Central Lancashire	81.1	75.5	35.2	127	60.4	81.4
45	Middlesex	80.8	77.1	41.2	110	62.5	81.3
46	Plymouth	84.6	79.3	26.5	128	59.5	81.2
47	Sunderland	72.9	64.5	49.8	123	60.2	80.1
48	London Metropolitan	83.9	76.6	42.2	121	51.0	79.9
=49	Birmingham City	83.5	78.1	31.2	128	53.8	79.8
=49	Arts University, Bournemouth	76.7	70.0	23.0	151	58.3	79.8
51	Anglia Ruskin	76.8	67.9	31.2	124	63.5	79.7
=52	University for the Creative Arts	80.1	69.6	41.2	138	50.5	79.6
=52	Greenwich	75.2	66.0	30.0	120	66.7	79.6
=54	Brunel	67.9	67.4	—	129	82.8	79.5
=54	Buckinghamshire New	90.1	82.8	41.2	115	45.1	79.5
56	Suffolk	96.1	94.5	—	121	53.3	79.2
57	York St John	81.9	77.0	5.8	116	68.7	79.1
58	West London	85.3	78.6	—	118	67.2	79
59	Chester	73.4	66.3	26.2	122	65.8	78.7
60	De Montfort	75.2	70.3	32.0	122	59.9	78.6
61	Leeds Beckett	77.1	66.5	29.2	108	64.7	78.4
62	Gloucestershire	69.1	59.4	45.0	125	59.5	78.1
63	Wolverhampton	81.6	71.2	35.2	116	53.2	78
=64	Worcester	75.9	72.2	19.2	118	63.8	77.9
=64	Leeds Arts	76.3	70.3	6.2	153	59.1	77.9
66	Salford	82.1	74.6	—	133	61.8	77.7
67	Northampton	83.8	73.9	12.2	118	58.7	77.4
68	Hertfordshire	79.9	72.0	24.2	110	58.2	77.1
69	London South Bank	81.7	71.2	—	106	69.4	77
70	Cumbria	69.7	62.1	23.2	136	57.7	76
71	Kent	71.7	66.3	—	115	71.0	75.6
72	Heriot-Watt	56.5	55.3	34.2	162	53.4	75.1
73	Bath Spa	72.4	61.1	18.5	132	53.7	74.4
74	Derby	79.2	73.7	19.5	119	46.8	74.1

75	Ravensbourne	72.4	62.9	13.5	115	58.9	73.8
76	Solent, Southampton	76.9	70.6	—	111	56.3	72.6
77	Bolton	67.3	58.8	17.8	113	57.8	72.3
78	East London	77.7	74.4	14.8	88	53.1	72.2
79	Wrexham Glyndŵr	74.5	60.7	3.2	128	51	71.6
80	Liverpool Hope	76.5	70.8	12.5	128	32.4	68.9
81	Bedfordshire	75.7	64.9	—	91	45.7	67
82	Chichester	62.0	58.7	—	122	43.8	65.6

Employed in high-skilled job	54%	Employed in lower-skilled job		31%
Employed in high-skilled job and studying	2%	Employed in lower-skilled job and studying		1%
Studying	4%	Unemployed		9%
High skilled work (median) salary	£22,000	Low/medium skilled salary		£19,000

Bioengineering and Biomedical Engineering

Oxford has overtaken Dundee at the top of our dedicated Bioengineering and Biomedical Engineering table, now in its second year of publication. Entry standards were highest at Oxford in 2021 while Imperial College London – which ties with Dundee in the runner-up spot – achieved the best results in the subjects in the new Research Excellence Framework 2021.

For student satisfaction with teaching quality, Nottingham Trent does best, followed by Reading, while for the wider experience Reading comes out top, with Sheffield behind it. At the opposite end of the scale, students at City expressed much lower rates of satisfaction in the latest National Student Survey (NSS), and the university comes bottom – by a clear margin – on both NSS-derived measures. The bioengineering and biomedical engineering table is unusual in being so dominated by older institutions. Only 21st-ranked Bolton, which gained university status in 1992, represents the modern sector.

Aging populations, the demand for new treatments for chronic conditions and the need to respond rapidly to evolving disease challenges have brought about growth in biomedical engineering and bioengineering among universities worldwide over the past two decades. The discipline collectively involves a range of engineering and scientific skills, including some of the newest areas of science in genomics, imaging, and computing to meet those challenges.

Graduate bioengineers may go on to develop prosthetics and biomedical implants, 3D medical imagine or image-guided and robot assisted surgery – among a range of career pathways. Some biomedical graduates apply for places on the Graduate Entry into Medicine programmes.

There is insufficient employment data so far for all but 10 universities, of which Queen Mary, London stands out for achieving the highest rate (93.4%) of graduates in high-skilled work or further study 15 months on from their degrees. In our graduate prospects ranking of 70 subject areas, bioengineering and biomedical engineering achieve a respectable 25th place. Full-time further study accounts for 20% of the 78% of graduates who were in high-skilled jobs or/and studying 15 months on from their degrees. The subjects rank in top-20 for starting salaries.

Bioengineering and Biomedical Engineering	Teaching quality %	Student experience %	Research quality %	Entry standards (UCAS points)	Graduate prospects %	Overall score
1 Oxford	—	—	69.5	216	92.5	100
=2 Dundee	75.7	81.0	78.0	195	—	98.1
=2 Imperial College	75.2	76.5	81.0	195	—	98.1
4 Leeds	76.4	75.5	64.8	193	—	93.7
5 Sheffield	79.1	81.2	70.2	160	85.9	93.1
6 Strathclyde	72.6	73.0	52.8	214	84.1	91.1
7 Loughborough	75.6	78.7	66.8	158	—	91
8 University College London	76.4	75.6	64.0	160	—	90.1
9 King's College London	76.3	79.4	50.0	150	87.9	87.9
10 Reading	81.2	82.0	54.0	124	—	86.1
11 Nottingham Trent	82.5	77.6	59.0	112	—	85.9
12 Surrey	79.8	77.5	55.2	124	—	85.3
13 Ulster	76.2	78.5	49.8	126	80.0	84.5
14 Queen Mary, London	62.1	68.0	50.5	144	93.4	84.4
15 Cardiff	69.2	74.4	54.0	144	—	83.9
16 Swansea	73.3	71.2	48.8	141	76.3	83.3
17 Birmingham	75.7	65.0	55.0	133	—	83.1
18 Essex	79.3	76.8	42.5	127	—	82.1
19 Salford	69.3	70.7	37.0	126	64.1	76.7
20 Bradford	77.8	80.1	—	126	56.5	70.6
21 Bolton	74.6	74.4	—	104	59.4	68.2
22 City	41.0	52.4	32.5	113	—	64.1

Employed in high-skilled job	56%	Employed in lower-skilled job	12%
Employed in high-skilled job and studying	2%	Employed in lower-skilled job and studying	0%
Studying	20%	Unemployed	10%
High skilled work (median) salary	£27,000	Low/medium skilled salary	£20,500

Biological Sciences

For the 18th year, Cambridge tops the Biological Sciences table, its tenure strengthened once more by fiercely high entry standards – with new undergraduates averaging 221 UCAS tariff points in 2021. Cambridge also boasts the third-best graduate prospects and second-highest research quality rating. But based on the outcomes of the Research Excellence Framework 2021, it is fourth-ranked Dundee that tops all 102 universities in our table for its strength in biological sciences research. Performing strongly across all measures Oxford moves into second position this year, up from fourth, while last year's runner-up Imperial slips to third.

The upper reaches of our table are dominated by universities with old foundations across the UK. For graduate prospects Queen's Belfast (in joint 19th place overall) comes out top, closely followed by 76th-ranked East London. Robert Gordon in Aberdeen is the top-ranked modern university, placing 35th. For teaching quality and the wider student experience, both measures derived from the National Student Survey, York St John (which ranks joint 41st overall) takes the lead, while Edinburgh Napier and Canterbury Christ Church are in the top three.

Of the specialisms within the grouping, biology is the most popular – with applications close to 25,000 and nearly 4,200 new students in 2021. It is followed by molecular biology, biophysics and biochemistry, which had over 3,700 enrolments in the same admissions round. Applications and enrolments to zoology rose in 2021, topping 10,000 and 2,000 respectively for the first time. Ecology and environmental biology also attracted higher rates of applications (up around 12% on the year before) and 2,110 students enrolled on courses.

With 46% of graduates in high-skilled jobs, 27% in postgraduate study and 4% combining both 15 months on from their degrees, the biological sciences have climbed up our employment measure, ranking from a middling position among the 70 subject areas to 26th place this year. For starting salaries, they place lower, at 46th.

Many of the leading universities will demand two sciences at A-level, or the equivalent – usually biology and chemistry – for any of the biological sciences.

Biological Sciences	Teaching quality %	Student experience %	Research quality %	Entry standards (UCAS points)	Graduate prospects %	Overall score
1 Cambridge	—	—	73.5	221	90.2	100
2 Oxford	—	—	69.5	197	87.9	95.7
3 Imperial College	74.5	79.7	63.2	188	90.1	95.2
4 Dundee	75.9	76.0	78.0	182	83.5	94.7
5 Glasgow	79.3	77.3	55.8	203	83.3	94.3
6 York	80.4	79.8	66.0	153	89.0	94.2
7 Strathclyde	73.8	72.6	65.8	200	82.1	93.2
8 Durham	82.4	78.9	44.0	180	85.7	92.8
9 Bath	80.6	81.7	49.2	164	86.4	92.5
10 Edinburgh	71.4	73.1	69.2	188	81.3	92.1
11 Lancaster	81.0	77.3	59.1	145	86.4	92
12 Glasgow Caledonian	73.4	76.9	61.0	185	81.7	91.9
=13 Bristol	80.7	79.2	67.2	161	77.4	91.8
=13 Surrey	78.4	81.2	58.0	138	88.4	91.8
15 University College London	68.6	69.5	64.0	177	89.0	91.7
16 St Andrews	80.5	78.6	49.5	201	73.5	91.2
17 Loughborough	80.2	80.4	66.8	148	77.4	90.8
18 Manchester	72.1	68.4	69.5	165	83.1	90.7
=19 Queen's Belfast	68.0	63.9	69.2	142	91.4	90
=19 Sheffield	75.5	74.7	70.2	150	78.5	90
21 Ulster	77.2	75.8	53.5	131	87.9	89.7
22 Warwick	73.5	73.8	46.5	155	86.2	89
23 Birmingham	74.2	73.8	57.0	151	80.5	88.6
24 Exeter	76.4	75.8	60.5	155	74.3	88.4
25 Bangor	76.2	73.1	67.5	116	79.5	87.7
26 Liverpool	67.3	67.0	68.2	145	80.5	87.2
27 Nottingham	74.0	71.4	50.2	138	82.3	87.1
=28 Newcastle	66.8	67.9	58.8	145	84.0	87
=28 Stirling	72.1	73.4	45.8	173	76.0	87

Biological Sciences cont.

		Teaching quality %	Student experience %	Research quality %	Entry standards (UCAS points)	Graduate prospects %	Overall score
30	Cardiff	70.9	68.5	53.5	148	81.5	86.9
31	East Anglia	75.1	72.3	56.0	125	80.6	86.8
32	Aberdeen	80.9	78.3	33.2	173	71.2	86.7
=33	King's College London	68.1	66.2	50.0	157	83.1	86.6
=33	Swansea	77.6	73.3	64.2	129	72.4	86.6
35	Robert Gordon	77.2	80.2	—	163	90.2	86.4
36	Leeds	71.4	73.1	52.0	153	76.3	86.3
37	Aberystwyth	83.9	84.2	48.8	117	71.5	86.2
38	Southampton	75.9	76.5	53.5	145	72.0	86.1
39	Royal Holloway, London	72.8	75.7	43.5	119	83.2	85.4
40	Teesside	77.2	77.0	35.0	104	85.5	85.1
=41	Northumbria	68.6	66.6	53.5	130	81.5	84.9
=41	York St John	90.0	86.9	—	112	83.9	84.9
43	Reading	75.8	77.0	54.0	120	72.2	84.6
44	Plymouth	78.7	76.7	42.9	125	73.0	84.5
45	Kent	71.2	70.4	50.0	120	77.6	83.8
=46	Coventry	74.6	73.2	47.2	112	76.4	83.7
=46	Queen Mary, London	68.8	70.7	50.5	141	73.5	83.7
48	Leicester	68.6	66.3	53.5	126	77.3	83.5
49	Hertfordshire	74.4	73.2	48.0	101	77.5	83.3
50	Sunderland	76.1	73.5	30.2	107	82.2	83.2
=51	Heriot-Watt	71.0	72.2	32.8	167	70.3	83.1
=51	Staffordshire	79.0	74.8	30.8	102	80.0	83.1
=51	West of England	82.2	82.5	42.8	113	66.0	83.1
=54	Abertay	84.6	80.9	—	151	73.3	82.9
=54	Edinburgh Napier	85.9	86.0	—	147	71.4	82.9
=56	Nottingham Trent	74.3	73.2	43.5	119	72.9	82.7
=56	Portsmouth	76.3	74.5	41.2	113	73.3	82.7
58	Canterbury Christ Church	85.6	86.2	9.5	71	85.0	82.5
=59	Essex	75.0	75.7	42.5	102	75.1	82.4
=59	Hull	77.3	74.5	42.0	115	70.6	82.4
=59	West of Scotland	83.8	81.7	30.8	135	62.2	82.4
=62	Keele	68.5	72.0	39.2	121	77.8	82.1
=62	Sussex	70.3	65.6	49.8	140	69.1	82.1
64	Manchester Metropolitan	74.8	71.9	44.8	118	69.9	82
65	Gloucestershire	77.5	75.5	25.8	105	78.2	81.9
=66	Liverpool John Moores	70.8	73.8	28.7	135	75.0	81.8
=66	St George's, London	60.9	55.9	50.2	140	79.8	81.8
68	Lincoln	82.9	79.1	—	119	77.5	81.2
69	Huddersfield	76.4	76.7	24.0	119	72.6	81.1
70	Anglia Ruskin	74.6	76.0	33.8	97	75.5	81
=71	Oxford Brookes	70.6	72.5	39.5	118	70.8	80.6

=71	South Wales	79.8	71.3	16.2	107	76.8	80.6
73	Liverpool Hope	79.0	80.3	—	117	78.0	80.4
74	Royal Veterinary College	79.8	72.3	—	120	79.2	80.2
75	Brighton	61.7	60.0	50.5	104	77.4	79.4
76	East London	70.6	71.5	—	90	91.2	79.2
77	Edge Hill	68.4	71.5	13.8	113	79.8	79
=78	Cardiff Metropolitan	72.7	72.0	—	117	79.5	78.5
=78	Kingston	71.9	69.0	38.5	98	68.5	78.5
=78	Leeds Beckett	68.6	71.2	38.0	102	69.9	78.5
81	Bournemouth	73.9	67.4	29.2	103	69.5	78.2
=82	Bedfordshire	81.6	82.9	—	104	69.6	78.1
=82	Central Lancashire	73.7	70.5	—	118	77.4	78.1
84	Worcester	73.6	79.2	7.8	103	73.6	77.9
85	Salford	73.5	69.7	37.0	119	59.5	77.7
86	Sheffield Hallam	71.9	66.4	16.8	108	73.6	77.5
87	Aston	69.8	70.1	—	118	75.9	76.7
88	Westminster	60.7	62.5	36.8	110	71.2	76.5
89	London Metropolitan	71.6	69.1	—	111	75.6	76.4
90	Roehampton	72.8	75.7	—	101	71.4	75.7
91	Greenwich	69.4	71.1	—	106	74.6	75.6
92	Chester	71.4	58.1	6.2	114	72.5	75.3
93	Bradford	64.4	68.4	—	114	77.0	75.2
=94	Derby	71.1	71.5	—	113	68.8	74.9
=94	Middlesex	69.2	70.0	—	103	73.5	74.9
96	Bath Spa	64.4	67.5	—	95	77.8	74.1
97	De Montfort	67.7	67.7	—	100	71.1	73.4
98	Brunel	67.4	61.2	—	119	66.9	72.8
99	London South Bank	75.8	67.8	—	96	60.6	72.2
100	Northampton	66.2	64.8	14.0	88	60.0	70.7
101	Wolverhampton	63.9	59.7	—	108	58.5	68.8
102	Cumbria	59.5	54.3	—	119	52.7	66.4

Employed in high-skilled job	46%	Employed in lower-skilled job		17%
Employed in high-skilled job and studying	4%	Employed in lower-skilled job and studying		1%
Studying	27%	Unemployed		6%
High skilled work (median) salary	£24,500	Low/medium skilled salary		£19,600

Building

Applications to study building courses increased by around 10% in 2021. The numbers starting degrees went in the other direction however – declining by about 8%, with 3,285 undergraduates enrolling on courses, which include surveying, construction, building services engineering and construction management. Graduate prospects look solid for those who do study building degrees: the subject ranks 11th in our employment table, in between general engineering and chemical engineering. The latest data shows that 79% of building graduates were in high-skilled work 15 months on from degrees, while a further 7% were either furthering their studies or combining it with a professional-level job. Starting rates of pay are also encouraging, the £27,000 median rate earned by building graduates in high-skilled jobs warranting the subject 17th place in our salaries index.

University College London tops our subject table for the second year running, bolstered by the second-best research rating and third-highest entry standards. It is separated by a hair's breadth (0.3%) from runner-up Heriot-Watt in Edinburgh, which had the highest entry standards among 2021's new students – though even here the UCAS tariff score is modest, at 159 points.

Students at Robert Gordon in Aberdeen were the most satisfied with their teaching quality, our analysis of the latest National Student Survey shows, followed by those at Brighton, Anglia Ruskin and Nottingham Trent. For the wider experience, Aston claims the highest rates of student satisfaction, with Brighton, Robert Gordon and Central Lancashire following it. Degree apprenticeships, although not included in our table, offer an increasingly popular route into the construction industry.

Building	Teaching quality %	Student experience %	Research quality %	Entry standards (UCAS points)	Graduate prospects %	Overall score
1 University College London	66.4	68.1	61.0	148	—	100
2 Heriot-Watt	67.8	67.7	59.0	159	83.6	99.7
3 Ulster	66.3	73.0	54.2	140	90.9	98.3
=4 Loughborough	51.3	59.1	72.0	138	97.3	97.8
=4 Nottingham	73.3	75.2	59.0	133	83.3	97.8
6 Northumbria	77.5	74.4	25.0	142	90.0	96.1
7 West of England	76.0	78.6	40.8	117	91.5	95.6
8 Reading	68.9	68.5	53.5	121	90.0	95.3
9 Robert Gordon	87.5	80.3	14.0	132	87.5	95
10 Sheffield Hallam	75.0	70.6	43.2	113	91.0	94.2
=11 Nottingham Trent	78.0	78.1	38.0	107	89.5	93.6
=11 Oxford Brookes	75.0	78.7	33.2	117	89.3	93.6
13 Edinburgh Napier	74.0	74.3	38.0	133	78.6	93.3
14 Glasgow Caledonian	66.2	63.5	30.2	149	81.8	92.2
15 Brighton	86.2	81.6	36.5	91	83.5	91.6
16 Liverpool John Moores	68.3	69.5	28.7	135	80.2	90.6
17 Salford	68.2	65.3	43.5	121	80.2	90.5
18 Plymouth	65.2	61.1	49.0	115	83.3	90.3
19 Coventry	71.0	69.7	23.5	112	90.6	89.8
20 Central Lancashire	77.0	80.1	—	119	90.9	89.4
21 Portsmouth	70.8	70.7	21.0	108	90.7	88.9
22 Anglia Ruskin	78.2	74.8	23.8	106	81.5	88.7
23 Westminster	63.9	61.4	38.2	121	79.4	88.1
24 Leeds Beckett	74.0	70.3	24.5	102	85.7	87.9
25 London South Bank	59.2	58.0	35.0	125	83.3	87.8
26 Greenwich	73.3	73.3	30.0	107	76.9	87.5
27 Birmingham City	66.1	64.1	34.8	114	72.5	85.6
28 Aston	77.6	86.1	—	127	63.0	84.2
=29 Kingston	63.0	60.1	17.2	97	70.4	78.6
=29 Wolverhampton	74.9	70.8	20.0	98	53.6	78.6

Employed in high-skilled job	79%	Employed in lower-skilled job	9%
Employed in high-skilled job and studying	4%	Employed in lower-skilled job and studying	0%
Studying	3%	Unemployed	5%
High skilled work (median) salary	£27,000	Low/medium skilled salary	£22,500

Business, Management and Marketing

Warwick has been closing in on the top spot of our Business, Management and Marketing table in recent years, rising from third place two editions ago to runner-up last year. It takes the lead in our new edition, boosted by the third-highest entry standards along with the fifth-best results in the subjects in the new Research Excellence Framework 2021 (REF 2021) – as well as strength across all other measures. Oxford – where new students averaged 207 UCAS points in 2021, the highest entry standards – has moved up to second place. St Andrews, which ranked at No 1 for several years running, settles for third place on this occasion, but still outdoes its top three rivals on rates of student satisfaction with both teaching quality and the wider experience. The London School of Economics, in joint fifth place overall, achieved the best results in the REF 2021 and therefore tops our research quality rating, followed by City (joint 16th) and Manchester (joint 11th).

The universities that nailed the highest scores for satisfaction with teaching quality rank in the middle to lower reaches of the table overall. The University of West London (in 68th place overall) came top for this measure, with London Metropolitan (joint 79th) close behind it. Bangor, however, does well to achieve third place for student satisfaction while also placing in the top 25 overall. Satisfaction with the wider experience is led by West London again, while students at Leeds Trinity (104th), South Wales (joint 58th), St Andrews and Loughborough expressed similarly high levels of satisfaction.

But graduate prospects are the most closely correlated aspect of the business ranking to the complete result. The top nine for this measure rank in the top-10 for business, management and marketing overall. Our analysis of graduate employment in high-skilled jobs or postgraduate study 15 months on from degrees showed that 94.8% of business graduates from Oxford achieved these outcomes, followed by Bath (91.8%), King's College London (91.3%) and Warwick (90.6%). By contrast, Cumbria is at the foot of our employment ranking with 42.8% of graduates in high-skilled work or study after 15 months.

Although salary data is not an ingredient of our subject ranking, students are naturally interested in them. The subjects occupying a middling position (33rd) in our earnings index, with graduates in high-skilled jobs making £25,000 on average.

The wide choice of institutions offering courses reflects the popularity of the various branches of business, management and marketing. There were 57,300 applications to business and management degrees in 2021; 73,515 to business studies; 39,240 to marketing courses; and 73,705 to management degrees. Reflecting the subjects' popularity, our dedicated tables ranks 119 universities this year. The huge number of places means there should also be plenty of opportunities to secure a place through Clearing. Some of the most famous business schools are absent from this table because they only offer postgraduate qualifications such as MBAs, whereas our *Guide* details undergraduate provision.

Business, Management and Marketing	Teaching quality %	Student experience %	Research quality %	Entry standards (UCAS points)	Graduate prospects %	Overall score
1 Warwick	80.3	82.8	65.2	194	90.6	100
2 Oxford	—	—	66.2	207	94.8	99.9
3 St Andrews	84.5	84.4	48.2	194	89.6	98.9
4 Bath	77.5	81.9	65.2	173	91.8	97.7
=5 King's College London	71.1	76.8	63.0	192	91.3	96.7
=5 London School of Economics	76.9	74.5	69.0	179	87.5	96.7
7 University College London	77.3	82.0	62.3	176	85.1	96.3
8 Exeter	80.6	77.9	63.5	157	88.4	95.8
9 Strathclyde	75.4	74.2	52.5	205	77.9	94.5
10 Loughborough	79.7	84.3	49.2	154	85.9	93.9
=11 Cardiff	—	—	56.0	144	80.6	92.4
=11 Durham	75.9	77.7	55.8	157	82.0	92.4
=11 Manchester	72.5	76.2	66.2	161	79.0	92.4
14 Glasgow	66.7	70.8	57.2	188	83.2	92.2
15 Lancaster	77.5	79.7	59.2	142	80.7	92
=16 City	68.6	72.5	67.2	176	76.5	91.9
=16 Leeds	72.5	74.9	62.3	156	81.7	91.9
18 Edinburgh	66.1	70.9	59.0	178	81.9	91.2
19 Aberdeen	77.5	81.6	32.2	177	74.7	90.6
20 Reading	77.4	78.7	46.2	127	84.9	89.8
=21 Birmingham	69.7	72.8	55.2	149	81.8	89.5
=21 Southampton	73.3	72.5	52.0	146	80.9	89.5
23 Bangor	86.6	81.4	32.2	123	76.5	88.7
24 East Anglia	72.3	72.2	57.8	133	79.7	88.6
25 Liverpool	69.1	72.6	58.0	141	77.5	88.2
=26 Surrey	74.6	78.0	54.8	135	70.1	87.9
=26 York	70.5	72.2	50.5	141	79.0	87.9
28 Bristol	67.5	68.8	46.0	157	80.3	87.6
29 Nottingham	67.0	71.6	46.8	142	82.2	87
30 Robert Gordon	84.4	79.5	19.0	155	64.4	86.6
31 Aberystwyth	84.9	79.0	22.8	127	73.0	86.5
32 Sussex	71.6	73.7	50.7	134	71.6	86.4
33 Stirling	75.4	77.2	38.2	166	57.9	86.2
=34 Nottingham Trent	78.1	78.7	34.2	122	72.9	85.8
=34 Ulster	78.0	78.5	45.8	127	63.8	85.8
36 Sheffield	69.4	71.0	48.8	137	72.9	85.7
37 Dundee	68.4	65.9	28.5	176	73.4	85.5
38 Queen's Belfast	70.6	69.9	40.5	141	74.4	85.4
=39 Aston	70.1	71.8	43.5	131	75.6	85.3
=39 Portsmouth	79.3	76.5	37.8	112	72.4	85.3
41 West of England	82.4	82.2	27.3	114	69.5	85.1
42 Queen Mary, London	68.1	68.8	53.2	153	62.6	85

43	Manchester Metropolitan	77.4	76.2	42.8	119	66.2	84.9
44	University for the Creative Arts	81.6	76.4	41.2	120	61.3	84.8
45	Central Lancashire	82.4	78.5	28.2	121	66.1	84.7
=46	Kent	73.0	72.9	37.2	126	73.5	84.6
=46	Swansea	71.9	71.5	38.8	132	72.7	84.6
48	Newcastle	62.6	64.0	40.5	144	82.1	84.4
49	Royal Holloway, London	71.4	72.6	43.0	131	68.3	84.3
50	Hull	74.0	74.6	29.5	122	76.0	84.2
51	Coventry	81.0	80.3	33.2	111	64.4	84.1
=52	Northumbria	74.3	72.7	28.2	133	72.0	84
=52	Queen Margaret, Edinburgh	81.4	80.9	7.5	143	66.7	84
54	Falmouth	79.0	72.6	48.8	114	59.6	83.9
55	Heriot-Watt	61.4	61.4	38.2	171	69.6	83.3
56	Lincoln	78.0	75.7	25.0	116	69.6	83.1
57	Bournemouth	73.7	74.2	23.0	110	79.1	82.9
=58	Buckingham	77.7	80.6	—	122	78.2	82.5
=58	South Wales	85.1	84.8	9.0	114	62.5	82.5
60	Sheffield Hallam	76.6	73.9	23.5	111	72.6	82.4
61	Anglia Ruskin	80.9	76.2	45.8	99	55.1	82.3
62	Teesside	68.6	70.4	49.2	110	67.0	82.2
=63	Chester	76.7	69.5	25.2	121	68.4	82.1
=63	Glasgow Caledonian	75.5	75.3	—	174	60.3	82.1
=63	Huddersfield	78.4	76.1	23.2	122	62.1	82.1
=63	Oxford Brookes	70.4	72.3	26.0	118	75.6	82.1
=63	Plymouth	75.6	73.1	28.7	117	66.7	82.1
68	West London	91.6	89.4	—	113	55.1	82
=69	Essex	70.7	74.1	39.8	107	67.8	81.9
=69	University of the Arts London	71.3	64.9	46.0	136	56.8	81.9
=71	Derby	80.4	77.4	18.0	115	64.0	81.8
=71	Liverpool John Moores	73.7	75.4	21.0	132	64.3	81.8
73	Chichester	82.3	81.0	1.2	104	73.7	81.6
74	Bradford	77.7	78.7	38.2	116	50.2	81.4
75	Edinburgh Napier	72.0	72.2	20.0	146	61.1	81.3
76	Salford	73.6	74.8	24.8	120	64.7	81.2
77	Gloucestershire	80.0	76.4	8.8	117	66.7	81.1
78	Bath Spa	79.2	74.8	23.8	101	63.0	80.6
=79	Edge Hill	77.3	76.7	21.0	124	55.6	80.5
=79	London Metropolitan	87.3	84.0	22.0	97	48.4	80.5
=79	Wales Trinity St David	80.1	78.2	—	143	57.1	80.5
82	Greenwich	74.3	70.7	33.2	115	57.5	80.2
=83	Brunel	70.6	71.5	30.2	122	59.5	80
=83	Keele	70.5	71.9	24.8	111	67.9	80
=83	Wolverhampton	83.1	83.6	20.2	96	53.2	80
=86	Brighton	71.0	65.9	28.5	107	70.3	79.9
=86	Cardiff Metropolitan	75.8	74.7	14.0	108	67.2	79.9
=86	Leicester	62.9	59.7	45.8	126	65.2	79.9

Business, Management and Marketing cont.

		Teaching quality %	Student experience %	Research quality %	Entry standards (UCAS points)	Graduate prospects %	Overall score
=86	York St John	82.8	77.8	9.8	98	63.0	79.9
90	Worcester	74.4	76.1	12.5	108	68.6	79.8
91	Hertfordshire	77.3	72.2	29.0	102	58.4	79.7
92	Abertay	70.9	74.1	—	139	67.1	79.3
93	Royal Agricultural University	72.5	75.1	—	114	73.1	78.9
=94	Kingston	73.3	72.3	24.0	109	58.3	78.6
=94	Middlesex	73.0	72.1	46.2	103	46.4	78.6
=96	Birmingham City	76.3	73.3	11.2	113	59.0	78.4
=96	SOAS, London	62.9	64.9	44.2	139	49.0	78.4
=98	Bolton	78.4	81.2	0.0	—	58.9	78.3
=98	Canterbury Christ Church	70.6	69.8	38.0	91	59.8	78.3
100	Roehampton	72.5	72.3	32.8	100	54.9	78.2
101	Westminster	67.4	71.0	37.5	119	49.9	77.9
=102	De Montfort	72.2	70.2	19.0	97	64.7	77.7
=102	Winchester	66.3	68.1	22.2	114	64.3	77.7
104	Leeds Trinity	83.6	85.9	—	99	50.6	77.6
105	West of Scotland	72.3	68.4	10.5	133	54.1	77.3
106	Goldsmiths, London	62.8	58.3	29.7	126	60.2	76.7
107	Leeds Beckett	70.2	67.4	8.2	102	68.4	76.6
108	Liverpool Hope	79.8	76.1	—	107	52.6	76.4
=109	Bedfordshire	70.0	68.0	22.0	99	57.1	76
=109	St Mary's, Twickenham	74.8	70.6	—	98	64.7	76
=111	East London	77.5	73.5	11.0	89	54.1	75.7
=111	London South Bank	75.6	74.0	21.5	95	46.4	75.7
113	Northampton	74.4	72.5	13.2	102	50.1	75.4
114	Suffolk	71.8	69.1	—	114	57.6	75.1
=115	Solent, Southampton	68.6	65.4	—	106	66.3	74.8
=115	Sunderland	77.8	75.7	—	103	48.5	74.8
117	Staffordshire	58.9	57.0	38.8	109	53.3	74
118	Cumbria	72.3	71.2	7.8	110	42.8	73.3
119	Buckinghamshire New	64.5	66.1	—	118	53.6	72.4

Employed in high-skilled job	55%	Employed in lower-skilled job	26%
Employed in high-skilled job and studying	4%	Employed in lower-skilled job and studying	1%
Studying	6%	Unemployed	7%
High skilled work (median) salary	£25,000	Low/medium skilled salary	£21,000

Celtic Studies

A shake-up to our Celtic Studies table this year brings Cardiff into the No 1 spot, while last year's leader Queen's Belfast is restricted to fifth place. Cardiff's rank has been boosted by attracting the highest entry standards in 2021, as well as its new research rating – which has rocketed off the back of much improved results in the recent Research Excellence Framework

(REF) 2021, compared with the previous REF 2014. Runner-up Bangor, in second place overall, also places second for research.

The content of courses within this grouping caters largely to each university's host Celtic nation. The four universities in Wales focus predominantly on degrees in Welsh history, culture and language, and those in Scotland and Ireland cover similar themes but with the focus on Gaelic, Scottish or Irish studies.

Cambridge, which has topped our Celtic Studies table eight times in the past, still offers its Anglo-Saxon, Norse and Celtic degree and accepts around 25-30 undergraduates each year. The small intake numbers mean that Cambridge did not have a tariff score in the data relevant to this year's Guide – hence its absence from our table.

Students who opt for Celtic studies report high levels of student satisfaction at the majority of universities in our table, led by Ulster, which does best for both measures derived from the National Student Survey (NSS): teaching quality and the wider experience. At the other end of the satisfaction scale is Glasgow, which places bottom for both NSS-derived metrics.

The subject area attracts a select group of students – and just 175 new undergraduates began degrees within the Celtic, Gaelic and Welsh studies areas in 2021. Career prospects are promising; placing in the top 20 of our employment ranking, 48% of Celtic studies graduates were in high-skilled jobs when surveyed 15 months on from their degrees and 28% were engaged in full-time postgraduate study, while 2% were combining the two. Just 2% of graduates were unemployed, one of the lowest unemployment rates of any subject. Median starting salaries of £25,000 for those in high-skilled jobs rank the subject 33rd out of the 70 in our table.

Celtic Studies	Teaching quality %	Student experience %	Research quality %	Entry standards (UCAS points)	Graduate prospects %	Overall score
1 Cardiff	85.8	86.7	55.5	172	81.4	100
2 Bangor	83.9	81.0	42.0	155	70.0*	89
3 Swansea	81.2	75.9	40.8	142	—	86
4 Ulster	90.5	86.8	37.0	126	—	84
5 Queen's Belfast	72.2	79.0	37.0	143	—	83.1
6 Glasgow	58.6	51.2	40.8	—	64.7	78.1

Employed in high-skilled job	48%	Employed in lower-skilled job		18%
Employed in high-skilled job and studying	2%	Employed in lower-skilled job and studying		2%
Studying	28%	Unemployed		2%
High skilled work (median) salary	£25,000	Low/medium skilled salary		£13,000

Chemical Engineering

Oxford leads our chemical engineering table this year, toppling Imperial from No 1 by the narrowest of margins (0.1%). Boosting its overall ranking, Oxford averaged the second-highest UCAS tariff scores in 2021 – at 216 points – and also ranks second in our research quality measure which is based on the Research Excellence Framework 2021 exercise.

Imperial College London as runner-up boasts the top employment record – with 94.5% of graduates working in high-skilled jobs or/and engaged in postgraduate study. It also has the top-rated research and highest levels of student satisfaction. Aston comes closest to Imperial for student satisfaction with teaching quality, while Sheffield leads on the broader undergraduate experience, followed by Hull.

Creating useful products from raw materials, chemical engineering combines natural sciences with life sciences, maths and economics. Cambridge claims the highest entry standards in the subject (222 UCAS tariff points, on average, in 2021). Chemical engineering students arrive with good grades; exactly half of the table have entry standards that equate to AAA or above at A-level (144 UCAS points), but less highly qualified applicants should not be put off as there are plenty of institutions with more accessible entry standards. Swansea, for instance, ranks a respectable 17th overall and averaged 128 UCAS points.

Maths is essential for chemical engineering degrees, and while chemistry or physics are required, the leading universities will usually expect both. Most courses offer industry placements in the final year and lead to Chartered Engineer status. Graduates are in-demand; more than seven in 10 (71%) had secured professional employment when surveyed 15 months after their degrees, and a further 14% were engaged in postgraduate study or combining it with a good job. Only 11 subjects do better in our employment ranking. Queen's Belfast, Oxford and Loughborough rank after Imperial for job prospects, while at the other end of the scale West of Scotland fares less well, with 61.5% of graduates having achieved the most desired outcomes.

Starting salaries stack up even better when compared with other subject areas, ranking seventh out of 70, with those in high-skilled jobs commanding £30,000 a year. Surprisingly for a subject with such a positive career outlook, applications and enrolments dipped for the second consecutive time in 2021's admissions round, and 2,340 students started courses.

Chemical Engineering	Teaching quality %	Student experience %	Research quality %	Entry standards (UCAS points)	Graduate prospects %	Overall score
1 Oxford	—	—	77.5	216	92.5	100
2 Imperial College	85.2	84.6	81.0	201	94.5	99.9
3 Cambridge	—	—	77.2	222	92.3	99.8
4 Strathclyde	81.2	83.1	52.8	207	85.2	93.3
5 Birmingham	78.1	82.5	63.7	175	85.2	91.9
6 Heriot-Watt	76.1	83.2	55.5	162	90.6	91.5
7 University College London	70.3	73.0	70.0	176	88.4	91
8 Aberdeen	81.2	84.1	35.8	187	84.7	90.1
9 Queen Mary, London	76.4	81.4	66.0	136	—	89.7
10 Leeds	74.6	75.7	64.8	162	84.6	89.6
11 Sheffield	81.8	87.3	66.8	147	76.9	89.5
12 Nottingham	79.9	81.7	59.0	158	81	89.4
13 Loughborough	73.9	77.8	46.5	146	92.4	89
14 Manchester	65.1	65.0	63.0	169	91.1	88.6
15 Bath	69.0	74.2	49.5	168	85.8	87.3
16 Queen's Belfast	63.3	66.9	51.0	148	92.6	86.2
17 Swansea	80.0	78.9	48.8	128	80.5	86
18 Edinburgh	56.8	64.2	55.5	194	86.1	85.9
19 Surrey	75.1	77.6	55.2	131	80.0	85.6
20 Ulster	75.3	74.8	49.8	127	—	85.3

=21 Lancaster	68.8	76.4	44.8	141	84.0	84.8
=21 Newcastle	66.6	68.2	58.5	132	85.1	84.8
23 Aston	82.1	83.7	35.2	117	77.6	83.9
24 Hull	81.1	85.4	36.2	111	75.9	83.2
25 Sheffield Hallam	75.3	70.3	30.0	115	—	80.7
26 Teesside	80.4	83.1	18.8	105	76.4	80.5
27 Bradford	75.2	74.8	27.0	103	79.4	80.3
28 Greenwich	74.5	72.2	31.5	93	—	79.2
29 London South Bank	74.7	75.8	27.3	95	76.1	78.9
30 Portsmouth	73.4	71.8	21.0	—	75.0	78.2
31 Huddersfield	72.7	69.6	18.5	107	—	77.4
32 Brunel	63.6	65.0	33.0	117	—	77.2
33 Chester	66.8	66.4	15.8	106	78.8	76.3
34 West of Scotland	63.8	74.0	16.5	—	61.5	69.8

Employed in high-skilled job	71%	Employed in lower-skilled job	9%
Employed in high-skilled job and studying	3%	Employed in lower-skilled job and studying	0%
Studying	11%	Unemployed	6%
High skilled work (median) salary	£30,000	Low/medium skilled salary	£22,000

Chemistry

Entry standards are generally high to study chemistry, and 23 universities averaged over 144 UCAS tariff points (equivalent to AAA at A-level) in 2021. They are led by Cambridge, which tops our table overall once again this year, where entrants arrived with 221 UCAS points, on average. The Chemistry table top 10 features almost all of the same institutions as it did last year (and the year before), albeit reshuffled. Shake-ups include Imperial rising from sixth to third place and Edinburgh (which does best on graduate prospects this year) slipping from second to fifth place overall. The older institutions tend to govern the upper end of the chemistry table, but they have been joined by Northumbria this year – which ties with Durham in tenth place. Boosting Northumbria up from 43rd place in our previous edition are the top rates of student satisfaction for both teaching quality and the wider experience.

Bristol, in 13th place overall, has pipped Cambridge to the top of our research quality rating, which is based on the results of the new Research Excellence Framework 2021. As evidenced by our table, entry standards are generally high.

Chemistry A-level, or equivalent qualification, is almost always a prerequisite and the leading universities will also look for maths and/or at least one other science – it is worth checking which second science individual institutions ask for, as these may differ. Courses include laboratory and experimentation work, alongside independent and group research projects and industry experience or placements.

Just under a quarter of chemistry graduates (24%) had progressed to postgraduate study when surveyed 15 months after their degrees, the latest data shows, which added to the 57% working in high-skilled jobs and 3% combining both. This ranks chemistry 13th out of 70 subject areas for graduate prospects. Median graduate salaries in high-skilled jobs of £25,500 put chemistry in the top 20 subjects for early career earnings.

Applications and enrolments have been declining in recent years and dipped by 7% and 8% respectively in 2021. But chemistry experienced a boom in numbers over the preceding decade or so, and options for aspiring undergraduates are broad: with 127 universities and colleges offering courses in 2023-24.

Chemistry

		Teaching quality %	Student experience %	Research quality %	Entry standards (UCAS points)	Graduate prospects %	Overall score
1	Cambridge	—	—	80.0	221	93.5	100
2	St Andrews	86.1	85.1	66.8	213	92.9	98.8
3	Imperial College	78.2	82.8	75.5	197	89.8	96.2
4	Oxford	—	—	74.0	198	92.4	95.9
5	Edinburgh	71.6	70.7	66.8	204	95.4	95.5
6	Strathclyde	85.7	84.1	56.8	197	84.6	93
7	York	80.2	74.4	71.0	170	86.9	92.4
8	Warwick	81.2	81.5	63.2	157	88.1	91.6
9	Aberdeen	74.9	78.0	39.5	185	94.9*	91.4
=10	Durham	75.7	70.1	55.0	189	89.5	91.3
=10	Northumbria	94.4	93.2	53.5	—	81.6	91.3
12	Bath	77.0	77.9	64.5	158	87.5	90.6
13	Bristol	70.8	68.6	80.5	153	86.4	90.3
14	University College London	69.9	70.1	76.0	169	84.6	90.1
15	Southampton	84.6	83.1	61.8	150	82.4	89.5
16	Birmingham	78.9	81.1	53.5	156	87.0	89.4
17	Surrey	85.1	83.0	55.2	136	86.4	89.2
18	Sheffield	74.4	76.2	62.7	144	85.8	88.3
19	Liverpool	63.5	61.5	72.8	146	87.2	87.2
20	Lincoln	91.0	89.9	42.2	113	85.4	87.1
21	Swansea	89.3	85.9	43.0	125	—	86.8
22	Manchester	58.9	59.0	72.2	165	84.9	86.6
=23	East Anglia	79.0	74.6	54.0	129	83.9	85.9
=23	Nottingham	71.2	70.4	58.2	140	84.8	85.9
25	Newcastle	65.8	67.9	62.7	131	86.4	85.5
=26	Brighton	80.8	76.5	50.5	—	80.5	85.4
=26	Glasgow	63.4	55.1	55.5	197	81.1	85.4
28	Lancaster	81.9	77.1	30.2	133	88.5	85.3
29	Queen's Belfast	59.8	62.6	48.8	156	90.3	85.2
=30	Hull	82.7	81.5	35.2	112	87.0	84.5
=30	Queen Mary, London	71.9	77.4	62.5	132	79.1	84.5
32	Leeds	65.6	61.4	50.2	152	84.4	83.8
=33	King's College London	61.5	57.4	74.2	149	77.4	83.3
=33	Plymouth	84.1	86.3	40.8	110	80.4	83.3
35	Cardiff	68.8	71.0	57.8	125	81.2	83.2
=36	Greenwich	84.4	87.0	32.8	116	—	83
=36	Leicester	77.4	79.2	51.2	119	78.7	83
=36	Loughborough	81.0	87.2	34.8	139	77.9	83
39	Keele	78.3	72.1	48.0	111	80.6	82.3

40	West of Scotland	88.3	92.1	28.7	130	75.0*	82.1
41	Heriot-Watt	68.7	67.4	32.8	171	79.7	81.8
42	Central Lancashire	86.4	84.9	—	115	87.5	80.8
43	Aston	89.6	88.8	—	115	83.3	80.1
44	Reading	67.9	68.0	36.0	116	83.1	79.8
45	Manchester Metropolitan	75.1	67.3	45.5	115	75.9	79.5
46	Nottingham Trent	70.5	70.4	59.0	108	73.1	79.4
47	Kent	73.9	73.0	40.2	107	77.9	79.3
48	Huddersfield	81.1	78.4	18.5	123	77.7	78.8
=49	Salford	74.9	73.4	37.0	114	75.8	78.7
=49	Sussex	68.9	66.4	43.5	141	72.9	78.7
51	Sheffield Hallam	80.8	81.8	—	102	83.0	77.1
52	Kingston	69.9	67.2	38.5	98	75.5	76.4
53	Bradford	72.6	73.8	25.0	102	71.1	74.1
54	De Montfort	61.2	69.5	—	100	80.4	71.6

Employed in high-skilled job	57%	Employed in lower-skilled job	10%
Employed in high-skilled job and studying	3%	Employed in lower-skilled job and studying	1%
Studying	24%	Unemployed	5%
High skilled work (median) salary	£25,500	Low/medium skilled salary	£21,000

Civil Engineering

Imperial College London retains the lead it first took in our civil engineering table last year when ousting Cambridge from the No 1 spot it had occupied for 16 years. In our analysis of the results of the recent Research Excellence Framework 2021 Imperial is peerless, and Oxford takes second place – as it does overall. While the older institutions dominate the upper end of our rankings, the highest rates of student satisfaction (as derived from the latest National Student Survey) are found at post-1992 university Northumbria, which comes top for teaching quality as well as the broader experience. The buoyant levels of student satisfaction have contributed to Northumbria's three-place rise to rank 11th overall this year.

Greenwich, Imperial and West London also place in the top three for student satisfaction measures, while civil engineering students at City are the least satisfied with their teaching quality and those at Anglia Ruskin place the university bottom for satisfaction with the wider experience.

A regular feature in the top 10 of our employment table, civil engineering ranks eighth this year. When surveyed 15 months on from their degrees, three-quarters of graduates were working in high-skills jobs 15 months on from their degrees and a further 12% were furthering their studies or doing so while also holding down a professional-grade job. Promising average starting salaries of £27,500, civil engineering sits 16th out of 70 subject areas for earnings.

As well as A-levels and Scottish Highers, BTEC qualifications are a popular means of entry into a civil engineering undergraduate degree, but applicants should check with individual universities as to their preferred entry requirements.

As the future brains behind the design, construction and maintenance of roads, bridges, pipelines, processing plants, buildings and harbours, civil engineering students learn how to apply physics, maths and mechanics to structural design. Some degrees in the subject are four-year courses leading to an MEng; others are sandwich courses that include a work placement.

Civil Engineering

		Teaching quality %	Student experience %	Research quality %	Entry standards (UCAS points)	Graduate prospects %	Overall score
1	Imperial College	84.6	89.1	81.0	191	100	100
2	Oxford	—	—	77.5	216	92.5	99.5
3	Cambridge	—	—	77.2	228	96.5	97.1
4	Bristol	82.4	79.6	68.0	181	93.6	94.5
5	Glasgow	69.1	72.7	61.5	205	100	94.1
6	Strathclyde	84.3	85.0	52.8	190	91.6	93.6
7	Leeds	81.3	78.7	64.8	177	92.4	93.2
8	Bath	81.0	83.7	49.5	176	95.5	92.6
9	Southampton	75.3	74.5	70.0	160	95.8	91.9
10	Sheffield	79.0	82.1	66.8	157	91.8	91.5
11	Northumbria	94.2	92.1	43.0	137	90.9	90.9
12	Nottingham	81.1	79.6	59.0	144	94.9	90.8
13	Birmingham	69.9	75.2	63.7	152	95.8	89.5
14	Loughborough	67.6	74.8	72.0	139	94.0	88.6
15	Heriot-Watt	70.8	72.0	55.5	167	92.2	88.5
16	University College London	75.1	76.5	70.0	158	83.3	88.3
17	Dundee	80.3	79.7	50.2	183	78.8	87.8
18	Surrey	78.3	83.0	55.2	132	88.4	87.3
19	Greenwich	89.1	89.8	31.5	125	—	87.2
20	Queen's Belfast	69.6	71.3	51.0	143	95.7	86.9
21	Ulster	81.0	77.7	49.8	129	89.9	86.8
22	Swansea	79.7	79.1	48.8	138	87.6	86.6
=23	Liverpool	68.1	71.2	57.0	133	95.2	86.4
=23	Manchester	69.7	70.6	63.0	157	85.7	86.4
25	Edinburgh	65.3	75.1	55.5	178	83.9	86.2
26	Aston	77.6	86.1	35.2	139	—	85.8
27	Exeter	74.6	71.5	47.0	142	89.7	85.6
=28	Aberdeen	73.3	71.4	35.8	161	—	85
=28	Cardiff	67.7	70.8	54.0	142	89.7	85
30	Glasgow Caledonian	68.8	64.7	12.8	168	96.7	83.7
31	Birmingham City	79.7	77.4	17.5	116	96.2	83.6
=32	Liverpool John Moores	69.5	69.8	45.5	129	88.2	82.9
=32	Nottingham Trent	71.4	76.0	38.0	122	90.0	82.9
34	Brighton	76.0	77.3	36.5	115	88.7	82.8
35	Edinburgh Napier	74.1	74.5	22.8	133	90.1	82.4
36	Newcastle	61.7	62.7	58.5	130	87.6	82.1
37	Plymouth	74.5	73.1	32.5	115	89.6	81.9
38	Salford	74.5	70.9	33.2	125	83.3	80.8
39	West of England	72.0	73.8	30.8	125	—	80.6
40	Derby	82.3	80.7	14.0	115	84.6*	80.5
41	Leeds Beckett	69.7	75.9	24.5	100	92.9	80.2
42	Abertay	75.8	69.9	24.2	—	83.9*	80.1

43 Brunel	66.2	70.3	33.0	137	82.4	79.7
44 Portsmouth	75.2	75.4	21.0	111	84.8	79.2
45 Coventry	72.5	73.5	23.5	118	81.9	78.5
46 Hertfordshire	70.0	68.4	33.0	112	—	78.4
47 West of Scotland	73.9	72.5	16.5	—	81.5	77.8
48 Bradford	74.4	79.6	27.0	112	75.9	77.7
49 West London	85.7	86.3	13.8	110	69.8	77
50 Teesside	70.5	69.3	18.8	125	79.4	76.9
51 Central Lancashire	64.1	61.9	23.0	128	—	76.1
=52 City	52.5	53.9	32.5	122	88.7	76
=52 London South Bank	75.8	74.3	27.3	123	68.0	76
=52 Wolverhampton	78.5	68.8	18.2	89	—	76
55 East London	73.4	74.6	21.2	105	71.2	74.4
56 Kingston	75.6	77.0	17.2	113	67.7	74.2
57 Bolton	55.0	61.1	22.0	100	—	70.6
58 Anglia Ruskin	53.3	48.8	23.8	111	—	70

Employed in high-skilled job	75%	Employed in lower-skilled job	7%
Employed in high-skilled job and studying	4%	Employed in lower-skilled job and studying	0%
Studying	8%	Unemployed	5%
High skilled work (median) salary	£27,500	Low/medium skilled salary	£21,000

Classics and Ancient History

Oxford takes the lead in our new classics and ancient history table, rising from fourth place in our previous edition and bringing Cambridge's 16-year reign at the top of the table to an end. Oxford's position is boosted by the best graduate prospects – with 86.5% of graduates working in high-skilled jobs and/or engaged in further study 15 months after their degrees, as well as the second-highest entry standards. St Andrews, in sixth place overall, outdoes it on this measure – its 2021 entrants having averaged 194 UCAS tariff points.

Results of the 2021 Research Excellence Framework see Warwick achieving the top research quality rating in the subjects, closely followed by King's College London and Manchester – which tie in our analysis of this measure. For student satisfaction with both the wider experience and teaching quality Roehampton (in 23rd place overall) is unbeaten, followed by Royal Holloway in each of these student-led categories. Conversely, Bristol finishes bottom for student satisfaction with teaching quality, while Manchester claims the same spot for the broader experience.

Classics takes in the broad literature, history and culture of Ancient Greek and Roman societies, and can include architecture, religion and philosophy. Some courses will want Latin or Greek A-level, while others will allow students to learn the languages from scratch once they have enrolled. Several universities teach the subjects as part of modular courses, but not on their own.

The numbers starting classical studies courses have been consistent in recent years, and 1,200 students enrolled on them in 2021. The more specialised degrees in Classical Greek studies attracted no new starters in the same year, while 10 Latin studies students began courses.

Classics and ancient history are confined to 48th position in our employment table of 70 subject areas, with 68% of graduates working in high-skilled jobs and/or engaged in postgraduate study when surveyed 15 months on from their degrees. However, 23% were employed in jobs deemed low-skilled and 10% were unemployed, while 1% were studying while holding down a low-skilled job. Although not an ingredient of our subject ranking overall, in our pay index the subjects place 53rd and graduates in high-skilled jobs command £25,000 salaries, on average.

Classics and Ancient History	Teaching quality %	Student experience %	Research quality %	Entry standards (UCAS points)	Graduate prospects %	Overall score
1 Oxford	—	—	60.0	192	86.5	100
2 Durham	80.9	72.6	57.8	181	85.3	97.5
3 Cambridge	—	—	48.8	185	84.1	97.4
4 Glasgow	83.7	79.3	62.5	168	—	97.3
5 Warwick	83.7	79.9	65.8	139	75.8	95.4
6 St Andrews	78.9	73.4	42.5	194	85.1*	94.1
7 University College London	83.5	76.9	44.2	169	81.4	93
8 Exeter	78.8	76.7	61.5	160	67.6	92.8
=9 Nottingham	86.4	81.8	51.5	134	75.0	91.8
=9 Royal Holloway, London	93.9	86.2	53.5	124	67.2	91.8
11 King's College London	75.8	72.3	65.5	146	65.1	91
12 Leeds	77.0	67.4	52.0	146	76.8	89.8
13 Birmingham	76.0	65.9	54.2	137	70.0	87.8
14 Manchester	71.9	61.9	65.5	144	58.5	87.5
=15 Bristol	65.6	66.9	52.8	144	70.9	86
=15 Swansea	87.5	83.8	45.2	111	63.1	86
17 Kent	79.2	74.0	58.8	110	58.0	85.6
=18 Liverpool	81.3	74.2	43.5	131	65.1	85.4
=18 Reading	84.6	78.6	43.2	118	65.3	85.4
20 Newcastle	79.7	74.2	42.0	127	68.7	85.1
21 Edinburgh	68.7	63.5	51.5	164	52.8	83.6
22 Cardiff	77.8	66.7	42.2	124	67.8	83.5
23 Roehampton	94.1	91.6	—	102	63.0	75.5
24 Leicester	78.4	74.1	—	117	56.0	70

Employed in high-skilled job	38%	Employed in lower-skilled job		23%
Employed in high-skilled job and studying	5%	Employed in lower-skilled job and studying		1%
Studying	23%	Unemployed		10%
High skilled work (median) salary	£25,000	Low/medium skilled salary		£20,000

Communication and Media Studies

A reordering of our table has placed Strathclyde at its top, while former winner Warwick slips 22 places to joint 23rd. Lancaster moves into runner-up position, up from tenth last year, and performs strongly across all measures. For research, Cardiff achieves the top score in our analysis of the new Research Excellence Framework 2021, followed by Goldsmiths, Loughborough and Southampton. In both National Student Survey-derived measures included in our table another Welsh university, Swansea, leads the field – achieving the best results for student satisfaction with teaching quality and for the wider experience. York St John and Strathclyde also fare well. At the other end of the scale is Goldsmiths, which places bottom for each of these student-led measures.

This subject table covers a wide range of courses; some focus on the history and theory of media and culture in society, while others range from practical production for TV, film and radio to script writing or journalism. Options are extensive; for 2023-24 entry, 196 universities and colleges were offering 1,788 courses classified by UCAS under the media studies banner – either as standalone degrees or as part of modular courses.

The Scottish universities of Strathclyde, Stirling and Glasgow Caledonian averaged the highest entry standards in 2021, with King's College London attracting the highest grades south of the border. Entry grades span a broad spectrum, from 204 UCAS points averaged by entrants to Strathclyde in 2021 down to 78 points at Bedfordshire – one of nine universities to average below 100 in the UCAS tariff.

With more than nine in 10 graduates (92.4%) working in high-skilled jobs and/or engaged in postgraduate study 15 months on from their degrees, City (eighth overall) does well to buck an otherwise lacklustre trend by media studies in our employment table – and does so for the second year running. The subject sits 59th out of the 70 listed, due to 30% of graduates working in low-skilled jobs at the point of survey, 8% being unemployed and 1% furthering their studies while working in a low-skilled job. Most communication and media studies students will be wise to the dearth of "professional"-level roles upon graduation, but career prospects vary considerably by university. Bedfordshire (90th overall) had just 37.5% of graduates in high-skilled work and/or further study 15 months on, and Aberystwyth (joint 81st) did almost as poorly, with just 44.8% achieving these desired outcomes. Median starting salaries of £21,500 in high-skilled roles place the subjects in the bottom four.

Communication and Media Studies	Teaching quality %	Student experience %	Research quality %	Entry standards (UCAS points)	Graduate prospects %	Overall score
1 Strathclyde	87.9	82.8	58.8	204	71.0	100
2 Lancaster	84.8	81.4	60.2	135	75.8	93.1
3 Loughborough	70.4	65.6	71.8	143	83.2	93
4 Sheffield	80.2	79.5	59.5	148	73.3	92.6
5 Stirling	84.8	82.3	44.5	173	65.2	92.2
6 Cardiff	70.7	70.2	77.0	143	71.0	91.2
7 Newcastle	70.4	70.1	60.8	147	78.7	91
8 City	71.2	70.3	42.8	134	92.4	90.7
9 Exeter	80.2	79.5	55.9	143	—	90.3
10 Leicester	78.4	81.8	68.6	127	63.9	89.1
11 Southampton	86.5	78.7	69.2	143	50.0	88.7
12 Leeds	68.7	64.9	50.2	158	73.8	88.5
13 Glasgow Caledonian	72.7	67.1	38.5	169	70.2	88
14 Edinburgh Napier	82.5	78.8	38.8	153	62.3	87.6
15 Teesside	83.2	80.8	49.2	114	69.1	87
16 Royal Holloway, London	74.9	70.4	63.7	138	61.2	86.9
17 Northumbria	82.1	80.8	45.8	130	64.5	86.7
18 Coventry	79.0	78.6	54.2	117	67.8	86.6
19 Swansea	91.2	84.6	31.5	132	61.9	86.5
=20 Nottingham	75.1	71.0	54.8	127	63.9	85.2

Communication and Media Studies
cont.

	Teaching quality %	Student experience %	Research quality %	Entry standards (UCAS points)	Graduate prospects %	Overall score
=20 Sussex	66.5	60.8	61.8	135	67.6	85.2
22 King's College London	66.6	63.9	64.5	160	52.9	84.9
=23 Kingston	75.9	72.5	45.0	102	76.5	84.5
=23 Warwick	87.2	77.4	—	154	69.7	84.5
25 Queen Margaret, Edinburgh	76.3	73.8	33.0	159	57.7	84.2
26 Liverpool	65.9	62.6	55.2	132	68.3	84
27 Keele	85.1	73.5	54.8	109	57.8*	83.9
28 Bournemouth	72.4	69.6	47.2	112	71.3	83.6
29 Robert Gordon	82.3	75.0	26.0	150	57.1	83.4
=30 Ulster	79.0	73.2	35.0	126	64.4	83.2
=30 Westminster	78.3	78.4	50.0	110	60.8	83.2
32 Nottingham Trent	80.5	77.7	42.5	115	61.2	83
33 Canterbury Christ Church	82.8	75.6	38.0	103	67.0	82.8
=34 Plymouth	73.9	73.5	49.8	—	58.8	82.5
=34 Salford	75.4	69.7	49.8	122	59.2	82.5
=36 Manchester Metropolitan	75.4	69.6	51.7	115	59.6	82.2
=36 University of the Arts London	74.4	66.2	46.0	122	62.4	82.2
=38 Birmingham City	73.7	67.4	40.8	117	67.1	82.1
=38 West London	87.2	83.5	45.5	111	49.5	82.1
40 Central Lancashire	81.0	74.6	31.8	114	64.6	82
41 Derby	80.5	78.4	24.0	113	66.7	81.5
42 Leeds Beckett	81.0	77.9	26.5	99	70.3	81.4
43 Sheffield Hallam	72.9	65.3	46.0	113	63.2	81.1
=44 Essex	70.6	70.5	49.8	115	—	81
=44 Falmouth	78.1	65.9	48.8	124	52.0	81
46 Gloucestershire	85.6	80.8	23.8	116	58.3	80.9
=47 Bath Spa	84.3	77.4	42.0	110	52.0	80.8
=47 East Anglia	68.8	63.8	50.2	127	58.2	80.8
=47 Hull	81.2	70.4	35.0	123	55.7	80.8
=47 West of England	81.0	75.3	48.2	114	50.3	80.8
=47 York	75.1	72.9	—	138	73.9	80.8
=52 Roehampton	70.0	65.9	53.0	99	64.3	80.3
=52 Staffordshire	80.6	72.8	31.5	114	58.9	80.3
54 Goldsmiths, London	50.2	42.1	72.8	129	65.2	80.1
55 Huddersfield	78.1	69.3	49.8	112	52.0	80
56 Liverpool John Moores	70.7	71.9	22.2	137	60.1	79.4
57 Plymouth Marjon	79.7	80.9	—	121	67.6	79
58 University for the Creative Arts	83.3	73.6	41.2	—	45.8	78.9
59 Bangor	—	—	33.2	118	57.9	78.8
60 Lincoln	74.6	65.0	33.5	116	59.2	78.7
61 South Wales	77.8	71.8	35.8	110	54.2	78.5
=62 Edge Hill	77.6	69.9	39.8	116	50.0	78.4

=62	Solent, Southampton	81.6	78.5	9.5	111	63.5	78.4
64	York St John	88.0	82.5	—	110	61.6	78.3
65	Anglia Ruskin	72.6	66.1	53.8	98	52.7	77.8
=66	Brighton	66.7	60.3	44.2	104	62.1	77.7
=66	Portsmouth	81.7	74.1	30.2	106	52.0	77.7
68	Sunderland	79.0	74.4	25.5	109	55.4	77.6
69	Oxford Brookes	74.3	70.8	21.5	116	59.1	77.4
70	Middlesex	76.1	68.8	26.0	106	55.7	76.2
=71	Wolverhampton	76.6	68.2	31.5	87	59.1	76
=71	Worcester	83.1	78.1	5.8	104	58.2	76
=73	De Montfort	68.3	64.5	24.0	107	61.1	75.3
=73	Winchester	62.3	64.3	29.2	104	64.0	75.3
=75	Greenwich	84.5	80.2	—	103	55.8*	74.9
=75	Liverpool Hope	84.4	77.1	—	115	52.0	74.9
77	East London	68.2	59.7	34.2	96	59.3	74.8
78	Leeds Trinity	80.8	74.6	—	102	59.7	74.5
79	London Metropolitan	74.9	71.4	—	102	65.3	74.3
80	Queen Mary, London	67.4	59.4	—	149	55.3	74
=81	Aberystwyth	82.3	78.6	—	124	44.8	73.8
=81	Hertfordshire	72.2	71.9	24.2	97	—	73.8
83	Chester	—	—	21.0	116	51.0	73.5
84	West of Scotland	75.6	69.9	19.2	—	50.0	73.1
85	London South Bank	72.1	47.3	35.8	94	52.5	72.6
86	Brunel	72.9	68.1	—	108	58.7	72.5
87	Kent	57.7	59.3	—	117	69.6	72.2
88	Northampton	72.2	65.3	—	101	61.6	72.1
89	Chichester	67.2	63.5	—	98	48.4	67.1
90	Bedfordshire	68.4	64.7	27.0	78	37.5	66.5

Employed in high-skilled job	53%	Employed in lower-skilled job		30%
Employed in high-skilled job and studying	3%	Employed in lower-skilled job and studying		1%
Studying	5%	Unemployed		8%
High skilled work (median) salary	£21,500	Low/medium skilled salary		£20,000

Computer Science

Cambridge returns to the top of the Computer Science ranking, having been knocked from it last year by St Andrews (in fourth place this year), breaking a five-year run at No 1. As well as leading on entry standards by averaging 225 UCAS tariff points among 2021's entrants, Cambridge is out in front on graduate prospects. But third-ranked Imperial secured the best results in computer science in our analysis of the recent Research Excellence Framework 2021, with second-place overall Oxford runner-up for research as well.

The computer science subject area is broad, taking in everything from artificial intelligence to computer games design, as reflected in our table – which is among the biggest of any subject. Further shuffling of positions at the top end of our new ranking include Warwick falling from joint seventh in our previous edition to joint 21st this year, due largely to reduced rates of student satisfaction. Edinburgh moves into the top-10 in seventh place, up from 19th. Students at Reading (in 23rd place overall) expressed the highest rates of satisfaction with their broad experience while those at East London (joint 77th) were the most satisfied with their teaching quality. London Metropolitan is in second place for both of these student-led measures.

Ranking 21st out of 70 subject areas, computer science offers promising job prospects. They are pretty good regardless of which university you attend, with only 15 out of the 111 universities tabled registering rates of high-skilled work/postgraduate study beneath 70%. Four universities, meanwhile, report more than 90% of their computer science graduates as being in high-skilled jobs or postgraduate study within 15 months. They are led by Cambridge, from which barely any (1.8%) computer science graduates failed to achieve these outcomes at the point of survey. Starting salaries are healthy, too, and graduates in high-skilled jobs can expect to earn around £27,500. Computer science places in the top 20 of our pay index – even though earnings are not an ingredient of our main subject ranking.

Computer Science	Teaching quality %	Student experience %	Research quality %	Entry standards (UCAS points)	Graduate prospects %	Overall score
1 Cambridge	—	—	78.2	225	98.2	100
2 Oxford	77.4	73.5	85.8	207	96.5	98.3
3 Imperial College	68.3	70.4	94.8	202	97.6	96.7
4 St Andrews	80.2	80.1	41.2	220	93.3	95.2
5 Southampton	80.5	82.8	70.8	170	88.7	93.5
6 University College London	70.1	72.8	82.2	189	89.4	93
7 Edinburgh	61.8	64.2	81.2	203	92.8	92
8 Durham	70.7	72.1	59.0	184	96.8	91.9
9 Birmingham	67.2	71.7	82.8	166	94.5	91.6
10 Sheffield	76.0	78.2	69.8	150	93.2	91.3
11 Glasgow	64.0	66.1	71.8	205	89.2	91
12 Strathclyde	72.1	73.5	46.2	198	91.7	90.9
13 Manchester	64.1	66.8	71.2	183	94.8	90.6
14 Bath	73.6	80.6	52.2	171	90.7	90.3
15 Bristol	65.1	64.6	76.0	178	92.5	90.1
16 Loughborough	79.9	81.8	46.5	152	92.1	90
17 Nottingham	69.7	74.6	63.5	158	90.1	88.8
18 Exeter	75.0	74.1	45.5	149	96.2	88.7
19 King's College London	62.6	67.6	68.0	167	94.5	88.6
20 Lancaster	69.4	71.5	64.8	145	94.5	88.5
=21 Warwick	53.9	51.7	81.8	190	94.7	88.3
=21 York	67.7	68.8	72.5	148	92.3	88.3
23 Reading	85.2	89.1	39.8	126	88.2	88.2
24 Surrey	73.4	77.3	50.5	133	94.6	87.5
25 Queen Mary, London	70.8	71.0	74.2	146	82.1	86.9
26 Aberystwyth	81.0	77.6	43.8	122	90.7	86.7
27 Cardiff	66.8	66.9	57.8	147	91.2	86
28 Heriot-Watt	66.8	67.3	39.5	171	90.5	85.8
=29 Dundee	70.2	66.3	53.5	172	80.6	85.7

=29	Newcastle	66.9	68.7	60.5	141	89.8	85.7
31	East Anglia	72.6	70.8	41.8	135	93.8	85.6
=32	Aberdeen	69.1	69.7	44.0	170	—	85.5
=32	Royal Holloway, London	66.2	66.8	65.0	132	91.5	85.5
=32	Sussex	74.6	74.3	59.2	137	81.1	85.5
=35	Kent	71.9	70.6	57.2	132	87.2	85.3
=35	Queen's Belfast	67.2	67.1	51.0	143	92.1	85.3
37	Edinburgh Napier	74.1	67.0	47.2	149	84.1	85
=38	Leicester	71.9	69.8	41.8	133	90.4	84.4
=38	Liverpool	70.4	71.5	61.0	137	81	84.4
40	Leeds	53.0	51.6	72.0	175	86.0	83.7
41	Plymouth	77.4	78.0	32.0	125	84.8	83.5
42	Swansea	72.3	68.9	46.5	133	84.0	83.4
43	Liverpool Hope	84.0	78.5	19.5	111	87.0	83.1
44	Aston	71.7	71.2	29.2	138	84.7	82.2
45	Robert Gordon	77.7	73.2	16.0	144	79.6	81.7
46	Essex	63.8	67.5	53.5	119	85.9	81.3
47	Bangor	74.6	71.8	40.2	109	81.4	81
=48	Manchester Metropolitan	76.0	70.4	29.2	125	78.8	80.6
=48	Northumbria	71.6	69.6	25.8	137	80.6	80.6
50	Staffordshire	79.1	74.1	25.5	122	76.3	80.5
51	Ulster	70.8	66.1	38.0	127	79.9	80.4
=52	Lincoln	64.3	67.4	44.0	127	82.3	80.3
=52	West of England	71.9	73.5	32.2	126	78.0	80.3
=54	City	64.3	66.4	47.5	124	81.2	80
=54	Huddersfield	70.0	68.5	26.5	133	80.9	80
=54	Hull	69.3	67.0	31.2	127	82.3	80
=57	Abertay	78.4	70.1	—	151	76.3	79.6
=57	Glasgow Caledonian	72.0	67.7	13.8	148	78.5	79.6
=57	South Wales	82.2	77.0	18.8	124	70.4	79.6
=60	Canterbury Christ Church	80.4	73.9	16.8	94	84.5	79.5
=60	Teesside	82.0	76.8	18.8	125	70.2	79.5
62	Greenwich	78.6	79.4	28.0	122	67.4	79.2
63	Salford	70.6	66.9	28.2	126	79.1	79.1
=64	Brunel	68.7	65.9	37.5	133	74.7	79
=64	Coventry	76.4	72.4	23.5	116	76.4	79
66	Nottingham Trent	72.9	65.4	26.0	126	77.5	78.8
=67	Birmingham City	78.6	72.7	23.2	120	71.4	78.7
=67	Liverpool John Moores	66.2	64.3	26.0	147	76.6	78.7
69	Bath Spa	82.5	76.3	—	106	80.4	78.5
=70	Portsmouth	72.1	69.3	32.8	113	75.9	78.4
=70	Arts London	80.8	74.0	46.0	100	64.0	78.4
=70	West of Scotland	81.0	73.2	18.0	134	65.2	78.4
73	Edge Hill	70.1	68.6	20.0	131	76.9	78.2
74	Sheffield Hallam	70.1	62.1	17.0	120	84.8	78.1
75	Leeds Beckett	81.1	72.9	18.2	109	71.6	77.9

Computer Science cont.

	Teaching quality %	Student experience %	Research quality %	Entry standards (UCAS points)	Graduate prospects %	Overall score
76 Oxford Brookes	65.7	68.1	24.2	116	83.2	77.8
=77 Brighton	74.0	68.8	32.5	94	77.2	77.5
=77 East London	86.6	85.3	28.7	90	60.8	77.5
=77 Stirling	64.9	55.8	24.0	144	79.1	77.5
=77 Sunderland	73.1	67.2	14.5	101	84.7	77.5
=81 Hertfordshire	67.8	67.5	41.2	115	71.1	77.1
=81 Worcester	81.1	75.8	12.5	103	71.6	77.1
83 London Metropolitan	85.8	87.9	13.2	91	65.0	77
84 Goldsmiths, London	64.6	56.2	28.5	131	78.4	76.8
85 Derby	76.5	71.5	15.8	114	71.0	76.7
=86 Falmouth	82.7	77.8	—	121	66.7	76.6
=86 West London	82.1	82.7	20.0	115	58.0	76.6
=88 Keele	57.8	62.1	20.8	123	86.8	76.4
=88 Westminster	67.4	68.1	24.0	116	75.8	76.4
=90 Central Lancashire	68.1	65.9	17.8	131	73.3	76.3
=90 Kingston	69.4	69.2	23.5	106	76.4	76.3
92 Bradford	72.8	69.9	20.5	125	66.2	76
93 Bolton	83.6	76.3	—	121	63.3	75.9
94 Middlesex	75.7	72.8	20.2	111	65.9	75.7
95 Bournemouth	64.3	59.9	22.2	120	77.3	75.3
96 Suffolk	73.1	69.2	—	117	75.0	75.2
97 Wales Trinity St David	69.5	62.4	—	148	70.2	75
=98 Chester	65.7	50.0	13.2	122	80.4	74.5
=98 York St John	72.9	66.4	—	107	77.3	74.5
100 Northampton	74.8	66.9	8.5	105	70.8	74.2
101 Buckinghamshire New	74.1	71.8	—	103	71.2	73.6
102 De Montfort	62.9	60.3	25.0	107	73.7	73.4
103 Norwich Arts	72.6	55.6	—	130	68.0	72.9
=104 Bedfordshire	64.4	63.0	15.2	114	68.8	72.5
=104 Solent, Southampton	74.9	65.3	—	104	68.5	72.5
106 Anglia Ruskin	64.8	62.2	10.0	108	73.2	72.4
107 Gloucestershire	59.2	55.9	6.2	118	72.3	70.6
108 Cardiff Metropolitan	61.3	59.6	—	117	70.5	70.4
109 Wolverhampton	70.5	65.7	12.5	92	60.6	70.1
110 Wrexham Glyndŵr	56.5	53.2	1.5	122	70.1	69
111 London South Bank	61.8	62.9	—	102	58.2	66.7

Employed in high-skilled job	71%	Employed in lower-skilled job	12%
Employed in high-skilled job and studying	3%	Employed in lower-skilled job and studying	0%
Studying	6%	Unemployed	9%
High skilled work (median) salary	£27,500	Low/medium skilled salary	£20,000

Creative Writing

Warwick returns to the top of our table after a year's hiatus during which Royal Holloway, London (now joint sixth), placed No 1. Entry standards are highest at Warwick, which also comes sixth for research and tenth for student satisfaction with teaching quality. Newcastle has the top research rating in our analysis of the latest Research Excellence Framework 2021, followed by Leeds.

Creative writing students tend to enjoy their studies, as represented by the high rates of student satisfaction with teaching quality throughout the table. These are topped by those at Nottingham Trent, which places 10th overall. Central Lancashire does best for students' feelings about the broader experience, while Hull is in the top three for each of these National Student Survey-led measures.

Creative writing has risen two places up our employment ranking of 70 subject areas, where it sits sixth from bottom this year. More than four in 10 graduates were in high-skilled work and/or further study when surveyed 15 months after their degrees, but a third were in jobs deemed "low-skilled" and 11% were unemployed – the second-highest unemployment rate of any subject ranked. But applicants to creative writing courses may not be motivated by immediate professional full-time employment upon graduation, which is perhaps why only 25 of the 45 universities tabled post a graduate prospects score.

Creative Writing	Teaching quality %	Student experience %	Research quality %	Entry standards (UCAS points)	Graduate prospects %	Overall score
1 Warwick	87.5	80.0	64.8	162	—	100
2 Newcastle	77.6	74.0	83.8	144	—	96.7
3 Birmingham	76.0	70.4	68.8	151	74.5	95.9
4 Liverpool John Moores	87.6	83.5	58.0	138	64.3	93.5
5 Leeds	69.9	54.5	73.2	160	—	93.2
=6 Lancaster	81.3	80.5	48.0	149	—	92.3
=6 Royal Holloway, London	79.3	71.0	60.5	145	—	92.3
8 East Anglia	70.4	62.4	67.0	148	69.6	92.1
9 Hull	92.3	86.8	55.5	120		91.9
10 Nottingham Trent	96.5	84.5	39.2	127	—	90.9
11 Kent	86.1	77.0	64.5	116	—	89.9
12 Birmingham City	91.4	67.2	65.5	112	—	89.7
13 Teesside	85.9	78.8	49.2	121	—	88.1
14 Bangor	84.8	81.7	44.2	125	55.6	86.7
15 Roehampton	91.3	85.7	50.5	109	54.4	86.6
16 Brunel	79.8	75.5	42.8	110	69.4	85.8
17 De Montfort	77.1	63.9	54.5	117	64.0	85.7
18 Kingston	83.0	81.2	47.0	114	—	85.5
19 Aberystwyth	90.1	83.6	25.5	126	55.4	85.3
20 Manchester Metropolitan	71.6	54.7	61.8	123	60.0	84.8
21 Essex	77.3	70.7	49.8	121	—	84.7
=22 Canterbury Christ Church	76.8	62.4	53.2	103	66.7	84
=22 Lincoln	86.3	75.7	36.0	115	—	84
=24 Anglia Ruskin	83.9	76.8	46.0	105	—	83.4

Creative Writing cont.

		Teaching quality %	Student experience %	Research quality %	Entry standards (UCAS points)	Graduate prospects %	Overall score
=24	Chichester	90.1	81.6	37.2	111	50.7	83.4
26	Central Lancashire	93.5	90.3	33.8	114	42.9	83
27	West of England	86.1	76.2	32.2	112	—	82.5
28	Edge Hill	82.3	79.9	32.8	121	50.4	82.4
29	Plymouth	67.8	59.5	60.5	119	—	82.3
30	Salford	76.5	77.0	26.5	122	59.0	82.2
31	Falmouth	76.4	67.0	48.8	118	50.7	81.9
=32	Bath Spa	73.9	68.1	51.7	104	58.5	81.7
=32	Greenwich	81.4	73.4	26.5	122	—	81.7
34	Arts Bournemouth	86.5	69.0	23.0	115	—	80.6
35	York St John	88.5	82.1	22.8	104	53.3	80.5
36	Portsmouth	79.9	69.5	30.8	103	60.7	80.3
=37	Liverpool Hope	83.0	71.7	36.0	104	—	80.2
=37	Worcester	77.8	65.0	19.2	109	67.3	80.2
39	Derby	79.0	64.8	—	114	73.0	79.8
40	Sheffield Hallam	86.1	78.8	50.7	106	33.8	79.5
41	St Mary's, Twickenham	81.6	70.9	30.2	—	44.4*	77.6
42	Bournemouth	65.7	63.9	22.5	—	65.5	77.5
43	Winchester	77.3	72.0	16.2	114	49.9	76.8
44	Brighton	72.9	59.3	44.2	98	—	76.3
45	Gloucestershire	66.1	55.6	32.8	109	51.9	75.2

Employed in high-skilled job	41%	Employed in lower-skilled job	33%
Employed in high-skilled job and studying	3%	Employed in lower-skilled job and studying	2%
Studying	9%	Unemployed	11%
High skilled work (median) salary	£21,000	Low/medium skilled salary	£18,000

Criminology

Bath finishes first for Criminology for the second year running, its ranking boosted by the best graduate prospects in the table – with 85% of graduates in high-skilled jobs and/or further study 15 months after finishing their degrees. Durham is runner-up, also for the second year running while Bristol comes out top for research in our analysis of the new Research Excellence Framework. Wrexham Glyndŵr, in 23rd place overall has the most satisfied criminology students, outdoing all others in the table for teaching quality and the broader experience – both measures derived from the National Student Survey. Rates of student satisfaction are next highest at Worcester. Entry standards were highest at Stirling in the 2021 admissions round – where entrants averaged 171 UCAS points, and reached down to 88 points in the UCAS tariff at London Metropolitan in the same cycle.

Now in its seventh year and stretching to 88 universities, our criminology table reflects this growing undergraduate field. The scientific study of crime and its causes, criminology is being offered by 161 universities and colleges across 1,304 courses for 2023-24, either by itself, as part of a joint honours degree, or within a broader social science degree.

The data in this table previously appeared under sociology and law. On its own, criminology finishes bottom of this year's employment, down from second to bottom last year. Holding it back is the higher proportion of graduates that start out in lower-skilled jobs (44%) than in high-skilled employment (34%). Career opportunities further down the line include in the police force, prison service, Home Office, charities or law practice. Starting salaries compare more favourably with other subject areas than job prospects do, and criminology ranks 58th out of 70, with graduates in high-skilled jobs earning £23,000 on average.

Criminology	Teaching quality %	Student experience %	Research quality %	Entry standards (UCAS points)	Graduate prospects %	Overall score
1 Bath	79.1	74.9	59.5	152	85.0*	100
2 Durham	80.0	77.4	53.0	151	75.0	96.8
3 Bristol	65.7	61.6	77.8	—	73.3*	93.3
4 Stirling	73.1	68.6	47.5	171	63.2	93.2
5 Cardiff	74.5	69.8	54.0	148	66.9	92.4
6 Edinburgh Napier	81.1	76.6	35.2	162	55.3	90.8
7 Southampton	73.9	67.5	66.8	142	57.9	90.7
8 Nottingham	67.7	68.5	54.0	135	73.8	90.6
9 Loughborough	68.1	68.4	55.8	148	63.5	90.1
10 York	71.4	70.5	58.0	137	61.5	89.4
11 Suffolk	84.0	72.8	21.8	105	84.8	89.1
12 Surrey	84.9	83.2	—	143	72.4	89
13 Leicester	73.0	72.9	52.2	125	65.4	88.6
14 Ulster	77.4	70.4	53.8	126	59.0	88.1
=15 Birmingham	76.1	69.6	61.0	144	47.2*	88
=15 Queen's Belfast	71.8	64.5	56.5	142	56.4	88
17 Manchester	67.1	58.7	40.8	148	66.4	87.5
18 Swansea	78.2	71.9	27.8	130	67.3	87.3
19 Kent	68.2	62.6	72.2	111	64.4	87.1
20 City	60.6	57.9	64.0	135	64.3	86.9
=21 Lancaster	71.8	69.4	48.0	144	52.5	86.6
=21 Sheffield	72.4	71.8	—	147	76.5	86.6
23 Wrexham Glyndŵr	96.5	93.0	20.5	103	57.5	86.3
=24 Essex	64.9	63.7	62.5	111	67.8	85.9
=24 Hull	74.4	72.8	53.8	117	57.4	85.9
26 Royal Holloway, London	70.8	70.6	38.0	124	63.7	85.2
27 Newcastle	59.4	49.8	53.8	—	72.2*	84.7
28 Manchester Metropolitan	76.5	74.1	32.8	118	60.7	84.5
29 Aberystwyth	86.3	76.3	34.2	117	50.5	84.4
30 Leeds	66.2	59.3	—	162	69.9*	84.2
31 Bedfordshire	77.6	73.6	50.2	107	54.7*	84.1
32 Salford	77.3	68.3	44.5	116	55.0	83.9
=33 Central Lancashire	70.6	62.2	51.5	122	55.3	83.8
=33 Lincoln	72.8	71.7	51.0	116	53.4	83.8
=33 West London	74.7	69.4	39.0	119	57.4	83.8

Criminology cont.

		Teaching quality %	Student experience %	Research quality %	Entry standards (UCAS points)	Graduate prospects %	Overall score
=36	Abertay	78.4	71.3	—	145	61.1	83.7
=36	Plymouth	77.4	74.9	50.5	116	48.0	83.7
=38	Edge Hill	75.8	73.8	17.5	126	61.7	83.5
=38	Staffordshire	86.8	79.5	18.2	103	61.8*	83.5
40	Worcester	89.0	84.2	12.8	121	51.0	83.4
=41	Portsmouth	74.8	69.6	33.0	122	56.7	83.1
=41	West of England	77.3	76.2	35.2	114	54.9	83.1
43	Keele	68.6	65.1	33.2	115	64.7	82.4
44	Liverpool John Moores	76.7	74.4	15.8	132	54.0	82.3
45	Nottingham Trent	75.6	72.3	29.5	112	58.7	82.2
46	Bangor	71.2	70.1	33.2	131	50.2*	82
47	Sunderland	75.4	65.8	39.5	106	57.2*	81.8
=48	Anglia Ruskin	74.5	68.7	35.5	105	57.1	81.2
=48	Derby	80.8	74.6	25.5	109	53.2	81.2
50	Bournemouth	76.9	73.9	10.2	110	64.0*	81
51	Liverpool	51.1	43.4	55.0	130	63.0	80.9
52	Sussex	66.3	58.2	41.0	132	48.9	80.5
53	Greenwich	77.2	72.6	37.0	118	42.5	80.3
54	Coventry	81.1	78.4	—	103	64.2	80.1
55	Sheffield Hallam	75.6	70.4	26.2	110	53.4	79.9
=56	Birmingham City	75.9	70.5	25.8	113	51.4	79.8
=56	Northumbria	58.3	50.2	42.0	136	54.0	79.8
58	Kingston	73.7	69.8	27.0	98	57.7	79
59	Oxford Brookes	75.3	68.7	28.2	113	47.2*	78.7
=60	Huddersfield	70.1	63.5	43.5	114	43.5	78.4
=60	South Wales	60.9	58.0	33.5	115	59.0	78.4
62	Solent, Southampton	75.4	70.7	9.5	106	58.5	78.3
63	Middlesex	69.4	63.9	27.8	104	54.7	77.5
=64	Teesside	74.1	68.5	18.2	108	51.3	77.4
=64	Westminster	75.8	76.4	31.5	113	36.7	77.4
66	Goldsmiths, London	56.5	40.6	48.0	121	53.7*	77.2
67	Chester	70.4	52.7	12.8	117	57.0	76.9
68	East London	68.0	57.4	40.0	94	53.8*	76.8
69	Brighton	64.6	53.5	34.0	102	57.5	76.7
70	Leeds Trinity	76.8	73.2	—	110	52.5	76.4
71	York St John	80.8	71.0	—	102	52.2	76
=72	De Montfort	64.2	57.3	43.2	97	50.6	75.9
=72	Winchester	66.2	64.3	16.5	104	57.2	75.9
74	London South Bank	71.5	65.4	27.8	98	47.1	75.5
75	West of Scotland	73.8	61.9	13.2	—	50.0*	75.2
76	Leeds Beckett	74.2	68.3	17.8	98	47.0	74.8
77	Bradford	67.5	64.9	—	109	54.8*	74

78	Gloucestershire	70.0	65.9	—	114	47.8	73.4
=79	London Metropolitan	74.2	68.6	—	88	54.5	72.9
=79	Roehampton	71.5	67.4	—	96	53.5	72.9
=79	Wolverhampton	69.2	68.8	12.2	96	—	72.9
82	Bath Spa	77.1	71.6	—	96	46.6	72.8
83	Canterbury Christ Church	73.5	67.8	—	93	50.8	72.3
84	Liverpool Hope	76.0	69.7	21.2	106	27.6	71.9
85	Cumbria	62.6	58.2	8.2	112	—	71.4
=86	Buckinghamshire New	68.8	61.0	12.5	—	43.9*	71.3
=86	Northampton	70.6	65.8	4.2	100	44.5	71.3
88	St Mary's, Twickenham	62.1	63.2	10.5	97	45.0*	69.8

Employed in high-skilled job	34%	Employed in lower-skilled job	44%
Employed in high-skilled job and studying	4%	Employed in lower-skilled job and studying	2%
Studying	9%	Unemployed	7%
High skilled work (median) salary	£23,000	Low/medium skilled salary	£19,550

Dentistry

With just 15 dental schools across the country, this is one of the smaller and more stable subject rankings. Glasgow remains the best place to study Dentistry, topping our subject ranking for the seventh successive year. The university's dentistry school welcomed students with the highest number of UCAS tariff points in 2021 (231, and 31 more than its nearest rival on entry standards, Dundee). Glasgow's strength across all five of our ranking measures includes top-three scores for student satisfaction with teaching quality, and with the broader experience.

Plymouth, one of two newer dental schools and in 13th place overall – comes top in its students' eyes for the quality of teaching and of the wider experience. At the other end of the student satisfaction scale is King's College London, which comes bottom for both of these measures. Four of last year's top five reappear, albeit reshuffled a little; only Manchester has dropped out, going from fourth place last year to joint tenth this. Bristol, meanwhile, has moved up one rank into fifth position. Birmingham has been replaced at the foot of the table, which it occupied in our previous edition, by Central Lancashire, the second of the two newer dental schools.

In common with other medical subjects, applications to dentistry are booming, up 9% on 2020 to almost 17,300 in 2021, and up 17% since 2019. Career prospects are good. Dentistry is the No 1 most lucrative option for graduates, with a median starter salary of £39,000, according to the latest data. Although graduate outcomes are not as consistently high as for medicine, almost all graduates (97%) from five-year dentistry courses are in a high-skilled job as a dentist or enrolled on postgraduate study within 15 months. Manchester tops the table, with 98.5% of graduates achieving these desired outcomes, while Leeds is not far behind. Liverpool is last but still has a respectable 85.4% of graduates hitting the mark.

		Teaching quality %	Student experience %	Research quality %	Entry standards (UCAS points)	Graduate prospects %	Overall score
1	Glasgow	90.6	88.3	63.5	231	93.8	100
2	Dundee	90.5	88.8	60.8	200	85.9	93.8
3	Queen's Belfast	88.0	87.5	66.2	180	92.3	91.4
4	Newcastle	85.4	82.6	65.8	169	96.6	88.6
5	Bristol	77.3	68.1	70.9	168	94.1	87.4
=6	Liverpool	87.1	81.2	63.2	157	85.4	85.9
=6	Sheffield	79.9	76.8	63.7	165	90.7	85.9
8	Cardiff	74.1	64.2	58.8	174	94.1	83.9
9	Queen Mary, London	74.4	71.0	54.8	175	86.4	83.5
=10	Birmingham	82.4	79.0	55.0	163	89.7	83.4
=10	Manchester	60.6	52.5	71.2	168	98.5	83.4
12	King's College London	46.7	40.6	76.2	177	92.8	83.2
13	Plymouth	94.7	94.6	39.5	164	89.9	82.2
14	Leeds	65.8	63.4	65.0	161	97.6	82.1
15	Central Lancashire	80.4	68.5	35.5	—	91.4	74.7

Employed in high-skilled job	89%	Employed in lower-skilled job	0%
Employed in high-skilled job and studying	7%	Employed in lower-skilled job and studying	0%
Studying	1%	Unemployed	3%
High skilled work (median) salary	£39,000	Low/medium skilled salary	—

Drama, Dance, Cinematics and Photography

Courses are broad-based within our Drama, Dance, Cinematics and Photography table, covering the four disciplines (although UCAS pairs photography with cinematics under the same grouping), and ranging from acting, theatre studies and performing arts to professional and commercial dance, film studies and photography. Joint honours courses, such as drama studies and English, are also incorporated.

Exeter tops the table for the second year running, buoyed by the top graduate prospects and strong performances in all other measures included in our table. Students at Coventry expressed the highest rates of satisfaction with their teaching quality in the most recent National Student Survey (NSS). Those at Liverpool Hope gave their university the best reviews for the broader experience. Buckinghamshire New comes in second place for each NSS-derived measure. Conversely, Goldsmiths (in joint 84th place overall) brings up the rear of the table for both.

Results of the new Research Excellence Framework 2021 put Manchester in front for research quality, closely followed by the Central School of Speech and Drama – which, in 21st place overall, ranks third among the four specialist institutions in our table, behind Guildhall (in ninth), the Royal Conservatoire of Scotland (18th) and in front of Trinity Laban (23rd).

The subjects as a whole occupy fourth from bottom of our employment ranking, up from second to last in our previous edition, with 45% in high-skilled jobs within 15 months of finishing their degrees, 2% enrolled in postgraduate study and 5% combining the two. Eight per cent were unemployed when surveyed, a big improvement on the 13% in the year before. Students are unlikely to be driven by hopes of hefty pay packets upon graduation, and the subjects rank 65th in our earnings index. Starting salaries range from £22,000 in high-skilled jobs down to £19,000 in medium-skilled work and £17,000 for jobs deemed low-skilled.

Glasgow leads on entry standards, averaging 189 UCAS points among 2021's entrants. Although 20 institutions averaged over 144 UCAS tariff points in 2020 (equivalent to AAA), performance or portfolio are often more important criteria for entry and there are plenty of courses with accessible entry standards.

Drama, Dance, Cinematics and Photography	Teaching quality %	Student experience %	Research quality %	Entry standards (UCAS points)	Graduate prospects %	Overall score
1 Exeter	77.5	72.2	62.3	155	76.2	100
2 Manchester	71.8	68.3	80.5	166	67.1	99.5
3 Warwick	83.9	83.9	68.8	152	65.2	99.4
4 Glasgow	70.7	70.1	60.5	189	59.9	97.9
5 Surrey	88.9	85.2	43.8	157	61.7	96.9
6 Queen Mary, London	71.9	66.7	76.4	135	74.6	96.7
7 Lancaster	81.0	79.4	59.5	150	—	96.3
8 Coventry	91.3	85.5	55.5	131	62.3	95.4
9 Guildhall School of Music and Drama	82.3	76.9	61.3	139	63.4	94.9
10 Royal Holloway, London	74.8	69.2	78.5	146	58.0	94
11 Leeds	64.6	69.7	56.8	156	67.3	93.7
12 York	63.2	63.9	58.2	157	68.9	93.6
13 Edinburgh Napier	75.7	72.3	8.5	169	71.7	93.3
14 Essex	86.3	84.5	34.2	155	55.9	92.9
15 Edinburgh	61.9	51.5	59.2	161	67.6	92.5
16 Birmingham	73.1	69.9	50.2	157	59.9	92.3
17 Kent	77.8	68.4	74.8	120	60.7	91.3
18 Royal Conservatoire of Scotland	76.7	66.7	35.2	157	60.0	90.9
19 Northumbria	85.4	77.9	45.8	140	54.1	90.8
20 Bristol	55.9	55.0	64.2	161	62.6	90.5
21 Central School of Speech and Drama	68.3	57.4	79.8	136	57.2	90.1
22 Queen Margaret, Edinburgh	82.2	78.8	—	182	52.6	90
23 Trinity Laban	65.9	67.7	38.0	135	72.0	89.7
=24 Nottingham	80.9	74.3	53.0	134	53.9	89.5
=24 West of England	76.8	70.9	48.2	142	55.9	89.5
=24 Westminster	63.5	60.0	75.5	131	61.9	89.5
27 Teesside	83.4	81.0	49.2	—	50.0*	89.1
28 Aberystwyth	82.9	79.5	44.5	129	54.9	89
29 Reading	66.3	67.9	59.0	123	65.0	88.6
=30 Hull	86.8	79.8	35.0	119	58.7	88.4
=30 Sunderland	79.1	74.6	49.8	125	57.1	88.4
=32 Manchester Metropolitan	75.3	66.2	61.8	139	50.2	88.2
=32 Roehampton	65.7	59.5	68.8	114	66.8	88.2
34 Birmingham City	79.3	71.0	46.5	129	56.3	88.1
35 Newcastle	73.1	54.3	59.2	135	—	87.9

Drama, Dance, Cinematics and Photography cont.	Teaching quality %	Student experience %	Research quality %	Entry standards (UCAS points)	Graduate prospects %	Overall score
=36 London Metropolitan	87.9	81.8	—	114	71.7	87.7
=36 West London	82.3	74.8	32.2	128	58.3	87.7
38 Falmouth	79.1	75.1	48.8	125	52.6	86.9
39 De Montfort	73.2	72.3	45.0	121	58.8	86.3
40 Queen's Belfast	67.2	64.8	46.8	139	55.9	86.2
41 West of Scotland	71.1	62.3	19.2	146	61.3	86.1
42 East London	89.3	86.2	13.0	115	58.2	86
43 Kingston	75.1	70.1	45.0	142	47.1	85.8
44 Liverpool Hope	88.9	91.0	17.5	118	53.6	85.7
=45 Lincoln	74.3	71.8	37.2	125	56.5	85.4
=45 Plymouth	77.1	66.8	49.8	124	52.0	85.4
=47 Bournemouth	74.9	69.7	38.5	117	59.7	85.3
=47 Wales Trinity St David	78.9	66.8	—	145	60.5	85.3
49 Arts University, Bournemouth	75.3	70.6	23.0	145	51.2	84.8
50 Salford	75.0	70.8	30.2	132	53.7	84.6
=51 Central Lancashire	81.1	72.6	19.0	125	56.3	84.5
=51 East Anglia	73.4	71.6	—	133	65.9	84.5
=51 Gloucestershire	73.2	72.0	45.0	122	52.7	84.5
=51 Sussex	71.8	68.5	48.0	142	44.4	84.5
55 Portsmouth	81.0	75.4	30.2	120	52.8	84.4
56 Brunel	66.6	62.5	38.0	119	62.2	83.9
57 Liverpool John Moores	75.9	73.6	22.2	145	47.3	83.8
=58 Bath Spa	87.1	82.9	26.0	122	45.6	83.7
=58 Edge Hill	82.0	76.1	—	133	56.5	83.7
=58 Ulster	80.3	75.8	49.0	119	44.0	83.7
61 Canterbury Christ Church	79.4	71.5	38.5	108	54.4	83.5
62 Anglia Ruskin	58.8	55.4	61.8	127	55.0	83.4
63 Huddersfield	81.7	78.4	20.0	128	48.4	83.2
64 Staffordshire	77.0	69.4	31.5	121	51.9	82.9
65 Creative Arts	70.1	63.5	41.2	133	48.5	82.8
66 University of the Arts London	69.2	57.7	46.0	130	50.1	82.7
=67 Winchester	81.0	79.4	32.5	108	50.4	82.5
=67 Leeds Arts	77.5	73.5	2.8	140	52.1	82.5
69 South Wales	75.1	67.7	35.8	123	49.0	82.3
70 Wolverhampton	81.5	77.2	6.8	109	58.5	81.8
=71 Northampton	71.7	64.7	30.2	114	55.9	81.4
=71 Worcester	83.0	79.8	5.8	116	52.5	81.4
73 Norwich University of the Arts	73.5	66.8	—	128	59.7	81.3
=74 Derby	80.8	75.7	—	122	54.2	81.1
=74 Oxford Brookes	76.9	75.0	21.5	115	—	81.1
76 Chester	65.7	59.3	21.0	127	57.6	81
77 Leeds Beckett	71.2	62.1	15.8	115	60.1	80.8

78 Middlesex	71.0	63.8	26.0	114	55.0	80.4
79 Hertfordshire	66.2	60.4	42.5	110	53.8	80.1
80 Sheffield Hallam	81.2	77.4	—	118	51.7	80
81 Rose Bruford	76.3	65.7	19.0	125	46.5	79.6
82 York St John	76.5	65.1	33.2	116	44.6	79.5
83 Wrexham Glyndŵr	74.1	62.8	3.2	—	56.9*	79.2
=84 Goldsmiths, London	49.5	42.1	46.8	131	54.9	78.8
=84 St Mary's, Twickenham	72.4	62.5	—	122	56.5	78.8
86 Bedfordshire	87.6	82.6	—	100	50.0	78.7
87 Greenwich	77.4	73.6	—	126	47.4	78.5
88 Chichester	73.6	69.5	13.2	129	43.6	78.3
89 Ravensbourne	65.7	50.2	—	116	61.4	77
90 Leeds Trinity	74.9	69.8	11.2	108	—	76.9
91 Buckinghamshire New	89.6	87.2	—	108	37.2	76.7
92 Bolton	68.1	64.0	—	119	49.9	75.6
93 Solent, Southampton	70.7	66.1	—	119	47.8	75.5
94 Cumbria	76.3	74.4	—	113	42.8	75.1
95 Brighton	60.3	49.9	44.2	113	42.3	74.8
96 London South Bank	73.8	66.4	—	109	45.7	74.1
97 Suffolk	76.8	68.5	—	111	39.3	73.2

Employed in high-skilled job	45%	Employed in lower-skilled job	38%
Employed in high-skilled job and studying	2%	Employed in lower-skilled job and studying	1%
Studying	5%	Unemployed	8%
High skilled work (median) salary	£22,000	Low/medium skilled salary	£19,000

East and South Asian Studies

Oxford tops this year's subject table, which encompasses Chinese studies, Japanese studies and South Asian studies. Ousting former No 1, Cambridge, Oxford performs strongly across all measures without coming first in any. Runner-up overall Cambridge has the edge on graduate prospects, as it does on entry standards. But results of the recent Research Excellence Framework put Oxford in second place, well ahead of Cambridge, which sits 11th for research this year. All other universities are outdone by East Anglia for research quality, however, moving it into third place overall, up from sixth in our previous edition.

Most undergraduates learn their chosen language from scratch, although universities expect to see evidence of potential in other modern language qualifications. Student numbers are modest, with Japanese studies attracting the highest number of applications and enrolments. In 2021, there were 100 new Chinese studies undergraduates, 260 in Japanese studies, 40 in South Asian studies, and 135 in other Asian studies.

Only four universities in the UK offer South Asian Studies: Central Lancashire, Leeds, Manchester and SOAS in London, which also offers a range of languages including Burmese, Indonesian, Thai, Tibetan and Vietnamese. Degrees in these subjects are afforded extra protection by the government because of their small size and their economic and cultural significance.

Results of 2021's National Student Survey revealed the best rates of student satisfaction with teaching quality to be found at Cardiff – by a clear margin – while Durham props up the opposite end of the teaching quality scale. The same two universities top-and-tail our measure for student satisfaction with the broader experience. East Anglia places second for each.

The subjects feature in the bottom 10 for graduate prospects, with six in 10 graduates occupied in high-skilled jobs and/or postgraduate study 15 months on from their degrees. Median starting salaries of £25,714 can be expected by graduates in high-skilled jobs.

East and South Asian Studies	Teaching quality %	Student experience %	Research quality %	Entry standards (UCAS points)	Graduate prospects %	Overall score
1 Oxford	—	—	62.3	191	73.8	100
2 Cambridge	—	—	45.2	201	85.0*	99.8
3 East Anglia	75.1	78.3	63.0	124	—	97.3
4 Edinburgh	70.4	63.2	45.8	191	77.7	97.2
5 Cardiff University	81.1	78.5	55.5	125	—	96.7
6 Manchester	70.0	62.1	52.5	153	68.8	93
=7 Leeds	67.9	72.4	52.0	153	66.3	92.8
=7 SOAS, London	68.3	60.1	60.0	146	64.8	92.8
9 Nottingham	67.1	61.5	62.0	139	64.3	92.5
10 Durham	50.6	42.1	46.0	176	79.2	88.9
11 Sheffield	72.3	69.2	48.8	149	51.0	88.5
12 Oxford Brookes	75.0	61.5	36.0	122	—	84.6
13 Central Lancashire	63.7	60.0	31.8	112	50.9	77

Employed in high-skilled job	41%	Employed in lower-skilled job	28%
Employed in high-skilled job and studying	4%	Employed in lower-skilled job and studying	3%
Studying	12%	Unemployed	12%
High skilled work (median) salary	£25,714	Low/medium skilled salary	£20,500

Economics

The trend for universities to trade the top spot of our Economics subject ranking continues this year with Warwick's relocation to No 1. Having placed fourth two years ago and second last year, Warwick moves up to first, its position driven by strength in all five areas measured in our ranking – including top-12 finishes for both measures of student satisfaction – without being unbeaten on any individually. For research quality and graduate prospects, Warwick achieves the second-best scores. The London School of Economics takes the lead on both but, due in large part to being bested on rates student satisfaction by Warwick, drops to second place overall from first last year – when, despite its name, the LSE topped our Economics table for the first time in a decade. Even so, the LSE ranks in the top 35 for both measures of student satisfaction, reflecting the remarkable upturn in this element of the student experience being achieved university-wide.

Cambridge, in third place overall, leads on entry standards with 220 UCAS points averaged by its 2021 cohort. St Andrews and Oxford also registered above 200 points in the same admissions cycle. Students at Hertfordshire (in 43rd place overall) are by a clear margin the most satisfied with their teaching quality and the wider experience. Those at Brighton (joint 35th) and Hull (31st) registered the second and third highest rates of student satisfaction across both measures. Conversely, economics undergraduates at Cardiff and City expressed the lowest rates of contentment with each.

Although we don't take account of salaries in our subject table, they are naturally of interest to applicants, who will likely be pleased to learn that economics graduates are among the most sought-after, commanding a median salary of £30,000 in high-skilled graduate jobs – only seven subjects place higher for earnings. For graduate jobs – which are an ingredient of our table – economics sits 17th out of 70 subject areas, with the latest data showing 81% of graduates were in high-skilled jobs and/or postgraduate study 15 months on from their degrees.

Applications increased by 6% in 2021 to nearly 95,000, while 14,200 new students began courses. Maths A-level (or equivalent qualification) is usually required by the leading universities, while philosophy, sociology, government and politics, further maths and economics may be useful.

Economics	Teaching quality %	Student experience %	Research quality %	Entry standards (UCAS points)	Graduate prospects %	Overall score
1 Warwick	78.8	79.2	76.5	191	95.5	100
2 London School of Economics	73.5	75.2	80.8	191	95.6	98.9
3 Cambridge	—	—	68.2	220	95.3	98
4 Oxford	—	—	62.0	207	94.4	96.6
=5 Strathclyde	80.0	79.7	52.5	198	87.6	95.6
=5 University College London	68.7	76.6	72.5	188	91.1	95.6
7 St Andrews	81.7	81.2	31.2	212	86.2	93.6
8 Glasgow	71.5	74.2	57.2	195	84.7	92.8
9 Durham	67.8	69.7	55.8	182	92.7	92
10 Exeter	72.0	78.1	44.8	163	92.1	90.9
11 Birmingham	73.8	75.9	55.2	149	88.4	90.8
=12 Leeds	65.6	68.4	62.3	170	88.6	90.6
=12 Loughborough	75.7	80.3	49.2	151	86.5	90.6
14 Nottingham	65.1	72.0	64.5	167	85.1	90.3
15 Liverpool	73.6	74.4	58.0	139	84.2	89.3
=16 Lancaster	69.2	69.9	59.2	140	88.3	88.9
=16 Surrey	73.2	76.3	54.2	132	86.4	88.9
18 Edinburgh	61.8	67.0	50.2	181	88.4	88.5
19 Southampton	77.0	79.1	42.0	140	83.0	88.1
20 East Anglia	81.0	79.9	46.2	129	78.5	88
21 Ulster	81.4	78.2	45.8	117	83.1	87.9
=22 Bath	66.3	75.4	25.2	173	94.9	87.7
=22 Stirling	78.1	72.7	38.2	156	—	87.7
24 Manchester	67.8	70.8	54.5	160	79.7	87.6
=25 Bristol	59.4	62.7	60.2	166	86.4	87.4
=25 Royal Holloway, London	77.4	81.9	53.8	116	78.1	87.4
27 Heriot-Watt	72.3	74.5	38.2	165	80.6	87.1
28 York	67.8	71.4	48.8	144	85.9	87
29 Queen Mary, London	67.9	68.3	60.5	151	77.0	86.9
30 Queen's Belfast	67.9	70.6	40.5	141	90.9	86.6
31 Hull	85.2	84.6	29.5	—	72.4	86.4
32 Reading	72.3	71.9	46.2	118	82.8	85.2
33 Newcastle	62.7	66.2	40.5	148	88.9	84.9

Economics cont.

		Teaching quality %	Student experience %	Research quality %	Entry standards (UCAS points)	Graduate prospects %	Overall score
34	King's College London	71.6	72.6	—	179	92.6	84.7
=35	Brighton	87.0	86.9	28.5	89	—	84.5
=35	Swansea	77.0	75.0	38.8	117	78.8	84.5
=37	Essex	76.5	77.1	59.5	104	64.5	83.7
=37	Kent	76.7	76.5	29.5	120	79.6	83.7
39	Manchester Metropolitan	79.1	82.3	42.8	113	66.8	83.6
40	Cardiff	58.3	57.7	56.0	140	83.0	83.3
=41	Nottingham Trent	79.2	79.4	34.2	115	70.5	82.9
=41	Sussex	63.5	66.3	52.0	130	76.7	82.9
43	Hertfordshire	95.7	95.5	29.0	88	54.0	82.3
44	Portsmouth	77.1	69.8	37.8	107	70.2	81.1
45	Sheffield	76.9	77.3	—	143	79.4	81
46	Westminster	69.4	76.8	37.5	105	—	80.8
47	Aberdeen	74.8	75.1	—	174	70.9	80.6
=48	Huddersfield	84.6	79.2	23.2	110	62.9	80.4
=48	Oxford Brookes	73.2	74.9	26.0	118	72.3	80.4
=48	West of England	78.6	75.6	27.3	106	69.6	80.4
=51	Bournemouth	78.2	71.7	23.0	106	72.3	79.8
=51	Dundee	65.5	62.3	—	175	83.5	79.8
=51	Plymouth	77.2	73.3	28.7	108	67.7	79.8
54	Coventry	71.5	73.5	33.2	97	72.6	79.5
55	Greenwich	74.3	70.4	33.2	101	66.5	78.7
56	Salford	68.5	73.5	24.8	114	—	78.3
57	Keele	66.6	71.0	24.8	100	75.4	77.7
58	Aston	71.6	70.2	—	119	81.0	77.6
59	Sheffield Hallam	74.5	73.5	—	102	71.4	75.3
60	Lincoln	76.8	76.9	—	110	61.5	74.6
61	SOAS, London	61.2	59.6	—	137	77.4	74.4
62	Kingston	75.7	72.4	24.0	84	55.8	74.3
63	Leeds Beckett	64.0	60.8	8.2	96	77.8	73.6
=64	City	49.7	58.5	32.5	120	68.6	73.4
=64	Leicester	62.3	68.8	—	122	71.1	73.4
=66	Middlesex	70.5	72.9	—	88	70.9	73.2
=66	Northampton	79.8	67.4	1.2	84	—	73.2
68	De Montfort	72.9	72.7	—	90	64.5	72.5
69	Goldsmiths, London	70.8	62.9	—	103	62.6	71.3
70	Birmingham City	75.1	78.7	—	107	47.5	71.2
71	Brunel	62.4	62.2	16.0	109	56.9	70.9

Employed in high-skilled job	60%	Employed in lower-skilled job	13%
Employed in high-skilled job and studying	8%	Employed in lower-skilled job and studying	1%
Studying	12%	Unemployed	5%
High skilled work (median) salary	£30,000	Low/medium skilled salary	£22,750

Education

An extra column populated by inspection data by Ofsted for universities in England is a distinctive feature of our Education ranking. Eleven universities tie for the best score (four) from Ofsted, and also all place within our table's top 26. These are, in descending order: Cambridge, Bristol, Durham, Warwick, Birmingham, Nottingham, University College London, Brighton, Winchester, St Mary's, Twickenham, and Brunel.

Teaching training BEd degrees – the most common route into primary teaching – had more than 55,900 applications in 2021 (up from 48,605 in 2020) and 10,035 new students enrolled on courses (down from 10,455 the year before). Academic Studies in Education degrees are also encompassed in our ranking and garnered 28,245 applications and 7,075 new undergraduates in 2021.

Secondary school teachers are more likely to take the Postgraduate Certificate in Education, or to train through the Teach First or Schools Direct programmes, which are not included in our table's statistics. Our focus exclusively on undergraduate provision explains the absence of some of the best-known education departments, which only offer postgraduate courses. Prime examples are University College London's Institute of Education, ranked top in the world for education by QS, and Oxford – which was the top-scorer in the Research Excellence Framework in this field.

Cambridge combines the academic study of education with other subjects, but does not offer Qualified Teacher Status. It returns to the top of the table this year in a tie with Glasgow – which moves up from fifth place. Last year's No 1, the Royal Conservatoire of Scotland, slips to 12th place overall but still has the highest entry standards of 212 UCAS points, on average, among 2021's entrants. The top five for entry standards is exclusively Scottish universities, which benefit from the favourable tariff conversion for Scottish secondary qualifications, while also performing strongly across our table's other measures.

For student satisfaction with teaching quality, Coventry has supplanted Aberystwyth in first place, while the Welsh university retains the lead it took last year for student satisfaction with the broader experience. Bangor, located further north in Wales than Aber, places at the foot of the same ranking, just below Oxford Brookes. For teaching quality Goldsmiths' students express the lowest rates of satisfaction – our analysis of the latest National Student Survey showed.

Education sits 31st in our employment ranking of 70 subject areas. The demands for new primary and secondary teachers vary across the country, creating differing graduate outcomes scores at universities. Edinburgh tops our ranking this year, 92.8% of graduates in high-skilled work and/or postgraduate study 15 months after their degrees. Reading, Stirling and Strathclyde also had over 90% of graduates achieving these outcomes. Though not an ingredient of our ranking, teachers' pay is of interest to many. Median graduate salaries of £25,000 for those in high-skilled jobs places education in the upper half of subject areas, at 30th place.

Education	Teaching quality %	Student experience %	Ofsted rating	Research quality %	Entry standards (UCAS points)	Graduate prospects %	Overall score
=1 Cambridge	—	—	4.0	67.8	179	—	100
=1 Glasgow	81.7	74.2	—	64.5	190	84.2	100
3 Edinburgh	75.7	70.9	—	51.0	195	92.8	99
4 Bristol	83.9	74.8	4.0	67.5	148	—	98.2
5 Stirling	72.1	67.0	—	53.2	192	91.1	97.2

Education cont.

		Teaching quality %	Student experience %	Ofsted rating	Research quality %	Entry standards (UCAS points)	Graduate prospects %	Overall score
6	Cardiff	—	—	—	72.0	151	78.7	97
7	Durham	72.7	68.0	4.0	73.2	156	87.2	96.7
8	Warwick	83.4	81.4	4.0	55.8	138	—	96.1
9	Birmingham	82.3	81.5	4.0	70.5	140	76.7	96
10	Strathclyde	76.2	71.6	—	20.8	202	91.0	95.5
11	Coventry	92.5	83.8	—	54.2	123	—	95.3
12	Royal Conservatoire of Scotland	71.7	57.4	—	—	212	100	95.2
13	Nottingham	76.8	75.3	4.0	61.5	133	—	94
14	University College London	81.2	79.6	4.0	68.8	154	61.8	93.5
15	Sussex	80.2	74.4	3.5	64.8	135	—	92.8
16	Brighton	83.6	77.0	4.0	37.5	119	86.8	92.6
17	Bath	78.3	82.0	3.5	47.8	145	—	92
18	Aberdeen	75.8	72.4	—	23.0	175	86.5	91.8
19	Winchester	82.6	81.3	4.0	28.0	123	83.1	91.4
20	Dundee	68.9	62.0	—	35.2	179	87.5	91.2
21	Southampton	87.5	90.8	3.0	41.0	160	70.3	91
22	Reading	81.9	79.7	3.0	41.8	130	91.4	90.9
23	West of Scotland	72.0	67.4	—	17.5	187	85.5	90.6
24	St Mary's, Twickenham	91.4	85.6	4.0	—	109	83.9	89.7
25	Liverpool John Moores	84.0	83.3	3.5	21.8	146	72.4	88.9
26	Brunel	85.6	83.0	4.0	20.8	115	73.2	88.7
27	Sheffield	77.3	72.6	3.0	62.0	149	65.8	87.7
=28	Leeds	75.3	68.8	—	44.2	150	71.8	87.6
=28	Sheffield Hallam	73.4	66.6	3.7	39.2	126	79.7	87.6
=30	Northumbria	72.6	62.8	3.0	42.0	144	84.2	87.2
=30	Swansea	73.8	71.2	—	46.5	134	—	87.2
=32	Derby	80.7	74.4	3.5	29.2	124	73.9	86.7
=32	West of England	77.1	71.6	3.0	48.5	127	77.1	86.7
34	Lincoln	82.4	83.0	—	28.5	119	—	86.6
35	Nottingham Trent	79.3	72.7	3.3	29.5	125	77.3	86.4
36	Plymouth Marjon	87.5	84.2	3.3	14.0	119	74.0	86.3
=37	York	64.8	63.5	3.0	70.8	130	76.4	85.9
=37	York St John	76.3	74.2	3.3	24.5	120	81.6	85.9
=39	Hull	80.9	79.4	3.0	31.5	125	74.2	85.6
=39	Newcastle	—	—	3.2	36.8	123	75.9	85.6
=41	Anglia Ruskin	89.6	87.7	3.0	16.2	115	72.7	85.3
=41	Roehampton	77.2	73.3	3.0	53.5	114	72.4	85.3
=43	Bath Spa	77.6	72.5	3.7	31.5	110	71.8	85.2
=43	South Wales	82.8	77.0	—	—	122	81.5	85.2
=45	Bedfordshire	85.1	79.6	3.1	21.0	112	75.8	85
=45	Chester	74.1	67.4	3.7	16.2	124	78.5	85
47	Portsmouth	82.4	71.8	3.3	51.7	110	60.3	84.5

=48	Edge Hill	77.5	75.6	3.0	30.8	129	72.5	84.4
=48	Wales Trinity St David	86.4	81.8	—	11.8	135	65.4	84.4
50	Sunderland	74.0	66.7	3.5	9.2	128	79.4	84
51	Bangor	66.3	54.4	—	42.0	147	74.5	83.9
52	Chichester	78.1	78.0	3.0	5.2	120	84.9	83.8
=53	Bishop Grosseteste	82.0	77.4	3.0	10.2	114	80.0	83.7
=53	Manchester Metropolitan	75.2	71.2	3.0	42.8	131	66.3	83.7
=53	Northampton	79.3	74.3	3.0	28.2	112	75.6	83.7
=53	Plymouth	69.9	64.7	3.0	39.2	125	78.4	83.7
57	Aberystwyth	92.2	91.3	—	—	117	61.9	83.5
58	Staffordshire	83.6	79.1	3.0	18.2	128	67	83.4
59	Oxford Brookes	65.3	55.3	3.0	36.0	121	85.8	82.8
=60	Keele	71.8	68.2	—	33.2	121	74.0	82.7
=60	Kingston	67.6	68.3	3.0	28.5	132	77.3	82.7
62	Greenwich	71.9	64.1	3.3	17.0	121	77.8	82.6
63	Birmingham City	79.4	76.0	3.0	11.8	125	71.2	82.2
=64	Central Lancashire	80.8	77.0	—	—	123	71.6	82.1
=64	Hertfordshire	81.0	74.6	3.0	9.5	112	75.8	82.1
=64	Huddersfield	82.0	74.7	3.1	31.2	127	55.6	82.1
67	Leeds Beckett	75.0	66.7	3.0	17.2	113	78.8	81.7
68	East Anglia	76.8	70.6	3.0	41.2	127	56.9	81.5
69	Canterbury Christ Church	69.9	62.6	3.0	29.5	106	80.8	81.4
70	Teesside	85.0	81.2	—	18.2	110	62.0	81.3
71	Liverpool Hope	81.8	72.6	2.0	23.8	123	75.6	80.5
72	Worcester	69.5	66.4	3.0	10.8	121	77.5	80.2
73	Leeds Trinity	73.1	73.0	3.0	8.0	114	74.9	80.1
=74	Gloucestershire	78.2	76.8	2.0	16.2	121	79.1	79.9
=74	Newman	70.3	68.7	3.0	4.8	118	78.6	79.9
76	Middlesex	74.8	68.4	3.0	15.5	113	68.2	79.4
77	Cardiff Metropolitan	68.1	66.4	—	17.5	122	71.7	79
78	Wrexham Glyndŵr	76.2	70.8	—	—	87	77.5	77.7
79	Wolverhampton	78.6	69.8	2.4	10.5	122	63.5	77.3
80	London Metropolitan	83.6	79.4	3.0	6.5	104	52.5	77.2
81	Cumbria	73.8	69.7	2.0	8.5	126	74.7	76.9
82	Bolton	77.2	78.5	—	7.8	107	60.0	76.7
83	East London	67.9	57.0	3.0	11.2	118	58.8	75
84	De Montfort	74.8	71.8	—	—	106	60.0	74.7
85	Goldsmiths, London	62.8	58.9	3.0	29.5	111	53.5	74.3
86	Suffolk	64.1	59.4	—	21.8	101	56.7	71.7
87	London South Bank	64.7	58.4	2.0	—	103	61.8	68.6

Employed in high-skilled job	66%	Employed in lower-skilled job	20%
Employed in high-skilled job and studying	3%	Employed in lower-skilled job and studying	1%
Studying	6%	Unemployed	5%
High skilled work (median) salary	£25,000	Low/medium skilled salary	£17,400

Electrical and Electronic Engineering

Led by our table's overall frontrunner Cambridge, where entrants in 2021 averaged 228 UCAS tariff points, 24 universities recorded over 144 points (equivalent to AAA at A level) for their electrical and electronic engineering degrees. With over five applications per place to study electrical and electronic engineering, competition can be stiff and entry standards at the leading institutions are high. Only at one university, Leeds Beckett, did new undergraduates arrive with less than 100 UCAS points.

Imperial, in third place overall, has the edge for research quality following results of the new Research Excellence Framework 2021, while Oxford sits second for research, as it does overall. The QS world rankings by subject put Cambridge and Oxford in the top 10 for the subject, but Imperial has slipped just outside to rank 11th in the latest list.

The best graduate prospects are found at Birmingham (in ninth place overall), where not far off a full house (96.9%) of graduates were working in high-skilled jobs and/or enrolled in postgraduate study when surveyed 15 months after their degrees. Birmingham is one of 13 universities to hit register above 90% for this measure and the subject places 16th out 70 areas in our employment ranking. It is in the top 10 for pay, based on median starting salaries of £28,560 in high-skilled jobs.

Taking 30th place in the main table, Royal Holloway tops both measures of student satisfaction derived from the National Student Survey – teaching quality and the wider experience, measures in which Cardiff (12th overall) is runner-up.

Maths A-level, or equivalent qualification, is required to study electrical and electronic engineering degrees, along with a second science such as physics, electronics or chemistry. The subject looks into how industry works and teaches the engineering skills and technological knowledge to design and improve electrical and electronic systems. It attracted the second-highest number of applications (27,515) among the engineering disciplines in 2021, and over 5,000 new students started courses.

Electrical and Electronic Engineering	Teaching quality %	Student experience %	Research quality %	Entry standards (UCAS points)	Graduate prospects %	Overall score
1 Cambridge	—	—	77.2	228	96.5	100
2 Oxford	—	—	77.5	216	92.5	98.3
3 Imperial College	70.7	75.1	81.0	198	94.6	97.7
4 Southampton	76.2	78.2	70.0	172	93.1	95.2
5 University College London	76.7	79.9	70.0	165	93.5	95.1
6 Edinburgh	67.4	73.0	55.5	203	100	94.6
7 Strathclyde	71.5	70.5	52.8	210	91.1	93.6
8 Sheffield	80.4	80.1	66.8	146	91.3	93.4
9 Birmingham	75.2	71.8	63.7	151	96.9	92.5
10 Nottingham	81.9	80.3	59.0	151	87.5	92.3
11 Queen's Belfast	79.9	77.0	51.0	156	90.4	91.3
12 Cardiff	84.8	87.6	54.0	133	85.3	91
=13 Bath	73.1	76.8	49.5	160	95.1	90.8
=13 Glasgow	61.4	63.2	61.5	206	88.9	90.8
15 Manchester	68.9	69.5	63.0	162	92.8	90.6
16 Surrey	77.1	78.2	55.2	140	90.5	90.1

17	Leeds	68.2	70.2	64.8	170	86.1	90
18	Heriot-Watt	71.7	70.4	55.5	180	83.6	89.8
19	Queen Mary, London	71.5	76.8	66.0	141	87.0	89.4
20	Liverpool	77.9	79.4	57.0	144	82.4	89.2
21	Exeter	78.1	78.3	47.0	146	85.9	88.6
22	Bristol	67.1	74.6	72.8	165	73.2	88.1
=23	Nottingham Trent	76.9	73.1	59.0	122	—	87.2
=23	Ulster	75.9	74.8	49.8	131	87.5	87.2
25	Loughborough	71.0	80.8	46.5	146	86.0	87.1
26	Lancaster	70.4	69.7	44.8	158	—	85.8
27	Aberdeen	71.1	74.2	35.8	164	—	85.6
28	York	69.4	69.2	49.8	129	88.6	85.1
29	Manchester Metropolitan	83.6	84.2	45.5	121	71.0	85
30	Royal Holloway	85.7	87.7	33.0	101	—	84.7
31	Swansea	71.9	70.3	48.8	130	83.3	84.6
32	King's College London	58.5	62.7	62.0	158	—	84.4
33	Bangor	79.8	76.9	40.2	128	75.0*	84
34	Huddersfield	76.3	81.3	32.5	—	76.6	83.7
=35	Newcastle	59.6	64.5	58.5	137	85.4	83.5
=35	Northumbria	74.2	77.5	43.0	128	76.7	83.5
37	Liverpool John Moores	67.5	64.7	45.5	128	88.4	83.4
38	Aston	67.8	73.7	35.2	131	84.8	82.4
39	Birmingham City	83.6	79.2	17.5	130	68.0	80.5
40	Plymouth	66.6	68.7	32.5	121	82.4	79.8
=41	Brighton	72.9	65.0	36.5	105	78.6	79.4
=41	West of England	69.4	67.8	30.8	—	77.1*	79.4
43	Robert Gordon	65.8	60.2	20.5	143	84.0	79.2
44	Brunel	66.4	63.9	33.0	135	75.0	78.9
45	Hertfordshire	73.6	67.9	33.0	101	—	78
46	Essex	57.6	57.3	53.5	120	—	77.5
47	Glasgow Caledonian	72.1	69.4	12.8	157	64.0	77.3
48	Teesside	78.8	80.4	18.8	116	62.5	77.2
49	Coventry	71.5	74.9	23.5	117	69.0	77.1
50	Portsmouth	67.4	66.7	21.0	101	83.9	76.8
51	De Montfort	71.9	73.4	21.8	103	—	76.2
52	Kent	54.1	62.1	41.5	118	76.4	75.8
53	South Wales	68.2	66.0	26.8	108	71.4	75.6
=54	Derby	77.3	74.4	14.0	118	61.3	75.4
=54	Sheffield Hallam	67.0	57.5	30.0	118	69.9	75.4
56	City	58.2	60.0	32.5	114	75.8	74.9
57	Leeds Beckett	69.7	75.0	18.2	99	—	74.6
58	Westminster	63.7	65.0	24.0	124	62.5	73.4
59	Ravensbourne	61.4	44.9	—	116	90.0	72.6
60	London South Bank	75.0	75.9	27.3	106	42.9	71.9
61	Salford	56.9	51.2	33.2	122	56.8	70.2

Employed in high-skilled job	70%	Employed in lower-skilled job	10%
Employed in high-skilled job and studying	3%	Employed in lower-skilled job and studying	1%
Studying	9%	Unemployed	7%
High skilled work (median) salary	£28,560	Low/medium skilled salary	£24,000

English

Oxford takes the top spot in our English table this year, ousting St Andrews into second place. The shift confirms an established pattern of the lead changing frequently in our English table. Entry standards are highest at Strathclyde, which averaged 202 UCAS points among its 2021 entrants.

There are also plenty of much lower-tariff options, with 10 universities registering less than 100 points in the same admissions round. Bishop Grossteste, in 42nd place overall, has the lowest entry standards (87 UCAS points) but comes second for student satisfaction with teaching quality. It is outdone by 55th-place Aberystwyth on this measure. Newcastle sits 15th overall but is peerless for its research in the subject, while Bedfordshire (joint 20th) achieves the second-best research quality score.

English literature is usually required for entry. Some English degrees offer an equal balance of literature and language, while others specialise in one or the other – a distinction usually clear in the course title. English is also frequently paired with other subjects in joint honours degrees. Sheffield Hallam hit the headlines in June 2022 when it announced plans to suspend its degree in English literature, amid pressure from government to ensure graduates go straight into well-paid jobs. English has not been immune to the declining popularity of humanities subjects in recent years, but there remains plenty of universities to study it at. The UCAS website showed 1,101 courses in English literature at 110 universities and colleges for 2023-24. For English degrees more broadly, there were 1,939 courses offered by 133 universities and colleges in 2023-24.

Such focus on the outcomes of English graduates makes the latest data especially of interest to those considering applying to study it. The new Graduate Outcomes survey showed 45% of English graduates to be in high-skilled jobs when it took its census 15 months on from degrees, while a further 21% were enrolled in postgraduate study or combining the two. Conversely, 26% were in low-skilled jobs, 1% were juggling such work with further study and 7% were unemployed. The outcomes rank English 49th out of 70 subject areas.

Graduate prospects vary considerably by university, ranging from 87% in high-skilled jobs/postgraduate study at Oxford to 50% at South Wales. Though not an ingredient of our ranking, English places 53rd in our earnings index, with median graduate salaries of £23,650 for those in high-skilled jobs.

English	Teaching quality %	Student experience %	Research quality %	Entry standards (UCAS points)	Graduate prospects %	Overall score
1 Oxford	—	—	69.8	190	87.0	100
2 St Andrews	85.0	79.8	61.8	196	82.2	98.8
3 Strathclyde	86.7	80.5	58.8	202	70.2	95.9
4 Stirling	84.7	80.4	47.5	175	84.1	95.5
5 York	82.1	76.9	70.2	156	80.2	95.3

6 Cambridge	—	—	65.0	189	79.4	95.1
7 Warwick	84.4	78.6	64.8	153	79.2	94.7
8 Aberdeen	82.0	79.2	53.8	173	80.0	94.4
9 Durham	75.7	61.3	55.5	188	85.7	94.2
10 University College London	84.7	75.0	61.5	182	69.7	93.6
11 Glasgow	76.7	70.9	61.8	187	74.0	93
=12 Exeter	82.2	78.3	59.5	160	74.6	92.7
=12 Lancaster	83.5	78.7	48.0	149	82.5	92.7
14 Surrey	81.0	75.5	63.0	123	83.0	92.1
15 Newcastle	79.1	70.5	83.8	142	69.1	91.7
16 Loughborough	76.1	79.2	54.5	147	81.3	91.4
17 Southampton	83.3	73.1	69.2	142	70.5	91.2
18 Edinburgh Napier	87.9	83.0	48.2	154	70.2	91.1
19 Edinburgh	68.6	60.9	74.5	177	73.5	91
=20 Bedfordshire	81.1	71.2	77.2	—	67.9*	90.9
=20 Hull	88.4	86.7	55.5	116	74.5	90.9
22 Nottingham	76.8	69.3	70.5	147	71.8	90.3
23 Liverpool John Moores	85.1	81.6	58.0	128	70.4	89.7
24 Birmingham City	84.7	79.9	65.5	111	71.9	89.6
=25 Sheffield	78.8	73.2	62.3	149	69.7	89.5
=25 Sussex	80.7	72.1	67.0	133	70.5	89.5
=25 Teesside	88.8	81.7	49.2	101	78.7	89.5
28 Leicester	86.2	77.8	67.8	123	65.8	89.4
29 Leeds	67.1	59.6	73.2	158	75.2	89.3
30 King's College London	72.0	61.0	70.8	154	71.9	89
31 Birmingham	71.6	68.0	68.8	149	72.1	88.9
32 Manchester	71.1	57.9	66.5	163	72.5	88.8
=33 Kent	75.6	75.2	64.5	120	75.2	88.6
=33 Oxford Brookes	82.2	74.3	72.8	107	69.4	88.6
=35 Cardiff	73.5	65.2	67.2	138	73.5	88.5
=35 Swansea	82.9	79.0	60.0	130	66.9	88.5
=37 Bristol	64.5	59.0	54.5	166	81.6	88.4
=37 Royal Holloway, London	74.5	66.3	60.5	136	76.4	88.4
39 Canterbury Christ Church	87.7	82.3	53.2	107	69.8	87.9
40 Edge Hill	91.0	89.7	32.8	125	68.3	87.4
41 City	90.0	83.1	43.8	109	—	87.3
42 Bishop Grosseteste	91.9	79.2	19.0	87	88.3*	87.2
43 Newman, Birmingham	89.3	81.3	43.8	96	73.3	86.9
44 Dundee	80.7	74.9	40.8	169	63.3	86.8
45 Plymouth	76.1	70.2	60.5	121	71.7	86.7
=46 Brunel	84.4	84.3	42.8	99	74.2	86.4
=46 Liverpool	74.8	65.1	65.5	134	67.2	86.4
48 Queen Mary, London	73.6	67.7	59.5	123	72.8	86.2
49 Coventry	85.1	78.6	54.2	104	67.3	86.1
50 Leeds Trinity	90.0	86.8	32.5	97	73.0*	86
51 Liverpool Hope	88.7	82.1	36.0	106	69.7	85.6

English cont.

		Teaching quality %	Student experience %	Research quality %	Entry standards (UCAS points)	Graduate prospects %	Overall score
=52	Falmouth	78.9	70.5	48.8	—	69.4	85.1
=52	Westminster	84.8	78.9	55.5	101	63.7	85.1
54	Queen's Belfast	77.4	70.4	47.5	145	64.0	84.9
55	Aberystwyth	93.3	92.3	25.5	119	60.7	84.6
=56	Anglia Ruskin	88.8	84.3	46.0	100	61.4	84.4
=56	East Anglia	70.9	62.9	67.0	139	61.8	84.4
58	Reading	79.1	73.0	51.0	122	64.1	84.3
=59	Chichester	90.5	80.8	37.2	112	61.8*	84.2
=59	Nottingham Trent	83.1	78.3	39.2	105	69.6	84.2
61	Worcester	90.8	76.6	19.2	107	72.7	84
=62	Lincoln	84.2	74.0	36.0	113	68.6	83.9
=62	Northumbria	80.7	72.0	54.0	124	59.5	83.9
=62	West of England	91.7	86.9	32.2	112	59.9	83.9
65	Huddersfield	75.1	74.6	60.0	110	63.9	83.8
66	Roehampton	83.9	80.0	50.5	104	60.8	83.6
67	Ulster	75.8	70.8	41.0	113	72.3	83.4
=68	Hertfordshire	82.3	79.3	42.5	99	65.2	82.9
=68	Manchester Metropolitan	75.2	65.8	61.8	113	62.1	82.9
=68	Wolverhampton	84.2	78.2	44.0	100	62.8	82.9
=71	Bath Spa	83.8	74.8	51.7	106	57.3	82.5
=71	Portsmouth	84.5	82.9	30.8	102	65.9	82.5
=71	Sheffield Hallam	81.8	73.2	50.7	106	60.0	82.5
=74	Gloucestershire	85.5	75.4	32.8	109	64.1	82.4
=74	Northampton	85.5	80.7	30.2	103	—	82.4
76	Bangor	82.7	80.4	44.2	116	54.1	81.6
77	Derby	89.4	85.5	—	117	68.9	81.4
78	Essex	76.5	72.1	49.8	112	59.3	81.3
=79	Aston	79.5	70.8	—	123	79.5	81.1
=79	Keele	72.2	67.3	54.8	115	60.7	81.1
81	Leeds Beckett	91.5	79.6	30.8	95	57.8	81
82	Winchester	79.0	71.7	16.2	113	73.3	80.9
83	De Montfort	71.9	69.6	54.5	100	62.3	80.6
84	Kingston	82.2	73.2	47.0	95	57.2	80.4
85	Bournemouth	80.0	71.9	22.5	106	69.0	80.3
86	Greenwich	85.5	81.1	26.5	110	57.2	80.1
87	Salford	81.3	77.5	26.5	114	59.7	79.8
88	Goldsmiths, London	72.0	54.6	46.0	116	63.4	79.4
89	Chester	75.8	64.7	25.0	110	68.6	79.3
90	Central Lancashire	78.7	76.4	33.8	111	56.9	79.1
91	Brighton	76.6	67.3	44.2	99	59.6	79
92	York St John	82.6	78.2	22.8	101	60.8	78.9
93	Sunderland	67.3	56.7	40.5	95	69.2	77.7

94 St Mary's, Twickenham	75.5	67.1	30.2	93	—	76.5
95 South Wales	—	—	39.8	103	50.0	74.9

Employed in high-skilled job	45%	Employed in lower-skilled job	26%
Employed in high-skilled job and studying	5%	Employed in lower-skilled job and studying	1%
Studying	16%	Unemployed	7%
High skilled work (median) salary	£23,650	Low/medium skilled salary	£19,000

Food Science

Glasgow Caledonian is No 1 in our new Food Science table, moving up from eighth last year. Strong performance across all measures within our ranking includes the highest entry standards (of 190 UCAS points among 2021's entrants), and the second-highest research rating. Glasgow Caledonian also features in the top-10 of both student satisfaction metrics: teaching quality and the broader experience.

Runner-up Surrey maintains the top-three record it has achieved in recent years. It does best for graduate prospects, with the latest data showing 94.7% of graduates were in high-skilled jobs and/postgraduate study 15 months after their degrees. King's College London (joint 15th this year, down from joint third) is not far behind, with 93.5% of graduates achieving the desired outcomes when surveyed 15 months on.

Queen's Belfast achieved the best results in the food science areas in the new Research Excellence Framework 2021, and tops our table's research measure. Abertay, in eighth place overall, has the best rates of student satisfaction with teaching quality while Bournemouth (joint 15th in the main table) came top for both last year and is unbeaten for the wider experience in our new ranking. At the other end of scale, students at Liverpool Hope reported the lowest rates of satisfaction, while those at Chester was only slightly more content.

Degrees under this grouping encompass a broad range of courses, from nutrition and dietetics – which offer opportunities to study alongside doctors, nurses and other health professionals in hospitals – to food manufacturing and professional cookery. There is even a BSc in Baking Science and Technology offered by London South Bank at its National Bakery School.

Food science courses consistently feature in the top-30 of our employment ranking and this year is no exception as the subject area places 24th out of 70, with almost eight out of 10 (79%) graduates in high-skilled jobs and/or further study within 15 months. Median graduate salaries of £25,000 in high-skilled jobs also rank food science in the top-30 for pay.

Food Science	Teaching quality %	Student experience %	Research quality %	Entry standards (UCAS points)	Graduate prospects %	Overall score
1 Glasgow Caledonian	84.2	86.3	61.0	190	87.0	100
2 Surrey	87.6	87.4	58.0	149	94.7	96.6
3 Queen's Belfast	84.3	84.4	69.2	149	84.6	95.8
4 Nottingham	76.3	76.5	52.0	148	89.6	91.1
5 Reading	86.6	87.8	42.5	132	89.0	90.5
6 Plymouth	72.7	66.3	58.2	146	86.0	89.6
7 Oxford Brookes	85.2	90.0	39.5	131	87.5*	89.5
8 Abertay	90.4	86.4	28.2	157	77.1	89.4

Food Science cont.

		Teaching quality %	Student experience %	Research quality %	Entry standards (UCAS points)	Graduate prospects %	Overall score
9	Newcastle	77.8	75.2	42.8	148	82.5	88.2
10	Ulster	79.2	82.0	53.5	131	77.9	88.1
11	Leeds	69.1	71.8	45.5	152	80.6	86.7
12	Manchester Metropolitan	86.2	83.3	36.0	127	78.3	86.1
13	Hertfordshire	86.0	85.3	42.5	120	73.3	85.6
14	Coventry	81.4	72.8	24.8	135	86.2	84.7
=15	Bournemouth	87.2	91.3	29.2	117	65.7*	82.1
=15	King's College London	69.1	70.5	—	161	93.5	82.1
17	Chester	64.4	60.8	31.0	119	100	81.8
18	Nottingham Trent University	80.3	76.5	30.8	120	—	81.5
19	Queen Margaret, Edinburgh	76.2	70.9	—	161	80.4	81.1
20	Liverpool John Moores	84.7	80.0	26.5	139	53.3	80.4
21	Cardiff Metropolitan	73.8	61.5	—	132	91.2	78.2
22	Sheffield Hallam	76.6	80.3	—	126	82.4	78.1
23	Harper Adams	79.5	83.4	19.5	102	71.5	77.3
24	Westminster	65.6	66.8	36.8	—	67.6	77.1
25	Kingston University	79.0	73.9	38.5	—	47.8	76.9
26	Leeds Beckett	71.2	65.7	—	120	74.1	73.2
27	Bath Spa	79.7	80.9	—	102	67.6	72.9
28	St Mary's, Twickenham	83.4	80.4	—	107	55.7	71.8
29	Edge Hill	65.0	71.6	—	113	64.7	69.8
30	Liverpool Hope	58.6	60.1	15.0	115	—	68.8

Employed in high-skilled job	65%	Employed in lower-skilled job		17%
Employed in high-skilled job and studying	3%	Employed in lower-skilled job and studying		2%
Studying	10%	Unemployed		4%
High skilled work (median) salary	£25,000	Low/medium skilled salary		£20,000

French

In a subject table that is almost entirely populated by some of the UK's older universities, Cambridge holds on to its lead. Some reshuffling at the top brings St Andrews up to second place, from third last year, and York enters the top three (a 13-place rise from joint 16th last year) in a tie with Oxford. Just Manchester Metropolitan represents the post-1992 institutions in our table this year, taking 28th place.

French attracts high entry standards; led by Strathclyde, more than two-thirds of the universities in our table averaged upwards of 144 UCAS tariff points (equivalent to AAA at A-level) among 2021's intake of students. No universities in our table averaged below 100 UCAS points. For research, York leads the field by a clear margin, following results of the new Research Excellence Framework 2021. Warwick, in tenth place overall, leads for student satisfaction with teaching quality while St Andrews is in front for students' evaluation of the wider experience – measures derived from the National Student Survey (NSS). Students at Queen Mary, London recorded the lowest scores under each of these student-led categories, however.

Bath, in 18th place overall, had the best-employed graduates 15 months on from their degrees, the latest data shows, with 89.1% working in high-skilled jobs and/or engaged in postgraduate study. As a whole, French sits 43rd in this year's employment ranking (down nine places from 34th in our previous edition), with just over seven in 10 (71%) graduates achieving those top outcomes, on average. For pay, which is not an ingredient of our ranking, it comes in at 33rd out of 70 subject areas, the latest data showing graduates in high-skilled jobs earn median salaries of £25,000.

The long decline in the popularity of modern languages is starkly evident in the case of French. The number of new students who enrolled on French degrees in 2021 was around a third of the amount that did so in 2012, following more than a decade of waning undergraduate numbers in the language. But applicants still have options; the UCAS website showed 998 courses in French offered by 68 colleges and universities in 2023-24.

French	Teaching quality %	Student experience %	Research quality %	Entry standards (UCAS points)	Graduate prospects %	Overall score
1 Cambridge	—	—	61.0	190	83.6	100
2 St Andrews	86.6	87.5	51.5	203	78.4	99.3
=3 Oxford	—	—	51.2	185	87.6	97.3
=3 York	80.7	80.0	74.8	144	—	97.3
5 University College London	86.2	79.0	56.0	162	82.4	96.4
6 Bristol	75.6	74.4	64.0	163	79.0	94.9
7 Surrey	87.3	86.7	63.0	133	—	94.6
8 Durham	74.7	71.7	46.0	182	86.1	94.3
9 Stirling	84.7	76.3	47.5	175	—	93.8
10 Warwick	88.8	83.3	46.2	158	79.0	93.6
11 Royal Holloway, London	87.0	80.6	60.0	132	—	92.8
12 Lancaster	68.2	64.5	68.5	151	—	91.3
13 Newcastle	72.0	71.3	61.8	150	75.2	91.1
14 Aberdeen	81.8	78.3	32.5	191	—	90.7
15 King's College London	73.6	64.3	51.2	159	79.6	90.5
16 Exeter	77.8	75.2	50.0	148	78.0	90.3
17 Nottingham	66.0	63.2	62.0	139	83.1	90.2
18 Bath	76.4	80.6	31.8	151	89.1	89.5
19 Cardiff	80.3	75.8	55.5	131	72.9	88.9
20 Liverpool	74.8	69.5	59.0	133	—	88.1
21 Southampton	87.4	83.0	47.8	163	53.4	87.1
22 Leeds	68.9	70.0	52.0	155	68.1	86.6
23 Manchester	66.6	54.4	59.5	155	67.6	86.4
24 Edinburgh	58.2	57.6	45.8	183	72.5	86.1
25 Birmingham	69.1	63.7	54.8	149	65.3	85.4
26 Queen's Belfast	79.7	78.9	37.0	150	64.1	84.3
27 Kent	78.1	72.5	57.5	120	60.6	84.1
28 Manchester Metropolitan	81.8	67.4	51.7	109	—	84
29 Glasgow	70.5	66.9	25.5	201	63.2	83.9

French cont.

		Teaching quality %	Student experience %	Research quality %	Entry standards (UCAS points)	Graduate prospects %	Overall score
30	Strathclyde	85.8	81.8	—	205	63.5	82.6
31	Queen Mary, London	52.0	39.6	51.1	132	74.8	79.9
32	Sheffield	67.0	58.1	35.8	—	63.5	77.2

Employed in high-skilled job	52%	Employed in lower-skilled job		24%
Employed in high-skilled job and studying	4%	Employed in lower-skilled job and studying		2%
Studying	13%	Unemployed		5%
High skilled work (median) salary	£25,000	Low/medium skilled salary		£20,500

General Engineering

As an undergraduate option, general engineering has undergone a popularity boom over the past decade – with applications in 2021 up by almost three-quarters since 2012 and enrolments almost 50% higher over the same decade. Students opting for the general strand of engineering gain the flexibility its breadth of the subject allows in their future careers, while degrees also provide opportunities to specialise in a specific area of interest.

Cambridge has overtaken Bristol at the top of our table, ending Bristol's three-year residency at No 1. The top entry standards at Cambridge – of 228 UCAS points on average among 2021's entrants – have helped boost its overall ranking. Cambridge also has the edge for graduate prospects, due to 96.5% of graduates achieving the desired career outcomes of a high-skilled job and/or postgraduate study when surveyed 15 months after their degrees.

General engineering makes a convincing choice for careers prospects. It places tenth in our employment ranking's top 10 this year and seventh for starting salaries, with graduates earning median pay rates of £29,070 per year in high-skilled roles – the type of job that nearly nine out of 10 (87%) were working in 15 months after graduating, according to the latest Graduate Outcomes survey.

Exeter is hitting all the right notes with its general engineering students, who returned the top scores for teaching quality and the broader experience in our analysis of the latest National Student Survey (NSS). Three universities (Cambridge, Oxford and Durham) averaged above 200 UCAS points in the 2021 admissions rounds and entry standards are higher than 144 points (equivalent to AAA) at 15 universities. But the subject can also be accessed with more modest entry standards, such as the 127 UCAS points averaged by entrants to Cardiff, which places tenth overall.

	General Engineering	Teaching quality %	Student experience %	Research quality %	Entry standards (UCAS points)	Graduate prospects %	Overall score
1	Cambridge	—	—	77.2	228	96.5	100
2	Bristol	95.6	88.8	68.0	196	90.0	99.1
3	Sheffield	95.9	92.5	66.8	178	—	98.8
4	Imperial College	82.8	85.9	81.0	192	90.9	98.2
5	Oxford	—	—	77.5	216	92.5	97.3
6	University College London	80.6	72.9	70.0	196	—	95.6
7	Durham	80.9	77.2	52.8	202	86.3	92.6

8 Exeter	98.8	96.0	47.0	144	—	92.1
9 Heriot-Watt	69.1	69.7	55.5	180	—	87.8
10 Cardiff	78.4	80.1	54.0	127	92.3*	87.7
11 Loughborough	75.8	79.1	46.5	156	88.6	87.5
12 Warwick	65.4	65.1	56.2	162	88.9	86.4
13 Strathclyde	69.1	71.8	52.8	185	74.7	85
14 Queen Mary, London	64.2	68.7	66.0	147	—	84.5
15 Aberdeen	75.0	76.8	35.8	164	—	84.3
16 Nottingham Trent	73.3	75.4	59.0	122	—	83.1
17 Liverpool John Moores	79.2	75.1	45.5	140	76.9	82.6
18 Leicester	72.7	72.6	39.8	—	76.2*	81.1
19 Ulster	69.1	68.3	49.8	128	81.0	81
20 Brunel	64.9	67.1	33.0	133	88.4	80.4
21 Glasgow Caledonian	71.2	69.9	12.8	145	86.5	79.4
22 Aston	71.6	74.1	35.2	132	—	79.2
23 Edinburgh Napier	70.5	68.9	22.8	—	81.5	79
24 Coventry	82.8	76.6	23.5	123	67.2	75.8
25 Bournemouth	69.3	67.7	14.0	114	83.8	75.5
26 Central Lancashire	64.1	61.9	23.0	127	—	73.1
27 Wolverhampton	70.7	63.5	18.2	—	65.0*	70.9
28 Northampton	73.1	60.7	8.5	—	66.7*	70
29 London South Bank	51.4	45.3	27.3	123	—	68.4
30 West of Scotland	48.9	40.1	16.5	—	65.2*	62.7

Employed in high-skilled job	77%	Employed in lower-skilled job	8%
Employed in high-skilled job and studying	2%	Employed in lower-skilled job and studying	0%
Studying	7%	Unemployed	5%
High skilled work (median) salary	£29,070	Low/medium skilled salary	£23,456

Geography and Environmental Sciences

Our table incorporates the different strands of geography – physical and human. The former focuses on physical processes and natural environments, the latter concerns human societies and the links between people and the planet. Environmental science studies the earth's physical, chemical and biological processes and looks at what impacts the planet in terms of social, political and cultural developments.

With the best-employed graduates, Oxford takes the lead in our Geography and Environmental Sciences table, up from second place last year. It swaps places with Cambridge after two consecutive years at the top. Further reshuffling of the top end of the table has brought the London School of Economics into third place (up from fifth) and seen Loughborough and Lancaster join the top-10. But Bristol, in joint 13th place overall, has the edge for research, following the recent Research Excellence Framework 2021, and is closely followed by Durham, Reading and Lancaster in this measure.

In joint 57th place overall, Derby outdoes all other institutions for student satisfaction with teaching quality and with the broad experience, as expressed in the National Student Survey. Fellow post-1992 universities also do well on these measures, notably Gloucestershire and West of England. Of the older universities, Aberytswyth places in the top-10 for both student-led measures.

Graduate outcomes are not far off the upper half of subjects this year, placing 37th out of 70. More than seven in 10 (72%) of graduates were working in high-skilled jobs (49%) and/or postgraduate study (23%) when surveyed 15 months on from their degrees. Performance in achieving these outcomes varies considerably by institution from 92.3% at Oxford down to 46.3% at Cumbria.

Entry standards do not reach the heights of some other subjects, with no universities averaging higher than the 192 UCAS points at St Andrews among their 2021 entrants, and 10 averaging 100 or less. Geography at A-level or equivalent is a requirement for geography degrees. For environmental science, the leading universities look for two subjects from geology, maths, psychology, physics, geography, biology or chemistry. Application and enrolment numbers vary between the disciplines, with human geography attracting the highest numbers of applications and enrolments (15,760 and 3,010 respectively in 2021), followed by physical geographical sciences (12,830 and 2,435), and environmental science (7,200 and 1,345).

Geography and Environmental Sciences	Teaching quality %	Student experience %	Research quality %	Entry standards (UCAS points)	Graduate prospects %	Overall score
1 Oxford	85.2	82.6	66.0	186	92.3	100
2 Cambridge	—	—	59.2	182	91.7	96.1
3 London School of Economics	79.7	81.3	63.0	165	88.7	95.5
4 St Andrews	83.8	78.2	48.2	192	82.7	95
5 Durham	74.9	71.6	68.8	173	88.0	94.7
6 University College London	76.6	76.7	59.2	174	84.7	93.6
7 Edinburgh	78.1	78.7	63.2	172	75.9	92.2
8 Loughborough	84.6	89.0	54.2	141	80.2	92
9 Lancaster	80.2	77.2	68.2	144	76.2	90.9
10 Exeter	74.6	77.4	67.2	151	78.2	90.6
11 Southampton	84.2	82.2	67.5	141	71.3	90.5
12 Glasgow	71.8	66.4	65.5	189	72.5	90.4
=13 Bristol	67.7	69.1	70.0	154	82.2	89.9
=13 Sheffield	81.0	80.2	51.0	142	80.0	89.9
15 Leeds	67.2	66.2	66.0	152	82.4	88.8
16 Aberystwyth	85.6	88.1	47.0	117	76.1	88.1
17 Manchester	75.0	71.1	49.0	156	76.9	87.8
=18 Northumbria	84.2	80.9	49.0	125	74.6	87.6
=18 Royal Holloway, London	83.5	83.1	64.0	125	67.0	87.6
20 York	78.7	76.3	65.5	134	69.3	87.4
21 Sussex	82.0	76.7	57.2	130	71.1	87.3
22 Birmingham	70.6	67.6	49.2	144	83.6	87.2
23 Aberdeen	79.7	79.3	—	186	80.1	86.9
=24 King's College London	68.9	68.6	58.8	146	77.0	86.6
=24 Reading	77.6	78.6	68.5	119	69.8	86.6
=24 Stirling	74.6	73.8	45.8	168	69.2	86.6
27 Dundee	76.8	75.6	46.2	172	62.7	86
28 West of England	91.2	91.5	40.8	104	67.0	85.5
29 Huddersfield	95.3	89.1	24.0	105	—	85.4

=30 Newcastle	70.7	63.9	53.8	135	76.5	84.8
=30 Nottingham	68.2	65.8	58.5	133	76.1	84.8
32 Bangor	78.2	76.6	67.5	113	63.0	84.1
33 Cardiff	73.4	70.9	38.2	131	76.2	83.8
=34 SOAS, London	73.4	68.7	29.8	155	73.1*	83.7
=34 Swansea	76.1	75.6	51.7	123	67.9	83.7
=34 Coventry	90.8	85.9	17.0	102	74.9	83.6
37 Gloucestershire	93.6	94.4	25.8	102	64.6	83.6
38 Queen's Belfast	78.2	76.9	35.5	130	70.3	83.5
=39 Leicester	80.6	75.7	28.7	116	74.6	82.9
=39 Ulster	82.6	79.2	43.0	116	64.3	82.9
=39 Hull	81.9	79.5	42.0	111	66.7	82.8
42 Manchester Metropolitan	78.7	77.7	44.8	106	70.5	82.8
43 Keele	78.2	75.0	35.2	111	71.6	82
44 Liverpool John Moores	83.7	83.0	28.7	116	64.6	81.8
45 Liverpool	65.8	63.5	45.2	128	75.5	81.7
46 Portsmouth	80.2	76.7	26.8	100	73.8	81.1
47 Salford	77.1	68.9	41.0	104	71.0	81.1
48 Brighton	82.0	77.6	31.8	92	70.6	80.7
=49 Canterbury Christ Church University	90.3	86.9	9.5	—	61.0	80.3
=49 Hertfordshire	82.8	80.5	42.5	92	61.9	80.3
=49 Leeds Beckett	88.8	87.6	24.5	104	58.9	80.3
52 Queen Mary, London	65.9	59.9	52.5	124	68.5	80.1
53 Lincoln	84.8	76.8	14.0	113	—	79.8
54 Plymouth	73.2	73.7	31.0	112	68.6	79.5
55 Liverpool Hope	83.0	84.2	9.5	111	—	79.3
56 Nottingham Trent	78.5	74.5	30.8	100	65.2	78.7
57 Derby	96.5	95.8	—	116	50.6	78.6
58 York St John	84.5	74.3	14.0	94	69.5	78.6
59 Edge Hill	79.0	77.5	15.2	113	64.9	78.3
60 Worcester	74.8	74.6	12.2	102	73.0	77.8
61 Oxford Brookes	70.4	71.6	34.8	101	65.0	77.3
62 Chester	83.2	75.6	7.2	107	63.6	77.2
63 East Anglia	71.5	74.4	—	124	71.8	77.1
64 Kingston	83.2	79.2	17.2	98	59.5	77
65 Northampton	84.9	78.7	12.0	97	60.7	76.9
66 University of South Wales	72.2	71.7	16.2	—	66.0	75.8
67 Bournemouth	77.4	74.3	31.2	99	52.2	75.1
68 Sheffield Hallam	73.2	63.3	—	103	71.2	74.4
69 Winchester	77.9	75.8	—	96	62.3	73.8
70 Bath Spa	73.0	69.1	19.2	95	56.0	72.7
71 Cumbria	60.2	51.7	16.5	113	46.3	66.7

Employed in high-skilled job	49%	Employed in lower-skilled job	23%
Employed in high-skilled job and studying	5%	Employed in lower-skilled job and studying	1%
Studying	18%	Unemployed	5%
High skilled work (median) salary	£25,000	Low/medium skilled salary	£20,000

Geology

For the third year running Cambridge tops our Geology table while its previous leader, Imperial, is runner-up. Cambridge leads for graduate prospects and entry standards, but Imperial has retained its leading edge in research, even as our research quality rating has been updated this year by results of the new Research Excellence Framework 2021. Imperial also places in the top three universities for both student satisfaction metrics: teaching quality and the wider experience.

However Aberdeen, in sixth place overall, outdoes all others for its students' evaluation of both these measures. Geology students in general tend to enjoy their degrees. Even at the bottom end of the scale Newcastle scores more than 70% for teaching quality and Leeds over 62% for the wider experience.

The leading universities require any two subjects, from: biology, chemistry, economics, further maths, geography, geology, maths, physics and psychology. Entry standards can be high; Cambridge has attracted even higher than the 221 points it averaged among 2021's entrants, and more than half of the universities listed attracted over 144 points in the UCAS tariff (equivalent to AAA at A-level).

Life after an undergraduate geology degree often involves postgraduate study, which 29% of graduates were engaged in 15 months on from their courses – the joint highest proportion of any subject. Combined with 44% working in high-skilled jobs, and 4% doing both, geology places 28th in our employment ranking of 70 subject areas.

The study of how the earth was formed and shaped, geology has applications in environmental research and oil and gas exploration as well as the water industries, mapping, remote sensing and engineering. Median graduate salaries of £25,000 for those in high-skilled jobs help rank geology 33rd in our pay index, though this is not an ingredient of the main subject table.

Geology	Teaching quality %	Student experience %	Research quality %	Entry standards (UCAS points)	Graduate prospects %	Overall score
1 Cambridge	—	—	79.5	221	93.5	100
2 Imperial College	86.8	85.7	81.0	168	92.2	98.3
3 St Andrews	84.9	83.8	68.2	185	87.7	96
4 Oxford	74.5	77.1	71.2	207	90.6	94.8
5 Edinburgh	79.1	78.1	63.2	208	78.6	92.8
6 Aberdeen	93.4	88.5	41.5	162	78.4	92.2
7 Exeter	85.9	82.4	69.8	145	78.0	92
8 Durham	79.0	77.8	60.2	156	89.0	91.3
9 University College London	74.5	74.8	63.0	158	87.7	90
10 Cardiff	80.3	81.8	67.8	126	77.2	88.9
=11 Birmingham	78.2	73.7	74.8	145	73.3	88.7
=11 Glasgow	79.8	76.4	39.5	191	78.2	88.7
13 Bristol	77.3	74.5	75.2	149	70.5	88.2
14 Leeds	73.2	62.4	68.2	156	82.5	87.9
15 Aberystwyth	84.8	86.1	47.0	—	69.2*	87.4

16	Liverpool	76.7	76.2	57.0	128	79.9	86.7
17	Southampton	77.9	74.4	71.0	148	64.6	86.6
18	Keele	79.9	77.7	35.2	109	90.3	85.9
19	Royal Holloway, London	77.8	77.4	42.0	121	83.6	85.5
=20	Manchester	73.1	67.3	69.8	152	65.2	84.7
=20	Newcastle	70.1	63.6	58.5	119	87.5	84.7
22	Hull	78.1	76.0	42.0	109	81.3	84.3
23	East Anglia	73.8	69.9	73.8	140	60.1	84
24	Portsmouth	80.4	76.2	40.8	103	77.3	83.6
25	Bangor	75.2	72.0	67.5	114	64.8	83.2
26	Leicester	77.8	80.9	50.5	126	62.3	83
27	Plymouth	79.2	77.2	40.8	115	71.5	82.9
28	Brighton	75.7	76.3	31.8	—	74.4*	81.6
29	Derby	78.3	82.5	28.0	109	68.2	80.6

Employed in high-skilled job	44%	Employed in lower-skilled job	18%
Employed in high-skilled job and studying	4%	Employed in lower-skilled job and studying	1%
Studying	29%	Unemployed	6%
High skilled work (median) salary	£25,000	Low/medium skilled salary	£20,000

German

Led by Cambridge, where entrants averaged 190 UCAS points in 2021, German attracts well-qualified undergraduates. Sixteen of the 21 institutions in our table averaged over 144 points (equivalent to AAA at A-level) among their 2021 intakes of students, and none averaged lower than the 127 UCAS points at Queen Mary. Cambridge tops the table overall this year and is the most regular incumbent of the No 1 spot. The small student numbers that German degrees attract create fluctuations elsewhere in the table, and almost all universities occupy different positions this year compared with last.

In third overall, Bristol is out front for research quality in our analysis of the new Research Excellence Framework 2021 results. Fourth-place Warwick has outdone all others for student satisfaction with teaching quality and the wider experience – both measures derived from 2020's National Student Survey, while St Andrews places just beneath it on each of them.

The subject's 20-year-plus ongoing decline continued in the 2021 recruitment cycle, when just 70 students started degrees – representing around 65% fewer enrolments than in 2012, a decade before. But there are still plenty of places to study German, either as a single honours degree or in combination with a wide range of subjects including law, film, accountancy and other languages. Most universities in the table offer German from scratch, as well as catering for those who took it at A-level.

The latest data shows that 54% of German graduates had found high-skilled jobs 15 months on from their degrees, while 14% were furthering their studies and 6% were combining both – outcomes that place the subject at the midpoint of our employment ranking, in 33rd place out of 70 subject areas. It occupies almost the same spot in our salary index, in 32nd place. Salaries range from £25,000 for graduates in high-skilled jobs down to £20,000 for those employed in work deemed "low-skilled".

German

	Teaching quality %	Student experience %	Research quality %	Entry standards (UCAS points)	Graduate prospects %	Overall score
1 Cambridge	—	—	61.0	190	83.6	100
2 St Andrews	88.3	84.3	51.5	189	—	99.3
3 Bristol	77.3	74.0	64.0	170	75.8	95.5
4 Warwick	91.8	85.9	46.2	162	77.0	95.1
5 Durham	74.7	71.7	46.0	182	86.1	95
6 Oxford	—	—	51.2	180	80.1	94.5
7 University College London	78.3	71.5	56.0	164	—	92.8
8 Newcastle	82.3	76.0	61.8	150	70.0	92.5
9 Exeter	77.8	75.2	50.0	148	78.1	91
10 Edinburgh	73.3	73.0	45.8	178	—	90.9
11 Cardiff	84.5	81.3	55.5	129	71.7*	90.2
12 Liverpool	77.3	69.9	59.0	129	—	88.2
13 Nottingham	70.9	67.4	62.0	139	69.0*	88.1
14 King's College London	65.2	63.3	51.2	170	—	88
15 Leeds	75.5	72.9	52.0	154	64.8	87.7
16 Bath	83.3	79.4	31.8	157	—	87.2
17 Manchester	63.3	59.2	59.5	158	68.3	87.1
18 Birmingham	69.8	64.1	54.8	149	64.8	85.9
19 Queen Mary, London	70.8	65.1	51.1	127	—	83.4
20 Sheffield	73.9	65.9	35.8	—	68.0	83
21 Glasgow	65.7	53.4	25.5	187	57.3	79.9

Employed in high-skilled job	54%	Employed in lower-skilled job	18%
Employed in high-skilled job and studying	6%	Employed in lower-skilled job and studying	1%
Studying	14%	Unemployed	8%
High skilled work (median) salary	£25,000	Low/medium skilled salary	£20,400

History

After closing the gap on Cambridge last year, St Andrews has overtaken it to place No 1 in our new history ranking. Strength across all five measures included in our table has secured St Andrews' position, including the second-best graduate prospects and entry standards just shy of the highest at Cambridge. With Oxford in third place, Durham in fourth and the London School of Economics (LSE) in fifth, the same universities populate our top five this year as last, albeit reshuffled a little.

Fifteenth-ranked Kent leads for research quality in our analysis of the Research Excellence Framework 2021 results, followed by Leicester and University College London. The best-employed graduates are produced by the LSE, with 92.1% employed in high-skilled jobs and/or postgraduate study 15 months on from their degrees according to the latest Graduate Outcomes survey. At the other end of the scale, 42% of South Wales' history graduates had secured the same outcomes 15 months after their degrees.

Of the top 20 universities, only St Andrews features in the top 25 of student satisfaction measures, which are dominated by post-1992 institutions. Bishop Grosseteste (49th overall) leads for teaching quality, and Derby is out in front for the wider experience. Conversely, Newcastle finishes bottom for both.

Placing 51st for graduate prospects, history is not a degree with an immediate utilitarian use. When surveyed 15 months after their degrees 40% of graduates were employed in high-skilled work, 19% were enrolled in postgraduate study and 4% were combining the two. Meanwhile nearly three in 10 (28%) were working in jobs deemed "low-skilled", 2% were combining this type of job with further study and 7% were unemployed. Graduate pay fares slightly better compared with other subjects; history ranking 48th and graduates in high-skilled jobs earning median salaries of £25,000.

Applications and enrolments to history degrees have been decreasing in recent years, although the trend seems to be confined to the lower- and medium-tariff institutions, according to analysis by UCAS.

History	Teaching quality %	Student experience %	Research quality %	Entry standards (UCAS points)	Graduate prospects %	Overall score
1 St Andrews	87.9	82.1	62.0	192	87.6	100
2 Cambridge	—	—	54.5	193	86	98
3 Oxford	—	—	61.3	192	87.2	96.6
4 Durham	80.6	71.4	59.2	188	84.5	95.7
5 London School of Economics	74.2	69.1	59.8	169	92.1	94.3
6 Warwick	84.2	80.0	61.3	154	81.5	94.2
7 University College London	74.4	68.2	67.8	177	81.9	93.6
8 Exeter	75.7	73.1	66.0	161	77.8	91.9
=9 Strathclyde	82.1	77.3	49.0	191	67.8	91.5
=9 York	83.1	75.4	64.8	154	71.0	91.5
=11 Birmingham	74.0	68.7	60.2	151	80.4	90
=11 Bristol	71.8	68.4	56.5	163	80.7	90
=11 King's College London	74.6	67.2	62.7	162	75.0	90
14 Southampton	81.4	80.8	59.5	142	70.5	89.8
15 Kent	82.4	75.9	77.2	126	65.0	89.5
16 Edinburgh	70.8	63.4	55.8	175	77.6	89.4
=17 East Anglia	80.1	69.7	67.5	125	74.6	89.2
=17 Leicester	81.7	79.2	71.5	124	67.2	89.2
=19 Aberdeen	84.5	78.8	38.5	177	65.9	89.1
=19 Manchester	72.4	62.8	67.0	159	73.7	89.1
21 Royal Holloway, London	80.9	74.3	53.5	133	73.8	88.3
22 Lancaster	78.8	72.6	51.7	146	72.9	88.2
23 Queen Mary, London	81.9	70.9	67.2	127	67.4	88.1
=24 Bournemouth	90.9	89.8	47.2	103	69.0	87.8
=24 Hull	88.3	82.2	60.8	109	64.5	87.8
26 Glasgow	71.9	65.5	62.5	182	62.0	87.7
27 Sussex	75.9	68.0	62.7	129	73.9	87.5
28 Leeds	71.9	66.4	49.2	161	75.5	87.4
=29 Lincoln	87.9	78.2	66.0	112	60.5	87.3
=29 Stirling	81.5	79.8	51.7	173	54.2	87.3

History cont.

		Teaching quality %	Student experience %	Research quality %	Entry standards (UCAS points)	Graduate prospects %	Overall score
31	Sheffield	76.8	73.0	49.0	150	71.0	87.2
32	Teesside	92.3	80.9	49.2	109	63.9	86.7
=33	Aberystwyth	89.8	81.6	36.8	118	70.1	86.6
=33	Loughborough	77.7	76.8	45.0	138	72.4	86.6
35	Portsmouth	84.6	78.2	51.7	93	75.9	86.5
36	Reading	83.0	80.8	42.2	119	72.4	86.3
37	Nottingham	73.1	65.7	52.5	142	74.1	86.2
38	Coventry	95.5	91.4	33.2	111	62.0	86
39	SOAS, London	77.7	69.5	47.5	141	68.2	85.4
40	Swansea	82.1	75.0	45.2	125	67.6	85.3
=41	Northumbria	79.4	71.7	49.5	125	65.9	84.5
=41	Roehampton	90.6	79.7	42.8	101	63.1	84.5
43	Hertfordshire	87.6	74.7	49.0	101	64.5	84.4
44	Cardiff	78.0	66.1	42.2	130	70.9	84.2
45	Greenwich	88.5	83.7	25.5	104	70.7*	83.9
46	Liverpool	71.3	63.3	52.8	135	68.7	83.7
47	Nottingham Trent	81.4	78.0	51.5	104	62.9	83.6
48	Queen's Belfast	75.2	66.3	54.2	138	60.3	83.4
=49	Bishop Grosseteste	96.9	92.0	16.0	96	64.6*	83.3
=49	Keele	76.1	70.2	41.5	110	74.3	83.3
=49	Salford	83.4	72.7	51.7	110	60.3	83.3
52	Anglia Ruskin	87.6	79.0	47.0	102	58.6	83.2
53	Dundee	81.1	75.4	23.8	178	54.3	83.1
=54	Bangor	82.4	71.8	33.2	118	68.0	82.8
=54	Liverpool Hope	88.8	77.7	24.2	107	68.4	82.8
56	Ulster	91.2	81.4	34.0	112	56	82.7
=57	City	84.5	76.8	40.8	101	—	82.6
=57	Liverpool John Moores	84.9	83.3	19.8	126	64.6	82.6
59	Newman, Birmingham	88.1	75.9	15.0	97	77.4	82.5
=60	Edge Hill	88.3	82.5	27.8	106	61.3	82
=60	Huddersfield	85.5	82.3	33.5	114	57.9	82
62	Plymouth	87.5	80.1	42.8	106	51.3	81.3
63	Derby	95.9	94.8	—	108	61	81.2
64	Leeds Beckett	89.5	84.9	13.8	93	68.3	81.1
65	Chichester	84.7	76.3	33.0	106	59.6	80.8
66	Northampton	83.2	81.5	31.2	96	—	80.5
67	Essex	80.8	74.7	40.2	106	57.6	80.3
68	Chester	80.2	69.7	28.7	102	67.8	80.1
=69	Central Lancashire	87.5	76.8	24.5	103	58.3	79.7
=69	Newcastle	63.3	56.2	33.5	142	72.1	79.7
71	Manchester Metropolitan	77.7	70.4	41.0	112	57.1	79.6
72	Worcester	79.3	69.3	30.2	112	61.4	79.3

73 West of England	88.8	78.2	15.0	105	58.1	78.9
74 Suffolk	92.6	82.9	—	106	60.0	78.7
75 Oxford Brookes	77.2	75.3	28.2	106	60.9	78.6
76 South Wales	92.8	74.0	30.5	113	42.0	78.5
77 Goldsmiths, London	75.2	56.4	41.5	111	60.7	78.4
=78 De Montfort	77.9	66.6	37.5	95	59.1	77.9
=78 Wolverhampton	84.0	79.0	23.8	101	54.0	77.9
80 Winchester	82.6	74.3	18.8	100	59.2	77.5
81 York St John	84.3	73.7	18.0	98	58.6	77.4
82 Brighton	82.3	73.3	44.2	98	44.5*	77.3
83 Sheffield Hallam	82.3	74.4	25.2	104	50.4	76.6
=84 Bath Spa	77.5	69.4	25.0	105	55.5	76.2
=84 Gloucestershire	89.4	81.4	8.2	92	53.1	76.2
=86 Brunel	79.9	76.0	—	103	65.1	76
=86 St Mary's, Twickenham	89.0	80.3	—	102	54.5	76
88 Canterbury Christ Church	83.8	70.0	17.8	89	54.1	75.1
89 Westminster	63.4	56.5	23.0	100	50.6	69.7

Employed in high-skilled job	40%	Employed in lower-skilled job	28%
Employed in high-skilled job and studying	4%	Employed in lower-skilled job and studying	2%
Studying	19%	Unemployed	7%
High skilled work (median) salary	£25,000	Low/medium skilled salary	£20,000

History of Art, Architecture and Design

St Andrews takes the lead in our new History of Art, Architecture and Design ranking. It has outdone all others for research quality in our analysis of the recent Research Excellence Framework 2021 results. The university where the Princess of Wales studied history of art, St Andrews also achieves high rates of student satisfaction with teaching quality as well as the broader experience. Only Sussex, in sixth place overall, does better on each of these measures, which are based on outcomes of the National Student Survey. University College London moves up to third place this year, from ninth last, boosted by the best graduate prospects in the table.

In this generally high-tariff subject area Oxford, in fifth place, averaged the highest entry standards in 2021, while Cambridge – formerly the longstanding No 1 – had the second highest at 192 points. In 11th place overall the Courtauld, a self-governing college of the University of London based in Somerset House, has previously topped our table. It is the only specialist institution to have done so in any subject ranking in our *Guide*.

While there are usually no essential subjects required for entry to a degree in history of art, essay-based subjects will prove useful, as the undergraduate course involves analysing and writing about art, architecture and design across styles, themes and techniques.

Applications and enrolments dipped by 5% and 6% respectively in 2021, in line with the wider pattern among humanities subjects. Career prospects may not be immediately gratifying; history of art, architecture and design ranks 57th out of the 70 subject areas in our employment ranking, with 42% of graduates in high-skilled jobs when surveyed 15 months after their degrees, 16% furthering their studies full-time and 4% combining both. Three in 10 were working in jobs classified as "low-skilled". The subjects rank slightly higher up our pay index in 53rd place (although this is not an ingredient of our subject ranking), with those employed in high-skilled jobs earning median salaries of £23,000.

History of Art, Architecture and Design	Teaching quality %	Student experience %	Research quality %	Entry standards (UCAS points)	Graduate prospects %	Overall score
1 St Andrews	88.8	87.2	78.2	178	77.8	100
2 Cambridge	—	—	65.8	192	82.6	97
3 University College London	83.7	79.4	64.7	170	82.8	95.4
4 Birmingham	82.6	83.0	70.2	156	81.4*	94.8
5 Oxford	—	—	61.3	200	—	93.2
6 Sussex	92.5	93.4	70.0	147	52.1	90.3
=7 Warwick	77.7	73.5	55.0	153	78.8	88.7
=7 York	72.4	67.6	77.0	138	71.1	88.7
9 East Anglia	79.2	74.4	67.0	143	64.3	87.5
10 Exeter	77.6	74.9	55.9	159	—	87
11 Courtauld	72.6	51.5	63.5	160	70.9	86.9
12 Glasgow	72.8	73.3	68.8	169	47.3	85.6
13 Manchester	71.9	61.9	70.8	153	57.7	85.4
14 Leeds	74.5	68.0	54.8	156	67.2	85.3
15 Nottingham	83.2	81.2	54.8	128	—	84.4
16 Edinburgh	66.1	54.2	54.0	158	72.4	83.5
17 Bristol	73.8	66.7	59.8	148	56.7	83
18 Goldsmiths, London	67.6	53.0	57.5	156	63.8	82.5
19 Manchester Metropolitan	59.5	54.2	51.7	156	—	77.8
20 Brighton	73.3	68.3	53.0	96	52.7	74.8
21 Oxford Brookes	80.2	77.4	25.5	117	55.2	73.7

Employed in high-skilled job	42%	Employed in lower-skilled job	30%
Employed in high-skilled job and studying	4%	Employed in lower-skilled job and studying	2%
Studying	16%	Unemployed	7%
High skilled work (median) salary	£23,000	Low/medium skilled salary	£20,000

Hospitality, Leisure, Recreation and Tourism

Birmingham tops our Hospitality, Leisure, Recreation and Tourism ranking for the seventh consecutive year. It has the top-rated research based on our analysis of the new Research Excellence Framework (REF) 2021 – just as it did in the previous REF 2014 exercise. Averaging 160 UCAS tariff points among 2021's entrants, Birmingham ties for the top entry standards with Edinburgh and Glasgow Caledonian.

The table incorporates a wide variety of courses, all of them directed towards management in the leisure and tourism industries. They include degrees in international hospitality management, and adventure tourism management. The post-1992 universities predominate more than institutions with older foundations.

The top-10 features many of the same universities this year as last, such as Liverpool John Moores, which was runner-up in our previous edition and takes third place this year, and Surrey – placing fourth for the second year running. Lincoln and Glasgow Caledonian are also consistent top-10 universities across recent years of our Hospitality, Leisure, Recreation and Tourism table.

Essex – in 13th place overall – has the top rates of student satisfaction with teaching quality, followed by Robert Gordon and Sunderland, while for students' evaluation of the wider experience Wolverhampton (14th overall) leads the field, with Ulster and Sunderland in second and third place respectively for this measure. Conversely, students at Staffordshire expressed the lowest rates of satisfaction with both teaching quality and the wider experience, our analysis of the latest National Student Survey shows. Somewhat paradoxically, Staffordshire also has the top graduate outcomes, with 72% of graduates in high-skilled jobs and/or further study 15 months on from their degrees.

As a whole, the subject area places third from bottom of our employment ranking – although this is an improvement on last year when it finished last. Slightly more graduates were in high-skilled jobs (44%) than "low-skilled' (40%) when the Graduate Outcomes survey took its 2019-20 census, and 7% were unemployed (much improved on the 12% unemployment rate in our previous edition). Salaries fare better: the subject area places 58th out of 70 subject areas and graduates in high-skilled jobs earn median salaries of £22,500, according to the latest data.

Hospitality, Leisure, Recreation and Tourism	Teaching quality %	Student experience %	Research quality %	Entry standards (UCAS points)	Graduate prospects %	Overall score
1 Birmingham	73.4	74.5	73.2	160	—	100
2 Edinburgh	69.0	73.4	55.0	160	67.9	95.9
3 Liverpool John Moores	84.0	85.5	60.8	137	56.7	95.6
4 Surrey	78.2	84.5	57.0	137	64.2	95.4
5 Portsmouth	79.9	77.2	57.5	—	57.8*	93.1
6 Glasgow Caledonian	83.1	80.3	38.5	160	47.6	92.1
7 Lincoln	82.5	82.0	30.8	128	67.1	91.3
8 Manchester Metropolitan	79.3	78.1	42.8	126	59.0	89.9
9 Sheffield Hallam	79.3	75.2	45.2	113	64.1	89.4
10 Northumbria	83.0	80.3	28.2	135	—	89.2
11 Leeds Beckett	79.4	79.6	49.2	104	61.5	88.7
12 Chester	86.2	82.7	25.2	133	52.5	88.3
13 Essex	89.3	85.7	32.5	109	55.6	88
14 Wolverhampton	86.4	88.4	25.2	118	56.4*	87.9
15 Bournemouth	71.5	70.5	41.8	117	65.4	87.5
16 Ulster	86.4	88.3	45.8	122	38.7	87.4
17 Edinburgh Napier	76.5	75.5	23.5	151	50.2	86.9
18 Cardiff Metropolitan	72.3	69.5	43.8	119	58.7	86.5
=19 Coventry	86.9	83.9	24.8	120	51.0	86.4
=19 Robert Gordon	89.0	86.7	—	146	50.6	86.4
21 Arts University, Bournemouth	83.0	78.6	23.0	111	59.3	85.4
=22 Sunderland	88.5	87.2	22.0	114	48.7	85.2
=22 Winchester	76.4	76.2	20.8	119	62.1	85.2
24 Gloucestershire	74.7	74.5	24.5	122	60.0	85.1
25 Westminster	76.2	73.1	37.5	126	47.1	84.7
26 Central Lancashire	84.1	81.6	19.2	122	49.2	84.4
27 York St John	81.5	81.7	27.5	110	—	84.1
28 Canterbury Christ Church	81.7	78.3	38.0	99	51.1	83.9
29 West of Scotland	81.1	74.3	29.0	126	43.1	83.6

Hospitality, Leisure, Recreation and Tourism cont.

		Teaching quality %	Student experience %	Research quality %	Entry standards (UCAS points)	Graduate prospects %	Overall score
30	West London	87.7	83.4	24.2	119	37.9	83
=31	Brighton	73.4	71.0	45.5	110	46.3	82.8
=31	Buckinghamshire New	74.3	71.2	22.8	102	64.6	82.8
33	Chichester	70.6	72.6	33.2	100	59.6*	82.3
34	Falmouth	80.4	76.5	—	115	59.8	81.6
35	Huddersfield	72.0	75.8	23.2	130	43.3	81.3
36	Plymouth	64.8	62.5	28.7	118	57.0	81.1
37	Derby	80.8	73.6	—	121	55.2	81
38	Queen Margaret, Edinburgh	73.8	72.1	—	136	51.5	80.4
=39	Greenwich	80.4	76.2	—	119	50.0	79.6
=39	Northampton	72.2	68.9	13.2	118	52.5	79.6
41	Wales Trinity St David	80.4	78.4	—	122	45.9	79.3
42	Oxford Brookes	68.9	69.1	—	124	58.2	79.1
43	Hertfordshire	75.0	70.0	29.0	103	44.6	79
44	Solent, Southampton	72.7	65.7	18.5	119	45.2	78.7
45	London South Bank	86.7	84.2	32.2	95	28.6	78.5
46	Bedfordshire	82.6	79.6	22.0	90	43.5	78.4
47	Salford	74.7	63.7	—	119	53.6	77.9
48	Middlesex	72.9	72.7	16.0	110	—	77.7
49	Staffordshire	55.8	51.6	—	112	72.0	76.1
50	East London	78.9	78.8	—	86	39.1	72.2

Employed in high-skilled job	44%	Employed in lower-skilled job	40%
Employed in high-skilled job and studying	2%	Employed in lower-skilled job and studying	2%
Studying	5%	Unemployed	7%
High skilled work (median) salary	£22,500	Low/medium skilled salary	£20,000

Iberian Languages

In a reordering of the top end of our Iberian languages table, St Andrews has moved up from fourth place last year to oust Cambridge from the No 1 spot this year. St Andrews benefits from strong performance across all five measures – including rates of student satisfaction with teaching quality and the broader experience that rank in the top three, as well as the second-highest entry standards. Third-place Stirling does even better for student satisfaction – topping our teaching quality measure, and placing second for the wider experience, behind Surrey (in eighth overall).

Among other reshuffles to our table, York rises six places to rank seventh this year, boosted by the top research rating following results of the new Research Excellence Framework 2021. Oxford slips from second place to fourth, but is out in front for graduate prospects, with more than nine in 10 (91.5%) employed in high-skilled jobs or further study 15 months after their degrees.

The Iberian languages of Spanish and Portuguese sit 39th out of the 70 subject areas in our employment ranking, with 53% of graduates in high-skilled jobs 15 months after their degrees, 12% furthering their studies and 6% combining both. Graduates in high-skilled command median salaries of £25,000 and the subjects rank in the upper half of our pay index, at 33rd – though earnings are an ingredient of our main subject ranking.

The waning popularity of modern language degrees has been well documented. The Iberian languages have suffered the decline along with other modern languages, despite Spanish overtaking French at A-level and closing the gap with it at degree level. The trend continued in 2021's admissions cycle, in which applications to Iberian studies courses decreased by 12% compared with the year before, and enrolments fell by 13% – with 1,000 students starting courses.

However, many more students take Spanish as part of a broader modern language degree or paired with diverse subjects as part of a joint honours programme. Portuguese has had zero single honours students since 2012 – but it can still be studied, and 22 universities were offering it for 2023-24 on the UCAS website, mostly as part of joint honours degrees or combined modern or Latin languages courses.

Iberian Languages	Teaching quality %	Student experience %	Research quality %	Entry standards (UCAS points)	Graduate prospects %	Overall score
1 St Andrews	90.1	86.2	51.5	193	—	100
2 Cambridge	—	—	61.0	190	83.6	99.6
3 Stirling	91.2	86.5	47.5	186	—	98.3
4 Oxford	—	—	51.2	186	91.5	97.9
5 University College London	84.9	73.2	56.0	167	83.9	96.7
6 Durham	74.7	71.7	46.0	182	86.1	94.5
7 York	79.4	70.0	74.8	135	—	94.4
8 Surrey	85.5	86.9	63.0	130	—	94.2
9 Warwick	89.5	83.7	46.2	159	77.4	93.7
=10 Bristol	73.8	72.3	64.0	158	71.3	91.3
=10 Newcastle	77.8	76.2	61.8	148	72.1	91.3
12 Leeds	72.3	69.1	52.0	155	81.2	91.1
13 Lancaster	69.0	66.2	68.5	146	—	90.9
14 Aberdeen	78.1	81.1	32.5	192	—	90.8
15 Exeter	77.8	75.2	50.0	148	77.9	90.6
16 Southampton	88.1	86.0	47.8	152	66.4	89.9
17 Bath	77.6	78.6	31.8	150	84.6	89.4
=18 Nottingham	65.8	62.4	62.0	144	76.8	88.8
=18 Royal Holloway, London	76.1	70.9	60.0	129	—	88.8
20 Manchester	68.0	60.1	59.5	152	74.2	88.5
21 Reading	78.9	77.7	54.5	120	—	87.7
22 Edinburgh	57.6	57.3	45.8	182	78.0	87.3
23 Cardiff	82.0	83.2	55.5	125	63.5	86.7
24 Queen's Belfast	79.1	76.3	37.0	145	71.0	85.8
=25 Chester	88.9	83.4	31.2	99	80.2	85.7
=25 King's College London	67.5	59.1	51.2	154	70.9	85.7
27 Liverpool	71.7	66.1	59.0	133	63.7	84.7
28 Birmingham	69.1	63.7	54.8	149	63.8	84.6
29 Strathclyde	84.7	83.6	—	191	71.7*	84.4

Iberian Languages cont.

		Teaching quality %	Student experience %	Research quality %	Entry standards (UCAS points)	Graduate prospects %	Overall score
30	Glasgow	70.0	68.7	25.5	199	64.2	83.9
31	Manchester Metropolitan	74.8	72.1	51.7	108	—	83.7
=32	Aston	75.5	67.7	38.0	—	64.2*	81.1
=32	Sheffield	74.3	69.3	35.8	—	65.9	81.1
34	Queen Mary, London	56.5	43.1	51.1	126	66.5	78.2
35	Westminster	73.7	65.4	24.5	113	—	75.7

Employed in high-skilled job	53%	Employed in lower-skilled job	21%
Employed in high-skilled job and studying	6%	Employed in lower-skilled job and studying	1%
Studying	12%	Unemployed	7%
High skilled work (median) salary	£25,000	Low/medium skilled salary	£20,000

Information Systems and Management

University College London tops our Information Systems and Management table by a clear margin and for the second consecutive year. It was the top scorer in the recent Research Excellence Framework 2021 and, with entrants in 2021 averaging 185 points in the UCAS tariff, it has the highest entry standards. Huddersfield, in joint 12th place overall, has the top rates of student satisfaction for teaching quality as well as the broader experience.

Our table includes all subjects to do with information curation and management. Formerly entitled Librarianship and Information Management, we first broadened and renamed this subject grouping in our previous edition. The courses encompassed range from information systems, data management and curatorial studies to bioinformatics, museum studies and systems analysis and design. The ranking also still takes in librarianship, which requires some postgraduate training after a first degree in order to enter the profession and has practically disappeared at undergraduate level.

Portsmouth, in sixth place overall, has the best-employed graduates, with almost nine in 10 (89.7%) working in high-skilled jobs and/or enrolled in postgraduate study 15 months on from their degrees. The subject group as a whole sits 42nd in our employment ranking, with 71% of graduates achieving the high-skilled work/postgraduate study outcomes. But the 12% of unemployed graduates 15 months after achieving their degree is the highest proportion in our table. For earnings it does much better, placing 20th out of 70 subject areas, with graduates commanding median salaries of £25,000 in professional-level jobs – although pay is not an ingredient of our main subject ranking.

Information Systems and Management		Teaching quality %	Student experience %	Research quality %	Entry standards (UCAS points)	Graduate prospects %	Overall score
1	University College London	76.4	82.1	56.8	185	—	100
2	West of England	74.2	73.9	48.2	—	83.2	91.5
3	Ulster	75.8	74.3	45.8	131	81.6	89.8
4	Northumbria	84.2	86.4	25.8	143	74.4	89.7
5	Leeds Beckett	80.7	74.7	26.5	—	82.1	88.8
6	Portsmouth	79.0	72.4	32.8	107	89.7	87.4

=7	Edinburgh Napier	76.0	69.7	38.8	—	73.3*	86.8
=7	West London	75.6	76.6	45.5	119	—	86.8
9	Edge Hill	71.8	69.4	39.8	139	—	86.3
10	Anglia Ruskin	67.0	63.4	53.8	133	—	86
11	Sheffield Hallam	70.4	62.7	46.0	—	74.6	85.9
=12	Greenwich	82.9	88.1	—	135	78.9	85.3
=12	Huddersfield	88.8	90.2	26.5	135	50.0	85.3
14	East London	80.1	76.3	34.2	—	62.5*	85
15	Solent, Southampton	79.4	73.6	9.5	—	82.9*	84.7
16	West of Scotland	79.7	72.4	19.2	—	75.0	84.5
17	Manchester Metropolitan	77.7	71.4	29.0	130	65.7	83.8
18	Hertfordshire	69.4	68.2	41.2	—	67.1*	83.1
19	Westminster	70.2	71.2	50.0	—	57.1*	82.9
20	Derby	78.7	75.0	24.0	—	65.1*	82.8
21	Wolverhampton	71.9	66.8	31.5	—	70.8*	82.7
=22	Bedfordshire	72.7	71.2	27.0	114	—	80.5
=22	Coventry	70.4	67.8	23.5	128	—	80.5
24	Middlesex	76.4	72.3	26.0	—	57.5*	80
25	South Wales	81.3	81.6	—	112	64.0	78.7
26	Gloucestershire	69.5	66.1	6.2	—	79.2	78.6
27	De Montfort	64.9	61.7	24.0	109	67.3	76.8

Employed in high-skilled job	63%	Employed in lower-skilled job		17%
Employed in high-skilled job and studying	3%	Employed in lower-skilled job and studying		0%
Studying	5%	Unemployed		12%
High skilled work (median) salary	£25,000	Low/medium skilled salary		£20,000

Italian

Led by Cambridge at No 1, the top three of our table is unchanged this year from last. Runner-up Durham has the edge on graduate prospects, with the latest Graduate Outcomes survey showing 86.1% in high-skilled jobs and/or further study 15 months after their degrees. Third-place Warwick is hitting all the right notes with its Italian students, coming top for student satisfaction with both teaching quality and the wider experience. Italian degrees attract small cohorts of undergraduates, which have made for plenty of movement further in our table, and most other universities occupy different positions this year to last. In a generally high-tariff subject, Glasgow leads on entry standards, its 2021 entrants averaging 207 UCAS points. Only two universities, Bath and Cardiff, averaged below below 144 points – equal to AAA at A-level.

Results from the Graduate Outcomes survey place Italian inside the upper half of our 70 subject areas, in 34th place, with 74% in high-skilled jobs and/or postgraduate study when surveyed 15 months after their degrees. For starting salaries, Italian occupies almost the same position (33rd) and graduates in high-skilled jobs command median pay of £25,000 per year, the latest data shows.

One modern language at A-level is required by the leading universities – and some of them require Italian specifically, while others allow it to be learned from scratch. Degree courses often include time spent abroad studying or teaching. Applications to study Italian dropped below 800 in 2021, and 150 new students enrolled on courses. But the UCAS website showed 37 colleges and universities were offering 585 courses in Italian for 2023-24, often as part of joint honours programmes.

Italian

	Teaching quality %	Student experience %	Research quality %	Entry standards (UCAS points)	Graduate prospects %	Overall score
1 Cambridge	—	—	61.0	190	83.6	100
2 Durham	74.7	71.7	46.0	182	86.1	94.9
3 Warwick	91.6	85.4	46.2	160	75.6	94.6
4 Bristol	80.0	79.6	64.0	154	69.4	93.5
5 University College London	78.3	71.5	56.0	164	—	93.2
6 Oxford	—	—	51.2	180	—	92.8
7 Exeter	77.8	75.2	50.0	148	77.5	90.8
=8 Cardiff	82.7	80.4	55.5	128	—	89.8
=8 Leeds	77.3	75.5	52.0	154	69.6	89.8
10 Manchester	68.0	60.1	59.5	156	—	89
11 Edinburgh	72.5	61.0	45.8	173	—	88.7
12 Birmingham	69.1	63.7	54.8	149	63.8	85.7
13 Bath	78.9	79.5	31.8	139	—	83.2
14 Glasgow	58.6	51.2	25.5	207	57.3	80.8

Employed in high-skilled job	48%	Employed in lower-skilled job	20%
Employed in high-skilled job and studying	4%	Employed in lower-skilled job and studying	1%
Studying	20%	Unemployed	6%
High skilled work (median) salary	£25,000	Low/medium skilled salary	—

Land and Property Management

Cambridge tops the Land and Property Management table once again this year. Its land economy degree encompasses law and economics along with aspects of the environment, business finance and resource management. The subject attracted six applications per place there in 2021 and 69 new students were accepted, averaging 188 points in the UCAS tariff – the highest entry standards by far in the table. Cambridge was also the top scorer in the recent Research Excellence Framework (REF) 2021, as it was in the previous REF 2014 exercise.

Real estate degrees are the biggest recruiters among the land and property management subject grouping, which also encompasses woodland ecology, surveying and conservation – among others. Reading, in fourth place, operates the Pathways to Property widening participation programme at its Henley Business School. Funded by property firms, it aims to attract greater numbers of state school-educated applicants into studying real estate.

Students were most satisfied at Ulster, which ties with Manchester in second place overall. For the third consecutive year, Ulster students gave the university the best ratings for both teaching quality and the wider undergraduate experience.

Property and land management ranks 30th out of 70 subject areas in our employment index this year, as it did in our previous edition. Two-thirds of graduates were employed in high-skilled jobs 15 months on from their degrees, the latest data shows, while a further 10% were continuing their studies or combining them with a professional-level job. Median salaries for graduates in high-skilled jobs are £25,000 and the subject grouping also places 30th for pay.

Land and Property Management	Teaching quality %	Student experience %	Research quality %	Entry standards (UCAS points)	Graduate prospects %	Overall score
1 Cambridge	—	—	74.8	188	—	100
=2 Manchester	76.4	78.5	59.2	158	—	94.1
=2 Ulster	90.0	86.5	54.2	124	—	94.1
4 Reading	71.6	76.1	53.5	132	88.5	89.9
5 Kingston	81.6	75.3	63.0	95	—	88.9
6 Sheffield Hallam	77.9	67.6	43.2	104	84.6	85.4
7 Salford	72.1	72.4	43.5	116	—	84.8
8 Harper Adams	76.7	76.4	—	112	91.7	83.2
9 Birmingham City	74.2	71.7	34.8	108	—	82.7
10 Nottingham Trent	74.9	73.6	38.0	107	75.7	82.1
11 Westminster	67.0	70.7	37.5	116	78.7	81.8
12 Liverpool John Moores	67.4	71.3	28.7	125	—	81.7
13 Royal Agricultural University	80.7	82.1	—	112	79.1	80.5
14 Leeds Beckett	63.0	56.9	24.5	106	—	75.8

Employed in high-skilled job	66%	Employed in lower-skilled job		18%
Employed in high-skilled job and studying	6%	Employed in lower-skilled job and studying		0%
Studying	4%	Unemployed		7%
High skilled work (median) salary	£25,000	Low/medium skilled salary		£20,700

Law

There is consistency at the upper end of our Law table, with eight of the same universities appearing in this year's top 10 as in our previous edition. Other than Cambridge, which continues its reign at No 1, the others have swapped ranks here and there. But only Edinburgh (in joint seventh) and Aberdeen (tenth) have moved into our new top-10 (from tying in 11th place last year) – and both were in it the year before last.

Fourth-place University College London achieved the best results in the recent Research Excellence Framework, while runner-up Glasgow attracted the highest entry standards among its 2021 entrants – a 225 UCAS tariff points. Entry to law degrees can be fiercely competitive at the leading universities and five universities averaged above 200 points in the UCAS tariff in 2021, while 30 averaged over 144 points – equal to AAA at A level. Conversely, 11 had entry standards beneath 100 UCAS points.

Led by Cambridge, which had 95% of graduates employed in high-skilled jobs and/or postgraduate study 15 months after finishing their degrees, the best universities for graduate prospects correlate with the top 10 universities overall, filling the top eight spots (only Aberdeen and Strathclyde place further down for graduate outcomes, in 24th and 34th place on this measure respectively). Queen's Belfast (in joint 22nd overall) ranks ninth for graduate prospects, with 87.4% of law graduates having secured the desired career outcomes within 15 months, and Dundee (15th) sits tenth, with 86.6% of graduates on the same trajectory.

Law graduates who want to become solicitors in England progress to the Legal Practice Course, while those aiming to be barristers take the Bar Vocational Course. In Scotland, most law courses are based on the distinctive Scottish legal system, which also has different professional qualification. About half of law graduates do not go into practise and, perhaps surprisingly, law ranks 46th out of the 70 subject areas in our employment ranking, with a rate of 70% for those in high-skilled work or postgraduate study 15 months after gaining their degrees. Our high-skilled employment measure falls below 60% at five universities: Roehampton, London South Bank, Wolverhampton, West London and Cumbria.

Training contracts for those that go into law keep pay in graduate-level jobs relatively low. But the median salary of £22,000 earned by legal trainees across all universities does not foretell the relative riches to come, and there is a strong case for the delayed career gratification posed by law.

Modern universities have the happiest undergraduates, according to data from the National Student Survey, which shows West London out front for student satisfaction with the broader experience, and Worcester top for students' evaluation of teaching quality. Applications and enrolments of 148,195 and 27,970 respectively were both up once again on the previous year.

Law	Teaching quality %	Student experience %	Research quality %	Entry standards (UCAS points)	Graduate prospects %	Overall score
1 Cambridge	—	—	59.2	199	95.0	100
2 Glasgow	72.2	74.6	66.8	225	88.0	98.6
3 Oxford	—	—	62.0	197	93.8	97.9
4 University College London	73.2	69.2	74.5	198	88.4	97.3
5 King's College London	78.3	69.4	56.2	202	87.6	96.3
6 Strathclyde	78.2	77.0	45.8	207	80.0	94.1
=7 Durham	71.2	65.1	59.5	190	87.6	93.6
=7 Edinburgh	62.8	65.3	64.2	210	87.5	93.6
9 London School of Economics	68.8	64.0	61.3	191	88.2	93.4
10 Aberdeen	76.6	77.6	43.2	195	82.6	93.2
11 Lancaster	82.4	79.4	48.0	142	86.2	92.5
12 Warwick	72.3	72.6	62.0	163	84.0	92.1
13 York	75.0	75.8	49.2	163	83.8	91.4
14 Bristol	66.8	61.9	67.5	175	83.7	91.1
15 Dundee	75.4	73.4	29.2	183	86.6	90.8
16 Leeds	68.1	65.8	66.5	167	81.3	90.5
=17 Exeter	69.4	70.5	54.8	159	84.4	90
=17 Stirling	74.8	70.0	38.5	182	81.1	90
19 Nottingham	72.0	67.5	53.5	159	80.3	89.1
=20 Glasgow Caledonian	77.0	79.7	25.8	202	71.4	88.8
=20 Kent	71.5	69.1	69.8	136	77.0	88.8
=22 Cardiff	67.6	62.8	60.5	150	83.6	88.6
=22 Queen's Belfast	63.1	56.8	62.3	157	87.4	88.6
24 Queen Mary, London	70.9	67.1	57.0	170	74.1	88.4
=25 Birmingham	66.1	65.1	61.5	157	80.6	88.3
=25 Southampton	71.8	72.2	46.5	146	82.7	88.3
27 Manchester	68.5	63.7	40.8	164	85.4	87.8
28 Sheffield	65.6	66.8	55.0	149	83.0	87.6
29 Surrey	75.2	76.4	41.5	127	81.8	87.3

30	Edinburgh Napier	85.7	82.9	5.5	166	76.2	87.2
31	Ulster	78.4	74.3	55.0	130	69.1	86.6
32	Nottingham Trent	77.5	74.7	53.0	115	74.2	86.3
=33	Leicester	74.1	70.6	32.0	132	84.3	86.2
=33	Newcastle	70.6	62.6	41.8	149	81.5	86.2
35	Swansea	79.5	76.8	27.8	131	77.2	85.7
=36	East Anglia	71.7	66.7	32.5	136	80.5	84.5
=36	Royal Holloway, London	69.1	66.7	38.0	125	83.0	84.5
38	Portsmouth	75.9	71.5	26.8	118	79.9	83.8
39	Liverpool	59.8	56.9	51.5	142	80.6	83.5
=40	Bournemouth	70.8	72.4	26.0	102	86.2	83.1
=40	Robert Gordon	76.7	71.1	—	163	77.8	83.1
=42	Essex	66.9	68.7	56.0	108	73.2	82.7
=42	Worcester	89.3	81.5	12.8	103	70.5	82.7
=44	Lincoln	73.5	73.0	32.8	114	74.6	82.6
=44	Northumbria	69.0	64.3	30.8	131	79	82.6
=44	Sussex	66.1	64.4	44.8	131	74.6	82.6
47	Oxford Brookes	—	—	32.5	104	81.1	82.5
48	SOAS, London	60.6	54.8	58.8	142	72.8	82.4
49	London Metropolitan	84.8	82.9	—	98	78.6	81.9
=50	Edge Hill	73.9	76.7	36.0	118	66.0	81.5
=50	Manchester Metropolitan	71.1	71.5	42.8	116	68.0	81.5
=50	Reading	66.4	64.9	33.8	124	77.6	81.5
53	Abertay	73.7	74.9	5.0	153	—	81.4
54	Aston	80.4	75.4	—	130	74.5	81.3
=55	Keele	68.4	64.6	29.5	112	79.9	81.2
=55	Plymouth	73.7	74.2	37.2	111	67.4	81.2
57	Buckingham	81.1	74.9	—	107	79.0	80.9
58	Sunderland	83.3	78.0	—	104	76.3	80.8
59	Brighton	75.0	71.0	28.5	100	72.8	80.6
60	South Wales	74.9	67.0	33.5	111	68.1	80.4
=61	Hertfordshire	74.9	72.2	29.0	99	71.3	80.3
=61	Teesside	78.7	75.7	18.2	105	70.2	80.3
63	Kingston	70.1	68.3	27.0	98	77.8	80.1
=64	Bedfordshire	73.8	70.8	—	104	83.6	79.7
=64	Chester	78.2	72.5	12.8	116	69.2	79.7
=64	Wolverhampton	85.5	84.2	27.8	97	55.3	79.7
=67	Hull	75.1	69.0	11.2	122	71.3	79.3
=67	West of England	64.0	61.8	46.5	111	69.7	79.3
69	Central Lancashire	75.4	71.4	13.2	122	68.7	79.2
70	City	66.2	59.0	34.8	132	68	79.1
71	Liverpool John Moores	73.3	73.6	9.0	127	69.6	79
72	Greenwich	63.8	59.1	37.0	111	74.4	78.9
73	Anglia Ruskin	76.0	69.9	9.8	93	76.5	78.7
74	Salford	68.3	65.4	24.8	115	71.3	78.6
75	Solent, Southampton	79.8	77.8	—	103	71.1	78.5

Law cont.

		Teaching quality %	Student experience %	Research quality %	Entry standards (UCAS points)	Graduate prospects %	Overall score
76	Westminster	69.3	69.6	29.0	109	67.0	78.3
77	Bangor	78.4	76.2	—	122	65.8	78
78	Coventry	72.1	69.9	33.2	103	62.1	77.9
79	De Montfort	72.2	69.5	13.5	95	72.2	77.2
80	Birmingham City	69.3	65.4	9.0	112	71.9	76.6
81	Winchester	69.3	63.1	11.5	103	72.9	76.3
82	West of Scotland	75.3	74.3	—	117	63.8	76.1
83	West London	87.6	84.2	—	104	51.2	75.9
=84	Brunel	57.3	54.8	34.5	117	69.8	75.8
=84	Cumbria	87.3	83.6	—	114	48.4	75.8
=86	Aberystwyth	59.1	58.5	34.2	109	68.8	75.7
=86	Northampton	68.9	60.9	—	105	77.3	75.7
88	Bradford	72.6	73.6	—	114	65.0	75.5
89	Leeds Beckett	70.0	68.5	11.8	103	65.5	75.2
90	Middlesex	65.6	61.2	26.0	99	63.0	74.3
91	St Mary's, Twickenham	76.6	70.6	—	88	64.3	74.1
=92	East London	—	—	17.8	95	66.7	73.9
=92	Sheffield Hallam	72.6	66.4	—	109	63.2	73.9
94	Huddersfield	63.8	58.4	15.2	121	63.6	73.8
95	Derby	70.9	64.4	—	119	61.6	73.6
=96	Canterbury Christ Church	68.9	61.5	16.8	93	61.9	73.1
=96	Gloucestershire	—	—	8.8	108	65.2	73.1
98	Staffordshire	57.2	51.1	18.2	105	69.2	72.1
99	Roehampton	73.2	72.2	—	95	57.1	72
100	London South Bank	71.7	64.9	—	102	56.7	71.2
101	Liverpool Hope	58.2	46.2	—	107	64.3	68.3

Employed in high-skilled job	48%	Employed in lower-skilled job	24%
Employed in high-skilled job and studying	7%	Employed in lower-skilled job and studying	2%
Studying	13%	Unemployed	6%
High skilled work (median) salary	£22,000	Low/medium skilled salary	£20,000

Liberal Arts

Now in its second year, our Liberal Arts table is topped by University College London (UCL), while last year's No 1, Warwick, is runner-up. UCL achieved the top scores in our analysis of the recent Research Excellence Framework 2021 and averaged the highest entry standards (197 UCAS tariff points) among 2021's entrants. Warwick has the most satisfied students however, topping both measures derived from the National Student Survey: teaching quality and the broader experience. At the opposite end of the scale, students at Bristol – in ninth place overall – recorded the lowest rates of satisfaction.

Interdisciplinary by design, liberal arts and humanities degrees encompass the arts, humanities and social sciences, although there is no set formula. They provide undergraduates with opportunities to hone their analysis, communication skills and critical thinking. As students progress through the courses they begin to specialise in areas of particular interest. Formerly the preserve of American universities, liberal arts programmes are a growing area in UK higher education, including Russell Group universities, and elsewhere globally.

The best-employed graduates were from Exeter at the time of the most recent Graduate Outcomes survey, with 79.1% employed in high-skilled jobs and/or postgraduate study 15 months after their degrees. Career paths include roles in the media, communications, PR, politics and art galleries. The subject as an entirety places 36th in our employment ranking of 70, with 54% of graduates employed in high-skilled jobs 15 months on from their degrees, and a further 16% enrolled in postgraduate study or combining it with a good job. Only 5% were unemployed – which is among the lower proportions. Graduates in high-skilled jobs command median salaries of £25,000 and the subjects sit 45th in our pay index – although this is not an ingredient of the subject ranking.

Liberal Arts and Humanities	Teaching quality %	Student experience %	Research quality %	Entry standards (UCAS points)	Graduate prospects %	Overall score
1 University College London	76.1	73.3	67.8	197.0	—	100
2 Warwick	89.7	86.3	61.3	163.0	—	97.5
3 Exeter	68.1	64.7	58.3	168.0	79.1	93.9
4 King's College London	65.6	59.1	62.7	179.0	72.9	93
5 Birmingham	70.4	73.9	56.8	174.0	71.6	92.4
6 Nottingham	84.7	73.7	58.2	148.0	—	92.1
7 East Anglia	—	—	67.5	147.0	65.6	91
8 Leeds	75.9	64.8	47.0	178.0	—	89.1
9 Bristol	59.8	44.2	58.7	167.0	65.2	85.9
10 Royal Holloway	67.8	57.6	53.5	128.0	69.8	84.6
11 Essex	83.2	78.5	40.2	104.0	67.3	81.9
12 Dundee	—	—	40.8	143.0	55.6	75.8

Employed in high-skilled job	54%	Employed in lower-skilled job	22%
Employed in high-skilled job and studying	3%	Employed in lower-skilled job and studying	2%
Studying	13%	Unemployed	5%
High skilled work (median) salary	£25,000	Low/medium skilled salary	£19,600

Linguistics

The scientific study of language, linguistics analyses how language is put together and how it functions, involving its form and meaning as well as how it works in context. The degree can lead to careers in speech therapy, or in the growing field of teaching English as a foreign language.

A reshuffling of our subject table has brought Cambridge into the top spot – boosted by the highest entry standards – up from fifth place last year, while Lancaster moves into second place (an eight-place rise on last year). Warwick has gone from third place last year joint 12th and University College London sits third, just one place off the runner-up spot it held last year. Oxford, formerly a regular incumbent at the top of the table, settles for fourth place for the second year running. For research quality York (in sixth place overall) leads the field in our analysis of the recent Research Excellence Framework 2021.

Students at West of England and Manchester Metropolitan (in that order) gave the most positive feedback for both teaching quality and the wider undergraduate experience in 2021's National Student Survey (NSS).

Jobs-wise, linguistics takes 60th position in our employment ranking of 70 subject areas. Although 42% of graduates were working in high-skilled jobs when surveyed 15 months after their degrees, and a further 19% were furthering their studies, a third of graduates were employed in jobs deemed "low-skilled". Graduates in high-skilled roles command median salaries of £25,000 and linguistics ranks 48th out of 70 in our pay scale.

Linguistics	Teaching quality %	Student experience %	Research quality %	Entry standards (UCAS points)	Graduate prospects %	Overall score
1 Cambridge	—	—	61.0	206	81.2	100
2 Lancaster	78.0	77.2	68.5	144	73.3	99.9
3 University College London	78.1	74.3	56.0	169	72.8	99.6
4 Oxford	—	—	44.0	187	—	99.4
5 Newcastle	77.7	75.3	61.8	152	68.1	97.7
6 York	80.1	77.2	74.8	142	59.3	97.6
7 Swansea	82.2	78.6	60.0	122	—	96.4
8 Edinburgh	66.1	57.6	45.8	184	80.0	96.3
9 Durham	75.6	60.7	46.0	—	82.3*	96.1
10 Manchester	77.8	69.4	59.5	161	62.1	95.9
11 Cardiff	80.4	74.9	55.5	127	—	94.8
=12 Essex	75.7	73.6	65.0	117	—	94.2
=12 Warwick	77.6	69.5	46.2	154	—	94.2
14 King's College London	64.6	58.7	51.2	156	79.2	94.1
15 Manchester Metropolitan	85.2	80.0	61.8	109	60.2	93.6
16 Leeds	75.8	70.4	52.0	144	65.4	93.3
17 West of England	92.6	90.5	32.2	113	—	93.1
18 Reading	74.9	73.3	54.5	126	66.7*	92.4
19 Kent	73.7	75.8	57.5	119	64.5	91.8
20 Sheffield	79.5	72.4	35.8	142	—	90.9
21 Queen Mary, London	73.7	66.6	51.1	124	58.7*	88.3
22 Southampton	67.0	63.7	47.8	—	64.5	87.6
23 Brighton	75.4	64.3	44.2	97	—	84.7
24 Bangor	73.7	66.0	42.0	111	50.6	82.9
25 Hertfordshire	82.3	79.3	9.5	—	58.1*	82.5
26 York St John	68.9	63.7	30.5	106	56.7	80.5
27 Ulster	63.2	61.3	37.0	122	50.0*	79.8
28 Huddersfield	58.9	64.8	25.5	110	—	76.2

Employed in high-skilled job	42%	Employed in lower-skilled job	33%
Employed in high-skilled job and studying	4%	Employed in lower-skilled job and studying	0%
Studying	15%	Unemployed	6%
High skilled work (median) salary	£25,000	Low/medium skilled salary	£19,000

Materials Technology

Courses in this table cover four distinct areas: materials science, mining engineering, textiles technology and printing, and marine technology. These highly specialised subjects attract relatively small student numbers. The prominent research-led universities require maths and physics at A-level, or equivalent, for entry and high grades are the norm.

These are led by Cambridge, also ranking No 1 overall in our table, where entrants in 2021 averaged 221 points in the UCAS tariff. Cambridge is also one of four universities where more than 90% of graduates were employed in high-skilled jobs and/or postgraduate study 15 months on from their degrees. These include Sheffield, Oxford and Birmingham. In our analysis of the recent Research Excellence Framework 2021, Imperial College London is in front for research quality in materials technology.

Swansea is in eighth place overall but has the highest rates of student satisfaction, its undergraduates giving the warmest evaluations of both their teaching quality and the wider experience in the 2021 National Student Survey.

Early career outcomes are promising; materials technology graduates command median salaries of £28,000 in high-skilled jobs and the subject sits 14th in our pay index (although this is not an ingredient of the subject ranking). Fifty-five per cent of graduates were employed in such professional-level work when surveyed 15 months after their degrees, while 20% were enrolled in full-time postgraduate study and 3% were doing both – which adding up to a top 20 place for materials technology in our employment list.

Materials Technology	Teaching quality %	Student experience %	Research quality %	Entry standards (UCAS points)	Graduate prospects %	Overall score
1 Cambridge	—	—	77.2	221	93.5	100
2 Imperial College	80.4	80.8	81.0	180	88.4	96.2
3 Oxford	—	—	77.5	208	92.9	95.9
4 Sheffield	81.0	82.0	66.8	159	93.3	94.2
5 Manchester	83.4	84.2	63.0	154	71.4	90.4
6 Loughborough	78.3	83.7	46.5	153	81.0	89.1
7 Birmingham	69.1	70.7	63.7	148	91.6	88.7
8 Swansea	86.5	87.0	48.8	126	66.7	86.9
9 Exeter	74.6	70.4	47.0	160	—	86.2
10 Queen Mary, London	60.8	76.8	66.0	136	85.1	86.1
11 Huddersfield	80.7	75.1	32.5	139	—	84.5
12 Staffordshire	78.4	74.8	25.5	—	63.8*	80.8
13 Birmingham City	84.4	75.1	17.5	130	61.3	80.7

Employed in high-skilled job	55%	Employed in lower-skilled job	13%
Employed in high-skilled job and studying	3%	Employed in lower-skilled job and studying	0%
Studying	20%	Unemployed	7%
High skilled work (median) salary	£28,000	Low/medium skilled salary	£21,000

Mathematics

Oxford has passed the baton to Cambridge at the top of our Mathematics table and takes the runner-up spot, in an ongoing to-and-fro between the two ancient universities. There is a hair's breadth – or more precisely 0.4% – between the two institutions' overall scores in our subject ranking. QS puts Cambridge and Oxford third and sixth respectively in its world ranking for maths.

Elsewhere in the top 10, the majority of universities feature this year as did in our previous edition. The London School of Economics, however, moves into eighth place (up from 20th) boosted by the top graduate prospects in the table – with 94.6% of its graduates employed in high-skilled jobs and/or postgraduate study 15 months after their degrees. Our analysis of the recent Research Excellence Framework 2021 puts Oxford top for research quality.

With an eye-watering 237 points averaged in the UCAS tariff among 2021's entrants, St Andrews leads on entry standards in a high-tariff table. Eight universities averaged over 200 UCAS points and 29 averaged 144 or higher (where AAA at A-level is equivalent to 144 points).

The leading universities will usually look for extra maths as well as maths at A-level, or equivalent. Courses tend to combine pure and applied maths, but some universities allow for specialising in one or the other.

The best rates of student satisfaction were found at Northumbria (18th in the main table) by the most recent National Student Survey. The university ranks first for both teaching quality and the wider experience. Aberystwyth (joint 35th) is in the top three for each of these student-led measures and Teesside is second for teaching quality. At the opposite end of the scale students at Kingston (68th in the main table) reported the lowest rates of student satisfaction across both metrics, while Leeds (34th overall) is second from bottom for the broader experience and Aston (66th) holds the same spot for teaching quality.

Maths adds up to a promising career for most. The subject is comfortably inside the top-20 of our employment index, with 81% of mathematics graduates in high-skilled employment or postgraduate study 15 months after finishing their degrees. Such expertise commands median starting salaries of £28,000 and the subject ranks 15th out of 70 in our pay index (although this is not an ingredient of our subject ranking).

Mathematics	Teaching quality %	Student experience %	Research quality %	Entry standards (UCAS points)	Graduate prospects %	Overall score
1 Cambridge	—	—	78.0	220	89.3	100
2 Oxford	77.5	68.5	83.2	205	91.5	99.6
=3 Imperial College	77.2	77.5	76.8	205	87.5	98.2
=3 Warwick	77.9	75.1	73.5	199	90.2	98.2
5 St Andrews	84.0	76.8	57.5	237	85.6	98.1
6 Bath	76.2	80.3	61.5	186	89.6	95.6
7 Heriot-Watt	73.1	73.1	66.0	188	90.5	95.4
8 London School of Economics	72.5	69.3	64.0	177	94.6	95.2
9 Glasgow	70.5	68.0	74.5	214	83.9	95
10 Bristol	73.8	71.6	77.0	177	84.5	94.1
11 University College London	74.8	77.6	57.5	186	87.2	93.6
12 Edinburgh	71.0	71.7	66.0	210	82.6	93.5

13 Durham	69.5	65.5	48.8	206	89.3	92.2
14 Lancaster	76.1	72.4	70.0	158	83.8	92.1
15 Manchester	71.6	67.2	66.0	177	83.8	91.4
16 Stirling	78.8	81.8	41.8	181	—	90.6
17 Strathclyde	76.7	76.0	43.2	205	79.3	90.4
18 Northumbria	95.0	93.1	49.0	135	74.6	90.2
19 Exeter	71.2	72.5	64.1	155	83.2	90
20 Loughborough	78.4	81.7	46.5	159	82.6	89.9
21 Nottingham	69.3	66.1	57.5	172	83.0	89
22 Southampton	75.0	73.2	61.5	161	77.2	88.8
23 York	77.2	71.8	55.0	151	80.4	88.6
=24 Birmingham	68.6	68.2	58.8	170	79.7	88.1
=24 East Anglia	83.5	76.9	44.5	143	80.1	88.1
26 Queen's Belfast	70.6	69.4	44.5	163	85.2	88
27 Sheffield	74.4	75.4	59.2	143	77.4	87.4
28 Aberdeen	73.8	72.7	40.0	172	—	87
29 Reading	73.8	68.6	51.5	125	84.3	86.7
30 King's College London	66.2	63.2	59.5	167	77.5	86.3
31 Dundee	74.5	71.5	55.2	183	68.6	86.1
32 Nottingham Trent	78.5	77.6	59.0	108	77.2	86
33 Swansea	72.6	70.9	58.2	138	75.7	85.6
34 Leeds	59.3	57.8	55.2	163	81.8	85
=35 Aberystwyth	89.9	87.6	22.5	136	74.0	84.8
=35 South Wales	87.7	83.8	24.5	—	74.3	84.8
37 Surrey	72.1	72.4	33.5	139	82.2	84.4
=38 Cardiff	69.9	71.2	45.5	144	77.5	84.3
=38 West of England	78.5	74.3	32.2	113	83.1	84.3
40 Kent	73.9	69.8	46.5	126	78.1	84.1
=41 Liverpool	68.3	71.2	43.2	142	78.8	84
=41 Plymouth	84.5	81.7	22.5	130	77.7	84
=43 Liverpool John Moores	83.1	86.1	26.0	123	75.8	83.6
=43 Queen Mary, London	66.9	65.6	51.5	138	77.6	83.6
45 Teesside	91.1	72.0	18.8	123	—	83.1
=46 Essex	72.5	74.8	29.0	115	83.1	82.9
=46 Lincoln	81.5	83.9	17.5	121	79.3	82.9
48 Huddersfield	84.0	77.9	26.5	113	—	82.6
49 Leicester	64.5	65.3	51.7	128	76.5	82.2
50 Newcastle	59.7	58.3	48.0	142	77.7	81.4
51 Keele	79.7	75.3	27.3	120	72.0	80.5
=52 Manchester Metropolitan	77.9	80.1	45.5	113	64.8	80.3
=52 Sussex	67.9	64.5	50.0	135	68.7	80.3
=54 Portsmouth	84.4	83.5	37.2	105	63.6	79.9
=54 Salford	73.1	62.4	33.2	123	—	79.9
=56 Greenwich	77.2	71.8	28.0	102	75.3	79.7
=56 Royal Holloway, London	77.0	72.3	30.2	132	68.5	79.7
58 Coventry	68.7	66.0	36.8	111	75.2	79.4

Mathematics cont.

		Teaching quality %	Student experience %	Research quality %	Entry standards (UCAS points)	Graduate prospects %	Overall score
59	Wolverhampton	89.6	86.7	—	103	74.1	79.3
60	Brunel	71.6	72.0	32.2	111	70.5	78.3
61	City	63.7	59.6	52.0	111	68.5	77.6
62	Brighton	66.4	64.3	32.5	99	75.5	77.5
63	Sheffield Hallam	70.4	69.7	—	104	83.2	77.2
64	Derby	70.3	68.2	—	117	79.6	76.6
65	Hertfordshire	67.0	64.5	45.5	95	64.6	75.4
66	Aston	55.3	58.1	—	115	86.1	74.8
67	Hull	65.7	58.2	—	117	77.4	74
68	Kingston	50.8	53.1	23.5	—	76.4	72

Employed in high-skilled job	59%	Employed in lower-skilled job	12%
Employed in high-skilled job and studying	6%	Employed in lower-skilled job and studying	1%
Studying	15%	Unemployed	7%
High skilled work (median) salary	£28,000	Low/medium skilled salary	£21,000

Mechanical Engineering

Mechanical engineering is the most in-demand strand of engineering by some distance and student numbers have stayed consistently buoyant across the past decade. There is stability careers-wise too; it sits a respectable 23rd in our employment ranking – with 79% of graduates in high-skilled employment and/or postgraduate study 15 months after their degrees. Such professional-level graduate jobs command median salaries of £28,000 and, although pay is not an ingredient of our subject ranking, applicants may be interested to know that the subject ranks 13th out of the 70 tabled in our *Guide* for starting salaries.

Oxford takes the lead in our table this year while last year's winner Cambridge drops one place to sit second – though it still has the highest entry standards of 228 UCAS tariff points among 2021's entrants. A high-tariff subject across the board, mechanical engineering also attracted over 200 UCAS points at Imperial, Oxford and Strathclyde in the same admissions round. But there are more accessible options too; Surrey, for instance, ranks 18th overall and its entrants averaged 132 tariff points, while Liverpool (19th overall) averaged 136 points.

Imperial, a former No 1 in our mechanical engineering table, secured the top research rating in our analysis of the new Teaching Excellence Framework 2021 results. But for rates of student satisfaction a modern university outdoes all others: Teesside is first for both teaching quality and the broader experience – measures derived from the National Student Survey. London South Bank, Sheffield and Bath also fare well in these student-led metrics.

Liverpool John Moores is the leading post-1992 university overall, in 29th position.

Mechanical Engineering

		Teaching quality %	Student experience %	Research quality %	Entry standards (UCAS points)	Graduate prospects %	Overall score
1	Oxford	—	—	77.5	216	92.5	100
2	Cambridge	—	—	77.2	228	96.5	99.3
3	Imperial College	78.3	80.9	81.0	216	90.7	97.9
4	Bath	80.5	82.3	49.5	187	91.6	92
5	Southampton	76.2	79.0	70.0	167	90.0	91.7
6	Sheffield	83.5	87.0	66.8	158	85.2	91.4
7	University College London	71.8	71.9	70.0	181	88.6	90.8
=8	Bristol	69.5	72.2	68.0	187	86.5	90
=8	Strathclyde	70.2	70.8	52.8	216	86.1	90
10	Leeds	68.7	70.1	64.8	177	87.2	88.6
11	Nottingham	70.1	70.0	59.0	148	90.2	86.5
12	Loughborough	71.8	76.7	46.5	154	89.7	86.1
13	Birmingham	71.3	73.6	63.7	154	81.5	85.9
14	Exeter	76.5	75.3	47.0	150	85.6	85.5
15	Glasgow	61.2	66.6	61.5	204	75.1	85.1
16	Manchester	72.1	73.9	63.0	166	74.4	85
17	Edinburgh	57.1	57.0	55.5	187	88.3	84.7
18	Surrey	77.6	77.5	55.2	132	79.7	84.1
=19	Heriot-Watt	62.8	61.0	55.5	172	83.8	83.8
=19	Liverpool	75.1	76.9	57.0	136	78.4	83.8
=21	Aberdeen	72.8	74.4	35.8	171	79.1	83.1
=21	Queen's Belfast	65.4	66.6	51.0	145	87.1	83.1
23	Ulster	73.2	72.7	49.8	127	84.4	82.9
24	Teesside	98.3	93.6	18.8	123	73.8	82.4
25	Lancaster	74.4	74.0	44.8	143	77.5	81.9
26	Newcastle	61.8	62.7	58.5	134	84.5	81.4
27	Cardiff	64.7	73.0	54.0	141	77.9	81.1
28	Nottingham Trent	71.1	72.9	59.0	112	—	80.8
29	Liverpool John Moores	70.5	73.0	45.5	125	80.0	80.4
30	Leicester	70.4	67.3	39.8	130	82.4	80.1
31	Queen Mary, London	59.5	65.5	66.0	136	74.3	79.6
32	Swansea	67.2	68.0	48.8	129	78.1	79.5
33	Robert Gordon	74.9	72.8	20.5	154	75.0	78.7
34	Edinburgh Napier	77.8	70.2	22.8	140	—	78.4
35	Hull	69.6	68.0	36.2	120	80.9	78.3
36	Dundee	56.2	62.3	50.2	175	69.2	78.2
37	Aston	65.7	67.3	35.2	135	77.4	77.5
38	West of England	71.5	71.1	30.8	134	73.8	77.3
39	Coventry	74.4	77.8	23.5	117	77.1	77.2
40	Manchester Metropolitan	71.9	69.9	45.5	123	64.6	76
41	Portsmouth	73.4	71.7	21.0	111	78.1	75.8
=42	Northumbria	53.0	59.0	43.0	134	79.1	75.6

Mechanical Engineering cont.

		Teaching quality %	Student experience %	Research quality %	Entry standards (UCAS points)	Graduate prospects %	Overall score
=42	Sussex	62.0	69.6	29.5	138	74.4	75.6
44	Harper Adams	83.2	78.5	—	120	74.3	75.2
45	London South Bank	83.9	83.7	27.3	110	60.7	75.1
=46	Glasgow Caledonian	68.8	68.2	12.8	156	69.8	74.7
=46	Hertfordshire	72.0	64.6	33.0	100	75.2	74.7
48	Bournemouth	76.2	80.8	14.0	104	—	74
=49	Huddersfield	68.5	65.3	32.5	103	73.4	73.9
=49	Plymouth	61.4	60.5	32.5	122	74.9	73.9
51	Sunderland	75.8	78.2	29.2	—	58.3	73.5
52	Bradford	74.4	71.8	27.0	116	64.3	73.4
53	Staffordshire	70.4	67.9	25.5	108	68.0	72.4
54	Brighton	66.7	63.4	36.5	97	69.2	72.3
55	Oxford Brookes	67.7	63.5	18.0	115	72.6	72.2
56	Greenwich	62.7	58.0	31.5	115	69.0	71.6
=57	Derby	70.0	68.6	14.0	123	65.6	71.3
=57	Lincoln	54.8	58.4	24.0	114	77.8	71.3
59	Brunel	57.4	57.9	33.0	126	67.4	71.1
60	East London	71.4	72.5	21.2	85	—	70.9
61	De Montfort	66.9	66.4	21.8	101	69.1	70.8
62	Sheffield Hallam	55.1	49.0	30.0	114	74.4	70.3
63	Central Lancashire	61.2	61.3	23.0	111	69.0	70.1
=64	Salford	44.5	49.8	33.2	132	69.4	68.8
=64	West of Scotland	65.6	67.1	16.5	—	63.6	68.8
=66	Birmingham City	64.5	64.2	17.5	119	59.6	68.4
=66	City	53.2	51.0	32.5	109	68.1	68.4
68	Chichester	60.9	57.6	12.5	109	—	67
69	Kingston	55.4	60.0	17.2	102	47.6	61.5

Employed in high-skilled job	65%	Employed in lower-skilled job		14%
Employed in high-skilled job and studying	3%	Employed in lower-skilled job and studying		1%
Studying	10%	Unemployed		7%
High skilled work (median) salary	£28,000	Low/medium skilled salary		£23,000

Medicine

Ever in demand, medicine posed an especially competitive field in 2022 following a unique set of circumstances. The number of places on undergraduate medical degrees in England is strictly regulated by the government, which, in light of higher demand and higher A-level grades in the pandemic, lifted the cap on numbers in 2020 and 2021, leading to more than 10,000 places being accepted. A number of students had to defer starting their training until 2022, while the cap on numbers was returned to the pre-pandemic level of 7,500. The upshot for applicants was that 85% of UK students who applied to study medicine to start in autumn 2022 were rejected outright. Only 15.6% of applicants were offered a place in 2022, down from 20.4% in 2021.

The opening of several new medical schools since 2019 at Sunderland, Lincoln, Edge Hill, Kent/Canterbury Christ Church and Anglia Ruskin has not been sufficient to meet demand for places. Those applying for 2023 entry, or deferred entry in 2024, should face a slightly less pressured environment, but high grades are a constant in medicine.

The Scottish universities dominate our Medicine table's entry standards measure, led by Dundee (in third place overall) with 244 points in the UCAS tariff among its 2021 entrants, followed by Aberdeen (which ranks six in the main table) with 240, and Glasgow with 236 points.

Oxford, which has topped the medicine ranking for more than a decade, is comfortably No 1 again, while Glasgow retains second place once again.

Medicine is unique among our 70 subjects for offering a guarantee of employment at the end of the course. Seven medical schools – Swansea, Bristol, Lancaster, Sheffield, Plymouth, Hull-York and Buckingham – report 100% graduate employment, and St Andrews, with the lowest rate, still reports 94.3% of medicine graduates in high-skilled jobs or further study after 15 months. The consistency of graduate prospects means we do not use the measure to help calculate our rankings to avoid small differences distorting positions (although the percentages are shown for guidance). Medicine tops our employment ranking of 70 subject areas and its starting salaries are second only to those offered by dentistry degrees, with medicine graduates commanding median pay of £34,000 a year.

In such a compressed ranking, with just two medical schools scoring less than 80 points overall, success in our tables other four metrics is spread around. Fourth-place Queen's Belfast has the highest rates of student satisfaction with teaching quality, while Aberdeen comes top for students' evaluation of the wider experience. Lancaster does well to rank second for both measures, which are derived from the National Student Survey. At the opposite end of the scale, students at Nottingham (32nd overall) and St George's (31st) reported the lowest rates of satisfaction.

Occupying ninth place in the main table, Cambridge was the top scorer in the recent Research Excellence Framework 2021, followed by Bristol (12th overall) , University College London (13th) and Leicester 10th).

Medicine	Teaching quality %	Student experience %	Research quality %	Entry standards (UCAS points)	Graduate prospects %	Overall score
1 Oxford	—	—	67.5	202	98.1	100
2 Glasgow	74.4	71.0	68.5	236	98.1	99.2
3 Dundee	75.1	77.1	57.0	244	97.4	98.4
4 Queen's Belfast	85.3	81.6	66.2	187	99.0	97.3
5 Swansea	79.1	70.7	66.8	—	100	96.2
6 Aberdeen	83.5	84.5	30.5	240	99.5	95.5
7 Edinburgh	70.2	66.8	64.0	227	99.1	95.4
8 Imperial College	76.9	78.2	68.5	190	99.0	95.3
9 Cambridge	—	—	76.2	212	99.6	94.8
10 Leicester	79.9	80.7	70.2	167	99.6	94.2
11 St Andrews	80.5	78.6	45.5	212	94.3	93.9
12 Bristol	75.8	71.7	71.8	180	100	93.8
13 University College London	69.9	69.6	70.8	188	97.8	92.6
14 Lancaster	84.6	82.3	55.0	164	100	92
15 Queen Mary, London	71.8	71.7	58.0	193	98.7	91.2

		Teaching quality %	Student experience %	Research quality %	Entry standards (UCAS points)	Graduate prospects %	Overall score
16	Cardiff	79.6	79.3	43.2	187	99.1	90.4
17	Keele	81.7	77.1	49.0	170	98.0	90
18	King's College London	70.6	65.8	65.5	174	99.7	89.5
=19	Birmingham	71.3	68.9	59.8	175	98.9	89
=19	Exeter	71.2	71.6	53.2	185	99.0	89
21	Sheffield	73.4	70.7	51.0	169	100	87.2
22	Newcastle	72.6	65.6	50.7	175	99.6	87.1
23	Manchester	65.5	59.3	61.3	179	98.9	87
24	East Anglia	70.5	72.1	50.0	172	98.8	86.7
25	Liverpool	72.9	73.7	46.8	169	99.6	86.5
=26	Hull-York Medical School	66.1	60.6	61.2	167	100	85.9
=26	Plymouth	78.0	75.7	38.2	165	100	85.9
28	Leeds	72.8	69.7	39.5	179	99.6	85.6
29	Brighton and Sussex Medical School	78.4	74.8	32.0	169	99.3	85
30	Southampton	64.1	59.3	49.5	166	99.5	82.5
31	St George's, London	59.9	56.6	50.2	175	98.9	82.3
32	Nottingham	59.9	52.6	54.0	168	99.7	81.8
33	Sunderland	69.8	69.1	30.2	162	—	80.7
34	Warwick	68.2	60.3	23.2	—	99.0	75.5
35	Buckingham	66.1	61.4	—	129	100	68.3

Employed in high-skilled job	92%	Employed in lower-skilled job	0%
Employed in high-skilled job and studying	5%	Employed in lower-skilled job and studying	0%
Studying	3%	Unemployed	0%
High skilled work (median) salary	£34,000	Low/medium skilled salary	£20,000

Middle Eastern and African Studies

Exeter takes the lead in our new Middle Eastern and African Studies table, its position boosted by being the top scorer in the recent Research Excellence Framework 2021. SOAS leads for student satisfaction with teaching quality, while Exeter does best in its students' eyes for the broader experience. Entry standards are by far the highest at Oxford.

The small student numbers on courses within this ranking make for big swings in the statistics, which in turn create plenty of movement in our table. This edition is a prime example, as no universities occupy the same rank this year as last.

Student numbers on single honours degrees are tiny and continuing to decline: 225 undergraduates began Middle Eastern studies courses in 2021 and none enrolled on single-honours African studies degrees. But modules from the courses in this grouping will have been taken by many students as part of broader-area studies courses. The subjects are afforded some official protection because they are of national importance and considered vulnerable.

The absence of graduate prospects scores for most universities in our table is due to student cohorts being insufficient to meet the response threshold for our employment ranking. As a grouping, however, the subjects occupy the midpoint of our jobs table, in 35th place, with 73% of graduates in high-skilled employment and/or postgraduate study 15 months after their degrees. They do better in our earnings ranking – placing 20th – with graduates in high-skilled jobs commanding median salaries of £27,000 a year.

Middle Eastern and African Studies	Teaching quality %	Student experience %	Research quality %	Entry standards (UCAS points)	Graduate prospects %	Overall score
1 Exeter	76.6	75.0	65.8	146	—	100
2 Oxford	—	—	62.3	191	—	97.2
3 Cambridge	—	—	45.2	201	—	96.4
4 SOAS, London	79.2	60.6	60.0	144	79.3	96
5 Edinburgh	66.0	68.8	51.7	168	—	93.7
6 Leeds	69.6	68.2	52.0	151	—	92.4
7 Manchester	58.7	52.8	52.5	153	72.1*	88.2

Employed in high-skilled job	58%	Employed in lower-skilled job	20%
Employed in high-skilled job and studying	7%	Employed in lower-skilled job and studying	1%
Studying	8%	Unemployed	7%
High skilled work (median) salary	£27,000	Low/medium skilled salary	—

Music

Reflecting music's many contrasting genres, courses in our subject ranking vary considerably in style and content – from the practical and vocational programmes in conservatoires to the more theoretical degrees in older universities, via sonic arts, creative sound design and everything in between elsewhere.

Oxford's strength in undergraduate music provision is the most eminent this year, buoyed by the second-best graduate prospects and the seventh-highest entry standards. Durham, a regular in the No 1, slips to 11th place this year while Royal Holloway moves up to second place from fifth, its ranking boosted by achieving the highest scores in our analysis of the new Research Excellence Framework 2021.

In 24th place overall, the Royal Northern College of Music ranks first out of the six specialist institutions, closely followed by the Royal Conservatoire of Scotland in joint 25th. Entry standards tip over the 200 UCAS tariff point mark at two universities, Glasgow and Edinburgh, while no universities averaged beneath 103 UCAS tariff points (at Canterbury Christ Church and Middlesex) among 2021's intake of students.

The best rates of student satisfaction are often found at post-1992 universities – in music's case at Huddersfield (joint 18th overall), where students regarded the teaching quality on their courses more highly than those at any other university. Bucking this trend though is 1495-founded Aberdeen (14th overall) which got the top scores for the wider undergraduate experience and the second-best for teaching quality.

Music ranks above the other performing arts in our employment table, in 54th place. When surveyed 15 months on from their degrees, 50% of graduates were working in high-skilled jobs and 13% were enrolled in postgraduate study or doing both. Conversely, nearly three in 10 graduates (29%) were being employed in work classed as "low-skilled", but only 6% were unemployed – no higher than degrees including chemical engineering and geology. Music places second to bottom on the earnings table, however.

Music

		Teaching quality %	Student experience %	Research quality %	Entry standards (UCAS points)	Graduate prospects %	Overall score
1	Oxford	—	—	49.2	185	89.8	100
2	Royal Holloway, London	75.2	74.7	78.5	167	79.3	99
=3	Cambridge	—	—	71.0	194	88.3	98.5
=3	Manchester	80.4	79.3	66.5	196	66.3	98.5
5	Southampton	80.0	79.2	58.8	169	81.1	98.2
6	Leeds	77.2	72.2	65.2	178	75.9	97.5
=7	Glasgow	72.5	70.0	60.5	207	69.6	96.9
=7	Sheffield	86.6	78.3	57.0	160	75.3	96.9
9	Bangor	87.6	83.0	42.0	134	91.9	96.8
10	Guildhall School of Music and Drama	81.8	77.8	61.3	144	82.4	96.5
11	Durham	72.0	64.5	59.5	198	74.1	96.2
12	Birmingham	75.8	75.1	50.2	169	82.6	95.9
13	Bristol	77.9	74.1	64.2	169	71.9	95.6
14	Aberdeen	89.3	86.4	31.0	179	69.8	95
15	York	80.4	79.9	54.8	149	77.8	94.7
=16	Edinburgh	64.8	70.5	59.2	203	69.0	94.3
=16	King's College London	64.7	63.5	72.2	160	82.1	94.3
=18	Huddersfield	89.6	84.5	71.5	124	66.0	94.2
=18	Surrey	85.7	79.9	43.8	155	75.1	94.2
20	Cardiff	79.3	74.3	50.5	155	73.5	92.8
21	Nottingham	75.3	69.9	62.7	135	76.0	91.8
22	Birmingham City	80.6	71.5	46.5	136	75.5	90.7
23	Ulster	83.4	83.9	49.0	119	73.0	90.6
24	Royal Northern College of Music	76.4	71.6	34.0	133	86.1	90.2
=25	Coventry	84.8	74.5	55.5	112	—	89.4
=25	Royal Conservatoire of Scotland	71.0	60.0	35.2	162	80.0	89.4
27	Newcastle	69.8	62.8	59.2	154	67.8	89.2
=28	City	67.5	58.1	66.5	142	—	88.3
=28	Sunderland	77.4	67.4	49.8	—	66.7*	88.3
30	West of England	85.4	77.0	48.2	118	65.8	88.2
31	Royal Academy of Music	78.0	73.4	20.0	127	86.6	88.1
32	Liverpool	80.3	78.9	43.8	156	55.4	88
33	Queen's Belfast	72.5	69.1	46.8	146	67.2	87.6
34	Westminster	66.6	63.5	75.5	125	65.9	87.4
35	Sussex	77.1	66.3	48.0	139	65.4	87.3
36	Edinburgh Napier	78.0	79.4	8.5	186	63.0	87.2
=37	Hull	86.0	79.7	35.0	124	64.4	87
=37	Salford	81.3	78.7	30.2	138	66.3	87
39	Portsmouth	86.2	83.5	30.2	117	—	86.7
40	Kingston	74.5	75.1	45.0	114	70.8*	86
41	Trinity Laban	71.3	67.6	38.0	124	75.6	85.6
42	Royal College of Music	78.8	72.2	45.5	125	61.8	85.5

43	York St John	84.2	77.9	33.2	106	67.6	85
44	South Wales	78.0	72.0	35.8	127	64.1	84.7
45	Brunel	80.2	74.8	38.0	113	—	84.6
=46	Gloucestershire	82.5	76.5	23.8	123	66.7	84.5
=46	Middlesex	82.7	78.4	26.0	103	72.1*	84.5
48	Winchester	85.2	84.7	32.5	122	54.8	84.3
49	Falmouth	78.3	71.9	48.8	109	61.8	84.2
50	East London	84.9	80.2	13.0	127	65.4	84
51	Leeds Arts	89.2	85.2	2.8	129	—	83.9
=52	Bournemouth	78.0	70.1	38.5	109	65.5	83.3
=52	Canterbury Christ Church	83.2	67.9	38.5	103	64.0	83.3
54	Manchester Metropolitan	69.7	62.8	51.7	—	59.3*	83.1
55	Brighton	71.8	62.4	53.0	110	—	82.8
56	Plymouth	69.2	59.2	49.8	120	—	82.3
57	Goldsmiths, London	57.7	45.4	46.8	135	72.6	81.9
58	Chester	74.7	61.1	21.0	141	63.2	81.7
59	Hertfordshire	80.1	74.3	24.2	109	63.4	81.6
60	Keele	71.8	65.1	30.5	129	—	81.3
61	De Montfort	81.3	65.6	45.0	117	48.7	81.1
=62	Bath Spa	73.0	66.1	26.0	124	63.6	81
=62	Lincoln	73.6	62.1	37.2	116	—	81
64	Leeds Beckett	79.9	74.9	15.8	114	63.2	80.7
65	Leeds Conservatoire	78.5	71.9	—	134	65.4	80.4
66	Staffordshire	86.7	82.7	31.5	128	36.4	80.2
67	West London	67.3	64.1	32.2	129	59.6	79.9
68	West of Scotland	69.4	55.9	19.2	148	59.8	79.6
69	Chichester	70.3	65.8	13.2	139	57.9	78.5
=70	Greenwich	79.5	70.3	—	136	52.7	77.4
=70	Liverpool Hope	70.6	76.4	17.5	116	56.2*	77.4
72	Wolverhampton	77.0	70.8	6.8	124	55.2	77.3
73	Anglia Ruskin	53.8	52.8	61.8	—	53.5	76.9
74	Oxford Brookes	68.8	66.6	21.5	110	—	76.1
75	Edge Hill	76.2	76.5	—	131	44.4	74.6
76	Solent, Southampton	70.9	70.5	—	112	54.7	73.5
77	Central Lancashire	53.4	51.8	19.0	122	57	72
78	Northampton	61.3	55.8	12.2	112	—	70.7
79	Kent	60.1	58.4	—	121	53.6	70.3

Employed in high-skilled job	50%	Employed in lower-skilled job	29%
Employed in high-skilled job and studying	5%	Employed in lower-skilled job and studying	2%
Studying	8%	Unemployed	6%
High skilled work (median) salary	£22,000	Low/medium skilled salary	£18,345

Natural Sciences

Natural sciences degrees give students the benefit of studying across different scientific disciplines as well as the flexibility to specialise in areas of specific interest as programmes progress. The subject's interdisciplinary approach should provide graduates with a breadth of knowledge and practical skills that will stand them in good stead for future careers in industry or for postgraduate research. Some universities offer the opportunity to transfer to a single science after a year, if a student decides their interests lie in one particular direction.

One of three new subject rankings to join our *Guide* last year, the first Natural Sciences table was topped by Cambridge, as is the second edition. Cambridge was by far the leading scorer in the recent Research Excellence Framework 2021 and, with 221 points averaged in the UCAS tariff by its 2021 entrants, it also has the highest entry standards. Runner-up Durham has the best graduate prospects, with almost all (94%) of graduates in high-skilled jobs or postgraduate study within 15 months.

Entry standards are high almost throughout the table, with no universities averaging lower than 167 points (East Anglia, in tenth place) in the UCAS tariff.

This is the first year that we have had sufficient data to include natural sciences in our employment and salaries rankings. The subject has joined with a splash – ranking seventh for career outcomes, with almost six in 10 graduates employed in high-skilled jobs 15 months after their degrees, a quarter enrolled in full-time postgraduate study, and 5% combining both. The subject places even higher for pay – in sixth place. Graduates in professional-level jobs command median salaries of £30,000 per year.

Natural Sciences	Teaching quality %	Student experience %	Research quality %	Entry standards (UCAS points)	Graduate prospects %	Overall score
1 Cambridge	—	—	73.5	221	92.1	100
2 Durham	78.1	73.0	53.0	207	94.0	92.4
3 York	83.8	79.2	66.0	187	79.8	90.6
4 University College London	69.6	68.6	64.0	184	89.5	89.2
5 Exeter	85.3	86.7	59.3	176	78.9	88.8
6 Bath	71.9	72.6	49.2	187	89.5	87.5
7 Nottingham	76.5	79.8	57.9	178	80.0	87
8 Loughborough	87.4	89.5	41.0	168	80.0	85.5
9 Leeds	70.8	73.0	50.2	182	—	85
10 East Anglia	70.2	66.0	56.0	167	78.9*	83
11 Lancaster	74.5	72.7	—	171	93.3	78.3

Employed in high-skilled job	59%	Employed in lower-skilled job	6%
Employed in high-skilled job and studying	5%	Employed in lower-skilled job and studying	0%
Studying	25%	Unemployed	5%
High skilled work (median) salary	£30,000	Low/medium skilled salary	£19,337

Nursing

Following the pandemic-induced boom in applications and enrolments to nursing degrees, new student nurse numbers fell by 10% in 2022, with 29,440 student nurses accepted onto programmes, down from 32,705 in 2021. The total number of applicants also decreased by 8%, from 9,140 in 2021 to 8,405 in 2022.

Reaching to 75 universities, our Nursing table shows there is breadth in options available to those considering nursing. Glasgow has taken the lead in our new subject ranking, up from second place in our previous edition. With 213 UCAS points among 2021's entrants it has the highest entry standards, and it also comes top for students' evaluation of teaching quality and the broader experience. Edinburgh, last year's winner has been overtaken by Sheffield this year. Sheffield's rank is boosted by achieving the second-best scores for teaching quality and the wider university experience – measures based on the outcomes of the National Student Survey.

In our analysis of the recent Research Excellence Framework 2021 results, King's College London (in joint 13th place overall) scores the highest, followed by Manchester (15th overall) and Southampton (10th).

In other subject rankings it is often the modern universities that lead scores for student satisfaction with teaching quality and the wider university experience, but in nursing there is a healthy mix of Russell Group and modern universities succeeding in these areas. For teaching quality, Greenwich (joint 31st) and Roehampton (joint 39th) come after Glasgow and Sheffield, and for the broad experience Ulster and Greenwich follow the same top two. At the opposite end of the scale nursing students at Birmingham are much less content, and the university comes bottom in each student-led measure, while Sheffield Hallam is second from bottom for both.

There is a near guarantee of employment on graduation and three universities – Liverpool, Queen Margaret and Manchester – record a perfect 100% score of graduates being employed in professional-level jobs or enrolled in postgraduate study 15 months after their degrees. Pay, though not an ingredient of our subject ranking, is a topic of hot debate in nursing. Graduates in professional-grade jobs command median salaries of £24,907, and the subject ranks 27th out the 70 featured in our *Guide*.

Nursing	Teaching quality %	Student experience %	Research quality %	Entry standards (UCAS points)	Graduate prospects %	Overall score
1 Glasgow	90.7	88.8	63.5	213	94.1	100
2 Sheffield	87.5	86.1	63.7	151	—	97.9
3 Edinburgh	85.0	82.4	55.2	185	96.8	97.3
4 Cardiff	78.2	67.7	58.8	168	98.3	95.4
5 Exeter	73.4	74.0	54.5	154	—	94.3
6 Surrey	79.1	75.6	58.0	147	98.6	94.2
7 Ulster	86.1	84.6	53.5	133	99.0	94.1
8= Bangor	77.1	68.3	59.8	146	98.5	93.6
8= Queen's Belfast	75.7	75.4	66.2	135	99	93.6
10 Southampton	73.3	65.9	69.8	147	97.6	93.5
11 Keele	76.6	67.5	66.2	140	97.9	93.3
12 York	77.2	73.4	65.0	140	97.3	93.1
13= King's College London	66.9	56.6	76.2	141	98.6	92.9
13= Swansea	64.8	54.6	66.8	154	98.7	92.9
15 Manchester	66.1	60.0	71.2	145	97.6	92.3
16= Dundee	77.8	66.5	60.8	128	98.7	92.2
16= Liverpool	74.7	73.3	46.8	134	100	92.2

Nursing cont.

		Teaching quality %	Student experience %	Research quality %	Entry standards (UCAS points)	Graduate prospects %	Overall score
18	Leeds	61.8	53.5	65.0	149	99.0	92.1
19	Edinburgh Napier	84.2	80.5	40.5	131	98.4	92
20	Nottingham	65.8	55.9	66.8	138	98.9	91.8
21	Glasgow Caledonian	69.9	62.0	61.0	140	97.9	91.7
22	Coventry	76.6	70.7	47.2	134	98.5	91.6
23=	Queen Margaret, Edinburgh	72.7	63.5	36.5	141	100	91.3
23=	West London	84.9	79.7	29.5	138	97.5	91.3
25	Hull	64.7	54.9	55.5	141	99.4	91.2
26	Northumbria	64.5	57.7	53.5	142	98.6	90.8
27	East Anglia	66.2	58.9	55.5	132	98.7	90.4
28	Derby	78.1	70.2	24.0	140	98.5	90.2
29=	Manchester Metropolitan	67.3	61.6	36.0	135	100	90
29=	Plymouth	67.6	57.9	39.5	141	98.7	90
31=	Greenwich	87.4	84.4	32.3	115	97.2	89.9
31=	Portsmouth	71.5	65.4	41.2	126	99.1	89.9
33=	Kingston	79.4	75.7	38.5	127	96.4	89.7
33=	Salford	66.8	57.7	37.0	140	98.9	89.7
35	Lincoln	58.9	60.0	55.8	136	97.5	89.4
36=	Hertfordshire	78.6	72.1	48.0	115	96.5	89.2
36=	Stirling	70.2	60.4	44.0	136	96.5	89.2
38	Teesside	70.1	61.3	35.0	126	99.3	89.1
39=	Brighton	65.5	58.9	50.5	125	98.1	89
39=	Roehampton	86.7	82.1	37.5	103	—	89
41=	Leeds Beckett	70.5	63.9	38.0	123	98.5	88.9
41=	South Wales	66.0	53.8	25.2	152	98.0	88.9
43	Oxford Brookes	72.1	63.3	37.8	128	97.4	88.8
44=	Birmingham City	68.0	61.9	37.8	130	97.8	88.6
44=	Liverpool John Moores	71.6	69.1	26.5	149	95.0	88.6
46=	Central Lancashire	63.6	52.3	35.5	140	97.8	88.3
46=	City	63.7	59.4	58.0	136	94.1	88.3
46=	London South Bank	73.9	67.2	34.5	120	97.6	88.3
49	Robert Gordon	76.5	66.8	24.5	130	96.9	88.2
50=	Bedfordshire	77.6	70.5	22.5	121	97.7	88.1
50=	Canterbury Christ Church	74.0	61.9	31.8	126	97.0	88.1
52=	Staffordshire	70.7	60.3	30.8	124	98.2	87.9
52=	West of England	59.6	48.7	42.8	132	98.4	87.9
54=	Birmingham	45.6	42.3	55.0	146	97.3	87.7
54=	Chester	66.5	52.9	31.0	126	98.9	87.7
56	Bradford	61.7	59.9	33.8	138	96.5	87.5
57=	Huddersfield	64.0	58.8	22.5	134	98.4	87.4
57=	De Montfort	68.7	60.6	20.8	123	99.1	87.3
59	Wolverhampton	65.7	57.7	24.2	133	97.6	87.2

60 Bournemouth	67.7	57.7	29.2	114	98.9	86.9
61 West of Scotland	73.5	59.5	30.8	141	92.8	86.8
62= Middlesex	74.5	70.2	22.5	111	97.3	86.6
62= Sheffield Hallam	55.8	48.6	29.8	128	99.5	86.6
62= Northampton	68.1	62.4	5.0	133	98.5	86.5
65 Essex	68.2	60.4	28.5	111	98.3	86.4
66 Worcester	62.4	55.4	24.2	124	97.5	85.9
67 Cumbria	67.3	59.7	18.5	128	96.2	85.7
68 Anglia Ruskin	81.2	73.0	33.8	119	90.5	85.5
69 Buckinghamshire New	81.8	77.8	16.8	107	94.5	85.4
70= Edge Hill	62.4	57.8	22.2	138	92.6	84.4
70= Gloucestershire	63.6	57.3	16.2	127	—	84.3
72 Suffolk	67.9	58.3	—	118	98.1	84.3
73 Sunderland	67.1	57.3	30.2	131	90.8	83.9
74 East London	59.3	58.2	25.5	111	—	82.8
75 Bolton	74.8	71.0	2.0	141	82.5	79.6

Employed in high-skilled job	95%	Employed in lower-skilled job	1%
Employed in high-skilled job and studying	3%	Employed in lower-skilled job and studying	0%
Studying	1%	Unemployed	1%
High skilled work (median) salary	£24,907	Low/medium skilled salary	£20,400

Pharmacology and Pharmacy

The disciplines of pharmacology and pharmacy are entirely different, leading to separate careers. Most English universities offer only one or the other, and courses are evenly split among institutions. The four-year MPharm degree is a direct route to professional registration as a pharmacist and the most popular option, or students can study three-year degrees in pharmaceutical science or as part of a broader degree. Pharmacology is available as a three-year BSc or as an extended course.

Strathclyde maintains its lead in our table for the second consecutive year. The university averaged the highest entry standards in 2021 (224 points in the UCAS tariff) and performs strongly across all other measures in our ranking. Strathclyde offers degrees in all three of subjects encompassed in this grouping: pharmacology – which is a branch of medicine concerned with drugs, their uses, effects and how they interact with the human body; pharmacy – which trains and licenses individuals to dispense prescription medicines as pharmacists; and toxicology – which is similar to pharmacology but focuses on the toxic rather than healing properties of venoms, poisons and drugs.

King's College London (in 21st place overall) has the edge for research quality in our analysis of the recent Research Excellence Framework 2021 results. Students at Ulster (placed joint third) were the most satisfied with teaching quality and the broader experience, results of the National Student Survey showed. St George's, London achieved the second-highest scores for teaching quality and Aberdeen for the broad experience.

Solid career prospects are in store for graduates. The subjects maintain a top-10 position in our employment table this year, as they are accustomed to, where they rank seventh this year. The latest data shows more than seven in 10 graduates employed in high-skilled jobs 15 months after their degrees, while 10% were enrolled in postgraduate study full-time and 6% were combining both. Pay offers early career rewards, with the subjects ranking third in our salaries index (behind dentistry and medicine), and with graduates in high-skilled roles commanding median salaries of £31,800.

Pharmacology and Pharmacy

		Teaching quality %	Student experience %	Research quality %	Entry standards (UCAS points)	Graduate prospects %	Overall score
1	Strathclyde	74.8	78.0	65.8	224	92.5	100
2	Queen's Belfast	80.4	85.8	66.2	155	99.1	98
=3	Glasgow	86.9	88.2	63.5	195	81.8	97
=3	Ulster	90.5	90.3	53.5	152	95.3	97
5	Bath	82.0	86.0	63.7	143	93.4	95.1
6	Lincoln	84.3	85.2	55.8	127	100	95
7	Nottingham	78.8	80.5	66.8	149	93.4	94.9
8	Cardiff	80.2	75.6	58.8	159	93.8	94.7
9	University College London	83.2	82.8	57.8	161	88.6	94.2
10	Glasgow Caledonian	79.4	87.4	61.0	159	87.0*	93.6
11	Queen Mary, London	80.9	85.4	54.8	141	—	92.6
12	Queen Margaret, Edinburgh	85.4	75.4	36.5	—	96.2*	92.4
13	Robert Gordon	72.2	71.5	24.5	195	96.3	91.7
14	East Anglia	79.0	75.6	55.5	126	94.5	91.3
15	Birmingham	75.4	78.4	55.0	136	92.5	91
=16	Manchester	68.1	63.9	71.2	152	88.4	90.7
=16	St George's, London	88.4	82.6	50.2	118	—	90.7
18	Newcastle	75.8	73.5	65.8	140	86.5	90.6
19	Leeds	77.3	77.5	52.0	147	86.7	89.9
20	Reading	75.0	77.8	54.0	123	91.9	89.4
21	King's College London	70.7	70.8	76.2	145	79.4	89.1
22	Aberdeen	85.8	88.6	—	172	90.3	88.4
23	Keele	63.5	63.0	66.2	136	90.1	88.2
24	Liverpool John Moores	79.3	80.5	26.5	130	94.5	88
25	Bradford	80.1	81.8	33.8	138	87.9	87.9
26	Sunderland	79.2	71.0	30.2	131	92.4	87.1
27	Swansea	58.8	67.7	66.8	137	—	86.6
28	Liverpool	69.4	70.3	46.8	148	84.9	86.5
29	Bristol	69.9	63.8	57.5	151	77.5	85.6
30	Aston	75.5	78.7	46.0	120	83.5	85.5
=31	Brighton	61.0	59.5	50.5	124	93.0	85
=31	Huddersfield	74.6	78.3	22.5	132	89.9	85
33	Portsmouth	77.8	77.8	41.2	104	86.3	84.7
34	Westminster	76.4	74.1	36.8	111	—	83.2
35	Nottingham Trent	75.3	73.9	43.5	115	77.1	82.2
36	Kent	69.4	67.9	36.8	122	—	81.9
37	Greenwich	73.9	50.7	32.3	121	84.4	81.2
38	Hertfordshire	66.6	66.5	48.0	109	80.1	80.9
39	Wolverhampton	75.8	74.8	24.2	116	80.2	80.6
40	Kingston	71.3	72.3	38.5	115	74.9	79.8
41	De Montfort	69.6	70.2	20.8	109	85.4	79.7
42	Central Lancashire	65.4	66.2	35.5	139	73.9	79.5

Employed in high-skilled job	71%	Employed in lower-skilled job	6%
Employed in high-skilled job and studying	6%	Employed in lower-skilled job and studying	0%
Studying	10%	Unemployed	7%
High skilled work (median) salary	£31,800	Low/medium skilled salary	£21,000

Philosophy

Unbeaten rates of student satisfaction with teaching quality have helped secure the No 1 spot for St Andrews in our philosophy table, for the second consecutive year. The university also achieves the third-best graduate prospects and second-highest entry standards among its strength across all five measures of our ranking. Oxford, which occupied the top of the table two years ago, attracted the highest entry standards in 2021 – with entrants averaging 202 points in the UCAS tariff.

The London School of Economics (LSE) is the runner-up for the second time in a row. With 93.1% of its philosophy graduates working in high-skilled jobs or enrolled in postgraduate study 15 months after their degrees, the LSE comes top for graduate prospects. Cardiff, in 18th place overall, was the top scorer in the recent Research Excellence Framework 2021. Eight of this year's top 10 universities appeared in last year's top-10 too. Only Southampton and York are new arrivals, each having risen from 21st and 20th place respectively in our previous edition.

Kent (joint 14th) does particularly well in the eyes of its students. No universities score higher for student satisfaction with the broad experience and Kent is second only to St Andrews for their evaluation of teaching quality.

Relatively few philosophy degrees require the subject at A-level, and some departments actively discourage it. Degrees involve more maths skills than many candidates expect, especially when the syllabus has an emphasis on logic.

The subject sits in the lower half of our jobs ranking, in 44th place, with 70% of graduates in high-skilled jobs or furthering their studies when surveyed 15 months after their degrees. For salaries – though not an ingredient of the ranking – philosophy compares more favourably with other subjects, placing 33rd.

Philosophy	Teaching quality %	Student experience %	Research quality %	Entry standards (UCAS points)	Graduate prospects %	Overall score
1 St Andrews	90.3	83.6	55.0	195	87.9	100
2 London School of Economics	76.0	74.7	60.0	186	93.1	97.3
=3 Cambridge	—	—	59.0	194	82.4	95
=3 Oxford	—	—	50.7	202	90.1	95
5 Warwick	82.1	77.6	55.8	173	78.6	93.5
6 Southampton	89.1	83.9	59.0	141	76.4	93.1
7 University College London	71.5	67.8	66.8	179	81.1	93
8 Durham	71.7	64.6	47.8	185	85.0	91
9 York	79.8	74.2	66.2	139	75.8	90,9
10 Birmingham	75.6	69.1	66.0	146	78.7	90.7
11 Exeter	76.8	71.8	46.8	164	82.2	90.4
12 King's College London	71.5	64.3	52.2	174	80.8	89.7
13 Edinburgh	69.2	64.7	49.0	170	81.7	88.7
=14 Bristol	67.5	62.1	54.8	162	78.8	87.6

Philosophy cont.

		Teaching quality %	Student experience %	Research quality %	Entry standards (UCAS points)	Graduate prospects %	Overall score
=14	Kent	90.1	86.9	57.2	109	64.3	87.6
16	Stirling	85.3	76.9	36.0	142	—	87.1
17	Aberdeen	86.5	77.9	22.8	164	—	87
18	Cardiff	76.4	68.4	67.2	127	65.0	86
19	Manchester	70.8	61.7	55.5	160	69.9	85.9
20	Sheffield	73.6	70.4	45.5	147	73.3	85.6
21	Reading	83.0	73.6	36.2	119	77.8	85.4
22	Newcastle	68.2	56.4	61.8	135	73.2	84.7
23	Dundee	78.5	73.7	17.8	174	—	84.1
=24	Lancaster	71.5	67.6	49.0	142	68.7	83.8
=24	Oxford Brookes	86.1	81.4	28.2	100	76.8	83.8
26	Nottingham	74.9	65.2	41.5	138	69.9	83.1
27	Glasgow	70.2	62.5	51.0	173	57.7	83
=28	Bangor	81.6	78.1	33.2	133	64.9	82.9
=28	East Anglia	80.2	70.2	38.2	123	69.4	82.9
30	Leeds	64.5	58.6	47.0	151	72.3	82.6
31	Liverpool	74.5	66.3	45.2	131	66.7	82.3
32	Hertfordshire	85.4	76.0	35.0	97	—	82
33	Hull	79.8	80.2	31.5	118	67.4	81.8
34	Sussex	64.5	62.8	49.0	132	69.2	81.1
35	Essex	72.0	67.5	46.5	110	65.6	80.2
36	West of England	79.5	75.9	35.2	104	63.2	79.7
37	Queen's Belfast	67.8	59.0	33.0	144	—	79.1
=38	Manchester Metropolitan	77.7	66.9	41.0	104	56.4	77.6
=38	Royal Holloway, London	69.4	64.6	26.5	125	67.5	77.6
40	Keele	79.6	68.6	9.5	110	70.3	77
41	Nottingham Trent	84.8	76.6	—	114	59.6	74.9

Employed in high-skilled job	44%	Employed in lower-skilled job	23%
Employed in high-skilled job and studying	5%	Employed in lower-skilled job and studying	1%
Studying	20%	Unemployed	7%
High skilled work (median) salary	£25,000	Low/medium skilled salary	£19,909

Physics and Astronomy

A shake-up to the rankings at the top end of our Physics and Astronomy table has ousted St Andrews from No 1 and replaced it with Cambridge. Durham and Oxford (the latter the leader for graduate prospects) have also swapped places this year, and a four-place rise has brought Lancaster into fifth position. Manchester has risen from 12th place last year to joint seventh this, its rank buoyed by the top scores in the new Research Excellence Framework 2021, in which regard it is closely followed by Sheffield and Birmingham.

Famous physicists and astronomers from Galileo Galilei to Marie Curie, Albert Einstein to Stephen Hawking, have helped earn the subjects a reputation for being the rarefied preserves of boffins. But student numbers in astronomy, in particular, have been rising in recent years – a trend dubbed the "Brian Cox effect", due to the University of Manchester particle physicist's work on television that has injected some accessibility and cool to the field.

Even so, entry standards are invariably among the highest in our *Guide* – as evidenced this year by seven universities averaging over 200 points in the UCAS tariff, led by St Andrews with 223 points. Only 18 institutions out of 47 average less than 145 (where 144 points is equal to AAA at A-level).

In a remarkable achievement Leicester (in 24th place overall) has outdone all other universities in the table for student satisfaction with both teaching quality and the wider undergraduate experience – for the second year running. Northumbria and Lancaster also perform strongly in these student-led measures. At the opposite end of the scale, Imperial College London ranks bottom for both – the low rates of student satisfaction holding back its overall ranking to 12th place, in spite of the second-best graduate prospects and entry standards outdone by only three universities.

The subjects translate into positive graduate job and salary outcomes. Occupying ninth place in our pay index (although wages are not an ingredient of our subject ranking), physics and astronomy graduates command median salaries of £28,000.

Physics and Astronomy	Teaching quality %	Student experience %	Research quality %	Entry standards (UCAS points)	Graduate prospects %	Overall score
1 Cambridge	—	—	72.8	221	93.5	100
2 St Andrews	87.1	81.9	65.8	223	84.2	98.8
3 Durham	84.7	78.9	57.2	211	87.8	96.8
4 Oxford	—	—	66.5	214	94.4	96.7
5 Lancaster	88.7	85.7	58.5	165	89.9	96.2
6 Birmingham	72.2	76.2	73.2	190	89.6	95.8
=7 Manchester	69.9	66.8	74.0	195	88.0	94.4
=7 Warwick	78.5	74.6	59.8	185	89.8	94.4
9 Glasgow	68.1	67.4	64.5	217	87.6	93.7
10 Edinburgh	67.1	64.1	62.7	211	89.3	93
11 Strathclyde	81.0	75.1	63.2	190	76.8	92.2
12 Imperial College	59.8	58.3	60.8	214	94.1	92.1
13 Bristol	72.3	67.6	70.5	172	85.1	92
14 Nottingham	78.4	72.9	68.8	169	79.1	91.7
15 Exeter	77.2	78.2	59.2	171	82.3	91.3
16 Cardiff	77.7	76.7	59.2	150	86.2	91
17 University College London	70.4	74.5	55.5	175	87.5	90.6
18 Sheffield	74.5	72.3	73.8	149	79.4	90.5
19 Bath	72.2	71.4	55.5	176	86.5	90.4
20 Heriot-Watt	76.4	81.4	65.5	167	74.0	90
21 York	73.2	72.9	62.7	153	83.1	89.7
22 Southampton	74.1	71.3	52.2	152	87.4	89
23 Queen's Belfast	69.6	66.7	46.8	165	90.2	88.3
24 Leicester	89.7	89.5	44.0	134	75.4	88.2
25 Leeds	65.3	66.7	64.5	158	83.4	88.1
26 Keele	80.5	82.1	49.5	120	84.2	88

Physics and Astronomy cont.

	Teaching quality %	Student experience %	Research quality %	Entry standards (UCAS points)	Graduate prospects %	Overall score
27 Surrey	75.1	68.8	45.5	142	88.2	87.4
28 Royal Holloway, London	70.8	67.0	48.0	140	87.4	86.4
29 Liverpool	68.5	65.1	61.5	140	80.8	86.2
30 Dundee	68.2	69.1	50.2	170	—	86.1
31 Coventry	87.5	85.7	36.8	109	—	85.4
32 Portsmouth	77.6	76.9	68.5	99	71.9	85.3
33 Central Lancashire	85.2	74.0	41.2	—	72.7	85.1
34 Hull	81.5	82.2	45.5	111	76.6	84.8
35 Nottingham Trent	80.7	80.9	59.0	109	69.5	84.7
36 Loughborough	77.7	74.7	39.2	146	77.1	84.6
37 Sussex	72.4	71.2	55.0	145	71.7	84.3
38 Northumbria	87.4	87.6	43.0	142	62.7*	84.2
39 Hertfordshire	73.9	74.5	45.5	96	84.2	83.6
40 West of Scotland	77.3	74.5	31.0	145	—	82.8
41 King's College London	62.1	65.1	49.2	157	73.4	81.7
=42 Newcastle	62.2	58.3	48.0	143	79.2	81.6
=42 Salford	80.3	71.6	33.2	118	75.8	81.6
44 Swansea	67.1	64.4	46.5	136	74.5	81.2
45 Lincoln	80.0	82.8	28.2	110	—	81.1
46 Queen Mary, London	69.1	63.6	48.8	138	67.4	80
=47 Aberystwyth	76.1	77.2	21.0	116	73.5	78.4
=47 Kent	76.2	69.6	32.5	126	67.0	78.4

Employed in high-skilled job	50%	Employed in lower-skilled job	9%
Employed in high-skilled job and studying	4%	Employed in lower-skilled job and studying	0%
Studying	29%	Unemployed	8%
High skilled work (median) salary	£28,000	Low/medium skilled salary	£20,000

Physiotherapy

Formerly part of the "Subjects Allied to Medicine" grouping, the Physiotherapy table is now in its tenth year. Glasgow Caledonian has taken the lead, rising four places since our last edition and boosted by the top entry standards of 208 UCAS points in 2021 – a tariff score shared by overall runner-up Robert Gordon. Strong performance across all other measures by Glasgow Caledonian includes one of the top-four scores in the new Research Excellence Framework 2021 (REF 2021), as well as the second-highest rates of student satisfaction with teaching quality and the wider experience. Based on the outcomes of the National Student Survey, Robert Gordon tops both of these measures.

King's College London (in joint 19th place overall) is top for research quality in our analysis of the REF 2021, where it is followed by Southampton – our table's former No 1, which now takes third place. The post-1992 universities feature prominently in our main physiotherapy ranking, four of them in the top-10.

In joint ninth place overall, West of England has the edge for graduate prospects, with 98.9% of graduates employed in high-skilled jobs and/or furthering their studies 15 months after their degrees.

The subject as a whole places sixth out of 70 in our employment ranking, behind only medicine, nursing, dentistry, radiography and veterinary medicine.

Applications and enrolments to physiotherapy are following an upward trend and increased again in 2021.

Physiotherapy	Teaching quality %	Student experience %	Research quality %	Entry standards (UCAS points)	Graduate prospects %	Overall score
1 Glasgow Caledonian	90.5	92.0	61.0	208	96.1	100
2 Robert Gordon	92.2	92.1	24.5	208	97.8	97.4
3 Southampton	79.7	82.0	69.8	160	96.7	95.8
4 East Anglia	65.2	62.1	55.5	165	100	94.7
5 Northumbria	81.6	85.4	60.5	145	97.7	94.5
6 Nottingham	76.6	67.7	56.0	146	100	94.3
7 Cardiff	74.8	70.0	58.8	161	97.0	94.1
8 Birmingham	67.3	62.9	55.0	168	97.9	93.9
=9 Liverpool	81.3	81.2	46.8	152	98.1	93.8
=9 West of England	84.4	83.3	42.8	148	98.9	93.8
11 Leeds Beckett	84.2	82.2	38.0	155	97.4	93
12 Bradford	80.5	72.1	33.8	149	100	92.9
=13 Brighton	88.6	83.4	50.5	134	96.0	92.1
=13 Salford	88.3	82.4	37.0	140	97.6	92.1
15 Central Lancashire	72.8	59.6	35.5	—	100.0*	92
16 Manchester Metropolitan	75.7	75.0	51.2	144	96.2	91.7
17 Worcester	86.5	87.1	24.2	131	100	91.4
18 Brunel	83.2	81.8	47.2	133	96.3	91.3
=19 King's College London	69.3	61.2	76.2	161	90.2	91.1
=19 Plymouth	84.0	76.6	39.5	152	94.7	91.1
21 York St John	80.3	81.0	13.8	142	100	90.5
22 Ulster	68.8	73.7	53.5	148	94.0	90.3
=23 Hertfordshire	87.2	78.1	48.0	127	94.5	90.1
=23 Keele	65.7	61.9	66.2	154	91.8	90.1
25 Coventry	64.8	61.5	47.2	140	97.1	90
26 Queen Margaret, Edinburgh	86.4	83.2	36.5	—	93.1	89.6
27 Wolverhampton	87.5	86.7	24.2	136	—	89.5
28 Bournemouth	68.9	58.7	29.2	127	100	88.9
29 Teesside	59.5	63.5	35.0	135	98.1	88.5
30 Huddersfield	86.4	84.4	22.2	132	93.6	87.5
31 Oxford Brookes	67.1	63.7	37.8	146	92.9	87.3
32 East London	84.9	87.8	25.5	131	92.5	87.1
33 Sheffield Hallam	61.9	49.6	29.8	146	95.1	86.8
34 Gloucestershire	68.0	60.1	24.5	143	—	86.7
35 Cumbria	54.4	48.2	18.5	134	96.6	84.7
36 London South Bank	45.1	37.7	34.5	121	—	81.7
37 St George's, London	52.6	45.1	—	152	92.0	81.4

Physiotherapy cont.

Employed in high-skilled job	91%	Employed in lower-skilled job	2%
Employed in high-skilled job and studying	3%	Employed in lower-skilled job and studying	0%
Studying	1%	Unemployed	2%
High skilled work (median) salary	£25,000	Low/medium skilled salary	—

Politics

In contrast to the leadership of the UK's current governing party, there is consistency at the top of our Politics table. For the fourth successive year St Andrews takes the No 1 spot, securing its lead by strong performances across all five measures in our table, while Oxford is in second place once more – joined this year by Warwick, which has moved up one place. Only two universities are new to the top-10, ninth-place Surrey – which is up from 19th last year, fuelled by the top rates of student satisfaction with the wider undergraduate experience, and tenth-place Exeter (up from 21st).

Strathclyde, in sixth place overall, was the top scorer in the recent Research Excellence Framework 2021, where it is followed by Royal Holloway, Edinburgh and London School of Economics. Oxford is unbeaten on graduate prospects – due to 93% of its politics graduates being employed in professional-level jobs and/or furthering their studies 15 months after their degrees.

The older universities dominate the upper end of our table. Northumbria – in 24th place – is the top-ranked post-1992 university. But another modern institution, Canterbury Christ Church (in 36th place overall), has outdone all others for student satisfaction with teaching quality and is second only to Surrey for students' evaluation of their wider experience. St Andrews ranks in the top three for both.

Politics ranks in the lower half of our employment table, in 45th place. When surveyed 15 months after their degrees, 48% of graduates were employed in professional-level jobs, 15% were enrolled in postgraduate study and 5% were combining both. These figures vary widely by institution – from Oxford, in the lead, down to Ulster where only 52.2% of graduates had achieved these outcomes in the same timeframe. Pay rates for politics graduates compare more favourably with other subjects, ranking 20th out of 70 subject areas.

Politics	Teaching quality %	Student experience %	Research quality %	Entry standards (UCAS points)	Graduate prospects %	Overall score
1 St Andrews	87.5	81.6	47.0	204	82.2	100
=2 Oxford	—	—	61.3	205	93	98.2
=2 Warwick	82.6	79.6	60.5	169	82.9	98.2
4 Cambridge	—	—	50.2	196	90.7	97.0
5 London School of Economics	71.1	69.1	65.8	180	86.0	96.4
6 Strathclyde	77.6	73.3	70.5	196	67.5	95.9
7 University College London	65.5	68.9	64.5	181	88.3	95.3
8 King's College London	74.1	69.2	52.2	182	84.1	94.7
9 Surrey	85.4	83.7	40.2	121	86.9	93.7
10 Exeter	74.3	72.9	57.5	156	81.3	93.4
11 Glasgow	72.5	68.6	50.2	195	72.5	92.1
12 Edinburgh	63.3	57.8	66.5	186	79.6	92.0
13 York	72.2	68.3	57.5	145	79.8	91.1

14 Bristol	69.2	61.3	50.7	166	83	90.9
15 SOAS, London	74.7	67.5	55.5	158	73.1	90.8
16 Manchester	70.3	62.2	60.5	158	77.2	90.7
17 Royal Holloway, London	74.5	70.2	67.2	124	71.7	89.9
18 Bath	70.9	70.8	31.8	159	86.5	89.8
19 Sheffield	73.8	62.5	58.0	148	72.7	89.5
=20 Durham	64.2	60.0	42.5	177	84.6	89.4
=20 Lancaster	73.2	68.7	49.0	144	77.2	89.4
22 Aberdeen	78.8	78.9	23.5	176	69.5	88.6
23 Aberystwyth	84.6	78.5	42.8	120	66.7	88.3
24 Northumbria	78.5	71.9	42.0	125	74.0	88.0
25 Essex	77.4	74.0	60.5	110	67.1	87.9
=26 Birmingham	68.7	65.3	51.5	148	74.0	87.8
=26 Cardiff	69.5	64.7	49.0	134	79.3	87.8
=26 Sussex	71.8	66.8	55.7	136	71.0	87.8
29 Nottingham	69.0	64.3	46.0	145	78.1	87.6
30 Queen Mary, London	68.8	59.1	61.3	140	70.5	87.2
31 Coventry	83.4	80.6	39.5	95	72.2	87.1
32 Leeds	69.4	66.4	35.8	153	77.8	87.0
33 City	73.3	69.6	40.8	117	79.3	86.8
34 Reading	75.3	73.2	49.2	119	68.6	86.6
35 Loughborough	73.7	73.8	29.5	139	76.2	86.5
36 Canterbury Christ Church	89.0	82.8	13.2	91	79.6	86.4
=37 Southampton	72.0	67.7	39.8	137	74.0	86.3
=37 Stirling	77.9	74.0	28.7	167	62.8	86.3
39 West of England	82.1	77.5	35.2	106	70.1	86.1
40 East Anglia	70.6	64.2	56.2	121	67.5	85.3
41 Plymouth	82.5	76.9	37.9	102	58.7	83.5
42 Leicester	73.0	68.5	36.8	117	68.6	83.4
43 Bournemouth	72.2	65.6	47.2	102	—	83.2
44 Newcastle	65.6	61.8	39.5	141	68.6	82.8
45 Hull	83.0	77.4	11.2	115	67.6	82.7
46 Portsmouth	73.6	66.9	51.7	102	60.8	82.6
47 Bradford	66.8	65.4	31.5	—	74.2*	82.1
48 Keele	72.6	69.4	28.0	108	71.3	82.0
49 Kent	70.0	61.7	41.0	110	66.8	81.5
=50 Huddersfield	79.0	67.7	43.5	107	53.2	81.4
=50 Salford	72.0	63.2	51.7	101	59.5	81.4
52 Westminster	76.5	74.0	41.5	106	54.1	81.3
53 Liverpool	67.0	60.0	39.8	131	63.5	81.1
54 Aston	74.9	70.7	—	116	79.1	81.0
55 Swansea	72.0	57.8	31.5	116	67.1	80.7
56 West of Scotland	83.3	76.2	13.2	—	58.0	80.5
=57 Lincoln	74.8	72.3	34.0	105	57.3	80.2
=57 Nottingham Trent	74.9	71.5	29.5	102	61.4	80.2
=57 Oxford Brookes	70.0	67.2	27.5	105	69.1	80.2

Politics cont.

		Teaching quality %	Student experience %	Research quality %	Entry standards (UCAS points)	Graduate prospects %	Overall score
=60	Brunel	74.2	68.3	35.0	92	62.3	80.0
=60	Manchester Metropolitan	76.5	67.8	29.0	108	58.9	80.0
=62	Chester	78.5	72.3	12.8	99	65.6	79.6
=62	Queen's Belfast	56.4	48.7	40.8	140	70.7	79.6
64	Ulster	70.4	58.8	53.8	107	52.2	79.5
65	Brighton	75.7	57.0	44.2	93	54.3	78.7
66	Sheffield Hallam	85.6	77.7	—	103	58.6	78.6
67	Dundee	69.8	68.4	—	177	56.5	78.3
68	Liverpool Hope	79.9	73.8	5.5	105	59.6	77.9
69	Leeds Beckett	79.2	74.8	15.5	89	57.4	77.7
70	Winchester	73.7	54.7	19.8	98	64.8	77.1
71	London Metropolitan	77.7	73.5	—	90	64.1	76.4
72	De Montfort	73.1	64.5	—	96	64.3	74.7
73	Goldsmiths, London	63.2	48.9	29.0	107	59.6	74.5
74	Northampton	77.1	64.3	1.2	94	—	74.4

Employed in high-skilled job	48%	Employed in lower-skilled job	23%
Employed in high-skilled job and studying	5%	Employed in lower-skilled job and studying	2%
Studying	15%	Unemployed	6%
High skilled work (median) salary	£26,000	Low/medium skilled salary	£21,000

Psychology

The London School of Economics (LSE) takes the lead in our Psychology table this year, while former No 1 Oxford settles for second place. Our analysis of the recent Research Excellence Framework 2021 shows the LSE to be the top scorer by a clear margin. Strength in research is comes in combination with remarkably high rates of student satisfaction at the LSE – which places in the top three universities for teaching quality as well as with the wider experience, measures which are derived from the National Student Survey.

The remainder of the top of the psychology table is stable this year, with eight of last year's top-10 universities featuring, albeit in a different order. The highest entry standards are at Glasgow, where entrants in 2021's cohort averaged 206 points in the UCAS tariff. Eighth-place Bath comes top for graduate prospects. While the older universities dominate the higher ranks of the main table, Cumbria (in joint 32nd place overall) outdoes all others for students' evaluation of the wider experience, while Wrexham Glyndŵr is top for teaching quality. Conversely, Goldsmiths gets the lowest ratings for both of these student-led metrics.

Psychology remains one of the most popular subjects offered by British universities, with 117 institutions represented in this year's table. Applications in 2021 hit 134,905, and have risen by nearly 50% since 2012. The number of new students starting courses dipped a little in 2021, year-on-year, but with 25,455 accepted applicants it was still 57% higher than the decade before in 2012.

Career prospects are unlikely to be what is attracting so many students. Across all universities, when surveyed 15 months after their degrees, the proportion of psychology graduates who were employed in professional-level jobs (34%) was less than the proportion working in jobs deemed low-skilled (37%).

Psychology	Teaching quality %	Student experience %	Research quality %	Entry standards (UCAS points)	Graduate prospects %	Overall score
1 London School of Economics	90.2	88.1	86.2	193	—	100
2 Oxford	—	—	75.5	192	76.4	96.3
3 Cambridge	—	—	75.0	194	75.5	93.7
4 King's College London	80.1	77.9	69.0	175	79.4	92.8
5 Glasgow	78.2	81.3	65.8	206	69.9	92.5
6 St Andrews	79.1	76.5	61.8	194	74.5	91.9
7 University College London	75.0	77.5	73.2	181	76.4	91.8
8 Bath	77.3	82.7	37.2	188	83.1	91.2
9 York	85.0	83.4	69.2	155	71.6	90.6
10 Exeter	70.1	73.7	62.7	165	81.9	89.3
11 Loughborough	73.6	77.7	66.8	154	75.5	88.3
12 Edinburgh	67.2	65.6	76.8	194	68.1	88.2
13 Strathclyde	76.5	75.0	65.8	194	61.6	88.1
14 Surrey	81.0	81.8	58.0	134	77.3	88
=15 Bristol	71.1	69.6	57.8	163	79.0	87.6
=15 Cardiff	70.4	71.6	68.8	165	73.8	87.6
=15 Warwick	77.8	80.6	57.5	151	73.4	87.6
=18 Birmingham	69.3	68.0	64.0	151	77.1	86.2
=18 Durham	66.6	65.5	50.0	172	79.4	86.2
20 Royal Holloway, London	70.7	72.2	74.0	139	71.4	85.4
21 Leeds	69.2	70.7	53.2	156	75.7	85.3
22 Southampton	74.9	75.1	60.5	147	69.1	85.1
23 Newcastle	72.0	72.5	55.2	154	71.6	85
24 Glasgow Caledonian	79.3	76.4	61.0	179	53.3	84.8
25 Stirling	81.0	78.1	47.2	163	59.9	84.2
26 Aberdeen	83.0	84.6	49.0	173	51.9	84.1
27 Lancaster	72.9	73.1	48.8	148	69.1	83.3
28 Nottingham	68.9	65.4	52.2	151	69.3	82.4
29 Bangor	82.4	82.4	47.0	119	63.7	82.1
30 East Anglia	73.2	72.1	60.8	132	64.6	82
31 Manchester	65.4	61.7	62.7	155	64.4	81.3
=32 Cumbria	90.7	88.7	—	119	69.6*	80.9
=32 Ulster	76.1	74.8	41.8	127	66.7	80.9
=34 Sheffield	62.8	60.6	62.7	141	67.4	80.4
=34 Sussex	68.2	68.5	59.5	141	61.9	80.4
36 City	73.3	74.6	36.0	137	64.7	79.9
37 Wrexham Glyndŵr	92.0	87.6	20.5	—	52.2	79.8
38 Essex	75.9	75.3	56.0	114	59.5	79.4
39 Portsmouth	81.5	76.9	40.8	119	58.9	79.3
40 Suffolk	81.7	75.0	—	101	79.8	78.7
41 Nottingham Trent	76.2	75.9	39.2	119	61.5	78.6
42 Leicester	68.5	70.2	55.0	126	60.5	78.5

Psychology cont.

		Teaching quality %	Student experience %	Research quality %	Entry standards (UCAS points)	Graduate prospects %	Overall score
43	West of England	79.1	77.8	35.2	120	59.2	78.4
44	Abertay	79.2	74.4	21.0	140	59.3	78.3
=45	Liverpool	61.7	58.6	65.5	139	60.7	78.2
=45	Oxford Brookes	81.4	77.7	39.0	119	55.3	78.2
=45	Reading	64.0	62.8	56.2	129	64.2	78.2
48	Northumbria	75.1	72.8	28.0	134	60.8	77.9
49	Wales Trinity St David	78.1	72.6	1.2	126	71.9	77.8
50	Queen's Belfast	73.1	71.4	31.0	149	56.2	77.7
51	Buckingham	79.1	71.8	—	110	75.5	77.5
=52	Dundee	69.8	67.9	39.0	172	48.9	77.4
=52	Hull	74.6	73.7	40.5	117	59.2	77.4
=52	Lincoln	69.5	71.2	39.5	125	62.2	77.4
=52	Staffordshire	80.2	72.4	30.8	109	61.8	77.4
56	Kent	55.7	56.4	50.7	137	69.2	77.2
=57	Plymouth	72.7	75.9	40.5	121	57.7	77.1
=57	West of Scotland	78.6	76.2	13.2	135	59.8	77.1
59	Swansea	67.6	60.6	30.0	129	68.6	77
60	Central Lancashire	72.8	72.2	30.0	119	62.4	76.7
61	Liverpool John Moores	77.2	72.0	16.2	134	59.3	76.5
62	Coventry	75.4	69.9	47.0	112	55.5	76.4
=63	Bolton	83.3	76.6	1.8	118	63.1	76.3
=63	Edinburgh Napier	84.0	81.7	—	155	49.7	76.3
=65	Derby	82.8	78.9	10.2	116	59.6	76.2
=65	Sunderland	82.6	72.8	30.2	110	55.6	76.2
=67	Greenwich	72.8	72.1	32.3	114	60.8	76.1
=67	Manchester Metropolitan	73.8	74.4	36.0	119	56.0	76.1
=67	Queen Margaret, Edinburgh	73.6	68.9	21.0	157	52.9	76.1
=70	Aston	75.3	73.5	—	126	67.5	76
=70	Canterbury Christ Church	82.5	78.5	24.0	103	57.1	76
=70	Edge Hill	76.3	79.1	18.8	127	56.5	76
73	Chichester	81.6	77.2	8.0	109	62.8	75.9
74	Winchester	73.8	72.3	16.2	108	66.1	75.5
75	Heriot-Watt	68.1	69.5	13.5	162	55.2	75.3
76	Keele	68.1	67.7	35.2	115	61.4	75.2
77	Birmingham City	74.3	72.3	18.2	111	62.4	75
=78	Aberystwyth	85.9	80.8	12.5	121	49.1	74.9
=78	Hertfordshire	72.9	70.2	39.8	102	57.7	74.9
=78	Queen Mary, London	71.3	72.8	—	143	61.5	74.9
=81	Chester	78.6	69.2	13.0	117	59.2	74.6
=81	Gloucestershire	73.9	73.1	5.0	118	64.3	74.6
=81	York St John	80.7	81.4	20.5	113	51.0	74.6
84	Anglia Ruskin	79.6	72.2	25.0	98	56.1	74

85	Bournemouth	72.3	70.6	22.8	108	59.5	73.9
86	Leeds Trinity	78.1	74.5	9.2	106	59.5	73.8
87	Westminster	71.6	71.1	24.8	108	58.0	73.5
88	Kingston	76.1	71.7	20.5	99	57.5	73.2
89	Sheffield Hallam	71.6	66.2	26.8	111	56.5	73.1
90	Huddersfield	76.4	74.3	22.0	117	49.2	73
91	London Metropolitan	84.1	78.6	—	91	57.7	72.7
92	Roehampton	68.4	66.0	37.5	99	56.4	72.6
93	West London	83.0	81.6	—	108	51.5	72.5
=94	South Wales	74.8	70.1	—	115	59.3	72.3
=94	Worcester	69.8	70.6	19.2	111	56.0	72.3
96	St Mary's, Twickenham	74.9	78.8	—	108	58.0	72.2
=97	Liverpool Hope	64.6	64.1	32.0	110	56.3	71.8
=97	Salford	62.3	53.9	37.0	118	57.1	71.8
99	Teesside	75.0	73.1	7.2	106	53.8	71.2
100	Middlesex	64.0	58.3	30.2	106	57.6	71
101	Bradford	67.9	67.9	8.2	114	56.4	70.6
=102	Leeds Beckett	72.9	67.9	21.5	102	50.1	70.4
=102	Wolverhampton	76.9	70.2	12.5	98	51.0	70.4
104	Brighton	65.1	60.0	34.0	107	51.4	70.2
105	Newman, Birmingham	77.4	79.3	3.5	96	50.5	70.1
106	Goldsmiths, London	50.8	48.2	35.5	117	62.2	69.9
107	Bath Spa	67.7	64.5	7.2	103	58.1	69.7
108	Brunel	61.4	60.0	23.2	109	56.2	69.6
109	Buckinghamshire New	82.3	85.4	—	90	44.4	69.2
110	De Montfort	65.6	61.1	20.5	101	52.2	68.5
111	Northampton	67.4	65.8	8.5	108	50.9	68.3
112	Bishop Grosseteste	61.7	53.4	6.2	95	64.6	68.2
113	London South Bank	63.6	57.5	18.0	106	52.9	68.1
114	Bedfordshire	70.1	66.8	—	104	51.3	67.8
115	Solent, Southampton	67.1	60.5	—	107	51.4	66.8
116	Cardiff Metropolitan	56.8	55.3	—	117	56.2	66.2
117	East London	60.4	54.2	23.2	105	46.2	65.8

Employed in high-skilled job	34%	Employed in lower-skilled job	37%
Employed in high-skilled job and studying	5%	Employed in lower-skilled job and studying	3%
Studying	15%	Unemployed	6%
High skilled work (median) salary	£23,000	Low/medium skilled salary	£18,900

Radiography

Glasgow Caledonian takes the lead in our tenth edition of a dedicated ranking for radiography degrees, which were previously listed among "Subjects Allied to Medicine" in the *Guide*. Leeds, last year's top university for the subject, settles for third place this year. In second place overall, Queen Margaret scored the highest with its students in the National Student Survey (NSS) and comes top for both NSS-derived measures: teaching quality and the wider undergraduate experience. Strength in research is unbeaten at fourth-place Keele, which achieved the top scores in the recent Research Excellence Framework 2021, followed by Leeds. Entry grades are led by Glasgow Caledonian, which averaged 181 points in the UCAS tariff among 2021's entrants, and no universities averaged lower than 111 points – at Suffolk and Hertfordshire.

Diagnostic courses usually involve two years of studying anatomy, physiology and physics followed by further training in oncology, psycho-social studies and other modules. Candidates need at least one science A-level, or equivalent, usually biology.

Graduates can feel confident that they will find professional-level work soon after university, with radiography rising to fourth in our employment ranking – up from fifth last year and sixth the year before. Salford and Canterbury Christ Church achieved perfect 100% graduate prospects scores, due to every one of their radiography graduates being employed in professional jobs and/or postgraduate study 15 months on from their degrees.

Radiography	Teaching quality %	Student experience %	Research quality %	Entry standards (UCAS points)	Graduate prospects %	Overall score
1 Glasgow Caledonian	85.0	80.1	61.0	181	96.5	100
2 Queen Margaret, Edinburgh	85.5	88.5	36.5	165	—	97.7
3 Leeds	76.1	67.8	65.0	156	97.0	96.7
4 Keele	77.1	85.0	66.2	132	—	96.5
5 Robert Gordon	81.4	72.5	24.5	176	—	95.2
6 Cardiff	69.2	60.5	58.8	146	98.9	94.9
7 Liverpool	75.8	74.8	46.8	136	98.6	94.3
8 Salford	70.1	66.9	37.0	146	100	93.5
9 Plymouth	78.0	74.2	39.5	138	—	92.7
10 Exeter	64.5	64.0	53.2	140	97.6	92.6
11 Ulster	84.1	87.0	53.5	142	89.1	92.4
12 Bangor	60.9	56.7	59.8	—	96.7*	91.7
13 West of England	75.3	73.3	42.8	126	96.2	91.6
14 Sheffield Hallam	69.6	61.3	29.8	140	98.4	91.1
15 Canterbury Christ Church	71.3	61.8	31.8	120	100	90.8
16 Portsmouth	78.2	66.1	41.2	122	94.9	90.5
17 Hertfordshire	74.3	71.6	48.0	111	95.0	90.1
18 Birmingham City	65.9	62.2	37.8	136	95.8	89.8
19 Bradford	63.9	62.7	33.8	148	94.6*	89.5
20 London South Bank	74.4	62.1	34.5	135	93.2	89.2
21 City	69.8	65.9	58.0	125	90.5	89.1
22 Teesside	68.0	72.5	35.0	122	95.1	88.9
23 Cumbria	75.8	73.5	18.5	130	93.2	87.9
24 Derby	59.8	52.0	24.0	133	97.4	87.5
25 Suffolk	71.1	63.5	—	111	96.1	84.6
26 St George's, London	68.9	64.9	—	127	92.6	83.9

Employed in high-skilled job	91%	Employed in lower-skilled job	2%
Employed in high-skilled job and studying	4%	Employed in lower-skilled job and studying	0%
Studying	2%	Unemployed	2%
High skilled work (median) salary	£25,000	Low/medium skilled salary	—

Russian and Eastern European Languages

Bristol takes the lead in the Russian and Eastern European Languages this year, bringing Cambridge's eight-year tenure at its top to an end. Securing its lead, Bristol has the highest rates of student satisfaction with teaching quality and the broader experience. It also out front on research, our analysis of the recent Research Excellence Framework 2021 shows, while Nottingham is not far behind it on this measure, and Cambridge ranks third for the metric. The highest entry standards – of 190 UCAS points in 2021 – are claimed by Cambridge by the narrowest of margins, with entrants to Oxford averaging 189 points in the same admissions round. In a tightly packed grouping, entry standards go no lower than 136 points at Nottingham.

Most undergraduates learn Russian or another Eastern European language from scratch, and while there are no required subjects for entry to degrees, a language is useful.

Unusually among our subject rankings, no post-1992 universities feature in our Russian and Eastern European Languages table, which is populated exclusively by institutions with older foundations. The subjects attract tiny student cohorts – ranging between 65 and 35 accepted applicants per year over the past decade. In 2021, just 205 candidates applied – although this was a jump up from the 175 that applied in 2020. Only 25 providers are offering programmes in Russian in 2023-24, some as part of broader modern language degrees, and 22 are listing courses that include Eastern European languages.

In third place overall, Durham comes out top for graduate prospects, with 86.1% of graduates employed in high-skilled jobs and/or enrolled in postgraduate study 15 months after their degrees. The subjects a whole sit inside the top half of our employment ranking and our pay index.

Russian and Eastern European Languages	Teaching quality %	Student experience %	Research quality %	Entry standards (UCAS points)	Graduate prospects %	Overall score
1 Bristol	90.7	86.3	64.0	162	—	100
2 Cambridge	—	—	61.0	190	83.6	98.9
3 Durham	74.7	71.7	46.0	182	86.1	95.4
4 Oxford	—	—	51.2	189	—	93.2
5 University College London	66.1	66.7	56.0	164	77.8	91
=6 Exeter	77.8	75.2	50.0	148	77.7	90
=6 Manchester	68.0	60.1	59.5	157	—	90
8 Birmingham	69.1	63.7	54.8	149	66.7	85.7
=9 Edinburgh	52.0	48.8	45.8	172	—	83.9
=9 Nottingham	54.5	58.2	62.0	136	—	83.9
11 Glasgow	64.7	59.6	25.5	183	64.6	82

Employed in high-skilled job	51%	Employed in lower-skilled job		17%
Employed in high-skilled job and studying	8%	Employed in lower-skilled job and studying		3%
Studying	14%	Unemployed		8%
High skilled work (median) salary	£25,714	Low/medium skilled salary		£22,000

Social Policy

Bath offers the top-ranked degree in social policy, knocking the London School of Economics off its long-held perch of our table. Moving up from fourth place in our previous edition, Bath's ascent is fuelled partly by unsurpassed graduate prospects; 87.9% of its graduates were in high-skilled employment or postgraduate study 15 months after their degrees. High rates of student satisfaction have also boosted Bath's ranking – it places in the top three universities for teaching quality and the wider experience, measures which are based on the outcomes of the National Student Survey (NSS). The London School of Economics takes second place overall but remains top for research in our analysis of the new Research Excellence Framework (REF) 2021 – as it was in the previous REF 2014 exercise.

The highest entry standards were at Glasgow among 2021's intake of students, the only cohort to average more than 200 UCAS tariff points. Only eight universities averaged above 144 UCAS points (equivalent to AAA at A-level) and there are usually no required subjects for entry. Staffordshire has moved into the top 10 at joint ninth place, up from 25th last year, and is clearly hitting the rights notes with its students – who registered unsurpassed scores for teaching quality and the wider experience in the NSS.

Not all social policy graduates progress immediately into top careers, and the 37% who were in jobs classed as low-skilled 15 months on from their degrees confines the subject to 66th place in our employment ranking of 70 subjects. Only marginally more (39%) had secured professional-level jobs within the same timeframe. Earnings compare better with other subjects, ranking 52nd in our pay index. Graduates in professional jobs command median salaries of £24,100.

Many students take joint honours degrees – such as pairings with politics or modern languages – or within wider social sciences programmes. Applications and enrolments in the subject have remained remarkably steady over the past decade.

Social Policy	Teaching quality %	Student experience %	Research quality %	Entry standards (UCAS points)	Graduate prospects %	Overall score
1 Bath	84.4	81.2	59.5	—	87.9*	100
2 London School of Economics	69.2	70.2	86.2	158	87.1*	98.3
3 Strathclyde	80.4	76.6	43.8	197	—	96.5
4 Southampton	73.7	67.8	66.8	—	76.6	93
5 Glasgow	68.9	66.1	62.0	203	55.2	91.7
6 Edinburgh	67.7	64.6	55.2	185	—	91.6
7 Bristol	63.5	61.6	77.8	145	75.4	90.5
8 Stirling	72.8	73.9	47.5	155	—	88.4
=9 Birmingham	71.7	66.7	61.0	142	65.8	87.7
=9 Staffordshire	95.4	89.1	18.2	—	62.1	87.7
11 Queen's Belfast	71.9	64.8	56.5	144	—	87.1
12 Swansea	81.5	73.4	46.5	130	—	87
13 York	69.8	66.3	58.0	133	70.8	86.9
14 Leeds	68.2	62.0	48.5	152	68.6	86
15 Nottingham Trent	84.5	81.0	29.5	134	—	85.9
16 Bangor	77.4	74.4	33.2	134	—	83.6
17 Kent	63.5	66.4	72.2	108	—	83

18 Lincoln	72.7	79.1	51.0	104	—	82.4
19 Salford	75.5	74.5	44.5	104	63.6	81.9
20 Liverpool Hope	83.2	76.6	21.2	—	58.7*	81.8
21 Nottingham	63.0	59.1	54.0	132	—	81.2
22 Ulster	77.4	70.4	53.8	111	46.6	80.6
23 Plymouth	73.2	71.0	50.5	116	43.4	78.9
24 Central Lancashire	60.9	52.6	51.5	112	64.5	78.4
25 Brighton	64.1	52.6	34.0	—	66.7	77.5
26 Hertfordshire	68.3	65.1	48.0	98	—	77.4
27 Bedfordshire	72.1	63.0	50.2	102	40.7	75.6
28 West of Scotland	77.1	62.8	13.2	135	39.3	73.9
29 Edge Hill	67.2	60.5	17.5	125	—	73.5
30 De Montfort	48.0	47.4	43.2	111	64.2	73.3
31 South Wales	61.2	58.3	33.5	107	—	72.3
32 Wales Trinity St David	57.3	48.1	11.8	127	59.2	70.9
33 Wolverhampton	71.2	71.0	12.2	95	41.0	69.1

Employed in high-skilled job	39%	Employed in lower-skilled job	37%
Employed in high-skilled job and studying	5%	Employed in lower-skilled job and studying	2%
Studying	9%	Unemployed	8%
High skilled work (median) salary	£24,100	Low/medium skilled salary	£20,000

Social Work

Edinburgh returns to the No 1 spot in our Social Work table this year, having placed second in our previous edition, and first the year before. Strong performance across the board includes the highest entry standards, with entrants at the university in 2021 averaging 181 points in the UCAS tariff.

In a table characterised by universities rising and falling in the rankings, Queen's Belfast moves into second place, from fifth, buoyed by high rates of student satisfaction with teaching quality and the third-best graduate prospects. Out in front on this measure however is Suffolk, in 38th place overall, with 97.3% of graduates employed in high-skilled work and/or postgraduate study 15 months on from their degrees. York (joint 13th in the main table) is not far behind it, with 96.2% achieving the desired career outcomes. Bristol is the top scorer in research quality the new Research Excellence Framework 2021, followed by Kent.

Worcester gets by far the warmest reviews by students, as expressed in the National Student Survey. Its exceptionally high scores for teaching quality (94.2%) and for broad undergraduate experience (92.4%) are unbeaten. At the opposite end of the scale, Oxford Brookes comes bottom for teaching quality (scoring 56%) and Sheffield Hallam fares worst for the broader experience (registering a 47.8% score).

Social work is a graduate career, and although the Frontline programme aims to attract graduates of other subjects to train in the profession, and degree apprenticeships have been developed in it (though these are not profiled here), social work degrees are still the main route into careers. Applications experienced something of a boom in 2021, increasing by around 12%, but the numbers starting courses were slightly lower than in the year before.

The subject maintains its top 10 rank in our salaries index, with median annual pay of £29,100 placing social work in ninth place – where it ties with electrical and electronic engineering, and physics and astronomy.

Social Work

		Teaching quality %	Student experience %	Research quality %	Entry standards (UCAS points)	Graduate prospects %	Overall score
1	Edinburgh	79.3	77.2	55.2	181	91.5	100
2	Queen's Belfast	88.5	80.3	56.5	146	95.8	97.8
3	Lancaster	81.3	74.5	60.2	147	94.3	96
4	Strathclyde	74.3	65.4	43.8	177	88	94.9
5	Nottingham	79.2	71.1	54.0	140	100	94.3
6	Dundee	86.8	79.3	28.5	142	100	93.7
7	Bath	84.8	79.5	59.5	138	81.1	93.4
8	East Anglia	70.0	58.0	69.8	134	100	92.2
9	Plymouth	83.5	72.0	50.5	133	85.7	91.3
10	Central Lancashire	78.4	70.5	51.5	134	89.4	90.9
11	Bristol	76.3	70.9	77.8	134	71.4	90.8
12	Salford	79.4	73.3	44.5	132	91.4	90.6
=13	Hertfordshire	77.6	66.1	48.0	140	87.5	90.4
=13	York	70.1	62.0	58.0	135	96.2*	90.4
15	Glasgow Caledonian	78.7	73.1	26.0	142	95.0	90
16	Anglia Ruskin	89.1	85.6	30.0	116	94.3	89.9
17	Ulster	84.8	80.8	53.8	120	79.7	89.8
18	Kent	72.9	59.7	72.2	126	87.0	89.7
19	Hull	74.7	72.6	53.8	139	78.2	89.4
20	Manchester Metropolitan	84.4	82.5	32.8	138	75.8	89.1
=21	Robert Gordon	89.6	80.6	—	143	90.4	89
=21	Teesside	86.9	87.8	18.2	125	91.7	89
23	Northumbria	79.7	74.0	42.0	148	69.9	88.9
24	Worcester	94.2	92.4	12.8	123	83.9	88.7
25	Wrexham Glyndŵr	89.5	78.9	20.5	—	83.7	88.6
26	Bournemouth	84.1	77.2	10.2	137	92.3	88.3
27	Goldsmiths, London	82.6	80.2	48.0	115	81.7*	88
28	Essex	72.3	63.7	62.5	117	89.9	87.8
29	Bedfordshire	76.7	68.7	50.2	113	93.0	87.5
30	West of England	68.4	61.0	35.2	134	100	87.4
31	Lincoln	76.3	70.2	51.0	128	73.8	86.6
32	Huddersfield	73.2	68.1	43.5	131	79.7	86.2
=33	Derby	87.4	83.2	25.5	121	74.6	86.1
=33	Swansea	78.4	65.0	46.5	130	72.3	86.1
=33	West of Scotland	78.8	70.6	13.2	146	80.2	86.1
36	Portsmouth	78.4	70.6	33.0	118	89.8	86
37	Liverpool Hope	78.0	75.6	21.2	126	88.8	85.8
38	Suffolk	77.0	58.6	21.8	—	97.3	85.7
39	Kingston	81.9	73.3	38.5	112	82.9	85.6
40	Greenwich	85.3	76.5	17.0	143	64.4	85.4
41	Staffordshire	80.9	78.4	18.2	119	85.7	84.7
42	Sunderland	86.9	83.3	39.5	120	57.0	84.5

43	Solent, Southampton	85.6	81.6	9.5	120	80.8	84.2
44	Keele	77.2	63.4	33.2	126	—	84
=45	Cumbria	82.1	79.2	8.2	123	83.0	83.9
=45	South Wales	82.0	75.0	33.5	112	75.9	83.9
47	Sussex	71.3	60.9	41.0	137	69.4	83.8
48	Brighton	73.6	65.9	34.0	116	85.7	83.6
49	Edge Hill	80.5	77.7	17.5	133	67.8	83.5
=50	Chester	84.1	73.9	12.8	129	71.0	83.3
=50	De Montfort	76.3	76.5	43.2	109	74.0	83.3
52	Sheffield Hallam	64.2	47.8	26.2	143	87.1	83.1
53	Birmingham City	77.1	73.3	25.8	117	78.7	82.9
54	Coventry	81.5	72.0	—	131	78.2	82.3
55	London South Bank	73.9	62.1	27.8	124	74.3	81.6
56	West London	80.2	79.9	39.0	110	58.5	81.3
57	Middlesex	69.2	64.3	27.8	121	79.1	81.2
58	East London	61.2	55.7	40.0	—	85.5	81
59	Winchester	81.4	71.0	16.5	111	74.5	80.7
60	Oxford Brookes	56.0	54.1	37.8	115	95.8	80.6
61	Bangor	70.7	65.8	59.8	—	50.0	80.4
=62	Leeds Beckett	75.4	72.0	17.8	108	80.0	80.1
=62	Liverpool John Moores	82.4	83.4	15.8	—	57.8	80.1
64	Gloucestershire	65.5	63.6	16.2	121	86.0	79.9
=65	Buckinghamshire New	82.9	72.4	12.5	—	62.2	79.3
=65	Cardiff Metropolitan	80.4	73.2	—	119	72.5	79.3
67	Nottingham Trent	81.1	78.1	29.5	114	50.2	79.2
68	Canterbury Christ Church	72.1	69.4	31.8	101	74.0	78.9
69	Chichester	80.6	78.1	3.0	103	76.5	78.5
70	Bradford	68.2	70.1	—	148	57.4	78.1
71	London Metropolitan	83.1	81.1	—	112	59.7	77.3
72	Leeds Trinity	76.9	76.5	—	108	58.8	74.7
73	Northampton	70.8	63.0	—	110	66.4	73.7
74	Wales Trinity St David	77.1	74.8	—	112	50.0	73.6
75	Newman, Birmingham	72.6	65.9	13.8	107	49.6	72.8
76	Wolverhampton	66.6	59.7	12.2	108	55.0	71.7

Employed in high-skilled job	62%	Employed in lower-skilled job		23%
Employed in high-skilled job and studying	4%	Employed in lower-skilled job and studying		1%
Studying	5%	Unemployed		5%
High skilled work (median) salary	£29,100	Low/medium skilled salary		£19,000

Sociology

Topping a subject ranking that stretches to 92 universities, Cambridge secures its position for the third consecutive year with the highest entry standards (of 198 UCAS points) and the best graduate prospects. Runner-up Oxford is close behind it, averaging just one less UCAS point among 2021's entrants and with the second-best results in the new Research Excellence

Framework (REF) 2021. For research strength however, Oxford is outdone by Loughborough, which moves up to eighth place overall this year from 11th in our previous edition.

Worcester (in joint 18th place) has the highest rates of student satisfaction, coming top in for both teaching quality and the broader undergraduate experience in our analysis of the National Student Survey. Seventh-place Surrey sits just behind Worcester on each of these student-led measures.

The study of human social relationships and institutions, sociology continues to attract increasing numbers of applications, which were up by around 5% in 2021 compared with 2020. In the decade since 2012 they have almost doubled, while the number of accepted students has risen by almost 80%. With entry standards ranging from 198 UCAS tariff points at Cambridge – to the 10 universities that averaged 100 points or lower, there are broad options for applicants.

Courses cover topics such as gender roles, multiculturalism, media and culture, and can include options to study criminology or social policy. The subject's academic breadth may the source of its popularity, as it tends to offer little immediate gratification in terms of graduate prospects. Sociology ranks 63rd in our employment table of 70 subject areas and 57th in our salaries ranking. The latest data shows 39% of graduates were employed in professional-level jobs 15 months after their degrees, while 13% were enrolled in postgraduate study and 4% were doing both. More than two-thirds (36%) were working in jobs deemed "low-skilled", however.

Sociology

		Teaching quality %	Student experience %	Research quality %	Entry standards (UCAS points)	Graduate prospects %	Overall score
1	Cambridge	—	—	69.2	198	90.6	100
2	Oxford	80.4	71.2	70.5	197	—	99.2
3	Durham	77.2	73.6	53.0	183	81.9	96
4	Bath	74.9	73.0	59.5	152	85.3	94.1
=5	Glasgow	75.5	69.4	62.0	198	66.7	93.9
=5	London School of Economics	82.2	78.7	61.0	157	71.8	93.9
7	Surrey	84.9	83.2	48.0	131	70.2	90.6
8	Loughborough	68.1	68.4	71.8	140	76.2	90.2
9	Warwick	74.5	70.9	53.8	143	72.7	89.1
=10	Aberdeen	76.8	76.5	37.0	177	63.2	88.8
=10	Exeter	74.2	74.9	46.8	150	71.3	88.8
12	King's College London	69.4	65.3	57.0	152	73.8*	88.7
13	York	71.4	70.5	68.5	135	63.2	87.1
14	Stirling	73.1	68.6	47.5	166	60.8	86.9
15	Swansea	78.2	72.2	46.5	132	66.7*	86.7
=16	Lancaster	71.8	69.4	60.2	146	61.3*	86.6
=16	Manchester	67.1	58.7	67.2	151	65.2	86.6
=18	Southampton	73.9	67.5	66.8	138	59.2	86.5
=18	Worcester	89.0	84.2	12.8	109	76.6	86.5
20	Hull	74.4	72.8	53.8	113	71.7	86.3
21	Cardiff	73.3	69.8	54.0	141	63.4	86.2
22	Glasgow Caledonian	82.2	76.7	26.0	179	52.0	86.1
23	Birmingham	76.1	69.6	61.0	145	53.7	85.9
24	Leeds	71.1	64.6	48.5	145	67.2	85.7

25	Edinburgh	65.8	58.4	53.5	184	58.0	85.6
26	Nottingham	67.7	68.5	54.0	132	70.2	85.5
27	Bristol	65.7	61.6	49.0	152	68.0	84.9
28	Suffolk	80.3	70.0	21.8	119	75.5	84.6
29	Leicester	73.0	72.9	48.0	117	66.6	84.2
30	University College London	70.6	69.6	—	175	74.8	84.1
=31	Plymouth	77.4	74.9	50.5	106	63.4	84
=31	Ulster	77.4	70.4	53.8	110	61.6	84
33	Sunderland	75.4	65.8	39.5	—	64.2	83.6
34	Queen's Belfast	71.8	64.5	56.5	135	56.1	83.2
35	Aston	68.7	64.7	42.5	120	70.0	82.6
36	Sussex	66.3	58.2	55.0	135	62.0	82.4
=37	Essex	64.9	63.7	62.5	116	63.1	82.2
=37	Sheffield	73.1	72.1	36.8	136	57.7	82.2
39	Nottingham Trent	75.6	72.3	29.5	110	68.1	82
40	Staffordshire	80.3	73.6	18.2	—	61.8	81.8
41	City	60.6	57.9	64.0	123	64.4	81.6
42	Salford	77.3	68.3	44.5	106	57.1	81
43	West of England	77.3	76.2	35.2	111	56.3	80.8
44	Bournemouth	76.9	73.9	10.2	106	72.7	80.7
45	Edinburgh Napier	81.0	76.3	—	148	54.9	80.2
46	Anglia Ruskin	74.5	68.7	35.5	112	58.7	80.1
=47	Coventry	81.1	78.4	39.5	100	48.9	79.8
=47	Manchester Metropolitan	76.5	74.1	29.0	117	54.9	79.8
49	Liverpool	51.1	43.4	55.0	129	74.7	79.5
50	Royal Holloway, London	70.8	70.6	38.0	115	56.4	79.4
51	Portsmouth	74.8	69.6	33.0	99	60.9	79.2
52	Roehampton	71.5	67.4	40.2	91	63.5	79
53	Edge Hill	75.5	74.2	—	121	65.3	78.6
54	Bedfordshire	81.4	76.8	—	109	62.3	78.5
55	Robert Gordon	80.0	79.9	—	147	47.4	78.3
=56	Brunel	73.6	67.9	30.8	104	58.1	78.2
=56	Newcastle	59.4	49.8	42.5	137	61.9	78.2
58	Birmingham City	76.2	70.9	21.0	112	54.1	77.6
=59	Chester	70.4	52.7	12.8	114	69.9	77.2
=59	Teesside	74.1	68.5	18.2	105	59.8*	77.2
61	Greenwich	77.2	72.6	—	109	62.7	77.1
62	Keele	68.6	65.1	33.2	110	55.2	76.8
63	Bangor	71.2	70.1	33.2	—	49.3	76.7
64	Kingston	73.7	69.8	27.0	96	55.9*	76.6
65	Liverpool John Moores	76.7	74.4	22.2	119	44.0	76.5
66	Huddersfield	70.1	63.5	43.5	116	44.1	76.2
67	Sheffield Hallam	75.6	70.4	—	107	60.8	75.8
=68	Leeds Beckett	74.2	68.3	17.8	99	56.2	75.7
=68	Northumbria	58.3	50.2	42.0	131	55.4	75.7
70	Liverpool Hope	76.0	69.7	—	114	57.0	75.5

Sociology cont.

		Teaching quality %	Student experience %	Research quality %	Entry standards (UCAS points)	Graduate prospects %	Overall score
71	York St John	80.8	71.0	10.0	102	49.6	75.3
=72	Central Lancashire	72.6	65.6	—	114	60.2	75
=72	Kent	68.2	62.6	—	115	66.1	75
=74	Canterbury Christ Church	73.5	67.8	13.2	96	56.2	74.6
=74	Lincoln	72.8	71.7	—	114	55.9	74.6
76	Oxford Brookes	75.3	68.7	27.5	104	42.0	74.3
77	Goldsmiths, London	56.5	40.6	52.5	115	54.8	74.1
78	Derby	80.8	74.6	—	108	45.7	74
79	East London	68.0	57.4	26.8	97	55.7	73.9
80	Abertay	78.2	70.3	13.5	—	44.1	73.8
81	London South Bank	71.5	65.4	—	100	61.7*	73.7
82	West of Scotland	68.1	60.4	13.2	127	48.8	73.5
83	Queen Margaret, Edinburgh	70.6	62.5	7.8	146	40.4	73.3
84	Bath Spa	75.5	69.3	—	102	52.2	73.1
=85	Brighton	64.6	53.5	34.0	101	52.0	73
=85	Wolverhampton	69.2	68.8	—	92	62.5	73
87	Northampton	70.6	65.8	4.2	98	57.0	72.8
88	Gloucestershire	67.7	62.8	24.5	113	44.1*	72.6
89	Westminster	75.8	76.4	—	104	44.8	72.2
90	Winchester	66.2	64.3	—	106	57.8	71.9
91	Middlesex	70.0	65.5	—	105	51.3	71.3
92	South Wales	60.9	58.0	—	103	52.6*	68.3

Employed in high-skilled job	39%	Employed in lower-skilled job	36%
Employed in high-skilled job and studying	4%	Employed in lower-skilled job and studying	1%
Studying	13%	Unemployed	6%
High skilled work (median) salary	£24,000	Low/medium skilled salary	£19,357

Sports Science

Sports science is one of our more competitive subject rankings, with the lead changing hands regularly in recent years. Since 2017, the table has been led by Birmingham, Bath (twice), Exeter and Loughborough and now – for a third successive year – Glasgow. The highest entry standards of 216 UCAS points combine with strong performances across the board to secure its position. In second place, also for the third year running, Bath – our University of the Year – benefits from outstanding sports facilities which provide the physical surroundings in which much world-leading and internationally excellent research takes place. The university ranks fourth on this measure. It also places second for student satisfaction with their broad undergraduate experience and fourth for graduate prospects.

The best sports facilities do not always equate to great outcomes in the academic discipline of sport science – but they can help, such as the laboratories in which performance, endurance and recovery are closely monitored. Placing eighth in our subject ranking, Durham wins this year's Sports University of the Year title.

Top for research in sports science by a clear margin is Exeter (in fifth place overall), following results of the new Research Excellence Framework 2021, with King's College London (third) and Bangor (35th) ranking second and third. For graduate prospects East Anglia is in front – with 88.2% of graduates employed in high-skilled jobs and/or postgraduate study 15 months after their degrees.

Nottingham, which benefits from excellent facilities at the £40m David Ross Sports Village, has suffered a huge fall in our Sports Science table, going from ninth place two years ago to 63rd in our previous edition, to this year sitting at the foot of the subject ranking in 82nd place. The lowest rates of student satisfaction contribute to its enormous slump, with students' rating it bottom for teaching quality and for the wider experience.

Lancaster, in sixth place overall, tops both measures of student satisfaction. Sports science is one of the subject areas where the modern universities compete on a level playing field with their older counterparts. York St John, Abertay, Edge Hill, Buckinghamshire New, Canterbury Christ Church and Coventry feature within the top five universities for measures of student satisfaction.

Applications for sports science degrees topped 71,000 in 2021 (up 7% year-on-year), and 15,660 new students were accepted onto courses. Forty-five per cent of graduates were in professional-level jobs when surveyed 15 months after their degrees, while a further 19% were enrolled in postgraduate study or doing both. The proportion unemployed is a low 4%, but more than three in 10 graduates were employed in jobs deemed low-skilled, and sports science ranks 52nd in our employment table. Graduates in high-skilled jobs command median starting salaries of £23,215, and sports science sits 58th in our pay index.

Sports Science	Teaching quality %	Student experience %	Research quality %	Entry standards (UCAS points)	Graduate prospects %	Overall score
1 Glasgow	80.2	79.8	68.5	216	—	100
2 Bath	85.0	88.5	73.2	161	78.9	96.5
3 King's College London	78.6	78.9	80.2	161	—	94.2
4 Loughborough	76.2	80.3	66.8	156	82.3	94.1
5 Exeter	76.3	78.9	84.0	160	74.2	93.4
6 Lancaster	92.0	90.7	55.0	139	—	92.4
7 Edinburgh	72.7	76.9	55.0	194	69.6	91
8 Durham	73.5	67.9	61.0	167	72.5	89.4
9 East Anglia	84.0	83.6	—	142	88.2	89.3
10 Stirling	82.6	79.5	36.5	172	69.7	88.9
11 Birmingham	69.0	70.8	73.2	148	73.5	88.8
12 Leeds	72.0	67.2	65.8	145	73.9	88
13 Northumbria	80.7	78.9	60.5	148	65.4	87.4
14 Surrey	81.4	81.3	58.0	139	66.7	87.1
15 York St John	89.5	87.5	27.5	122	73.3	86.5
16 Oxford Brookes	82.4	80.5	37.8	127	73.9	86.4
=17 St Mary's, Twickenham	85.3	82.8	46.0	116	71.9	86.3
=17 Teesside	85.6	77.3	35.0	132	72.6	86.3
=19 Newcastle	75.5	72.3	50.7	145	—	86.1
=19 Portsmouth	76.0	73.8	57.5	122	73.3	86.1
21 Liverpool John Moores	74.8	75.2	60.8	155	62.9	85.8
22 Abertay	89.3	79.3	19.8	148	68.8	85.7

Sports Science cont.

		Teaching quality %	Student experience %	Research quality %	Entry standards (UCAS points)	Graduate prospects %	Overall score
23	Essex	78.3	76.8	32.5	131	74.6	85.3
=24	Cardiff Metropolitan	76.3	76.5	43.8	135	70.3	85
=24	Edge Hill	86.2	85.4	32.5	140	64.9	85
=26	Brighton	76.9	67.2	45.5	118	75.7	84.7
=26	Chichester	80.3	80.5	33.2	127	71.7	84.7
=28	Salford	84.6	78.2	37.0	134	66.7	84.6
=28	Swansea	78.0	72.2	48.2	133	68.6	84.6
=30	Nottingham Trent	83.3	81.9	36.8	128	67.4	84.3
=30	Ulster	76.2	73.4	43.2	143	67.2	84.3
32	South Wales	83.4	82.3	45.8	115	67.4	84.2
=33	Coventry	85.9	87.3	24.8	133	65.4	83.8
=33	Strathclyde	78.8	78.1	—	195	62.5	83.8
35	Bangor	70.6	70.1	73.8	124	64.5	83.6
36	Newman, Birmingham	82.9	81.5	13.2	101	80.0	83.5
=37	Brunel	76.2	73.6	50.5	133	65.0	83.4
=37	Worcester	85.4	84.9	15.2	123	71.1	83.4
39	Manchester Metropolitan	80.4	77.8	51.2	133	60.8	83.2
40	Hertfordshire	80.9	78.3	48.0	110	66.9	82.9
41	Hull	81.9	79.9	47.2	141	57.4	82.8
42	Lincoln	78.7	76.2	30.8	125	69.1	82.6
=43	Leeds Beckett	75.6	73.5	49.2	116	67.5	82.4
=43	Sheffield Hallam	75.6	68.6	45.2	125	67.6	82.4
=45	Hartpury	81.4	75.4	15.8	125	71.7	82.3
=45	Northampton	84.8	81.0	5.0	106	77.0	82.3
47	Bedfordshire	75.9	70.8	22.0	112	77.1	82.2
48	Buckinghamshire New	88.4	82.7	22.8	116	65.8	82.1
49	Anglia Ruskin	83.7	81.5	18.5	111	71.0	82
50	West of Scotland	71.8	66.9	29.0	142	67.9	81.5
51	Canterbury Christ Church	86.9	81.7	38.0	95	65.9	81.4
52	Robert Gordon	77.5	72.3	—	165	65.9	81.3
53	Central Lancashire	81.2	76.8	19.2	127	66.5	81.2
54	Chester	74.9	66.2	15.8	131	72.4	81.1
=55	Birmingham City	86.3	82.7	—	126	68.2	81
=55	Gloucestershire	74.1	74.8	24.5	122	70.2	81
57	Aberystwyth	72.2	70.3	48.8	114	—	80.9
58	Solent, Southampton	78.5	76.0	18.5	124	67.8	80.6
=59	Roehampton	80.9	81.6	—	102	76.0	80.4
=59	Wolverhampton	80.0	75.1	25.2	112	67.6	80.4
61	Kingston	86.6	80.3	38.5	109	59.1	80.3
62	Sunderland	82.7	80.0	22.0	121	62.3	80
=63	Bournemouth	71.0	71.4	41.8	121	62.5	79.2
=63	Middlesex	81.2	80.0	16.0	118	63.6	79.2

65	Liverpool Hope	80.2	78.5	13.8	122	63.7	79.1
66	Plymouth Marjon	78.2	75.9	20.0	122	63.3	79
67	Greenwich	61.8	50.3	32.3	124	73.5	78.7
68	Kent	73.7	70.3	37.2	132	57.6	78.5
=69	Huddersfield	76.1	75.9	22.2	131	58.8	78.1
=69	Staffordshire	76.3	70.1	30.8	117	61.1	78.1
=71	Edinburgh Napier	69.9	72.0	23.5	153	55.8	77.9
=71	Wales Trinity St David	72.3	62.1	11.8	138	65.3	77.9
73	London South Bank	75.4	71.8	32.2	102	—	77.8
74	Bolton	70.8	65.5	—	117	71.4	76.9
75	Leeds Trinity	72.7	75.1	18.0	114	62.8	76.8
76	Winchester	72.4	69.3	20.8	111	63.7	76.4
77	Derby	79.2	77.0	—	121	61.5	76.3
78	London Metropolitan	70.4	75.4	—	108	69.1*	76
79	East London	75.8	70.7	—	109	67.0	75.9
80	Suffolk	63.4	66.3	—	117	71.0	75.4
81	Cumbria	64.7	67.1	—	115	70.1	75.2
82	Nottingham	37.6	46.3	61.0	141	—	74.6

Employed in high-skilled job	45%	Employed in lower-skilled job	31%
Employed in high-skilled job and studying	6%	Employed in lower-skilled job and studying	2%
Studying	13%	Unemployed	4%
High skilled work (median) salary	£23,215	Low/medium skilled salary	£18,500

Subjects Allied to Medicine

Our table for the group of Subjects Allied to Medicine encompasses a wide range of degrees. They include audiology, complementary therapies, counselling, health services management, health sciences, nutrition, occupational therapy, optometry, ophthalmology, orthoptics, osteopathy, podiatry and speech therapy. Physiotherapy and radiography have rankings of their own. Not all the universities that feature in this table offer all of the subjects that fall under the broad "allied to medicine" heading, and performance in our ranking is naturally influenced by which specialisms are offered.

In a Scottish university top-three, Dundee takes the lead in this year's table, buoyed by the third-highest entry standards among strong performance across the board. Strathclyde, which has topped our table for the past six years, sits third this year, while Glasgow Caledonian is up seven places to rank second.

King's College London sits 21st overall but its strength in research is unsurpassed, according to results of the new Research Excellence Framework 2021. Manchester, Southampton and Bristol follow it, in that order.

Entry standards of 207 UCAS points put Glasgow in front on this measure. Based on the outcomes of the National Student Survey (NSS), Buckinghamshire New is rated top for teaching quality by its students, in a ranking that sees Bolton and Edinburgh Napier fill second and third place respectively. For the wider undergraduate experience, also derived from the NSS, Buckinghamshire New is unbeaten, with Edinburgh Napier runner-up and St Mary's, Twickenham in third place.

Applications in 2021 saw increases in most of the subjects – including complementary medicine, counselling and occupational therapy – as well as the much larger group classified "others" by UCAS. Early career prospects are solid. When surveyed 15 months after their degrees, more than six in 10 graduates were employed in professional-level jobs and a further two in 10 were enrolled in postgraduate study, or combining it with professional work – ranking the grouping 14th in our employment index.

Subjects Allied to Medicine	Teaching quality %	Student experience %	Research quality %	Entry standards (UCAS points)	Graduate prospects %	Overall score
1 Dundee	76.5	76.1	60.8	188	91.7	100
2 Glasgow Caledonian	77.9	76.9	61	186	90.5	99.8
3 Strathclyde	72.7	70.2	65.8	193	89.2	99.2
4 University College London	72.4	77.7	57.8	172	86.1	95.5
5 Cardiff	71.7	70.0	58.8	156	94.6	95.4
=6 Lancaster	84.6	77.9	55	143	90.3	95.3
=6 Manchester	69.8	67.8	71.2	157	89.9	95.3
=8 Edinburgh Napier	90.8	90.5	40.5	137	—	95.2
=8 Northumbria	81.5	65.6	53.5	146	95.5*	95.2
10 Glasgow	68.7	71.4	63.5	207	72.4	95
11 City	78.8	77.3	58	132	95.6	94.8
12 Surrey	74.8	77.5	58	146	89.7	94
13 Swansea	71.6	70.7	66.8	145	89.9	93.8
14 Bangor	80.3	68.3	59.8	123	96.7	93.7
=15 Southampton	59.6	63.6	69.8	137	100	93.2
=15 Ulster	79.6	80.3	53.5	140	87.8	93.2
=17 Birmingham	74.0	73.2	59.8	151	84.6	92.7
=17 Bristol	63.0	63.6	68.7	165	85.1	92.7
=19 Nottingham	82.1	74.2	57.9	143	81.5	92.4
=19 Robert Gordon	73.8	74.9	24.5	164	95.2	92.4
21 King's College London	65.8	63.6	76.2	156	81.2	92.1
22 East Anglia	68.2	65.8	55.5	138	94.6	91.7
23 Queen Margaret, Edinburgh	73.2	69.3	36.5	171	85.9	91.6
24 Sheffield	72.3	71.3	63.7	149	79.4	91
25 Newcastle	66.1	70.0	61.8	153	82.0	90.6
=26 Abertay	84.6	80.9	19.2	151	—	90.5
=26 Exeter	74.4	74.5	53.2	150	79.8	90.5
28 Hull	76.9	72.9	55.5	129	83.3	89.8
29 Teesside	79.3	75.4	35	121	93.4	89.6
30 Reading	71.0	72.9	56.2	125	87.6	89.5
=31 Liverpool	69.6	65.9	46.8	138	90.1	89.4
=31 West of England	75.3	71.0	42.8	134	88.0	89.4
33 Cardiff Metropolitan	76.4	73.3	20.5	147	91.1	89.1
=34 Buckinghamshire New	100.0	96.8	16.8	104	—	88.7
=34 Plymouth	70.8	68.3	39.5	133	91.6	88.7
=36 Aston	69.8	69.4	46	127	90.4	88.4
=36 Wrexham Glyndŵr	84.1	76.7	20.5	—	86.8	88.4
=38 Leeds	65.7	61.9	65	151	75.5	88.1

=38 Portsmouth	73.9	73.1	41.2	122	89.3	88.1
40 Bradford	74.3	72.1	33.8	145	83.1	87.9
=41 Coventry	71.6	69.3	47.2	131	84.1	87.7
=41 Greenwich	75.5	71.9	32.3	122	91.3	87.7
=41 Hertfordshire	75.5	71.3	48	112	88.2	87.7
44 Northampton	83.3	81.4	7.5	116	96.9	87.5
45 Queen Mary, London	69.0	69.9	54.8	145	75.7	87.4
46 Keele	67.9	71.7	66.2	121	76.5	86.5
47 Bournemouth	77.8	69.5	29.2	111	90.6	86
=48 Lincoln	78.9	74.4	55.8	121	71.3	85.9
=48 Liverpool John Moores	73.4	75.5	26.5	144	79.5	85.9
50 Cumbria	69.0	56.2	18.5	136	95.5	85.7
51 Sussex	68.6	62.7	54.2	140	74.3	85.6
52 Birmingham City	74.0	66.4	37.8	120	84.9	85.5
=53 Bolton	94.4	81.9	2	121	—	85.2
=53 York St John	86.2	80.1	13.8	118	83.9	85.2
55 Salford	75.3	72.2	37	122	80.3	85.1
=56 Manchester Metropolitan	71.8	69.4	36	119	83.3	84.5
=56 Oxford Brookes	65.6	62.8	37.8	128	85.3	84.5
58 Derby	81.7	76.0	24	125	75.9	84
59 London South Bank	79.2	69.2	34.5	122	76.0	83.9
60 Canterbury Christ Church	66.7	55.9	31.8	120	90.7	83.8
61 Staffordshire	74.5	67.4	30.8	122	—	83.7
62 Leicester	73.9	74.1	—	123	93.3	83.6
=63 Huddersfield	73.6	65.0	22.5	127	83.4	83.5
=63 West of Scotland	77.8	79.2	30.8	134	69.0	83.5
65 Brunel	52.8	53.0	47.2	126	89.6	83.4
66 Brighton	62.5	60.0	50.5	114	82.6	83
=67 Anglia Ruskin	70.5	69.0	33.8	103	86.2	82.8
=67 Nottingham Trent	67.6	69.3	43.5	125	74.2	82.8
69 Central Lancashire	76.0	70.3	35.5	132	69.2	82.7
70 Sheffield Hallam	65.5	60.3	29.8	121	86.1	82.5
71 South Wales	68.3	59.7	25.2	130	81.2	82
=72 Edge Hill	70.2	64.6	22.2	129	—	81.7
=72 St George's, London	67.8	62.3	—	139	88.1	81.7
=72 Sunderland	69.6	64.9	30.2	120	79.2	81.7
75 Leeds Beckett	69.4	70.6	38	109	76.0	81.2
76 Chester	70.3	59.5	31	116	77.8	80.6
77 St Mary's, Twickenham	87.7	89.2	—	123	65.0	79.6
78 Roehampton	70.8	72.2	37.5	105	70.8	79.5
79 Suffolk	54.5	44.6	—	131	97.0	79
=80 Bedfordshire	77.2	53.5	22.5	124	70	78.9
=80 East London	73.9	71.4	25.5	96	76.6	78.9
82 De Montfort	71.8	69.3	20.8	110	74.1	78.6
=83 Essex	66.8	60.4	28.5	121	70.8	78.2
=83 Wolverhampton	68.6	64.3	24.2	118	71.7	78.2

Subjects Allied to Medicine cont.

		Teaching quality %	Student experience %	Research quality %	Entry standards (UCAS points)	Graduate prospects %	Overall score
85	Middlesex	70.3	69.7	22.5	105	74.6	78.1
86	Gloucestershire	65.7	56.2	16.2	127	—	78
87	Worcester	52.3	53.2	24.2	131	78.9	77.6
88	Westminster	54.9	58.1	36.8	111	69.9	75.3

Employed in high-skilled job	62%	Employed in lower-skilled job	12%
Employed in high-skilled job and studying	4%	Employed in lower-skilled job and studying	1%
Studying	16%	Unemployed	5%
High skilled work (median) salary	£24,907	Low/medium skilled salary	£18,813

Theology and Religious Studies

Looking at how different beliefs have influenced society historically and their roles within the contemporary world, Theology and Religious Studies courses draw on students' critical thinking and textual analysis, encouraging intellectual curiosity and articulate communication. Not all who take theology or religious studies degrees go on to work for the Church, but the vocation is among the career pathways that contribute to the subjects ranking 41st out of 70 in our employment table. For pay they place 33rd (though salaries are not an ingredient of our ranking). Other career routes include the civil service, law, international development, the arts, banking, investment, teaching, research, the media, and communications.

Student numbers in theology and religious studies are following a similar pattern to the size of congregations filling pews on Sundays. In 2021's admissions round the subjects attracted 2,705 applications (down 12%, year-on-year) and just 620 students were accepted onto courses – a 17% decline compared with 2020, and less than half the number of a decade before in 2012.

Cambridge holds on to its lead in our subject ranking and claims the top graduate prospects – with 94.3% of graduates employed in professional-level jobs and/or postgraduate study 15 months after their degrees. Exeter moves up to second place from seventh, elevated by the highest-scoring results in the new Research Excellence Framework 2021. Oxford, in fifth place overall, has the highest entry standards with 187 UCAS points averaged among its 2021 entrants.

Based on the outcomes of the National Student Survey, Chester (15th overall) is top for student satisfaction with teaching quality and the wider undergraduate experience, measures in which Kent (joint fifth) is runner-up.

Theology and Religious Studies		Teaching quality %	Student experience %	Research quality %	Entry standards (UCAS points)	Graduate prospects %	Overall score
1	Cambridge	—	—	58.5	184	94.3	100
2	Exeter	82.4	82.7	75.0	139	88.5	96.7
3	Durham	80.0	76.7	55.0	162	82.7	93
4	Glasgow	82.2	78.0	62.5	171	69.6	92.6
=5	Kent	90.3	86.6	65.8	125	71.7*	92.4
=5	Oxford	—	—	44.8	187	86.5	92.4

=5 St Andrews	87.3	83.4	36.5	168	—	92.4
8 Edinburgh	79.5	76.5	51.2	159	82.2	92
9 Birmingham	82.4	75.6	67.2	141	75.6	91.9
10 St Mary's, Twickenham	88.1	84.4	31.0	—	76.2	88.7
=11 Bristol	78.1	72.7	48.5	144	73.3	87.5
=11 King's College London	69.1	61.6	67.0	145	75.0	87.5
13 Leeds	69.7	69.1	52.0	134	83.2	87.1
14 Lancaster	77.3	71.5	49.0	137	—	86.6
15 Chester	93.0	90.4	44.5	105	63.7	86.5
16 Cardiff	80.1	70.3	42.2	129	75.3	85.9
17 Manchester	74.1	64.2	39.5	146	74.2	84.7
18 Nottingham	73.8	61.5	51.5	130	69.4	83.7
19 Roehampton	89.2	81.6	31.5	101	63.1	82.3
20 Liverpool Hope	75.9	74.7	30.5	112	—	79.9
21 Canterbury Christ Church	81.9	77.2	25.0	101	55.0	77.2
22 York St John	82.9	76.8	15.8	93	60.8	76.6

Employed in high-skilled job	48%	Employed in lower-skilled job	24%
Employed in high-skilled job and studying	6%	Employed in lower-skilled job and studying	1%
Studying	16%	Unemployed	5%
High skilled work (median) salary	£25,000	Low/medium skilled salary	£18,250

Town and Country Planning and Landscape

University College London returns to the top of our table this year, after spending the past two years as runner-up. Its position is secured by strong performance in all five measures that make up our ranking – from research, where it places fourth, and the second-highest entry standards, to top-four finishes in both measures of student satisfaction: teaching quality and the wider experience.

Averaging 182 points in the UCAS tariff, Edinburgh leads on entry standards by a clear margin, just as Newcastle does on graduate prospects – with 90.2% of graduates in professional-level employment and/or postgraduate study 15 months after their degrees. In our analysis of the new Research Excellence Framework 2021 results Loughborough leads the field, closely followed by Sheffield. Students at West of England reported the highest rates of satisfaction with the broad undergraduate experience, while those at Sheffield felt the most positive about their teaching quality.

Cambridge topped the Town and Country Planning and Landscape ranking for the past two years but is absent from it this year. This is due its land economy degree now being included in our Land and Property Management table instead.

Degrees in planning include surveying techniques, computer-aided design, plan drawing, report writing and negotiation skills. Various planning courses being offered in 2023 include urban studies, sustainable development and rural enterprise management. Applications rose by 10% in 2021 and have surged by 80% in the decade since 2012, while the numbers starting courses has gone up by around 44% over the timeframe, with 830 applicants being accepted in 2021. Student numbers are lower on landscape and garden design degrees, which accepted 170 new students in 2021.

Around two-thirds of graduates of the various courses encompassed within the planning and landscape grouping had secured professional-level jobs when surveyed 15 months after finishing their degrees, helping to place the subjects 22nd in the employment table. They are also in the top-20 for pay, with graduates in professional-level work earning median starting salaries of £25,000.

Town and Country Planning and Landscape	Teaching quality %	Student experience %	Research quality %	Entry standards (UCAS points)	Graduate prospects %	Overall score
1 University College London	80.7	79.3	61.0	169	—	100
2 Edinburgh	78.7	71.6	59.0	182	—	99.8
3 Sheffield	84.8	82.0	71.8	147	81.5	98.4
4 Leeds	79.2	83.3	64.8	142	—	97.9
5 Manchester	69.4	75.2	59.2	158	85.0*	96
6 Loughborough	70.4	70.1	72.0	137	83.3	94.9
7 Heriot-Watt	73.7	73.3	59.0	166	79.4	94.7
8 Newcastle	66.8	61.2	56.0	126	90.2	94.1
9 Liverpool	81.4	73.8	45.2	127	84.3	93.8
10 Ulster	74.5	77.0	54.2	132	—	93.3
11 West of England	78.3	83.9	40.8	125	81.7	92
12 Birmingham	74.0	67.9	49.2	135	—	91.8
13 Queen's Belfast	80.7	78.7	36.5	131	80	91.3
14 Cardiff	70.2	64.5	38.2	136	82.1	89.8
15 Oxford Brookes	69.5	69.2	33.2	112	79.5	86.4
=16 Gloucestershire	64.8	64.0	24.0	—	80.8	84.5
=16 Leeds Beckett	77.7	70.6	24.5	108	75.0	84.5
18 London South Bank	67.9	57.3	35.0	107	—	84.1
19 Westminster	63.8	60.9	38.2	99	—	83.1

Employed in high-skilled job	64%	Employed in lower-skilled job	18%
Employed in high-skilled job and studying	4%	Employed in lower-skilled job and studying	1%
Studying	10%	Unemployed	3%
High skilled work (median) salary	£25,000	Low/medium skilled salary	£21,000

Veterinary Medicine

In a shake-up to our Veterinary Medicine table, Glasgow has secured the No 1 spot, up from second place, while former winner Edinburgh sits third. Entrants to Glasgow's veterinary medicine degree averaged 213 points in the UCAS tariff in the 2021 admissions cycle – the top entry standards. Liverpool moves into the runner-up position from sixth place, its rank supercharged by achieving the top results in the recent Research Excellence Framework 2021.

Nottingham is hitting all the right notes with its students, achieving exceptionally high scores for teaching quality and the broad student experience in the National Student Survey. Even more remarkable is that this is the second consecutive year the university has topped both measures of student satisfaction.

Led by Cambridge, which has a 100% rate of graduate employment in high-skilled jobs and/or postgraduate study, and reaching no lower than 88.5% at the Royal Veterinary College, employment rates in veterinary medicine are so tightly bunched that they do not form part of the calculations which determine universities' positions, although the scores are still shown in our table. Veterinary medicine is in the top four subjects for earnings in professional jobs, as it also is in this year's employment table.

The norm for veterinary science degrees is five years, but the Cambridge course takes six years and both Bristol and Nottingham offer a gateway year. Edinburgh and the Royal Veterinary College also run four-year courses for graduates. The subject is offered by very few universities – none of them in Wales or Northern Ireland – and student numbers are centrally controlled. Although not featured in our table yet as there is not enough data to include it, the University of Surrey opened the UK's eighth vet school in 2013. A ninth launched in 2020, a joint venture between Keele and Harper Adams, which will also be included in our table once it has sufficient statistics to populate the rankings.

Some veterinary schools demand high grades in chemistry and biology, while others require chemistry and one or two additional science subjects, such as biology, maths or physics. Cambridge also sets applicants an admissions test and all vet schools require candidates to have proven their commitment to the course by completing some form of relevant work experience before applying. Ever a competitive subject, in the 2021 admissions cycle there were nearly 11,500 applications for 1,700 places. The deadline for applications is October 15, earlier than for most other subjects to allow extra time to process the high demand for courses.

Veterinary Medicine		Teaching quality %	Student experience %	Research quality %	Entry standards (UCAS points)	Graduate prospects %	Overall score
1	Glasgow	85.9	85.2	64.8	218	93.1	100
2	Liverpool	85.5	81.9	68.2	172	97.2	96.3
3	Edinburgh	83.7	79.5	50.2	213	98.9	93
4	Cambridge	—	—	60.2	197	100	92.6
5	Nottingham	95.5	94.5	52	155	97.4	92.1
6	Surrey	83.3	82.8	58	168	97.1	91.6
7	Bristol	79.3	78.5	60.2	171	97.9	91.4
8	Royal Veterinary College	75.6	69.3	55	180	96	88.5

Employed in high-skilled job	95%	Employed in lower-skilled job	2%
Employed in high-skilled job and studying	1%	Employed in lower-skilled job and studying	0%
Studying	1%	Unemployed	1%
High skilled work (median) salary	£31,000	Low/medium skilled salary	£29,000

13 Applying to Oxbridge

Known collectively as Oxbridge, the two ancient universities of Oxford and Cambridge continue to dominate the academic rankings. Oxford tops our league table this year while Cambridge – which led our academic table for eight years until 2021 – sits third. Only once has Oxbridge been ousted from the head of our rankings; a distinction claimed by St Andrew's – last year's top university and this year's runner-up.

On the international stage, Oxbridge's tenure as the UK's top-ranked universities remains unchallenged. In the 2023 edition of *Times Higher Education's* global league table, Oxford takes first place and Cambridge third. But it is Cambridge with the lead over its old rival in the 2023 QS World University rankings – where it takes second position, while Oxford sits fourth.

Enduring academic big hitters though these universities are, it is their admissions arrangements that warrant a separate chapter in our *Guide*. Oxford and Cambridge are part of the UCAS system but there are three significant peculiarities to the process of applying to them:

1. The deadline for applications is October 15 at 6pm – three months earlier than for other universities for entry in 2024 or deferred entry in 2025.
2. You can only apply to one or the other university in the same year, so you need to choose between the two.
3. Selection is in the hands of the colleges rather than the university centrally. Most candidates apply to a specific college, although open applications can be made if you are happy to go to any college.

What are the chances of getting in?

For anyone with Oxbridge in their sights, this is a "starter for 10" question. Competition intensifies every year and Oxbridge is continuing to broaden its intake. Cambridge typically receives six applications per place on average across all subjects, while Oxford received around seven per place in 2021. But these ratios vary noticeably, as the tables on pages 285-6 and page 287 show.

In the 2021 admissions cycle, Cambridge received 22,795 applications (up from 20,426 in 2020), made 4,260 offers (down from 4,710 year on year), and accepted 3,660 new undergraduates (down from 3,997). This follows 2020's exceptional year in which there were over 450 additional acceptances to Cambridge, due to the Covid-19 pandemic.

Oxford's response to the pandemic also resulted in a larger cohort than usual being admitted. In 2021, Oxford received 24,338 applications (up from 23,414 in 2020), made 3,555 offers (down from 3,932) and admitted 3,298 new undergraduates (down from 3,695).

Entry standards are famously formidable. While three A grades is Oxford's minimum standard offer, many courses – particularly in the sciences – require at least one A* grade. At Oxford, more than 77% of 2021's UK applicants and almost 95% of admitted students were awarded A*AA or better at A-level, while 68.1% achieved three A* grades. The picture is very similar at Cambridge, where the typical conditional A-level offer is A*AA or A*A*A. Of home students accepted to Cambridge in the 2021 cycle, 98.6% achieved the equivalent of A*AA or better.

Such statistics should not put bright, academically driven students off from applying. What is the worst that can happen? One wasted option out of five on a UCAS form, perhaps. One thing to be mindful of, though, is that selectors have to be confident that applicants will cope with the demands of an undergraduate course at Oxbridge. At only eight weeks long, Oxbridge terms are intensive.

Student satisfaction?

Both universities boycott the National Student Survey (NSS). But going by a report by the Higher Education Policy Unit, published in 2018 and based on six years of survey results, Oxbridge students were more content with university life than their Russell Group peers. The analysis found they students were more satisfied with their courses, believed that they got better feedback and enjoyed greater wellbeing, although they studied for longer hours.

Job prospects for those with Oxbridge degrees are reliably promising. Cambridge ranks second this year, with 92.6% of graduates employed in high skilled jobs or engaged in postgraduate study 15 months on from their degrees. Oxford is in fourth place, with 91.6% of graduates having achieved these desired outcomes.

Cambridge: The Tompkins Table

The 2022 Tompkins table ranks by college the results of all Cambridge students in their end-of-year Tripos examinations this summer

College	2022**	2019	2018	2017	College	2022**	2019	2018	2017
Christ's	1	1	1	2	Sidney Sussex	16	13	17	17
Trinity	2	2	3	1	Robinson	17	21	24	25
St Catharine's	3	9	10	19	Magdalene	18	18	18	16
Jesus	4	14	6	14	Trinity Hall	19	10	12	15
Pembroke	5	3	2	4	Fitzwilliam	20	17	19	21
St John's	6	15	8	3	Wolfson	21	27	29	27
Gonville & Caius	7	16	14	11	King's	22	12	5	8
Churchill	8	5	7	5	Hughes Hall	23	25	25	26
Corpus Christi	9	11	15	12	Newnham	24	22	22	23
Queens'	10	6	13	7	Girton	25	20	23	24
Emmanuel	11	7	9	6	Homerton	26	26	27	28
Clare	12	24	16	13	Murray Edwards	27	19	26	29
Downing	13	23	20	20	St Edmund's	28	28	21	22
Selwyn	14	8	11	9	Lucy Cavendish	29	29	28	18
Peterhouse	15	4	4	10					

*Published by Varsity. Based on degree classifications: 1st=5pts; 2:1=3pts; 2:2=2pts; 3rd=1pt.
**The Tompkins Table was not published in 2020 or 2021 because of the pandemic.
Source: Peter Tompkins, 2022

Diversity

Progress to widen access to Oxbridge is accelerating. Professor Stephen Toope, the vice-chancellor of the University of Cambridge, told The Times in May 2022: "I would say we have to keep making it very, very clear we are intending to reduce over time the number of people who are coming from independent school backgrounds into places like Oxford or Cambridge."

In 2021, the proportion of students joining Oxford from state schools was 68.2%, up from 58% five years earlier. Our social inclusion ranking confirms this dynamic, although our social inclusion index measures admissions from non-selective state schools only, which stood at 52.2% in the latest data, up from 45.6% the before – and a rise from 39.4% in 2018 when we first launched it. The proportion of students from ethnic minorities (23.7%) ranks Oxford 61st (up from 63rd year on year) among the 116 universities in England and Wales.

The proportion drawn from deprived areas has almost doubled at Oxford to 15.9% over the past five years. The number of those who come from areas of low progression to higher education has risen from 11.4% to 15.6% over the same period.

The university's flagship access programme, UNIQ, has extended its reach by transferring online and the university has grown its bridging programme, Opportunity Oxford, from 116 offers in 2020 to 231 in 2022. In 2023, Oxford will welcome its first 50 Astrophoria Foundation Year students. The one-year programme for UK state school students with significant academic potential, who have experienced severe personal disadvantage and/or disrupted education, offers them full financial support.

Cambridge is also working hard to diversify its student community. State school pupils represented 71.6% of the 2021 intake (up from 70.6% in 2020). The proportion from non-selective-only state schools was 48.5%.

Oxford: The Norrington Table

The 2021 Norrington table ranks by college the performance of 3,072 undergraduates who completed their finals last summer

College	2021	2020	2019	2018	College	2020	2019	2018	2017
Merton	1	5	1	4	Keble	16	24	23	23
St John's	2	8	6	1	Mansfield	17	29	5	20
Lincoln	3	10	21	26	Wadham	18	6	20	8
Brasenose	4	7	16	7	St Hugh's	19	15	30	28
New College	5	1	2	5	Oriel	20	9	8	12
St Catherine's	6	2	4	3	Christ Church	21	28	15	11
Worcester	7	14	24	=13	Magdalen	22	20	3	2
Balliol	8	16	9	9	Trinity	23	12	26	10
Harris Manchester	9	21	11	30	St Edmund Hall	24	25	29	29
St Anne's	10	22	28	24	Exeter	25	26	19	18
Queen's	11	3	7	19	Somerville	26	30	22	22
Corpus Christi	12	23	12	15	Hertford	27	11	14	27
St Peter's	13	4	25	16	Pembroke	28	19	17	25
University	14	13	13	17	St Hilda's	29	17	18	=13
Jesus	15	18	10	6	Lady Margaret Hall	30	27	27	21

*Published by Cherwell. Based on degree classifications: 1st=5pts; 2:1=3pts; 2:2=2pts; 3rd=1pt. Score shown is the percentage of total points available. Where tied, the overall number of first-class degrees and then 2:1s are used as separators

Oxford applications and acceptances by course

Arts	Applications			Acceptances			Success rate %		
	2021	2020	2019	2021	2020	2019	2021	2020	2019
Ancient and modern history	98	100	94	26	19	24	26.5	19	26
Archaeology and anthropology	103	113	103	19	30	22	18.4	27	21
Classical archaeology and ancient history	121	84	110	29	28	17	24.0	33	15
Classics	252	278	278	106	119	115	42.1	43	41
Classics and English	35	35	40	13	16	12	37.1	30	26
Classics and modern languages	13	20	9	5	7	3	38.5	33	38
Computer science and philosophy	151	175	149	12	16	13	7.9	9	9
Economics and management	1,732	1,540	1,529	87	93	85	5.0	6	6
English language and literature	942	901	1,058	229	247	223	24.3	27	21
English and modern languages	99	117	104	32	31	24	32.3	26	23
European and Middle Eastern languages	31	39	51	15	14	18	48.4	36	35
Fine art	264	219	231	29	29	26	11.0	13	11
Geography	458	448	538	79	97	84	17.2	22	16
History	933	1,078	1,127	229	278	223	24.5	26	23
History and economics	172	167	168	17	15	19	9.9	9	11
History and English	121	112	110	13	13	13	10.7	12	12
History and modern languages	83	113	98	23	27	19	27.7	24	19
History and politics	463	415	403	49	51	36	10.2	12	9
History of art	121	119	131	18	18	14	14.9	15	11
Law	1,674	1,611	1,566	209	234	178	12.5	15	11
Law with law studies in Europe	304	274	303	31	29	30	10.9	11	10
Mathematics and philosophy	158	120	137	20	21	13	12.7	18	9
Modern languages	371	406	414	166	170	156	44.7	42	38
Modern languages and linguistics	86	77	96	34	31	32	39.5	40	33
Music	146	185	198	74	87	70	50.7	47	35
Oriental studies	156	150	205	41	45	40	26.3	30	20
Philosophy and modern languages	63	66	78	16	21	23	25.4	32	29
Philosophy and theology	146	140	149	29	29	30	19.9	21	20
Physics and philosophy	174	182	179	14	15	17	8.0	8	9
Philosophy, politics and economics (PPE)	2,300	2,233	2,338	232	256	242	10.1	11	10
Theology and religion	112	133	92	43	56	35	38.4	42	38
Religion and Oriental studies	11	9	7	3	2	2	27.3	22	29
Total Arts	**11,893**	**11,659**	**12,093**	**1,942**	**2,144**	**1,858**	**23.6**	**18.4**	**15.4**

The university's new free and fully-funded Foundation Year for study in the arts, humanities or social sciences welcomed its first 52 students in autumn 2022. No tuition fees are charged for the year and scholarship funding covers accommodation and living costs. Entry requirements are BBB at A-level (120 UCAS tariff points) and five applicants chased each place in the inaugural year through a rigorous process of interviews and assessments. Foundation Year

Oxford applications and acceptances by course cont.

Sciences	Applications			Acceptances			Success rate %		
	2021	2020	2019	2021	2020	2019	2021	2020	2019
Biochemistry	738	707	752	107	114	96	14.5	16	13
Biology	677	739	700	99	122	110	14.6	17	16
Biomedical sciences	558	449	418	43	49	39	7.7	11	9
Chemistry	862	774	637	183	220	179	2.2	28	28
Computer science	843	682	693	33	42	44	3.9	6	6
Earth sciences (Geology)	111	142	116	37	40	35	33.3	28	30
Engineering science	1,097	1,159	1,040	172	189	174	15.7	16	17
Experimental psychology	469	496	427	57	68	56	12.2	14	13
Human sciences	233	220	186	29	39	30	12.4	18	16
Materials science	178	147	188	45	47	47	25.3	32	25
Mathematics	1,849	1,829	1,656	169	196	184	9.1	11	11
Mathematics and computer science	603	502	424	46	36	40	7.6	7	9
Mathematics and statistics	262	232	225	9	8	12	3.4	3	5
Medicine	2,054	1,768	1,795	151	165	161	7.4	9	9
Physics	1,630	1,646	1,405	166	181	185	10.2	11	13
Psychology and philosophy (PPL)	281	263	265	30	35	30	10.7	13	11
Total Sciences	**12,455**	**11,755**	**10,927**	**1,342**	**1,551**	**1,422**	**11.9**	**13.2**	**12.9**
Total Arts and Sciences	**24,338**	**23,414**	**23,020**	**3,298**	**3,695**	**3,280**	**17.8**	**16**	**14.1**

students who achieve 65% in their exams can move on to a full degree course on one of the university's 18 courses in the arts, humanities or social sciences

Among other outreach activities, Cambridge works with social mobility charities such as the Sutton Trust and Target Oxbridge, while individual colleges have links with different areas with low records of sending students to Russell Group universities. Since its launch in 2018, the Stormzy Scholarship has provided financial support to 19 UK black students at Cambridge. This began with two students each year, before the scheme was expanded in 2021 to benefit at least 10 black students starting their studies in autumn 2022.

Stating the case: public or private

According to an Independent Schools Council (ISC) census in 2022, the proportion of pupils getting into Oxford and Cambridge from the UK independent sector was at 4.3% in 2021, down from 5.3% the year before and 6.5% in 2016. To put this in context, the independent sector educates around 5.8% of all schoolchildren in the UK.

As Oxbridge works to broaden its intake, independent schools' coaching of pupils to excel at applications and interviews is proving less effective than it once was. "We want to select the academically most able – the really strong candidates versus those that are average but have been well-prepared," Samina Khan, Oxford's director of undergraduate admissions, has said.

While Oxbridge is making progress, the universities continue to prop-up the bottom of our social inclusion index of universities in England and Wales – which looks at nine measures of social

Cambridge applications and acceptances by course

Arts, Humanities and Social Sciences	Applications			Acceptances			Success rate %		
	2021	2020	2019	2021	2020	2019	2021	2020	2019
Anglo-Saxon, Norse and Celtic	45	44	60	24	26	19	53.3	59.1	31.7
Archaeology	39	57	58	20	24	22	51.3	42.1	37.9
Architecture	370	471	455	53	51	53	14.3	10.8	11.6
Asian and Middle Eastern studies	108	117	143	41	51	43	38	43.6	30.1
Classics	107	138	134	54	73	66	50.5	52.9	49.3
Classics (four years)	53	66	57	26	33	21	49	50.0	36.8
Economics	776	1,364	1,143	102	165	156	13.1	12.1	13.6
Education	62	140	153	26	44	42	41.9	31.4	27.5
English	654	730	766	172	232	189	26.3	31.8	24.7
Geography	386	351	297	88	116	93	22.8	33.0	31.3
History	522	632	616	172	217	174	33	34.3	28.2
History and modern languages	64	94	92	20	33	25	31.3	35.1	27.2
History and politics	225	261	223	51	62	41	22.7	23.8	18.4
History of art	67	105	122	28	25	26	41.8	23.8	21.3
Human, social and political sciences	819	1,075	1,089	129	210	185	15.8	19.5	17.0
Land economy	222	363	314	44	69	50	19.8	19.0	15.9
Law	1,097	1,537	1,498	169	262	221	15.4	17.0	14.8
Linguistics	80	98	100	34	40	24	42.5	40.8	24.0
Modern and medieval languages	319	378	417	148	187	159	46.4	49.5	38.1
Music	154	138	172	65	70	65	42.2	50.7	37.8
Philosophy	206	222	251	47	49	47	22.8	22.1	18.7
Theology and religious studies	91	131	124	37	55	39	40.7	42.0	31.5
Total Arts, Humanities and Social Sciences	**6,466**	**8,512**	**8,284**	**1,550**	**2,094**	**1,760**	**33.4**	**24.6**	**21.2**

Sciences	2021	2020	2019	2021	2020	2019	2021	2020	2019
Computer science	955	1,465	1,330	77	119	116	8.1	8.1	8.7
Engineering	1,545	2,518	2,250	220	363	329	14.2	14.4	14.6
Mathematics	921	1,633	1,518	140	251	253	15.2	15.4	16.7
Medicine	1,369	1,817	1,584	246	295	281	18	16.2	17.7
Medicine (graduate course)	42	485	552	3	37	43	7.1	7.6	7.8
Natural sciences	1,796	3,042	2,922	410	663	608	22.8	21.8	20.8
Psychological and behavioural sciences	476	547	527	65	96	71	13.7	17.6	13.5
Veterinary medicine	297	407	392	58	79	67	19.5	19.4	17.1
Total Science and Technology	**7,401**	**11,914**	**11,075**	**1,219**	**1,903**	**1,768**	**14.8**	**16.0**	**16.0**
Total	**22,795**	**20,426**	**19,359**	**3,660**	**3,997**	**3,528**	**24.1**	**19.6**	**18.2**

Note: the dates refer to the year in which the acceptances were made.
Mathematics includes mathematics and mathematics with physics

inclusion: state school entrants (non-grammar); ethnic minorities; black attainment gap; white working-class males; low participation areas; low participation areas dropout gap; first-generation students; disabled students; mature students. Oxford finishes second from bottom at 115th (as it did the year before) and Cambridge is in last place at 116th (as in our previous edition).

Choosing the right college

Undergraduates at Cambridge are admitted to 29 colleges, each with its own distinctive history, atmosphere and location. It is worth visiting before applying to help you decide on a college that most suits, though it is possible to make an open application. Oxford has 30 colleges that accept undergraduates, and applicants should likewise do their research.

That said, both universities work to find a college for those who either make an open application or who are not taken by their first choice. At Oxford, subject tutors put candidates into bands, using the results of admissions tests as well as exam results and references. Applicants may not be seen by their preferred college if the tutors think their chances are better elsewhere.

The "pool" at Cambridge gives the most promising candidates a second chance if they were not offered a place at the college they applied to. Cambridge still interviews around 80% of applicants, whereas Oxford interviews around 40% to 45% of candidates.

The tables in this chapter give an idea of the relative strengths of the colleges, as well as the levels of competition for a place in different subjects. But only individual research will help you uncover where you will feel most at home.

The application process

Both universities have made concerted efforts to demystify the application process.

Cambridge requires most applicants to take a written pre-interview admission assessment at the beginning of November. Some subjects administer tests at interview and some applicants are asked to submit examples of their written work. The Cambridge website lists the pre-interview assessments, which may include a reading comprehension, problem-solving test; or thinking skills assessment; in addition to a paper on the subject itself.

Applicants to Oxford must also take an admissions test for many courses, and written work may be a requirement. Those who are shortlisted are invited to interview in early to mid-December.

Applicants to Cambridge must also complete an online Supplementary Application Questionnaire (SAQ) by October 22 (6pm UK time) in most cases. However, there is an earlier deadline of September 27 for international applicants.

Interviews for 2023 entry to Cambridge (or deferred entry in 2024) took place online, except for UK-based applicants to Trinity College. Oxford also decided to continue holding undergraduate admissions interviews (2022-23) online. At the time of writing the interview format for 2024 entry (or deferred entry in 2025) remained up for review at each university. Applicants receive either a conditional offer or a rejection in the new year.

For more information about the application process and preparing for interviews, visit **www.undergraduate.study.cam.ac.uk/** or **www.ox.ac.uk/admissions/undergraduate**.

Oxford College Profiles

Balliol

Oxford OX1 3BJ   01865 277 765   www.balliol.ox.ac.uk
Undergraduates: 390   Postgraduates: 385   undergraduate@balliol.ox.ac.uk

While maintaining its reputation since 1263 as the oldest academic site in the English-speaking world co-founded by a woman, Balliol also has one of the liveliest junior common rooms (known as JCRs) of all Oxford colleges. Named after John de Balliol, who was ordered by Henry III to perform a substantial act of charity, the "House of the Scholars of Balliol" was established formally by his widow, Dervorguilla. It is the only Oxford college to boast the triple "threat" (to study) of a student-run bar, popular café and excellent theatre – the Michael Pilch Studio. Academics are still a priority, and the college consistently falls within the top 10 on the Norrington Table, ranking eighth in the latest table, see page 284. Finalists and tutors inhabit the beautiful front quad, now equipped with a ramp to make the college accessible. Undergraduates are guaranteed accommodation for their first and final years, while graduate students are typically lodged in beautiful Holywell Manor. The impressive mediaeval library hosts 70,000 books and periodicals. Friendly librarians buy any texts necessary for the vast 32 courses on offer, and also host popular quizzes and ghost tours throughout the year. With access programmes for Year 12 students, Balliol also runs interview and admissions tests workshops for prospective applicants.

Brasenose

Oxford OX1 4AJ   01865 277 510   www.bnc.ox.ac.uk
Undergraduates: 375   Postgraduates: 235   admissions@bnc.ox.ac.uk

Brasenose is renowned as friendly, accessible and forward-thinking, focusing primarily on welfare and reducing its environmental impact through its EESG – an environmental strategy steering group, which meets twice a term. The diversity and equality committee (D&E) runs a diversity week each Michaelmas (the first of three terms at Oxford). Freshers' events feature LGBTQ+ and CRAE (Campaign for Racial Awareness and Equality) workshops. Throughout the year there is excellent support, with an on-site counsellor, yoga classes, welfare walks, sexual health advice and trained peer supporters. Results have soared in recent years: Law, PPE, and history are traditional strengths. This academic year, all biochemists and physicists achieved firsts. The annual Arts Week is very popular, celebrating varied art forms – from a poetry reading brunch to a stage-combat workshop. Generous sports grants encourage participation in university teams, and the prestigious Brasenose boat club is one of the oldest in the world. The Brazen Nose door knocker, after which the college is named, was placed on the wall in 1890 and hangs above the high table. Served in the beautiful sixteenth-century dining hall, the food is delicious, affordable and always includes vegetarian and vegan options. Unusually, college accommodation is guaranteed for all undergraduates in the city centre – with first and third-years housed in college; and second and fourth-years in either the Frewin or Hollybush Row annexes nearby.

Christh Church

Oxford OX1 1DP — 01865 286 583 — www.chch.ox.ac.uk
Undergraduates: 470 — Postgraduates: 235 — admissions@chch.ox.ac.uk

Christ Church remains one of the most imposing sites in the university and boasts the largest quad in Oxford. The impressive scale, beautiful meadow and religious foundations of Christ Church continue to attract students, academics and tourists in large swathes. Founded by Cardinal Wolsey in 1525, it is also the Cathedral of the Oxford diocese. The well-publicised and costly employment tribunals with its former dean, the Very Reverend Martyn Percy, came to a close in April 2022 as he left both the college and the Church of England. A new dean is yet to be announced. Undergraduate politics are likewise renowned since Christ Church's student body disaffiliated from the students' union in 2021 – a move colloquially referred to as "ChChexit" (the college is referred to as "ChCh"). Bowler-hatted porters, a listed eighteenth-century library, daily formal dining and wooden-panelled shared "sets" (double rooms), characterise the overall feel of student life here. Accommodation covers all four years and ranges from the Blue Boar 1960s concrete block (for first-years), to the beautiful rooms in Peck quad (the domain of second-years) and the impressive Meadows and Old Library rooms (mostly for third- and fourth-years). The infamous *Harry Potter* hall hosts two servings every evening, one informal and one formal. Students choose between two student bars: The Buttery, open daily, and The Undie, from Wednesday to Saturday. Extracurriculars are a notable feature of college life, with an impressive choir, music and drama societies.

Corpus Christi

Oxford OX1 4JF — 01865 276 693 — www.ccc.ox.ac.uk
Undergraduates: 275 — Postgraduates: 105 — admissions.office@ccc.ox.ac.uk

Corpus Christi describes itself as an inspiring oasis for study and friendship. The tight-knit community and friendly atmosphere are nurtured within beautiful buildings between Christ Church meadow and the High Street. Over its 500-year history, the college has prioritised philanthropy. Founded in 1517 by Richard Fox, Bishop of Winchester – whose coat of arms shows a pelican in a selfless act of charity – Fox's focus on humanist learning had a strong influence on its impressive sixteenth-century library. The original bookstacks sit alongside more modern reading rooms, which contain 70,000 volumes. Recent exhibitions have showcased Corpus's very own *Magna Carta* and *King James Bible* manuscripts. Small but mighty, the college provides one of Oxford's most generous bursary schemes which bestows travel, book and vacation grants. Academic expectations are high; medicine, English, classics and PPE are especially well-established. Corpus's postgraduate community represents 25 countries. Quirky extracurriculars include the Cheese Society and an annual tortoise race. The large and modern Al Jaber Auditorium is used for music, drama, art exhibitions and film screenings. Corpus's drama club, The Owlets, is highly regarded.

Exeter

Oxford OX1 3DP — 01865 279 668 — www.exeter.ox.ac.uk
Undergraduates: 375 — Postgraduates: 275 — admissions@exeter.ox.ac.uk

The fourth oldest Oxford college, Exeter is situated in the heart of town on Turl Street, between the High Street and Broad Street. It has occupied its current site since 1315 – one year after it was founded. One of Exeter's many enviable features is its spectacular view from the Fellows' Garden, which overlooks the beautiful Radcliffe Camera and impressive All Souls' College.

Most undergraduates are guaranteed in-college accommodation, though many second-years choose to live out. Modern Cohen Quad, located on Walton Street and nearer Worcester college, provides 90 en-suite bedrooms. With a large number of postgraduates, the college has a distinctly international feel. The Williams at Exeter Programme maintains links to Williams College, Massachusetts and gives 26 American students full college membership. The college is supporting four carbon emission reduction programmes, while simultaneously helping communities in Rwanda, Kenya and Bulgaria. Exeter hosts essay competitions for prospective undergraduates and is part of the Oxford for South West Consortium with Lady Margaret Hall and Merton, focusing on Bristol and the southwest of England. The college counts many prominent twentieth-century writers among its alumni including Martin Amis, Alan Bennett, Phillip Pullman and JRR Tolkien. Arts-based extracurriculars are strong, particularly the annual Arts Festival, in partnership with neighbours Lincoln and Jesus.

Harris Manchester

Oxford OX1 3TD   01865 271 009   www.hmc.ox.ac.uk
Undergraduates: 105   Postgraduates: 205   admissions@hmc.ox.ac.uk

The only college solely for mature students aged over 21, Harris Manchester is known for its inclusivity and openness – attracting students from across the globe. The college's Principal, Jane Shaw, fosters a vision for an internationally and ethnically diverse community, erasing age barriers so that students can gain a first, second or third chance at higher education. All members of the MCR (middle common room) are also members of the JCR (junior common room), which creates a close-knit community. Close to the Bodleian, Harris Manchester's own library is excellent, and boasts the best student-to-book ratio of any college. Its small size, however, means many sports teams join other colleges and degree course offerings are relatively limited. The college was originally founded in Manchester in 1786 to provide education for non-Anglican students; and after stints in both York and London it finally settled in Oxford in 1889, moving to its current central site in 1996 where it enjoys beautiful buildings and grounds just off Holywell Street. All accommodation is on the main site: the 2017 student building provides additional en-suite rooms, a lecture hall, music practice rooms and a gym. The college hosts a range of extracurriculars centred around diversity: weekly language nights over dinner; a liberations working group relating to black, Asian and ethnic minority members, LGBTQIA+, women and disability communities; and a refugee language programme provides tutoring and companionship to Syrian families.

Hertford

Oxford OX1 3BW   01865 279 404   www.hertford.ox.ac.uk
Undergraduates: 435   Postgraduates: 255   undergraduate.admissions@hertford.ox.ac.uk

With its ambitious new project, Hertford 2030, the college has announced a period of transformational change and is raising £16million to build a new library. The *Future Fund* aims to create a sustainable fundraising model for the college to maintain its ethos of inclusivity, outreach and diversity. Known as "the college with the bridge" – after the breath-taking Bridge of Sighs which links two of its buildings opposite the Bodleian Library – Hertford also provides educational bridges for prospective and current students. The John Porter Diplomacy Centre will support scholarships, research and peace-making. A new residential course for second-year undergraduates, *Head, Hand & Hertford*, focuses on developing skills often missed from formal education – featuring an introduction to ethics, how to understand power and how to find purpose. Granted full college status in 1740, Hertford provides means-tested bursaries to

UK undergraduates studying for a first degree. It also partners with Opportunity Oxford, which supports talented offer-holders from underrepresented backgrounds. Hertford is proud that 77% of its new students are from state schools, higher than the college-wide average of 68%. The college provides accommodation across all years: first-years live on site, while second- and third-years are in catered halls near Folly Bridge. Hertford's strong music scene includes a jazz band, wind band, choir and orchestra.

Jesus

Oxford OX1 3DW   01865 279 721   www.jesus.ox.ac.uk
Undergraduates: 385   Postgraduates: 260   admissions.officer@jesus.ox.ac.uk

Having undergone the largest transformation of the college since the seventeenth century with the £40million Cheng Yu Tung Building, named after its principal donor, the Cheng Kar Shun Digital Hub events programme has drawn in an array of impressive panel speakers to demystify the digital age. Visible from central Cornmarket Street, the new building also contains 64 en-suite rooms, a ground floor retail space and the Tower Room for events and exhibitions. The lower ground floor houses an NHS Primary Care Centre. The college maintains strong links with Wales, having been founded by Elizabeth I at the request of a Welsh churchman in 1571. Tucked away on a small site off Turl Street, Welsh dragons sit proudly at the entrances to staircases in Second Quad – now an appropriate nod to the well-funded outreach programme across Wales and flagship summer school programme to encourage Welsh state school students to apply. A generous range of financial support includes book and vacation grants. The lively JCR is housed in modern accommodation with a conservatory and snack bar where students play pool. Offsite, Jesus has squash courts and extensive playing fields with hockey, cricket, football and rugby pitches, grass tennis courts, netball courts, a boathouse and a sports pavilion. It holds a shared ball with Somerville every three years.

Keble

Oxford OX1 3PG   01865 272 708   www.keble.ox.ac.uk
Undergraduates: 460   Postgraduates: 525   admissions@keble.ox.ac.uk

The "holy zebra" stripy brickwork of Oxford's most distinctive Victorian college, Keble, was intended to mark the college from its predecessors and attract attention and funding. Keble is still marking itself out from the crowd: the second exhibition of Keble portraits, with two more planned in 2023 and 2024, currently hangs in the longest dining hall in Oxford. The collection of 28 individuals by portrait photographer Fran Monks, also digitised on Twitter, showcases tales of resilience and tenacity from different genders, disabilities, ethnicities and socioeconomic backgrounds. Each figure was nominated by peers for making a positive difference to Keble, Oxford and the world. The sheer size of the dining hall reflects Keble's 1870s foundational premise that students should eat together regularly. Café Keble and the Red Brick Oven, the college pizza bar, are both open all day. Student productions run from the O'Reilly Theatre every fortnight, making Keble one of the best places for drama. Student magazine *Strangeway* celebrates undergraduate literature and writing. The annual Keble Ball is arguably the most popular black-tie event in Oxford. Undergraduate accommodation is provided for three years; some students live out in their second or fourth year. The graduate community is based a short distance from the main site at the HB Allen Centre with 250 new rooms. Keble's sporting facilities and record are exemplary, with a sports ground for football, cricket and tennis 15 minutes away, as well as shared squash courts and a boat house.

Lady Margaret Hall

Oxford OX2 6QA   01865 274 310   www.lmh.ox.ac.uk
Undergraduates: 410   Postgraduates: 305   admissions@lmh.ox.ac.uk

In October 1879, nine women entered Lady Margaret Hall (LMH): the first women to receive an Oxford education. The new principal of LMH, Professor Stephen Blyth, is committed to continuing this trend by reducing barriers to higher education. The college was the first to establish a Foundation Year for students from underrepresented groups and paved the way for Foundation Oxford, a new university-wide scheme. Situated just north of the city centre, LMH has an enviable expanse of green space compared to more central colleges. Beautiful gardens back onto the Cherwell River and the grounds include a punt house and tennis courts. The college has a strong reputation in PPE (philosophy, politics and economics) with Nobel Peace Prize laureate Malala Yousafzai among its graduates. The college's art scene is supported by its library's extensive collections in the arts and humanities. The library is spread across three floors and contains 75,000 books. Music has become a strong focus at the college: there is a concert series, several student-run ensembles and visits by guest artists. Accommodation is guaranteed for first, second and third-year students in the Pipe Partridge, a graceful neo-classical building with 64 en-suite bedrooms, the theatre and JCR.

Lincoln

Oxford OX1 3DR   01865 279 836   www.lincoln.ox.ac.uk
Undergraduates: 320   Postgraduates: 315   admissions@lincoln.ox.ac.uk

Third in the Norrington Table and with Prime Minister Rishi Sunak as an alumnus, Lincoln is an up-and-coming smaller college which prides itself on academia as well as extracurriculars. Warm, friendly and dynamic, Lincoln won a sustainability award and launched a West Midlands access programme called Pathfinders in 2022. Located centrally on Turl Street, next to Exeter and Jesus, Lincoln is largely comprised of ivy-covered mediaeval buildings. It is home to one of the most beautiful libraries in Oxford, a converted Queen Anne Church. The supportive environment includes a welfare team, "cookie fairies" and tutors who are renowned for checking in on wellbeing. College food is excellent; the dining hall serves three meals a day during term-time – a rarity among older colleges. Deep Hall, the college bar, is popular with students and serves lighter food. The college has generous subsidies for food and accommodation, with a large number of bursaries and hardship awards. Lincoln has many scholarships available for graduates and also rewards undergraduates who perform well in examinations. City centre accommodation is provided for all undergraduates; graduate students are housed in Bear Lane or Little Clarendon Street nearby. Drama and music are popular: the Oakeshott Room in the recently refurbished Garden Building is a well-used venue for screenings and performances – especially during the Turl Street Arts Festival.

Magdalen

Oxford OX1 4AU   01865 276 063   www.magd.ox.ac.uk
Undergraduates: 430   Postgraduates: 185   admissions@magd.ox.ac.uk

One of the oldest, largest and most beautiful colleges, Magdalen rivals Christ Church in terms of renown. Choir boys sing from its stunning bell tower to mark May Day. Its breath-taking grounds are thought to have inspired CS Lewis's depiction of Narnia as he strolled around them; they host a deer park, punting house, riverside walkway and even a college dog. Tutors are known for their worldwide research and encourage applicants with a strong interest in their chosen subject and excellent academic ability. Magdalen typically sits within the top five on the Norrington Table and tends to attract students who have rarely dropped a grade, although has fallen to around 20th place in the last couple of years and ranks 22nd in the latest table. More than a quarter of students receive financial support – from travel grants to funding for creative projects. College diversity initiatives include packages for care-experienced students, as well as financial grants and welfare support from counselling to mentoring. A huge appeal of Magdalen is access to beautiful in-college rooms, which all cost the same, though its double "sets" (two rooms with a drawing room in between) can be impressive to the point of austerity. The Magdalen Players host a production in the gardens every summer, and the Florio Society (poetry) and Atkin Society (Law) are among extensive extracurricular options.

Mansfield

Oxford OX1 3TF   01865 282 920   www.mansfield.ox.ac.uk
Undergraduates: 265   Postgraduates: 210   registrar@mansfield.ox.ac.uk

As around 80 undergraduate students at Mansfield enter the college for the first time, Principal Helen Mountfield quotes poet Mary Oliver to ask: "Tell me what it is you plan to do with your one wild and precious life?" This is an aspirational and exceptionally high-achieving college, with the highest intake of state-sector applicants from a wide variety of social and educational backgrounds. Opened in Oxford in 1886, Mansfield's original purpose in educating non-conformist ministers is echoed in its current commitment to access: the college began outreach work before many Oxford colleges with the Access to Excellence scheme established in 2000. Mansfield has extensive facilities considering its size, with four 24-hour libraries, the popular Crypt Café and the sun terrace open during Trinity term. Undergraduates live in throughout their degree, either on site in Victorian buildings or in an East Oxford annexe. The Hands Building is home to the law faculty's Bonavero Institute of Human Rights; it provides a lecture space, and additional accommodation with 73 en-suite rooms. Proximity to University Parks encourages sporting enthusiasm. The JCR committee, called the Bench, is responsible for running social events and welfare provision. The "entz reps" (entertainment officers) co-ordinate a full timetable of open mic and comedy nights, sports days and charity auctions.

Merton

Oxford OX1 4JD   01865 286 316 (admissions)   www.merton.ox.ac.uk
Undergraduates: 320   Postgraduates: 220   undergraduate.admissions@merton.ox.ac.uk

Merton's wide range of subjects goes some way to explaining its breadth of achievement. Its luminous roll of alumni includes TS Eliot, physicist Sir Antony Leggett, the chemist Frederick Soddy and former Prime Minister Liz Truss – the first Mertonian to hold this post. This is also where the Emperor of Japan, Naruhito studied and creator of *Lord of the Rings*, JRR Tolkien, was an English professor. One of Oxford's most ancient and prestigious colleges, founded in 1264 by Walter de Merton, Lord Chancellor of England, Merton houses Europe's oldest academic library in continuous use. Some of the cheapest accommodation across Oxford colleges is guaranteed for all three years of study, alongside generous bursaries and grants. Although dubbed as the college "where fun goes to die" by its undergraduates, Merton's extracurriculars now include the Merton Floats drama society and the Bodley Club for literary speakers. A charity rounders match raised money to support Ukraine and long-form pieces are published in its magazine, *Postmaster & the Merton Record*. The white-tie Merton Winter Ball and the annual Merton Society Garden Party are highlights of the social calendar. The choir is renowned, with its Girl Choristers drawn from the local Oxfordshire community.

New College

Oxford OX1 3BN | 01865 279 272 | www.new.ox.ac.uk
Undergraduates: 430 | Postgraduates: 315 | admissions@new.ox.ac.uk

With spectacular gardens and huge stretching buildings set against the thirteenth-century medieval city wall, despite its name, New College is one of the older Oxford colleges. It is also one of the few with its own sports ground and pavilion, as well as a famous ornamental mount. Founder William of Wykeham was the first to build a college as an integrated complex in 1379 – set with Hall, Chapel, Library and Muniment Tower – and New became a model for the Oxford college layout. Just as important as its impressive academic record, New has a fun and relaxed community compared to its rivals in the top five of the Norrington Table. Both music and drama are prominent, aided by excellent facilities. The Clore Music Studios house the orchestra, chamber groups and a world-class male choir which sings a Choral Evensong six nights a week during term. There is also a well-equipped band room and a 120-seat, fourteenth-century performance space, the Long Room. The antechapel holds opera performances in Michaelmas term, while Trinity term sees productions in the ancient cloisters – which feature in *Harry Potter and the Goblet of Fire*. The renovated Gradel Quadrangles on the Savile Road site contain 99 new student rooms, a flexible study and working space and a multi-purpose arts and performance area.

Oriel

Oxford OX1 4EW | 01865 276 555 | www.oriel.ox.ac.uk
Undergraduates: 335 | Postgraduates: 220 | admissions@oriel.ox.ac.uk

Slightly smaller than the average Oxford college, Oriel's central location, unusual portico and immaculate front quad continue to attract tourists and students alike. The college is primarily known for its rowing prowess, but also offers archery, badminton and even cheerleading. Accommodation is guaranteed for the duration of study, graded from A* to D, with varying rents. Formal dining in the small yet impressive mediaeval hall is a popular feature, with Latin grace providing a traditional atmosphere. All years live, eat and socialise together: there are formal and informal options to dine in hall six days per week, with brunch at the weekends. Undergraduates maintain a strong presence in the Oxford University Conservative Association. The board's decision not to remove the controversial Cecil Rhodes statue over the High Street is yet to be overturned, despite the JCR standing resolutely in disagreement in hustings (JCR votes). Graduate housing is off the popular Cowley Road a mile away and includes several recently renovated flats. The college usually appears at the upper end of the Norrington Table, although fell to the lower third this year. Facilities include a sports ground, multiple gyms, a boathouse and squash courts – and a play is performed in the quads each summer.

Pembroke

Oxford OX1 1DW | 01865 276 412 | www.pmb.ox.ac.uk
Undergraduates: 400 | Postgraduates: 250 | admissions@pmb.ox.ac.uk

Located just off St Aldates, Pembroke sits opposite Christ Church in a quieter part of the city centre. Promoting a supportive and down-to-earth approach to college life, its community is nevertheless lively and ambitiously intellectual. Founded by King James I in 1624, the current site contains four quads: Old, Chapel, North and The Rokos; two new quadrangle spaces; and five recently developed buildings. Pembroke offers a range of joint honours undergraduate courses – from PPL (psychology, philosophy and linguistics) to European and Middle Eastern languages. History is both a strong subject and strong presence around college: there are tributes to the Pembroke fallen, such as war memorial plaques in the Damon Wells Chapel; and just outside it a three-figure sculpture, *Mourning Women*. Applicants from disadvantaged and non-traditional backgrounds are encouraged to apply. The *BlackPembroke Stories* series in October 2022 shared stories from across the college community. Pembroke's outreach work has expanded from London to northwest England, including Heywood, Rochdale and Middleton. The McGowin Library is open 24/7 and its special collections include works by alumnus Samuel Johnson. Rowing is strong, as are talks and panels by high-profile media figures. Living on site requires pre-payment for a minimum of six dinners a week.

Queen's

Oxford OX1 4AW   01865 279 161   www.queens.ox.ac.uk
Undergraduates: 365   Postgraduates: 195   admissions@queens.ox.ac.uk

Located just off the High Street, the imposing neo-classical buildings and bell tower of Queen's College create a grand entrance. With a large, supportive and stimulating community, Queen's is strong in a range of subjects and offers a diverse array of degrees – including fine art, Asian and Middle Eastern studies, biomedical sciences and psychology. A budget of £90,000 is set aside each year for student support, with grants and loans awarded by a student finance committee. Music awards (including choral, organ and instrumental) are given annually to offer-holders following auditions. The impressive Queen's website and the *Access Podcast* provide excellent information about applications, teaching, welfare and sport. Facilities are splendid, with accommodation offered throughout undergraduate courses – some in annexes around central Oxford and a third on the main site, mostly en-suite. The lecture theatre is used for concerts and screenings. Two refurbished squash courts are said to be the best in Oxford. Sport, drama and music are all important parts of the community, particularly the Trinity term garden play. The beer cellar is popular and JCR facilities are extensive; afternoon tea is a daily highlight. The college is fully catered, providing three subsidised meals a day. The Upper Library is one of the most beautiful reading rooms in Oxford.

St Anne's

Oxford OX2 6HS   01865 274 840 (admissions)   www.st-annes.ox.ac.uk
Undergraduates: 470   Postgraduates: 350   admissions@st-annes.ox.ac.uk

St Anne's aims to be the home of choice for the brightest and most ambitious students of every background. It gained full college status in 1952 but has been widening access since 1879, when it was founded as the Society of Oxford Home-Students – allowing women to study in affordable halls without having to pay for college membership. Each year it funds 40 "Study Abroad" visiting students and it is also the only college to offer paid internships for its students – based in the UK, India, Serbia and Japan. Like its motto, *Consulto et audacter* (purposely and boldly), St Anne's is bold and modern. Rooms in its purpose-built complex are decided by ballot and accommodation is guaranteed over three-year courses. The new library and academic centre on Woodstock Road is a point of pride, with 2,000 books added every year. The college is particularly strong for music: a student-led society encompasses various ensembles and hosts a termly showcase for all abilities. St Anne's Swingers perform jazz, swing and soul. The college Arts Week includes drama, talks, film and dance classes. Although closer to the suburb of Jericho (north of the city) than central Oxford, the college is near University Parks. Many students cycle to the university sports ground, although there is an on-site gym and nearby sports field.

St Catherine's

Oxford OX1 3UJ   01865 271 700   www.stcatz.ox.ac.uk

Undergraduates: 515   Postgraduates: 400   admissions@stcatz.ox.ac.uk

Up-and-coming "Catz" is the youngest of any Oxford college and contains the most undergraduates. The college offers a vast 36 undergraduate subjects and houses more than 60,000 books in its modern and spacious library. Positioned right by the English, law and social science faculties, Catz is characterised by a laidback atmosphere but achieves excellent results. Established in 1962, its modern design and progressive JCR allow for a less traditional feel. Facilities include a theatre, an on-site boathouse, squash courts, a water garden, an amphitheatre, a gym (free after a one-off £3 induction) and car park – a rare feature among Oxford colleges. With the largest bar in Oxford, it has a sociable reputation and hosts popular "bops" (big organised parties) four times a term. Increased welfare support in recent years has seen the appointment of a college counsellor and a fund for transgender students. Large student numbers and generous sporting funds bring strength in extracurriculars – particularly in men's rugby, women's football and drama. Catz students also take active roles in writing, directing and acting. The annual Cameron Mackintosh Chair of Contemporary Theatre has seen visiting professorships held by Arthur Miller and Sir Tom Stoppard. Rooms are small, but warmer than in older colleges – and are available on site for first-, second- and third-years.

St Edmund Hall

Oxford OX1 4AR   01865 279 009   www.seh.ox.ac.uk

Undergraduates: 395   Postgraduates: 310   admissions@seh.ox.ac.uk

St Edmund Hall's mediaeval crypt, now a converted library beneath the church, is one of many hidden gems at SEH or Teddy Hall (two of its common nicknames). Termly exhibitions are housed in the seventeenth-century Old Library – which recently showcased author Kevin Crossley-Holland's work. The college hosts a writer in residence, journalism prizes, weekly student-run writers' workshops and an annual publication. SEH is among the oldest Oxford colleges, dating back at least to 1317; and likely to the 1190s when St Edmund of Abingdon taught on the site. Located just off the High Street on the quieter Queen's Lane, the undergraduate community is known for being lively, social and sporty. It is typically in the lower segment of the Norrington Table, the latest results ranking it 24th, but at the top of the inter-college sports tournaments. A two-part college bar houses the Buttery, a hub for sports teams or societies, and the lively Well bar – known for its darts matches. Food is excellent, though expensive. The college blog showcases the breadth of research fellowships and travel bursaries. Exchange partnerships with Lingnan University College in Guangzhou, China, provide opportunities for international study. Undergraduate accommodation is offered for two years; offsite rooms are at Norham Gardens, close to the University Parks. First-years live in the mediaeval college quads.

St Hilda's

Oxford OX4 1DY   01865 286 620   www.st-hildas.ox.ac.uk

Undergraduates: 400   Postgraduates: 175   undergraduate.admissions@st-hildas.ox.ac.uk

St Hilda's maintains a campus feel due to its location, just beyond Magdalen bridge and towards Cowley. Founded in 1893 as an all-female college, Hilda's started admitting men in 2006 and now has an equal gender split. Professor Dame Sarah Springman, appointed Principal in February 2022, is focusing on sustainability. The college now owns Radley Large Wood and through this aims to improve the area's biodiversity – and its own carbon footprint. It has excellent facilities: an exceptionally well-stocked library; one of the busiest JCR-run student bars; the new Anniversary Building with 52 student bedrooms; beautiful gardens instead of the more typical Oxford quads; and the impressive Jacqueline du Pré Music Building and recording studio. The riverside setting is ideal for punting season, during which students can use St Hilda's own punts. Round tables in the dining hall encourage a friendly atmosphere. The college prides itself on inclusivity: a "class liberation officer" represents those who self-identify as being from working-class backgrounds; and St Hilda's has its own multifaith room. Sport is particularly strong, with excellent hockey, football, and cross-country teams topping their respective Cuppers tournaments. The Hilda's College Ball is Oxford's most affordable. Second-year students typically live out, but on-site undergraduate accommodation is now available for the full three years.

St Hugh's

Oxford OX2 6LE   01865 274 910   www.st-hughs.ox.ac.uk
Undergraduates: 440   Postgraduates: 460   admissions@st-hughs.ox.ac.uk

St Hugh's seeks to make a home away from home in its extensive facilities, with 14 acres of green space. Students often cycle into the city centre. Like St Hilda's, there is an independent campus feel; listed red-brick Edwardian buildings combine with more recent additions, such as the Maplethorpe Building. Renowned for humanities subjects, there is an array of essay prizes and competitions for Hugh's students – as well as for prospective applicants, and university-wide undergraduates and graduates. Its Howard Piper Library is one of the best in Oxford, containing seven reading rooms and more than 70,000 books. Welfare is taken seriously and there is an extensive suite of support for students. The food is excellent and hall costs are subsidised. Hugh's highlights include brunch at weekends and a popular café; themed formal dinners on special occasions; a croquet lawn, tennis courts and areas for frisbee and football. Undergraduate accommodation is guaranteed; the Dickson Poon University of Oxford China Centre Building houses 63 graduates in en-suite bedrooms. The complex has five spacious floors, 60,000 volumes, a lecture theatre, language laboratory and an ecologically efficient roof terrace. There is a relaxed approach to academia, but the college has climbed up the Norrington Table in recent years and currently sits in 19th place.

St John's

Oxford OX1 3JP   01865 277 317   www.sjc.ox.ac.uk
Undergraduates: 420   Postgraduates: 260   admissions1555@sjc.ox.ac.uk

The wealthiest Oxford college, enabling cheaper rent and food for students, St John's has a reputation for both academic and sporting success. It ranks second in the latest Norrington Table. The college provides generous academic prizes and book grants, while the unique St John's discount scheme is the envy of other colleges and gives students money off at many nearby eateries. John's also enjoys a prime spot – a few minutes' walk from the Bodleian and the High Street. Founded by London merchant tailor, Sir Thomas White, in 1555, the college traditionally produced Anglican clergymen. Its early history prioritised medicine and law, though it has expanded into the arts and humanities over the past half-century. The college buildings combine traditional limestone quadrangles (the Front and Canterbury Quads) with modern accommodation blocks (Kendrew Quad and the Beehive Building) and the spacious new Library & Study Centre. Women's rowing is a particular sporting strength, and there is a squash court and two free gyms. Other extracurriculars include a chapel choir, drama society and orchestra. Music practice rooms are equipped with keys, drums and piano. The St John's *Inspire Programme* is divided into pre- and post-GCSE support for non-selective state-school applicants and has launched an Inspire Year 13 twilight session for interview preparation.

St Peter's

Oxford OX1 2DL   01865 278 863   www.spc.ox.ac.uk
Undergraduates: 370   Postgraduates: 260   admissions@spc.ox.ac.uk

St Peter's takes an equal number of undergraduates and graduates every year (about 100 of each), with 20 visiting students who make up a significant part of the international community. Granted college status in 1961, it has since fostered an open community, averse to pomposity and stuffiness with a team of welcoming porters. The site is close to the Westgate shopping centre and its buildings are an eclectic mix of mediaeval, Georgian and nineteenth-century styles. It was founded as St Peter's Hall in 1929 to offer an Oxford education to students with limited financial means. Peter's still dabbles in more typical Oxford traditions – including formal hall, held twice a week. It generally sits in the middle of the Norrington Table. Facilities are impressive given it has one of the smaller endowments: the recently renovated JCR and popular student-run bar are favourite haunts. Undergraduate accommodation is available for first- and third-years and ranges from traditional to purpose-built rooms – the latter a few minutes' walk away. Music is well represented, with a tuneful college choir and popular open mic nights every two weeks. The college library is open 24/7, with two floors and over 53,000 books. Rugby and rowing contribute to Peter's growing sporting reputation.

Somerville

Oxford OX2 6HD   01865 270 619   www.some.ox.ac.uk
Undergraduates: 435   Postgraduates: 245   academic.office@some.ox.ac.uk

Located just off St Giles and close to the beautiful Taylor Institution Library, dedicated to studying the languages of Europe, Somerville has committed to supporting sanctuary-seeking students and academics since the 1930s. It prides itself on progressive values, fierce intelligence and empathy – enshrined by its Sanctuary Scholarships and a visiting scholarship for black, Asian and ethnic minority early-career academics. Named after Mary Somerville, the astronomer and pioneering academic, Somerville, founded in 1879, was one of the first two Oxford colleges to admit women (along with Lady Margaret Hall). Eminent female Somervillians include author Dorothy L Sayers, Booker Prize-winning novelist AS Byatt, Nobel Prize-winning scientist Dorothy Crowfoot Hodgkin and economist Alison Wolf. The college has an impressive 100,000-volume library and its arts budget funds one of the best Arts Week programmes in Oxford; Somervillians are prominent in both journalism and drama. Food is great value and there are independent student kitchens in all buildings. College rooms are provided for three years to most undergraduates and all first-year postgraduates. Extracurriculars include an excellent chapel choir, a baking society and boat club although – ranked 26th in the latest results – it tends to fall towards the bottom of the Norrington Table. Somerville remains one of the most international colleges. Its Twitter page demystifies the undergraduate application process and encourages state school applicants, particularly those from the southeast.

Trinity

Oxford OX1 3BH   01865 279 874   www.trinity.ox.ac.uk
Undergraduates: 310   Postgraduates: 135   admissions@trinity.ox.ac.uk

Minutes from the Radcliffe Camera and High Street, Trinity is in the heart of the city – though its long drive, friendly porters and renowned lawns lined with 14,000 new bulbs make it a peaceful haven. The new Levine Building, overseen by President Dame Hilary Boulding and inaugurated by the then Prince of Wales in May 2022, has modernised the college. It contains the de Jager Auditorium, five new teaching rooms, 46 student bedrooms, an informal study space and popular café. The first public event in auditorium hosted novelist Alan Hollinghurst. Trinity food is renowned – especially Monday's steak-and-brie night and weekend brunches. Formal hall is held three times a week, though new student kitchens provide a social space for informal dining. Access and outreach have gained momentum to counterbalance Trinity's traditionally high public-school intake. Milton Keynes is a new link region. Trinity's biochemistry, maths, English and history departments are strong – and so are its extracurriculars. The boat club and the chapel choir are the largest societies; the Trinity Players stage a garden play every summer; and Trinity Arts Week is well-established. First- and second-years live in college, with "sets" (double rooms) popular with second years. Third- and fourth-years mostly live out, either in "Stav" (on Staverton Road), on Woodstock Road or in privately rented Cowley properties. Trinity's Commemoration Ball, held every third year, sells out in minutes.

University College

Oxford OX1 4BH   01865 276 677   www.univ.ox.ac.uk
Undergraduates: 430   Postgraduates: 215   admissions@univ.ox.ac.uk

University College is known as "Univ" and is thought to be the oldest Oxford college. According to the generally accepted legend, it was founded by King Alfred in 872 – although, more likely, its origins lie with William of Durham in the thirteenth century. Despite its ancient roots, Univ is one of the most forward-thinking colleges. The Opportunity Programme, launched in 2016, paved the way for a university-wide scheme called Opportunity Oxford. Baroness Valerie Amos, the Labour life peer and former United Nations official, became Oxford's first black head of house in 2019, and just the second black woman to lead an Oxbridge college. A generous bursary scheme includes travel grants for study trips abroad, while 10% of undergraduate spaces are reserved for applicants from low-income backgrounds. Strong in both academic results and research, Univ excels in the sciences, PPE and law. First- and third-years live in college – either in flats, sets, or single rooms – with second-years housed in a comfortable annexe near Summertown. Both men's and women's rowing continue to excel. College members have access to a chalet in the foothills of Mont Blanc. Two 24-hour libraries and proximity to the Bodleian make Univ ideal for book lovers. The chapel choir is excellent, and students put on an annual Comedy Revue.

Wadham

Oxford OX1 3PN   01865 277 545   www.wadham.ox.ac.uk
Undergraduates: 460   Postgraduates: 235   admissions@wadham.ox.ac.uk

Wadham's impressive new "Back Quad" buildings were opened by Lord Patten, Chancellor of the University of Oxford, in October 2022 as the first built specifically for access. Over £17million funding was raised by Wadham's Access to Excellence programme; the college has reached 37,782 pupils across 991 access events in the past seven years. Overseen by Wadham's warden Robert Hannigan, two more building complexes – the William Doo Undergraduate Centre and the Doctor Lee Shau Kee Building – will consolidate the college's impressive commitment to improve every step of the journey into higher education. Known for its leftist politics and activism, Wadham prides itself on a liberal and laidback atmosphere. It occupies an imposing and attractive site opposite Trinity on Parks Road and offers more languages than any other college. The JCR has rebranded itself as a students' union (combining the JCR and MCR) and prioritises welfare for minority groups. Queerfest is a highlight of Wadham's colourful social calendar, as is Wadstock – an open-air music festival in Hilary (spring) term. The Holywell Music Room is the oldest purpose-built European music room. Weekday dinners are served in the seventeenth-century hall, though there are no gowned formal sittings. Undergraduates are guaranteed on-site rooms in their first and final years; other years are offered modern offsite accommodation.

Worcester

Oxford OX1 2HB   01865 278 391   www.worc.ox.ac.uk
Undergraduates: 450   Postgraduates: 190   admissions@worc.ox.ac.uk

As one of Oxford's most popular colleges, Worcester maintains beautiful grounds and a strong academic reputation. Undergraduates live in college for all three years and sports fields are on site – thanks to the fact it was on the edge of the city in the eighteenth century. Before the dissolution of the monasteries, 15 abbeys had lodgings in Gloucester college, which was re-founded as Worcester college after the benefaction of Sir Thomas Cookes (a Worcestershire baronet) in 1714. The famous Hall and Chapel, with interiors by James Wyatt, were completed in approximately 1770. Worcester's horticulture is the subject of a blog by its gardeners, and croquet on the extensive lawns is popular. The Sultan Nazrin Shah Centre – containing lecture theatres, rehearsal spaces and a dance studio – looks over the college's very own lake. Arts and humanities lovers enjoy the Arts Week and summer Shakespeare performances by the Buskins dramatic society. There are two libraries: the modern reading rooms contain 65,000 volumes; the impressive Old Library houses important European manuscripts, special collections, prints, drawings and early printed books. The college hosts a popular Commemoration Ball every three years. Good food is served at the nightly formal hall, where students stand at the entrance and exit of tutors, accompanied by Latin grace.

Cambridge College Profiles

Christ's

Cambridge CB2 3BU   01223 334 900   www.christs.cam.ac.uk

Undergraduates 441   Postgraduates 272   admissions@christs.cam.ac.uk

Christ's students are just a stone's throw from the city centre's attractions but enjoy tranquil grounds, including a Darwin garden named after its famous alumnus and an outdoor swimming pool – one of the few colleges to offer one. Most undergraduates live in college, although some are nearby in row houses on King's Street and Jesus Lane. About 40% of rooms are en-suite. This includes small, single bedrooms in the Modernist "Typewriter" building (New Court) and large, double bedrooms in Second Court. More traditional rooms and sets (a study room and bedroom) are in First Court. There is plenty to keep student life vibrant, from the Yusuf Hamied Theatre, which hosts student productions, to Christ's Cinema, and an art society. Students can borrow art for their rooms through the Picture Loan Scheme. Christ's has plenty of its own sports clubs from rowing to mixed lacrosse, while some sports share teams with other colleges. The Bridging Course, launched in 2020 in collaboration with Gonville & Caius and King's, provides new students from underrepresented backgrounds with academic support and an introduction to university life. In 2021, Christ's welcomed a new master: the former diplomat Lord Simon McDonald of Salford. The college has a reputation for being academically intense and in 2022 was the highest performing college according to the newly reinstated Tompkins Table, see page 283.

Churchill

Cambridge CB3 0DS   01223 336 000   www.chu.cam.ac.uk

Undergraduates 485   Postgraduates 390   admissions@chu.cam.ac.uk

Churchill, a "hill college" outside of the city centre, offers the perks of a 45-acre site and has more than 1,000 trees. The location is a quick commute to the West Cambridge site, where many science departments are based – particularly useful for the 70% of undergraduate Churchillians who study STEM (science, technology, engineering, mathematics) subjects. Famed for its Brutalist architecture, the Churchill campus also houses a gym, theatre, music centre, squash and tennis courts and grass pitches. College sport is popular and in 2022 the badminton team won both finals in the open and mixed intercollegiate Cuppers. Accommodation is not bad, either: students are promised on-site rooms for the entirety of their undergraduate degrees. More than 40% of them are en-suite. Cowan Court offers some of the most luxurious accommodation, complete with double beds. Churchill is one of the least traditional colleges: students are welcome to walk on the grass and they do not wear academic gowns to formal dinners. The state school intake was 75% in 2022. The college has also achieved a more even gender split in the past few years, with 49% of 2022's intake female. Funding has been secured for the Bill Brown Creative Workshops, a new interdisciplinary facility for innovation and co-operation which is to open at the start of the 2023 academic year.

Clare

Cambridge CB2 1TL   01223 333 200   www.clare.cam.ac.uk

Undergraduates 520   Postgraduates 314   admissions@clare.cam.ac.uk

Cambridge's second-oldest college, Clare dates from 1326 and fields delightful garden views leading out onto the Backs and the River Cam. Much of Clare has been a construction site in recent years, however, as the college has been transforming Old Court by refurbishing existing rooms and adding bathrooms. There will also be a River Room Café with a terrace by the river and space for students to meet. These developments are due to be completed by the start of the 2023-24 academic year. Clare is renowned for music, with a famous choir and recitals, as well as intimate gigs in the iconic Clare Bar in the crypt under the College Chapel. Rooms in Old Court offer a traditional experience, while Memorial Court, across the river, is close to the university library and both humanities and science departments. All freshers live in Memorial, Thirkill or Lerner Court. Students in their second year often live at "Clare Colony", closer to the boathouse on the slopes of Castle Hill, a 13-minute walk from the main site. Clare has its own punts, a boat club and good sports facilities just beyond the botanic garden – a 10-minute cycle ride away. Sir David Attenborough is among famed alumni. The college has a popular, non-partisan Politics Society, drawing high-profile speakers, as well as *Clareification*, a student-run newsletter.

Corpus Christi

Cambridge CB2 1RH 01223 338 000 www.corpus.cam.ac.uk
Undergraduates 328 Postgraduates 237 admissions@corpus.cam.ac.uk
In the heart of Cambridge, Corpus Christi is a small bustling college with a welcoming feel. Tourists flock to its famous clock, the Chronophage, displayed on the outside of the Taylor Library in Kwee Court. The Parker Library houses a collection of mediaeval manuscripts and is also home to the college's ancient drinking horn – given to it upon its 1352 founding and made from the horn of an auroch, an extinct cattle species. Some students are housed in ancient rooms, others are accommodated away from, but close to, the main site, in the Beldam, Bene't Street and Botolph Court buildings. There is also a cosy underground bar for socialising. All undergraduates are guaranteed accommodation with a "ballot" for selecting rooms after first year, although some "prize rooms" are allocated based on exam results. The college has its own gym, playing fields and an open-air pool, located at its postgraduate campus at Leckhampton, just over a mile away, which turned 60 in 2022. The Old Court is said to be the oldest continually inhabited court in either Cambridge or Oxford, while renovations to the medieval Old Hall were shortlisted for a RIBA award. To expand the sports offering, Corpus joins with King's and Christ's colleges to form collaborative "CCK" teams. Its small but much-used theatre, the Corpus Playroom, is where students university-wide stage performances and comedy nights. In 2022, the college accepted its third cohort of Bridging Course students from underrepresented groups. It will continue to offer approximately 10 places each year. Corpus also participates in the STEM Smart widening participation initiative and the Pelican Programme, which supports arts and humanities applicants.

Downing

Cambridge CB2 1DQ 01223 334 800 www.dow.cam.ac.uk
Undergraduates 510 Postgraduates 485 admissions@dow.cam.ac.uk
Built in a neo-classical style in the 19th century, Downing has a different appearance to any other college. Grand buildings open on to the Paddock lawn – a popular spot for relaxing in the post-exam period. Students at Downing throw themselves into plenty of extracurriculars. On the sports front the college is known as a fearsome opponent. For arts and culture there is the 160-seat Howard Theatre, a vibrant drama society that hosts a festival of student writing each year, and the Heong Gallery, opened in 2016 and dedicated to modern and contemporary art. It hosted the well-reviewed Hockney Eye exhibition in 2022 in collaboration with the Fitzwilliam Museum. Downing has some plush accommodation with double beds, while more than half of rooms are en-suite and laundry services are free. It also has its own termly student-run magazine, *The Griffin*. A lively social scene centres on the comfy Butterfield Café and Bar. In 2022, Downing opened a new

wellbeing centre, to promote and support student health. Originally founded for the study of law and natural sciences and while still popular with scientists, lawyers and geographers – thanks to its fall-out-of-bed-and-into lectures proximity to their faculties – Downing is now home to an eclectic body of students. More than half (51%) of 2022's new undergraduates came from state schools. Through the Downing 360 Campaign, the college aims to raise £40million by 2027 to increase the number of fellows, remove accessibility barriers and fund renovations.

Emmanuel

Cambridge CB2 3AP   01223 334 200   www.emma.cam.ac.uk
Undergraduates 470   Postgraduates 220   admissions@emma.cam.ac.uk

Nicknamed "Emma", students love the college for its central location, friendly atmosphere and the weekly load of laundry included in their rent. The large Paddock lawn is a space to study and socialise, while the open-air pool is a boon in the summer. Ducks – as well as students – enjoy the college pond and beautiful gardens. Extensive renovations are underway at Emma as it builds new residential facilities on the main site with 50 rooms, with the aim that all undergraduates may be accommodated on-site throughout their degrees. Students currently move off-site in their second and third years. Emma is also converting Furness Lodge into a three-part facility: an education centre, a bar and an event space. They can now enjoy the new Fiona's Cafe and the entire project was set to be completed by January 2023. Founded by Puritans in the 1580s, Emma strives to maintain a forward-thinking and egalitarian atmosphere. Societies and sports focus more on inclusion than competition and activities are diverse. The elegant Christopher Wren chapel hosts concerts organised by the music society.

Fitzwilliam

Cambridge CB3 0DG   01223 332 000   www.fitz.cam.ac.uk
Undergraduates 494   Postgraduates 336   admissions@fitz.cam.ac.uk

The occasional goat figurine or drawing around college attests to Fitzwilliam's mascot: the billy goat. Many "Fitzbillies" enjoy the quieter surroundings of their Castle Hill locale and the camaraderie of the 10-minute walk into town. Fitzwilliam's commitment to widening access is born out by the 83% of its undergraduate intake drawn from the state sector in 2022 – one of the highest proportions in Cambridge. It participates in the Foundation Year programme for students from disadvantaged backgrounds. A friendly feel is enshrined at the busy café-bar. While Fitzwilliam lacks ancient architecture, its gardens are beautiful, and its dining hall boasts an eye-catching Brutalist lantern roof. Students are accommodated throughout their degrees in one of the 627 rooms on site or in houses minutes from the campus. Good facilities also extend to a large auditorium, a two-storey gym, squash courts and the college's own sports ground five minutes' walk from the main site. While there are sports clubs to cater to all levels, standards can also be high at Fitzwilliam, whose men's football team won the inter-college Cuppers for the sixth year in a row in 2022. The college's cultural life is also rich. Rehearsal rooms, along with the chapel and crypt, are available for musicians. As well as a choir, there are two *a cappella* singing groups, an opera company and the long running Fitz Swing band.

Girton

Cambridge CB3 0JG   01223 338 999   www.girton.cam.ac.uk
Undergraduates 553   Postgraduates 427   admissions@girton.cam.ac.uk

Since its inception in 1869 as the UK's first residential college offering higher education to women, Girton has had a storied history. Boasting Virginia Woolf as an alumna, it is now co-educational and home to a dynamic community of scholars. The quiet surrounds of Girton village with its Victorian architecture, the college pond and 50 acres of natural woodland and orchards are enjoyed by many. However, students tend to be well-acquainted with the cycle or bus route into town as their college is the furthest from the city centre. Top-notch facilities include three gyms and various hard courts as well as football, rugby and cricket pitches, as well as the only indoor heated pool of any college. A café-bar serves as a social hub and another cellar bar hosts JCR (a students' union for the undergraduate community) events. As a low-carbon college, Girton has won awards for energy efficiency and has an eco-friendly green roof. Student rooms range from the atmospheric Victorian to modern en-suite in Ash Court. Off-site accommodation is in college-owned houses or at Swirles Court, at Eddington. Just over a third of undergraduate rooms are en-suite. One accommodation corridor in the main building is reserved for women and non-binary students. Girton has its own museum and an artsy extracurricular scene – supported by a permanent Peoples' Portraits exhibition. The college participates in the Foundation Year programme for students from disadvantaged backgrounds, which started with the 2022 admissions round – in which 70% of new undergraduates came from the state sector. In 2022, Girton elected the academic Dr Elisabeth Kendall as the new college mistress.

Gonville & Caius

Cambridge CB2 1TA   01223 332 400   www.cai.cam.ac.uk
Undergraduates 630   Postgraduates 275   admissions@cai.cam.ac.uk

Founded as Gonville Hall in 1348, Caius (pronounced "keys") is one of the oldest colleges and its undergraduate population is among the largest. Its main site, Old Courts, features five peaceful courtyards in the heart of town and a lovely view of Senate House. Caius also has a beautiful nineteenth-century library and a chapel with a claim to being the oldest purpose-built in Cambridge, with walls dating back to 1390. Unlike other colleges, Caius serves a three-course meal, six nights a week, in hall. There is a brisk first sitting at 6pm and for the second students are required to wear their formal blue gowns (often with jeans or sports kit underneath) to file into hall. A unique dining policy obliges undergraduates to pay for 31 dinners a term in advance, with the aim of encouraging students to dine together. There is plenty to get involved with – the college has 40 clubs and societies. Most freshers live on West Road by the Sidgwick Site. This includes the Stephen Hawking Building, which offers 75 modern, en-suite rooms. There is also the Brutalist Harvey Court with its own JCR, where some rooms have balconies. Many second-years live in rooms overlooking shops in the city centre or in houses near the Fenners cricket ground. More traditional rooms and sets are in the Old Courts, and these often host third-years. Caius has a boathouse and gym. In the past the college had some of the lowest state school intakes (just 57% in 2020) but it appears to have turned a corner, with that figure rising to 73% in 2022.

Homerton

Cambridge CB2 8PH   01223 747 111   www.homerton.cam.ac.uk
Undergraduates 626   Postgraduates 775   admissions@homerton.cam.ac.uk

Homerton is one of the furthest colleges from the city centre, and it is also the biggest – with 626 undergraduates. The 25 acres of college grounds have plenty to keep students busy, which can give the impression of a self-contained university campus. Homerton officially became a college in 2010, making it Cambridge's youngest, although it was initially founded more than 250 years ago as a "dissenting academy". Close to the railway station, a 15-minute cycle ride brings students into town. The benefit of space means accommodation is mainly en-suite and of a high standard. There is an orchard and extensive lawns that may be walked upon – contributing to the friendly and unpretentious atmosphere. Plenty of facilities have been upgraded recently including the £8million new dining hall, which opened in May 2022. There is an on-site gym and the college shares a sports ground with St Mary's school – launched in 2020, it accommodates hockey, cricket, netball, tennis and many other sports. A new auditorium and 18 en-suite bedrooms in North Wing are further additions. There is more to come in the form of a new lantern-shaped Porter's Lodge and library extension. Homerton has many education Tripos students, in line with its history as a teacher training college. In October 2021, the new master, Lord Simon Woolley, became the first black man to head an Oxbridge college. Homerton has a high state school intake at 80% of new undergraduates, with five Foundation Year students. It hosts 90 nationalities across its student body.

Hughes Hall

Cambridge CB1 2EW   01223 334 898   www.hughes.cam.ac.uk
Undergraduates 203   Postgraduates 738   admissions@hughes.cam.ac.uk

A small number of undergraduates aged over 21 are welcomed to Hughes Hall, the oldest graduate college at Cambridge. Known for being very international, 57% of its students come from outside the UK and the marigolds on the gate to Gresham Court represent the different countries from which alumni hail. The college enjoys commanding views over the Fenners cricket ground from its roof terraces, and sits alongside Mill Road, a hub for independent businesses. Hughes Hall has a strong record on the sports pitch and the river, with its rowing club historically performing very well in the intercollegiate "Bumps" competition. There are 358 student rooms, 58% of them en-suite, and undergraduates are guaranteed accommodation throughout their degrees. First-years are generally given rooms in the central college site. Some students can live in couples' flats, which tend to be in high demand. There are 85 single en-suite rooms along with a bike store and study rooms in the new Gresham Court building. The college is aiming for carbon neutrality by 2030 and has been awarded gold by the NUS Green Impact programme in the past three years – 100% of its electricity provision is renewable. In 2022, former diplomat Sir Laurie Bristow became the new Hughes Hall president.

Jesus

Cambridge CB5 8BL   01223 339 339   www.jesus.cam.ac.uk
Undergraduates 538   Postgraduates 426   undergraduate-admissions@jesus.cam.ac.uk

Jesus enjoys acres of picturesque grounds close to the city centre as well as the open green space of Jesus Green. Many of its red brick buildings date back to its foundation in the 1500s, while the twelfth-century chapel outdates the college by 350 years. There are modern facilities, too, such as the West Court complex which has student common rooms, a games room, a swanky café commonly called "Waff" that doubles as a popular bar in the evenings, and a terrace. The West Court Gallery often hosts impressive exhibitions, including the student-run John Hughes Arts Festival. Jesus also has on-site pitches for football, rugby and cricket, as well as squash and tennis courts and in 2022 it won the ladies' netball Cuppers. Students can showcase their musical abilities in the Blues and Chill evenings hosted in the chapel, or at the college's 2022-launched song-writing competition with the Centre for Music Performance. All undergraduates are accommodated for every year of their degree, not just the first three – a feature especially welcome for medical students. Other accommodation facilities include a kosher staircase and free washing machines and dryers. The college hall and kitchens, known as "caff", have been undergoing renovations which are now almost complete. Jesus's current master, former media executive Sonita Alleyne, is the first black woman to lead an Oxbridge college. The much-loved grounds are punctuated by a permanent modern sculpture exhibition and the college's own collection contains work by Sir Antony Gormley and John Bellany, among others. Students are permitted to roam on most – but not all – the lawns. The May Ball is glamorous and usually popular. In 2021, Jesus recruited more than 80% of its UK students from state schools for the second year running – one of the highest proportions of all Cambridge colleges.

King's

Cambridge CB2 1ST   01223 331 100   www.kings.cam.ac.uk
Undergraduates 480   Postgraduates 356   undergraduate.admissions@kings.cam

An iconic landmark, King's Chapel's grandeur of scale and vaulted ceilings rivals many cathedrals. One of the biggest draws for visitors to Cambridge, the chapel hosts the choir's famous carols – which students and parents snap up tickets for weeks before they are broadcast on television. College life is less staid than the imposing surroundings would suggest. King's has a modern outlook, and the student community can be quite alternative, as evidenced by the King's Affair May Week event, which typically features techno music and avant-garde dress. The college is aiming to raise £100million to preserve its buildings and develop access efforts. A bridging programme before term starts provides support for students from schools in disadvantaged areas. King's has an art studio space for students to use and punts for them to rent. In the summer, they can sit in the beautiful Fellows' Garden along the riverbank and wander through the meadow behind the chapel – with a view of the Backs that often includes cows. Accommodation ranges from the archetypal Cambridge rooms in old buildings to en-suite rooms in newer hostels off-site. First-years are housed in the more modern Keynes building or in the older Webb's Court or the renovated Bodley's Court, though this set-up can change depending on the year. Garden Hostel, on the other side of the river, has been renovated to provide 70 contemporary en-suite rooms and in 2022 the college opened new accommodation on Barton Road for graduate students and families. King's renovated its bar in recent years and plans to add a new auditorium.

Lucy Cavendish

Cambridge CB3 0BU   01223 332 190   www.lucy.cam.ac.uk
Undergraduates 385   Postgraduates 544   admissions@lucy.cam.ac.uk

Historically a college only for mature, female students, Lucy Cavendish has firmly entered a new chapter as the fastest growing and most diverse college. It welcomed its first mixed-gender intake in 2021 and also accepts students from age 18. Efforts to widen access are showing success: in 2022, Lucy Cavendish became the first college to admit more than 90% of its students from state schools, and one in four are the first in their family to go to university. The college also held its fourth free bridging week for all its new undergraduate intake to help them adjust to Cambridge. Accommodation is provided for all for at least three years, subject to availability. Housing is either in college or in nearby houses, close to those of fellow "hill" colleges St Edmunds and Fitzwilliam. There is also an attractive apartment complex in Histon Road. Students can stay in women-only sets if preferred for religious or cultural reasons. There are also some flats for couples. In 2022, the college opened a new accommodation facility, providing 72 en-suite bedrooms and a ground floor café in a building meeting top sustainability standards. One hundred per cent of the college's electricity is supplied by renewables. The college's Fiction Prize, in its 13th year in 2023, has helped launch the publishing career of successful authors, including Gail Honeyman and Laura Marshall. Many students participate in university-level sports clubs, while the college has its own boat club and shares badminton, football and netball teams with other colleges. In 2021, two new student bursaries were launched: one for British-Bangladeshi students and one for women studying STEM subjects.

Magdalene

Cambridge CB3 0AG   01223 332 100   www.magd.cam.ac.uk

Undergraduates 368   Postgraduates 220   admissions@magd.cam.ac.uk

With historic courts situated alongside the River Cam, Magdalene's river frontage is the longest of any college and goes back nearly 600 years, while its chapel was built in the 1470s. Tradition means the college still hosts one of the university's few white-tie summer balls every other year, while its modern outlook makes Magdalene a firmly 21st century seat of learning. Its airy new library, unveiled in 2021, features study spaces for 90 as well as an archive centre and art gallery and won the RIBA stirling prize in 2022. The college's most famous alumnus, Samuel Pepys, is immortalised in the Pepys Building that houses a collection of 3,000 of the diarist's books and manuscripts. In 2021, almost 50 books and pamphlets belonging to Mary Astell, sometimes considered the "first English feminist", were also found in the library. The theatre society, called MDS, is very active and students can hold theatre productions at Cripps Auditorium, a space with 142 seats. The sports pitches are shared with St John's (both colleges have a sporty reputation) and Magdalene also has its own Eton fives court. Students live either in the main courts, in the village on the other side of Magdalene Street, or in college-owned houses a few minutes' walk away. All undergraduates are guaranteed accommodation for all three or four years of their course. The college came second in the BBC's University Challenge contest in 2021.

Murray Edwards

Cambridge CB3 0DF   01223 762 100   www.murrayedwards.cam.ac.uk

Undergraduates 408   Postgraduates 185   admissions@murrayedwards.cam.ac.uk

Students at women's college Murray Edwards enjoy the supportive atmosphere at its architecturally Brutalist campus on Castle Hill, as well as the brunch served at weekends in hall, whose dome roof inspired the "dome is home" refrain among its students – often referred to as "Medwards". The college is also home to the second largest collection of women's art in the world, including work by Dames Barbara Hepworth and Paula Rego, and Tracey Emin, and hosts regular and hosts regular exhibitions. Women's achievements are encouraged, and the Gateway programme provides workshops on academic leadership and career development. Seventy-four per cent of new students in 2022 came from state schools and the college is participating in the university's Foundation Year scheme. The laidback feel extends to the gardens where students can grow herbs and vegetables in their allotments, as well as walk on the grass. All freshers are housed in one building where kitchens and freezers are available. A new three-storey Art Cafe has just opened overlooking Fountain Court and there is a new wellbeing service. Sport is strong and everything from badminton to hockey is catered for. The college often provides Blues players to the university teams. In 2020, Dorothy Byrne, the former Channel 4 editor, became the new college president.

Newnham

Cambridge CB3 9DF   01223 335 700   www.newn.cam.ac.uk

Undergraduates 430   Postgraduates 325   admissions@newn.cam.ac.uk

Newnham celebrated its 150th anniversary as an all-women's college in 2021, having sought to champion women's academic success and help them to realise their potential since 1871. The idyllic grounds stretch across 18-acres and feature sports pitches, tennis courts and beautiful gardens. The college is ideally located for arts students, given it is just across the road from the Sidgwick Site. Upgrades to the estate mean that Newnham students can now enjoy 90 new en-suite rooms, as well as a new porters' lodge, gym, café, and some of the plushest student kitchens in Cambridge. Rooms for conferences and supervisions are in the Dorothy Garrod building, named after Cambridge's first ever female professor. The Iris café-bar is a light-filled space whose popular sandwiches create a daily lunchtime rush of students, fellows and visitors from other colleges. There is also a well-stocked art room open to students. Newnham has many of its own sports clubs, including badminton, football, netball and lacrosse. Alumni include Mary Beard, who is a fellow, Sylvia Plath, Diane Abbott and Emma Thompson. One criticism levelled against Newnham is that rooms can be expensive as they all cost the same despite their varying quality. The college has introduced rent bursaries for students from lower income backgrounds.

Pembroke

Cambridge CB2 1RF   01223 338 100   www.pem.cam.ac.uk
Undergraduates 488   Postgraduates 295   admissions@pem.cam.ac.uk

Pembroke is Cambridge's third-oldest college, and within its walls there are tranquil gardens including a wild orchard, and Christopher Wren's first chapel. It has remained in its original location (on what is now Trumpington Street) for centuries, having been founded by Marie St Pol on Christmas Eve of 1347. Its food is popular – particularly brunch – and formal dinner is traditionally served every night. Alumni include Ted Hughes, and the actors Naomie Harris and Tom Hiddleston. Renovations to the Mill Lane site across the road will enlarge the college's footprint by a third and create 110 bedrooms. The college is also gaining a new café, auditorium and gathering spaces. The project's phased opening begins with a lecture, gallery space and other facilities in spring 2023. Resources including the Ray and Dagmar Dolmar court accommodation and leisure spaces are due to open in spring 2025. Most first-years live in the modern Foundress Court and in New Court, and should be prepared to share bathrooms as en-suites are uncommon. Currently, many second-years tend to move away to Selwyn Gardens behind the Sidgwick Site, or to Lensfield Road near the station. Many desirable third-year rooms are in terraced houses on Fitzwilliam Street. Pembroke students make the most of an arty extracurricular scene, including the Pembroke Players, one of the largest college drama societies. Other clubs include the Music Society, the Stokes Scientific Society and Pembroke Politics. There are plenty of sports teams, an on-site gym and sports grounds 10 minutes away by bicycle. Around two-thirds of 2021 undergraduate entrants were state-school-educated.

Peterhouse

Cambridge CB2 1RD   01223 338 223   www.pet.cam.ac.uk
Undergraduates 311   Postgraduates 187   admissions@pet.cam.ac.uk

Peterhouse retains some traditional idiosyncrasies – such as hosting a white-tie ball every other year and formal hall dinners that glow atmospherically by candlelight every night. Cambridge's oldest college and one of its smallest, Peterhouse is also one of the wealthier colleges and as such can offer travel grants, academic awards and high-standard accommodation. Students are housed either on site or not more than five minutes away for all years of their degree. Most freshers live in St Peter's Terrace – grand Georgian houses on Trumpington Street, or in the William Stone building, an eight-floor high-rise dating from the 1970s. Though it shares sports grounds with Pembroke, Peterhouse has its own squash court and a modern gym. It also has one of Cambridge's wilder outdoor spaces, known as the Deer Park – where no deer live but plenty of students roam in summer. The college is well located for both the science and arts faculties and is particularly strong in the arts. Two libraries, the Perne and the Ward, provide plenty of quiet learning space. Rooms in Fitzwilliam Street were renovated in summer 2021, its old brewhouse has been converted into a music facility, and Peterhouse has plans to landscape its outdoor spaces around Cosin Court to create courtyard gardens with a focus on health and wellbeing.

Queens'

Cambridge CB3 9ET   01223 335 540   www.queens.cam.ac.uk
Undergraduates 552   Postgraduates 464   admissions@queens.cam.ac.uk

The Queens' campus sits on both sides of the River Cam, and is connected by the striking, wooden Mathematical Bridge, a much reproduced Cambridge image. Walking through it provides a quick course in architectural history via buildings that hail from every era since its 1448 foundation. A lively, outgoing atmosphere is especially felt in the new courts. The active BATS dramatic society puts drama centre stage. Sport is also strong – Queens' tends to field several Blues team players and its own clubs cover everything from chess to water polo, with strong men's and women's football teams. Its biennial May Ball is a popular fixture that welcomes big-name bands. A popular annual Arts Festival features student work and a range of events and it has a non-audition choir called MagSoc. Most first-year students are housed in the modern Cripps Building, while second- and third-years are allocated accommodation through a ballot system. Queens' is also one of the few colleges to host all undergraduates on site for three years. Students have the option of sharing a set of rooms or have their own bedsit.

Robinson

Cambridge CB3 9AN   01223 339 143   www.robinson.cam.ac.uk
Undergraduates 394   Postgraduates 299   apply@robinson.cam.ac.uk

Robinson's is next to the university library and students can reach the city centre in a few minutes by bicycle. Most humanities and science departments are also within easy reach. The college's 1970s architecture might not fit the Cambridge stereotype but there are beautiful gardens – that have the bonus of students being allowed to walk on the lawns – and a buzzing social life. Around half of undergraduate accommodation is en-suite. Freshers tend to live in the centre of college and later they can opt for houses bordering the campus. The Garden restaurant and the Red Brick café-bar serve delicious food and in October 2021 the college opened a new wellbeing centre. Aspiring dramatists can organise productions with the Brickhouse Theatre Company. The sports grounds, shared with Queens', Selwyn and King's, are a 10-minute walk away and Robinson is close to the university rugby ground. Its teams frequently do well: returning to the pre-pandemic swing of things, Robinson won the 2021 intercollegiate athletics Cuppers between its men and women's teams. In 2022, 65% of new entrants were from state schools, a big improvement since 2020 – when Queens' was the only Cambridge college to admit fewer than half of undergraduates (48%) from the maintained sector.

Selwyn

Cambridge CB3 9DQ   01223 767 839   www.sel.cam.ac.uk
Undergraduates 450   Postgraduates 340   admissions@sel.cam.ac.uk

Given the Sidgwick Site is practically the college's back garden, Selwyn is in an ideal location for humanities students who value a short commute. West Cambridge is also a quick cycle away for STEM students. Selwyn enjoys an impressive range of freshly renovated facilities after extensive fundraising. The completed Ann's Court development features a 140-seat auditorium and the Bartlam library opened in 2021. The sleek, recently renovated café-bar buzzes in the evenings and makes a popular study space during the day. Selwyn consistently has one of the highest intakes of home students from state schools – 80% in 2022. All students are accommodated for every year of their undergraduate degree. First years are guaranteed en-suites and tend to live together in Cripps Court. Selwyn has a strong musical tradition, and the chapel choir has recorded numerous albums and toured the world. In the arts, the Selwyn Mighty Players helps fund and produce student theatre both in and out of college. Long-standing sports clubs known as the Hermes and Sirens fund grants for various teams. Selwyn shares sports and tennis grounds around a mile away. It also shares its boathouse with King's and Churchill. At the end of first term, the college hosts a popular winter event called the Selwyn Snow Ball.

Sidney Sussex

Cambridge CB2 3HU   01223 338 872   www.sid.cam.ac.uk
Undergraduates 402   Postgraduates 269   admissions@sid.cam.ac.uk

Study snacks are within easy reach at Sidney, which has the distinction of being 10 steps away from Sainsbury's in the centre of town (a fact valued by undergraduates, though it can deter them from going to the Aldi on Castle Hill). Sidney is also just moments from the ADC student theatre. It is one of the smaller colleges by population, and its bijou grounds mean many students are housed off-site. A bridge over the shops of Sussex Street connects the college to Sussex House accommodation. There are some atmospheric rooms to be had, a few of which even include en-suite facilities, but the furthest away have a 15-minute walk. Sidney is a musical college with an award-winning chapel and a recently inaugurated organ. More bizarrely, it is also where the head of Oliver Cromwell is buried, given he was among the college's first students. The student-run bar is a social hub, thanks to its affordability and rowdy "bops" – cheesy dance nights held every other Friday in term time. The extensive grounds make it a popular choice for May Week garden parties. Sports teams are more enthusiastic than competitive, and grounds are shared with Christ's, a 10-minute cycle ride away. In October 2021, a new dining space opened. Sidney is one of the colleges participating in the Foundation Year programme and in 2022 offered a preparation week to freshers to help them transition to college life.

St Catharine's

Cambridge CB2 1RL   01223 338 319   www.caths.cam.ac.uk
Undergraduates 474   Postgraduates 414   undergraduate.admissions@caths.cam.ac.uk

The flock of cyclists flying past King's and St Catharine's on Trumpington Street on the way to their 9am lectures is among the quintessential Cambridge sights. Students at "Catz" can take advantage of a central location and thriving community. Mid-size Catz has two libraries, having been founded by benefactor Robert Woodlark in 1473 with a library of 84 manuscripts and three printed books. In 2021, two new health and wellbeing roles were created while in 2022 the central spaces building project was completed, including a new dining hall and a central lift and atrium. Catz students live on site in their first year and undergraduates are guaranteed accommodation for their three or four-year courses. Second-years usually live a few minutes away in the St Chad's accommodation, which is currently being renovated. There is also the McGrath Centre, which houses an auditorium, junior common room and bar, plus a refurbished boathouse and hockey pitch. The literary society, the Shirley Society, is Cambridge's oldest. Catz holds a May Ball every other year, and students can attend one at Corpus during the "off" years. The David and Claudia Harding Foundation made a £25m donation to Catz in 2019 – one of the largest in Cambridge's history – which will support postgraduates and encourage applications by students from underrepresented backgrounds. In 2022, almost 77% of UK students came from the maintained sector. In 2023, St Catharine's will celebrate its 500th anniversary.

St Edmund's

Cambridge CB3 0BN   01223 336 086   www.st-edmunds.cam.ac.uk

Undergraduates 200   Postgraduates 600   admissions@st-edmunds.cam.ac.uk

Home to graduates and mature undergraduates from all over the world (more than 80 countries at last count) "Eddies" has a convivial and laidback atmosphere on the hill away from the centre of town. Eddies also participates in the university's Foundation Year programme, which provides a fully funded year of study (before starting a degree) for students from less-advantaged backgrounds. The college's cheap and cosy bar, which remains entirely student-run, is a popular choice for socialising. Many of the university's top athletes go to Eddies. The college aims to be particularly supportive of student parents through its St Teddy's Club, featuring family lunches and gatherings. Accommodation and food can be pricey, as St Edmund's does not enjoy the big endowments of some of the larger colleges. Its Mount Pleasant halls opened in September 2019 with 136 comfortable en-suite bedrooms and 64 studio flats. St Edmund's is unique among Cambridge colleges for having a Catholic chapel and takes a relaxed approach to traditions. There is no fellows' high table in hall, and students and academics are encouraged to mingle.

St John's

Cambridge CB2 1TP   01223 338 703   www.joh.cam.ac.uk

Undergraduates 658   Postgraduates 312   admissions@joh.cam.ac.uk

St John's enjoys a fairy-tale setting, with the River Cam snaking under the Bridge of Sighs, past grand ivy-covered buildings. Inside, the college hosts a vibrant community with myriad sporting and cultural activities. A large and wealthy college, St John's offers some generous financial support to its students. From 2023, its Free Places programme will completely cover the costs of up to 40 low-income undergraduates at a time – including all tuition fees, accommodation and living expenses – allowing them to graduate debt-free. The college's state school intake increased to 71.7% in 2021 from 48% in 2017. St John's prowess on the sports field includes the "Red Boys" rugby team – which won the inter-collegiate Cuppers for the 12th time since 2005 in 2022. "Maggie", as the boat club is known, is another force to reckon with. In 2021, the college choir made the decision to start admitting women and girls. The Picturehouse is the college's student-run cinema. Food in the Buttery Dining Room is delicious and well-subsidised. St John's May Week Ball is known as one of the most fabulous. On the night, punts fill the river to watch the fireworks display. In 2022, the college was granted permission to build 245 rooms in 39 townhouses on the Grand Lane development.

Trinity

Cambridge CB2 1TQ   01223 338 422   www.trin.cam.ac.uk

Undergraduates 720   Postgraduates 350   admissions@trin.cam.ac.uk

Arguably Cambridge's most famous college, Trinity boasts vast grounds on the Cam and an alumni list that ranges from Sir Isaac Newton to Eddie Redmayne. It has retained some of its quirkier traditions, including the Great Court Run, where students try to run around the court faster than the clock can strike 12 (made famous by *Chariots of Fire*). Trinity has by far the largest undergraduate population in Cambridge and is the richest college, which is reflected in the resources (including bursaries) and high-quality accommodation available. At last count around 60% of its undergraduates were studying STEM subjects. A mentoring scheme called *Track to Trin* aims to widen access for black students. The Tudor-Gothic buildings of New Court have been renovated to provide 169 student rooms, and nearly half the accommodation is now en-suite. A two-storey gym is minutes from the main gate, along with pitches for netball, football, rugby and cricket. There are also hockey pitches and courts for badminton, tennis and squash. The college punts are popular on summer afternoons. The famed chapel choir has toured extensively. The JCR takes up two floors and there is a bar that serves as a café during the day. Trinity also hosts candlelit formals in its stunning hall. The college takes on a studious atmosphere in exam time and is consistently high-performing. In 2019, Trinity installed its first female master: former chief medical officer Dame Sally Davies.

Trinity Hall

Cambridge CB2 1TJ 01223 332 535 www.trinhall.cam.ac.uk
Undergraduates 419 Postgraduates 223 admissions@trinhall.cam.ac.uk

Home to Cambridge's smallest college chapel, year groups are also relatively small which creates an intimate atmosphere at Trinity Hall (nicknamed "Tit Hall"). Compact, with plenty of charm and not be mistaken for its larger neighbour Trinity, the college's Jerwood Library has enviable views of the River Cam. A short walk across Garrett Hostel Bridge offers access to Sidgwick Site and the university library. Market Square is also just a few minutes away. All first-years are housed on the central site, where the cafeteria, coffee shop, bar, library, chapel and main music room are also located. The Thompson's Lane off-site accommodation is also central. There are en-suite rooms in WYNG Gardens, while there are also more affordable single rooms in Bishop Bateman Court. Many students live at the Wychfield site further afield. The chapel choir's recordings are well-received, and off-site there are squash and tennis courts, plus football, hockey, rugby, cricket and netball facilities. Alumni include the scientists Stephen Hawking and Nobel Prize-winner David Thouless, actor Rachel Weisz and Olympic medal-winning cyclist Emma Pooley. In June 2022, the college opened its new WongAvery Music Gallery with rehearsal spaces and in October 2022 former BBC World Service editor Mary Hockaday was appointed the new master.

Wolfson

Cambridge CB3 9BB 01223 335 918 www.wolfson.cam.ac.uk
Undergraduates 206 Postgraduates 973 ugadministrator@wolfson.cam.ac.uk

Wolfson's postgraduate-heavy balance of students creates a grown-up feel to social life. Forward-thinking and welcoming, Wolfson has a small intake of mature undergraduates annually (it accepted 21 in 2021). It is very international college, too, with students from 96 different countries. Wolfson does not shy away from breaking some Cambridge conventions, with no "high table" – meaning academics and students share their dinners. The college was originally founded in 1965, and at the time was unique in Cambridge in accepting both women and men as part of the fellowship and the student body. Wolfson may not have the medieval buildings of many central colleges, but it boasts serene gardens and a fast commute to the Sidgwick Site and the university library. Undergraduates are guaranteed accommodation on the college campus for their first three years. Wolfson raised £7million in donations when it celebrated its 50th anniversary in 2015. It has one of the university's best gyms as well as a court for basketball and tennis. The college's Howler comedy nights draw an audience from across Cambridge to catch professional and student stand-up at its lively bar.

14 University Profiles

The full university experience has returned to UK campuses, as higher education emerges from the pandemic that restricted students to virtual learning environments. Results of the National Student Survey (NSS), published in summer 2022, revealed that students' satisfaction with their courses had recovered compared with the year before – to an extent – but remained lower than pre-Covid-19. The UK-wide poll of 325,000 students found that 76.3% of respondents were satisfied with the quality of their course overall, up from 74.4% in 2021. Even so, the overall scored was still below the previous lowest figure for overall satisfaction of 80.3%, recorded in 2006.

The NSS results reflect the views of final-year students who were at the sharp end of the pandemic, with much of their time at university affected by lockdowns and other restrictions. Evidently, there is more to do if students' views of the quality of their course and time at universities is to improve further. But the advances in online learning necessitated by lockdowns have proved helpful, and with campuses buzzing with action once more, students can hope for a best-of-both worlds blend.

This chapter looks at the NSS and much more. It provides profiles of all 132 universities that feature in *The Times* and *Sunday Times* league table. It also has profiles of the Open University, which supplies the country's most part-time degrees; Birkbeck, University of London, which specialises in evening courses; and the University of the Highlands and Islands. Because of their special course or geographical circumstances, none of these appear in our main ranking. University College Birmingham withheld data for our table and is therefore not profiled, although it is listed at the end of the book.

Specialist colleges, such as the Royal College of Music (**www.rcm.ac.uk**) or institutions that only offer postgraduate degrees, such as Cranfield University (**www.cranfield.ac.uk**), are omitted. This is not a reflection on their quality, it is simply due to their particular roles. A number of additional institutions with degree-awarding powers are listed at the end of the book with their contact details.

Dating back to 1836, the University of London (**www.london.ac.uk**) is Britain's biggest conventional higher education institution by far, with a total of more than 240,000 students studying over 3,700 courses. A federal university, it consists of 17 self-governing colleges, and most of its students are based in the capital. Further afield it also offers degrees at the Institute in Paris, and its global prestige attracts more than 50,000 students in 190 countries to take University of London degrees via distance learning. Its School of Advanced Study comprises eight specialist institutes for research and postgraduate education (details at **www.sas.ac.uk**).

The following University of London colleges have their own entries in this chapter: Birkbeck, City, Goldsmiths, King's College London, London School of Economics and Political Science, Queen Mary, Royal Holloway, SOAS, St George's and University College London. Contact details for its other constituent colleges are given on page 586.

Guide to the profiles

Our extensive survey of UK universities provides detailed, up-to-date information for their profiles. The latest campus developments, results from the National Student Survey, trends in application and social data, financial help available to undergraduates, research reputation and findings from the government's Teaching Excellence Framework inform their content. You can also find contact details for admission enquiries along with postal addresses and open day information.

We also include data under the heading "Where Students Come From" in Chapter 6. This is taken from our latest table on social inclusion that gives details of student recruitment and the socioeconomic and ethnic mix of each institution. The methodology for its data can be found on page 91-101.

In addition, each profile provides information under the following headings:

» ***The Times and Sunday Times*** **rankings:** For the overall ranking, the figure in bold refers to the university's position in the 2024 *Guide* and the figure in brackets to the previous year. All the information listed below the heading is taken from the main league table. (See Chapter 1 for explanations and the sources of the data).
» **Undergraduates:** The number of full-time undergraduates is given first followed by part-time undergraduates (in brackets). The figures are for 2020-21 and are the most recent from the Higher Education Statistics Agency (HESA).
» **Postgraduates:** The number of full-time postgraduates is given first followed by part-time postgraduates (in brackets). The figures are for 2020-21 and are the most recent from HESA.
» **Mature students:** The percentage of undergraduate entrants who were 21 or over at the start of their studies in 2021. The figures are from UCAS.
» **International students:** The number of undergraduate overseas students (both EU and non-EU) as a percentage of full-time undergraduates. The figures are for 2020-21 and are from HESA.
» **Applications per place:** The number of applications per place for 2021, from UCAS.
» **Accommodation:** The information was obtained from university accommodation services, and their help is gratefully acknowledged.

Tuition fees

Details of tuition fees for 2023-24 are given wherever possible. At the time of going to press, a number of universities had not published their international fees for 2023-24. In these cases, the fees for 2022-23 are given. Please check university websites to see if they have updated figures.

It is of the utmost importance that you check university websites for the latest information. Every university website gives details of the financial and other support available to students, from scholarships and bursaries to study support and hardship funds. Some of the support will be delivered automatically but most will not, and it is up to applicants to explore the details on university websites, including methods of applying and deadlines, to get the greatest benefit.

In addition, in England the Office for Students (**www.officeforstudents.org.uk**) publishes "Access Agreements" for every English university on its website. Each agreement outlines the university's plans for fees, financial support and measures being taken to widen access to that university and to encourage students to complete their courses.

University of Aberdeen

A "revolutionary" science teaching hub has opened at Aberdeen, designed to transform how chemistry, medical, biological and geosciences students work together.

The £35million building has digitised teaching spaces alongside flexible laboratory areas for cross-disciplinary projects. The new hub joins other modern developments such as the Sir Duncan Rice Library, opened 10 years ago by the Queen, at the Old Aberdeen campus, founded in 1495, while the historic King's buildings provide an imposing backdrop.

When the original King's College opened it had 36 staff and students who studied only the arts, divinity and law. Fast-forward more than five centuries and theology and religious studies was at the forefront of the university's successful submission to the latest Research Excellence Framework (REF 2021). Aberdeen slips 20 places in our research quality index, however, against stronger performances from rival institutions across the sector.

These days the curriculum covers 12 teaching schools and the opportunity to follow a special interest is built into degrees, allowing students to add contrasting courses to their main subject area.

The Aberdeen Employability Boost Award for students and graduates has been introduced to enhance readiness for work, offering live workshops and employer-led sessions to find out how to stand out in job applications.

The university has been associated with five Nobel laureates in the fields of chemistry, medicine, physics and peace. At Foresterhill, life sciences and medical students share Europe's largest health campus, run by the university and NHS Grampian.

Applications and admissions to Aberdeen hit a five-year peak in 2021's recruitment round. New entrants will find in-person lectures, tutorials and practical teaching supplemented by virtual learning services. Lecture capture is an established tool, and some staff use a "flipped classroom" approach, requiring students to study a topic before in-person sessions where they can explore ideas with peers and tutors.

In our analysis of the latest National Student Survey, published in summer 2022, Aberdeen reaches the top 10 for student satisfaction with the overall experience, rising from 12th in 2021 to ninth place. The university is 14th for satisfaction with teaching quality, up from =31. Students are offered support for their mental health including a free counselling service, therapy pets and free mindfulness sessions.

AFG College with the University of Aberdeen is the first campus to open in Qatar in partnership with a UK institution. It offers bachelor's degrees in accounting and finance and business management. Aberdeen also has partnerships in Sri Lanka and an alliance with Curtin University in Perth, Western Australia.

King's College
Aberdeen AB24 3FX
01224 272 000
study@abdn.ac.uk
www.ausa.org.uk
www.abdn.ac.uk
Open days: see website

The Times and The Sunday Times **Rankings**
Overall Ranking: 19 (last year: 20)

Teaching quality	79.4%	14
Student experience	78.6%	9
Research quality	38.7%	=63
Entry standards	185	8
Graduate prospects	79.9%	=33
Good honours	88.3%	=13
Expected completion rate	89.9%	=41
Student/staff ratio	15	=39

The university has longstanding links with Aberdeen's offshore oil and gas industries. Its facilities include the National Decommissioning Centre in Newburgh, Aberdeenshire, a global research centre that has engineering laboratories and hangar space for the design and development of oil and gas decommissioning technology, as well as environmental commercial testing facilities.

At the Oceanlab research centre just north of the city, Aberdeen's engineering experts test subsea equipment. The university also nurtures strengths across the life sciences and medicine, the arts and social sciences, and business – with an emphasis on co-curricular experiences and collaborative teaching and learning.

Different bursaries and scholarships – from means-tested access payments to merit-based awards for those entering with top grades – are offered according to whether applicants are from Scotland, the rest of the UK or abroad. The university makes contextualised offers for students who have left care or are estranged from their parents, or who come from a deprived area. Aberdeen is third among Scottish universities for its black achievement gap (11.1%), improved from 12.3% last year.

All first-years are guaranteed one of the 2,184 rooms in halls if they apply by the deadline. A £225,000 development at the Hillhead Student Village has created a new social area with decking and a canopy for performances and get-togethers. There is also an outdoor gym,

facilities and a community garden with plants from the university's Cruickshank Botanic Garden – an 11-acre oasis of greenery on the King's College campus. Accommodation starts at £92 a week, or £155 for 148 catered spaces.

Students at Aberdeen can choose from more than 100 sports clubs and societies. Aberdeen Sports Village, across the road from the main campus, features Olympic-standard sports and exercise facilities, from a diving pool to indoor and outdoor athletics arenas. More sports facilities are to be found around the city: there is a boathouse on the River Dee and a climbing bothy in Royal Deeside. At the King's Pavilion there are outdoor playing fields, tennis courts and an artificial cricket wicket.

The university also has the oldest shinty club in the world, established in 1861, and students play the Scottish game – similar to field hockey – at Balgownie. There is no excuse for taking a breather in the great outdoors. The region has 150 miles of coastline and the university is within striking distance of the Cairngorms National Park and the Glenshee Ski Centre.

Tuition fees

»	Fees for Scottish students	£0–£1,820
	RUK fees	£9,250
»	Fees for International students 2023–24	£19,800–£22,800
	Medicine	£47,500
»	For scholarship and bursary information see	
	www.abdn.ac.uk/study/undergraduate/finance.php	
»	Graduate salary	£26,000

Student numbers

Undergraduates	9,164	(688)
Postgraduates	3,407	(2,819)
Applications/places		19,435/3,105
Applications per place		6.3:1
Overall offer rate		70.5%
International students – EU		18.7%
Non-EU		8.2% %

Accommodation

University provided places: 2,184
Catered: £155 per week
Self-catered: £92–£156 per week
First-years guaranteed accommodation
www.abdn.ac.uk/accommodation

Where do the students come from?

State schools (non-grammar)	81.1%	First generation students	30.7%	
Grammar schools	2.8%	Low participation areas	7.9%	
Independent schools	16.1%	All ethnic minorities	14.2%	

Social inclusion ranking (Scotland): 11

White working class males	n/a
Black achievement gap	-11.1%
Mature (over 21)	15.8%

Abertay University

Abertay's cyberQuarter opened in June 2022. An £18million hub for cybersecurity research will provide a bridge between academia and industry growth. The centre is in the newly opened Annie Lamont Building, where students will find a social and networking space with a café. The university was the first to offer degrees in ethical hacking and the cyberQuarter has already attracted NHS Scotland's cyberteam as a tenant.

Dundee is the UK's only Unesco City of Design and Abertay's School of Design and Informatics carries the baton in a digital direction. Its Emergent Technology Centre houses teaching and research into mixed-reality technologies, with facilities such as a development studio for experimental games design and hacking projects. Students also use eye-tracking equipment, specialist cameras and an extended reality lab with room-scale virtual reality. Sony chose Abertay as the site for the largest teaching laboratory in Europe for its PlayStation consoles, which opened in 2014.

David Jones, the creator of the hit Grand Theft Auto video game, is an Abertay graduate and the university heads the InGAME research and development project at the forefront of the renowned Dundee video games cluster. Abertay also hosts the national Centre for Excellence in Computer Games Education. All games students become members of UK Interactive Entertainment (UKIE), the gateway to a bespoke programme of industry mentorship and support. There is more to come: the university is one of the partners in a project to bring Scotland's first e-sports arena to the regenerated waterfront in Dundee by 2024.

The university's global reputation in experimental design is again reflected in the latest Research Excellence Framework (REF 2021), where one of its strongest performances was in art and design – covering work in digital games. Research in engineering also did well, including the fields of cybersecurity, computing and environmental engineering. However, Abertay's overall submission was relatively small, covering eight subject areas, and the university has fallen 10 places in our research quality index (101st).

Abertay's superb record in the National Student Survey (NSS) earned it University of the Year for Teaching Quality in The Good University Guide 2021. However, the pandemic dealt a huge blow to student satisfaction. The university has climbed one place on student satisfaction with teaching quality (17th) and fallen three for satisfaction with the overall experience (=46). Hybrid in-person and remote teaching continues to be the model post-pandemic. Individual programmes decide the best balance of on-campus teaching and online delivery for their students.

Eight new online programmes in business and computing subjects began in 2022. Designed

Kydd Building
Bell Street
Dundee DD1 1HG
01382 308 080
sro@abertay.ac.uk
www.abertay.ac.uk
Open days:
see website

The Times and The Sunday Times **Rankings**
Overall Ranking: =89 (last year: =94)

Teaching quality	78.7%	17
Student experience	73.2%	=46
Research quality	24.6%	101
Entry standards	148	= 32
Graduate prospects	70.5%	81
Good honours	78%	61
Expected completion rate	76.3%	=121
Student/staff ratio	24.2	127

to appeal to students who hope to combine their studies with a job or with caring responsibilities, the courses offer flexible start dates and a pay-per-module finance structure. Abertay plans to extend the subjects offered in this format.

Seven new degrees are being introduced in 2022 and 2023. Criminology can be combined with policing or sociology, and psychology with development and education, forensic and investigative psychology, or forensic scene investigation. Degrees in food science, nutrition and wellbeing, and social care management will also add breadth to the curriculum.

Abertay was rated silver in the latest Teaching Excellence Framework in 2017, commended for embedding employability within the curriculum.

Most courses have a work placement built in. Abertay offers Scotland's first accelerated degrees – which take three years, rather than the standard four in the Scottish system.

Students from the School of Business, Law and Social Sciences benefit from Abertay's longstanding links with Heineken to be offered the opportunity to create marketing solutions for a real-world brief. Student enterprise is funded by Santander. According to our analysis of graduate prospects, the university is 81st, based on the proportion of graduates in highly skilled work or postgraduate study 15 months after leaving.

Abertay is once again No 1 in our Scottish social inclusion index, for the third successive year. The first university north of the border to introduce contextual offers, Abertay also runs its own part-time access programme.

About half of Abertay's students qualify for some form of scholarship or bursary. The university's sports science research scholarships enable students and staff to work with clubs such as Dundee Rugby, Dundee United Football Club, Fife Flyers Hockey Club and the World Karate Federation. A link with the leading mobile games company Ninja Kiwi Europe provides scholarship funding as well as support for Abertay's games design competition.

About 500 study rooms are available from £65 per week in a twin room. New students who apply by August 1 are guaranteed accommodation. During freshers' week, students must take a compulsory training module to make sure they understand sexual consent. The university's mental health service is free.

Promising a more personal undergraduate experience than bigger universities can offer, Abertay has just over 4,000 students in Scotland's fourth-largest city.

Tuition fees

- » Fees for Scottish students   £0–£1,820
  RUK fees   £9,250
- » Fees for International students 2023–24   £14,000–£15,500
- » For scholarship and bursary information see www.abertay.ac.uk/study-apply/money-fees-and-funding/tuition-fees/
- » Graduate salary   £23,000

Student numbers

Undergraduates	3,993	(157)
Postgraduates	204	(219)
Applications/places		5,280/1,220
Applications per place		4.3:1
Overall offer rate		83.5%
International students – EU		11.3%
Non-EU		1%

Accommodation

University provided places: 500
Self-catered: £65–£133 per week
https://www.abertay.ac.uk/accommodation/

Where do the students come from?

State schools (non-grammar)	94.8%	First generation students	46.5%	White working class males	n/a
Grammar schools	0.9%	Low participation areas	16.8%	Black achievement gap	n/a
Independent schools	4.4%	All ethnic minorities	8.7%	Mature (over 21)	40.5%

Social inclusion ranking (Scotland): 1

Aberystwyth University

Aberystwyth's gothic Old College on the seafront is to have a new lease of life. The university's original building, opened in 1872, is being transformed into a cultural and creative centre – making its heritage accessible to students, staff, the community and visitors alike.

The £27million development will offer new study areas and lifelong learning facilities along with space for art exhibitions, music performances and a centre for new entrepreneurs. The plans also include the UK's first Centre for Dialogue, which aims to help young people to express themselves better as they enter the working world.

The last academic departments moved from Old College to the university's purpose-built Penglais campus overlooking the town in 2014. The refurbished Hugh Owen Library is at Penglais, plus the National Library of Wales, one of the UK's copyright libraries.

A serial winner in our University of the Year awards – for teaching quality in 2018 and 2019 and named Welsh University of the Year in 2020 – Aberystwyth continues to flourish. In 2021 it ranked third for student satisfaction with teaching quality and sixth for the overall experience, even after one of the toughest years that students and universities had known. In our analysis of the latest National Student Survey, published in summer 2022, it remains third for

satisfaction with teaching quality and rises to joint second for satisfaction with the wider undergraduate experience.

Rated gold in the Teaching Excellence Framework (TEF) in 2016, Aberystwyth was found to have "outstanding levels of stretch", ensuring that all students were significantly challenged to achieve their full potential. Substantial investment in e-learning was another plus point, as was the integrated approach to Welsh-language teaching. Just under a third of existing students come from Wales and Welsh-medium teaching is flourishing.

The university's new School of Veterinary Science has welcomed its second cohort of students taking a Bachelor of Veterinary Science (BVSc) degree in collaboration with the Royal Veterinary College. They spend the first two years of the five-year course in Aberystwyth before transferring to the RVC's Hawkshead campus in Hertfordshire to complete their degree. It is the first veterinary school in Wales, and one of only 11 across the UK. Facilities include a European Union-funded veterinary hub and the Centre of Excellence for Bovine Tuberculosis is based there.

The new veterinary science degree and new nursing degrees are credited with contributing to a small rise in applications, according to a snapshot of the application cycle at the end of March 2022. This consolidates a 9% increase in applications in 2021, resulting in their highest level in eight years. However, the numbers

---

Penglais Campus
Aberystwyth SY23 3FL
01970 622 021
ug-admissions@aber.ac.uk
www.abersu.co.uk
www.aber.ac.uk
Open days:
see website

The Times and The Sunday Times **Rankings**
Overall Ranking: 41 (last year: 38)

Teaching quality	83.7%	3
Student experience	80.5%	2
Research quality	38.7%	=63
Entry standards	121	=77
Graduate prospects	66%	113
Good honours	72.5%	=103
Expected completion rate	85.2%	=67
Student/staff ratio	15.6	51

seeking a place have yet to be restored to their peak in 2011, 40% higher than in 2021.

From 2023, a degree in veterinary nursing will also join the curriculum. The Aberystwyth Innovation and Enterprise Campus (AberInnovation), a £40.5million facility providing world-leading facilities in food, biorefining and agritech, is based on the university's Gogerddan campus.

Agriculture produced some of the best results for Aberystwyth in the latest Research Excellence Framework (REF 2021). Food science, geology, sports science, and Celtic studies were also prominent. King Charles III learnt Welsh at Aberystwyth in 1969. Overall, three-quarters of the university's research was rated as world-leading or internationally excellent, the top two categories. Its performance represented an improvement since the previous REF in 2014 but it has fallen 18 places in our research quality index to =63 against sector-wide gains.

Efforts to improve social inclusion at Aberystwyth continue. Although its performance has sunk from 36th in 2021 to 50th, the university is seventh in England and Wales according to our new measure for the recruitment of white working-class male students, now the most underrepresented group in higher education. The university runs a contextual offers scheme and those eligible include students from schools in the lower 40% of A-level achievement, those who have spent time in care, or those whose school participates in the Pathway to Success programme in Wales.

Aberystwyth supports about half of its UK entrants with some form of financial aid and the university offers assistance for Welsh-speakers and those who have left care or are estranged from their family.

Sports facilities are excellent, with 48 acres of pitches. A pool and saunarium is complemented by a sundeck – no, the rain is not nonstop, whatever people may say about Welsh weather. Unusually, the university offers stabling for students' horses.

The Penglais and Gogerddan campuses are about a mile apart. All first-years are guaranteed one of more than 3,000 places ranging from the newly refurbished, Welsh-speaking Pantycelyn hall of residence to the modern blocks of Fferm Penglais and Pentre Jane Morgan.

No one can dispute the attraction of Aber's seaside setting and jaw-dropping sunsets – although it is a long journey from many parts of the UK. Once part of the Aberystwyth community, students are immensely loyal to their university.

Tuition fees

» Fees for UK students £9,000
» Fees for International students 2023–24 £15,375–£17,575
» Veterinary Medicine £17,575
» For scholarship and bursary information see https://www.aber.ac.uk/en/undergrad/before-you-apply/fees-finance/tuition-fees/#-
» Graduate salary £20,907

Student numbers

Undergraduates	5,409	(1,196)
Postgraduates	666	(768)
Applications/places	9,345/1,855	
Applications per place	5:1	
Overall offer rate	97.6%	
International students – EU	12.8%	
Non-EU	5.8%	

Accommodation

University provided places: 3,145
Self-catered: £88–£165 per week
www.aber.ac.uk/en/accommodation/

Where do the students come from?

State schools (non-grammar)	91%	First generation students	37.1%	White working class males	n/a
Grammar schools	4.4%	Low participation areas	12.1%	Black achievement gap	n/a
Independent schools	4.5%	All ethnic minorities	6.5%	Mature (over 21)	15.7%

Social inclusion ranking: 50

Anglia Ruskin University

Anglia Ruskin continues to be the main provider of essential staff in the east of England, including social workers, operating department practitioners and teachers. Many will be trained at the new ARU Peterborough site, where students on more than 72 new degree courses walked through the doors in September 2022. The £30million campus has a mission to raise academic attainment in the region and the courses have been co-created with regional organisations to meet local demand for skills.

Longer term, Anglia Ruskin expects to invest more than £100million in the Peterborough site, the centrepiece of a university quarter in the city. It aims to have 12,500 students by 2030.

New degrees and degree apprenticeships offered in Peterborough span business and marketing, computing and games development, education, engineering, food and environment, health and social care, nursing and midwifery, law, construction and surveying.

Degree apprenticeship numbers have already reached about 2,000 in 25 programmes training students for roles in policing, business and management, building, digital, data and technology, and nursing and healthcare.

Anglia Ruskin's world-leading research in music therapy for patients with dementia was recognised in February 2022 with the award of the Queen's Anniversary Prize, presented by (the then) Prince Charles. The honour – the highest in UK further and higher education – singles out innovative work that delivers significant public benefit.

Nine subject areas at Anglia Ruskin were judged to have a world-leading impact, according to results from the latest Research Excellence Framework (REF 2021): allied health professions; business and management studies; communication; cultural and media studies; language and literature; history; music; drama; dance; performing arts; psychology; social work and social policy; and sociology. The university rises five places in our research quality ranking this year to 84th place.

Anglia Ruskin's strong tradition in healthcare education is backed up by simulated hospital wards and clinical skills facilities at the Young Street Building in Cambridge. The university was shortlisted for the Nursing Times pre-registration Provider of the Year award in 2019 and 2020. The £20million medical school, opened in 2018, is at the riverside Chelmsford campus. The Cambridge campus is the base for students taking degrees from the Cambridge School of Art. Hands-on learning facilities at the Cambridge site include crime scene rooms in the Science Centre, a mock law court and gaming laboratories.

Anglia Ruskin also has two London bases – in the City and Docklands – mainly for business and law students.

Even before ARU Peterborough opened, there had been a spike in applications to

---

Bishop Hall Lane
Chelmsford CM1 1SQ
01245 686 868
answers@aru.ac.uk
www.aru.ac.uk
www.angliastudent.com
Open days: see website

The Times and The Sunday Times **Rankings**
Overall Ranking: 109 (last year: 115)

Teaching quality	76.8%	=37
Student experience	71.4%	73
Research quality	30.2%	84
Entry standards	110	=115
Graduate prospects	67.4%	=104
Good honours	76%	=80
Expected completion rate	79.3%	106
Student/staff ratio	19.4	=110

Anglia Ruskin. Applications exceeded 19,000 in the 2021 admissions cycle and enrolments were at their highest level since 2016.

As well as the new courses at Peterborough, the university introduced degree courses in creative writing; fashion communication and branding; computer games (both design and programming); media production; television production and biological sciences with sustainability in September 2022.

Rated silver in the Teaching Excellence Framework (TEF), Anglia Ruskin was commended for its strong support for students at risk of dropping out.

Ruskin Modules were incorporated into most degree courses from September 2021, teaching skills such as problem-solving, teamwork and creative thinking. For students whose degree structure does not include a formal work placement, Anglia Ruskin makes sure students have real-world experience through industry links and live briefs. However, the university has fallen from 63rd to =104 in our analysis of the Graduate Outcomes survey comparing the proportion of students in highly skilled work or further study 15 months after leaving university.

Widening access is part of the university's mission. In 2021, almost 23% of offers made by Anglia Ruskin were contextual, a proportion expected to be similar in 2023. Unusually, Anglia Ruskin does not require maths A-level for some of its engineering programmes as part of its efforts to diversify its intake.

More than half of Anglia Ruskin's students are the first in their family to go to university and more than two-thirds are over 21 (the sixth-highest proportion). Although the university has fallen seven places year-on-year to rank joint 24th in our overall analysis of social inclusion, it remains in the top 25 for its record on recruiting students from underrepresented backgrounds.

At the university's foundation year centre, ARU College, Navitas, students develop study skills and aim to progress to a degree programme. There are courses available in computing and digital technology, business, animal sciences, health and medical sciences, art and design, psychology and public health.

Anglia Ruskin's financial support includes the ARU Bursary of up to £300 per year for UK and eligible European Union students from low-income households and international merit scholarships of £1,000–£2,000 for international students.

Accommodation in Cambridge and Chelmsford is guaranteed for all first-years who apply by the July deadline.

Tuition fees

» Fees for UK students £9,250
» Fees for International students 2023–24 £14,300–£15,000
» For scholarship and bursary information see https://aru.ac.uk/student-life/preparing-for-university/help-with-finances/scholarships
» Graduate salary £24,395

Student numbers

Undergraduates	22,138	(2,171)
Postgraduates	4,022	(3,850)
Applications/places		19,015/4,380
Applications per place		4.3:1
Overall offer rate		71.2%
International students – EU		8.8%
Non-EU		4.4%

Accommodation

University provided places: 2,136
Self-catered: £112–£152 per week
First-years in Cambridge and Chelmsford guaranteed accommodation
www.aru.ac.uk/student-life/accommodation

Where do the students come from?

State schools (non-grammar)	93%	First generation students	53.5%	
Grammar schools	3.8%	Low participation areas	16.3%	
Independent schools	3.2%	All ethnic minorities	31.5%	

Social inclusion ranking: =24

White working-class males	5.1%
Black achievement gap	-21.5%
Mature (over 21)	71.9%

Arts University Bournemouth

Arts University Bournemouth (AUB), which sits between Bournemouth and Poole on the Jurassic Coast, has its buildings painted in pops of bright colour – reflecting the creative endeavours within.

Teaching is based on a single site and facilities include the CRAB drawing studio, the first to be built at an art school for more than a century and designed by Sir Peter Cook, an alumnus. The Photography Building has flexible teaching spaces and IT suites, and TheGallery is AUB's own exhibition space, where the work of students and other contemporary artists is showcased. The library's Museum of Design in Plastics exhibits thousands of mass-produced design icons.

All undergraduate courses have their own studio space, but students are encouraged to work together across disciplines on campus. The Campus Halls student accommodation development, featuring curated artworks in the communal areas, is the latest addition.

Digital support has been a focus of investment, with students benefiting from software such as the Adobe Creative Cloud Suite, Microsoft Office 365 and access to LinkedIn learning courses. Digital capability is assessed at the start of the academic year and those in digital hardship receive support such as long-term laptop loans and financial help.

However, rates of student satisfaction have yet to recover from the huge falls they suffered in pandemic-hit 2021. AUB was in the top five for our measures derived from the National Student Survey (teaching quality and student experience) only two years ago. But it ranks =48 for satisfaction teaching quality in our analysis of the NSS outcomes published in summer 2022, and =81 for satisfaction with the wider experience.

Recent feedback by students is at odds with the findings of the Teaching Excellence Framework (TEF) in 2017, when AUB was rated gold, the highest standard. The TEF panel praised the contributions of practising artists and creative professionals to teaching and the curriculum.

AUB climbs 14 places up our research quality index following its best outcomes yet in the latest Research Excellence Framework REF 2021. More than 12% of AUB's research was classified as world-leading (4*) and a further 42% was rated internationally excellent (3*). Architecture and history of art and design were among the strongest subjects in the university's submission.

Boasting the largest film school outside London (Bournemouth Film School, founded more than 50 years ago) AUB is able to offer courses covering all aspects of film-making. Its partnership with Crowdfunder – an alliance that shows students how to source funding and also boosts their own graduate film budgets – is in its sixth year. In 2021, AUB's 16 graduate films raised more than £103,000.

The university is restoring the Palace Court

Wallisdown
Poole BH12 5HH
01202 363 228
admissions@aub.ac.uk
www.aub.ac.uk/life-aub/
students-union
www.aub.ac.uk
Open days: see website

The Times and The Sunday Times Rankings
Overall Ranking: 76 (last year: =79)

Teaching quality	76.2%	=48
Student experience	70.3%	=81
Research quality	23%	104
Entry standards	145	=38
Graduate prospects	57.4%	131
Good honours	70.4%	=114
Expected completion rate	88.5%	51
Student/staff ratio	14.5	=29

Theatre in Bournemouth town centre, renovating the Art Deco venue to include a teaching space alongside the 400-seat auditorium, interval bar and rehearsal studio. It will provide a university outpost less than five minutes' walk from the beach and is scheduled to open in late 2023.

Applications and enrolments increased in the 2021 admissions round, year-on-year, and very few entrants (3%) secured their places via Clearing. A foundation degree launched in September 2022 provides students with the skills required in live music production, studio recording and media-based contexts.

Graduate prospects are a challenge for institutions with an art and design focus and AUB is near the foot of our table for its proportion of students who are in highly skilled work or further study 15 months after finishing their degree.

Professor Paul Gough, AUB's vice-chancellor since 2020 and an art historian, broadcaster and expert on Banksy, plans to rebuild the curriculum to better embed equality, diversity and inclusion as well as the United Nations sustainability goals.

About 70% of entrants receive some form of financial assistance and tuition fees include standard course materials costs – typically a big expenditure for those on creative courses.

The university has launched a new post-16 access scheme, All Access AUB. Participants attend a residential summer school on campus and part in creative workshops to boost their artistic confidence. Their work is then put in a two-week exhibition at TheGallery and their families invited to a private view.

Those who complete All Access AUB qualify for additional consideration from the admissions team and a reduced conditional offer. The new outreach programme may help to boost AUB's position in our social inclusion index, where it sits 92nd.

The Small Things Matter is a Students' Union-run campaign promoting mindful self-care tools and more than 200 staff have been trained in mental health first aid.

For £15 a term the union offers social sports sessions such as yoga, jogging and hockey through the Give it a Go programme (regular attendees get a free hoodie). AUB does not have its own sports facilities. Instead, a subsidy allows students to share the neighbouring University of Bournemouth's extensive gym, courts, pitches and fitness studios. An Olympic-sized velodrome 10 minutes away is free for students to use.

There are 1,131 study bedrooms, with tenancies released in waves from March to July to avoid any first-come, first-served scrum. All first-year full-timers can live in.

Tuition fees

» Fees for UK students	£9,250
Foundation years	£5,421
» Fees for International students 2023–24	£17,950–£19,950
» For scholarship and bursary information see www.aub.ac.uk/fees/	
» Graduate salary	£21,000

Student numbers

Undergraduates	3,334	(0)
Postgraduates	118	(68)
Applications/places	7,180/1,435	
Applications per place	5.1	
Overall offer rate	63.5%	
International students – EU	7.7%	
Non-EU	7.9%	

Accommodation

University provided places: 1,131
Self-catered: £165–£227 per week
First-years guaranteed accommodation
www.aub.ac.uk/accommodation

Where do the students come from?

State schools (non-grammar)	91.9%	First generation students	38.8%	White working-class males	4%
Grammar schools	2.9%	Low-participation areas	9%	Black achievement gap	−28.5%
Independent schools	5.2%	All ethnic minorities	12.2%	Mature (over	11.5%

Social inclusion ranking: 92

University of the Arts London

The world needs creativity, declares a 10-year strategy for the University of the Arts London (UAL). James Purnell, the institution's president and vice-chancellor, now in his second year of tenure, has outlined bold plans to double student numbers over the next decade.

The expansion is planned not only for the curriculum at UAL's London campuses but more significantly via online delivery. UAL intends to use its experience of digital provision during the Covid-19 pandemic as a springboard. A former Labour cabinet minister and BBC director of strategy and digital, Purnell has been described as the "architect" of Tony Blair's 50% participation target for higher education. He believes that UAL has the capacity to respond to high demand for its courses while also widening access, making the institution more inclusive.

UAL is one institution comprised of six distinct colleges founded in the 19th or early 20th centuries. Each has a unique identity and specialism: Camberwell College of Arts, Central St Martins College of Art and Design, Chelsea College of Arts, London College of Communication, London College of Fashion, and Wimbledon College of Arts.

Since becoming a university in 2003, UAL has established a reputation for innovation across the creative fields and has produced more than half of the nominees for the Turner prize since it was first awarded in 1984. The artist Grayson Perry – who won the Turner prize in 2003 – is UAL's chancellor. His Grayson's Robes competition challenges UAL students to design what he will wear at graduation ceremonies as an unconventional alternative to a formal black academic gown.

Superb facilities are found on all UAL's sites. Central Saint Martins' award-winning £200million campus at King's Cross is a defining feature in the area's regeneration. The London College of Fashion is moving its operations to its new single campus at Queen Elizabeth Olympic Park in east London in September 2023. It will join Sadler's Wells, the V&A and the BBC at its new home

The Greencoat Building opened in Camberwell, south London, in May 2022, as the base for UAL's incubation programme for graduates of Camberwell, Chelsea and Wimbledon Colleges of Arts. The new facility also provides space for the UAL Creative Computing Institute's growing cohort of staff and students at Wimbledon College of Art the theatre has been refurbished to improve lighting and add wheelchair-accessible facilities. Eagle Wharf is UAL's new Digital Hub in Peckham, south London. Student accommodation is also due to open on the site in September 2022.

UAL made the largest submission for art and design in the latest Research Excellence Framework (REF 2021) – far eclipsing the next-largest contribution by the Royal College of Art.

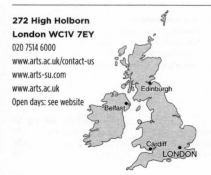

272 High Holborn
London WC1V 7EY
020 7514 6000
www.arts.ac.uk/contact-us
www.arts-su.com
www.arts.ac.uk
Open days: see website

The Times and The Sunday Times **Rankings**
Overall Ranking: 56 (last year: =52)

Teaching quality	72.6%	101
Student experience	63%	126
Research quality	46%	47
Entry standards	139	=43
Graduate prospects	59.3%	130
Good honours	75.4%	=83
Expected completion rate	86.4%	=56
Student/staff ratio	11.9	7

It climbs 25 places to reach the top 50 in our latest research quality index (47th), with 85% of its work judged world-leading or internationally excellent, the top two categories.

On a global scale, UAL is second for art and design in the QS World University rankings 2022 for the fourth year running, behind only the Royal College of Art, a postgraduate institution.

The university was rated silver in the national Teaching Excellence Framework (TEF), praised for its immersive, inquiry-led curriculum with plenty of opportunity for work placements and employer involvement via live briefs.

Arts London is aiming to reach its net zero target for carbon emissions by 2040. Students are taught to develop sustainable practices and business models.

Recruitment remains strong at UAL. As the curriculum continues to become broader, undergraduate applications rose 9% by the end of March 2022 compared with the same point in the previous admissions cycle. Seven degree programmes begin in September 2023, in data science and artificial intelligence, creative robotics, design for climate justice, service design, commercial photography, computer animation and visual effects, and fashion marketing and content creation.

UAL is in the top half of our table for social inclusion. It aims to increase the proportion of black, Asian and minority ethnic students to one third and staff to 30% by 2024, building on a steady increase over recent years.

Graduate prospects tend to present a hurdle for institutions dedicated to art and design and UAL is near the bottom of our analysis of the proportion of graduates in highly skilled work or further study after 15 months. UAL's internal recruitment service, Arts Temps, teams up with employers to find temporary jobs for UAL students in the creative and non-creative sectors. Links with global brands are built into the curriculum – either via live briefs, work placements or other project-based work. UAL also runs about 150 consultancy projects with companies such as Microsoft, Levi's and Unilever.

UAL has 21 full-time mental health professionals whose diversity reflects the student body, as well as 80 staff trained in mental health first aid.

First-year international students are guaranteed accommodation, as are under-18s and disabled students. UAL's prime London locations make for student-friendly downtime, with clubs and vintage shops, great food and galleries on the doorstep.

Tuition fees

»	Fees for UK students	£9,250
	Foundation courses	from £5,420
»	Fees for International students 2023–24	£20,940–£23,610
»	For scholarship and bursary information see	
	https://www.arts.ac.uk/study-at-ual/fees-and-funding/tuition-fees	
»	Graduate salary	£23,000

Student numbers

Undergraduates	16,343	(0)
Postgraduates	4,134	(627)
Applications/places	26,270/4,510	
Applications per place	5.8:1	
Overall offer rate	43.8%	
International students – EU	14.1%	
Non-EU	35.2%	

Accommodation

University provided places: 3,281
Self-catered: £154–£454 per week
No accommodation guarantee
www.arts.ac.uk/study-at-ual/accommodation

Where do the students come from?

State schools (non-grammar)	88.7%	First generation students	37.6%	
Grammar schools	3.2%	Low-participation areas	7.5%	
Independent schools	8.1%	All ethnic minorities	31.2%	

Social inclusion ranking: 53

White working class males	4.2%
Black achievement gap	-20.5%
Mature (over 21)	18.5%

Aston University

Every degree at Aston in Birmingham has work-based modules or a placement year. Most students choose integrated placements, organised by a university team, in the UK or abroad. Alternatively, students can set up and run their own business.

Placement years may also be used to study overseas at one of Aston's partner universities, or undergraduates can create a combination of options for a 12-month tailor-made experience. Students on some courses – pharmacy and optometry, for example – take a pre-registration year to gain work experience.

The university's accent on work-ready skills has long distinguished Aston, which began as a college of advanced technology and has grown into a multi-faculty institution encompassing five schools: business, medicine, engineering and applied science, life and health sciences, and languages and social sciences.

Aston has forged productive partnerships with local and global small and medium-size enterprises as well as strong links with large organisations such as BMW, HSBC, Greater Birmingham Chambers of Commerce and the National Crime Agency.

Employability skills are embedded in degrees, one of the factors that earned Aston a gold rating in the Teaching Excellence Framework. Assessors also admired the involvement of professional bodies and employers in course design and delivery. This pays off in a strong showing in the Graduate Outcomes survey: Aston is 35th in our analysis of the proportion of graduates in highly skilled work or further study after 15 months, a slight decline from 2021.

Based on a self-contained 60-acre site not far from the centre of Birmingham, Aston offers a campus experience within a big city. Its popularity is on the rise: a third consecutive year-on-year increase in applications brought them to a record high in the 2021 admissions cycle, up 8% on the year before. New student enrolments have remained steady.

Aston's students record rising levels of satisfaction in the latest National Student Survey. In our analysis, the university rises 12 places to rank joint 50th for satisfaction with the undergraduate experience. It is =97 for satisfaction with teaching quality.

Modern teaching facilities include a redeveloped library and an up-to-date home for the highly rated business school, the base for almost half of all Aston's students. Extra social learning spaces have been added and a new students' union opened at the heart of the campus in 2019.

There are many pockets of greenery where students can relax: the campus is

---

Aston Triangle
Birmingham B4 7ET
0121 204 3030
ugadmissions@aston.ac.uk
www.astonsu.com
www.aston.ac.uk
Open days: see website

The Times and The Sunday Times Rankings

Overall Ranking: =45 (last year: 45)

Teaching quality	72.8%	=97
Student experience	72.8%	=50
Research quality	40.9%	57
Entry standards	128	=57
Graduate prospects	79.6%	35
Good honours	84.3%	28
Expected completion rate	91.1%	=35
Student/staff ratio	17	=76

dotted with outdoor sculptures and there are geese to watch on the redesigned Chancellor's Lake.

The pioneer of degree apprenticeships in the UK, Aston offers 16 programmes across the IT, business, technology, transport, science and healthcare sectors. Since September 2022, new programmes cover digital marketing, business-to-business sales, research science, and leadership and management, healthcare, supply chains and engineering.

Aston doubled the number of staff taking part in its submission to the latest Research Excellence Framework (REF 2021) compared with the previous national assessment in 2014, and 79% of the team's work was assessed as world-leading or internationally excellent, the top two categories, almost the same as last time around.

The university hosts research centres in enterprise, healthy ageing, Europe, and neuroscience and child development, among others. Pharmacy, another strength at Aston, was awarded a prestigious Regius Professorship to celebrate the Queen's 90th birthday in 2016.

Aston has lost ground as one of the best-performing pre-1992 universities in our social inclusion index in recent years (72nd). It has the UK's second-highest proportion – 85.6% – of students drawn from ethnic minority backgrounds and 87.8% of its students are from non-selective state schools.

A women-only gym is among facilities at the Sir Doug Ellis Woodcock Sports Centre on campus, which also include a swimming pool and sports hall with indoor courts. Six miles away, the Outdoor Recreation Centre has pitches for football, cricket and hockey.

One of the country's leading student cities, Birmingham's bright lights are walking distance from campus.

First-years are guaranteed student accommodation and while no halls of residence are catered, a termly meal deal at campus catering outlets provides sustenance to cookery-shy students.

Tuition fees

»	Fees for UK students	£9,250
»	Fees for International students 2023–24	£16,300–£20,200
	Medicine	£43,650
»	For finance information see www2.aston.ac.uk/study	
»	Graduate salary	£25,000

Student numbers

Undergraduates	11,530 (1,079)
Postgraduates	1,523 (2,664)
Applications/places	20,230/3,520
Applications per place	5.7:1
Overall offer rate	81.7%
International students – EU	1.8%
Non-EU	6.4%

Accommodation

University provided places: 1,500
Self-catered: £144–£150 per week
First-years guaranteed accommodation
www2.aston.ac.uk/accommodation/

Where do the students come from?

					Social inclusion ranking: 72	
State schools (non-grammar)	87.8%	First generation students	53.6%	White working-class males	1.9%
Grammar schools	8.8%	Low-participation areas	11.6%	Black achievement gap	-14.2%
Independent schools	3.4%	All ethnic minorities	85.6%	Mature (over 21)	4.7%

Bangor University

Bangor's research profile is growing stronger. The university climbs nine places in our research quality ranking to reach the top 40 after 85% of its submission to the latest Research Excellence Framework (REF 2021) was assessed as world-leading or internationally excellent, the top two categories. Some of the best results were in sports sciences, earth systems and environmental science, and allied health professions.

The university's highly rated School of Ocean Sciences has its own research vessel, the Prince Madog, while teaching and research at the School of Natural Sciences benefits from the university's 18-hectare botanic gardens on the shores of the Menai Strait. Bangor has a research farm, animal care facilities, aquariums and greenhouses and a natural history museum.

Bangor is also investing in research on low-carbon energy – bringing opportunities for students to gain experience in the field. The university is based in Gwynedd, the county with more Welsh speakers than any other. It holds its own on teaching, as the only university in Wales to be rated gold in the Teaching Excellence Framework. Assessors commended its bilingual learning in Welsh and English as well as the personalised support for students and strategic approach to assessment, coupled with very good physical and virtual learning resources.

No university has more students who study through the medium of Welsh. At Bangor, they can also opt for Welsh language modules alongside an English-medium degree.

Bangor enjoys a spectacular setting, with the mountains of Snowdonia on one side and the Menai Strait on the other. Originally located in an old coaching inn, it was established in 1884, funded by quarrymen. Now the university encompasses 14 academic schools across the arts, humanities and sciences.

Rates of student satisfaction have returned to their usual high levels at Bangor in 2022, having dipped during the pandemic. In our analysis of the latest National Student Survey the university ranks =20 for satisfaction with teaching quality, leaping 48 places year-on-year, and =31 for the wider undergraduate experience, up 41 places.

The prospects are improving for Bangor graduates, according to our analysis of the latest Graduate Outcomes survey, in which the university climbs 16 places to =74. Students can choose to do a year's work placement at the end of their second year and the Bangor Employability Award accredits activities that are valued by employers such as volunteering, learning a new language and part-time work. Graduates can take paid internships within the university's academic schools and services.

Bangor continues to expand its curriculum. New degrees lined up to begin in September 2023 include tourism management, marine science and conservation, pharmacology (with

College Road
Bangor LL57 2DG
01248 383 717
admissions@bangor.ac.uk
www.undebbangor.com
www.bangor.ac.uk
Open days: see website

***The Times and The Sunday Times* Rankings**

Overall Ranking: =45 (last year: 64)

Teaching quality	78.5%	=20
Student experience	74.5%	=31
Research quality	51.3%	38
Entry standards	123	=72
Graduate prospects	71%	=74
Good honours	75.3%	85
Expected completion rate	82.3%	91
Student/staff ratio	15.1	=41

or without a foundation year), astudiaethau plentyndod ac leuenctid a Chymraeg (childhood and youth studies and Welsh), and drama, theatre and performance. The university offers an increasing range of joint honours degrees, too. Programmes combining philosophy, ethics and religion, modern languages and Cymraeg, film studies and production, and English literature and journalism are new from 2022.

Degree apprenticeships at Bangor cover cybersecurity, mechanical engineering, electrical/electronic engineering, data science and software engineering. So far they have attracted only small numbers – 38 at last count. The first part of the courses is delivered through Grŵp Llandrillo Menai, a group of local colleges. Links with further education partners across north Wales are considered a special strength by the university.

Bangor University is central to the development of a proposed North Wales Medical School. For the time being, it is delivering the four-year MBBCh graduate entry to medicine programme, C21, in collaboration with Cardiff University's School of Medicine.

The university offers about 40 merit scholarships each year, worth up to £3,000 in the first year of study and awarded to entrants who excel in Bangor's annual entrance scholarship exam. Sports scholarships – up to £3,000 a year – go to those who will represent the university in the British University and Colleges Sport (BUCS) competitions.

Bangor remains in the middle reaches in our analysis of social inclusion measures (=58). A contextual admissions scheme which accounted for about 15% of Bangor's offers in 2021. Non-selective comprehensive state school students make up 94% of the intake, with 8.8% from ethnic minority backgrounds.

The sports centre at Ffriddoedd, Canolfan Brailsford, is named after the cycling coach Sir Dave Brailsford, who grew up nearby. There is also a fitness room at St Mary's and gym membership is included in the fees for halls.

The Pontio arts and innovation centre houses the students' union and links the university with the town. Membership to all clubs and societies is free and there are about 200 sports and other activities to choose from.

Both student villages, St Mary's and the larger Ffriddoedd, are within walking distance of university buildings. Accommodation is guaranteed for first-years who book by the July 31 deadline. A small city with a high proportion of students, Bangor has a lively atmosphere.

Tuition fees

»	Fees for UK students	£9,000
»	Fees for International students 2023–24	£15,250–£18,250
»	For scholarship and bursary information see www.bangor.ac.uk/studentfinance/info	
»	Graduate salary	£22,000

Student numbers

Undergraduates	6,716	(187)
Postgraduates	1,181	(920)
Applications/places		9,365/2,290
Applications per place		4.1:1
Overall offer rate		85%
International students – EU		4.6%
Non-EU		10.2%

Accommodation

University provided places: 2,403
Self-catered: £103–£200 per week
First-years guaranteed accommodation
www.bangor.ac.uk/student-life/accommodation

Where do the students come from?

SState schools (non-grammar)	94%	First generation students	44.3%	White working-class males	7.5%
Grammar schools	3.7%	Low-participation areas	13%	Black achievement gap	-24.7%
Independent schools	2.2%	All ethnic minorities	8.8%	Mature (over 21)	33.6%

Social inclusion ranking: =58

University of Bath

Improvements on almost every measure make Bath our University of the Year. Making a steady march up our academic league table, it ranks eighth overall – up from ninth in 2021 and 2020, and 11th in 2019.

Students are on board with the direction of travel. Bath is fourth for satisfaction with the wider undergraduate experience in our analysis of outcomes from the latest National Student Survey, and fifth for graduate prospects, with more than 90% of graduates in highly skilled jobs or further study within 15 months. Its course completion rate (96.2%) is the sixth best in the country.

Record numbers of applicants (almost 31,000) sought places at Bath in the 2021 admissions cycle and the upward trend continues. The numbers continued to go up by the end of March 2022, when a snapshot of the latest cycle showed a 6% increase compared with the same point a year before. Enrolments also rose to more than 4,000 in 2021.

Bath offers courses in engineering, humanities, management, science and social sciences. At the Claverton Down campus, where the university was established in 1996, the £70million School of Management is the latest flagship development, opening in time for the 2022-23 academic year. Its new research and learning facilities include a student entrepreneurship hub and a behavioural research laboratory, eight modern lecture theatres and an auditorium.

Bath's high-quality physical and digital resources were highlighted by assessors from the government's Teaching Excellence Framework (TEF) when the university was awarded gold – the highest standard. The university's successful teaching methods and students' engagement with developments at the forefront of research also drew praise.

The TEF panel also commended Bath's strong orientation towards employment. The university's work placement scheme has links with more than 3,000 organisations around the world and two-thirds of undergraduates spend a year gaining real-world work experience in the private, public or not-for-profit sectors.

Bath's history of collaborations with regional and national industry partners is reflected in its teaching and research. For more than 40 years, the institution's strength in automotive propulsion research has contributed to the development of cost-effective electric motors and improvements in fuel consumption.

In the latest Research Excellence Framework (REF 2021), Bath's best results were in sports science, hospitality and tourism, accounting; and business studies. The university's submissions in subjects allied to health, nursing, dentistry and social policy also did particularly well, as did

---

Claverton Down
Bath BA2 7AY
01225 383 019
admissions@bath.ac.uk
www.thesubath.com
www.bath.ac.uk
Open days: see website

The Times and The Sunday Times Rankings
Overall Ranking: 8 (last year: 9)

Teaching quality	76.7%	=41
Student experience	79.7%	4
Research quality	53%	31
Entry standards	170	=14
Graduate prospects	90.9%	5
Good honours	90%	10
Expected completion rate	96.2%	6
Student/staff ratio	15.4	=47

those in social work, criminology, pharmacology and pharmacy, and chemistry. Overall, 92% of Bath's submission was rated world-leading or internationally excellent, the top two categories (up from 87% in the previous national assessment in 2014). Other universities did even better, however, so Bath falls seven places in our research excellence index to 31st place.

Student satisfaction with teaching quality has fallen five places to joint 41st. Bath committed to in-person teaching on campus again from the 2022-23 academic year.

Social inclusion remains a weak point for Bath and the university is in the bottom five in our analysis overall. Its efforts to reduce the black achievement gap, however, achieve a top-20 place, at 10.8%.

The university helps prospective students from underrepresented backgrounds to seize the opportunity of higher education through its contextual admissions scheme, Access to Bath. Those who complete its preparatory module qualify for a one-grade discount on the typical offer — accounting for about 30% of offers in 2021-22. More generally, the university takes notice of contextual information about an applicant's background.

Nearly one third of Bath's UK and international students gained scholarships and bursaries in 2022-23 and the university expects to help about the same proportion in 2023-24. A past winner of our Sports University of the Year award, Bath has a £35million Sports Training Village in the heart of the campus. The multi-sport facility is a national training centre for several Olympic and Paralympic sports and students have free use of most of its facilities. An Olympic-sized London 2012 legacy swimming pool, indoor and outdoor tennis courts, more than 20 sports pitches and a fitness centre featuring nearly 200 workout stations are available. The Sulis Club about a mile from campus has extra grass pitches.

Pre-paid food and drink credits can be added to students' library cards. A small number of Bath's student rooms are fully catered and all first-years who apply in time are guaranteed a room.

A student wellbeing service is in place providing therapeutic groups, short-term individual therapy and specialist mental health support. A 24/7 phone, video or live chat service supplements help available from qualified mental health professionals.

Although small, Bath's reputation is hard to beat for students.

Tuition fees

»	Fees for UK students	£9,250
	Foundation	£7,710
»	Fees for International students 2023–24	£19,800–£24,500
»	For scholarship and bursary information see www.bath.ac.uk/topics/tuiton-fees/	
»	Graduate salary	£29,500

Student numbers

Undergraduates	13,537	(50)
Postgraduates	2,845	(2,123)
Applications/places		30,765/4,030
Applications per place		7.6:1
Overall offer rate		62.7%
International students – EU		10.4%
Non-EU		12.7%

Accommodation

University provided places: 4,740
Catered costs: £205–£250 per week
Self-catered: £120–£220 per week
First-years guaranteed accommodation
www.bath.ac.uk/professional-services/student-accommodation

Where do the students come from?

State schools (non-grammar)	56.2%	First generation students	23.7%	White working-class males	3.6%
Grammar schools	16.7%	Low-participation areas	5.3%	Black achievement gap	-10.8%
Independent schools	27.1%	All ethnic minorities	17.9%	Mature (over 21)	2.7%

Social inclusion ranking: 112

Bath Spa University

Bath Spa has been expanding its course offering in recent years. After the introduction of seven degrees including architecture, business psychology and professional humanities in the 2022-23 academic year, more options are on the way in sports management, sport and exercise nutrition, multimedia sports production, marketing and biomedical science for 2023-24.

The popularity of new and existing courses has contributed to a rise in applications, which were at their highest in five years in 2021, and up by 24% in March 2022 compared with the same point the year before. Cybersecurity, games development and forensic psychology are among the courses causing a spike in applications, the university notes.

Of Bath Spa's four campuses in and around the city, Newton Park is one of the UK's most picturesque, with grounds landscaped by Capability Brown. Located four miles outside the Unesco World Heritage city, it features an imposing Georgian manor house owned by the Duchy of Cornwall and a 14th-century gatehouse is among the teaching facilities. Contemporary developments include the Michael Tippett concert hall and the Commons building.

The Locksbrook Road arts and design campus opened in 2019. With views over the River Avon, the city centre building features technical workshops, flexible studio spaces and social areas in a redeveloped factory close to the Lower Bristol Road and Oldfield Park student accommodation. The Sion Hill campus is within walking distance of Bath city centre and houses studios and workshops for fashion and textiles, plus a specialist art and design library. Corsham Court, another historic manor house, is the university's postgraduate centre near Chippenham.

Bath Spa was rated silver in the government's Teaching Excellence Framework (TEF), winning praise for its course design and assessment practices "that provide high levels of rigour and stretch". The TEF panel also noted the personalised teaching, the availability of a personal tutor, peer mentoring and independent study at Bath Spa.

Having had a chance to digest the relative merits and pitfalls of blended online learning, developed during the Covid-19 pandemic, Bath Spa is hosting all seminars and workshops on campus. Lectures, meanwhile, are taking place either online or on campus – and recorded in most cases. The location of tutorials and dissertation supervision is similarly fluid, depending on the student's preference. The university did away with traditional-style, unseen exams under exam hall conditions for 2022-23, replacing them with alternative methods of assessment.

One in four entrants to Bath Spa are on a professional placement-year-added route. The

---

Newton Park
Newton St Loe
Bath BA2 9BN
01225 876 180
admissions@bathspa.ac.uk
www.bathspasu.co.uk
www.bathspa.ac.uk
Open days:
see website

The Times and The Sunday Times **Rankings**
Overall Ranking: 77 (last year: =103)

Teaching quality	77.7%	30
Student experience	71.5%	=71
Research quality	29.3%	89
Entry standards	112	=108
Graduate prospects	61.9%	127
Good honours	79.1%	=55
Expected completion rate	83.7%	=79
Student/staff ratio	16.6	=73

university also helps students to secure internships at local and national businesses. In spite of these efforts, Bath Spa remains in the bottom 10 for graduate prospects, according to our analysis of the Graduate Outcomes survey comparing the numbers in highly skilled work or further study 15 months after finishing a degree.

Bath Spa recorded its best research results yet in the latest Research Excellence Framework (REF 2021), increasing the amount of its world-leading work by 60%. However, it falls 16 places in our research rankings this year to 89th against strong competition across the sector.

Although 93.7% of undergraduates are from non-selective state schools, Bath Spa lies in the bottom half of our table for social inclusion overall (=85).

The university awards about 500 undergraduate bursaries per year, which range in value from £2,500 to £4,000 (plus £750 for care-leavers), paid over three or four years to students from areas with low participation in higher education, where household incomes are less than £42,875. Talent and Excellence scholarships of £500 are paid in the first year to students who achieved results better than their predicted grades, or who display outstanding talent in the creative arts – and to all students who enter Bath Spa with AAB or equivalent grades.

Support for student mental health and wellbeing includes mental health practitioners, a chaplaincy and accessibility advisers who provide information and practical help to students who identify as disabled and neurodiverse. Wellbeing advisers offer guidance around matters such as budgeting, homesickness, family estrangement and caring responsibilities and Bath Spa operates a 24/7 wellbeing and mental health service for students online and by telephone. All students complete compulsory training on sexual consent as part of induction activities.

A gym, netball and tennis courts, and games pitches are among the sports facilities located across the university's campuses. Bath Spa has also acquired the Bath Spa Sports ground close to town, which has a cricket pitch and floodlights. The university fields about 15 teams in the British Universities and Colleges Sport (BUCS) league and has nearly 25 sports societies and clubs.

First-years who apply by the deadline are guaranteed student accommodation within a housing stock of almost 1,700 rooms. Spaces are allocated so that everyone gets the same chance of their preferred option, regardless of which stage in the cycle they applied.

Tuition fees

»	Fees for UK students	£9,250
	Foundation courses	£6,000–£9,000
»	Fees for International students 2023–24	£14,400–£16,075
»	For scholarship and bursary information see	
	www.bathspa.ac.uk/students/student-finance	
»	Graduate salary	£20,000

Student numbers

Undergraduates	6,290	(269)
Postgraduates	1,301	(1,373)
Applications/places		13,685/2,240
Applications per place		6.1:1
Overall offer rate		80.1%
International students – EU		3.4%
Non-EU		2.4%

Accommodation

University provided places: 1,969
Self-catered: £122–£194 per week
First-years guaranteed accommodation
www.bathspa.ac.uk/be-bath-spa/accommodation

Where do the students come from?

State schools (non-grammar)	93.7%	First generation students	41.7%	White working-class males	5.3%
Grammar schools	2.1%	Low-participation areas	15.4%	Black achievement gap	-30%
Independent schools	4.2%	All ethnic minorities	8.6%	Mature (over 21)	17.7%

Social inclusion ranking: =85

University of Bedfordshire

Student contentment is improving at the University of Bedfordshire although the institution remains at the bottom of our academic rankings for the second year in a row. Bedfordshire gains 34 places for satisfaction with teaching quality in our analysis of the results of the latest National Student Survey, published in summer 2022, reaching 46th place. For satisfaction with the wider undergraduate experience, the university has risen 15 places to rank =71.

Bedfordshire withstood the impact of the disruption of the pandemic better than many institutions in our analysis of student satisfaction over the period 2020-21 at its five campuses in the southeast of England, from where famous alumni have emerged including the Radio 1 presenters Melvin Odoom and Rickie Haywood-Williams. They broadcast their BBC show live from the Luton campus during graduations in June 2022.

At Luton, the largest base, a £40million, 6,000 sq m building for STEM subjects (science, technology, engineering and maths) opened recently as part of the university's £180million investment in its estate across six years. More recent upgrades have included improved simulated learning in the Faculty of Applied Social Sciences, as well as dynamic interactive and traditional course resources

from Harvard Business School for those within the University of Bedfordshire Business School. Aviation and airport management courses have acquired simulated business planning and operations experiences, along with industry-standard Global Flight information and database sources.

The Bedford campus, in a leafy setting a 20-minute walk from the town centre, houses the education and sports faculty as well as courses in performing arts, law and business management. The university is one of the UK's largest providers of training for physical education teachers.

The Aylesbury campus at the Stoke Mandeville Hospital, home of the highly regarded National Spinal Injuries Centre, is Bedfordshire's newest, opened in 2020. The university's Health and Social Care Academy was launched in 2021, in partnership with local councils and NHS Trusts with the aim of developing the health, social work and social care workforce across Bedfordshire and the UK.

At the Milton Keynes campus, courses range from human resource management to professional social work practice. The Putteridge Bury campus, a neo-Elizabethan mansion on the outskirts of Luton, doubles as a management centre and conference venue.

Applications for the 2022 admissions cycle had increased by almost 13% by the end of March 2022, compared with the same point in the applications cycle the year before. However,

University Square
Luton LU1 3JU
01582 743 500
admissions@beds.ac.uk
www.bedssu.co.uk
www.beds.ac.uk
Open days: see website

The Times and *The Sunday Times* **Rankings**

Overall Ranking: 132 (last year: 132)

Teaching quality	76.4%	46
Student experience	71.5%	=71
Research quality	30%	=85
Entry standards	107	=119
Graduate prospects	68.5%	96
Good honours	64.8%	129
Expected completion rate	56.2%	130
Student/staff ratio	27.4	131

across the decade from 2011 to 2021, applications have more than halved, although enrolments have decreased less sharply, by about 30%.

New degrees have been introduced to appeal to more students. Degrees in English, sports coaching and development, and special educational needs and disability launched in September 2022 – with options to take a foundation or professional practice year or to study part-time. A top-up course in make-up for fashion and media also accepted its first students. From 2023-24, degrees in architectural technology, construction management, and financial technology will accept their first students – again with foundation or placement years. The university's teacher training provision has added a degree in primary education (3-7) with Qualified Teacher Status (QTS), and English (secondary) with QTS scheduled to start in September 2023.

Bedfordshire has slipped eight places in our research quality index to =85, but there were considerable successes in its performance in the latest Research Excellence Framework (REF 2021). Overall, 60% of the university's research was assessed as world-leading or internationally excellent, the top two categories. It gained silver in the Teaching Excellence Framework.

The university ranks =26 in our social inclusion table despite a fall of 16 places. In the five years that this index has been published, this is the first time that Bedfordshire has ranked lower than 11th.

The financial support extended by Bedfordshire to its students is among the most inclusive in the country. Every undergraduate home entrant receives a minimum bursary of £1,500 over the duration of their course. Merit scholarships are given to students who achieve 112 UCAS tariff points at A-level, or equivalent qualifications, worth £2,400 over three years.

Students have free access to sports and fitness activities through the Get Active membership scheme. Shuttle buses take students to playing fields and a multipurpose sports hall. At Luton, students benefit from discounted access to a wealth of sports and leisure facilities at Venue 360.

First-years are guaranteed a space in student accommodation on the Luton and Bedford campuses. The university ranks eighth out of 154 institutions in the People and Planet University Green League, and also holds platinum People and Planet certification. It markets its proximity to London as a big draw, although the social scene is lively closer to home, too. Trains to the capital take 30 to 40 minutes.

Tuition fees

- » Fees for UK students £9,250
  Foundation courses £6,165–£9,250
- » Fees for International students 2023–24 £13,500–£14,975
- » For scholarship and bursary information see www.beds.ac.uk/howtoapply/money/fees/
- » Graduate salary £24,000

Student numbers		
Undergraduates	11,944	(1,497)
Postgraduates	3,647	(892)
Applications/places		9,285/3,030
Applications per place		3.1:1
Overall offer rate		76.2%
International students – EU		19.4%
Non-EU		8.2%

Accommodation
University provided places: 1,369
Self-catered: £112–£199 per week
First-years guaranteed accommodation
www.beds.ac.uk/accommodation

Where do the students come from?

State schools (non-grammar)	98.5%	First generation students	58.8%	White working-class males	2.1%
Grammar schools	0.2%	Low participation areas	7.6%	Black achievement gap	-31.8%
Independent schools	1.4%	All ethnic minorities	56.1%	Mature	71.3%

Social inclusion ranking: =26

Birkbeck, University of London

Home-working plus limited time on campus has always been the modus operandi at Birkbeck, University of London. Evening classes – between 6pm and 9pm – at the campus in fashionable and historic Bloomsbury are central to the student experience. Libraries and food outlets open late to cater to the Birkbeck day. As the prospectus says: "You don't have to choose between getting a job or going to university – you can do both."

Birkbeck has been expanding its teaching reach across the capital. After a partnership with the University of East London that established a presence in Stratford, close to the Queen Elizabeth Olympic Park, a new teaching facility has opened at 373 Euston Road, a 15-minute walk from the main campus. The building houses one of the university's largest lecture theatres and new classrooms, as well as a co-learning space in which students can prepare for lectures and share ideas.

Foundation years continue to be added to a range of degrees, in line with Birkbeck's founding cause to widen access to higher education. The course portfolio is also being expanded to include plenty of conventional three-year full-time degrees, although it remains best known for its evening-class degrees that can be taken over four years full-time or six years part-time.

New options from September 2022 include marketing with a foundation year; English with linguistics; theatre studies and arts management; and theatre, film and media studies. But the 2023 intake will have a huge swathe of options to choose from, as Birkbeck overhauls its curriculum with about 20 new degrees in subjects such as sociology with criminology; law with business; planetary exploration with astronomy and astrobiology; psychosocial studies with principles of psychodynamic counselling; financial economics with data science; and journalism and language. Most are offered with the option of a foundation year.

Birkbeck withdrew from our league table in 2019 on the grounds that our measures place a heavily part-time university at a disadvantage compared with traditional, residential institutions. We continue to include it in our listings because of its unique place in British higher education, where it sets a high bar for widening participation.

Outcomes of the latest Research Excellence Framework (REF 2021), showed that 83% of research at Birkbeck was rated world-leading (4*) or internationally excellent (3*), the top two categories. Some of the best results were in art and design; English language and literature, biological sciences; computer science and informatics; earth systems and environmental science; economics and econometrics; history (classics and archaeology); psychology; psychiatry and neuroscience; and sociology.

Malet Street
London WC1E 7HX
020 3907 0700
studentadvice@bbk.ac.uk
www.bbk.ac.uk/su
www.bbk.ac.uk
Open days: see website

The Times and The Sunday Times **Rankings**
Overall Ranking: n/a
No data available

The university was in the top 40 in our 2021 analysis based on the previous national assessment (REF 2014), rating institutions for the quality and quantity of its output. But it is not included in our new research quality index, based on REF 2021 results.

Specialist research facilities include the Wohl Wolfson ToddlerLab in Torrington Square. This is the world's first purpose-built centre for the study of brain development in toddlers as they interact with their natural environment. It builds on the renowned research conducted in Birkbeck's BabyLab and hopes to advance the understanding of conditions such as autism, ADHD, Fragile X and Williams Syndrome.

Birkbeck does well in the QS World University Rankings: at =343 it is in the top 40 in the UK, and fifth in London. In the government's Teaching Excellence Framework, Birkbeck is rated silver, having impressed assessors with its initiatives to support students from diverse backgrounds to achieve their full potential.

Furthering its work to break down barriers to higher education, Birkbeck's support for refugee students has been recognised with University of Sanctuary status. The university has also become the first to join the New University in Exile Consortium, whose members host an exiled or persecuted scholar.

Applications to Birkbeck boomed during the pandemic, rising by about 16% between the admissions cycles of 2020 and 2021. Enrolments decreased by 24% over the same period, however, in a recruitment round when 33% of undergraduates entered via Clearing.

Many Birkbeck students are already well into their careers when they enrol, so the university has always performed well on graduate employment measures. A string of collaborations with businesses provide pathways to industry through career workshops, opportunities for entrepreneurship, and course programmes co-created with sector leaders such as Goldman Sachs, Facebook, Santander and Le Cordon Bleu.

The college welcomes applications from people without standard qualifications and continues to attract non-traditional learners of all ages and backgrounds.

A new initiative in partnership with Goldman Sachs has broadened support programmes, particularly for students of colour, boosting scholarships, extending outreach in low participation communities and working to address the black attainment gap.

Most Birkbeck students live at home in the capital, but places are available in University of London intercollegiate halls.

Tuition fees

» Fees for UK students	£9,250
» Fees for International students 2023–24	£14,280
» For scholarship and bursary information see https://www.bbk.ac.uk/student-services/financial-support	
» Graduate salary	n/a

Student numbers

Applications/places	6,045/1,285
Applications per place	4.7:1
Overall offer rate	n/a

Accommodation

www.bbk.ac.uk/student-services/accommodation

Where do the students come from?
No data available

University of Birmingham

Outstanding research has sent the University of Birmingham shooting up our rankings and it was shortlisted for our University of the Year award.

In our analysis of the latest Research Excellence Framework (REF 2021) the institution has risen to tenth – up 16 places – with brilliance in a broad range of subjects. The best performers included American, Celtic studies, East and South Asian, and Middle Eastern and African studies. Hospitality, leisure, recreation and tourism, education and sports science also did well, plus a broad range of sciences and social sciences.

Britain's first "civic" university, founded at the turn of the 20th century, is halfway through a 10-year, £600million transformation of its original redbrick buildings, completed in 1909. Its landmark tower Old Joe – said to be the world's tallest freestanding clocktower at 100 metres – stands among new developments on the 260-acre campus in leafy Edgbaston.

Pioneering projects include the Collaborative Teaching Laboratory – designed to change the way STEM subjects (science, technology, engineering and maths) are taught – featuring wet, dry and e-labs with learning space for 1,000 students. The Green Heart is a 12-acre space in the middle of Birmingham's campus where students can study and socialise or watch performances.

In 2021 the new School of Engineering opened, bringing together the university's engineering disciplines in 12,000 sq m over five floors. The department has a strong record in rail research and the £46.5million centre has a full-size set of railway points and a test track for the university's scaled hydrogen-powered train. Next door is a research centre of excellence in digital systems, opened in 2020, which focuses on railway control and cybersecurity.

In 2023 a Life Sciences Park will open at the Selly Oak campus, two miles from Edgbaston. Drama courses are also based in Selly Oak, where the BBC Drama Village on campus offers opportunities for student placements. In 2024 the School of Chemistry will open a new Molecular Sciences building on the former Munrow Sports Centre site on the main campus.

Expanding its reach, Birmingham is the first Russell Group university to open an outpost in Dubai. It offers courses in business, economics, computer science, mechanical engineering and teacher training on a new campus, which opened in 2021.

Seven new degree courses will be introduced in 2023: social anthropology; digital media and communications; film and creative writing; psychology and religion; environmental and engineering geoscience; human sciences; and global environmental change and sustainability.

Edgbaston
Birmingham B15 2TT
0121 414 3344
www.guildofstudents.com
www.birmingham.ac.uk
Open days: see website

The Times and The Sunday Times **Rankings**
Overall Ranking: =20 (last year: 25)

Teaching quality	71.3%	112
Student experience	70.4%	=79
Research quality	61.9%	10
Entry standards	154	25
Graduate prospects	84.2%	18
Good honours	88.3%	=13
Expected completion rate	95.4%	10
Student/staff ratio	14.9	=36

The full campus-based, in-person teaching experience has returned at Birmingham, where rates of student satisfaction took a big hit in the pandemic-affected National Student Survey of 2021. It has clawed back to =79 for satisfaction with the overall experience.

Outshining several Russell Group rivals to be rated gold in the Teaching Excellence Framework (TEF) in 2016, Birmingham won praise for a strategic focus on research-informed teaching which is highly valued by employers. "All student outcomes are excellent," the TEF panel acknowledged.

Birmingham's enduring popularity with undergraduates hit new heights in the 2020 admissions round, in which more than 56,000 students applied – a 5% increase on 2019 and 30% up in a decade. Enrolments are also on the rise, up 13% from 2019-20 and 40% higher in a decade.

Birmingham topped the 2021 High Fliers report, tracking which graduates are targeted the most by top employers, and is consistently in the top five. In our analysis of the latest Graduate Outcomes survey recording the numbers in highly skilled work or further study after 15 months, Birmingham has climbed eight places to enter the top 20 (18th).

A degree apprenticeship in computer science with digital technology – run in partnership with PwC – has taken the earn-as-you-learn route to the next level. The company pays apprentices' tuition fees as well as salaries throughout the four-year course. A graduate job awaits at the end, subject to performance.

Birmingham is in joint 100th place overall in our social inclusion index and continues its efforts to improve the diversity of its intake. The Pathways to Birmingham programme for Year 12-13 pupils encourages applications from those from underrepresented backgrounds and provides bursaries that do not need to be repaid.

Bursaries are available to help fund internships, and scholarships may be provided for travel projects even if they are not linked to the student's main degree.

An official partner of the 2022 Commonwealth Games, the university hosted hockey and squash events and its halls of residence at the Vale became the largest of the athlete villages. One of the UK's most vibrant cities, Birmingham has earned a reputation as a leading student destination. Rooms in halls are guaranteed for first-years who meet the criteria and 12% of places are catered.

Tuition fees

» Fees for UK students £9,250
» Fees for International students 2023–24 £10,650–£27,932 Medicine £27,540–£46,320; Dentistry £25,860–£46,320
» For scholarship and bursary information see https://www.birmingham.ac.uk/study/undergraduate/fees-funding/tuition
» Graduate salary £26,000

Student numbers

Undergraduates	23,835	(689)
Postgraduates	7,880	(5,347)
Applications/places	56,850/7,865	
Applications per place	7.2:1	
Overall offer rate	64.6%	
International students – EU	3.1%	
Non-EU	16.3%	

Accommodation

University provided places: 6,420
Catered costs: £91–£287 per week
Self-catered: £135–£230 per week
First-years guaranteed accommodation
www.birmingham.ac.uk/study/accommodation/Index.aspx

Where do the students come from?

State schools (non-grammar)	70.6%	First generation students	32.6%	White working-class males	2.5%
Grammar schools	13.6%	Low participation areas	8.4%	Black achievement gap	-14.5%
Independent schools	15.9%	All ethnic minorities	34.1%	Mature (over 21)	4.5%

Social inclusion ranking: =100

Birmingham City University

The doors of the £70million STEAMhouse innovation centre opened in November 2022, completing the transformation of a Victorian factory into a Birmingham City University (BCU) campus for computing and digital technology students. They will be on the spot for creative collaborations with entrepreneurs based at the centre on real industry-based projects.

The development on the City Centre campus in Birmingham's up-and-coming Eastside – the site of the Curzon Street HS2 rail station, due to open in 2026 – is part of a £340million university expansion programme.

The Royal Birmingham Conservatoire's 500-seat concert hall, rehearsal rooms and teaching spaces are also based at the City Centre campus, overlooking Eastside City Park. Courses taught here include music, business, English, social sciences, acting and media.

Facilities for healthcare students at the City South Campus in Edgbaston are also being improved with a £3.57million investment in hands-on training resources enabled with 5G technology. BCU's world-renowned School of Jewellery, founded in 1890, is based in the city's Jewellery Quarter, while the Birmingham Institute of Fashion and Creative Art is the university's outpost in Wuhan, China, in partnership with Wuhan Textile University.

BCU more than doubled its submission to the latest Research Excellence Framework (REF 2021), compared with the previous national assessment in 2014. Creative writing and English produced the best results, while land and property management, building, and town and country planning also did well. Birmingham City moves up seven places in our research quality index to rank 91st.

Rated silver in the Teaching Excellence Framework (TEF), the university gained accolades for its consistency in retaining students most at risk of dropping out. The TEF panel also praised personalised learning and the use of peer mentors, including a black and minority ethnic support scheme.

The university has set up the Centre for Equality, Diversity and Inclusion in the Arts, which holds public lectures and workshops. The Sir Lenny Henry Centre for Media Diversity, named in honour of the BCU chancellor, opened in 2020.

Scores have slipped year-on-year for student satisfaction with teaching quality and the wider undergraduate experience. Our analysis of the latest National Student Survey, published in summer 2022, shows that satisfaction with teaching has fallen 19 places to =62. Contentment with the overall experience has cooled by 11 places (=81).

Student mentoring, summer schools and interactive workshops under the Aimhigher scheme contribute to BCU's work to widen

University House
15 Bartholomew Row
Birmingham B5 5JU
0121 331 6295
admissions@bcu.ac.uk
www.bcusu.com
www.bcu.ac.uk
Open days: see website

The Times and The Sunday Times Rankings
Overall Ranking: 94 (last year: =83)

Teaching quality	75.4%	=62
Student experience	70.3%	=81
Research quality	29%	91
Entry standards	120	=81
Graduate prospects	70.3%	=82
Good honours	72.8%	101
Expected completion rate	84%	76
Student/staff ratio	17.2	=81

participation in higher education. The university also provides advice and guidance talks to pupils and parents, as well as study skills sessions. BCU Forward, a new attainment-raising initiative with partner schools, engages pupils from Year 7-13. The university is in the top 20 for its proportion of first-generation students (56.2%) and 36th for social inclusion overall.

Applications to study at BCU rose by 6% in 2021 and enrolments nudged up by about 3%.

Three degrees will begin in September 2023: computer science with artificial intelligence, digital animation, and creative advertising. A foundation degree in sports coaching and development will also welcome its first students.

In 2023, a package of specialist courses for those with combined hearing and sight loss is being introduced in partnership with national charities, leading to a certificate or diploma in deaf-blind studies.

About 50 professional accreditations are embedded within BCU's courses, recognised by professional bodies such as the Nursing and Midwifery Council and the Royal Institute of British Architects. Students can also build experience through the Graduate+ range of extracurricular, employment-related activities, recording their achievements in an online e-portfolio.

BCU has also teamed up with industry partners to launch I Built It – a networking and training initiative for the construction industry that aims to fill skills shortages in the West Midlands. The university falls 13 places in our analysis of graduate prospects to =82, however, based on the proportion of students in highly skilled work or further study within 15 months of leaving.

A wide-ranging portfolio of 21 higher and degree apprenticeships – providing training for nearly 1,500 students – includes three programmes new from 2022: fire safety engineer, speech and language therapist, and senior healthcare support worker. Two more are in development in diagnostic and therapeutic radiography. The university expects to have 1,700 degree apprentices by September 2023.

Students have access to an 80-station fitness suite, eight-court sports hall and workout and spinning studios at the Doug Ellis Sports Centre at Perry Barr. There is also a sports pavilion with an all-weather pitch, 12 football pitches and two rugby pitches.

All first-years are guaranteed accommodation if they apply in time, but most students commute to classes. The UK's second-biggest city has a total of 80,000 students and its vibrant, affordable lifestyle will not disappoint.

Tuition fees
- » Fees for UK students £9,250
- » Fees for International students 2023–24 £13,980–£27,325
- » For scholarship and bursary information see www.bcu.ac.uk/student-info/finance-and-money-matters
- » Graduate salary £24,000

Student numbers	
Undergraduates	20,658 (1,462)
Postgraduates	4,536 (2,338)
Applications/places	36,875/6,950
Applications per place	5.3:1
Overall offer rate	64.1%
International students – EU	2.5%
Non-EU	5.6%

Accommodation
University provided places: 2,060
Self-catered: £125–£171 per week
First-years guaranteed accommodation
www.bcu.ac.uk/student-info/accommodation

Where do the students come from?

				Social inclusion ranking: 36	
State schools (non-grammar)	96.6%	First generation students	56.2%	White working-class males	3.3%
Grammar schools	1.7%	Low participation areas	16%	Black achievement gap	-20.3%
Independent schools	1.7%	All ethnic minorities	59.3%	Mature (over 21)	24.2%

Bishop Grosseteste University

Bishop Grosseteste University (BGU) takes pride in offering students "a real family feel" – with fewer than 1,700 full-time undergraduates on the roll call at its campus just a few minutes' walk away from Lincoln Cathedral.

Our analysis of the results of the latest National Student Survey shows that students agree: the university takes fourth place for satisfaction with teaching quality and 13th for the wider student experience. The results represent an extraordinary turnaround in rates of student satisfaction, which nosedived more than most in pandemic-affected 2021 but have recovered 52 places in our teaching quality measure and shot up 77 places in our wider experience ranking.

Lectures have returned to full in-person delivery and the prevalent teaching model at BGU is face-to-face. Rated gold in the Teaching Excellence Framework, BGU was commended for an "outstanding learning environment and a personalised approach with high-quality support maximising retention, attainment and progression". Course design and assessment were highlighted for providing outstanding levels of stretch, ensuring students are consistently challenged and engage with developments from the forefront of research, scholarship or working practice.

Teaching degrees are the focus at BGU, which was founded as an Anglican teacher-training college for women in 1862 and named after Robert Grosseteste, a thirteenth-century bishop of Lincoln. The university now offers a range of degrees to people of all genders, and of all faiths and none.

Theology produced by far BGU's best results in the latest Research Excellence Framework (REF 2021). The university increased its submission to eight subject areas submitted by four times more staff than were assessed in the previous REF in 2014.

Graduate prospects have fallen out of the top 50 to 65th. Our analysis of the Graduate Outcomes survey examined the proportion in highly skilled work or further study 15 months after finishing their degree.

New degrees in business (finance) and business (marketing) joined the curriculum in September 2022 – both offered either with or without a foundation year. A portfolio of three degree apprenticeships – in business-to-business sales, chartered management, and career development – has resulted in a steady increase in student numbers. More than 200 apprentices are expected to be signed up by September 2023.

The leafy campus in historic Lincoln features two on-site halls of residence, one of them with modern teaching and learning facilities attached after a £2.2million extension that doubled the teaching space.

Longdales Road
Lincoln LN1 3DY
01522 583 658
enquiries@bishopg.ac.uk
www.bgsu.co.uk
www.bishopg.ac.uk
Open days: see website

The Times and The Sunday Times **Rankings**
Overall Ranking: 75 (last year: 82)

Teaching quality	82.5%	4
Student experience	77	13
Research quality	11.3%	129
Entry standards	107	=119
Graduate prospects	73.4%	65
Good honours	70.4%	=114
Expected completion rate	88.6%	50
Student/staff ratio	19.8	113

An extended library houses student advice and learning development teams.

At the heart of the campus is the Venue, mostly used as a theatre during the daytime by drama and performing arts students. By night it transforms into a cinema, with Dolby surround sound and the latest film releases.

The campus grounds have a peace garden where students can relax. A round-the-clock mental health and wellbeing service has been introduced, linking students with counsellors over the phone or in structured sessions. The chaplaincy is another source of support.

Underpinned by the belief that every student has the right to consider higher education, BGU focuses its outreach work on school students in Years 9-12. It provides presentations, campus visits and help with study skills. Students who complete the Year 12 programme and apply to BGU qualify for a contextual offer under a reduced UCAS tariff – also extended to those from low-participation backgrounds and to those who have been in care.

About half of BGU's 18-year-old applicants each year qualify for a contextual offer. The same proportion of entrants qualify for some form of financial help, such as bursaries or scholarships ranging from £600 to £3,600. A £150,000 budget annually supports students in need – including student parents and carers, mature students and those from low-income families.

The university's initiatives to widen participation pay dividends in our social inclusion ranking, where BGU is in the top four overall. Breaking down the figures, it is also fourth for recruiting students from areas with low take-up of higher education (28.2%), in the top five for the number of students in receipt of Disability Support Allowance (15.9%) and sixth for the recruitment of students who are the first in their family to attend university (60.7%).

BGU's sports facilities include a sports hall, gym and acres of outdoor fields, offering opportunities to take part in activities from fitness classes and indoor tennis to hockey, volleyball and rugby.

All first-years are guaranteed student accommodation, although not necessarily on campus. The university has more than 300 spaces spread across Wickham Hall, Constance Stewart Hall and Cloud Houses.

A friendly city, Lincoln has a more lively nightlife than you might think, boosted by the presence of the much larger University of Lincoln.

Tuition fees

»	Fees for UK students	£9,250
	Foundation courses	£6,935
»	Fees for International students 2023–24	£12,445
»	For scholarship and bursary information see www.bishopg.ac.uk/apply-now/fees-funding/	
»	Graduate salary	£23,343

Student numbers

Undergraduates	1,707	(0)
Postgraduates	506	(251)
Applications/places		1,715/650
Applications per place		2.6:1
Overall offer rate		95.1%
International students – EU		0.3%
Non-EU		0.6%

Accommodation

University provided places: 319
Self-catered: £113–£135 per week
First-years guaranteed accommodation
www.bishopg.ac.uk/student/accommodation

Where do the students come from?

State schools (non-grammar)	94.5%	First generation students	60.7%	White working-class males	5.8%
Grammar schools	4.7%	Low participation areas	28.2%	Black achievement gap	n/a
Independent schools	0.9%	All ethnic minorities	3.7%	Mature (over 21)	32.9%

Social inclusion ranking: 4

University of Bolton

Expansion of the curriculum at Bolton is contributing to a surge in applications – up 19% year-on-year according to a snapshot of the latest admissions cycle at the end of March 2022.

Six new degree programmes were scheduled to begin in September 2022 with 14 more listed for 2023. The degree apprenticeship offering is set to double by September 2023 from 15 subject areas to 30. New degree courses for 2022 include digital content creation, fashion photography, and photojournalism and documentary photography. In 2023, students will be able to study subject combinations featuring immersive arts, artificial intelligence, virtual, augmented and mixed realities and aerospace technology.

Foundation years and/or industrial placements are offered on all of the new courses and getting students ready for the world of work has been a longstanding focus at Bolton. Its degree programmes in special effects are connected with some of the biggest SFX houses in the world, associated with *Harry Potter*, Disney, Marvel and *James Bond* films.

The spike in applications follows a record set in 2021, up 22% compared with the previous year. Enrolments also reached their highest level, increasing by 18%.

Bolton is consistently popular with students, according to the National Student Survey (NSS). Our analysis of the latest NSS results ranks the university 12th for satisfaction with teaching quality, down from fifth place in 2021.

Rated silver in the Teaching Excellence Framework (TEF), Bolton was commended for an institutional culture that "facilitates, recognises and rewards excellent teaching", as well as providing excellent support for students from disadvantaged backgrounds. Bolton ranks seventh in our social inclusion index (slipping just two places year-on-year), with the biggest proportion of students from non-selective state schools of any university (99%) and 57.5% who are the first in their family to experience higher education (12th).

The TEF panel blamed "the student demographic and the challenging local employment context" for the university's above-benchmark dropout rate and relatively poor graduate employment record, and praised Bolton's initiatives to address these challenges. The latest data on course completion shows that Bolton has reduced its dropout rate below the expected benchmark, given the background of its students and the subject mix – a marked improvement from when almost one in three Bolton students abandoned their course.

Bolton has bolstered its careers service with an employer engagement team, which works with local, regional and national employers to source work placements, live project briefs and internships for students, and advertises graduate job vacancies. In our analysis of graduate prospects, Bolton has

---

Deane Road
Bolton BL3 5AB
01204 903 394
UGadmissions@bolton.ac.uk
www.boltonsu.com
www.bolton.ac.uk
Open days: see website

The Times and The Sunday Times Rankings
Overall Ranking: 124 (last year: =89)

Teaching quality	80.8%	12
Student experience	76.8%	15
Research quality	10.6%	130
Entry standards	117	=93
Graduate prospects	64.9%	=117
Good honours	66.1%	128
Expected completion rate	76.3%	=121
Student/staff ratio	16.4	70

gained two places but remains in the bottom 20 for the proportion in highly skilled work or further study within 15 months.

Founded as the Bolton Mechanics Institute in 1824, the university merged with the local further education provider Bolton College in 2018 and wholly owns Alliance Learning, one of the northwest's largest independent apprenticeship training providers. The university has branched out to establish an outpost in Salford through a training partnership.

In the past decade, Bolton has opened the city centre Institute of Management and the £31million Bolton One health, leisure and research centre on the main Deane campus. Here, students have access to a multi-sports hall, climbing wall and a sports and spinal injuries clinic, as well as a 25m competition swimming pool and a therapeutic hydrotherapy pool, fitness suite and community gym.

Near Dubai, in the United Arab Emirates, the university has a campus at Ras al-Khaimah with space for 700 students on courses identical to those in Bolton.

Research facilities include the Centre for Islamic Finance and the National Centre for Motorsport Engineering, opened in 2017, which incorporates the renowned Centre for Advanced Performance Engineering (CAPE) training base. The university helps to run a professional motor racing team in conjunction with a motorsports company and students work and learn alongside its engineers and mechanics as they study for degrees in automotive performance engineering or motorsport technology.

In the latest Research Excellence Framework (REF 2021), Bolton submitted a broader body of work from a third more academics compared with the previous national assessment in 2014. Art and design, allied health professions, and business and management studies were new additions, while English and engineering produced the best results. However, as results improved across the sector, Bolton fell 16 places in our research quality ranking to the foot of our table.

Bolton has developed the Life Lounge on the main campus, made up of a team of experienced mental health and wellbeing professionals. Trainees in cognitive behavioural therapy offer free sessions to students.

The 381 rooms available in Bolton's Orlando Village are allocated on a first-come, first-served basis. Many students live locally and commute to university. Bolton has a reputation as one of the UK's friendliest towns and students are a 20-minute train ride from the big-city attractions of Manchester.

Tuition fees

»	Fees for UK students	£9,250
»	Fees for International students 2023–24	£12,950
»	For scholarship and bursary information see www.bolton.ac.uk/student-life/fees-and-funding	
»	Graduate salary	£22,000

Student numbers

Undergraduates	7,674	(726)
Postgraduates	1,342	(835)
Applications/places		7,380/1,575
Applications per place		4.7:1
Overall offer rate		59.3%
International students – EU		2.5%
Non-EU		5.1%

Accommodation
University provided places: 381
Self-catered: £99–£131 per week
https://orlandovillage.co.uk

Where do the students come from?

State schools (non-grammar)	99%	First generation students	57.5%	White working-class males	4.2%
Grammar schools	0.3%	Low participation areas	17.5%	Black achievement gap	-23.2%
Independent schools	0.6%	All ethnic minorities	29.4%	Mature (over 21)	74.8%

Social inclusion ranking: 7

University of Bournemouth

Bournemouth continues to expand its provision of media courses. New degrees in virtual and augmented reality and in immersive media are on the way in September 2023.

The university has developed specialist facilities to consolidate its international reputation as one of the leading institutions for computer animation, TV and media production, music and sound production. The Poole Gateway Building, opened in 2020, has industry-standard features in 5,000 sq m. Students taking the university's flagship media courses have access to two television studios with ultra-high-definition cameras, a film studio and sound stage, green screen, edit suites and a motion-capture studio for animation.

The university also hosts the National Centre for Computer Animation and students also have access to Games PC and Mac laboratories, a critical listening lab and seminar and workshop facilities.

Research in communication, cultural and media studies, and leisure and tourism — two of Bournemouth's most well-regarded areas – performed well in the latest Research Excellence Framework (REF 2021). The breadth and volume of the university's submission was substantially increased since the previous assessment in 2014 and involved three times as many staff. However, Bournemouth has dropped 16 places to rank 80th in our research quality rating based on the latest results, against stronger gains at other universities.

Health students practise their burgeoning skills in simulation suites in another Gateway building recently opened on the main Lansdowne campus – replicating an operating theatre, hospital wards, a birthing room and a residential flat for practising at-home care.

Bournemouth pledges to provide a professional work placement during every undergraduate degree in the UK or abroad. Dedicated university staff help students to find the ideal posting from four weeks to a year in a range of workplaces.

The university has cultivated links with more than 70 institutions worldwide, enabling Bournemouth students to have opportunities to study abroad too. The Skills Development Programme – an extracurricular activity with a focus on employer-led skills and achievements – is tailored to help students shine as graduates anywhere in the world.

The university has gained eight places year-on-year to enter the top 50 for graduate prospects, reaching 48th place. Our analysis examined the proportion of students in highly skilled work or further study 15 months after finishing their degree.

Talbot Campus
Poole BH12 5BB
01202 961 916
futurestudents@bournemouth.ac.uk
www.subu.org.uk
www.bournemouth.ac.uk
Open days: see website

The Times and The Sunday Times **Rankings**
Overall Ranking: =89 (last year: =106)

Teaching quality	71.8%	109
Student experience	68.7%	=103
Research quality	30.7%	80
Entry standards	112	=108
Graduate prospects	76.9%	48
Good honours	78.7%	58
Expected completion rate	82.9%	=86
Student/staff ratio	19.2	=108

Good progression to highly skilled employment contributed to a silver rating for Bournemouth in the Teaching Excellence Framework. Assessors highlighted student retention and the success of the university's mentoring programme, which ensures that all first-years are offered advice from student representatives who are further along in their chosen course.

Bournemouth was using remote teaching technology before the Covid-19 pandemic struck, having installed the £6million Brightspace virtual learning environment in 2017. This did not stop a huge slump in student satisfaction during the pandemic, contributing to a 38-place tumble in our academic table in 2021. Although the university has recovered somewhat in our analysis of student satisfaction, derived from the latest National Student Survey, published in summer 2022, it remains outside the top 100: it ranks =103 (up 21 places) in terms of the wider undergraduate experience, and 109th (up 18 places) for satisfaction with teaching quality.

In-person teaching has now returned, supplemented by recorded lectures and seminars to which students may listen back remotely.

Applications to study at Bournemouth rose 14% year-on-year in the 2021 admissions cycle, restoring them to former levels. The university's subject mix, seaside location and promising graduate prospects are a reliable drawcard. Enrolments have remained fairly steady over the past decade and edged up a little in 2021.

Bournemouth is in =66th place overall in our social inclusion index measuring efforts to widen participation for underrepresented groups. The AccessBU contextual offer system makes allowances for the most disadvantaged students, who may be accepted with lower grades.

On the Talbot campus, students can get in shape with pole fitness, yoga, boxercise, Zumba and spin. Bournemouth runs a huge range of activities including basketball drop-in sessions, courses in the martial art jiu-jitsu, surfing and kayaking.

Chapel Gate is the university's recently acquired 65-acre sports facility near the airport, where students can compete in football, rugby, hockey, table tennis, cricket, archery and rifle shooting.

First-years are guaranteed one of 3,640 study bedrooms allocated on a first come, first served basis, not far from Bournemouth's seven-mile sandy beach.

Tuition fees

»	Fees for UK students	£9,250
	Foundation courses	£8,200
»	Fees for International students 2023–24	£15,250–£16,500
»	For scholarship and bursary information see	
	www.bournemouth.ac.uk/study/undergraduate/fees-funding	
»	Graduate salary	£24,000

Student numbers		
Undergraduates	12,955	(855)
Postgraduates	2,538	(1,352)
Applications/places	22,455/4,795	
Applications per place	4.7:1	
Overall offer rate	74.9%	
International students – EU	3.5%	
Non-EU	3.5%	

Accommodation
University provided places: 3,640
Self-catered: £144–£215 per week
First-years guaranteed accommodation
www.bournemouth.ac.uk/why-bu/accommodation

Where do the students come from?					**Social inclusion ranking: =66**	
State schools (non-grammar)	91%	First generation students	48%	White working-class males	7.6%
Grammar schools	4%	Low participation areas	12.6%	Black achievement gap	-26.8%
Independent schools	4.9%	All ethnic minorities	15.4%	Mature (over 21)	20.8%

University of Bradford

Bradford is seeking to decarbonise its campus and decolonise its curriculum so that equality is at the core of teaching and learning – giving impetus to the university's wider aim to help to create fairer societies. It is already among the most socially inclusive universities in the UK (fifth). Bradford succeeds in recruiting the largest proportion of students from ethnic minority backgrounds (86.3%) in the UK, the latest figures show. Our University of the Year for Social Inclusion in 2020, Bradford has the third-highest proportion of students who are the first in their family to attend university (67.4%).

A successor to local technical college forerunners, Bradford became a university in the 1960s. It was awarded silver in the Teaching Excellence Framework (TEF), praised for its "strategic and systematic commitment to diversity and social mobility that enables the majority of students, including a very high number from black, Asian and minority backgrounds, to achieve excellent outcomes". The latest data on course completion gives Bradford a 14-place gain on this measure: its 6.6% dropout rate is well below the expected level of 10.6% based on the socioeconomic backgrounds of its intake and subject mix.

The TEF panel also commended the curriculum for stretching students to achieve their full potential and for its work-based learning. The physiotherapy and sport rehabilitation team was singled out for recognition with a teaching excellence award from Advance HE in 2019.

A degree in psychology and criminology welcomed its first students in September 2022, as did degrees in architectural technology and in architectural engineering. An option in pharmaceutical and cosmetic science begins in 2023. Bradford offers four degree apprenticeships: healthcare science practice; chemistry; nursing associate; and advanced clinical practice.

Work experience or placements are offered and many courses are designed with input from industry partners such as the BBC, the NHS, Jaguar Land Rover, Amazon, the Civil Service, Wm Morrison Supermarkets, PwC and Fujitsu. Bradford is 49th in our analysis based on the Graduate Outcomes survey, recording the proportion of students who find highly skilled work or enrol in postgraduate study 15 months after finishing their degree. It is a rank far above its position in our main academic table (95th).

Just minutes from the centre of Bradford, the university's self-contained City Campus has facilities on site for accommodation, entertainment and sport as well as teaching and learning. To encourage biodiversity there are edible gardens and buildings made from hemp, while student beekeepers keep beehives.

Among Bradford's specialist developments

Richmond Road
Bradford BD7 1DP
01274 233 081
enquiries@bradford.ac.uk
www.bradfordunisu.co.uk
www.bradford.ac.uk
Open days:
see website

The Times and The Sunday Times **Rankings**
Overall Ranking: 95 (last year: =89)

Teaching quality	70.6%	116
Student experience	70.2%	=83
Research quality	29.9%	87
Entry standards	125	=63
Graduate prospects	76.8%	49
Good honours	83%	35
Expected completion rate	86.1%	=59
Student/staff ratio	19.1	=106

is the purpose-built Digital Health Enterprise Zone, which hosted one of the first mass Covid-19 vaccine trials. The Lady Hale mock court opened in 2020, while the university's Wolfson Centre for Applied Health Research opened at Bradford Royal Infirmary in 2019 in a partnership with the University of Leeds and Bradford Teaching Hospitals NHS Foundation Trust.

New facilities for students within the Faculties of Health and Life Science include clinical skills suites, CT, X-ray and virtual reality simulation facilities as well as world-class optometry resources. An Innovation Lab has been established to nurture entrepreneurs.

Having fared better than most in terms of student satisfaction during the pandemic, Bradford lost ground in the latest National Student Survey (NSS), published in summer 2022. Our NSS analysis reveals a 48-place fall for satisfaction with teaching quality (now 116th), and a 39-place descent for the wider undergraduate experience (=83). The prevalent teaching model from 2022 is in-person delivery.

Bradford's new Space Centre for artificial intelligence is tasked with advancing the region's capabilities within automation, advanced communications and sensing. Elsewhere, the world-renowned Peace Studies and International Development department has more than 40 years' experience. It collaborates with the United Nations, the UK Ministry of Defence and development banks in Africa and China, and lately its expertise has been quoted in the media since the outbreak of war in Ukraine.

The latest Research Excellence Framework (REF 2021) highlighted strengths in archaeology, engineering, accounting and allied health. Bradford increased the number of academics who contributed to the university's submission, compared with the previous national assessment in 2014, and 73% of their work reached the top two categories, classified as world-leading or internationally excellent. However, against improvement across the sector, Bradford's gains were not enough to prevent a 25-place drop to 87th in our research quality index.

More than 3,000 cash bursaries are awarded to students with a household income below £30,000. Four in 10 entrants in 2021 received a contextual offer – a high proportion that the university expects to remain similar in future admissions rounds.

Unique Fitness and Lifestyle on the City Centre campus has a swimming pool, climbing wall and squash courts. Accommodation at the Green, the student village on campus, is near the students' union and library. It is allocated on a first-come, first-served basis.

Tuition fees

»	Fees for UK students	£9,250
»	Fees for International students 2023–24	£16,895–£20,843
	Foundation years	£12,800
»	For scholarship and bursary information see	
	www.bradford.ac.uk/money/fees/	
»	Graduate salary	£24,000

Student numbers

Undergraduates	7,470	(296)
Postgraduates	1,276	(1,305)
Applications/places		12,465/2,575
Applications per place		4.8:1
Overall offer rate		81.7%
International students – EU		3.3%
Non-EU		8.8%

Accommodation

University provided places: 1,002
Self-catered: £75–£102 per week
www.bradford.ac.uk/accommodation

Where do the students come from?

State schools (non-grammar)	95%	First generation students	67.4%	White working-class males	1.9%
Grammar schools	3.4%	Low participation areas	10%	Black achievement gap	-9.5%
Independent schools	1.6%	All ethnic minorities	86.3%	Mature (over 21)	28.7%

Social inclusion ranking: 5

University of Brighton

The four-year Big Build at Brighton came to an end with the opening of a pedestrian bridge in September 2022 to connect parts of the busy Moulsecoomb campus. The transformation of the campus – the base for the schools of applied sciences, business and law, and architecture – includes landmark design features.

New accommodation blocks for 800 students are shaped to reflect the undulating South Downs while the façade of Elm House, the new base for business and law, has geometric tiles that will catch the light and suggest movement, inspired by the murmuration of starlings along the Brighton seafront.

The Big Build has also added a students' union venue, gym and fitness studios at Moulsecoomb. The campus development is a key element of a wider regeneration project in this part of Brighton, creating a bold contemporary gateway to the city.

By the start of the 2023 academic year Brighton plans to open a building at Moulsecoomb for the School of Humanities and Social Sciences, which at present runs courses on the university's City and Falmer campuses.

Brighton's wide range of creative courses are based at the City campus on Grand Parade. Falmer is where students study sports science, English, criminology and nursing. The university plans to expand the site to bring together all courses under the School of Sport and Health Sciences. About 3,000 students in these subject areas are based at Eastbourne.

The Brighton and Sussex Medical School is run in a long-standing partnership with the University of Sussex, also based in nearby Falmer. One of the first medical schools awarded to a post-1992 university, the school accepts 200 trainee doctors each year.

Expansion at Falmer will pave the way for Brighton to close the Eastbourne campus by September 2024, bringing all university activity within a more manageable radius. The move – and many new facilities – should bolster student satisfaction in future. Poor showings in the National Student Survey have contributed to Brighton's loss of ground in our main academic league table in recent years but the university has retrieved 11 places for satisfaction with teaching quality (111th) in our analysis of the latest NSS results, published in summer 2022.

Our inaugural University of the Year in 1999, Brighton has also been penalised in the rankings by a dropout rate of 13.1%, significantly higher than its expected level (9.6%), based on its course and student profile.

Results of the Graduate Outcomes survey, however, provide a more positive narrative. Brighton has held its own in the top 60 in the country for the past two years and is now just outside it in 64th place for graduate prospects.

Work experience is built into all courses, ranging from short to long placements, assessed

Mithras House
Lewes Road
Brighton BN2 4AT
01273 644 644
enquiries@brighton.ac.uk
www.brightonsu.com
www.brighton.ac.uk
Open days: see website

The Times and The Sunday Times **Rankings**

Overall Ranking: =98 (last year: 117)

Teaching quality	71.4%	111
Student experience	64.8%	125
Research quality	41.4%	55
Entry standards	111	=112
Graduate prospects	73.6%	64
Good honours	72.2%	=106
Expected completion rate	83.9%	77
Student/staff ratio	17	=76

voluntary work and live project briefs. Step-Up, a paid internship and skills training programme introduced in 2020, places students with local employers for six weeks.

The university also runs five mentoring programmes to help students to prepare for the workplace. The *LGBT+* programme, run by Uni-Amex, links students with a mentor sharing their sexual or gender identity. Another, *Men in Primary*, aims to shift the gender imbalance in the education sector and offer support.

In the Teaching Excellence Framework in 2017, Brighton gained silver, winning praise for its relationships with professional bodies, employers and local community groups and its personalised learning and support, particularly for first-year students. The university has improved its standing in our analysis of measures to increase social inclusion, rising 13 places year-on-year to 61st place.

Applications leapt up by about 25% in 2021 compared with the year before, halting three years of declining numbers, and enrolments increased by 10%. Three new degree apprenticeships started in September 2022 – providing training for diagnostic radiographers, solicitors and accountants – adding up to 19 programmes already on the books in fields as diverse as teaching, social work and podiatry. Diagnostic radiography is also offered as a degree course for the first time in 2022, alongside politics options

including environmental politics, politics and social change, and politics, sexuality and gender. A degree course in aerospace engineering will start in 2023.

Brighton is one of the most successful post-1992 universities for research. Results from the latest Research Excellence Framework (REF 2021) showed it has maintained its position in the top half of UK universities. Brighton climbs 11 places to 55th in our research quality index, shining in hospitality and tourism, nursing, architecture and building.

The university expects about a fifth of the student intake in 2023 to qualify for one of its bursaries. Payments of £500 a year are available for students from low-income households, rising to £1,000 per year for those who have left care or are estranged from their families. Merit-based scholarships include awards for law students from low-income backgrounds and 30 for sport.

Student-friendly Brighton is a magnet for trendy bars and clubs and the seaside community is welcoming and diverse. Rooms are guaranteed to first-years who apply in time.

Tuition fees

» Fees for UK students	£9,250
» Fees for International students 2023–24	£13,842–£17,892
Medicine	£39,158
» For scholarship and bursary information see	
www.brighton.ac.uk/studying-here/fees-and-finance/index.aspx	
» Graduate salary	£24,500

Student numbers

Undergraduates	12,976	(1,513)
Postgraduates	1,624	(1,671)
Applications/places	31,100/4,550	
Applications per place	6.8:1	
Overall offer rate	71%	
International students – EU	4.4%	
Non-EU	8.2%	

Accommodation

University provided places: 3,026
Self-catered: £83–£218 per week
First-years guaranteed accommodation
www.brighton.ac.uk/accommodation-and-locations/Index.aspx

Where do the students come from?

State schools (non-grammar)	90.1%	First generation students	45.4%	White working-class males	6.9%
Grammar schools	4.9%	Low participation areas	14.2%	Black achievement gap	-18%
Independent schools	5%	All ethnic minorities	22.3%	Mature (over 21)	29.2%

Social inclusion ranking: 61

University of Bristol

Bristol is in our top 10 for research quality after an outstanding performance in the latest Research Excellence Framework (REF 2021). The university is sixth in England and Wales after 94% of the work of 1,500 eligible staff was rated world-leading or internationally excellent, the top two categories.

The university's research pedigree means that students have the opportunity to be taught by academics at the cutting edge of their field. Work across a broad range of subjects performed well, including geography and chemistry, Russian, social policy, social work and criminology. Good results in law, natural sciences, mathematics, modern languages (French, Iberian languages and Italian), geology, dentistry, physics and astronomy, veterinary medicine and four engineering disciplines confirmed Bristol's strength in research.

Most teaching takes place on Bristol's main campus in the desirable enclave of Clifton, where Georgian buildings are set against the rolling green spaces of the Downs and the Avon Gorge – straddled by the Clifton Suspension Bridge.

Standout campus facilities include the £56million Life Sciences Building, with its chemistry laboratories certified as a Centre for Excellence in Teaching and Learning. Eight of Bristol's nine libraries are at the Clifton site. A modern humanities hub features a lecture theatre, social learning zone, gallery space, virtual museum and cinema.

The Richmond Building, a few minutes away, houses the students' union, two theatres and one of the city's largest gig venues. Further afield, in Stoke Bishop, the university has a botanic garden with more than 4,500 plant species.

On a seven-acre site near Temple Meads train station, Bristol is building the Temple Quarter Enterprise Campus which will focus on digital, business and social innovation. Work was due to start on the new car-free £300million development in summer 2022, with a view to a 2025 opening date. The former schools of management, accounting and finance have united from September 2022 under one roof at the new University of Bristol Business School.

The merger will also bring opportunities for interdisciplinary research, building on another strong showing in REF 2021: 88% of the business and management submission (covering accounting and finance research) was placed in the top two categories, world-leading and internationally excellent.

Links with more than 150 universities – including the University of Copenhagen, the National University of Singapore and the University of California – create opportunities for students to go abroad. More than 20 degree programmes incorporate a year in industry or professional placements.

Beacon House
Queens Road
Bristol BS8 1QU
0117 394 1649
choosebristol-ug@bristol.ac.uk
www.bristolsu.org.uk
www.bristol.ac.uk
Open days: see website

The Times and The Sunday Times **Rankings**
Overall Ranking: 15 (last year: 14)

Teaching quality	71.2%	113
Student experience	69%	=100
Research quality	66.2%	6
Entry standards	165	18
Graduate prospects	84.7%	13
Good honours	91.2%	9
Expected completion rate	95.9%	=7
Student/staff ratio	14.1	=24

A degree from Bristol carries weight in the jobs market: graduates from the university were the third most sought-after by top employers, according to the latest High Fliers graduate market report. The university is 13th in our analysis of graduate prospects, with nearly 85% of students in professional jobs or postgraduate study within 15 months.

In the Teaching Excellence Framework (TEF) in 2017, Bristol won praise for encouraging independent learning. However, low scores in the National Student Survey (NSS) for assessment and feedback, and academic support meant the university had to settle for a silver rating.

After further falls in the latest NSS, published in summer 2022, Bristol is only just in the top 100 for student satisfaction with the wider undergraduate experience and is 113th for satisfaction with teaching quality.

The university has, however, stepped up provision for student wellbeing as it continues to analyse the contributing factors behind a cluster of suicides in recent years. Same-day mental health appointments are available at the university's GP surgery. Students can opt in to allow the university to contact a designated parent, guardian or friend if there are serious concerns about their wellbeing.

A pioneer of contextual offers, now the norm across the university sector, Bristol makes offers up to two grades lower than standard to students from backgrounds that are underrepresented in higher education. There is also a generous bursary and scholarship scheme: about a quarter of the annual intake qualifies for some form of financial award.

However, the university remains close to the bottom of our social inclusion index (113th). Forty per cent of Bristol's intake is from independent or selective state schools, the second-largest proportion. Only about a quarter of students are the first in their family to go to university.

Sports facilities are spread across five sites with the 38-acre Coombe Dingle sports complex, the site of most training and competition, three miles north of the main campus. The university boathouse is at Saltford on the River Avon.

Bristol guarantees accommodation to first-years, as long as they apply by the deadline. Not too big and not too small, diverse and charming Bristol is hard to leave for some graduates. Many put down roots in the city and there is a wealth of professional jobs available in the region.

Tuition fees

» Fees for UK students £9,250
» Fees for International students 2023–24 £20,100–£24,700
  Foundation years £5,150
  Dentistry £43,100; Medicine £39,700;
  Veterinary Medicine £36,300
» For scholarship and bursary information see
  www.bristol.ac.uk/study/undergraduate/fees-funding/
» Graduate salary £28,000

Student numbers

Undergraduates	21,252	(255)
Postgraduates	6,888	(1,390)
Applications/places	58,185/7,650	
Applications per place	7.6:1	
Overall offer rate	64.6%	
International students – EU	4.7%	
Non-EU	14%	

Accommodation

University provided places: 8,613
Catered costs: £158–£262 per week
Self-catered: £90–£199 per week
First-years guaranteed accommodation
www.bristol.ac.uk/accommodation/undergraduate/

Where do the students come from?

State schools (non-grammar)	60.3%	First generation students	24.3%	White working-class males	2.9%
Grammar schools	12.6%	Low participation areas	6.9%	Black achievement gap	-8.9%
Independent schools	27.1%	All ethnic minorities	20.1%	Mature (over 21)	6.4%

Social inclusion ranking: 113

Brunel University, London

The capital's newest medical school opens at Brunel's campus in Uxbridge, west London, in September 2022. Initially it is only accepting international students but hopes to extend admissions to UK students soon. At the heart of the university's single, self-contained campus, the Quad North Building features simulated hospital wards and clinical skills laboratories for the new cohort of medical students.

The delayed opening of the medical school and the introduction of new nursing courses have contributed to a rise in applications by the end of March 2022, according to the university, after a dip of 8% in 2021. Enrolments have fluctuated between 2,820 and 3,675 over the past decade.

Hands-on learning has been Brunel's approach since it was founded in 1966. Almost all degree courses offer the option of work placements and Brunel students may find themselves gaining clinical experience at King's College Hospital in south London or getting into the swing of business at IBM.

Brunel was rated silver in the government's Teaching Excellence Framework (TEF), winning praise for opportunities for work experience. The TEF panel also highlighted Brunel's analytical approach to addressing attainment gaps within its diverse student body.

Up to 30 interns a year are recruited from Brunel through a strategic alliance with the Environment Agency while Jaguar Land Rover, Disney, L'Oréal, and Morgan Stanley are among employers with links to the university. More than 700 students undertook work placements of six to 12 months in 2021.

In our analysis of the latest Graduate Outcomes survey, however, Brunel has slipped five places to joint 90th for the proportion of graduates in highly skilled work or further study within 15 months.

Brunel became the first UK university to host a live Chelsea Challenge when the football club initiative began in 2022. Students work in small teams to solve a real-life business challenge set by the Chelsea FC Foundation. The three-week intensive challenge was such a success that it will become an annual fixture.

Brunel's growing degree apprenticeship programme adds another dimension to the focus on readiness for the workplace. So far, 469 students are enrolled on courses for clinical practitioners, nurse associates and digital technology solutions. The university also offers a police constable degree apprenticeship in partnership with the Metropolitan Police, as well as a graduate-level entry programme for the service. Brunel plans to almost double the numbers to 850 on degree apprenticeships by the start of the 2023-24 academic year.

For 2022-23, Brunel has decided on a hybrid teaching model with some in-person

---

Kingston Lane
Uxbridge
UB8 3PH
01895 265 265
admissions@brunel.ac.uk
https://brunelstudents.com/
www.brunel.ac.uk
Open days:
see website

The Times and The Sunday Times Rankings
Overall Ranking: =110 (last year: 121)

Teaching quality	68.3%	126
Student experience	66.8%	115
Research quality	34%	72
Entry standards	120	=81
Graduate prospects	69%	=90
Good honours	77.1%	=68
Expected completion rate	88.1%	53
Student/staff ratio	17.9	=93

lectures on campus and others live online.

In common with many universities with a focus on practical courses, Brunel suffered in the 2021 National Student Survey. In 2021 it fell outside the top 100 in our survey analysis and remains there in 2022, although it has clawed back 11 places for satisfaction with the wider undergraduate experience (ranking 115th) and four for teaching quality (126th).

Degrees in criminology, history and international relations began in September 2022. There are also new degree programmes in design, industrial design and product design engineering.

Hospitality, leisure, recreation and tourism produced good results for Brunel in the Research Excellence Framework (REF 2021), along with sports science, anthropology and radiography. Overall, 72.7% of Brunel's submission was assessed as world-leading or internationally excellent, an increase from 61% in the previous national assessment in 2014. However, against sector-wide improvement, Brunel drops 23 places in our research quality index to rank 72nd.

More than 500 scholarships and bursaries were awarded in 2021, a level expected to have been repeated for 2022.

Brunel has been among the most socially inclusive of the pre-1992 universities over the years, in the top 50 in all four of our social inclusion rankings published to date, although it now slips six places to 54th. Brunel ranks sixth for its relatively high proportion of students from black and ethnic minority backgrounds (76.7%).

Superb sports facilities distinguish Brunel. Recent additions include a World Rugby-approved artificial pitch and strength and conditioning gym, via a partnership with Ealing Trailfinders Rugby. Opposite the campus, the Sports Park's facilities include an FA-registered 3G pitch and there are sports scholarships for elite student athletes. Brunel was the first university to introduce a sports hijab to boost participation among its female Muslim students.

The multimillion-pound Indoor Athletics Centre was refurbished in 2021 and remains a jewel in Brunel's sporting crown. The university is a regional training centre for UK Athletics. The rower James Cracknell (MSc sport science 1999) is among a number of Olympians who have studied at Brunel.

Accommodation is plentiful in new and refurbished rooms. All first-years are guaranteed a live-in place, and all campus facilities are within a 10-minute walk – a rarity among London universities. The West End is 45 minutes away on public transport.

Tuition fees

- » Fees for UK students — £9,250
- » Fees for International students 2023–24 — £16,825–£20,450
  Medicine — £44,908
- » For scholarship and bursary information see www.brunel.ac.uk/study/undergraduate-fees-and-funding
- » Graduate salary — £25,000

Student numbers

Undergraduates	11,727	(194)
Postgraduates	4,661	(1,162)
Applications/places		17,375/3,210
Applications per place		5.4:1
Overall offer rate		81.4%
International students – EU		6.2%
Non-EU		17%

Accommodation
University provided places: 4,359
Self-catered: £125–£225 per week
First-years guaranteed accommodation
www.brunel.ac.uk/life/accommodation

Where do the students come from?

State schools (non-grammar)	93.2%	First generation students	50.8%	White working-class males	3.6%
Grammar schools	3.2%	Low participation areas	3.5%	Black achievement gap	-16.8%
Independent schools	3.6%	All ethnic minorities	76.7%	Mature (over 21)	12.5%

Social inclusion ranking: 54

University of Buckingham

Condensed courses focus the mind for students at Buckingham, the university believes. Most students study for two-year degrees at Britain's first – and largest – private university. A 40-week teaching year has two advantages: students save money on tuition fees and living costs and enter the employment market a year ahead of their peers.

While still small, with just over 1,600 students on campus, Buckingham offers traditional courses matching the range at other UK universities. Degree courses begin in January or September – providing appealing flexibility for many students, including those who switch to Buckingham. Students on two-year courses also qualify for up to £900 extra in loans to cover living expenses during a longer term. Three-year degrees are also offered in the humanities at Buckingham, and other faculties are beginning to follow suit.

The leafy main campus has the River Ouse running through it and some historic buildings, such as a former friary and military barracks, are used as academic facilities.

A second campus opened in 2020 in Crewe, 120 miles from Buckingham, after the university took over the former Manchester Metropolitan University campus there in a joint venture with the Indian private healthcare company Apollo Hospitals. Crewe offers medicine and podiatry courses and hopes to add other medical and allied health degrees in future.

Buckingham's finances took a hit over the Crew venture, reporting a £17million deficit in 2019, but have since recovered. Student numbers remain buoyant, in spite of a dip from European Union applicants post-Brexit. Buckingham's medical school is a popular choice for home and overseas students. Medical students finish their courses in a shorter time than they would elsewhere with a 4.5-year MBChB – modelled on the one offered by the University of Leicester.

The university's School of Computing has opened an Artificial Intelligence and Innovation Centre as the first phase of a £3.2million investment. There are new computer suites and specialist equipment such as Birdly, an immersive virtual reality flying machine that simulates soaring over landscapes and cities around the world. Students also plan projects using Spot, a robotic dog.

The student refectory at the Buckingham campus has been extensively refurbished with the addition of extra social learning space. The university has had an excellent track record in our student satisfaction rankings over the years, derived from the National Student Survey, but has nosedived 45 places year-on-year for satisfaction with teaching in the latest analysis. For teaching quality it ranks =60, down from 15th last year, and it is =74 for the overall undergraduate experience, down from 29th.

Hunter Street
Buckingham MK18 1EG
01280 820 227
admissions@buckingham.ac.uk
su.buckingham.ac.uk
www.buckingham.ac.uk
Open days: see website

Edinburgh
Belfast
BUCKINGHAM
Cardiff
London

The Times and The Sunday Times Rankings
Overall Ranking: 85 (last year: =89)

Teaching quality	75.5%	=60
Student experience	71.3%	=74
Research quality	n/a	
Entry standards	117	=93
Graduate prospects	79.9%	=33
Good honours	69.1%	119
Expected completion rate	85.7%	63
Student/staff ratio	n/a	

Every Buckingham student has regular meetings with a personal tutor and one-to-one appointments with staff in the university's wellbeing, skills and diversity team are always available. Buckingham achieved a gold rating in the government's latest Teaching Excellence Framework (TEF) in 2017. The panel praised personalised learning as a result of teaching in small groups. Buckingham's rigorous monitoring of attendance was also commended, making for the best rates of retention, attainment and progression.

Sixth for graduate outcomes in 2021, Buckingham has fallen to =33 in our analysis of the proportion of graduates in highly skilled work or further study 15 months after finishing their degree.

Students can complete a number of Microsoft certifications for free to help them prepare for the workplace. An initiative run jointly with the Home Office allows law students to opt for a one-year paid work placement. B Enterprising, a scheme offered by the university's careers and employability service, places students of any discipline in start-ups and small businesses for paid experience that they can undertake alongside their studies.

With four in 10 UK-domiciled recruits drawn from ethnic minorities and nearly four in 10 mature students (aged over 21 on entry), Buckingham scores well in some of our social inclusion measures. However, it continues to have the lowest proportion (0.9%) of white working-class male students (the most underrepresented group in higher education) of any university. Overall, it is 111th for social inclusion.

Buckingham has 91 degree apprentices on two programmes: digital and technology solutions, and teaching (level 6). New Level 7 degree apprenticeships for senior leaders and sustainability business specialists will begin in 2023.

Students from the UK and Ireland who achieve AAB or better in their A-levels (or equivalent qualifications) automatically get high-achiever scholarships of £2,000 – providing they make Buckingham their firm choice or accept an offer. The scholarship is not available for medical students.

The main campus has a bar and fitness facilities, and events are hosted at the nearby Radcliffe Centre. All first-years who want to live in can. Buckingham's pretty and rural environs provide calm: those in search of bright city lights will need to explore further afield

Tuition fees

» Fees for UK students (2-year degree)	£12,672
(3-year degree)	£8,448
» Fees for International students 2023–24	£40,464–£55,638
(2-year degree)	
Medicine (all students 4.5-year degree)	£38,000
» For scholarship and bursary information see	
https://www.buckingham.ac.uk/admissions/fees	
» Graduate salary	£25,200

Student numbers

Undergraduates	1,601	(45)
Postgraduates	1,121	(443)
Applications/places		1,035/460
Applications per place		2.3:1
Overall offer rate		n/a
International students – EU		5%
Non-EU		38.8%

Accommodation

University provided places: 476
Self-catered: £121–£205 per week
First-years guaranteed accommodation
www.buckingham.ac.uk/life/accommodation

Where do the students come from?

State schools (non-grammar)	87.5%	First generation students	31.1%	White working-class males	0.9%
Grammar schools	3.4%	Low participation areas	8.5%	Black achievement gap	-39.9%
Independent schools	9.1%	All ethnic minorities	42%	Mature (over 21)	36.7%

Social inclusion ranking: 111

Buckinghamshire New University

The 2023 intake at Buckinghamshire New University's High Wycombe campus will benefit from a contemporary refectory and roof garden, more green spaces outdoors and improvements to communal areas and exhibition spaces. The upgrades follow already impressive gains in rates of student satisfaction at BNU. In our analysis of the latest National Student Survey – published in the summer of 2022 – the university ranks 11th for its students' evaluation of teaching quality, a 42-place rise on 2021, when scores slumped nationwide as a result of the pandemic. The university ranks =21 for satisfaction with the wider undergraduate experience, climbing 61 places.

Teaching has returned to in-person delivery, with online technologies deployed to enhance this method of learning. Room-based lecture capture is set to expand in 2022-23. As a result of feedback, BNU now offers online learning support packages. Bucks Anywhere allows remote access for students and staff.

Originally founded as a School of Science and Art in 1891, BNU gained university status in 2007. The main campus is in High Wycombe, where £100million has been invested over the past decade and a Gateway Building is a focal point in the town centre. There is a second base in Uxbridge, northwest London, and a third – the newest – in Aylesbury, hosting nursing and other healthcare courses.

BNU, which has added about 60 new courses over the past five years, will launch a new curriculum for September 2023 after a review of all full-time undergraduate courses. New programmes in paramedic science and midwifery – which opened part-way through the previous academic year – have contributed to a 37% surge in applications in the latest admissions cycle according to a snapshot at the end of March 2022. Other new programmes such as physiotherapy have also proved popular and international applications have bounced back after the easing of Covid travel restrictions. BNU also makes effective use of Clearing, the admissions route used by 23% of first-year students in 2021.

Degree apprenticeship provision extends to 12 programmes with more than 1,000 learners on courses including product design and development, nursing; social work, and academic practice. From September 2023 there are plans to deliver nine new degree apprenticeships in subjects including construction site management, civil engineering, and express delivery management. For more than 15 years, BNU has worked with Thames Valley Police to deliver policing programmes, which include a bachelor's degree in police studies with criminal investigation, a police constable

Queen Alexandra Road
High Wycombe HP11 2JZ
01494 605 060
advice@bucks.ac.uk
https://www.bucksstudentsunion.org
www.bucks.ac.uk
Open days: see website

The Times and The Sunday Times **Rankings**
Overall Ranking: 121 (last year: =119)

Teaching quality	81.1%	11
Student experience	75.9%	=21
Research quality	17.6%	118
Entry standards	111	=112
Graduate prospects	66.5%	=108
Good honours	57.9%	132
Expected completion rate	72.3%	126
Student/staff ratio	15.4	=47

degree apprenticeship and a new pre-join professional policing programme.

Film and television degree courses boast the advantage of teaching on location from industry professionals at nearby Pinewood Studios. Courses are run via BNU's partnership with Pinewood's CMS training platform.

Travel and aviation courses include the chance to study for a pilot's licence while working towards a degree. The quality of aviation provision has been rubber-stamped by the United Nations special agency, the International Civil Aviation Organisation, which chose BNU as its partner in an aviation security master's degree introduced in 2020.

The Teaching Excellence Framework (TEF) upgraded BNU's bronze rating to silver in the second round of assessments in 2018. The university has fallen out of the top 100 for graduate prospects, however, in our analysis of the proportion in highly skilled work or postgraduate study within 15 months (=108).

BNU moves up five places in our research quality rankings (118th), boosted by an improved performance in the latest Research Excellence Framework (REF 2021). Art and design, history of art, geology, and sports sciences produced some of the best results. Overall, 44% of BNU research was judged to be world-leading or internationally excellent, the top two categories.

BNU performs well across measures of social inclusion, rising nine places to =17. It has the third-highest proportion of mature students (74.9%) in the UK and succeeds in attracting one of the higher proportions of white working-class male students – now the most underrepresented group in higher education. Most students went to non-selective state schools and more than three in 10 come from ethnic minority backgrounds. To widen access, contextual offers are made to eligible students with either a 12 or 24 UCAS tariff point reduction – which benefited 63% of the 2021 intake, a proportion BNU expects to remain stable.

Sports facilities include one of only five swimming performance centres approved by Swim England. BNU owns or endorses 881 student bedrooms, a large proportion of them renting from just £79 per week. First-years who want to live in are guaranteed a space.

London is within easy reach of High Wycombe, which has its own student pubs and clubs, too. The university funds free access to recreational and sporting activities through the students' union's Big Deal programme.

Tuition fees

» Fees for UK/EU students	£9,250
» Fees for International students 2023–24	£14,250
» For scholarship and bursary information see www.bucks.ac.uk/applying-to-bucks/undergraduate/fees-and-funding	
» Graduate salary	£24,206

Student numbers

Undergraduates	15,071	(1,523)
Postgraduates	516	(861)
Applications/places		7,890/2,550
Applications per place		3.1:1
Overall offer rate		77.1%
International students – EU		4.5%
Non-EU		0.8%

Accommodation

University provided places: 881
Self-catered: £79–£180 per week
First-years guaranteed accommodation
www.bucks.ac.uk/life/accommodation

Where do the students come from?

State schools (non-grammar)	94.3%	First generation students	47.8%	White working-class males	6.9%
Grammar schools	2%	Low participation areas	11.6%	Black achievement gap	-8.3%
Independent schools	3.7%	All ethnic minorities	30.7%	Mature (over 21)	74.9%

Social inclusion ranking: =17

University of Cambridge

Cambridge slips to No 3 after an eight-year reign at No 1 until 2021 – but the ancient university leads in 21 of our subject rankings – more than any other university. Cambridge also demands the highest entry standards: its last intake averaged 206 UCAS tariff points.

Overall, the university is just one percentage point behind St Andrews, which has high levels of student satisfaction – not measured at Cambridge, which boycotts the National Student Survey. The Cambridge Students' Union has decided to lift the six-year boycott, however, so more students may decide to provide their views in future.

Cambridge outperforms all other British universities to achieve second place in the latest QS World University rankings, which emphasise research. In our league table, the university is second only to Imperial College London for research quality, according to our analysis of the latest Research Excellence Framework (REF 2021). Cambridge remains ahead of all other institutions which share its broad academic range across the sciences and arts.

Graduates have glittering prospects. Almost 93% were in professional-level jobs or further study 15 months after the end of their degree, the latest Graduate Outcomes survey found, ranking Cambridge second on this measure, again behind Imperial.

Cambridge's 31 colleges dominate the city centre, providing a more intimate setting than Oxford, its bigger-city counterpart. Although open applications are allowed, it is better to visit Cambridge before applying to decide which college most appeals.

Most lectures are returning to in-person delivery. Students are expected to spend between 42 and 46 hours a week on their studies during high-pressure eight-week terms. But social life thrives, regardless.

State sector admissions are rising overall (reaching 71%) but Cambridge remains at the bottom of our social inclusion index, which considers only the numbers arriving from non-selective state schools (48.5%, the second-lowest proportion). Only Imperial College London accepted more students from independent or selective state schools. However, the academic giant continues to work hard to diversify its intake.

A new foundation year for disadvantaged students may be a game-changer. The first 52 students begin next month, with fees and living costs covered. Five applicants chased each place through a rigorous process of interviews and assessments. Entry requirements are BBB at A-level (120 UCAS tariff points) reduced from the standard A*A*A or A*AA. Professor Stephen Toope, the university's vice-chancellor (and the role's 346th incumbent), said: "It is an innovative programme that aims to reach an entirely new field of Cambridge candidates, and to transform lives." The extensive eligibility

Cambridge Admissions Office
Student Services Centre
New Museums Site
Cambridge CB2 3PT
01223 333 308
admissions@cam.ac.uk
www.cusu.co.uk
undergraduate.study.cam.ac.uk
Open days: see website

The Times and The Sunday Times **Rankings**

Overall Ranking: 3 (last year: 3)

Teaching quality	n/a	
Student experience	n/a	
Research quality	69.7%	2
Entry standards	206	1
Graduate prospects	92.6%	2
Good honours	93.5%	3
Expected completion rate	99%	=1
Student/staff ratio	11.6	4

criteria cover free school meals, household income below £25,000, the loss of a parent or carer while at secondary school, moving secondary school two or more times, and late diagnosis of special educational needs such as dyslexia, dyspraxia and autism.

Foundation year students who achieve 65% in their exams can move on to a full degree course on one of the university's 18 courses in the arts, humanities or social sciences – or an undergraduate course elsewhere. The university also works with social mobility charities such as the Sutton Trust and Target Oxbridge while individual Cambridge colleges have links with different areas with low records of sending students to Russell Group universities. Their work focuses on breaking down admissions barriers.

But it took the Stormzy Scholarships, launched in 2018, to help Cambridge attract more applications from black students, a traditionally underrepresented group. The number of black British students rose to 137 in 2020, up from 58 in 2017.

Financial support is extensive. In 2020-21 the university spent £9.3million on Cambridge Bursaries of £3,500 a year for UK students. These are offered to students from homes with annual incomes of £25,000 or less, tapering to £100 for households with an income of up to £62,215. The bursary is in some cases supplemented by individual awards from colleges. About one in four students received some sort of financial aid in 2021 and the university expects to provide a consistent level of support in future.

A new "design Tripos" degree – bringing together architecture, engineering and materials science in a single degree – will be introduced in 2024. Cambridge has refined its course offering to just 30 undergraduate courses across about 65 subject areas. After the rise in admissions in 2020 as a result of the pandemic, the number of students starting courses in 2021 decreased by about 9% against rising applications (up about 12% year-on-year).

Despite a heavy workload, students throw themselves into extracurricular activities. There is a thriving student media and sports facilities are outstanding, especially for popular rowing and cricket.

Catering is available but not compulsory in college accommodation. What is compulsory, however, is that throughout their studies, students are required to live during term-time within the university "precincts" – defined as being within a three-mile radius of Great St Mary's Church.

Tuition fees

» Fees for UK students	£9,250
» Fees for International students 2023–24	£24,507–£37,293
Medicine and Veterinary Medicine	£63,990
» For scholarship and bursary information see	
www.undergraduate.study.cam.ac.uk/fees-and-finance	
» Graduate salary	£30,000

Student numbers

Undergraduates	12,972	(576)
Postgraduates	7,057	(1,549)
Applications/places	22,795/3,660	
Applications per place	6.4:1	
Overall offer rate	21.6%	
International students – EU	7.9%	
Non-EU	13.8%	

Accommodation

See: www.undergraduate.study.cam.ac.uk/why-cambridge/student-life/accommodation

College websites provide accommodation details

See Chapter 13 for individual colleges

Where do the students come from?

State schools (non-grammar)	48.5%	First generation students	16.3%	
Grammar schools	21.4%	Low participation areas	5%	
Independent schools	30%	All ethnic minorities	29.1%	

Social inclusion ranking: 116

White working-class males	1.7%
Black achievement gap	-7.2%
Mature (over 21)	4%

Canterbury Christ Church

Diamond jubilee celebrations in 2022 mark 60 years since Canterbury Christ Church (CCCU) began as a teacher training college. It opened its doors with 75 students and now has more than 9,000 11,500 undergraduates on a broad range of courses.

While most are based at the main Canterbury campus, the university also has outposts in Chatham and Broadstairs and a postgraduate centre in Tunbridge Wells. Courses in commercial music, digital media, photography and early childhood studies are based in the purpose-built campus at Broadstairs, while the Medway site has recently expanded at Chatham's historic dockyard and specialises in education and health programmes.

The university has invested £150million in its main campus, where the library won a design award in 2013. The £65million Verena Holmes Building opened in 2021, named after a pioneering female engineer from Kent, housing courses in science, technology, health, engineering and medicine. It sits next to St Augustine's Abbey, a World Heritage site a few minutes from Canterbury Cathedral.

The university has set a goal of attracting 35% female engineering students to turn around the traditional male domination in the subject, and 40% from less-advantaged communities. CCCU has risen eight places to enter our top 50 for social inclusion (=43). It has a strong record for attracting students from underrepresented groups through working with more than 50 schools and colleges in Kent and Medway to widen access.

The institution is in the top 20 for the proportion of students recruited from deprived areas (19.3%) and for those who are the first in their family to go to university (56.7%). Graduate prospects have improved year-on-year to be just outside the top 50 (51st, up from 67th in 2021).

A string of collaborative projects helped to drive up applications by a sharp 39% by the end of March 2022, compared with the same point in the admissions cycle a year earlier. One such partnership is with Global Banking School (GBS), which introduced a BSc in business and tourism management in 2021, delivered at GBS campuses in Greenford, west London, Birmingham and Manchester and accredited by CCCU.

In the latest Research Excellence Framework (REF 2021), more than twice as much of CCCU's work was assessed as world-leading than reached the top category in the previous national assessment in 2014. Overall, 61% of its submission achieved the top two categories.

Although the university's dropout rate is improving, it is among the factors holding back CCCU's ranking in our main league table. For student satisfaction, measured by

---

North Holmes Road
Canterbury CT1 1QU
01227 928 000
courses@canterbury.ac.uk
https://ccsu.co.uk
www.canterbury.ac.uk
Open days: see website

The Times and The Sunday Times **Rankings**
Overall Ranking: 119 (last year: =119)

Teaching quality	74.9%	=71
Student experience	66.9%	114
Research quality	26.1%	100
Entry standards	101	=130
Graduate prospects	76.1%	51
Good honours	68.5%	121
Expected completion rate	79.5%	=104
Student/staff ratio	18.2	101

our analysis of the latest National Student Survey, the university has climbed 13 places to reach =71 in terms of teaching quality.

It has also edged up its score for satisfaction with the overall undergraduate experience, but still lies outside the top 100 (114th). The university has promised enhanced provision to help to reverse the damage caused by the pandemic to the student experience.

Peer mentors and wellbeing advisers are part of a wide-ranging team offering support. The Safezone app alerts university security staff if a student needs urgent assistance.

At Discovery Park in Sandwich, the university has set up the Life Sciences Industry Liaison Lab, which is also used by local businesses

The Kent and Medway Medical School, a partnership with the University of Kent, opened in 2020 offering 100 places each year on its five-year undergraduate programmes. Foundation years are offered as a way in to a number of degree courses.

The curriculum is gaining three new degrees — food science and nutrition, geography, and wildlife ecology and conservation science. The choice of degree apprenticeships is growing. At the last count there were 445 apprentices across 10 degree programmes and one higher apprenticeship. Courses include chartered management, social work, occupational therapy and diagnostic radiography. By September 2023, when a course for enhanced clinical practitioners will begin, the university expects to have 700 student apprentices.

More financial support is being put in place and the university expects a rising proportion of students to qualify for new awards households with incomes under £25,000. Sports and choral scholarships are also available. A modern sports centre is close to the Canterbury campus and there are playing fields a mile away in the Kent countryside at Stodmarsh, and at Polo Farm Sports Club two miles away.

The university works with local clubs to provide access to facilities. Canterbury Rugby Club allows free membership to students, and they can use Canterbury Golf Club and an athletics track at a local college. The Verena Holmes Building features high specification provision for sport and exercise science.

There is enough residential accommodation to guarantee a place for all foundation and first-year students who apply by the end of July. The cobbled streets of Canterbury are home to a large student population and there is a lively choice of entertainment in the city.

Tuition fees

» Fees for UK/EU students	£9,250
» Fees for International students 2023–24	£14,500
Medicine	£48,200
» For scholarship and bursary information see www.canterbury.ac.uk/study-here/fees-and-funding	
» Graduate salary	£24,373

Student numbers

Undergraduates	11,853	(1,617)
Postgraduates	1,320	(1,563)
Applications/places		11,010/8,490
Applications per place		1.3:1
Overall offer rate		85.7%
International students – EU		2.4%
Non-EU		0.7%

Accommodation

University provided places: 1,214
Self-catered: £118–£190 per week
First-years guaranteed accommodation
www.canterbury.ac.uk/study-here/student-life/accommodation

Where do the students come from?

State schools (non-grammar)	91.9%	First generation students	56.7%	White working-class males	6.7%
Grammar schools	5.7%	Low participation areas	19.3%	Black achievement gap	-37.5%
Independent schools	2.3%	All ethnic minorities	28%	Mature (over 21)	64%

Social inclusion ranking: =43

Cardiff University

Cardiff is our Welsh University of the Year for the second year in a row and is the best-performing institution in Wales in our academic rankings, climbing 10 places to 25th.

Students and staff had their say on the design of the Abacws Building – the new home for the schools of computer science and mathematics. The six-storey building pioneers Cardiff's collaborative emphasis for the future and is part of a £600million campus upgrade – its biggest for a generation. The university's Bute Building, housing the Welsh School of Architecture, has reopened after a £17million refurbishment. The wood and metal workshop has been enlarged and there is more space for the school's robotic arm, and digital fabrication technology to produce laser-cut models, as well as 3D printing and CNC (computer numeric control) equipment.

Post-pandemic, Cardiff's students can now make the most of the £50million Centre for Student Life at the heart of the Cathays Park campus. The new student resources are one attempt to lift rates of student satisfaction. Like most other research-led institutions, Cardiff has tended to struggle in the National Student Survey, although it has returned to the top 100 for satisfaction for teaching quality (=94) and the overall undergraduate experience (=85) in our latest analysis.

Most academic schools are based at Cathays Park, where the university's elegant pale stone buildings stand on tree-lined avenues in the city's civic centre. The healthcare schools share a 53-acre campus at Heath Park with the University Hospital of Wales, with teaching facilities in the £18million Cochrane Building. The School of Dentistry is the only one in Wales and offers students some of the UK's most modern training facilities. Cardiff is the only Russell Group university in Wales and counts two Nobel Prize-winners and 13 Royal Society Fellows on staff. Its new Translational Research Hub adds 129,000 sq ft of hi-tech laboratory space from September 2022 and will house the renowned Cardiff Catalysis Institute and the Institute for Compound Semiconductors.

In the latest Research Excellent Framework (REF 2021), 90% of the university's submissions was classified in the top two ratings (world-leading or internationally excellent). Philosophy led the way, along with communication and media studies, education and architecture. Overall, Cardiff rises 13 places to rank 21st in our research quality index this year.

The demand for places at Cardiff is on the up, rising by 15% in the 2021 admissions cycle to another new high. Enrolments also increased, by a more modest 6%. A snapshot

---

Cardiff
CF10 3AT
029 2087 4455
enquiry@cardiff.ac.uk
www.cardiffstudents.com
www.cardiff.ac.uk
Open days: see website

The Times and The Sunday Times **Rankings**
Overall Ranking: 25 (last year: =35)

Teaching quality	73%	=94
Student experience	70.1%	=85
Research quality	56.7%	21
Entry standards	146	=35
Graduate prospects	84.3%	17
Good honours	83.2%	34
Expected completion rate	92.8%	26
Student/staff ratio	14.5	=29

of the 2022 recruitment cycle at the end of March revealed that applications were up again by 7% in a year.

New programmes introduced in 2021-22 are behind the rise, according to the university. Popular new courses include an environmental sustainability science degree and a BEng integrated engineering degree apprenticeship. Cardiff remains in our top 20 for graduate prospects (17th, down one place from =16 in 2021).

Strategic partnerships with industry and public or third sector organisations include collaborations with the Office for National Statistics, the Airbus Centre of Excellence for Cyber Security Analytics and the insurer Admiral – which offers internship opportunities.

Cardiff's silver award in the government's Teaching Excellence Framework (TEF) was attributed in part to the support that personal tutors provide. The university's outreach activities aim to dispel any negative myths about what it is like to study at an elite Russell Group university.

Cardiff falls just outside the top 100 (102nd) in our analysis of social inclusion, and 12th out of the 21 Russell Group universities. The university is near the bottom of our table for England and Wales for its proportion of students from homes where neither parent went to university (31.6%, 105th).

Contextual admissions are available on most programmes except medicine and dentistry – for which applicants may be given extra points in the interview selection process. In the 2021-22 academic year, almost 22% of all offers made were contextual – more than 26% of UK applicants. The university expects the proportion to be similar this year.

About 4,000 new students received some form of financial support in 2021-22. In collaboration with the Cowrie Scholarship Foundation (CSF), Cardiff has introduced a new award for financially disadvantaged black British students from September 2022.

The university has a three-floor fitness centre at Senghennydd Road and Studio 49 offers a range of fitness classes. The Sports Training Village is at the Talybont campus and further afield students can use more than 33 acres at the Llanrumney sports fields.

University accommodation is guaranteed to first-years and there are a small number of catered and part-catered places – rarely found at UK universities these days. Reasonable private rents, lively nightlife and sporting events within easy reach of beaches and countryside add up to a strong student city package for Cardiff.

Tuition fees

» Fees for UK/EU students £9,050

» Fees for International students 2023–24 £18,700–£23,450
 Medicine £39,700; Dentistry (first year pre-clinical) £25,450

» For scholarship and bursary information see
 www.cardiff.ac.uk/study/undergraduate/tuition-fees

» Graduate salary £24,907

Student numbers

Undergraduates	21,162	(2,186)
Postgraduates	7,101	(3,059)
Applications/places		44,155/7,915
Applications per place		5.6:1
Overall offer rate		70.3%
International students – EU		3.1%
Non-EU		10.3%

Accommodation

University provided places: 5,530
Catered: £133–£152 per week
Self-catered: £108–£150 per week
First-years guaranteed accommodation
www.cardiff.ac.uk/study/accommodation

Where do the students come from?

				Social inclusion ranking: 102	
State schools (non-grammar)	77.3%	First generation students	31.6%	White working-class males	4%
Grammar schools	8.6%	Low participation areas	9.1%	Black achievement gap	-16.5%
Independent schools	14.1%	All ethnic minorities	19%	Mature (over 21)	11.7%

Cardiff Metropolitan University

Demand for places to study at Cardiff Met increased by almost 14% in the 2021 admissions round. A snapshot of the 2022 cycle at the end of March showed another 7% year-on-year increase compared with the same point 12 months earlier. The university credits its success in league tables such as ours (in which it won Welsh University of the Year 2021) with the upturn.

A range of new courses have also proved attractive to a growing number of applicants; since 2019 more than 40 further degree programmes have been introduced at Cardiff Met, and over 30 existing programmes have been revalidated. Joining the roster in the present academic year are a degree in business law and management and an aviation management degree being co-delivered with Cardiff airport and the US-based Embry-Riddle Aeronautical University.

Two degree apprenticeships, in cybersecurity and in applied software engineering, also welcomed their first students this year. They fall under the university's School of Technologies, where options in robotics engineering, virtual and augmented reality and computing with creative design are among the curricular offerings. Cardiff Met will offer a degree in criminology from September 2023.

Across both of Cardiff Met's campuses at Llandaff and Cyncoed, close to Cardiff city centre, the university has pledged to invest £80million in new and repurposed academic buildings, as well as further sport and health facilities. A new cycleway is also in the pipeline, stretching as far as Cardiff Bay. The university's sound financial position, as evidenced by its increased turnover over recent years, is enabling the developments.

Sport, the university's best-known feature, is based at the Cyncoed campus. The £7million National Indoor Athletics Centre has a six-lane 140m straight, and competition-standard long jump, high jump and pole vault pits as well as physiotherapy and sports medicine facilities. Performance and elite sport scholarships offer tailored support and Cardiff Met teams and individuals compete at the highest level of BUCS (British University & College Sport) competitions.

Cardiff Met was one of only four Welsh universities awarded silver in the government's Teaching Excellence Framework (TEF). Assessors noted that its personalised learning secured high levels of commitment from students, including those studying in the Welsh language. An enhanced personal tutor system gives students greater access to academic guidance.

Across all five of the university's schools (Art and Design; Education and Social Policy; Management; Sport and Health Sciences; and Technologies) degree programmes are linked

---

Western Avenue
Llandaff
Cardiff CF5 2YB
029 2041 6010
askadmissions@cardiffmet.ac.uk
www.cardiffmetsu.co.uk
www.cardiffmet.ac.uk
Open days: see website

The Times and The Sunday Times **Rankings**

Overall Ranking: 93 (last year: =79)

Teaching quality	72.3%	=104
Student experience	69.2%	=97
Research quality	32%	78
Entry standards	124	=70
Graduate prospects	71.6%	=71
Good honours	75.1%	87
Expected completion rate	80%	=101
Student/staff ratio	18.1	=99

with industry partners. The university is an accredited provider of Initial Teacher Education in Wales, for instance, and is degree in professional policing has links with South Wales Police. Degrees within tourism, hospitality and events offer opportunities such as work experience at Glastonbury Festival and mentoring by The Ivy restaurant chain.

Via the MetHub platform, students and graduates can access help with job applications, work placements and internships. Appointments with the careers team are bookable online. Graduate start-ups are on the rise, and support is offered through the Centre for Entrepreneurship.

The university is among the biggest risers in our research quality index, jumping 29 places this year. In our analysis of the results of the latest Research Excellence Framework (REF 2021), Cardiff Met climbs to 78th from 107th in 2021. Four times as many staff submitted work for assessment and 79% was judged world-leading or internationally excellent. Sport, a strength, produced the best results alongside art and design: 88% of sports research reached the top two categories.

Graduate prospects have edged up four places to =71 in our analysis of the proportion in highly skilled work or further study within 15 months.

Cardiff Met is in the top 30 in our social inclusion index overall. The university succeeds in recruiting more working-class white male students than most (ranking 13th), and almost half of students are the first in their family to go to university. The approach to widening access targets those from the lowest two quintiles of the Welsh Index of Multiple Deprivation, who have not previously had access to higher education, as well as carers, care-leavers, unemployed people, asylum seekers, refugees and ex-offenders. A University of Sanctuary since 2016, Cardiff Met has pledged £400,000 over two years in fellowships for academic staff and scholarships for students, as well as accommodation for those fleeing Ukraine.

There are 1,737 bed spaces in university-owned or endorsed accommodation, and first-years who meet the eligibility criteria are guaranteed a spot. Before being given their key, students must complete a compulsory halls induction, which includes sections on consent, alcohol and drugs. A leading student city, Cardiff offers music, culture, sport and nightlife by the bucketload.

Tuition fees

» Fees for UK/EU students	£9,000
» Fees for International students 2023–24	£15,000
» For scholarship and bursary information see www.cardiffmet.ac.uk/study/finance/Pages/ Undergraduate-Students.aspx	
» Graduate salary	£22,000

Student numbers

Undergraduates	7,687	(475)
Postgraduates	2,515	(757)
Applications/places		10,760/3,210
Applications per place		3.4:1
Overall offer rate		90.2%
International students – EU		1.7%
Non-EU		4.5%

Accommodation

University provided places: 1,737
Catered: £173–£197 per week
Self-catered: £109–£140 per week
First-years guaranteed accommodation
http://www.cardiffmet.ac.uk/accommodation/Pages/default.aspx

Where do the students come from?

State schools (non-grammar)	94.2%	First generation students	45.7%	
Grammar schools	1%	Low participation areas	16%	
Independent schools	4.8%	All ethnic minorities	12.9%	

Social inclusion ranking: 29

White working-class males	8.1%
Black achievement gap	-15.4%
Mature (over 21)	21.7%

University of Central Lancashire

The University of Central Lancashire (UCLan) has opened the UK's 11th veterinary school. Based at the university's Preston campus, it is offering courses at foundation, undergraduate and postgraduate level from September 2022. As well as veterinary medicine, options include bioveterinary science, veterinary clinical practice, veterinary sciences, veterinary physiotherapy and rehabilitation and clinical animal behaviour and training.

The first intake of UK and international students will begin veterinary science degrees and foundation courses, while the Bachelor of Veterinary Medicine and Surgery (BVMS) degree course will begin in 2023.

Under the university's £200million masterplan, a £35million Engineering Innovation Centre opened in 2019. UCLan's £60million student centre, at the Preston campus, opened in 2021. Featuring a rooftop garden, the centre houses all student services from mental health provision to careers advice and housing assistance. A large pedestrianised public square has been developed alongside, forming a new gateway into Preston.

The student-centric facility should help to improve UCLan's satisfaction scores in future National Student Surveys (NSS). In our analysis of the results of the latest NSS,

the university has slipped further outside the top 100 for satisfaction with the wider undergraduate experience this year (102nd), while it has improved slightly to =84 for satisfaction with teaching quality.

One of Britain's bigger universities, with more than 17,000 undergraduates and close on 5,000 postgraduate students, UCLan operates on multiple sites – including its Larnaka campus in Cyprus, offering UK degrees in a Mediterranean setting. Students on a wide range of UK-based courses have the opportunity to spend a year there.

Courses based at UCLan's Burnley campus promise small class sizes, and the Pennine site has a students' union hub, a moot court and science laboratories. The Westlakes campus in West Cumbria focuses on nursing and other health subjects.

Enrolments in the 2021 admissions cycle dipped by about 17%, but applications to study at UCLan reached their highest since 2017. International relations and education and English were among seven new courses to begin in September 2022.

Rated silver in the Teaching Excellence Framework in 2019, UCLan was commended for embedding employability skills across the curriculum and for extensive engagement with local employers. All students can take advantage of work placements and other opportunities to boost their work-readiness upon graduation and the university has links with the NHS,

Preston PR1 2HE
01772 892 400
cenquiries@uclan.ac.uk
www.uclansu.co.uk
www.uclan.ac.uk
Open days: see website

The Times and The Sunday Times **Rankings**
Overall Ranking: 107 (last year: =108)

Teaching quality	74%	=84
Student experience	68.9%	102
Research quality	30.4%	=82
Entry standards	125	=63
Graduate prospects	72.9%	66
Good honours	73.3%	96
Expected completion rate	74.8%	124
Student/staff ratio	16.2	=65

BBC, Lancashire Constabulary, Wigan Warriors and Royal Mail, among other organisations. Graduate prospects have improved by 16 places year-on-year, ranking 66th, based on the proportion in highly skilled jobs or postgraduate study 15 months after leaving UCLan.

Extensive degree apprenticeship provision at UCLan spans 30 subject areas across the fields of engineering, professional services and health and wellbeing. The university expects to increase its number of earn-as-you-learn programmes from 1,800 to about 2,500. Youth worker and fire safety engineer courses were set to begin in September 2022.

Physics, maths and astronomy research at UCLan has longstanding research links with NASA. Under the partnership, UCLan scientists unveiled in December 2020 the highest-ever resolution images of the Sun from NASA's solar sounding rocket mission. Two-thirds of UCLan's submissions to the latest Research Excellence Framework (REF 2021) were rated world-leading or internationally excellent, the top two categories. The university has done well to gain four places in our research quality index (=82) against sector-wide improvements compared with the previous national assessment in 2014.

UCLan remains in the top 50 in our social inclusion index (=43). Of its student population, 40.2% are aged over 21.

Foundation years are offered in a wide range of subjects, while about 30% of applicants benefit from UCLan's contextual offers, which cut grade requirements by eight UCAS points for disadvantaged students.

The university's portfolio of 14 undergraduate bursaries and scholarships includes medical scholarships which cover all tuition fees for the duration of the five-year course. Other awards include bursaries of £1,000 a year for young people leaving care or estranged from their parents.

The Sir Tom Finney Sports Centre at the Preston campus and the UCLan Sports Arena two miles away provide facilities such as grass rugby and football pitches, floodlit tennis/ netball courts, artificial pitches, an eight-lane athletics track and a 1.5km cycle circuit. Cycle hire is also offered.

Students are drawn to Preston's generally safe environment and lower cost of living than nearby Liverpool or Manchester. Accommodation is guaranteed for first-years and there are 377 rooms costing £79 per week – among the lowest rent for halls of residence in the country.

Tuition fees

»	Fees for UK/EU students	£9,250
	Foundation courses	£6,000
»	Fees for International students 2023–24	£14,250
	Foundation courses	£10,000
	Medicine £46,000; Veterinary Medicine £23,000–£48,000	
»	For scholarship and bursary information see www.uclan.ac.uk/study/fees-and-finance	
»	Graduate salary	£24,000

Student numbers

Undergraduates	17,291 (1,851)
Postgraduates	4,825 (3,977)
Applications/places	21,575/4,925
Applications per place	4.4:1
Overall offer rate	68.9%
International students – EU	2.4%
Non-EU	10.2%

Accommodation

University provided places: 1,356
Self-catered: £79–£135 per week
First-years guaranteed accommodation
www.uclan.ac.uk/accommodation

Where do the students come from?

State schools (non-grammar)	97%	First generation students	51.9%	
Grammar schools	1.5%	Low participation areas	14.2%	
Independent schools	1.4%	All ethnic minorities	34.6%	

Social inclusion ranking: =43

White working-class males	6.7%
Black achievement gap	-27.5%
Mature (over 21)	40.2%

University of Chester

Founded more than 180 years ago as a teacher-training college by William Gladstone, who went on to become the prime minister, and others, Chester predates all other English universities except Oxford, Cambridge, Durham and London. Today's university is structured around seven academic faculties at sites throughout the city and at centres in Birkenhead, Reaseheath, Shrewsbury and Warrington.

A rich digital infrastructure and ethos is central to a "digital-first" approach. Core texts are available digitally as are a vast number of e-books and e-journals. In addition, there are an estimated 32,000 physical books that students can get their hands on. A laptop loan scheme supports flexible working and the Recap centre provides recorded lectures on demand.

The original Exton Park (Parkgate Road) campus is a 32-acre site a 10-minute walk from Chester city centre. The Queen's Park campus, once the wartime headquarters of the army's Western Command, now houses Chester Business School. At the Riverside campus, the Faculty of Health and Social Care has invested in facilities that include an anatomy suite with human cadaveric plastinated prosections and digital anatomy tables — among other fresh provision.

Courses in education and children's services are also based at Riverside and the Riverside Innovation Centre hosts business start-ups generated by Chester students and graduates.

The Kingsway creative campus houses arts and media courses. The merger of the departments of performing arts and media into the Department of Music, Media and Performance Acting has brought about opportunities for acting students to collaborate with those on the new media and TV production degree.

The expanded Warrington centre has moved from its out-of-town Padgate base into new town centre premises, where it occupies a shopfront building in Time Square. There are more facilities five minutes' away in Barbauld Street's Sarah Parker Remond Centre, home to programmes in business, policing, social work, nursing and teaching. As with other Chester developments, students were involved in designing the spaces. Elsewhere, the new Design and Manufacturing Suite at Exton Park has brought workshop space with manufacturing facilities.

Students receive mentoring by a personal academic tutor throughout their degree, however student satisfaction scores have yet to recover since the pandemic in our measures derived from the latest National Student Survey (NSS). Chester has slipped 30 places to 124th for satisfaction with the wider undergraduate experience, near the foot of our table, and has fallen 21 places to =79 for satisfaction with teaching quality. Just three

Parkgate Road
Chester CH1 4BJ
01244 511 000
admissions@chester.ac.uk
www.chestersu.com
www.chester.ac.uk
Open days: see website

Belfast, Edinburgh, CHESTER, London, Cardiff

The Times and The Sunday Times Rankings
Overall Ranking: 97 (last year: 68)

Teaching quality	74.4%	=79
Student experience	65.2%	124
Research quality	21.1%	110
Entry standards	120	=81
Graduate prospects	72%	70
Good honours	74.1%	=92
Expected completion rate	83.2%	85
Student/staff ratio	15.1	=41

years ago Chester ranked in the top 30 on both measures.

The university expects to double its number of student apprentices (565, at the last count) by September 2023. A programme to train senior leaders is new to the portfolio of degree apprentices, joining existing programmes that include healthcare assistant practitioner, police constable, registered nurse and chartered manager.

The first fashion communication marketing (social media) students started courses in September 2022. Course delivery mirrors the fashion communication marketing industry for social media, with students becoming interns mentored by industry professionals. The degree's innovative structure delivers 75% online and 25% face-to-face over two years.

A graduate entry medicine degree is also new, as are programmes in philosophy, ethics and religion; and in banking and finance. From 2023, degrees will be launched in criminology and cybersecurity; and social justice and community action. Theology, health subjects and sports and exercise science produced some of the best results in the latest Research Excellence Framework (REF 2021). Overall, 51% of research was assessed as world-leading or internationally excellent, while the number of staff who submitted research almost doubled.

Chester's silver award in the Teaching Excellence Framework (TEF) brought praise for its students' employability skills. About two-thirds of undergraduates take work-based learning modules. More than two-thirds of the academic staff hold Higher Education Academy fellowships. Evening classes in a foreign language are offered to all students, and students can beef up the contacts and references in their e-portfolio through work placements and industry events.

Chester's graduate prospects have declined slightly, down six places year-on-year to 70th, according to our analysis of the latest Graduate Outcomes survey. The institution has fallen seven places in our social inclusion index but remains in the top 25 for its efforts to recruit students from underrepresented groups.

First-years are guaranteed student accommodation, about a fifth of which is fully catered. Most sports facilities are near the Exton Park site. Shrewsbury students are entitled to free membership at the town's sports village.

Liverpool and Manchester are within easy reach, while Chester is one of those places beloved by students seeking the security of a smaller city but with plenty of entertainment, too.

Tuition fees

»	Fees for UK students	£9,250
»	Fees for International students 2023–24	£12,950
	Foundation courses	£9,250
»	For scholarship and bursary information see http://www1.chester.ac.uk/finance	
»	Graduate salary	£23,000

Student numbers

Undergraduates	8,311	(682)
Postgraduates	2,591	(2,627)
Applications/places	16,485/2,880	
Applications per place	5.7:1	
Overall offer rate	75.8%	
International students – EU	1.1%	
Non-EU	5%	

Accommodation

University provided places: 1,800
Catered costs: £160 per week
Self-catered: £99–£149 per week
First-years guaranteed accommodation
www1.chester.ac.uk/departments/accommodation-office

Where do the students come from?

State schools (non-grammar)	94.5%	First generation students	54.3%	White working-class males	7.9%
Grammar schools	3.1%	Low participation areas	20%	Black achievement gap	-14.6%
Independent schools	2.4%	All ethnic minorities	7.2%	Mature (over 21)	38.1%

Social inclusion ranking: =24

University of Chichester

With the goal of providing hundreds of healthcare workers by 2025, the University of Chichester launched the new School of Nursing and Allied Health in 2021. A three-year Bachelor of Science honours degree in adult nursing joined pre-existing degrees in physiotherapy, while health-related degree apprenticeships are planned for the future.

The 1,600 sq ft facility, run with University Hospitals Sussex NHS Foundation Trust, is housed on the university's Bishop Otter campus, next to St Richard's Hospital. Students have access to mock wards and simulation suites to develop their clinical skills.

An expanded course offering – in psychology as well as nursing and allied health subjects – has contributed to a rise in applications to study at Chichester, which were up by nearly a quarter in 2021, year-on-year. Enrolments rose by 15% during the same period. A snapshot at the end of March 2022 showed another 10% increase in applications.

A degree in aeronautical engineering will be available to students from September 2023, joining options first offered in 2022-23 in digital film production, childhood with therapeutic play, and e-sports and sports media. The new options further broaden the academic focus at Chichester, long known for its strong arts and teacher training provision.

In 2018 the university's £35million Tech Park at the Bognor Regis campus was officially opened by the Duke and Duchess of Sussex on the day of their first – and only – joint visit to the county of their titles.

Degree courses in STEAM subjects (science, technology, engineering, arts, mathematics) are housed at the Tech Park, facilitated by resources such as a machinery workshop, fabricating laboratory, specialist 3D printers and an engineering centre.

Chichester's Department of Creative Digital Technologies features a TV production studio, a special effects room and a media operation centre. First established as a teacher-training college in 1839, in memory of William Otter, a bishop of Chichester and a passionate educationalist, it became a women-only college in 1873 until male students returned from 1957.

Chichester has slipped 16 places since entering our overall top 50 in 2020. Although the institution performed well in the pandemic-hit National Student Survey (NSS) of 2021, it has dropped out of the top 10 in our analysis of the latest NSS results, published in summer 2022. It remains in the top 30, however, ranking 27th for satisfaction with teaching quality and =29 for satisfaction with the wider undergraduate experience.

Rated silver in the government's Teaching Excellence Framework, Chichester was commended for its outstanding support for disadvantaged students. Recruitment of

Bishop Otter Campus
College Lane
Chichester PO19 6PE
01243 816 002
admissions@chi.ac.uk
www.ucsu.org
www.chi.ac.uk
Open days: see website

The Times and The Sunday Times **Rankings**
Overall Ranking: 66 (last year: 50)

Teaching quality	78%	27
Student experience	74.6%	=29
Research quality	20.1%	114
Entry standards	125	=63
Graduate prospects	64.9%	=117
Good honours	77.1%	=68
Expected completion rate	86.4%	=56
Student/staff ratio	5.4	44

students from the most deprived areas is in the top 20, according to our latest analysis, although Chichester is in 89th place overall for social inclusion.

The latest dropout figures for Chichester (7.5%) show that far fewer students give up than the expected level (10.6%) based on the course and student profile. Almost all of its students come from non-selective state schools (93.6%, ranking 48th), and nearly half are the first in their family to go to university (46.8%, 57th).

The university's portfolio of eight degree apprenticeships had more than 300 learners on programmes at the last count. Courses cover training for areas such as social work, manufacturing engineering, digital marketing and senior leadership.

Graduate prospects are in the bottom 20, according to our analysis of the latest Graduate Outcomes survey, tracking how many students find highly skilled work or take up further study 15 months after finishing their degree (=117).

The Mathematics Centre has an international reputation and has become a focal point for curriculum development in England and elsewhere.

Nearly twice as many of Chichester's academic staff contributed to the latest Research Excellence Framework (REF 2021) as in the previous national assessment in 2014. Sport, history, and English and creative writing produced the best results.

Students sign a charter committing to respect the diversity of their community. In addition, the students' union runs activities covering the importance of sexual consent, mental health support and inclusion.

The university owns and manages all of its 1,238 residential places, which are fairly equally divided between the Bognor Regis and Chichester (Bishop Otter) campuses. First-years are guaranteed a room if they made the university their first choice and get housing applications in on time.

Chichester's sports resources are all on campus, where facilities include indoor and outdoor climbing walls, a grass rugby pitch and a three-court sports dome. The sports hall has four courts and students can also use Astro pitches, a fitness suite and a multi-use games area. Between 20 and 25 gifted athlete scholarships are awarded per year across three levels: elite, development and BUCS (British Universities and Colleges Sport).

An intercampus bus service links Bognor and Bishop Otter, which each have students' union bars, while the towns have their own social scenes as well as seaside pursuits.

Tuition fees

»	Fees for UK/EU students	£9,250
	Foundation courses	£5,500
»	Fees for International students 2023–24	£14,500
»	For scholarship and bursary information see www.chi.ac.uk/study-us/fees-finance	
»	Graduate salary	£22,000

Student numbers

Undergraduates	4,108	(455)
Postgraduates	479	(804)
Applications/places		8,415/1,765
Applications per place		4.8:1
Overall offer rate		77.2%
International students – EU		2%
Non-EU		2.5%

Accommodation

University provided places: 1,238
Catered costs: £167–£189 per week
Self-catered: £111–£157 per week
First-years guaranteed accommodation
www.chi.ac.uk/student-life/accommodation

Where do the students come from?

State schools (non-grammar)	93.6%	First generation students	46.8%	White working-class males	6.5%
Grammar schools	3.2%	Low participation areas	19.1%	Black achievement gap	−34.1%
Independent schools	3.2%	All ethnic minorities	6.8%	Mature (over 21)	22%

Social inclusion ranking: 89

City, University of London

City has restructured its academic departments to reflect its distinctive specialisms and longstanding commitment to business and the professions.

There are now six schools: the School of Policy and Global Affairs; Bayes Business School; the School of Communication and Creativity; the School of Health and Psychological Sciences; the School of Science and Technology; and the City Law School.

Rooted in the heart of the capital since its foundation more than 125 years ago, the university has invested more than £140million in developing its sites since 2012. Most of it has gone on improvements to the main campus at Northampton Square in Clerkenwell, which now also houses the Law School's new home. Elsewhere, journalism students have access to a dedicated learning space, modelled on a broadcast newsroom.

The Bayes Business School's site on Bunhill Row is the latest facility to benefit from redevelopment in summer 2022. This follows the refurbishment of the school's newest building on Finsbury Square in the heart of the City of London. The MBA from Bayes – formerly known as Cass Business School – is ranked sixth in the UK by the Financial Times and attracts high-profile visiting lecturers.

City was rated silver in the Teaching Excellence Framework, thanks to strong engagement with students and the students' union. However, outcomes of the latest National Student Survey (NSS) fell short. In our NSS analysis, City is down three places to 127th for student satisfaction with teaching quality (fourth from bottom in our table). The university is =116 (down from 88th) for how students rate their wider undergraduate experience. The low rates of student satisfaction have contributed to a 14-place fall for City in our main academic rankings this year (now 69th).

Teaching includes a mixed model of blended learning in the 2022-23 academic year, with in-person teaching prioritised in small group settings.

Graduate prospects remain one of City's strongest suits in our league table, although the university has slipped out of the top 25 to rank =45 in our analysis of the proportion of graduates in highly skilled work or postgraduate study within 15 months.

For emerging entrepreneurs, the university's CityVentures Team and Launch Lab run a three-month accelerator programme to kickstart student and graduate start-ups. The incubator has created more than 1,000 jobs and secured £13million in investment to date.

There was good news for City in the latest Research Excellence Framework (REF 2021). Eighty-six per cent of the university's research

---

Northampton Square
London EC1V 0HB
020 7040 8716
ugadmissions@city.ac.uk
www.citystudents.co.uk
www.city.ac.uk
Open days:
see website

The Times and The Sunday Times Rankings
Overall Ranking: 69 (last year: 55)

Teaching quality	67.5%	127
Student experience	66.7%	=116
Research quality	51.5%	37
Entry standards	132	52
Graduate prospects	77.6%	=45
Good honours	80.5%	46
Expected completion rate	90.2%	40
Student/staff ratio	19.4	=110

was rated as world-leading or internationally excellent (the top two categories) in the national exercise – an improvement on REF 2014, triggering a 14-place rise to 37th in our research quality rating.

Applications and enrolments increased for the fourth consecutive year in 2021, in which 28% of new entrants gained their places through Clearing. Applications were up by 8% by the end of March 2022 compared with the same point the year before. A suite of eight engineering-based degrees join the curriculum from September 2023, among them aerospace engineering; energy and sustainability engineering; and biomedical and healthcare engineering. The portfolio of degree apprenticeships is also gaining two programmes in 2023, which will make seven in total with about 800 student apprentices.

The university introduced a contextual offers scheme for the first time in 2022-23, in which eligibility is based on two criteria: being the first in the family to attend university and having been in care. City is already one of the more socially inclusive institutions within the University of London, ranking 71st in our analysis. It has the fourth highest proportion of UK-domiciled students drawn from ethnic minorities (81.3%) and is in the top 10 for the proportion of students who are the first in their family to go to university (58.5%).

City nurtures its students to stick with their courses, rising into the top 40 for its course completion rate. The dropout rate (4.1%) is comfortably below the expected level (7.1%) when the students' background and the university's mix of subjects is taken into account.

Financial help includes the newly launched Bayes Undergraduate Scholarship for Black British students, a means-tested award that covers home-level tuition fees and pays a £6,000 annual stipend for three years of study to 10 students per year. Up to 50 Lord Mayor of London scholarships are awarded annually, worth £4,625 to first-years who outdo their conditional offer entry grades.

Students get discounted access to the CitySport gym and to the Saddlers sports hall. New entrants who accept an offer by the end of June are guaranteed a space in student accommodation. Some of London's most fashionable and fun neighbourhoods surround City, making it easy for students to explore the delights of Old Street, Islington, Clerkenwell and beyond.

Tuition fees

» Fees for UK students	£9,250
» Fees for International students 2023–24	£16,230–£27,860
» For scholarship and bursary information see www.city.ac.uk/prospective-students/finance	
» Graduate salary	£26,000

Student numbers		
Undergraduates	11,396	(1,105)
Postgraduates	6,647	(2,179)
Applications/places		26,625/4,265
Applications per place		6.2:1
Overall offer rate		53.7%
International students – EU		7.8%
Non-EU		18.8%

Accommodation
University provided places: 999
Catered costs: £216–£306 per week
Self-catered: £165–£232 per week
First-years guaranteed accommodation
www.city.ac.uk/prospective-students/accommodation

Where do the students come from?

					Social inclusion ranking: 71	
State schools (non-grammar)	88.7%	First generation students	58.5%	White working-class males	1.8%
Grammar schools	4.5%	Low participation areas	2.9%	Black achievement gap	-13.4%
Independent schools	6.8%	All ethnic minorities	81.3%	Mature (over 21)	12.8%

Coventry University

The university's recent acquisition of the learning experience platform Aula reinforces Coventry's pioneering attitude to education technologies. Students began using Aula in 2020 during the Covid-19 pandemic and the university says the result has been a more engaged and social approach to teaching and learning. Aula also allows the flexibility to combine online and on-campus semesters within degrees.

Such a resource is especially valuable to Coventry, which usually attracts more European students than any other British university, although it has been pipped to the top spot by University College London in the latest figures.

International experiences are part of Coventry's ethos, with overseas opportunities for UK students ranging from field trips to a semester or year abroad studying, working or both.

An overhaul of undergraduate provision for the September 2023 cohort has increased teaching and learning hours in the first year of courses and enhanced hands-on experiences. A "common first year" is being introduced to enable students to mix and learn with those from other related courses. There will be an option to switch courses at the end of the first year.

Success coaches have been introduced, working one-to-one and identifying where students might need extra support. Students continue to give their university the thumbs-up in the National Student Survey (NSS). In our analysis of the latest NSS results, Coventry ranks in the top 20 for student satisfaction with teaching quality (=18) and the wider undergraduate experience (16th), improving on top-25 rankings in 2021.

The university was awarded gold in the Teaching Excellence Framework for "consistently outstanding" student support services, especially for those from disadvantaged backgrounds, which aid retention and progression. It has won plaudits in our guide as well, having scooped our Modern University of the Year award three times between 2014 and 2016, and University of the Year for Student Experience in 2018. Coventry was also shortlisted for our University of the Year 2021.

At the city centre campus a £64million redevelopment of facilities at the Faculty of Arts and Humanities will give students access to a hyper-studio for cross-disciplinary projects and immersive studios with virtual and mixed-reality technologies. Scheduled to open fully in early 2023, it will also bring high-quality workshops for film, photography, printmaking, metal and ceramic fibre clay among other creative disciplines.

It follows the opening of the Beatrice Shilling Building for the Faculty of Engineering, Environment and Computing and a revamp of the Lanchester Library. The Starley Gardens open-air urban space was unveiled in May 2021. A Bloomberg trading

Priory Street
Coventry CV1 5FB
024 7765 2222
ukadmissions@coventry.ac.uk
www.cusu.org
www.coventry.ac.uk
Open days: see website

The Times and The Sunday Times Rankings

Overall Ranking: 55 (last year: 51)

Teaching quality	78.6%	=18
Student experience	76.7%	16
Research quality	33.8%	73
Entry standards	115	=101
Graduate prospects	71%	=74
Good honours	76.8%	73
Expected completion rate	80.1%	=99
Student/staff ratio	13.8	=15

floor, hospitality suite and fashion studio are among facilities at the London campuses.

The curriculum is growing across the UK campuses: degrees in health and social care at Greenwich, sport performance and coaching at Scarborough and architectural engineering, philosophy and forensic science at Coventry are among 28 new options. Coventry offers 42 apprenticeships from Levels 4 to 7, with about 2,000 learners on Level 6 (degree) and 7 (postgraduate) programmes. Options cover roles in business and administration, care services, construction, digital, education and childcare, engineering and manufacturing, environmental, health and science, legal, finance and accounting, and protective services.

There was evidence that Coventry's investment in research had paid off in the results of the latest Research Excellence Framework (REF 2021), in which 70% of its submission was classed as world-leading or internationally excellent, the top two categories. The best results were in architecture; education; linguistics; and communication and media studies. The university rises 35 places from =108 to 73rd in our research quality index on the back of considerable improvement since the previous national assessment in 2014, when 61% of its submission reached the top two categories. Coventry has expanded its research centres, increased research and doctoral staff and developed purpose-built facilities.

Coventry ranks =74 for graduate prospects, based on the proportion of graduates in highly skilled work or further study within 15 months.

More than 60% of Coventry's students are from ethnic minorities, a top-20 ranking, while the university is steady in joint 56th place on our measures of social inclusion overall.

The university's indoor Sport and Recreation Centre in Coventry city centre features a dance studio, two sports halls and a fitness suite among its resources. Students can access the Westwood Heath outdoor facilities, five miles away by public transport.

Applicants who make Coventry their firm choice and request accommodation by mid-July are guaranteed a room in halls of residence.

All students can take part in a training course called *I Heart Consent*, delivered in sexual health and guidance week. Support for mental wellbeing is extensive.

Student-oriented nightlife creates a lively atmosphere in Coventry, while the £14million Scarborough seaside campus is close to beaches and the North Yorkshire Moors.

Tuition fees

» Fees for UK students	£9,250
Foundation courses	£6,800–£9,250
» Fees for International students 2023–24	£16,800–£24,050
» For scholarship and bursary information see www.coventry.ac.uk/study-at-coventry/finance/	
» Graduate salary	£24,000

Student numbers

Undergraduates	27,612	(3,191)
Postgraduates	5,198	(3,142)
Applications/places		27,535/5,575
Applications per place		4.9:1
Overall offer rate		91.3%
International students – EU		11.1%
Non-EU		20.1%

Accommodation

University provided places: 2,579
Catered costs: £99–£185 per week
First-years guaranteed accommodation
www.coventry.ac.uk/life-on-campus/accommodation

Where do the students come from?

State schools (non-grammar)	94.4%	First generation students	46.8%		
Grammar schools	3.2%	Low participation areas	13.1%		
Independent schools	2.4%	All ethnic minorities	62.3%		

Social inclusion ranking: =56

White working-class males	4%
Black achievement gap	-18.4%
Mature (over 21)	22.1%

University for the Creative Arts

The University of the Creative Arts (UCA), one of Britain's seven arts universities, paints a bright trail 56 places up our research quality index to rank 56th. Its performance in the latest Research Excellence Framework (REF 2021) far outdid its results in the previous national assessment in 2014.

UCA's submission from 72 researchers included 115 entries including sculpture, ceramics, photographic collections, films, essays and books. It had more world-leading research than any other UK university: overall, 78% of the work was rated world-leading or internationally excellent, the top two categories. The improvement in research quality has triggered a six-place boost in our main academic league table, too.

A wide-ranging development programme has revamped UCA's campuses across Kent and Surrey. The School of Fashion and Textiles at UCA Epsom now has all courses under one roof, with the latest facilities. Graphics and music courses are also based in Epsom.

UCA's Business School for the Creative Industries is the first of its kind in the country and offers degrees such as event and promotion management, and international buying and merchandising.

A £2million funding boost from the Office for Students has provided motion capture and virtual reality studios at the new School of Games and Creative Technology, based at UCA Farnham. Teaching and research spaces have also been improved along with IT infrastructure.

More than 2,000 students are based at Farnham, which also hosts courses such as advertising, film production and journalism. UCA Farnham's £4million Film and Media Centre consolidates its strong reputation in the industry, and graduates of the university's film production degree have gone on to work on movies such as the *Harry Potter* franchise, *Mission Impossible* as well as Marvel's Disney+ television spinoff *Loki*.

As one of only two architecture faculties remaining within a specialist art and design institution, the Canterbury School of Architecture promotes collaboration between student architects, designers and fine artists. On a modern site close to the city centre, the UCA Canterbury campus also hosts degree courses in fine art, interior design, graphic design, and illustration and animation.

The purpose-built UCA Rochester campus – formerly the Medway School of Arts, whose graduates include the fashion designer Dame Zandra Rhodes, the university's chancellor emirata – will close in September 2023 and its courses will shift to Farnham, Canterbury and Epsom. Karen Millen, the fashion designer, and the jeweller Stephen Webster also studied at Rochester, which has hosted further education

UCA Farnham
Falkner Road
Farnham GU9 7DS
01252 416 110
admissions@uca.ac.uk
http://ucasu.com
www.uca.ac.uk
Open days: see website

The Times and The Sunday Times Rankings
Overall Ranking: 63 (last year: 69)

Teaching quality	77.2%	=33
Student experience	68.7%	=103
Research quality	41.2%	56
Entry standards	134	=50
Graduate prospects	52.2%	132
Good honours	78.3%	60
Expected completion rate	84.7%	73
Student/staff ratio	13.8	=15

and postgraduate programmes. Some undergraduate television production classes were held there, although most were already mainly based at Maidstone TV Studios, the largest independent studio complex in the UK.

Student satisfaction held up during the pandemic at UCA better than it did at many institutions and the university was third in our analysis of the impact of Covid-19 from 2020-21. The latest results of the National Student Survey show a rise of five places to =33 for satisfaction with teaching quality. In-person lectures, studio and workshop sessions have returned in full for the 2022-23 academic year. Satisfaction with the wider undergraduate experience has improved slightly to =103.

UCA launched the Institute of Creativity and Innovation in southeastern China in 2020, in partnership with Xiamen University. Closer to home, those on the Royal School of Needlework's hand embroidery degree, which is accredited by UCA, are based in apartments designed by Sir Christopher Wren at Hampton Court Palace.

The UCA undergraduate curriculum is expanding. Six new degrees – including interior architecture, visual communications and comic and concept art – welcomed their first students in September 2022. Another 14 courses are on the way in 2023-24 including computer science, music and sound production, architectural technology, and user experience design.

The university achieved a gold rating in the Teaching Excellence Framework, reflecting its outstanding levels of stretch for students, driving them to achieve their full potential.

A concerted effort to boost graduate employability is behind UCA's recent guarantee of work placements for all undergraduates. Universities serving the creative industries have struggled in our analysis of graduate prospects and UCA has been at the bottom of all three Graduate Outcomes surveys to date. In our analysis of the latest results, the university records a slight improvement of one percentage point, with 52.2% of graduates in highly skilled jobs or postgraduate study 15 months after leaving UCA.

The university's dropout rate is lower than expected, given its course profile and the background of its student intake.

New student halls of residence at the Farnham campus bring the number of bed spaces to 1,190 and the university makes an accommodation guarantee to all first-years.

Tuition fees

»	Fees for UK students	£9,250
	Foundation courses	£5,420
»	Fees for International students 2023–24	£16,950
	Foundation courses	£15,540–£16,950
»	For scholarship and bursary information see www.uca.ac.uk/study-at-uca/fees-finance/	
»	Graduate salary	£20,000

Student numbers

Undergraduates	5,491	(1,732)
Postgraduates	997	(202)
Applications/places		5,195/1,115
Applications per place		4.7:1
Overall offer rate		92.4%
International students – EU		5.9%
Non-EU		11.5%

Accommodation

University provided places: 1,190
Self-catered: £125–£187 per week
First-years guaranteed accommodation
www.uca.ac.uk/study-at-uca/accommodation/

Where do the students come from?

State schools (non-grammar)	92.9%	First generation students	48%	White working-class males	5.1%
Grammar schools	3.4%	Low participation areas	12.4%	Black achievement gap	-12.4%
Independent schools	3.7%	All ethnic minorities	25.3%	Mature (over 21)	38.4%

Social inclusion ranking: 32

University of Cumbria

Cumbria is expanding its foothold in Barrow-in-Furness, where operations have until now focused on delivering nursing and health practitioner courses in partnership with Furness College. The planned Barrow Learning Quarter – a collaboration with partners including BAE Systems, Lancaster University and Barrow borough council – will establish a Cumbria campus in its own right.

Adjacent to the BAE Systems Submarine Academy for Skills and Knowledge, the new campus is due to welcome its first students in 2024. The Barrow site will house Cumbria's Institute for Engineering, Computing and Advanced Manufacturing, with degrees including project management, digital and cybersecurity, advanced manufacturing, and supply chain and logistics. Creating a full university presence in Barrow, home to one of the few shipyards in the world capable of designing and building nuclear submarines, is expected to attract and retain high-skilled graduates pursuing careers in the new campus's specialised fields.

The institution has seven campuses, reaching from Ambleside, on Lake Windermere in the Lake District National Park – which offers the UK's biggest programme of outdoor education courses plus conservation and forestry degrees – to its newest campus in Canary Wharf, east London, its base for health, education and business courses.

The main campus in Lancaster is set in parkland a short walk from the city centre and caters for courses in education, health, sport and business. The £9million Sentamu teaching and learning building has a 200-seat lecture theatre and the restaurant has panoramic views towards Morecambe Bay. The library has bookable study rooms, individual booths and laptops for loan. Teaching facilities include sport performance labs, ambulance simulators and teacher training rooms.

The Workington campus provides graduate courses in decommissioning, reprocessing and managing nuclear waste and has specialist facilities. The university is a partner in the National College for Nuclear and the Project Academy for Sellafield.

The Fusehill campus in Carlisle is in a former First World War military hospital and offers courses in health, science, conservation, education, business, law and policing. A second site in Carlisle, close to Hadrian's Wall, is home to the university's Institute of Arts.

Applications increased by about 13% in 2021's admissions round, after six consecutive years of decreasing demand for places at Cumbria. Enrolments also rose in 2021, by 7%, to reach their highest level in five years.

Eight new degree options launched in the 2022-23 – including psychology with counselling and psychotherapy, outdoor education

Head Office
Fusehill Street
Carlisle CA1 2HH
01228 242 932
ugadmissions@cumbria.ac.uk
www.ucsu.me
www.cumbria.ac.uk
Open days: see website

The Times and The Sunday Times Rankings
Overall Ranking: 129 (last year: 125)

Teaching quality	72.7%	=99
Student experience	67.5%	111
Research quality	13.6%	124
Entry standards	121	=77
Graduate prospects	68.2%	=98
Good honours	66.6%	127
Expected completion rate	82.8%	88
Student/staff ratio	18.7	105

(accelerated degree), and graphic design with a work placement. Four more options join the curriculum from September 2023: animation and visual effects, commercial photography, education studies with placement (accelerated degree), and youth work in the digital age.

Cumbria was one of a small number of universities rated bronze in the Teaching Excellence Framework in 2017. It was marked down for a low graduate employment rate in high-skilled jobs, but the university pointed out that such roles are in short supply in the northwest compared with the national average. The Barrow campus should in time contribute to improved employability in the region.

The university ranked in the middle reaches of our graduate prospects measure in 2021 but has fallen 25 places to =98 in our latest analysis of the numbers in highly skilled work or undertaking further study 15 months after graduation. Cumbria's portfolio of degree apprenticeships has grown to 14, with about 1,700 trainees on courses in health, business and industry. It delivers degree apprenticeships and a supply chain academy for BAE Systems, and project management programmes for Sellafield. Other partners include Defra, the NHS, the BBC and Rolls-Royce.

The university has maintained its 124th place in our research rankings. Work submitted on history of art, art and design, and geography produced the best results.

In our measures of student satisfaction —

derived from the National Student Survey – Cumbria has fallen 15 places to =99 for teaching quality and 111th for the wider undergraduate experience.

Cumbria is in the top 50 according to our analysis of measures of social inclusion (47th). About one in five admissions in 2021 met one or more of the eligibility criteria to be made a contextual offer – at the lower end of the UCAS tariff range for the course. As Cumbria broadens its contextual data to include carers, estranged students and those who qualify for free school meals, it expects 25% to 30% of offers to qualify for lower entry requirements in September 2023.

Sports facilities are available at the Lancaster, Carlisle and Ambleside campuses – ranging from a fitness suite, sports hall and swimming pool in Lancaster to a large sports hall and fitness facilities in Carlisle and a gym with classes and small group training in Ambleside.

Accommodation is guaranteed to first-years within Cumbria's stock of about 500 bed spaces – some housed within attractive stone cottages at the Ambleside campus.

Tuition fees

»	Fees for UK students	£9,250
	Foundation courses	£6,125
»	Fees for International students 2023–24	£13,250–£16,000
	Foundation courses	£12,800–£13,250
»	For scholarship and bursary information see	
	www.cumbria.ac.uk/study/student-finance	
»	Graduate salary	£24,500

Student numbers

Undergraduates	4,777 (2,161)
Postgraduates	960 (1,383)
Applications/places	4,790/1,565
Applications per place	3.1:1
Overall offer rate	74.5%
International students – EU	1.6%
Non-EU	1.3%

Accommodation

University provided places: 500
Self-catered: £80–£120 per week
www.cumbria.ac.uk/student-life/accommodation/

Where do the students come from?

State schools (non-grammar)	95.3%	First generation students	55.2%	White working-class males	4.1%
Grammar schools	2.3%	Low participation areas	16.3%	Black achievement gap	-17.6%
Independent schools	2.4%	All ethnic minorities	12.7%	Mature (over 21)	64.9%

Social inclusion ranking: 47

De Montfort University

A campus university – unusually located in a city centre – De Montfort has invested £136million in teaching and learning spaces to inspire students. Its flagship Vijay Patel Building – named after the leading pharmacist and donor, a graduate – brings together art and design courses and includes the Gallery, the city's largest display space. There are printmaking, casting and photographic facilities and workshops for glass, ceramics and rapid prototyping.

The development echoes the history of DMU, which opened in 1870 as an art school to provide education and training for workers from Leicester's booming industries.

Another recent improvement is the Yard – a £5.5million four-storey extension to the learning space for the Faculty of Business and Law. The wing adds to the same faculty's teaching space in the regenerated Great Hall of Leicester Castle Business School.

The pandemic spurred a large-scale overhaul of audiovisual equipment, enabling DMU to transform almost all of its classrooms and laboratories to be hybrid learning spaces. In another development, students from September 2022 are the first to experience DMU's Education 2030 programme, which introduces flexible block learning. Modules will be delivered in 30-credit blocks running one after the other, allowing students to study and be assessed on one subject at a time. The system has been shown to improve outcomes for widening participation students in particular, DMU has found.

The review of teaching and learning patterns may help DMU improve its rates of student satisfaction, as expressed in the National Student Survey (NSS). These have tumbled in recent years and contribute to the university dropping down our league table – having ranked as high as 53rd seven years ago. In our analysis of the latest NSS results, DMU has improved to 115th for satisfaction with teaching quality and 110th for the wider undergraduate experience.

DMU scored better in the government's Teaching Excellence Framework (TEF), where it holds a gold rating. The TEF panel commended "optimum" levels of contact time between students and staff and "outstanding" support for learning.

In the latest Research Excellence Framework (REF 2021), more than 60% of De Montfort's research was judged as world-leading or internationally excellent (the top two categories). The university entered the largest number of academics yet and featured more research carried out by women and ethnic minority academics than it has before. Land and property management produced the best results, followed by building, and town and country planning.

However, DMU has fallen 29 places in our

The Gateway
Leicester LE1 9BH
0116 270 8443
enquiry@dmu.ac.uk
www.demontfortsu.com
www.dmu.ac.uk
Open days:
see website

The Times and The Sunday Times **Rankings**		
Overall Ranking: =122 (last year: 126)		
Teaching quality	70.8%	115
Student experience	67.6%	110
Research quality	27.4%	96
Entry standards	106	=126
Graduate prospects	69.3%	89
Good honours	73.7%	95
Expected completion rate	81.6%	94
Student/staff ratio	18.5	103

research rankings to 96th place against greater improvements across the sector. Good performance in research used to be one of DMU's strongest contributors to its overall academic ranking.

All DMU students are guaranteed work experience and participating organisations include Disney, Asos, HSBC, KPMG, L'Oréal, Microsoft and the NHS. Some courses offer the chance to take part in industry showcases, such as engineering's Formula Student competition at Silverstone motor racing circuit and Graduate Fashion Week.

Graduate outcomes have improved slightly, year-on-year. DMU now ranks 89th on our measure for graduate prospects.

More than half of students are from black, Asian and ethnic minority backgrounds at DMU, which won our first University of the Year for Social Inclusion award for 2019. The university remains in the top 40 overall (35th) in our social inclusion ranking for the fifth successive year.

Higher and degree apprenticeships are a growing area for DMU, which offers 13 programmes – up from 11 in 2021 – and has another six in development. Nursing, operations department managing, hearing aid dispensing, police constable, and cybersecurity technical professional are among the options already available, while chartered surveying, creative digital design professional, and data scientist will be new

additions to the portfolio for those considering a degree apprenticeship.

Applications fell by about 8% in 2021, although new student numbers rose somewhat. Nine degrees have been introduced, such as music production, business economics, and photography. From 2023-24 another two begin: accounting and finance, and accounting with business management.

Buses are provided to Beaumont Park, DMU's outdoor sports facilities which have had a £3.4million upgrade. Your DMU, the university's pre-induction programme, contains guidance on initiatives such as *No Space for Hate* and the Mandala Project, which provides help for students who have experienced sexual violence, domestic abuse and sexual harassment. The university advises students to view the content before they start at university.

Students like Leicester's size – not too big, not too small – and affordable private-sector rents. In previous years all those who wanted to live in were able to claim a place if they met application deadlines.

Tuition fees

» Fees for UK students	£9,250
Foundation courses	£6,165
» Fees for International students 2023–24	£14,750–£16,336
» For scholarship and bursary information see	
www.dmu.ac.uk/study/fees-and-funding/index.aspx	
» Graduate salary	£23,000

Student numbers

Undergraduates	20,881	(1,386)
Postgraduates	3,015	(2,252)
Applications/places	21,600/5,925	
Applications per place	3.6:1	
Overall offer rate	89.5%	
International students – EU	8.4%	
Non-EU	10.2%	

Accommodation
University provided places: 4,100
Self-catered: £99–£186 per week
www.dmu.ac.uk/study/accommodation/index.aspx

Where do the students come from?

State schools (non-grammar)	96%	First generation students	49.8%	White working-class males	4.3%
Grammar schools	2.1%	Low participation areas	16.1%	Black achievement gap	-25.8%
Independent schools	1.9%	All ethnic minorities	53.4%	Mature (over 21)	19.3%

Social inclusion ranking: 35

University of Derby

Derby has joined forces with local employers and higher education providers on a £13million plan to create the East Midlands Institute of Technology (IoT). Its focus will be on the engineering, manufacturing and digital skills required by employers to drive eco-friendly business growth and a data-driven economy.

The IoT – set up in partnership with Loughborough University, Loughborough College and the Derby College Group – will be based in Loughborough with linked sites across the region. It is one of 21 institutes being created across the country under the government's levelling-up agenda, offering more high-quality, flexible education and training and supporting more people into higher-skilled, better-paid jobs.

A new business school is scheduled for completion in 2024, built to net zero carbon standards and set to become the study base for 6,000 students by 2030.

Kedleston Road is the biggest of Derby's three sites in the city. It hosts most teaching subjects as well as the students' union, a multifaith centre and the main sports facilities. The Markeaton Street site is the base for arts, design, engineering and technology courses, while courses including fine art and social care are based at Britannia Mill.

Nursing has a school of its own in the market town of Chesterfield. Engineering and IT are also taught in Chesterfield. In the spa town of Buxton, the university's Devonshire Dome, formerly the Devonshire Royal Hospital, hosts courses including hospitality management.

Derby got a gold rating in the government's Teaching Excellence Framework (TEF), winning praise for its personalised learning and support. The university's teaching scores well with its own students, too: Derby is 16th for student satisfaction with teaching quality in our analysis of the results of the latest National Student Survey. The top-20 ranking represents a rise of five places year-on-year. For satisfaction with the wider undergraduate experience, Derby ranks 36th, climbing three places since 2021.

Students benefit from hands-on learning in "real world" simulation environments. Facilities include a crime scene house for forensic science students, a replica crown court, a Bloomberg financial markets lab and an NHS-standard hospital ward. Hospitality courses use industry-standard kitchens and a fine dining restaurant. The Devonshire spa is an award-winning commercial day spa that doubles as a classroom for spa management students.

A 6% year-on-year dip in applications in 2021 brought them to their lowest level in nine years. Enrolments decreased twice as steeply. Numbers joining the university have fluctuated between 3,130 and 4,070 in the past decade.

Links with local industry help to prepare students for the workplace, with internships available at Microsoft, IBM, Porsche, Bentley,

Kedleston Road
Derby DE22 1GB
01332 590 500
admissions@derby.ac.uk
www.derby.ac.uk
www.derbyunion.co.uk
Open days:
see website

The Times and The Sunday Times **Rankings**
Overall Ranking: 96 (last year: =94)

Teaching quality	78.8%	16
Student experience	74%	36
Research quality	21%	=111
Entry standards	118	=89
Graduate prospects	68.9%	93
Good honours	68.4%	122
Expected completion rate	80.1%	=99
Student/staff ratio	15.8	=54

Rolls-Royce and the locally-based Toyota, among others. However, Derby has fallen seven places to 93rd in our analysis of graduate prospects.

A new "omics" laboratory – covering a range of biological sciences – has been created to extend the university's cutting-edge research. In an example of the collaborative work that the university nurtures with a range of regional partners, students at a Derby laboratory joined a drive to develop a 10-minute Covid-19 test that is now used worldwide.

Education and geology produced some of the best results for Derby in the latest Research Excellence Framework (REF 2021) and have contributed to a six-place rise to =111 in our research quality index. More than two-thirds of the university's submission in earth systems and environmental sciences was assessed as world-leading or internationally excellent, the top two categories. The equivalent figure for education research was 63%, and for allied health subjects and art and design it was 60%.

Derby is in the top 20 according to our analysis of measures of social inclusion overall (19th). More than half (53.7%) of new students are the first in their family to go to university.

Derby bursaries of up to £1,000 are awarded according to a sliding scale of household income and paid as £100 e-cards for study resources plus up to £900 cash. Students who achieve or exceed their course's published UCAS tariff point requirements qualify for £1,000 academic achievement scholarships. There are also scholarships for international students and sports scholarships for student athletes competing from high county level up to senior internationals.

The sports centre at Kedleston Road has a HiPAC (high-performance analysis centre).

Students who are experiencing problems with their mental health can book appointments with a mental health practitioner or adjust their study schedule. Those with a long-term physical or mental health condition are offered support meetings with a specialist mentor.

Derby's halls of residence earned shortlisting in six categories in the National Student Housing Awards 2021, including Best Student Halls, Best Student Wellbeing and Best Value for Money, and won the Best Environmental Management award. First-years who apply by the end of July are guaranteed a place in the university's stock of 1,962 bed spaces.

Located in the heart of England, Derby makes a legitimate case for being within easy reach of Manchester, London and Birmingham. The breath-taking scenery of the Peak District is on its doorstep.

Tuition fees

» Fees for UK students £9,250
» Fees for International students 2023–24 £14,045–£14,700
» For scholarship and bursary information see www.derby.ac.uk/undergraduate/fees-and-finance/
» Graduate salary £23,813

Student numbers

Undergraduates	12,316	(3,865)
Postgraduates	1,948	(3,158)
Applications/places		16,395/3,130
Applications per place		5.2:1
Overall offer rate		81.9%
International students – EU		4.7%
Non-EU		5%

Accommodation

University provided places: 1,962
Self-catered: £115–£164 per week
First-years guaranteed accommodation
www.derby.ac.uk/life/accommodation

Where do the students come from?

State schools (non-grammar)	96.1%	First generation students	53.7%	White working-class males	6.3%
Grammar schools	2.2%	Low participation areas	24.7%	Black achievement gap	-26.7%
Independent schools	1.8%	All ethnic minorities	27.1%	Mature (over 21)	38.7%

Social inclusion ranking: 19

University of Dundee

The outbreak of war in Ukraine prompted Dundee to establish a Ukraine Crisis Fund to support 26 incoming Ukrainian students with their tuition fees and living costs. Dundee has experience in this area, having supported scholars from around the world via its Humanitarian Fund, which has helped Afghan scholars to continue their studies in the UK after the Taliban takeover. The university has also introduced an Oversight Board to help students and staff fleeing war and other crises who often face a time lag between escaping conflict and settling in a new country before being ready to recommence their studies.

The global outlook at Dundee, which is in the midst of increasing demand from international students, extends to its new joint education institute in China with the Central South University. The Dundee International Institute of Central South University expects 300 students per year to enrol on courses in maths, computer science, civil engineering and mechanical engineering with transportation. At the Dundee campus, a China support hub launched in early 2022.

Dundee's self-contained city campus has benefited from about £200million of redevelopment investment. The £50million Discovery Centre encourages interaction between disciplines. Away from the city centre, the medical school is on a 20-acre site, while nursing and midwifery students are 35 miles away in Kirkcaldy. The highly rated design courses are taught at the Duncan of Jordanstone College of Art and Design, one of the university's 10 schools. Dundee also offers a joint degree with the National Union of Singapore.

The prospects have improved for graduates of Dundee – up eight places to =26 in our analysis of the Graduate Outcomes survey, which tracks how many students find highly skilled work or begin postgraduate study 15 months after the end of their degree course.

Three years ago, Dundee won our University of the Year for Student Experience award, but satisfaction ratings took a significant hit in the pandemic-affected National Student Survey last year. They have fallen further still, by 36 places for student satisfaction with the wider undergraduate experience (=85) and by 15 places for teaching quality (=77). On-campus activity has resumed, with no restrictions on class sizes, although the prevalent teaching model will vary between subjects.

Dundee was one of three Scottish universities to earn a gold rating from the Teaching Excellence Framework (TEF) panel. Assessors commended the opportunities students are given to develop work-ready skills and knowledge, and said Dundee's courses encourage ideal levels of stretch and

Nethergate
Dundee DD1 4HN
01382 383 838
contactus@dundee.ac.uk
www.dusa.co.uk
www.dundee.ac.uk
Open days:
see website

The Times and The Sunday Times Rankings
Overall Ranking: 32 (last year: =35)

Teaching quality	74.5%	=77
Student experience	70.1%	=85
Research quality	51.1%	=39
Entry standards	178	=11
Graduate prospects	82%	=26
Good honours	79.7%	=52
Expected completion rate	89.4%	46
Student/staff ratio	14.9	=36

student engagement. Students from all backgrounds achieve outstanding outcomes at Dundee, the TEF report found.

In the latest Research Excellence Framework (REF 2021) Dundee did well in biological sciences, a strength which attracts students to the university from all over the world, and rising to =39 overall in our research quality index.

Building on its reputation in this area, the university is creating a Life Sciences Innovation District in Dundee, which will support the creation of new businesses. The hope is that they will mirror the success of Exscientia, a spin-out company from the university that has grown into a significant pharmaceutical success in the UK.

For those taking humanities, social sciences and law degrees the university has integrated three former schools (education and social work, humanities and social sciences) into a single School of Humanities, Social Sciences and Law. The union has been designed to foster a modern, dynamic school that builds on its constituents' strengths.

Dundee's programmes to attract applications from students from underrepresented backgrounds make it sixth in Scotland for social inclusion, according to our analysis. It has whittled down its black achievement gap to the second-smallest in Scotland.

Dundee offers one of the most generous financial support packages among UK universities. While Scottish students do not pay tuition fees at universities north of the border, and qualify for the Scottish government's funding package, the university helps others with uncapped numbers of awards based on academic merit and/or financial need. In the 2021-22 academic year, 74% of international students had an award of some sort while about 80% to 85% of Rest of the UK students tend to receive one.

Sports facilities on campus and at the Riverside sports ground on the banks of the River Tay are excellent and the university is a partner in Eden Project Dundee, an attraction being built on the former gasworks on East Street overlooking the Tay.

Scottish students who apply before June 30 are guaranteed student accommodation, and the application deadline is extended to August 25 for those with further to travel from the rest of the UK or abroad. The main campus is just two minutes' from the centre of student-friendly Dundee, where one in every seven people in the population is in higher education.

Tuition fees

» Fees for Scottish students	£0–£1,820
RUK fees	£9,250
» Fees for International students 2023–24	£18,495–£24,495
Medicine £50,100; Dentistry £38,150 for Level 1	
» For scholarship and bursary information see	
https://www.dundee.ac.uk/collections/tuition-fees	
» Graduate salary	£25,000

Student numbers

Undergraduates	10,487 (1,066)
Postgraduates	2,506 (2,170)
Applications/places	19,905/2,865
Applications per place	6.9:1
Overall offer rate	53.9%
International students – EU	7.3%
Non-EU	6.8%

Accommodation

University provided places: 1,924
Self-catered: £132–£174 per week
First-years guaranteed accommodation
www.dundee.ac.uk/accommodation

Where do the students come from?

State schools (non-grammar)	84.7%	First generation students	41.4%		
Grammar schools	4.9%	Low participation areas	16.4%		
Independent schools	10.3%	All ethnic minorities	12.2%		

Social inclusion ranking (Scotland): 6

White working-class males	n/a
Black achievement gap	-7%
Mature (over 21)	31.2%

Durham University

Durham's collegiate structure leads to intense sporting rivalry and participation rates are high. Durham is our Sports University of the Year, a title it last held in 2015. The university is second overall in the BUCS (British University and Colleges Sport) league for the 2021-22 season and is No 1 for producing the most professional sports stars with 141, compared with its nearest rival Oxford, with 86. It has invested £32million in its Sports and Wellbeing Park and offers sports scholarships.

Extracurricular life at Durham has gone up a gear via Game Changer – a programme that pits real-world problems to students, who work in teams to solve them. Each challenge is linked to at least one of the United Nations' Sustainable Development Goals (SDG) and teams use "design thinking" (the creative problem-solving methodology) to come up with innovative solutions. Students pitch their ideas to win a share of a cash prize. The programme caught the eye of the UN, which has included Game Changer in its SDG Best Practices, a compilation of successful SDG implementations.

The scheme is one of a range of employability initiatives at Durham, whose graduates are among the most sought-after.

The university fares well in our graduate prospects measure, rising three places year-on-year to rank seventh.

Durham's purpose-built space for entrepreneurship – the Hazan Venture Lab – provides facilities for students or graduates working on new ventures or enterprise projects. Experienced entrepreneurs and sector professionals help to deliver its start-up programmes, and the number of students working on business ideas with the potential to scale is growing, the university notes.

Based around the cobbled cathedral city of Durham, the university is England's third-oldest and has a collegiate structure similar to Oxford and Cambridge. Unlike Oxbridge, however, teaching takes place centrally rather than within the colleges – although these provide an important social hub, each with its own characteristics. University College (Castle) and Collingwood remain the most popular options. The former is part of the Cathedral and Castle Unesco World Heritage Site at the heart of the historic peninsula ringed by the River Wear; the latter is at the heart of the hill colleges to the south of the city centre and close to the science site and the main university library.

Durham is in demand. Application numbers first exceeded 30,000 in the 2019 admissions cycle and have not looked back. New student enrolments increased by about 8% in the 2021 admissions round, year-on-year, to their highest yet.

The Palatine Centre
Stockton Road
Durham DH1 3LE
0191 334 1000
www.durham.ac.uk/study/askus
www.durhamsu.com
www.dur.ac.uk
Open days:
see website

The Times and The Sunday Times **Rankings**
Overall Ranking: 6 (last year: 6)

Teaching quality	74.9%	=71
Student experience	70.8%	=77
Research quality	55.9%	23
Entry standards	183	9
Graduate prospects	87.3%	7
Good honours	92.6%	=4
Expected completion rate	97.2%	4
Student/staff ratio	13.7	=12

Durham was one of the winners in our analysis of the impact of the Covid pandemic on Britain's campuses in 2021, with improvements in student satisfaction with teaching quality and the wider undergraduate experience. However, the university has lost ground on both measures, according to outcomes from the latest National Student Survey, published in summer 2022. It sits =71 (down 28 places) for student satisfaction with teaching quality and =77 (down 21 places) for the wider undergraduate experience.

Durham has introduced a range of initiatives designed to widen participation. The university teamed up with a local sixth-form centre to establish the newly opened Durham Mathematics School, following the model of similar schools with input from King's College London and the University of Exeter. It is hoped that the school will provide a stream of students into Durham's maths, science and engineering departments.

Increased recruitment from within the northeast – the English region with the lowest participation rates in higher education – should help to diversify the student population, which is among the least inclusive in England and Wales. The university stands eight places off the bottom in our latest social inclusion index. Durham is one of three universities where less than half the student intake is drawn from non-selective state schools.

Contextual offers are part of Durham's determination to change the student profile.

Last year, 19% of applicants were made a contextual offer of at least one A-level grade below the standard offer for a given course.

A member of the research-led Russell Group of universities, Durham's top 100 global university status remains secure in the 2023 QS world rankings. In our domestic research quality index, which is based on results of the latest Research Excellence Framework (REF 2021), Durham is 23rd. The best results in REF 2021 were in education and geography, archaeology and forensic science. Classics and ancient history, theology, and sports science also did well.

All new students must take a one-hour online course called *Consent Matters: Boundaries, Respect and Positive Intervention*. Colleges can offer accommodation for all first-years, with almost 7,500 places available.

Despite the small size of the city, there is no shortage of private landlords and private university accommodation blocks for those who "live out" in their second and third years.

Tuition fees

» Fees for UK students	£9,250
» Fees for International students 2023–24	£22,500–£28,500
» For scholarship and bursary information see www.durham.ac.uk/study/undergraduate/ fees-and-funding/tuition-fees	
» Graduate salary	£28,000

Student numbers

Undergraduates	16,082	(31)
Postgraduates	3,584	(948)
Applications/places	32,570/6,160	
Applications per place	5.3:1	
Overall offer rate	71%	
International students – EU	3.6%	
Non-EU	19.9%	

Accommodation

University provided places: 7,472
Catered costs: £232–£245 per week
Self-catered: £149–£187 per week
First years guaranteed accommodation
www.dur.ac.uk/colleges-and-student-experience/ accommodation-and-catering/costs/

Where do the students come from?

State schools (non-grammar)	49.1%	First generation students	23.4%	White working-class males	3.3%
Grammar schools	12.4%	Low participation areas	7.6%	Black achievement gap	-7.3%
Independent schools	38.4%	All ethnic minorities	13.7%	Mature (over 21)	3.1%

Social inclusion ranking: 109

University of East Anglia

The University of East Anglia (UEA) climbs 15 places in our research quality index to arrive in the top 20 (17th). Excellent results in a broad range of subjects saw 91% of the university's submission classified as world-leading or internationally excellent, the top two categories. The best results included research in agriculture, food and veterinary sciences, development studies; anthropology, history, earth systems and environmental sciences, and social policy and social work.

UEA's success builds on a strong history as a research-led institution and appears to support the university's statement that "not all great universities are in the Russell Group".

After graduation, the prospects are good for UEA students. In our analysis of the latest Graduate Outcomes survey, tracking the proportion in highly skilled work or further study within 15 months of finishing their degree, UEA is 24th, a rise of 15 places.

UEA, founded in 1963, occupies a 360-acre self-contained campus just outside Norwich. Modern teaching facilities are among further contemporary resources that blend with listed buildings from UEA's 1960s origins, including the iconic Denys Lasdun-designed Ziggurat accommodation blocks.

UEA has become the first university to offer 360-degree virtual reality headsets to all medical students, who benefit from resources at the university's £19million Biomedical Research Centre. When awarding UEA gold (the top rating), assessors from the government's Teaching Excellence Framework noted that investment in high-quality physical and digital resources has had a "demonstrable impact on the learning experience".

Focusing on the wider student experience, UEA's Student Information Zone is a new base in the heart of the campus, while a 24/7 online student wellbeing service is also offered. Weekly pulse surveys have been introduced, to capture how students are feeling on a range of topics. The university is likely to hope the student-facing services will improve rates of student satisfaction. In our analysis of the latest National Student Survey results, East Anglia plunges 52 places year-on-year to =97 for the wider undergraduate experience, and falls 27 places to =99 for teaching quality.

From September 2023, the curriculum gains a suite of six education degrees as well as Bachelor of Science in mathematics with statistics. Placement years have been added to established degrees in philosophy; modern history; English literature; and history of art with gallery and museum studies. New student enrolments dipped by about 12% in the 2021 admissions round but remain more than 15% higher than they were a decade ago.

Most degrees have opportunities for work experience and UEA has embraced degree

Norwich Research Park
Norwich NR4 7TJ
01603 591 515
admissions@uea.ac.uk
www.uea.ac.uk
www.uea.su
Open days:
see website

The Times and The Sunday Times **Rankings**
Overall Ranking: 27 (last year: 27)

Teaching quality	72.7%	=99
Student experience	69.2%	=97
Research quality	58%	17
Entry standards	134	=50
Graduate prospects	82.4%	24
Good honours	86.7%	19
Expected completion rate	89.7%	=44
Student/staff ratio	14.2	=26

apprenticeships. There are about 700 student apprentices on eight programmes – soon to grow to 10, with the addition of social worker and psychological wellbeing practitioner options.

Environmental science is one of UEA's flagship subject areas. The Climatic Research Unit and the Tyndall Centre for Climate Change Research based on the Norwich Research Park and the £75million Quadram Institute on the same site has the remit of improving health and preventing disease through innovations in microbiology, gut health and food.

On the main campus the Sainsbury Centre for the Visual Arts houses a priceless collection of modern and tribal art in a building designed by Lord (Norman) Foster of Thames Bank. More recently the crime author Lee Child donated his archive of work to UEA.

UK students do not need to formally apply for university bursaries because all are automatically considered using household income information from Student Finance England. In 2021-22 East Anglia awarded 23% of home students a bursary or scholarship, a proportion likely to remain similar going forwards.

UEA works with schools in outreach projects across disadvantaged areas in Norfolk and North Suffolk. In 2021, 5% of admissions received contextual offers, a proportion the university hopes to increase in future years. Medicine with a Gateway Year is a programme aimed at widening access to UEA's medical school. UEA gains one place in our social inclusion index to rank 83rd.

UEA's Sportspark and Colney Lane Sports Pavilion facilities include an Olympic-sized swimming pool. Students can get fit off-site with provision for sailing, scuba, rowing and golf. Sports scholarship packages are offered to student athletes from developing to elite level. There are also more than 250 societies.

UEA has signed the Students' Minds new University Mental Health Charter Programme. Accommodation is guaranteed to first-years who apply by the end of July and prices start at £86.38 a week for a space in a standard twin Ziggurat room. UEA's bucolic setting has earned Green Flag status for five years running. Named as the best place to live in the East of England by The Sunday Times in 2022, Norwich is a student-friendly city. Beaches, the Broads and rural idylls are within easy reach.

Tuition fees

»	Fees for UK students	£9,250
»	Fees for International students 2023–24	£19,250–£24,400
	Medicine (Norwich Medical School)	£39,550
»	For scholarship and bursary information see	
	www.uea.ac.uk/study/fees-and-funding/	
»	Graduate salary	£24,700

Student numbers

Undergraduates	13,426	(615)
Postgraduates	3,284	(1,652)
Applications/places		19,215/4,050
Applications per place		4.7:1
Overall offer rate		77.7%
International students – EU		3.5%
Non-EU		9.2%

Accommodation

University provided places: 4,327
Self-catered: £86–£178 per week
First-years guaranteed accommodation
www.uea.ac.uk/uea-life/accommodation

Where do the students come from?

State schools (non-grammar)	83.2%	First generation students	39.6%	White working-class males	6.3%
Grammar schools	8.8%	Low participation areas	12.8%	Black achievement gap	-13.8%
Independent schools	8%	All ethnic minorities	23%	Mature (over 21)	14.2%

Social inclusion ranking: 83

University of East London

More than £20million is being invested through the University of East London's (UEL) Connected Campus programme to improve its three sites.

"Campus Hearts" hubs at Docklands, Stratford and University Square provide welcoming focal points for learning and socialising. The second of three strands to the development programme enhances UEL's visual identity with new signage and the liberal application of its phoenix logo in murals. The third creates fresh destinations where students can meet and relax, including Pump House, a new vegan café/bar and student-led venue.

Investment has also gone into teaching and learning facilities, including practical resources such as a mock courtroom, a trading floor and a hospital and primary care training hub.

When the Docklands base was completed in 1999 as London's first new campus for 50 years, its striking architecture was described as "poetry" and design plaudits followed. Free buses connect the waterside buildings with headquarters in Stratford, where UEL has taken over the University Square Stratford development, built in partnership with Birkbeck, University of London add facilities for the Royal Docks School of Business and Law.

UEL became a university in 1992 but traces its history back to the establishment of the West Ham Technical Institute 100 years earlier. The forging of industry links is a point of pride for the university, which counts Amazon Web Services, Asos, Siemens and Ford among the organisations it works with. Initiatives to equip graduates for today's world of work include the flagship Professional Fitness and Mental Wealth programme, which puts soft skills such as critical thinking and practical skills such as digital proficiency into every course. Achievements are recorded in a digital career passport and count towards final results.

UEL's career focus has yet to translate into buoyant results in the Graduate Outcomes survey, where UEL ranks 121st. Low graduate employment rates were the main stumbling block in its failed appeal to be upgraded from bronze to silver in the Teaching Excellence Framework. UEL remains one of only a few universities in our table with a bronze rating.

UEL has introduced the hybrid teaching model Dual Delivery 2.0 to continue using remote learning, ensuring that face-to-face opportunities allow opportunities to collaborate with peers.

Having fared better than most universities in the pandemic-hit National Student Survey (NSS) in 2021, rates of student satisfaction have dwindled, however. In our analysis of the outcomes of the latest NSS, published in summer 2022, UEL has slipped 21 places for student satisfaction with teaching quality (=89) and 24 for the wider experience (=92).

Docklands Campus
University Way
London E16 2RD
020 8223 3333
study@uel.ac.uk
www.uelunion.org
www.uel.ac.uk
Open days:
see website

The Times and The Sunday Times Rankings
Overall Ranking: 131 (last year: 130)

Teaching quality	73.6%	=89
Student experience	69.6%	=92
Research quality	22.8%	105
Entry standards	101	130
Graduate prospects	64.3%	121
Good honours	72.1%	=109
Expected completion rate	77.3%	117
Student/staff ratio	26.2	130

As an agent of social mobility, the university achieves much more success, in 12th place in our social inclusion index. Two-thirds of undergraduates are from ethnic minority populations and more than 56.7% are the first in their family to go to university. The proportion of mature students (57.1%) is in 14th place. UEL's projected dropout rate, although relatively high at 11.8%, is well below the expected level of 13.8% based on its student and subject profile.

Many students choose to start their course in January rather than the autumn. The university's pre-entry programmes offer those aged 19 and above who have no formal qualifications the opportunity to convert their skills into academic competencies during a 10-week course, accepted as an entry qualification.

Applications rose by about 17% in the 2021 recruitment cycle – bringing the demand for places to its highest in eight years. A snapshot of the present admissions cycle at the end of March 2022 showed an even bigger increase of more than 34% compared with the same point in the cycle the year before. The university puts the rise down to easing Covid travel restrictions for international students and targeted recruitment strategies. Enrolments have yet to experience such a turnaround, however, instead decreasing a little for the second year running in 2021 to a level about 31% lower than a decade before. More than a third of entrants in 2021 gained their place at East London via Clearing.

New courses include airline and airport management, social media, game programming, and football business. Twenty-four degree apprenticeships are offered, in fields including nursing, teaching and digital technology.

In the latest Research Excellence Framework (REF 2021), computer science, allied health, and social work and social policy delivered UEL's best results. Although research performance improved markedly, so did many other universities: UEL falls outside the top 100 in our research rankings, slipping from 76th in 2021 to 105th.

The university's prestigious sports scholarship is worth up to £6,000. SportsDock, the multimillion-pound facility on the Docklands campus, has upgraded its equipment.

Campus social life centres around the Docklands student village, while students have some of London's hippest enclaves on their east London doorstep. Unusually for a London university, UEL has two halls of residence on campus, in standout waterside buildings. First-years who want to live in are guaranteed a room.

Tuition fees

- » Fees for UK students   £9,250
- » Fees for International students 2023–24   £13,740–£16,200
- » For scholarship and bursary information see www.uel.ac.uk/undergraduate/fees-and-funding
- » Graduate salary   £24,000

Student numbers

Undergraduates	10,196	(583)
Postgraduates	5,169	(1,445)
Applications/places		18,135/3,800
Applications per place		4.8:1
Overall offer rate		74.3%
International students – EU		3.6%
Non-EU		8.8%

Accommodation

University provided places: 1,169
Self-catered: £148–£198 per week
First-years guaranteed accommodation
www.uel.ac.uk/study/accommodation

Where do the students come from?

State schools (non-grammar)	96.9%	First generation students	56.7%	White working-class males	3%
Grammar schools	0.6%	Low participation areas	6.4%	Black achievement gap	-15.9%
Independent schools	2.6%	All ethnic minorities	66.1%	Mature (over 21)	57.1%

Social inclusion ranking: 12

Edge Hill University

Edge Hill gained university status in 2005 and has since forged a successful path as one of the country's leading post-1992 universities. Investment of £300million at the 160-acre campus near Ormskirk has transformed this former teacher training college.

Following the addition of a medical school, Edge Hill is continuing to focus on STEM (science, technology, engineering and mathematics) subjects, recently adding more computer science courses to the curriculum. New engineering degrees are scheduled for 2023. Graduate prospects have held up, improving six places to 78th in our analysis of the numbers in highly skilled work or postgraduate study 15 months after finishing a degree.

A year on from winning our Modern University of the Year title in 2021, Edge Hill has toppled 20 places to rank 78th overall, after declining performance over a range of measures. Faith in teaching quality has faded: our analysis of the latest National Student Survey shows a fall of 20 places to =84, although the university is rated gold in the government's Teaching Excellence Framework. The panel noted that "students from diverse backgrounds achieve consistently outstanding outcomes".

The return of face-to-face teaching in 2022 may lift the mood on campus. In our research quality index, Edge Hill has also recorded a 20-place fall year-on-year. Results of the latest Research Excellence Framework (REF 2021) showed that 62% of the work submitted achieved the top two ratings: world-leading or internationally excellent. Hospitality, leisure, recreation and tourism, and information systems and management produced the best results, while submissions within law, sports science and natural sciences also did well.

The university was granted research degree-awarding powers in 2008 and its postgraduate provision is growing: a range of new master's programmes will be launching in 2022 and 2023 in diverse subject areas such as creative arts, psychology, and sport and activity.

Edge Hill's recently added £13million Tech Hub has biotechnology laboratories for research into disease prevention, DNA sequencing, cloning and genetic treatments. The medical school houses England's only bioethics unit, as well as facilities for clinical skills and a simulation centre where students can apply their learning.

When the £27million Catalyst building opened in 2018, bringing together student support services and the university library, study spaces increased by half. Creative Edge, a £17million complex for the departments of media and computing, has studios for television, animation, sound, photography and radio. There is also a multimedia laboratory.

Although Edge Hill has fallen 20 places in our index measuring social inclusion, almost all

St Helens Road
Ormskirk L39 4QP
01695 650 950
admissions@edgehill.ac.uk
www.edgehillsu.org.uk
www.edgehill.ac.uk
Open days:
see website

The Times and The Sunday Times **Rankings**
Overall Ranking: 78 (last year: =58)

Teaching quality	74%	=84
Student experience	71.9%	=64
Research quality	26.3%	99
Entry standards	128	=57
Graduate prospects	70.9%	78
Good honours	74%	94
Expected completion rate	86.7%	55
Student/staff ratio	15.5	=49

of its students are recruited from non-selective state schools, and more than half (51.8%) are the first in their family to go to university.

Edge Hill's ambition for widening participation in higher education is demonstrated in its approach to offering medical degrees. Breaking down the subject's elite reputation, the university offers a widening access to medicine courses and a foundation year in medicine. Students from the northwest of England from secondary schools with below average pupil performance and who meet widening access criteria qualify for entry requirements of BBB at A-level – three grades lower than for direct entry to the five-year programme.

A completion rate that places Edge Hill within the upper half of universities nationally is evidence that the support package offered to students from non-traditional backgrounds who join is effective. The university invests £1.4million a year in a range of scholarships and bursaries.

A degree in children's learning in development welcomed its first students in September 2022, as did electrical engineering and the new intelligent automation and robotics degree. On top of next year's engineering degree launches, the university is introducing degrees in film and broadcast production and in education and special educational needs.

To the east of the main Ormskirk campus, Edge Hill's £30million sports centre has an eight-court sports hall, 25m swimming pool, 80-station fitness suite, aerobics studio and health suite with sauna and steam rooms. Outdoors, there is a trim trail with exercise stations, a competition-standard running track, rugby, hockey and football pitches, an athletics field and netball and tennis courts.

Student accommodation in the elegant 1930s-designed Main Building has been refurbished, providing en-suite accommodation on campus. The Backs Halls accommodation is in line for demolition, to make way for further modern student bedrooms in the centre of campus. First-years who apply by the housing deadline are guaranteed a place.

Edge Hill is a certified hedgehog-friendly campus and also welcomes its resident ducks on two lakes. Students can relax at La Plage, a man-made sandy beach on campus. Those in search of brighter lights than those offered by characterful Ormskirk can reach all that Liverpool has to offer within a 30-minute train trip.

Tuition fees

»	Fees for UK students	£9,250
	Foundation courses	£6,165
»	Fees for International students 2023–24	£15,000
	Foundation	£13,000
»	For scholarship and bursary information see www.edgehill.ac.uk/departments/support/registry/ fees-scholarships-and-bursaries	
»	Graduate salary	£23,000

Student numbers

Undergraduates	10,197	(522)
Postgraduates	1,573	(2,285)
Applications/places	17,415/3,715	
Applications per place	4.7:1	
Overall offer rate	68.1%	
International students – EU	0.5%	
Non-EU	0.4%	

Accommodation

University provided places: 2,340
Self-catered: £75–£140 per week
First-years guaranteed accommodation
www.edgehill.ac.uk/study/accommodation

Where do the students come from?

SState schools (non-grammar)	96.7%	First generation students	51.8%	White working-class males	7.4%
Grammar schools	1.8%	Low participation areas	20%	Black achievement gap	-27.4%
Independent schools	1.6%	All ethnic minorities	8.3%	Mature (over 21)	22.7%

Social inclusion ranking: 63

University of Edinburgh

Established in 1583, the University of Edinburgh has enduring appeal. In 2021, applications (up 13%) and enrolments (up 16%) reached record levels. Another top-20 finish in the QS World University rankings in 2022 adds clout.

One of the UK's research giants, Edinburgh is 11th in our research quality index, falling one place year-on-year. Fifty-five per cent of its submission to the latest Research Excellence Framework (REF 2021) was assessed as world-leading, the highest category, and a further 41% was internationally excellent. Results were excellent in psychology, biological sciences, English, politics, pharmacology and pharmacy, anatomy, and computing.

In common with many leading research-led institutions, student satisfaction is a persistent bugbear for the university, however. Our analysis of the latest outcomes in the National Student Survey (NSS) puts Edinburgh in the bottom 10 for satisfaction with teaching quality. Edinburgh's new student support model is intended to improve things. Student advisers are being introduced as the first point of contact for study-related queries across the university, replacing the personal tutor system. Students will continue to be able to get support for their studies from academic staff and senior tutors but will also be able to turn to wellbeing advisers for help with their health and personal life.

The university buildings span the historic Old Town and newer territory. An £8million Health and Wellbeing Centre opened in 2020 on Bristo Square, near the grand McEwan Hall, offering counselling and disability services and the chance to grab a calm moment in the wellbeing lounge. A couple of miles out of the city centre at the 115-acre King's Buildings campus, the Nucleus Building opened in October 2022, adding teaching and learning facilities such as a laboratory, shops and restaurants plus social and study spaces.

The university hosts the £79million national supercomputer, Archer2, and its expertise in data science is behind its establishment of six data-driven innovation hubs under the Edinburgh and South East Scotland City Deal. Two – the £45million Bayes Centre and the Edinburgh International Data Facility – are already open, while the National Robotarium, Edinburgh Futures Institute, Agritech Hub and Usher Institute are under development.

Helping to meet its commitment to achieve net-zero carbon emissions by 2040, Edinburgh has completed is divestment from fossil fuel investments – a substantial undertaking for the university with the third-largest endowment fund of any UK institution, behind Oxbridge. It has also built a large solar farm at the Easter Bush campus, home of the Royal (Dick) School of Veterinary Studies and the Roslin Institute.

Undergraduate provision is broad, extending across 58 subjects and almost 400

Old College
South Bridge
Edinburgh EH8 9YL
0131 650 4360
futurestudents@ed.ac.uk
www.ed.ac.uk
www.eusa.ed.ac.uk/
Open days:
see website

The Times and The Sunday Times Rankings
Overall Ranking: 10 (last year: 13)

Teaching quality	68.6%	124
Student experience	67%	=112
Research quality	61.5%	11
Entry standards	188	7
Graduate prospects	84.6%	14
Good honours	91.5%	7
Expected completion rate	93.4%	14
Student/staff ratio	11.5	3

degrees. New courses are offered in sport management and in Arabic with Islamic and Middle Eastern studies in 2022. Fine art will be introduced in 2023. Lecture capture has been commonplace at Edinburgh since pre-pandemic times and the university is keen to continue using digital learning where it enhances the experience, with an appropriate balance of in-person learning.

An early convert to contextual offers, Edinburgh has worked hard to lose its exclusive tag and prioritise widening participation. In partnership with the University of Glasgow, it has launched three learning centres that provide extra support to young people aged seven to 18 in some of Scotland's most deprived areas. The university met a government target for admissions from the most deprived areas early, but does not shine in national measures for social inclusion, coming last in Scotland in our analysis.

The Access Edinburgh Scholarship provides up to £5,000 per year of study to full-time undergraduates. The exact sum depends on circumstances and household income, with awards assessed automatically when students apply for funding. The financial assistance is especially valuable to those from England, Wales and Northern Ireland facing four years of full tuition fees in Scotland. The university prospectus notes that Edinburgh awarded £10million in undergraduate financial support in 2020-21.

Edinburgh's sports programmes are among the best in the UK, producing past Olympic champions such as the cyclist Sir Chris Hoy and the rower Dame Katherine Grainger. The university has an outdoor centre 80 miles from Edinburgh in a beautiful setting in the southern Highlands. There is a network of student gyms in and around the city with membership packages starting at just £15 a year. Students have a choice of 65 sports clubs and can take part in the full range of fixtures from informal games to competitive tournaments.

There are 6,448 residential places reserved for undergraduates, more than a third of which come with breakfast and evening meals included. All first-years who come from outside Edinburgh's city limits are guaranteed a room.

Students here have enviable access to the cultural hangouts of one of the world's most exciting cities. Edinburgh is ranked the tenth best student city in Europe according to QS Best Student Cities 2023.

Tuition fees

» Fees for Scottish students £0–£1,820
  RUK fees £9,250
» Fees for International students 2023–24 £24,500–£32,200
  not £23,100–£30,400
  Medicine £35,000–£49,900; Veterinary Medicine £35,200
» For scholarship and bursary information see
  www.ed.ac.uk/student-funding
» Graduate salary £27,450

Student numbers

Undergraduates	24,066	(629)
Postgraduates	8,875	(3,528)
Applications/places	72,365/8,455	
Applications per place	8.6:1	
Overall offer rate	39.3%	
International students – EU	9.4%	
Non-EU	23.5%	

Accommodation

University provided places: 9,464
Catered: £216–£294 per week
Self-catered: £92–£193 per week
First-years guaranteed accommodation
www.accom.ed.ac.uk

Where do the students come from?

State schools (non-grammar)	57.8%	First generation students	19.5%	
Grammar schools	6.7%	Low participation areas	9.1%	
Independent schools	35.5%	All ethnic minorities	12.8%	

Social inclusion ranking (Scotland): 15

White working-class males	n/a
Black achievement gap	-11.4%
Mature (over 21)	23.5%

Edinburgh Napier University

The demand for places to study at Edinburgh Napier University reached new heights in 2021. Applications increased to their highest level since 2018, although enrolments fell slightly.

The prospects for graduates from Edinburgh Napier's career-driven courses have improved year-on-year. It is up 17 places to =43 in our analysis of the latest Graduate Outcomes survey, and buoyant rates of student satisfaction have contributed to the university's ascent of our academic league table. Although it has fallen out of the top 20 for satisfaction with teaching quality (32nd) and the wider undergraduate experience (33rd), it remains around the top third in our latest analysis.

The university took student feedback into consideration to develop a hybrid system of teaching and learning according to course content. Aspects of blended learning are being used in the 2022-23 academic year.

There are three campuses across the city, each with a distinct focus. Beside the sixteenth-century tower marking the birthplace of John Napier, the mathematician from whom the university takes its name, the Merchiston campus hosts creative arts subjects. Screen Academy Scotland, run in partnership with Edinburgh College of Art (now part of the University of Edinburgh), also operates from the campus in trendy Bruntsfield.

The 500-seat computer centre, based at Merchiston and open 24/7, has a Cyber Academy, cyberattack simulation suite and computer games laboratory. Students have the opportunity for a year-long, credit-bearing work placement in their third year. The undergraduate degree in cybersecurity and forensics was the first in the UK to be fully certified by the National Cyber Security Centre. Its parent organisation is GCHQ, the Government Communications Headquarters.

Overlooking Edinburgh, the Craiglockhart campus hosts the Business School, featuring a curved lecture theatre known as the Egg. Sighthill, 20 minutes away by tram, has splendid views of the city and is the base for the schools of nursing, midwifery and social care.

Many other courses at Edinburgh Napier include work placements of varying duration through extensive industry links, including BBC Scotland, while a microplacements scheme offered by the School of Applied Sciences places students within bioscience and social science organisations. Overseas, the School of Health and Social Care provides professional training and research in neonatal services in Vietnam and delivers professional training for nurses in Singapore.

The university more than doubled the number of academics whose work was submitted to the Research Excellence Framework (REF 2021). The proportion of work achieving the top two ratings (world-leading or internationally

Sighthill Court
Edinburgh EH11 4BN

0333 900 6040
ugadmissions@napier.ac.uk
www.napierstudents.com
www.napier.ac.uk
Open days:
see website

The Times and The Sunday Times Rankings
Overall Ranking: 59 (last year: 57)

Teaching quality	77.3%	32
Student experience	74.4%	33
Research quality	32.9%	=74
Entry standards	150	=28
Graduate prospects	77.7%	=43
Good honours	81.3%	41
Expected completion rate	82.7%	89
Student/staff ratio	22.1	122

excellent) rose, too, from 53% in 2014 to 68%. Edinburgh Napier has risen 21 places in our research quality rankings — one of the biggest increases. Building, land and property management, and town and country planning produced some of the best results.

A top-up degree in animation for games began in September 2022, as did degrees in user experience (UX) design, information for business, and electrical and electronic engineering. New for 2023 will be computer science (artificial intelligence), informatics (with three options: business, eHealth and fintech) and a top-up course in law/legal studies. The university offers 11 graduate apprenticeships (known as degree apprenticeships in the rest of the UK) with 432 students enrolled on programmes in the fields of architecture, building and planning, business management, engineering, computing, and informational technology.

Edinburgh Napier sits in fifth place in our Scottish social inclusion index, down from third in 2021. In its 2022-23 intake, 92.8% of students attended non-selective state schools and 40% were aged 21 or over at the start of their studies.

While undergraduates from Scotland qualify for the national scheme for financial help, students from the rest of the UK and Ireland qualify for the university's eye-catching financial packages – paying tuition fees for only three years of their four-year degree course and cash awards of up to £3,000. About 80% of students from England, Wales and the island of Ireland qualify for some form of financial aid.

All sports facilities at the Sighthill campus are wheelchair accessible. Edinburgh Napier is the official training partner of four teams in Scottish Rugby's Super6 league, as well as Cricket Scotland. It is the only university in Scotland to offer a football coaching programme performance and development degree in collaboration with the Scottish Football Association.

Student accommodation is in three halls: Bainfield, where most students aged under 20 live, Slateford Road, for nursing students and postgraduates, and Orwell Terrace. First-years from outside Edinburgh who apply by the deadline are guaranteed a place. All new students take the online course *Consent Matters*. Those in positions of responsibility – society and sports club leaders, student representatives and resident assistants – are invited to participate in active bystander training.

Tuition fees

» Fees for Scottish students	£0–£1,820
RUK fees	£9,250
» Fees for International students 2023–24	£14,170–£16,425
» For scholarship and bursary information see www.napier.ac.uk/study-with-us/undergraduate/fees-and-finance	
» Graduate salary	£24,000

Student numbers

Undergraduates	10,097	(819)
Postgraduates	2,743	(1,211)
Applications/places	20,145/3,585	
Applications per place	5.6:1	
Overall offer rate	58.4%	
International students – EU	9.1%	
Non-EU	3.3%	

Accommodation

University provided places: 1,240
Self-catered: £110–£186 per week
www.napier.ac.uk/study-with-us/accommodation

Where do the students come from?

State schools (non-grammar)	92.8%	First generation students	39.6%	White working-class males	n/a
Grammar schools	1%	Low participation areas	12.5%	Black achievement gap	-14.9%
Independent schools	6.2%	All ethnic minorities	10.2%	Mature (over 21)	40%

Social inclusion ranking (Scotland): 5

University of Essex

The six accommodation tower blocks on Essex University's main campus are a landmark of quintessential 1960s architecture – but only on the outside. Students moving in to two of them in September 2022 will find modern living quarters after a £22million makeover, and a £10.3million project will transform a third tower in 2023.

The newest halls of residence – the Pastures – will open in time for students enrolling in September 2023, adding 1,204 rooms and 58 studio apartments to the university's accommodation stock.

Academic facilities are also being upgraded. The School of Health and Social Care opened a new therapy suite hub in September 2022. The School of Life Sciences has extended its marine biology and aquatic sciences laboratory and is planning new Growth Rooms, a research facility where the internationally acclaimed Plant Productivity Group will continue to study how to improve crop photosynthesis.

The campus improvements should help to keep rates of student satisfaction on their upward trajectory. Having lost ground during the pandemic, Essex rises 33 places in our analysis of satisfaction with the wider undergraduate experience to rank 53rd, based on results from the latest National Student Survey. The university also gains 25 places for student satisfaction with teaching quality, now ranking =92.

Social sciences are the longstanding strongest suit at Essex. In the latest QS global rankings 2022, the university is in the top 50 for politics and the top 55 for sociology. In the most recent Research Excellence Framework (REF 2021), politics, sociology, economics and a number of modern languages performed strongly. Across all subject areas, 83% of the submission from academics at Essex was rated world-leading or internationally excellent, the top two categories. Although it had edged up from almost 80% in the previous national assessment in 2014, other institutions did even better this time around: Essex drops 16 places to 41st in our research quality index.

In 2021, the university was 43rd in our main academic rankings, and now sits in 54th place. In 2017, it was in our top 25 and shortlisted for our University of the Year award.

Essex received a gold rating in the Teaching Excellence Framework (TEF), commended for its use of student feedback to develop "rigorous and stretching teaching that is tailored to student needs".

Most undergraduates are based in Colchester at the main campus in the historic 200-acre Wivenhoe Park. There are also university sites in Southend-on-Sea and Loughton in Essex. A new nursing laboratory is in development at Southend.

The £19million Parkside phase of the

Wivenhoe Park
Colchester CO4 3SQ
01206 873 666
admit@essex.ac.uk
www.essexstudent.com
www.essex.ac.uk
Open days:
see website

The Times and The Sunday Times **Rankings**
Overall Ranking: 54 (last year: 43)

Teaching quality	73.3%	=92
Student experience	72.5%	53
Research quality	50%	41
Entry standards	114	=103
Graduate prospects	72.6%	68
Good honours	79.7%	=52
Expected completion rate	87.6%	54
Student/staff ratio	16	=59

university's Knowledge Gateway research and technology park in Colchester will incorporate the new Institute of Public Health and Wellbeing. The East 15 Acting School, which was founded more than 60 years ago and counts the actress Alison Steadman and director Stephen Daldry among its alumni, merged with the university in 2000.

Essex enjoyed seven years of consistent growth in enrolments until 2020. But they decreased by about 22% year-on-year in the 2021 admissions cycle. Applications fell less sharply, by about 8%.

New courses may go some way to attract more students. The first global sustainability students started degree courses in September 2022 and eight other programmes have been added to the curriculum, with options for a foundation year, a year abroad or a work placement, including ecology and environmental biology, artificial intelligence, journalism and film, drama and creative writing, business administration and supply chain management, social work, and politics with criminology.

Essex remains determined to maintain its longstanding European links post-Brexit. As a member of the Young Universities for the Future of Europe (YUFE) alliance of 10 research-intensive universities – alongside Maastricht in the Netherlands and Bremen in Germany – it is also involved in plans for a European university.

Essex's student population is unusually diverse for a pre-1992 university, and climbs 24 places in our social inclusion chart to rank 30th. The university runs a range of outreach programmes for students from backgrounds that are underrepresented in higher education. Under the V16 Project, four local sixth forms use the Essex campus to teach A-levels they otherwise could not offer to small student cohorts.

The student development team works with employers of all sizes to help students gain career insights, work experience and commercial awareness. The university's graduate prospects ranking has improved by 15 places to 68th.

Every student is allocated a wellbeing adviser throughout their studies. There is a drop-in service for concerns about mental health and counselling is available.

The £12million Essex Sport Arena has seating for 1,655 spectators and hosts the university's professional basketball teams, the Essex Rebels. The arena is part of a 40-acre sports area that includes an 18-hole frisbee-golf course, all-weather tennis courts and room for five-a-side football.

Tuition fees

- » Fees for UK students £9,250
- » Fees for International students 2023–24 £18,585–£27,500
- » For scholarship and bursary information see https://www.essex.ac.uk/undergraduate/fees-and-funding
- » Graduate salary £24,000

Student numbers

Undergraduates	13,218	(526)
Postgraduates	2,839	(1,880)
Applications/places	16,945/3,245	
Applications per place	5.2:1	
Overall offer rate	74.5%	
International students – EU	13.7%	
Non-EU	14%	

Accommodation

University provided places: 5,383
Self-catered: £108–£243 per week
First-years guaranteed accommodation
www.essex.ac.uk/life/accommodation

Where do the students come from?

State schools (non-grammar)	92.6%	First generation students	46.9%	White working-class males	5.4%
Grammar schools	3.6%	Low participation areas	14.7%	Black achievement gap	-3.9%
Independent schools	3.8%	All ethnic minorities	44.4%	Mature (over 21)	26.7%

Social inclusion ranking: 30

University of Exeter

Rising popularity has spurred significant growth at Exeter, runner-up for our University of the Year award. Applications rose 9% year-on-year to nearly 41,700 in 2021 among prospective students seeking a Russell Group university experience in a beautiful part of the world. In the decade since 2011, enrolments have nearly doubled to reach 8,175.

Most students are based at the main Streatham campus, an attractive hillside site yet close to the city centre. About £20million is being invested in campus improvements, mainly to upgrade engineering facilities in the Harrison Building, and 1,182 new student bedrooms have been added at East Park.

Contentment has grown year-on-year within the student body, according to our analysis of the latest National Student Survey. Exeter has risen 35 places to reach the top 25 for student satisfaction with the undergraduate experience and 28 places to =66 for how students rate teaching quality.

Graduate prospects have soared into the top 20 (=19), up nine places from its performance in 2021 according to our analysis of how many students find highly skilled work or embark on further study within 15 months of finishing their degree course. Exeter has set out its 10-year plan in Strategy 2030, vowing to pour its energy into addressing the challenges of our time: climate change, healthcare provision and social justice.

The university claims to have Britain's five most influential climate scientists on staff.

Exeter was rated gold in the Teaching Excellence Framework, attracting praise for "optimum" contact hours and class sizes and for involving business, industry and professional experts in its teaching.

Nearly half of Exeter's extensive submission in the latest Research Excellence Framework (REF 2021) was assessed as world-leading and the university has maintained its 18th place in our research quality index. The university has conducted leading research on dementia, diabetes and the impact of the environment on human health, and has made strong contributions to the arts, humanities and social sciences. Its submission to the REF excelled in sports sciences, theology, and hospitality, leisure and tourism, a growing focus for jobs in the region.

A purpose-built Centre for Resilience Environment, Water and Waste is being built at Streatham. A new undergraduate degree in environmental humanities will be introduced in 2023 with options to study abroad or work placements in the UK or overseas.

Less than two miles away from the main campus, St Luke's campus houses the medical school, which also has a health education and research centre at the Royal Devon and Exeter Hospital and a smaller base in Truro,

Northcote House
The Queen's Drive
Exeter EX4 4QJ
0300 555 6060
www.exeter.ac.uk/enquiry
www.exeter.ac.uk
Open days:
see website

The Times and The Sunday Times **Rankings**
Overall Ranking: 13 (last year: 21)

Teaching quality	75.3%	=66
Student experience	75.5%	24
Research quality	57.5%	18
Entry standards	157	23
Graduate prospects	83.8%	=19
Good honours	88.8%	12
Expected completion rate	94.9%	11
Student/staff ratio	15.8	=54

Cornwall. The Graduate School of Education and programmes in sport and health sciences are also based at St Luke's.

At Exeter's Penryn campus in Cornwall, shared with Falmouth University, the Exchange Courtyard opened in 2020 as part of a £4.4million project to create social and flexible learning spaces. Penryn also hosts the Renewable Energy Engineering Facility, which provides specialist teaching facilities.

A relatively low proportion of recruits from non-selective state schools (53.6%) keeps Exeter in the lower reaches of our social inclusion index. But the university is determined to focus on widening access, as well as supporting lifelong learning to adapt to the jobs of the future.

Unlike many other Russell Group members, Exeter has embraced degree apprenticeships and at last count had 1,733 students following one of six undergraduate programmes – which include civil engineering, diagnostic radiography and digital and technology solutions – and seven postgraduate courses. The university is a partner in the new Institute of Technology, which has a £3.2million facility on the Streatham campus featuring artificial intelligence technology and a computer learning laboratory.

One in six new entrants in 2021 received a contextual offer and the university expects that to rise after tweaking the eligibility criteria. All state school-educated applicants who live or go to school in the most deprived postcodes will qualify for a contextual offer,

typically one A-level grade (or equivalent qualification) below the standard offer. A contextual offer to study medicine can be reduced to ABB at A-level.

There is also a generous bursary and scholarship scheme. Sports performance bursaries of up to £3,000 are awarded to student athletes who compete internationally in one of Exeter's Athletics Union clubs. Other awards include the global excellence scholarship, which provides financial help to high-achieving international students.

Exeter has introduced mandatory training for new students on equality, diversity and inclusion, and on sexual consent.

Sports facilities at Exeter are some of the best in the country, boosted by recent investment of more than £12million. All first-years who apply in time are guaranteed a room. At the main Streatham campus there are 6,482 places and almost 20% are catered. Another 831 rooms are available at Penryn, 10% of them catered.

Although the city has a sleepy side, sandy beaches are only 20 minutes away and Exeter offers live music and festivals aplenty.

Tuition fees

» Fees for UK students	£9,250
» Fees for International students 2023–24	£21,500–£27,000
Medicine	£41,500
» For scholarship and bursary information see www.exeter.ac.uk/undergraduate/fees/	
» Graduate salary	£26,500

Student numbers

Undergraduates	21,695	(660)
Postgraduates	5,204	(2,691)
Applications/places		41,695/8,175
Applications per place		5.1:1
Overall offer rate		79.2%
International students – EU		5.4%
Non-EU		15.8%

Accommodation

University provided places: 7,313
Catered costs: £159–£285 per week
Self-catered: £116–£193 per week
First-years guaranteed accommodation
www.exeter.ac.uk/accommodation

Where do the students come from?

State schools (non-grammar)	53.6%	First generation students	26.3%	White working-class males	3.4%
Grammar schools	11.9%	Low participation areas	5.7%	Black achievement gap	-9.5%
Independent schools	34.5%	All ethnic minorities	10.6%	Mature (over 21)	6.7%

Social inclusion ranking: 108

Falmouth University

Marking its 10-year anniversary as a university in 2022, Falmouth is also celebrating leaps forward in our league table, where it has jumped 45 places to rank joint 42nd this year.

Contributing to the remarkable rise are Falmouth's excellent results in the latest Research Excellence Framework (REF 2021), in which 63% of the university's art and design submissions were rated world-leading or internationally excellent. The results represent a significant improvement on Falmouth's performance in REF 2014 and have spurred a huge 53-place rise in our research quality rating.

Originally the Falmouth School of Art, founded in 1902, the university's research centres on the fourth industrial revolution and how human-centred design, innovation and storytelling can bring meaningful value to digital technologies. Such academic direction reflects the breadth of courses, which have grown from a wide range of art and design options to encompass film, performance, business entrepreneurship and marketing, journalism, game development, and architecture.

Light-filled creative spaces and subtropical gardens distinguish the campus at Falmouth, near the town centre and a short walk from the popular Gyllyngvase beach. Teaching facilities for photography include an in-house photo agency that takes on live industry projects.

The purpose-built Penryn campus nearby is shared with the University of Exeter. It gained a social space in 2021, positioned for views down the Penryn River, built sustainably and featuring workspace alongside a bar and café.

Performing arts students have the Academy of Music and Theatre Arts at Penryn, where facilities include a cinema, motion-capture studio, video-editing suites with animation software, fully sprung dancefloors, rehearsal studios and theatre space.

Awarded gold in the Teaching Excellence Framework (TEF), Falmouth impressed assessors with students' personalised learning. The majority of teaching is practice-based in studios, workshops or industry-based environments. All of this takes place in-person, and the university notes that less than 7% of teaching and learning happens within a traditional lecture format. That said, lectures are captured for playback.

Falmouth's students expressed their agreement with the TEF panel, results of the latest National Student Survey suggest – with Falmouth ranking 15th for teaching quality in our analysis this year (up 23 places). Scores for satisfaction with the wider undergraduate experience rose, too, and Falmouth ranks 25 places higher in our student experience measure this year.

The TEF panel also praised the university for stretching students and ensuring that they acquire the knowledge, skills and understanding

Woodlane
Falmouth TR11 4RH
01326 254 350
futurestudies@falmouth.ac.uk
www.thesu.org.uk
www.falmouth.ac.uk
Open days:
see website

The Times and *The Sunday Times* Rankings		
Overall Ranking: =42 (last year: 87)		
Teaching quality	79%	15
Student experience	72.9%	49
Research quality	48.8%	=42
Entry standards	125	=63
Graduate prospects	60.6%	128
Good honours	77.6%	=62
Expected completion rate	n/a	
Student/staff ratio	14.8	35

most highly valued by employers. In line with its "Doing it for real" ethos the university interviews all applicants and asks them to prove their potential via their portfolio or audition. Once enrolled, students across all academic departments have opportunities to work on live briefs with industry partners.

However, Falmouth appears near the bottom of our graduate prospects ranking again this year, in 128th place. This is in common with most specialist arts institutions and is unlikely to be a surprise to those in creative fields, many of whom settle into professional life later than the Graduate Outcomes survey's measure 15 months after graduation.

Falmouth's growing curriculum acquired seven new degrees in 2022, with media production, architectural design and technology, e-sports and interior design (online) among them. From September 2023, another two undergraduate options will be offered, in music business and sound design.

Applications were 8% higher by the end of March in 2022's admissions cycle, compared with the same point the year before.

Around one in five students qualified for financial aid in 2022's incoming cohort. Help with the cost of materials (a significant outgoing for arts students) is offered to 400 students and worth £100. Up-to-date details on talent-based scholarships can be accessed via the university website.

The sports centre on the Penryn campus has a four-court sports hall, fitness studio and gym, as well as multi-use pitches and outdoor gym. Spinning, yoga and Zumba are some of the classes offered. Water sports on the Cornish coast are a huge part of the Falmouth student experience and part-time jobs in the tourist trade help with living costs.

There are residential places on both campuses and accommodation is guaranteed to all full-time first-years who apply in time.

Cornwall's star is in the ascendant, its coastal charms having attracted pandemic-hit city dwellers to its different pace of life. In terms of student-friendly social scenes think pop-up bars, clubs on farms, contemporary galleries and arthouse cinemas. Jam, a shop on Falmouth's High Street, offers the twin appeal of vinyl records and Monmouth coffee.

Students can opt in to having their meals catered at the Glasney Student Village accommodation. A place in halls of residence is guaranteed to all first-years who apply by the deadline.

Tuition fees

» Fees for UK students	£9,250
	£11,100 for 2-year courses
» Fees for International students 2023–24	£10,400–£17,460
for 2-year courses	£19,570
» For scholarship and bursary information see www.falmouth.ac.uk/study/tuition-fees	
» Graduate salary	£20,000

Student numbers

Undergraduates	4,978	(23)
Postgraduates	262	(908)
Applications/places		5,585/2,095
Applications per place		2.7:1
Overall offer rate		75.9%
International students – EU		1.4%
Non-EU		2.1%

Accommodation

University provided places: 1,676
Catered costs: £167–£208 per week
Self-catered: £122–£210 per week
First-years guaranteed accommodation
www.falmouth.ac.uk/accommodation

Where do the students come from?

					Social inclusion ranking: 94	
State schools (non-grammar)	92%	First generation students	33.8%	White working-class males	7.3%
Grammar schools	1.7%	Low participation areas	10.3%	Black achievement gap	-32.5%
Independent schools	6.3%	Ethnic minorities	7.6%	Mature (over 21)	19.1%

University of Glasgow

One of Scotland's four ancient universities and founded in 1451, Glasgow was the first in Britain to have a school of engineering and the first in Scotland to have a computer. A pioneer still, Glasgow unveiled the largest project of a £1bn, 10-year investment in its estate in June 2022. The Mazumdar-Shaw Advanced Research Centre (ARC) is the university's new flagship research facility, the fruits of a £166.5million investment on the Western campus.

Designed to accommodate about 500 academics, postdoctoral researchers and PhD students, the ARC's focus for research is across five main themes: creative economies and cultural transformation, digital chemistry, international development, quantum and nanotechnology, and technology touching life. The building's ground floor is open to the wider university and the community.

One of only two Russell Group universities in Scotland, Glasgow burnished its golden research reputation in the latest Research Excellence Framework (REF 2021). Excellence in food science, agriculture, medicine, classics, and mathematics helped to keep its 12th place in our research quality index. The university secured 73rd place in the 2022 QS World University rankings.

Our Scottish University of the Year in 2021, Glasgow's ambitious development plan is making space for a growing student community. The demand for places increased by 16% in the 2021 admissions round, year-on-year. Enrolments edged up by just 2% in the same cycle but are up by half in the past decade.

Providing plenty of legroom for studying, the £90.6million James McCune Smith learning hub opened in 2021. The building can accommodate more than 2,500 students.

Glasgow's imposing gothic revival buildings on the Gilmorehill campus are a landmark in the city's fashionable West End, where the university has been based since 1871. Glasgow has its own museum – the Hunterian – at Gilmorehill, with collections of art, zoology and anatomy.

The spacious Garscube campus, four miles from Gilmorehill hosts the veterinary school and outdoor sports pitches. Liberal arts and teaching courses are delivered in Dumfries.

Glasgow scored highly with its students during the pandemic, compared with most other institutions, boosting its scores for student satisfaction with the wider undergraduate experience to 24th place in our analysis of the National Student Survey in 2021. A year on, however, Glasgow falls to =67 on that measure and =92 for satisfaction with teaching quality.

The university's only graduate apprenticeship (known as degree apprenticeships south of the border) is a four-year programme in software engineering designed with local employers to create a talent pipeline of graduates with skills tailored to industry needs.

University Avenue, Glasgow G12 8QQ
0141 330 2000
ruk-undergraduate-enquiries
@glasgow.ac.uk;
scot-undergraduate-enquiries
@glasgow.ac.uk
study@abdn.ac.uk
www.guu.co.uk
www.glasgow.ac.uk
Open days: see website

GLASGOW
Edinburgh
Belfast
London
Cardiff

The Times and The Sunday Times Rankings
Overall Ranking: 14 (last year: 12)

Teaching quality	73.3%	=92
Student experience	71.7%	=67
Research quality	61.2%	12
Entry standards	203	3
Graduate prospects	81.4%	29
Good honours	86.1%	20
Expected completion rate	89.9%	=41
Student/staff ratio	13.7	=12

Glasgow's Internship Hub works with more than 150 organisations to provide placements. Many students are kept on afterwards. The university's School of Culture and Creative Arts, Scotland's leading centre for music research, also offers opportunities for placements within the city's legendary music scene.

The university has improved its graduate prospects year-on-year to reach the top 30 for the proportion of those in highly skilled work or postgraduate study after 15 months (29th). More than a quarter of undergraduates are from outside the UK and Glasgow has a branch campus in Singapore, working with the Singapore Institute of Technology, and a joint graduate school with Nankai University in northeastern China.

Four-year courses are the norm in Scotland but students from the rest of the UK will find their fourth-year tuition fees waived on the majority of degree courses. There are access bursaries of £1,000 to £3,000 per year of study for students from England, Wales and Northern Ireland from low-income households.

Social inclusion is a challenge for Glasgow, which has a relatively low proportion of students from non-selective state schools (78.3%). However, it boasts the lowest black achievement gap in Scotland.

One-to-one counselling appointments are available and a peer wellbeing support scheme is in place linking trained students with those seeking help for mild mental health issues. The university's SafeZone app is at the ready for students who get lost, need to report an emergency or require first aid.

Given the shortage of student housing in Glasgow – which led to a number of students being housed in hotels by the university in autumn 2022 – applicants are advised to take heed of all criteria and deadlines governing the guaranteed allocation of one of 3,400 residential places intended to first-years.

Glasgow's sports union supports more than 50 clubs and activities and there are purpose-built sports facilities on the Gilmorehill and Garscube campuses. The Stevenson Building at Gilmorehill includes a 25m pool, indoor cycle studio and squash courts. At Garscube students have access to all-weather and grass pitches as well as a cricket oval and tennis courts.

Scotland's biggest metropolis has five universities and was crowned the world's friendliest and most affordable city by Time Out in 2019. It was also the first in the UK to be named a Unesco City of Music.

Tuition fees

»	Fees for Scottish students	£0–£1,820
»	RUK fees	£9,250
»	Fees for International students 2023–24	£19,920–£27,930
	Medicine £53,460; Dentistry £48,960;	
	Veterinary Medicine £33,500	
»	For scholarship and bursary information see	
	www.gla.ac.uk/undergraduate/fees	
»	Graduate salary	£26,000

Student numbers		
Undergraduates	19,813	(1,988)
Postgraduates	11,635	(3,711)
Applications/places	42,180/6,605	
Applications per place	6.4:1	
Overall offer rate	56.3%	
International students – EU	9.3%	
Non-EU	12.1%	

Accommodation
University provided places: 3,508
Catered: £168–£198 per week
Self-catered: £91–£245 per week
First-years guaranteed accommodation
www.glasgow.ac.uk/myglasgow/accommodation

Where do the students come from?				Social inclusion ranking (Scotland): 13	
State schools (non-grammar)	78.3%	First generation students	25.6%	White working-class males	n/a
Grammar schools	5.5%	Low participation areas	14.8%	Black achievement gap	-0.1%
Independent schools	16.2%	All ethnic minorities	12.3%	Mature (over 21)	13.9%

Glasgow Caledonian University

The Sir Alex Ferguson Library at Glasgow Caledonian University (GCU) now has a Relax and Renew zone where students and staff can take a break from their studies, or work in a contemplative space. There is literature available on self-care, hobbies and non-academic fiction. Focusing on welfare, GCU has also appointed a vice-principal for staff and student wellbeing.

The Glasgow campus occupies a single site, where the centrepiece of a £32million redevelopment is the Heart of the Campus building. The modern university's reach extends further than its home city, however. GCU was the first Scottish university to open a base in London, where postgraduate fashion students are based in the hip enclave of Spitalfields.

Across the Atlantic in New York's SoHo, GCU was the first foreign university to be granted a charter to award its own degrees in fashion and business. The institution has helped to set up the African Leadership College in Mauritius, where the first students embarked on GCU degrees in 2017. It also co-founded the Grameen Caledonian College of Nursing in Bangladesh, and has links with institutions across the world, including in Oman, China, India and South America.

With a stated mission to be a "university for the common good", CGU has set out a vision to be a world leader in social innovation in its Strategy 2030 document and aims to drive sustainable economic and social development in line with the United Nations' Sustainable Development Goals. The university is ranked 70th out of 1,406 institutions globally in the Times Higher Education's Impact rankings 2022, and first in the UK for promoting gender equality.

It is already setting an example in the UK for social inclusion and ranks fourth among Scotland's 15 universities. In the latest social inclusion data, GCU records 96.4% of its intake from non-selective state schools and is third in Scotland for its proportion of white working-class male students (8.4%), the most underrepresented demographic in universities.

Outreach initiatives target local communities and schools with a low progression rate to university, providing campus visits, skills training, careers guidance and taster days. Improving completion rates – with a projected dropout rate of 6.6%, below the 7.9% expected, based on the course and student profile – show that the university's academic, social and financial support for those at risk of dropping out is bearing fruit.

GCU is one of the largest providers of graduates to the NHS in Scotland and its facilities include a virtual hospital. It trains 90% of the country's eyecare specialists

Cowcaddens Road
Glasgow G4 0BA
0141 331 8630
studentenquiries@gcu.ac.uk
www.gcustudents.co.uk
www.gcu.ac.uk
Open days: see website

The Times and The Sunday Times **Rankings**
Overall Ranking: 52 (last year: 60)

Teaching quality	75.1%	=69
Student experience	72.2%	=57
Research quality	38.5%	66
Entry standards	168	17
Graduate prospects	78.6%	39
Good honours	82.5%	37
Expected completion rate	86.4%	=56
Student/staff ratio	22.9	124

and is the only Scottish university offering optometry degrees.

Nursing and allied health subjects produced some of GCUs best work in the latest Research Excellence Framework (REF 2021). GCU moves up 11 places in our research quality index to rank 66th.

The School of Engineering and Built Environment teaches three-quarters of Scotland's part-time construction students. The Glasgow School for Business and Society offers highly specialised degrees, having pioneered subjects such as entrepreneurial studies and risk management, with its first cohort of economic policy undergraduates welcomed in September 2021. A new degree in artificial intelligence and data sciences began in September 2022.

GCU is Scotland's leading provider of graduate apprenticeships (known as degree apprenticeships south of the border). So far there are nine programmes and GCU expects more than 750 apprentices to have enrolled by September 2023. Subject areas include civil engineering, cybersecurity and accountancy – a new addition from 2022.

The university's MINT (mentoring, internships, networking and talks) employment programme pairs students with GCU alumni, offers paid internships and industry talks.

GCU's graduate prospects remain in the top 40 according to our analysis tracking those in highly skilled work or further study 15 months after leaving university (39th).

Student satisfaction with the wider undergraduate experience has slipped 21 places to =57, according to our analysis of the latest National Student Survey. Fashion courses are a flagship programme and GCU's British School of Fashion has teamed up with companies including Marks & Spencer, which has a design studio at the London campus and funds scholarships. The university's purpose-built studio in Glasgow, the Fashion Factory, has industry-standard machinery for designing and making clothing.

Known for its friendliness and culture, Glasgow is Scotland's largest city. GCU facilities include the Arc sports centre and 24-hour computer labs. There are only 654 residential places, with priority given to those aged under 19, international or disabled students. The historic West End's redbrick flats are popular for off-campus student living.

Tuition fees

» Fees for Scottish students	£0–£1,820
» RUK fees	£9,250
» Fees for International students 2023–24	£14,500
» For scholarship and bursary information see www.gcu.ac.uk/study/tuitionfees	
» Graduate salary	£24,600

Student numbers

Undergraduates	13,168	(1,775)
Postgraduates	2,504	(1,583)
Applications/places		21,710/3,860
Applications per place		5.6:1
Overall offer rate		51.8%
International students – EU		4.6%
Non-EU		1.7%

Accommodation

University provided places: 654
Self-catered: £100–£118 per week
www.gcu.ac.uk/study/undergraduate/accommodation

Where do the students come from?

State schools (non-grammar)	96.4%	First generation students	43.1%	
Grammar schools	0.4%	Low participation areas	23%	
Independent schools	3.1%	All ethnic minorities	14.5%	

Social inclusion ranking (Scotland): 4

White working class males	8.4%
Black achievement gap	-36.8%
Mature (over 21)	41.2%

University of Gloucestershire

A former Debenhams store in the centre of Gloucester is being transformed into the University of Gloucestershire's City Campus, opening in autumn 2023, a short walk from Gloucester Cathedral and the train station.

Staff and students from the School of Health and Social Care will be among the first to move to the site, where a new arts, health and wellbeing centre will be open to the public as well as students. The library and café will also be shared. The development is the centrepiece of the King's Square regeneration, under Gloucester city's successful £20million bid to the government's Levelling Up Fund.

The new campus will be the university's second in Gloucester, and it has three in Cheltenham, seven miles away. The main Park campus, a mile from the centre of Cheltenham, houses the business, education and professional studies faculty. Art and design facilities are closer to the town centre at Francis Close Hall. Nearby Hardwick has photography and fine art studios as well as its own gallery. Recent upgrades at the Cheltenham sites have added a biomedical laboratory as well as an architecture studio and community teaching space. The purpose-built Oxstalls campus in the centre of Gloucester caters for business, healthcare, sport and exercise sciences.

On the edge of the Cotswolds' Area of Outstanding Natural Beauty, Gloucestershire became a university in 2001, having begun as a teacher-training college. Its primary and secondary teacher-training courses are rated "outstanding" by Ofsted. It was rated silver in the Teaching Excellence Framework for its integrated approach to enhancing employability through volunteering and placements. The Your Future Plan team operates at all of the university's campuses, offering careers and employability services such as a mentoring programme, placement opportunities and keynote speakers.

Having fared better than many other universities in terms of student satisfaction during the pandemic, Gloucestershire has tumbled downhill in our analysis of the results of the latest National Student Survey, published in summer 2022. It topples 50 places to 103rd for student satisfaction with teaching quality and falls 44 places to 106th for satisfaction with the wider undergraduate experience.

Gloucestershire's curriculum gains nine new degrees in September 2023, including audio engineering, nutrition, sport coaching and performance analysis, zoology, and construction project management. Face-to-face teaching is back as the main delivery system, after the university canvassed student opinion. Recordings of lectures and presentations are also available on a virtual learning platform.

The university's degree apprenticeship provision was rated "good" by Ofsted in

The Park
Cheltenham GL50 2RH
03330 141 414
admissions@glos.ac.uk
www.uogsu.com
www.glos.ac.uk
Open days:
see website

Edinburgh
Belfast
CHELTENHAM
Cardiff
London

The Times and The Sunday Times Rankings
Overall Ranking: 112 (last year: =96)

Teaching quality	72.4%	103
Student experience	68.6%	106
Research quality	21%	=111
Entry standards	118	=89
Graduate prospects	67.4%	=104
Good honours	72.2%	=106
Expected completion rate	81.1%	98
Student/staff ratio	17.2	=81

March 2022. Its portfolio of options spans 21 programmes, with about 1,000 learners enrolled. Among them are programmes to train cybersecurity technical professionals, healthcare science practitioners (ophthalmology), registered nurses, and digital marketers.

The university offers diplomas in environmentalism, sustainability research and development projects that bring together researchers from around the world, undertaking work for agencies such as Unesco. Its Countryside and Community Research Institute on the Oxtalls campus is the largest rural research centre in the UK and produced some of Gloucestershire's best results in the latest Research Excellence Framework (REF 2021). Art and design also performed well. Overall, 47% of the university's submission was rated as world-leading or internationally excellent, the top two categories. Gloucestershire doubled the number of subject areas assessed, compared with the previous REF in 2014. The university slid three places to =111th in our research rankings in a year of improving performance across the sector.

About half of each year's entrants qualify for some form of financial aid, from the academic merit scholarship of £400 a year awarded to new students who achieve 128 UCAS tariff points or better, to the care-leavers scholarship of up to £6,625 per year for three years.

The university sits in 31st place in our social inclusion rankings for England and Wales, with an intake overwhelmingly from non-selective state schools (92.8%). The intake includes 47.2% of students who are the first in their family to attend university.

More than 20 sports scholarships are awarded each year, not only to student athletes but also to talented student coaches and officials. A strong sporting tradition is supported by extensive facilities at Oxstalls Sports Park and in Cheltenham. Students have the run of an indoor and outdoor tennis centre, a cold-water therapy pool, playing fields, international-standard 3G pitches for rugby and football, fitness suites, a sports hall and cricket pavilion. The university's sporting alumni include Lizzie Yarnold, the double Olympic skeleton gold medallist, and Ruaridh McConnochie, the former England rugby international.

Gloucester makes an accommodation guarantee to all first-years, including those who arrive via Clearing (about 15% of the intake in 2021). Spa town Cheltenham offers nightlife within a honey-toned Cotswold setting and the Gloucestershire countryside hosts more than 45 music, arts and science and festivals each year, such as the Wychwood, 2000 Trees and the Cheltenham Literature Festival.

Tuition fees

» Fees for UK students	£9,250
» Fees for International students 2023–24	£15,000
» For scholarship and bursary information see www.glos.ac.uk/finance/fees-and-loans	
» Graduate salary	£21,450

Student numbers

Undergraduates	6,157	(277)
Postgraduates	799	(958)
Applications/places		8,630/2,305
Applications per place		3.7:1
Overall offer rate		80.7%
International students – EU		1.7%
Non-EU		3.6%

Accommodation

University provided places: 1,685
Self-catered: £119–£213 per week
First-years guaranteed accommodation
www.glos.ac.uk/accommodation

Where do the students come from?

State schools (non-grammar)	92.8%	First generation students	47.2%	White working-class males	7.6%
Grammar schools	3.5%	Low participation areas	13.1%	Black achievement gap	-16.7%
Independent schools	3.7%	All ethnic minorities	8.1%	Mature (over 21)	35.2%

Social inclusion ranking: 31

Goldsmiths, University of London

Goldsmiths has some of London's best facilities for the creative arts. Dedicated studio space is set aside for all design students and there are nine specialist research laboratories – and even a university yarn shop. Media and communications students have access to digital video and audio editing hardware and software; music studios provide industry-standard equipment for students enrolled on a range of music degrees.

A member of the University of London, Goldsmiths is based in New Cross, in the southeast of the capital, with all undergraduate teaching and support on one site. Building on its history, the themes of environmental and social justice run through the university's latest initiatives. These include the Green New Deal, in which Goldsmiths is aiming to be carbon-neutral by 2025, and incorporating the climate change crisis into its research and curriculum.

The Goldsmiths Centre for Contemporary Art is housed in the Grade II listed former water tanks for the Laurie Grove public baths, while the university's £2.9million performance studios and 200-seat theatre are used by the public as well as students.

In the QS World University Rankings by subject, published in 2022, Goldsmiths ranks 18th in the world for art and design and in the top 100 for the performing arts. Its international stature is further bolstered by the many famous creatives who have studied at Goldsmiths, from Mary Quant in the 1950s to numerous Turner prize winners, including Damien Hirst and the Oscar-winning director Sir Steve McQueen.

Another celebrated Goldsmiths alumnus is Bernardine Evaristo, whose novel Girl, Woman, Other shared the Booker prize in 2019; she graduated with a PhD in creative writing in 2013.

Goldsmiths' degree portfolio extends beyond the creative arts, however, encompassing the humanities, management, law, social sciences and computing. The university is one of just 24 to be granted an Alan Turing Institute Network Development award, which is based on the quality of its research in the fields of data science, artificial intelligence and related fields.

In the latest Research Excellence Framework (REF 2021), 79% of work submitted by Goldsmiths was rated world-leading or internationally excellent, the top two categories. Anthropology; art, design and visual cultures; media, communications and cultural studies; social therapeutic and community studies; and sociology produced some of the best results. Goldsmiths is comfortably in the top half of universities in our analysis of research quality (49th) although it has fallen 13 places in a year against rising standards sector-wide.

A new partnership with Algebra University College in Zagreb will allow students in Croatia

New Cross
London SE14 6NW
020 7078 5300
Course-info@gold.ac.uk
www.goldsmithssu.org
www.gold.ac.uk
Open days:
see website

Edinburgh
Belfast
Cardiff
LONDON

The Times and The Sunday Times Rankings
Overall Ranking: 108 (last year: 61)

Teaching quality	63.8%	130
Student experience	54.7%	130
Research quality	45.5%	49
Entry standards	127	=60
Graduate prospects	65.5%	=115
Good honours	83.6%	=32
Expected completion rate	78.6%	=108
Student/staff ratio	13.9	=21

to study design, computing and marketing courses in English and validated by Goldsmiths.

In the Teaching Excellence Framework (TEF) Goldsmiths managed only bronze, its accreditation dragged down by poor student satisfaction, a common problem in London, and low levels of graduate employment, often a challenge for arts-dominated institutions.

Initiatives to prepare students for future employability include live briefs set by companies such as Kodak and Microsoft for those on design, computing and management degrees. Goldsmiths also has connections with Tate Modern, Universal Music, Home Office and the Lewisham Refugee Network, among others.

Low rates of student satisfaction continue to beleaguer Goldsmiths, which trails our rankings derived from the National Student Survey (NSS) – on both satisfaction with teaching quality and the wider undergraduate experience – as it did in 2020. These outcomes continue to hold back Goldsmiths' overall standing in our main academic table, where it has suffered a huge 47-place fall to 108th this year.

Goldsmiths does better in our social inclusion index, once again ranking in the top 30 in England and Wales (=26). More than half of its students come from ethnic minority backgrounds and it has one of the 35 lowest black achievement gaps.

About 15% of entrants receive one of Goldsmiths' range of scholarships and bursaries.

The university has lost ground on undergraduate completion rates, however. The latest figures show that the 21.1% dropout rate is more than nine percentage points higher than the expected level, based on the social and academic background of Goldsmiths students, and the subject mix.

On campus there is a large college green along with tennis and netball courts for hire. Loring Sports Ground, half an hour away, is the home ground for men and women's football, rugby and cricket.

The university owns or endorses nearly 1,400 study bedrooms, most very local to the university and none further than a 30-minute commute. First-years are prioritised and international students who apply by the deadline are guaranteed a space.

Central London can be reached in 10 minutes by train, while the area has hip enclaves such as Peckham, known for its artistic atmosphere and rooftop bars, while east London is easily accessible via the Overground train line.

Tuition fees

» Fees for UK students £9,250

» Fees for International students 2023–24 £17,560–£24,590

» For scholarship and bursary information see www.gold.ac.uk/ug/fees-funding/

» Graduate salary £24,000

Student numbers

Undergraduates	5,987	(158)
Postgraduates	2,473	(1,212)
Applications/places	10,820/2,085	
Applications per place	5.2:1	
Overall offer rate	72%	
International students – EU	7.8%	
Non-EU	13.9%	

Accommodation

University provided places: 1,395
Self-catered: £157–£336 per week
www.gold.ac.uk/accommodation

Where do the students come from?

State schools (non-grammar)	87.7%	First generation students	45.9%	White working-class males	4.3%
Grammar schools	3.3%	Low participation areas	5%	Black achievement gap	-15%
Independent schools	9%	All ethnic minorities	51.5%	Mature (over 21)	28.4%

Social inclusion ranking: =26

University of Greenwich

Investment in teaching facilities and student-facing resources appears to be hitting the right note, as student satisfaction rates are on the rise at Greenwich, according to our analysis of the outcomes of the latest National Student Survey, published in summer 2022. For student satisfaction with teaching quality, the university in southeast London ranks =41 (up 23 places) while their evaluation of the wider undergraduate experience ranks it =42 (up 18 places).

At the Avery Hill campus on the outskirts of southeast London, a makeover of the Victorian mansion adds three clinical skills laboratories and a new library. It enables student nurses, midwives and paramedics to train for real-life emergencies using augmented-reality technology and lifelike manikins. Three manikins were built for the university and the most complex, Lucina, can even simulate birth.

Greenwich was awarded silver in the Teaching Excellence Framework (TEF) for investing in high-quality physical and digital resources to enhance learning. Assessors praised course design and assessment practices that stretch students, and noted that personalised provision was rewarded with good engagement and commitment to learning. Lecture-capture facilities are in place, although the main teaching model is face-to-face.

The Greenwich campus occupies a World Heritage site overlooking the Thames, with the completion in 2018 of a £23million refurbishment of the historic Dreadnought building centralising many services, including the students' union, and flexible teaching spaces.

The prizewinning Stockwell Street development, also in Greenwich, was designed partly by the university's specialists in architecture and has a landscaped roof terrace, large architecture studio, model-making workshop, and television and sound studios as well as the main library and other facilities.

At Chatham, in Kent, Greenwich shares the Medway campus with the University of Kent and Canterbury Christ Church University. The schools of pharmacy, science and engineering are based at Medway and the campus also has nursing and some business students. The listed redbrick buildings, a former Royal Navy base, house a student hub with study spaces as well as a restaurant, bar and nightclub.

Greenwich moves 19 places up our research rankings to =74th place after an improved performance in the latest Research Excellence Framework (REF 2021) compared with the previous assessment in 2014. Double the number of academic staff were entered (400) and agriculture, building and food science produced some of the best results.

The Natural Resources Institute at Medway was awarded a Queen's Anniversary Prize in 2019 for developing smart solutions to tackle pests that cause plague, famine and disease.

Maritime Greenwich Campus
Old Royal Naval College
Park Row
London SE10 9LS
020 8331 9000
courseinfo@gre.ac.uk
www.greenwichsu.co.uk
www.gre.ac.uk
Open days:
see website

The Times and The Sunday Times **Rankings**
Overall Ranking: 84 (last year: =89)

Teaching quality	76.7%	=41
Student experience	73.4%	=42
Research quality	32.9%	=74
Entry standards	117	=93
Graduate prospects	70.2%	=84
Good honours	77.5%	65
Expected completion rate	83.4%	=81
Student/staff ratio	19.5	112

Through its partnership with SEGi College in Malaysia and FPT University in Vietnam, Greenwich is broadening its course offering at outposts in Kuala Lumpur, Subang Jaya and Ho Chi Minh City, among other Asian locations. New options for degrees include: accounting and finance; human resource management; graphic and digital design and computing. In London, food science and nutrition joins the curriculum from September 2023.

The portfolio of degree apprenticeships spans 20 programmes across the faculties of engineering and science, education, health and human sciences, and liberal arts and science. By 2023, Greenwich expects to have 500 degree apprentices, one of the larger contingents in British higher education. Graduate employability initiatives include opportunities to interact with employers at the campus and through virtual events such as hackathons, a mentoring scheme and networking events. High-quality internships and other opportunities are also available. Pfizer, Northern Trust, BAE Systems, Soho House, the Dorchester and Warner Media are among companies tapping into the university's talent stream.

Abiy Ahmed, a Greenwich graduate, became prime minister of Ethiopia aged 42 in 2018. Africa's youngest leader, Ahmed won the Nobel peace prize in 2019 for his efforts to achieve international co-operation. The university has a second Nobel laureate in the late Dr Charles Kao, who won the prize for physics in 2009 for his work in fibre optics. Baroness (Doreen) Lawrence of Clarendon, the mother of the murdered black teenager Stephen Lawrence, killed in a racially motivated attack, is another former student, noted for her campaign for justice and equality of opportunity.

The university has a strong record in our social inclusion table. With 55.3% of undergraduates from ethnic minorities, Greenwich is in the top 25 universities in the country on this measure. More than 57% of students are the first in their family to go to university, putting Greenwich in 13th place.

There are gyms at all three campuses. Sports halls at Avery Hill and Medway are suitable for badminton, basketball, netball, futsal and volleyball. Avery Hill's facilities include four grass football pitches, a 3G pitch for football and rugby, a hockey pitch, tennis courts, and an indoor 3G training facility that is shared with Charlton FC. First-years are guaranteed a room in halls of residence if they apply before the August 21 deadline, although latecomers can usually be accommodated, too.

Tuition fees

»	Fees for UK students	£9,250
	Foundation courses	£6,165
»	Fees for International students 2023–24	£15,100–£17,000
»	Pharmacy	£21,200
»	For scholarship and bursary information see www.gre.ac.uk/finance	
»	Graduate salary	£25,000

Student numbers

Undergraduates	15,028	(1,163)
Postgraduates	4,683	(1,885)
Applications/places	27,930/6,590	
Applications per place	4.2:1	
Overall offer rate	65.1%	
International students – EU	10.3%	
Non-EU	10.8%	

Accommodation

University provided places: 2,185
Self-catered: £118–£291 per week
First-years guaranteed accommodation
www.gre.ac.uk/accommodation

Where do the students come from?

State schools (non-grammar)	94%	First generation students	57.3%	
Grammar schools	4.4%	Low participation areas	7.4%	
Independent schools	1.6%	All ethnic minorities	55.3%	

Social inclusion ranking: 22

White working-class males	5.5%
Black achievement gap	-18.4%
Mature (over 21)	34.9%

Harper Adams University

Developing sustainable farming methods and helping UK agriculture to achieve net-zero carbon emissions are the primary goals of Harper Adams's new School of Sustainable Food and Farming. A UK first, it is a collaboration with Morrisons supermarket, McDonald's UK and Ireland and the National Farmers' Union.

Harper Adams offers undergraduate courses to train new sustainable farmers and short courses and apprenticeships for agricultural workers to upskill. The school is also a hub for research and will aid policy-making to ensure that the farming sector benefits from support and advice.

The new school marks another milestone in the history of Harper Adams – long renowned as the UK's leading specialist agricultural institution. The university still occupies a single site on the Shropshire country estate where it was founded in 1901.

Harper Adams is under the new leadership of Professor Ken Sloan, the vice-chancellor, previously deputy vice-chancellor of Monash University in Australia and formerly chief operating officer at the University of Warwick. An advocate for social inclusion and equality in education, he also provides mentorship and leadership in the LGBTQ+ community.

Sloan joins a university that underwent a period of growth under his predecessor,

Dr David Llewellyn, during which it became one of only two institutions to achieve gold in successive years in the government's Teaching Excellence Framework (TEF). Having earned gold in 2017, it did not need to be reassessed – but the university wanted to test its performance against the latest measures. The TEF panel praised course design, delivery and assessment practices, which challenged students to achieve their full potential, and gain knowledge and skills valued by employers.

However, Harper Adams has tumbled 23 places for student satisfaction with teaching quality to rank =37, according to our analysis of the results of the latest National Student Survey, published in summer 2022. Satisfaction with the wider undergraduate experience has fallen less sharply from 11th in 2021 to =21. It may prove to be a bump in the road: the university ranked in the top 10 for both measures before the pandemic and largely maintained its seal of approval from students in 2021.

In June 2021, the Princess Royal, the university's chancellor, officially opened the Harper & Keele Veterinary School. The school, a joint venture with the University of Keele, has been accepting students since 2020.

Campus facilities include the modern Bamford Library and the Weston teaching and learning building. Students also get to learn "in the field" at the university's 627-hectare farm.

Students have placement years and accredited part-time programmes in industry,

Edgmond
Newport
Shropshire TF10 8NB
01952 815 000
admissions@harper-adams.ac.uk
www.harpersu.com
www.harper-adams.ac.uk
Open days:
see website

The Times and The Sunday Times Rankings
Overall Ranking: 47 (last year: 29)

Teaching quality	76.8%	=37
Student experience	75.9%	=21
Research quality	19.5%	116
Entry standards	123	=72
Graduate prospects	71.6%	=71
Good honours	73.2%	97
Expected completion rate	92.2%	33
Student/staff ratio	13.8	=15

meaning that only about half of them are on campus at the same time. The university maintains links with four agricultural universities in China and one in the Netherlands.

The demand for undergraduate places at Harper Adams reached a record high in the 2021 admissions round, up 26% year-on-year, while student enrolments swelled by 29% in the same cycle – returning them to a level last seen in 2016. A curriculum review is underway at the university, with new degrees in the fields of engineering, business and food science. Six new degrees will be rolled out in September 2023, including food science and innovation – with specialisms in product development, nutrition, food technology, marketing, and business, agribusiness management, and food quality with retail management.

Harper Adams offers four degree apprenticeships in rural surveying (offered as Level 6 and Level 7 qualifications), food and drink engineering, food industry technical professional, and senior leader (food business management). Programmes for vet technicians (livestock) and a Higher Level programme in food and drink engineering are in development, which should bring the number on courses to about 300 by September 2023.

Harper Adams, granted full university status in 2012, is building its research pedigree. Sixty per cent of the body of research submitted to the latest Research Excellence Framework (REF 2021) was rated world leading or internationally excellent (the top two categories). However, even greater improvement elsewhere means that Harper Adams now falls outside our top 100 for research quality, ranking 116th.

Scholarships funded by philanthropic and industry donations totalling over £500,000 were awarded to more than 130 students in 2020-22. None are made at admission: instead, students qualify for awards as they study.

Student accommodation, more than half of it catered, is guaranteed on campus to those from abroad, or who are disabled or have left care.

The rural setting does not diminish the vigour of the social scene and the campus has its own local, the Welly Inn, as well as the students' union Main Bar. Sports facilities include a shooting ground as well as a gymnasium, heated outdoor swimming pool, rugby, cricket, football and hockey pitches, tennis courts and an all-weather sports pitch. A rowing club operates from nearby Shrewsbury.

Tuition fees

» Fees for UK students	£9,250
» Fees for International students 2023–24	£11,250
» Veterinary Medicine	£19,250–£33,000
» For scholarship and bursary information see www.harper-adams.ac.uk/apply/finance/	
» Graduate salary	£24,000

Student numbers

Undergraduates	2,375	(1,894)
Postgraduates	103	(765)
Applications/places		3,310/765
Applications per place		4.7:1
Overall offer rate		83.1%
International students – EU		1.2%
Non-EU		2.6%

Accommodation

University provided places: 774
Catered costs: £140–£171 per week
Self-catered £130–£139
First-years given priority for accommodation
www.harper-adams.ac.uk/university-life/accommodation

Where do the students come from?

State schools (non-grammar)	77.2%	First generation students	35.3%	White working-class males	4.8%
Grammar schools	6.7%	Low participation areas	8.3%	Black achievement gap	n/a
Independent schools	16.1%	All ethnic minorities	4.1%	Mature (over 21)	15.1%

Social inclusion ranking: 79

Hartpury University

Founded in 1948 as an agricultural institute, Hartpury makes its second appearance in our academic league table. University life centres around a Gloucestershire farming business based at five sites spanning 360 hectares. The main Home Farm on campus occupies 72 hectares while the other four are nearby. Students learn how to farm cows, calves, sheep and arable land, and the business supplies Sainsbury's, Müller and Glencore among others.

As well as offering a broad land-based selection of courses, the curriculum has grown to encompass animal, equine, sport and veterinary nursing degrees.

Hartpury was awarded gold in the Teaching Excellence Framework in 2018, just before gaining university status. The panel praised the institution for course design and assessment practices that provided a high level of stretch and challenge. It also highlighted the "inquiry-based" approach to teaching and learning and its "optimum contact hours, which secure high levels of engagement and commitment to learning and study from students".

Students receive 15 hours per week of teaching contact time, and the university pledges that no more than two hours will be online. Most degrees include a work placement and many students have the option of an integrated placement year as part of their studies – compulsory on some courses.

The university has been ploughing plenty of investment into facilities. Equine students have access to a new £500,000 water treadmill facility, with fresh teaching and stabling resources, as well as the new equine and animal assisted activity area – a £730,000 arena for equine and canine research and training. The arena also hosts Hartpury's international horse trial and dressage events – among them the FEI (Fédération Equestre Internationale) Dressage and Eventing European Championships for Young Riders and Juniors. There is stabling for 230 horses – used by students for their learning and by equestrian athletes in training.

Students can even bring their own horse to university (not many places can say that). Hartpury also has a rider performance centre and equine therapy centre among provision.

Facilities for bovine studies include a dairy bull-beef rearing unit and a 296-cubicle dairy unit. An advanced dairy parlour on campus reduces milking times and improves hygiene and welfare for its 250-strong award-winning herd, while also providing hands-on experience for students. A herd of 50 pedigree Guernsey cattle are a recent addition and allow students to carry out research into the breed within an applied, commercial setting.

As part of a 10-year vision to turn its commercial Home Farm into an agritech

---

Hartpury House
Gloucester
GL19 3BE
01452 702 244
admissions@hartpury.ac.uk
www.hartpury.ac.uk
hsu.unioncloud.org
Open days:
see website

The Times and The Sunday Times **Rankings**
Overall Ranking 105 (last year =112)

Teaching quality	82.2%	6
Student experience	76.9%	14
Research quality	15.8%	120
Entry standards	121	=77
Graduate prospects	66.2%	111
Good honours	62.5%	131
Expected completion rate	n/a	
Student/staff ratio	23.6	126

pioneer, the university launched a dedicated Agri-Tech Centre in 2019 and has more recently opened the first of its Tech Box Park workshops for local agritech businesses, which also provide collaborative opportunities for students.

A strong record in student satisfaction has been re-established after a wobble last year as a result of the Covid-19 pandemic – understandable, given the practical courseload. In our analysis of the latest National Student Survey (NSS), Hartpury ranks sixth for student satisfaction with teaching quality and 14th for the wider undergraduate experience.

Partnerships with more than 3,000 employers across agriculture, animal, equine, sport and veterinary nursing provide opportunities for students to benefit from field trips, careers events, work placements and live briefs. Two hundred events take place on campus, too, from a qualifying dog agility competition to agricultural community events – offering opportunities for students to volunteer and get behind-the-scenes insights.

Nine out of every 10 students come from a non-selective state school. Nearly half (45.3%) are the first in their immediate family to go to university and 6.8% have an ethnic minority background.

On campus, the £9.8million Graze student centre is a hub for food and drink outlets, social spaces and flexible learning areas. The ULH (University Learning Hub) is set to open in the 2023-24 academic year and will bring group work pods, open-plan social areas and quiet study zones as well as being the base for the library and careers services.

A £10million sports academy opened in the centre of campus in 2019, and houses biomechanics and human performance laboratories, an anti-gravity treadmill, an altitude chamber, and high-speed cameras and digital mirrors to map body movement. There are also medical and physiotherapy rooms, a rehabilitation suite and a large multisports hall. A new performance gym opened in 2022. The sports academy is surrounded by eight grass and two rubber crumb pitches, while a golf driving range is by the entrance to campus. Hartpury University RFC recruits many students as players.

Most student bedrooms are on site and Hartpury endeavours to allocate student accommodation for first-years and international students, but does not offer a guarantee.

Tuition fees

» Fees for UK students	£925–£9,250
» Fees for International students 2023–24	£13,000
» For scholarship and bursary information see www.hartpury.ac.uk/university/facilities/life-at-hartpury/finance/	
» Graduate salary	£20,000

Student numbers

Undergraduates	1,916	(25)
Postgraduates	51	(207)
Applications/places		3,480/875
Applications per place		4.1
Overall offer rate		n/a
International students – EU		4.1%
Non-EU		3.8%

Accommodation

University provided places: 1,202
Catered costs: £136–£153 per week
Self-catered: £136–£155
First years-given priority for accommodation
www.hartpury.ac.uk/university/facilities/life-at-hartpury/accommodation

Where do the students come from?

State schools (non-grammar)	90.9%	First generation students	45.3%	Social inclusion ranking: 68	
				White working-class males	7.2%
Grammar schools	2.9%	Low participation areas	14%	Black achievement gap	n/a
Independent schools	6.3%	All ethnic minorities	6.8%	Mature (over 21)	17.9%

Heriot-Watt University

Heriot-Watt University is home to the UK's first National Robotarium, due to open in autumn 2022. The purpose-built facility on the Riccarton campus, a joint partnership with the University of Edinburgh, will explore how robotics and autonomous systems can address real-life issues. Delivering research and support for business, as well as data skills and new undergraduate and postgraduate programmes, the aim is to be a leading innovation hub for the practical application of these technologies, to drive economic growth and transform lives worldwide.

The new centre augments existing facilities which include laboratories in ocean systems, human robotic interaction, and assisted living. The recently-opened GRID (Global Research, Innovation and Discovery) centre has collaborative learning spaces which feature augmented reality, virtual reality and gaming studios. Its enterprise hub promotes emerging technology and inventions, where staff and students are encouraged to pursue the commercial potential of creative ideas.

Elsewhere at the Edinburgh campus, the library's £6million refurbishment has increased capacity to more than 1,000 study spaces. A virtual learning environment has been introduced, bringing online learning materials to complement in-person teaching. The primary teaching model is on-campus, with students expected to participate in learning opportunities in person – albeit while reaping the benefits of online resources and support, connecting with Heriot-Watt students globally and getting the best out of self-directed study.

Named after George Heriot and James Watt, two giants of industry and commerce, Heriot-Watt began as the world's first institute for mechanics in 1821. As well as the main campus, the university has a site in the Scottish Borders, 35 miles south of Edinburgh in Galashiels, which specialises in textiles, fashion and design. An Orkney campus in Stromness caters exclusively for postgraduates and specialises in renewable energy. A former winner of our International University of the Year award, Heriot-Watt also has campuses in Malaysia and Dubai – the latter with the capacity for up to 4,000 students. The university's Go Global programme offers students the chance to move between campuses for a semester, a year, or longer.

The prospects for graduates are improving, reflecting a long focus on graduate employability at Heriot-Watt. In our analysis of the latest Graduate Outcomes survey, published in summer 2022, the university climbs 10 places to =36 with 79.3% of students in highly skilled jobs or postgraduate study 15 months after leaving Heriot-Watt. Many degree programmes include industry placements or projects and carry professional accreditation.

Options for graduate apprenticeships (known as degree apprenticeships outside

Edinburgh EH14 4AS
0131 451 3376
studywithus@hw.ac.uk
www.hwunion.com
www.hw.ac.uk
Open days:
see website

EDINBURGH
Belfast
London
Cardiff

The Times and The Sunday Times **Rankings**

Overall Ranking: =57 (last year: =30)

Teaching quality	66.5%	128
Student experience	66.7%	=116
Research quality	48.7%	44
Entry standards	172	13
Graduate prospects	79.3%	=36
Good honours	81.9%	38
Expected completion rate	86%	61
Student/staff ratio	18	=95

Scotland) are broader here than at most other Scottish universities, with 500 students enrolled. The university plans to add 220 more places across the nine existing programmes: engineering, design and manufacturing, IT management for business, IT software development, civil engineering, built environment (quantity surveying), business management, data science, and instrumentation measurement and control.

A new degree in sport and exercise science welcomed its first students in September 2022, and an accelerated three-year version begins in the 2023-24 academic year. Enrolments were up by 19% in 2021, year-on-year, although applications have dipped a little each year for the past six admissions cycles.

Rated silver in the Teaching Excellence Framework, Heriot-Watt drew praise for course design that was "directly informed by research activity".

Physics was a strength for Heriot-Watt in the results of the latest Research Excellence Framework (REF 2021), with 97% of the university's submission in the subject rated world-leading or internationally excellent (the top categories). Mathematical sciences; architecture, built environment and planning; and engineering – where Heriot-Watt made joint submissions with the University of Edinburgh – also did well. In our research quality index, based on sector-wide improvements on the previous national assessment in 2014, the university has dropped out of the top 30 to rank 44th.

In our analysis of the latest National Student Survey, published in summer 2022, Heriot-Watt is in the bottom 10 for satisfaction with teaching quality (128th). It has also tumbled a startling 83 places for how students feel about the wider undergraduate experience to rank =116.

A generous bursary system makes financial awards to about 30% of the intake of students from England, Wales and Northern Ireland. Students living in Scotland may be eligible for the HWU Bursary of £1,000 per year.

The main Riccarton campus hosts Oriam, Scotland's national centre for performance in many sports, where world-class facilities are available to Heriot-Watt students. The £33million complex features a Hampden Park replica pitch, plus medical facilities.

All first-years who apply by the housing deadline are guaranteed one of 1,823 spaces in the conveniently placed Edinburgh halls of residence. Regular bus services link the 380-acre parkland campus to the city centre's cultural hotspots and thriving nightlife.

Tuition fees

- » Fees for Scottish students   £0–£1,820
- » RUK fees   £9,250
- » Fees for International students 2023–24   £16,000–£20,584
- » For scholarship and bursary information see www.abdn.ac.uk/study/undergraduate/finance.php
- » Graduate salary   £25,000

Student numbers

Undergraduates	7,258	(390)
Postgraduates	2,389	(1,161)
Applications/places	8,745/1,650	
Applications per place	5.3:1	
Overall offer rate	84.3%	
International students – EU	4.7%	
Non-EU	15.5%	

Accommodation

University provided places: 1,823
Self-catered: £154–£215 per week
First-years guaranteed accommodation
https://www.hw.ac.uk/uk/edinburgh/accommodation.htm

Where do the students come from?

State schools (non-grammar)	85.3%	First generation students	33.1%	White working-class males	n/a
Grammar schools	4.4%	Low participation areas	13.4%	Black achievement gap	-18.5%
Independent schools	10.3%	All ethnic minorities	13.2%	Mature (over 21)	23.4%

Social inclusion ranking (Scotland): 10

University of Hertfordshire

Hertfordshire's research performance has improved in the latest Research Excellence Framework (REF 2021), propelling the university 26 places up our research rankings to reach 60th place. The university submitted work by a team of 346 academic staff – up 58% compared with the previous national assessment in 2014 – including more early-career researchers. The best results were in allied health subjects, followed by computer science and psychology.

Among the fruits of the university's investment in facilities is the £61million science building on the College Lane campus, benefiting undergraduate teaching and learning as well as research. The SPECS building, a multimillion facility for physics, engineering and computer science, is scheduled to open in 2024. This will give students access to hands-on learning resources, such as a robotics lab, advanced cybersecurity facilities, an electric vehicle centre, flight simulator and wind tunnel.

College Lane, Hertfordshire's original campus, is a 20-minute walk from the purpose-built £120million De Havilland base and the two are linked by a free shuttle bus, footpaths and cycle lanes. The Hutton Hub has student services on the College Lane site, where there is also an art gallery and the Automotive Centre – home of engineering teaching. Many of its graduates have gone on to work in Formula One teams.

When upgrading Hertfordshire to a gold award in 2018, the Teaching Excellence Framework (TEF) panel commended the strong emphasis on work-based learning.

Professional accreditations or approvals are often built into courses at Hertfordshire, and students leave with CV extras such as Microsoft qualifications or City & Guilds awards. Most courses offer work placements and the university's careers team supports students for four years after graduation. The chance to study at one of more than 170 universities around the world is promoted to students – for a term, a summer or a year.

The De Havilland campus houses Hatfield's £12million Enterprise Hub. The top floor's teaching space is for students on courses including degree apprenticeships and MBAs. The Institute of Sport opened at De Havilland in 2021, bringing modern facilities for students and researchers in the School of Life and Medical Sciences.

The university has its own teaching observatory. Bayfordbury Observatory, which was opened by Sir Patrick Moore, offers hands-on learning in astronomy and astrophysics six miles from Hatfield.

Rates of student satisfaction have been consistently sound at Hertfordshire. Our analysis of the latest National Student Survey (NSS) shows the university rising 13 places to rank 59th for satisfaction with teaching quality. Hertfordshire has slipped year-on-year from

---

College Lane
Hatfield AL10 9AB
01707 284 000
ask@herts.ac.uk
www.hertfordshire.su
www.herts.ac.uk
Open days:
see website

The Times and The Sunday Times **Rankings**
Overall Ranking: 91 (last year: =96)

Teaching quality	75.6%	59
Student experience	71.8%	66
Research quality	39.2%	60
Entry standards	106	=126
Graduate prospects	72.4%	69
Good honours	70.6%	=112
Expected completion rate	83.4%	=81
Student/staff ratio	16.5	=71

=56 to 66 for how students feel about the wider undergraduate experience.

More than 700 higher and degree apprentices are enrolled on Hertfordshire's 12 apprenticeship programmes. Fields include engineering (electronics and mechanical), nursing and sports management. A degree apprenticeship in enhanced clinical practice is to begin in September 2023.

Demand for places at Hertfordshire is prone to fluctuate. Fewer new students started courses in 2021 than in any other year in the past decade, with numbers down 23% year-on-year. Applications fell much less sharply in 2021, however, by about 5%, but after six consecutive years of declines they reached their lowest level for 10 years. Four new degrees launched in 2022, in business and human resource management; fashion communication; psychology in education; and data science – which may boost student numbers going forwards.

Few universities have more students drawn from ethnic minorities than Hertfordshire, where nearly six in 10 are in that category, unusual outside a big city in southern England. Few can beat its recruitment from non-selective state schools (96.3%). More than half of Hertfordshire's students are the first in their family to go to university. Hertfordshire has links with schools across the county to encourage wider participation and the university runs outreach events such as GCSE booster workshops,

student shadowing and summer schools.

For new students from households with incomes of less than £25,000 and who come from areas with a low progression rate to university, Hertfordshire offers an undergraduate bursary worth £1,000 (paid in two £500 instalments in the first year of study only).

The £15million Hertfordshire Sports Village features a 110-station health and fitness centre, 25m pool, physiotherapy and sports injury clinic and a multipurpose sports hall.

With 4,600 study bedrooms across both campuses, the university can guarantee a place for all first-years. Trains to King's Cross take 25 minutes, although there is also plenty to do in the network of local Hertfordshire towns, including St Albans, Watford and Broxbourne, as well as Hatfield itself.

The redevelopment of the Forum nightclub on the College Lane campus has created two socialising areas – an informal bar and a second-floor nightclub, each with 530-person capacities. A student wellbeing team offers counselling, mental health support and disability support.

Tuition fees

» Fees for UK students	£9,250
Foundation courses	£6,165
» Fees for International students 2023–24	£14,000–£20,085
» For scholarship and bursary information see www.herts.ac.uk/study/fees-and-funding	
» Graduate salary	£24,907

Student numbers

Undergraduates	15,492 (2,886)
Postgraduates	7,015 (4,706)
Applications/places	18,760/3,485
Applications per place	5.4:1
Overall offer rate	67.8%
International students – EU	4.4%
Non-EU	12.5%

Accommodation

University provided places: 4,600
Self-catered: £106–£214 per week
First-years guaranteed accommodation
www.herts.ac.uk/life/student-accommodation

Where do the students come from?

State schools (non-grammar)	96.3%	First generation students	51.7%	
Grammar schools	2.2%	Low participation areas	7%	
Independent schools	1.5%	All ethnic minorities	58.4%	

Social inclusion ranking: =45

White working-class males	3.6%
Black achievement gap	-16.4%
Mature (over 21)	24.9%

University of the Highlands and Islands

Undergraduate life for students at the University of the Highlands and Islands (UHI) is unique in the UK. The university's buildings – spanning 13 campuses and more than 70 local learning centres – are set amid some of Scotland's most stunning locations.

UHI has sites stretching from Shetland in the far northeast to Campbeltown in the southwest, from Lews Castle College (set in 600 acres of parkland) on the Isle of Lewis in the northwest to Perth College in the east. Some colleges are relatively large and located in centres such as Perth, Elgin and Inverness; others are smaller, including some where the primary focus is research. There are a dozen specialist research facilities in total.

The university recorded a strong performance in the latest Research Excellence Framework (REF 2021). Nearly three-quarters of the work submitted achieved the top two categories: world leading or internationally excellent. Within the research area of earth systems and environmental sciences, 84% of research reached the top two categories.

UHI Sabhal Mòr Ostaig, on the Isle of Skye, is the only Gaelic-medium centre of higher and further education in the world. Across the university, many courses can be studied in the language. UHI was the first in Scotland to produce a Gaelic Language Plan, which includes proposals to enhance the Gaelic curriculum, produce more bilingual resources for students and hold more Gaelic events.

With students often in far-flung locations, blended learning has always been the norm at UHI. Options, depending on the course taken, include online, face-to-face, practical, fieldwork and self-study. Some courses were already exclusively online, while for other students the shift in delivery was a welcome change – and as a result is now here to stay, even as other programmes have returned to their in-person elements. The university recognises the need to bolster the wider student experience with on-campus activities, too, be they academic, social or support.

More than half the students are aged over 21 at the start of their courses, and more than 3,000 undergraduates study part-time, often juggling studies with work and childcare. Nevertheless, about 5,500 study full-time, attached to one of the campuses or learning centres.

Just as part-time and distance learning help UHI serve its region and country, they make comparison with other universities a challenge. UHI was withdrawn from our rankings in 2017 on account of its dissipated nature and the large numbers of part-time staff and further-education students within its colleges.

Offers are set at the minimum level required to successfully complete a course, rather than "standard" and "minimum".

12b Ness Walk
Inverness IV3 5SQ
01463 279 190
info@uhi.ac.uk
www.uhi.ac.uk/en/students/
get-involved/students-association
www.uhi.ac.uk
Open days:
see website

The Times and The Sunday Times **Rankings**
Overall Ranking: n/a
No data available

This supports its remit to widen access to higher education with additional consideration given to applicants from Scottish postcodes with the highest areas of social deprivation, those who have been in care, those who have taken part in a Schools for Higher Education programme, such as ASPIRENorth, or those who have attended a school that has a low progression rate to university studies.

UHI attracts the second-highest proportion of students from non-selective state schools among Scottish universities (98%). The university is No 1 in Scotland on our new measure of social inclusion covering the recruitment of white working-class males, the most underrepresented group in higher education. About one in nine students at UHI come from this demographic.

The course portfolio reflects the needs of the locality of each campus. UHI works with organisations as diverse as the Crown Estate, Scottish Land and Estates, the Cairngorms National Park Authority, the Dounreay Partnership and SSE, the Perth-based energy company. A partnership with IBM has spawned the innovative BSc in applied software development, giving students access to the latest technologies replicating modern software development practices, guest speakers, industry mentors from around the world, and enhanced IBM Cloud access.

Boeing, Lockheed Martin and Liberty have been partners in developing STEM (science, technology, engineering and mathematics) subjects, including aerospace and advanced technology. The optometry sector, including Specsavers, has been a collaborative partner in developing UHI's optometry degree, designed to support employment demand in rural areas. There are two graduate apprenticeship programmes supporting the civil engineering and childcare sectors in Scotland, via a BEng (Hons) in civil engineering and a BA (Hons) in early learning and childcare.

All students and graduates have access to FutureMe, UHI's online platform to help manage career paths. This incorporates the JobShop, for job and placement opportunities. For graduate prospects, UHI is =36th in our analysis based on the Graduate Outcomes survey, looking at the proportion in highly skilled work or postgraduate study 15 months after finishing their degree.

Most students live locally to the colleges, but the university offers just over 600 places in student accommodation, about half of them at UHI Inverness College.

Tuition fees

» Fees for Scottish students	£0–£1,820
RUK fees	£9,250
» Fees for International students 2023–24	£13,020–£14,310
» For scholarship and bursary information see www.uhi.ac.uk/en/studying-at-uhi/first-steps/how-much-will-it-cost	
» Graduate salary	£24,500

Student numbers

Undergraduates	5,946	(2,998)
Postgraduates	445	(1,020)
Applications/places	4,550/2,340	
Applications per place	1.9:1	
Overall offer rate	59.7%	
International students – EU	2.5%	
Non-EU	0.4%	

Accommodation

University provided places: 612
Catered: £120–£161 per week
Self-catered: £109–£143 per week
www.uhi.ac.uk/en/studying-at-uhi/first-steps/accommodation

Where do the students come from?

State schools (non-grammar)	98%	First generation students	42.5%	White working-class males	n/a
Grammar schools	0.3%	Low participation areas	8.6%	Black achievement gap	n/a
Independent schools	1.6%	All ethnic minorities	3.3%	Mature (over 21)	57.6%

Social inclusion ranking (Scotland): 7

University of Huddersfield

The £30million Barbara Hepworth Building, named after the sculptor and West Yorkshire native, is among the purpose-built facilities at Huddersfield's single-site campus, a short walk from the town centre. Equipped for the study of art, design and architecture, the building features creative studios and technology resources that combine digital and physical innovation – all overlooking the Narrow Canal, which runs through the campus.

The university's £31million Joseph Priestley Building caters for science subjects, providing students with teaching spaces, workshops and laboratories, as well as its own student hub and social area. Next on the horizon is the institution's National Health Innovation campus, due to open in 2024.

Huddersfield is the largest provider of apprenticeships in nursing and allied health in Yorkshire and the Humber, as well as being one of only two universities contracted to deliver Health Education England's distance learning nursing degree, launched in 2021. The university's portfolio of degree apprenticeships gains a programme in enhanced clinical practice in September 2023, which will bring the number of courses offered to 12.

An academic restructure in 2021 merged the university's School of Art, Design and Architecture with the School of Music, Humanities and Media to create the School of Arts and Humanities. The new department encompasses the university's Yorkshire Film and Television School. The school's latest degrees include film-making; television studies and production, performance for screen, and screenwriting. From September 2023, the portfolio of drama-related courses will gain a performance element.

The constant refreshing of the curriculum is evidence of Huddersfield's commitment to maintaining the same level of teaching and learning experience for students that earned it gold in the government's Teaching Excellence Framework (TEF).

Student feedback in the National Student Survey (NSS) backs up the TEF's warm review. Our analysis of the results of the latest National Student Survey, published in 2022, ranks Huddersfield =52 for satisfaction with teaching quality, rising 53 places on 2021. Teaching has returned an in-person, on-campus model. The university has also improved from 112th place to =59 for how students feel about their wider experience.

Having done well in the previous Research Excellence Framework (REF 2014), when the arts and social sciences flourished, Huddersfield falls 18 places to 79th in our research quality index, based on the results of the latest national assessment, REF 2021, although strong performances were noted in music, creative writing, building, land and

Queensgate
Huddersfield HD1 3DH
01484 472 625
study@hud.ac.uk
www.huddersfield.su
www.hud.ac.uk
Open days:
see website

The Times and The Sunday Times Rankings
Overall Ranking: 73 (last year: 75)

Teaching quality	75.9%	=52
Student experience	72.1%	=59
Research quality	31.1%	79
Entry standards	122	76
Graduate prospects	67.6%	=102
Good honours	77.2%	67
Expected completion rate	84.5%	=74
Student/staff ratio	14.7	=33

property management, and town and country planning. The university's Institute of Railway Research won a coveted Queen's Anniversary Prize in 2019.

A link with Santander promotes internship opportunities that have often resulted in permanent positions for graduates, the university notes. All undergraduates may undertake work-related experience during their studies. Other employability initiatives include an alliance with the Chartered Management Institute (CMI) that provides all students with a CMI leadership qualification. Companies at which Huddersfield students undertook work placements in 2021-22 include boohooMan, Jaguar Land Rover, Bank of America and HMRC.

A strong record in our social inclusion index continues for Huddersfield, which rises three places to rank =17. More than half (57.2%) of new students are the first in their family to go to university and 95% are educated at non-selective state schools.

About three in 10 new undergraduates qualify for financial aid through a bursary or scholarship. Huddersfield has a range of outreach activities including the year-long Progression Module, a skills-boosting programme worth 12 UCAS tariff points. The points can be used towards entry requirements at Huddersfield, Leeds Beckett and Leeds Trinity universities.

There is also the Aspire to Uni 10-year outreach programme for pupils from target primary schools, designed to improve their results and progression from SATs up to post-16 courses. Headstart Huddersfield offers applicants who qualify under widening participation criteria an extra eight UCAS points, plus support including guaranteed interviews and help deciding where to apply.

Digs is Huddersfield's preferred accommodation provider. It has 1,367 rooms in the Storthes Hall Park student village where prices start at just £82.50 per week per person for those willing to share a twin room. First-years are guaranteed a space and can make requests such as living with friends, or for a single-gender flat or in a quieter area. Where possible, Digs allocates at least two students on a similar course in the same flat.

At the £22.5million Student Central building, sports facilities include an 80-station gym, two multi-purpose studios, a physiotherapy treatment room and a double sports hall with seating for 500 spectators. The town's leisure centre is within 10 minutes' walk of campus.

Huddersfield offers a lively social life for its student body of nearly 20,000, while Leeds and Manchester are accessible by train.

Tuition fees

- » Fees for UK students £9,250
- » Fees for International students 2023–24 £15,000–£20,000
- » For scholarship and bursary information see www.hud.ac.uk/undergraduate/fees-and-finance
- » Graduate salary £23,000

Student numbers

Undergraduates	11,916 (4,363)
Postgraduates	2,662 (1,671)
Applications/places	17,910/3,480
Applications per place	5.1:1
Overall offer rate	76%
International students – EU	2.5%
Non-EU	11%

Accommodation

University provided places: 1,367
Self-catered: £82.50–£115 per week
First-years guaranteed accommodation
www.hud.ac.uk/uni-life/accommodation

Where do the students come from?

State schools (non-grammar)	95%	First generation students	57.2%		
Grammar schools	4%	Low participation areas	16.1%		
Independent schools	0.9%	All ethnic minorities	46.3%		

Social inclusion ranking: =17

White working-class males	5.8%
Black achievement gap	-12.4%
Mature (over 21)	23.4%

University of Hull

Hull, founded in 1927, has its sights set on the future. Its education strategy 2020-25 sets out a path to provide courses to prepare students for the challenges of the fourth industrial revolution and a global community. In tandem with these goals, the two themes of environmental sustainability and social justice are to the fore of the wider strategic mission at Hull – which aims to become carbon-neutral by 2027.

As well as thinking big, the university has been investing in teaching and learning facilities at the redbrick campus on England's east coast. For those on media-related degrees a media centre has been brought together on one site and gained the augmented/virtual reality equipment required for games-design degrees.

Elsewhere, a crime scene investigation house – which simulates the inside of a domestic home – has been created to give students hands-on experience. For those on law courses, a second court has been built to enhance the established university moot court. Hull has also relaunched its legal mediation centre, which provides final-year law students with real-world experience of mediation within civil law disputes. At the Nidd Building, a newly installed business lounge is facilitating business networking among students and external partners.

The first computer science (artificial intelligence) students began their studies in September 2022. Computer science facilities include dedicated labs and hi-tech equipment such as gigabit networking and immersive virtual networks. The Turing Lab has high-specification desktop PCs and the Superlab's 150-plus workstation space has been refurbished. Engineering students now have access to a racing car simulator of a standard to match those supplied to Formula One teams and a FabLab with the latest 3D printing technologies.

For biology students, facilities have been upgraded in a new molecular genomics teaching laboratory. Hull also has industry-standard recording and performance facilities in Middleton Hall and an art gallery in the £30million Brynmor Jones library.

Having secured £86million funding in April 2022, the university now plans to invest in sustainable facilities and infrastructure to accelerate its carbon-neutral campus ambitions. These build on its efforts to create green skills and training through its £12million Aura Innovation Centre in East Yorkshire, which specialises in offshore wind energy.

Hull was awarded silver in the Teaching Excellence Framework, commended for course design and assessment practices that stretch and challenge students.

Having achieved one of the stronger performances in the National Student Survey (NSS) in 2021, Hull has remained in the top half of UK universities in our analysis of the latest NSS results, albeit slipping to 50 for

Cottingham Road
Hull HU6 7RX
01482 466 100
admissions@hull.ac.uk
www.hullstudent.com
www.hull.ac.uk
Open days:
see website

***The Times and The Sunday Times* Rankings**
Overall Ranking: =67 (last year: =52)

Teaching quality	76.1%	50
Student experience	72.1%	=59
Research quality	42.4%	52
Entry standards	125	=63
Graduate prospects	75.2%	55
Good honours	76%	=80
Expected completion rate	81.5%	=95
Student/staff ratio	16.2	=65

satisfaction with teaching quality and =59 for the wider undergraduate experience. Environmental research projects place it at the heart of the wider Humber region's push towards a low-carbon economy.

In the latest Research Excellence Framework (REF 2021) Hull doubled its research graded world-leading (the highest category) compared with the previous assessment in 2014. Across all subjects, 82% of Hull academics' work achieved the top two categories, lifting the university two places in our research rankings to 52nd place. The university won a Queen's Anniversary Prize for its research into slavery and played a key role in shaping the UK's Modern Slavery Act.

Hull's strength in politics is reflected in a steady flow of graduates into the House of Commons. The Westminster-Hull internship programme offers a year-long placement for British politics and legislative studies students.

Now in its fourth year, the university's partnership with Team GB – the nation's Olympic competitors – has resulted in a variety of opportunities for Hull students. During Black History month, students heard a talk by Kye Whyte, the Tokyo 2020 BMX rider and silver medallist, and there is a continuing research project exploring the heritage of the Olympic Games.

Based in the £25million Allam Medical Building, the medical school offers a gateway year programme for students from underrepresented backgrounds as well as alternative or contextual offers for its five-year medicine degree.

Hull achieves one of the highest rankings among pre-1992 universities in our social inclusion index – where it ranks among the top 20 most socially inclusive universities this year. Hull makes contextual offers reduced by up to 16 UCAS points to students who qualify under its widening participation criteria.

The university has teamed up with Attitude, the UK's bestselling gay magazine, to launch a new LGBTQ+ scholarship. Supporting six students from the LGBTQ+ community with £1,000 towards the cost of their studies at Hull, it follows the success of the Jeremy Round scholarship, named in memory of the Hull alumnus, cookery writer and journalist

First-years are guaranteed a place in halls of residence. The city itself is student wallet-friendly and there is plenty of local nightlife. On campus, students can get from their halls of residence to their lectures in 10 minutes.

Tuition fees

»	Fees for UK students	£9,250
	Foundation courses	£7,500
»	Fees for International students 2023–24	£15,400–£18,300
	Medicine (Hull-York Medical School 2022, annual increases capped at 2%pa)	£38,500
»	For scholarship and bursary information see www.hull.ac.uk/choose-hull/study-at-hull/money	
»	Graduate salary	£24,000

Student numbers

Undergraduates	10,780 (1,060)
Postgraduates	1,470 (1,306)
Applications/places	11,885/3,350
Applications per place	3.5:1
Overall offer rate	77.1%
International students – EU	2%
Non-EU	10.6%

Accommodation

University provided places: 2,312
Self-catered: £140–£225 per week
First-years guaranteed accommodation
www.hull.ac.uk/choose-hull/student-life/accommodation

Where do the students come from?

State schools (non-grammar)	93.9%	First generation students	53%	White working-class males	8.5%
Grammar schools	3.6%	Low participation areas	28.8%	Black achievement gap	-16.7%
Independent schools	2.5%	All ethnic minorities	13.6%	Mature (over 21)	32.6%

Social inclusion ranking: =17

Imperial College London

Imperial is our University of the Year for Graduate Employment for the second time in three years. The career prospects of Imperial graduates are the best in the country, proving the talent pipeline to industry is unsurpassed from its courses specialising in science, medicine, engineering and business.

Private-sector partners engage academic staff as consultants, send experts to give guest lectures and fund scholarships and prizes. The links enable Imperial to offer integrated years in industry in most departments and many students find jobs through these networks upon graduation. Employers also visit careers fairs to recruit Imperial students. The latest national Graduate Outcomes survey shows that 95.2% of graduates had moved on to high-skilled jobs or further study within 15 months.

Imperial is fifth in our rankings overall and rises to first for research quality. Its results in the latest Research Excellence Framework (REF 2021) are outstanding. Fifty-five per cent of its work submitted to the national assessment was classed as world-leading, the top category. Almost all (96%) achieved the top two categories. The stellar outcomes put Imperial ahead of Cambridge, the No 1 university in the previous national REF assessment in 2014.

Success in the latest REF comes after the global spotlight was turned on Imperial's research during the pandemic, when its academics spearheaded efforts to model the spread of the disease, develop new vaccines and treat Covid-19 patients.

Confirming its reputation on a global stage, Imperial ties in sixth place with California Institute of Technology in the 2023 QS World University rankings. The university counts 14 Nobel prize winners among its alumni — including Sir Alexander Fleming, who discovered penicillin. Many of Imperial's researchers are involved in teaching and the breadth of research allows the university to offer some advanced modules in the later stages of degree programmes.

Teaching at Imperial was awarded gold in the government's Teaching Excellence Framework, praised for providing an "exceptionally stimulating and stretching academic, vocational and professional education that successfully challenges students to achieve their full potential".

Imperial was named our University of the Year in 2021, as one of only two universities where student satisfaction improved under the intensely challenging conditions of the pandemic. However, in our analysis of the latest National Student Survey (NSS) results, Imperial falls from third place to 12th for satisfaction with the wider undergraduate experience and has plummeted 43 places to =71 for how its students rate

---

South Kensington Campus
Exhibition Road
London SW7 2BU
Engineering.admissions@Imperial.ac.uk
Medicine.ug.admissions@Imperial.ac.uk
Ns.admissions@Imperial.ac.uk
bs.recruitment@imperial.ac.uk
www.imperialcollegeunion.org
www.imperial.ac.uk
Open days: see website

The Times and The Sunday Times **Rankings**
Overall Ranking: 5 (last year: 4)

Teaching quality	74.9%	=71
Student experience	77.2%	12
Research quality	73.9%	1
Entry standards	197	6
Graduate prospects	95.2%	1
Good honours	92.4%	6
Expected completion rate	97.9%	3
Student/staff ratio	11.7	5

teaching quality. Teaching for the present academic year is by "multi-mode" delivery — combining on-campus and online learning. Assessment formats vary by department.

The university's 23-acre White City campus in west London is in the midst of rapid development that in 2023 will bring the new £100million School of Public Health building into use. This joins the 13-storey Sir Michael Uren building, opened in 2020 and dedicated to biomedical engineering research, and Scale Space – a building designed for life sciences and tech firms to grow their businesses.

The latest chapter in Imperial's history, the ambitious White City campus brings together academia, business, the third sector and the community on the same site. Undergraduates in most subjects are based at the original South Kensington campus, however, which is home to the business school and the Dyson School of Design Engineering. The university's strength in engineering is renowned and Imperial is the only UK university to provide teaching and research in the full range of engineering disciplines.

Imperial's footprint across the capital includes teaching bases attached to a number of hospitals in central and west London. The Faculty of Medicine is one of Europe's largest in terms of staff and student numbers. A partnership with a medical school in Singapore, run jointly with Nanyang Technological University, began in 2017 and will conclude 2028, but the two institutions remain committed to collaborating in education and research.

Imperial's record on social inclusion is improving in some areas. Notably, it has the second-lowest black achievement gap and is in the top 20 for its proportion of students from ethnic minorities (17th). Imperial continues to attract the largest cohort of students from private and grammar schools, with just 45.5% from non-selective state schools.

The Imperial bursary is a generous one, offering eligibility on a sliding scale from £2,000 to £5,000 for undergraduates with annual household incomes up to £60,000. In 2021, 36% of British students at Imperial received the bursary and almost four in 10 qualified for the maximum amount. The university expects a similar proportion to benefit in 2023-24.

Students pay £30 a year to belong to the Ethos sports centre on the South Kensington. Imperial's outdoor facility, Harlington Sports Ground near Heathrow airport, hosts Queen's Park Rangers Football Club's training centre and a training venue for England rugby teams.

All first-years are guaranteed a space in halls as long as they meet the application deadline.

Tuition fees

»	Fees for UK students	£925–£9,250
»	Fees for International students 2023–24	£37,900–£39,100
	Medicine	£50,400
	www.imperial.ac.uk/study/ug/fees-and-funding	
»	Graduate salary	£33,000

Student numbers

Undergraduates	11,252	(1)
Postgraduates	8,443	(1,674)
Applications/places	28,700/3,305	
Applications per place	8.7:1	
Overall offer rate	32.5%	
International students – EU	14.8%	
Non-EU	34.6%	

Accommodation

University provided places: 2,861
Self-catered: £125–£331 per week
First-years guaranteed accommodation
www.imperial.ac.uk/study/campus-life/accommodation/

Where do the students come from?

State schools (non-grammar)	45.5%	First generation students	25.7%		
Grammar schools	20.3%	Low participation areas	4.5%		
Independent schools	34.2%	All ethnic minorities	61.6%		

Social inclusion ranking: 114

White working-class males	1.9%
Black achievement gap	-2.5%
Mature (over 21)	7.6%

Keele University

Keele's new Global Challenge Pathways introduce elective study options for students to take alongside their core degree. Introduced in 2022 and designed to add experiences that will help them to stand out as graduates, each pathway lasts all three years of undergraduate study. Students will engage with a global issue or challenge connected to societal issues. Those on the pathways can take part in research-driven and external-facing projects that address current debates, linking their studies to the UN Sustainable Development Goals, building a digital showcase of their achievements and presenting to employers, organisations and communities.

A broad-based interdisciplinary approach has been part of Keele's DNA since its foundation in 1949 as an "experiment" in post-war university education by Lord Lindsay, whose words still resonate: "If we are going to try and keep a democratic country and maintain understanding of one another, we have to send out people from our universities who can do the technical stuff and who at the same time have an understanding of political and social problems and of the values that lie behind them."

The university, which offers the interdisciplinary liberal arts and natural sciences degrees as well as dual honours programmes, was awarded gold – the highest standard – in the Teaching Excellence Framework (TEF). The judging panel praised the Keele Curriculum, introduced in 2012, which covers voluntary and sporting activities as well as the academic core. It contributes to the Keele University Skills Portfolio, accredited by the Institute of Leadership and Management.

A former winner of our University of the Year for Student Experience, Keele comes a cropper in our analysis of the latest National Student Survey (NSS), plummeting 61 places for satisfaction with the wider undergraduate experience to rank =90. It also falls 53 places for satisfaction with teaching quality, now ranking =104. Campus-based teaching has returned, the university reports.

Based in 600 acres of parkland in the heart of England, near Stoke-on-Trent, Keele continues to refresh its self-contained campus landscape. The university's low carbon energy generation park became fully operational in 2021 – a significant milestone in Keele's ambition to be carbon-neutral by 2030. Known affectionately as the "Keele bubble", the campus has all the amenities of a small town.

The newly opened 150-room Courtyard by Marriott hotel is the latest addition to on-site amenities, nestled in the university's Science and Innovation Park. A new Digital Society Institute opened in summer 2022, its purpose to drive local business growth by sharing Keele's research expertise with relevant industries including health, business, energy and computing.

Keele ST5 5BG
01782 734 010
admissions@keele.ac.uk
www.keelesu.com
www.keele.ac.uk
Open days: see website

The Times and The Sunday Times Rankings		
Overall Ranking: 64 (last year: 48)		
Teaching quality	72.3%	=104
Student experience	69.9%	=90
Research quality	42%	53
Entry standards	123	=72
Graduate prospects	79.3%	=36
Good honours	78.9%	57
Expected completion rate	89.2%	47
Student/staff ratio	15.3	=45

Now in its third year, the veterinary school – a joint venture between Keele and Harper Adams universities – features a hospital and a clinical skill centre among its teaching and learning facilities, opened in 2022.

Sir David Attenborough opened the life sciences laboratories and, elsewhere, the Keele Business School has a big-data laboratory and a business incubator. The £34million Central Science Laboratory brings together practical teaching across a range of disciplines.

The demand for undergraduate places increased by 16% in the 2021 admissions round, year-on-year, to a level last seen five years ago. New student enrolments also swelled in the same entry cycle, but by a more modest 3%. Keele's popular health programmes attract a significant number of applications, the university notes, and enjoy teaching and facilities on campus as well as at sites including University Hospitals of North Midlands – one of the largest acute hospitals in the country.

Research at Keele's Institute for Sustainable Futures is focused on issues such as food security, climate change and clean energy. Keele was awarded Sustainability Institution of the Year at the 2021 Green Gown awards, which celebrate such efforts within higher education institutions.

In the latest Research Excellence Framework (REF 2021), 80% of the work submitted by Keele was placed in the top two categories of world-leading or internationally excellent, an improvement on results from the previous national assessment in 2014. The university also increased the number of academics put forward to the REF by 25%. Some of the best results were in allied health; dentistry; agriculture; communication and media studies; archaeology; and general engineering.

Keele is more successful than many other pre-1992 universities in our social inclusion index, where it ranks 39th, up one place on last year. In further efforts to widen participation, about 10% of applicants in the 2021 cycle received a contextual offer. The medical school runs a widening participation scheme to support students from underrepresented groups.

Sports facilities include a full-size 3G football pitch suitable for all-weather play. The university has about 2,800 residential spaces – enough to guarantee a space to first-years. Renowned for its safe, friendly atmosphere, Keele was ranked No 1 Best UK University in the Student Crowd Awards 2022, which are based on student feedback.

Tuition fees

» Fees for UK students	£1,850–£9,250
» Fees for International students 2023–24	£15,500–£25,400
Medicine £41,000; Veterinary Medicine	
(Harper & Keele Veterinary School)	£19,250–£33,000
» For scholarship and bursary information see	
www.keele.ac.uk/study/undergraduate/	
tuitionfeesandfunding/	
» Graduate salary	£24,000

Student numbers

Undergraduates	8,313	(539)
Postgraduates	760	(1,893)
Applications/places	16,805/2,870	
Applications per place	5.9:1	
Overall offer rate	69.4%	
International students – EU	2.3%	
Non-EU	4.4%	

Accommodation

University provided places: 2,778
Self-catered: £92–£174 per week
First-years guaranteed accommodation
www.keele.ac.uk/discover/accommodation/

Where do the students come from?

State schools (non-grammar)	83.8%	First generation students	43.7%	White working-class males	5.5%
Grammar schools	9.6%	Low participation areas	18.6%	Black achievement gap	-12.4%
Independent schools	6.6%	All ethnic minorities	35.2%	Mature (over 21)	17.5%

Social inclusion ranking: 39

University of Kent

Kent's 300-acre Canterbury campus is benefiting from £1.148million of funding from the Office for Students to upgrade facilities for its natural sciences division. Hi-spec teaching laboratories for computing are among the new developments. For forensic science students, new facilities include a taphonomy farm (for the examination of decomposition) along with a superglue fuming chamber for developing fingerprints, two cars for crime scene training and a comparison microscope for ballistic and trace evidence.

Students on courses within the school of architecture and planning will also be able to use new facilities, thanks to more studio space in the Marlowe Building in line with Kent's creation of a 21st-century studio culture.

The Kent and Medway Medical School, a collaboration with Canterbury Christ Church University, opened in September 2020. The school's Pears building provides undergraduates with a GP simulation suite, a 150-seat lecture theatre, seminar rooms and social spaces.

A strong performance by Kent in the latest Research Excellence Framework (REF 2021) has nudged it up a place to joint 32nd in our research quality index, holding its own against improving results sector-wide. The best results were in architecture, classics, history, law, philosophy, social work and social policy, theology, music, drama, dance, performing arts, film and screen studies.

Kent is one of a handful of UK universities to have a collegiate system. Every student is attached to a college, the epicentre of social life, especially in the first year, with academic as well as residential facilities. The Canterbury campus has six colleges and there is one at the university's Medway campus on the old Chatham naval base, which is shared with Greenwich and Canterbury Christ Church universities. The £50million School of Pharmacy and the purpose-built Centre for Music and Audio Technology are at Medway too, with the refurbished business school.

Kent's colleges drew praise in the Teaching Excellence Framework, which gave the university a gold rating. Assessors said the collegiate system was a vital element underpinning a "flexible and personalised" approach to academic support. They also commended Kent's "outstanding" Student Success project, which identifies trends in results and completion rates, and acts to help those likely to fall behind.

In-person teaching returned as the default model in the 2022-23 academic year, supported by lecture capture technology which has been in place at Kent since 2018. The return to an on-campus experience may help to improve declining rates of student satisfaction at Kent. In our analysis of the results of the latest National Student Survey, published in summer 2022, Kent fell 33 places to rank =107

The Registry
Canterbury CT2 7NZ
01227 768 896
www.kent.ac.uk/contact-us
www.kentunion.co.uk
www.kent.ac.uk
Open days: see website

for satisfaction with teaching quality, and dropped 42 places to rank =97 for what students think of their wider experience.

Kent has embraced degree apprenticeships. At last count it had about 1,250 learners on 17 programmes, studying for roles such as senior journalist; clinical trials specialist; social worker; chartered manager and operational research specialist. The university expects to expand the subject range and predicts the number of degree apprentices to reach between 1,500 and 1,800 by September 2023.

About 3,500 of 2021-22's new students received some form of scholarship or bursary, an admissions year that welcomed 4,715 first-year students, according to UCAS figures. Among merit-based awards is the Kent Scholarship for Academic Excellence – a single £2,000 payment that is not means-tested, awarded to new entrants with at least A*AA at A-level, or equivalent qualifications.

Scholars may combine an academic award with the Kent Financial Support Package (KFSP), which is worth £1,500 in the first year of study and £1,000 annually in years two to five, to state-educated students from households with incomes up to £30,000 and whose homes fall within areas of deprivation. Other means-tested bursaries are available, too.

A modern £3million hub in the Park Wood student village on the Canterbury campus includes a shop, café/bar and dance studios. The Pavilion outdoor playing fields complex opposite is also the site of the cycle hub. All first-year undergraduates living in university accommodation get free access to sports facilities. The Sports Centre near the heart of the Canterbury campus has a fitness suite, strength and conditioning training area and three multipurpose sports halls among its provision. The Medway Park Premier membership gives students access to local sports and leisure centre.

With 5,233 residential spaces at the Canterbury campus and a further 1,106 at Medway, Kent is one of the best-provided universities for accommodation and can guarantee a space to all first-years who apply by the deadline. Kent students have a compulsory *Expect Respect* module that covers sexual consent.

Student-centric venues populate Canterbury's cobbled streets and the charming seaside resorts of Whitstable and Margate are easily reached by public transport. During term time a free shuttle bus connects the campuses at Canterbury and Medway.

Tuition fees

»	Fees for UK students	£9,250
»	Fees for International students 2023–24	£18,000–£21,200
	Medicine	£48,200
»	For scholarship and bursary information see	
	www.kent.ac.uk/courses/undergraduate/fees-and-funding	
»	Graduate salary	£24,000

Student numbers

Undergraduates	14,139	(877)
Postgraduates	2,349	(1,219)
Applications/places		21,440/4,715
Applications per place		4.5:1
Overall offer rate		90.2%
International students – EU		5.6%

Accommodation

University provided places: 6,339
Catered costs: £151–£279 per week
Self-catered: £129–£220 per week
First-years guaranteed accommodation
www.kent.ac.uk/accommodation/

Where do the students come from?

State schools (non-grammar)	79.8%	First generation students	46.6%	**Social inclusion ranking: 78**		
				White working-class males	5.2%
Grammar schools	15.9%	Low participation areas	11.5%	Black achievement gap	-15.7%
Independent schools	4.3%	All ethnic minorities	45.8%	Mature (over 21)	9.7%

King's College London

The Quad, which has been at the heart of the Strand campus at King's College London (KCL) for nearly 200 years, is being given a new lease of life. Set to complete in late 2022, the redevelopment creates a new home for the Department of Engineering and adds 3,000 sq m to the thoroughfare, framed by the historic King's Building and the East Wing of Somerset House. The engineering facilities will include experimental laboratory space.

The extra capacity will help to absorb rising student numbers. Applications hit a record high in 2021, when more than 67,300 students applied to the university – up 17% on 2020 and the fourth consecutive year-on-year rise. More places were awarded than ever before, with 8,460 new student enrolments in 2021 – up about 7% in a year. The university credits growing interest in courses across the curriculum, especially from overseas students.

One of the oldest and largest colleges of the University of London, KCL has more than 30,000 students – just over a third of them from outside the UK. Four of its five campuses are within a square mile of each other, near the banks of the Thames at London Bridge and Waterloo. The fifth is in Denmark Hill, in south London, the base for the Institute of Psychiatry, Psychology and Neuroscience, and dentistry teaching facilities.

The Strand site and the Waterloo campus house most of the university's non-medical departments. Facilities for film studies have been enhanced by the addition of new industry-standard equipment. The Dickson Poon School of Law has expanded into the East Wing of the striking London landmark Somerset House. Bush House, the former headquarters of the BBC World Service and another historic London building, is the latest acquisition, housing KCL's business school, the Faculty of Social Science and Public Policy and some student services.

Nursing and midwifery and some biomedical subjects are based at Waterloo, while medicine and dentistry are mainly at Guy's Hospital, near London Bridge, and the St Thomas' Hospital campus, across the river from the Houses of Parliament. A £3million upgrade to dentistry facilities at Guy's has added 70 "phantom head" simulators for practising dental surgery and 12 haptics technology units using virtual reality.

More than 300 employers visit KCL each year to recruit students – including JP Morgan, Meta, Clifford Chance and PwC. King's graduates do well in the jobs market – resulting in 11th place in our analysis of the latest Graduate Outcomes survey.

KCL's links with employers contributed to a silver rating in the Teaching Excellence Framework.

Fourteen KCL staff and alumni have been awarded the Nobel prize. The university continues its research-intensive tradition,

Strand
London WC2R 2LS
020 7848 5454
Admissions@kcl.ac.uk
www.kclsu.org
www.kcl.ac.uk
Open days: see website

The Times and The Sunday Times Rankings
Overall Ranking: 26 (last year: 18)

Teaching quality	69.6%	120
Student experience	66.3%	=121
Research quality	64.2%	8
Entry standards	164	19
Graduate prospects	86.2%	11
Good honours	87.3%	17
Expected completion rate	92.6%	28
Student/staff ratio	13.9	=21

climbing one place to eighth in our research quality index this year after 55.1% of the work submitted to the latest Research Excellence Framework (REF 2021) was judged to be world-leading – the top category. KCL's best results were in allied health subjects, business and management, classics, clinical medicine, sport and exercise sciences, chemistry, modern languages, engineering and theology.

The university does less well on rates of student satisfaction – in common with many London and research-led institutions. KCL has fallen to the bottom 10 for how students rate teaching quality and their wider experience in the latest National Student Survey, published in summer 2022 — contributing to its disappearance from the top 20 in our main academic league table.

A dual award master's degree leading to registration as an adult nurse and mental health nurse has been added to the curriculum for 2022-23. Medical students are now able to pursue a chosen field in greater depth during an intercalated BSc (iBSc). A one-year cardiovascular medicine iBSc is welcoming its first cohort of students, taught by one of only six British Heart Foundation Centres of Excellence in the UK. From 2023, KCL will offer degrees in classics and the ancient world, and liberal arts (with international development).

KCL is more successful in our social inclusion index (80th) than most other Russell Group universities, behind only Queen Mary, University of London and Sheffield. Two-thirds of students are from ethnic minorities and the university's narrow black achievement gap is the sixth-best. Course completion rates have improved to 28th: KCL's dropout rate is lower than expected in light of the course profile and the background of the student intake.

Contextual admissions are made to students enrolled on KCL's schemes to widen participation and who meet other criteria. About 30% of entrants in 2021 qualified for KCL's wide range of bursaries and scholarships and the university expects to continue a similar level of financial assistance.

KCL's sports grounds are a train ride away in south London. There are facilities for all the main sports, plus rifle ranges, two gyms and a swimming pool. Accommodation is guaranteed to all first-years who apply by the late May deadline. More than 1,100 rooms are at the lowest end of the rent scale (£155-£169 a week). Only 11 rooms are available at the maximum price of £465 a week. Halls are spread out across the capital but each has its own community and events.

Tuition fees

» Fees for UK students	£9,250
» Fees for International students 2023–24	£31,260
Medicine £45,420; Dentistry £50,760	
» For scholarship and bursary information see www.kcl.ac.uk/study/undergraduate/	
» Graduate salary	£30,000

Student numbers

Undergraduates	20,316 (1,041)
Postgraduates	11,253 (5,883)
Applications/places	67,390/8,460
Applications per place	8.1
Overall offer rate	52.9%
International students – EU	14.8%
Non-EU	24.9%

Accommodation

University provided places: 5,670
Catered costs: £318 per week
Self-catered: £155–£465 per week
First-years guaranteed accommodation
www.kcl.ac.uk/accommodation

Where do the students come from?

State schools (non-grammar)	70.6%	First generation students	38.8%	White working-class males	1.9%
Grammar schools	12.2%	Low participation areas	4.6%	Black achievement gap	-5.6%
Independent schools	17.1%	All ethnic minorities	66.4%	Mature (over 21)	17.2%

Social inclusion ranking: 80

Kingston University

Kingston boasts Britain's best new building: the award-winning Town House at its Penrhyn Road campus. The £50million centre won the 2021 Royal Institute of British Architects (RIBA) Stirling prize – the highest accolade in British architecture. Since opening in 2020, Town House has fast become a focal point, offering an auditorium and informal learning spaces as well as a studio theatre, dance studios and a library on the campus close to Kingston town centre.

At the nearby Knights Park campus, where the Kingston School of Art is based, the Mill Street Building has been transformed by a £29million project to create more than 9,000 sq m of creative teaching, workshop and studio space.

A total of £118.7million has been invested to enhance the student experience, including £55million to upgrade halls of residence at the Seething Wells and Kingston Hill campuses. Students at Seething Wells are set to benefit from modern, energy-efficient bedrooms from September 2022, with listed buildings earmarked to transform into a café and events space. At Kingston Hill the kitchens were planned to be expanded, with shared social spaces in line for a facelift, too.

It is paying off, with satisfaction in the overall student experience rising 14 places to rank =59 in our analysis of the results of the latest National Student Survey.

Applications climbed by 20% in the 2021 admissions round, while enrolments swelled by about 9% year-on-year. Another 12% increase in applications was evident in a snapshot of the 2022 cycle by the end of March. Courses in business and the social sciences, art and design, and science, engineering and computing have grown in popularity, according to the university.

Kingston's creative courses are among its most successful. In our analysis of improvements in research performance in the latest Research Excellence Framework (REF 2021) the university rose 20 places to rank 71st.

The university fared less well in the government's Teaching Excellence Framework (TEF) in 2017, earning bronze — lowest rating. The TEF panel highlighted the its award-winning focus on black and other ethnic minority students.

Kingston's Elevate accelerator programme for UK-based black students was named the best initiative to widen participation in higher education in March at the National Undergraduate Employability Awards 2022.

Kingston's student population is one of the country's most diverse, with 65.1% from ethnic minorities, and the programme seeks to equip black students with commercial awareness and skills, providing practical

Holmwood House
Penrhyn Road
Kingston upon Thames
KT1 2EE
020 3308 9932
admissionsops@kingston.ac.uk
www.kingstonstudents.net
www.kingston.ac.uk
Open days: see website

The Times and The Sunday Times Rankings
Overall Ranking: 92 (last year: =101)

Teaching quality	75.4%	=62
Student experience	72.1%	=59
Research quality	34.6%	71
Entry standards	118	=89
Graduate prospects	70.3%	=82
Good honours	72.5%	=103
Expected completion rate	82.5%	90
Student/staff ratio	17	=76

advice on job applications and how to start a business as well as inspiration from black entrepreneurs. The university has improved its graduate prospects in our rankings, by 28 places to =82, in our analysis of the proportion in highly skilled work or further study after 15 months.

The TEF panel also noted that the course completion rate at Kingston was in line with the national average for the university's courses and student profile.

Degree apprenticeships are a relatively small but growing area: Kingston introduced a programme in social work in 2022, as well as three options in construction and courses in nursing, and environmental science.

Kingston expects to have more than 600 student apprentices enrolled by September 2023. The curriculum has also gained an integrated master's degree in chemistry with medicinal chemistry with intakes in 2022 and 2023.

Kingston has four campuses: Penrhyn Road and Knights Park are near the town centre, with Kingston Hill a couple of miles away. The purpose-built Roehampton Vale, in a former aerospace factory a short bus ride away, is the base for engineering. The university is the UK's largest provider of undergraduate aerospace education, with its own Learjet and flight simulator.

The Tolworth Court outdoor sports facilities are three miles from the main campus and the university recently added a new sports pavilion designed to make use of green technologies including a ground source heat pump and solar thermal panels for hot water heating.

The 65-station gym on the Penrhyn Road site offers student rates and its fitness studio provides aerobics, dance and wellbeing classes – from Bollywood dancing to Pilates – to suit people of all abilities and interests.

All new entrants are guaranteed one of Kingston's 2,340 residential places. The suburban riverside location and its relative proximity to London's bright lights are a big selling point.

Tuition fees

» Fees for UK students	£9,250
Foundation courses	£6,000–£7,800
» Fees for International students 2023–24	£13,500–£16,800
» For scholarship and bursary information see www.kingston.ac.uk/undergraduate/fees-and-funding/	
» Graduate salary	£25,000

Student numbers

Undergraduates	12,076	(790)
Postgraduates	4,271	(1,363)
Applications/places	25,795/5,040	
Applications per place	5.1:1	
Overall offer rate	72.6%	
International students – EU	3.5%	
Non-EU	8.7%	

Accommodation

University provided places: 2,340
Self-catered: £115–£220 per week
First years guaranteed accommodation
www.kingston.ac.uk/accommodation/

Where do the students come from?

State schools (non-grammar)	95.5%	First generation students	51.5%	White working-class males	3.1%
Grammar schools	1.8%	Low participation areas	5.4%	Black achievement gap	-18.6%
Independent schools	2.7%	All ethnic minorities	65.1%	Mature (over 21)	27.4%

Social inclusion ranking: 60

Lancaster University

Lancaster, now 12th in our main academic league table, has featured consistently near the top in recent years, joining Warwick as the most successful of the 1960s generation of universities.

A former winner of our University of the Year title, and our International University of the Year in 2019, Lancaster's global outposts include a joint institute near Weihai, in Shandong province in China, a branch campus in Ghana and another in Leipzig, Germany. An academic partnership with Sunway University in Malaysia paves the way for students on a range of undergraduate programmes to graduate from both universities.

At home, the university is set within a 560-acre parkland campus on the outskirts of Lancaster in the northwest of England. The Margaret Fell lecture theatre – the biggest on campus – is among the latest buildings to open. In 2020, Lancaster opened a hi-tech architecture studio providing specialist facilities for up to 48 students.

The Management School has also undergone a revamp, extending into a five-storey West Pavilion. The school also recently signed up to the Principles of Responsible Management Education action plan – a United Nations initiative to achieve its Sustainable Development Goals through responsible management education.

Student numbers have swelled in the past decade. Enrolments in 2021 were about 43% higher than they were in 2011. Applications were at their highest in the 2020 recruitment cycle and, although they dipped a little in 2021, they remained 24% higher than they had been a decade before. Fifteen per cent of 2021's new entrants gained their place via Clearing. The curriculum gains a new degree in international management from 2023.

A strong performance in the latest Research Excellence Framework (REF 2021) resulted in 91% of Lancaster's research being assessed as internationally excellent or world-leading (the top two categories) – up from 83% in 2014. Of this, 46% achieved the highest (4*) category. Against even bigger rises elsewhere, Lancaster loses four places to rest 19th in our research quality index.

Lancaster also performs well in the eyes of its students. It remains in the top 20 (17th) for satisfaction with the wider student experience, according to our analysis derived from the latest National Student Survey, published in summer 2022. It ranks 31st for what students think of the university's teaching quality.

Contented students tend not to drop out. Lancaster is 15th in our analysis of the latest course completion figures, with a dropout rate well below the level expected in light of its course and student mix. All students belong to one of nine colleges at Lancaster, each with its own advisory team dedicated to student support.

Bailrigg
Lancaster LA1 4YW
01524 592 028
ugadmissions@lancaster.ac.uk
www.lancastersu.co.uk
www.lancaster.ac.uk
Open days: see website

The Times and The Sunday Times **Rankings**

Overall Ranking: 12 (last year: 11)

Teaching quality	77.6%	31
Student experience	76.6%	17
Research quality	57.4%	19
Entry standards	146	=35
Graduate prospects	82.6%	23
Good honours	82.9%	36
Expected completion rate	94.1%	15
Student/staff ratio	14.1	=24

Alan Milburn, the chancellor, who is the former chairman of the Social Mobility Commission and a Lancaster alumnus, said he "got lucky" in finding his way to the university from one of the most deprived comprehensives in Newcastle. His time at Lancaster then set him on the path to top jobs in the Labour government between 1998 and 2003.

The university continues its efforts to widen participation and introduced contextual offers two A-level grades (or equivalent) lower than the published entry standards in 2021. It is also a member of the Realising Opportunities programme for research-intensive universities and has pledged its support to students from military families and care-leavers.

The university ranks 93rd in our social inclusion ranking for England and Wales, with 19.6% of students from an ethnic minority. Only 5.4% of the intake are white working-class boys, the most underrepresented group.

About a third of the intake is expected to qualify for some form of financial assistance – such as a £1,000 annual bursary for UK students with a household income of less than £30,000, or a £2,000 Lancaster scholarship awarded to all UK entrants with at least AAA at A-level (or the equivalent) and five GCSEs at grade A/7 or above. There is a sanctuary bursary of £2,000 per year for two applicants classed as refugees or with humanitarian protection.

The university's links with industry span relationships forged with corporations; small to medium-sized enterprises and entrepreneurs; and the public, private and third sectors. In our graduate prospects ranking, Lancaster slips four places to 23rd.

The sports centre has four sports halls, a swimming pool, strength and conditioning room and a "human performance lab" among its facilities, while a trim trail and woodland walk make use of the campus countryside. Off campus, Lancaster has a boathouse on the River Lune.

The university's eco-friendly student residences have won best halls awards in the National Student Housing Survey. First-years who make Lancaster their firm choice and who apply by the early August deadline are guaranteed a room. The city of Lancaster might be small but it tends to charm those who visit, and the nightclubs are said to be decent. The Lake District is an hour away and transport links to Manchester and Liverpool bring their bright(er) lights within reach.

Tuition fees

» Fees for UK students	£9,250
» Fees for International students 2023–24	£21,980–£26,550
Medicine	£41,195
» For scholarship and bursary information see	
www.lancaster.ac.uk/undergraduate/courses/fees/	
» Graduate salary	£25,000

Student numbers

Undergraduates	12,548	(13)
Postgraduates	3,428	(1,482)
Applications/places		22,210/4,115
Applications per place		5.4:1
Overall offer rate		88.2%
International students – EU		10.5%
Non-EU		19.2%

Accommodation

University provided places: 10,634
Catered costs: £183–£205 per week
Self-catered: £111–£172 per week
First-years guaranteed accommodation
www.lancaster.ac.uk/accommodation/

Where do the students come from?

State schools (non-grammar)	78.3%	First generation students	34.7%	White working-class males	5.4%
Grammar schools	10.9%	Low participation areas	8%	Black achievement gap	-18.8%
Independent schools	10.8%	All ethnic minorities	19.6%	Mature (over 21)	3.9%

Social inclusion ranking: 93

University of Leeds

One of the most popular universities in the country, Leeds attracted more than 66,000 applicants last year: only Manchester, Edinburgh, University College London and King's College London had more. Admissions reached a record high, too, with nearly 9,000 new students starting.

Impressive results in the latest Research Excellence Framework (REF 2021) may further boost the university's appeal. Leeds advances seven places in our research quality index to reach the top 20. Ninety per cent of a hefty submission by Leeds academics across 28 subject areas achieved the top two categories (world-leading or internationally excellent), up from 80% in the previous national assessment in 2014. Some of the best results were in creative writing, English, information and systems management, architecture, and law. The engineering disciplines, dentistry, economics, sports science, and town and country planning also scored highly.

Based on a campus a 10-minute walk from the city centre, the university's investment in its facilities continues. The Esther Simpson Building opened in 2022 as part of an expansion by the business and law schools. The Faculty of Biological Sciences has received a significant refurbishment, too.

These developments follow the recently opened Sir William Henry Bragg Building for engineering and physical sciences. The Laidlaw Library and the refurbished Edward Boyle Library are among the modern resources, while a £17million upgrade to the students' union building, once famed for having the longest bar in the country, improved social spaces and performance venues.

The biggest investment, £174million over the next decade, is to put its Climate Plan into action – aiming to support climate change mitigation and adaptation locally and globally. Most of the budget, £150million, is being put toward the university's goal of achieving net-zero carbon emissions by 2030. The university was an "official observer" at the Cop26 summit in Glasgow in 2021.

Leeds secured gold in the Teaching Excellence Framework (TEF), impressing its panel with an emphasis on education inspired by "discovery, global and cultural insight, ethics and responsibility, and employability". The university has risen six places in the QS World University Rankings to reach 86th place in the 2023 edition.

There are more than 500 undergraduate programmes and the university supports more than 1,000 students each year to complete work placements with organisations locally, nationally and globally. Leeds advertised more than 9,000 vacancies including 2,500 internships in 2021.

For graduate prospects, Leeds has slipped slightly but remains in the top 30 in our analysis based on the numbers in highly skilled work or postgraduate study 15 months after leaving university.

Woodhouse Lane
Leeds LS2 9JT
0113 343 2336
study@leeds.ac.uk
www.luu.org.uk
www.leeds.ac.uk
Open days: see website

The Times and The Sunday Times Rankings
Overall Ranking: 23 (last year: 15)

Teaching quality	69%	122
Student experience	66.7%	=116
Research quality	57%	20
Entry standards	160	22
Graduate prospects	81.6%	28
Good honours	89%	11
Expected completion rate	94%	16
Student/staff ratio	13.8	=15

Leeds continues to channel its research expertise into tackling Covid-19. In 2022 it teamed up with the World Health Organisation on a global strategy to protect future generations against similar threats. The Leeds Cancer Research Centre opened in 2021.

The university's Vulnerability and Policing Futures research centre has opened in partnership with the University of York, exploring how policing can prevent and reduce the risk of harm to the vulnerable.

Leeds has had a digital education service since 2013. In-person teaching is the key focus, however, and there are no plans to deliver programmes on campus and online within the same cohort, the university points out.

Even so, Leeds has crashed out of the top 100 for each of our two measures of student satisfaction, our analysis of the latest National Student Survey shows. For satisfaction with teaching quality, Leeds has plunged 40 places year-on-year to rank 122nd, while it is =116 for how students feel about the wider undergraduate experience, a fall of 49 places.

Two-thirds of Leeds students come from families with a history of university education and three in 10 are drawn from independent or selective state secondary schools. This means that Leeds has one of the lower proportions of students from non-selective state comprehensive schools in the UK.

Among the university's widening participation schemes are contextual offers of a two-grade reduction on published entry requirements, which benefited 26% of entrants in 2022. Leeds' financial package of scholarships and bursaries is one of the biggest in UK higher education, aiding 30% of admissions.

Those living in halls get free access to the Edge sports centre. The facility is complemented by the Brownlee Centre, the UK's first purpose-built triathlon training base, housed at Sports Park Weetwood, three miles from the main city centre campus. The centre is named after Jonny and Alistair Brownlee, the Leeds alumni and Olympic medal-winning brothers.

Although the university's 98-acre site is close to the city centre, much of the accommodation is further out. Support for students' mental health is embedded. Same-day drop-in appointments are available remotely and the number of counselling staff has been increased.

Friendly, multicultural and renowned for fun-packed social options, Leeds is one of the UK's leading student cities.

Tuition fees

» Fees for UK students		£9,250
» Fees for International students 2023–24		£22,250–£27,500
Medicine		£39,750
» For scholarship and bursary information see		
www.leeds.ac.uk/undergraduatefees		
» Graduate salary		£25,000

Student numbers

Undergraduates	26,730	(380)
Postgraduates	8,014	(1,717)
Applications/places	66,200/8,885	
Applications per place	7.5:1	
Overall offer rate	64.5%	
International students – EU	4.2%	
Non-EU	14.1%	

Accommodation

University provided places: 9,294
Catered costs: £166–£216 per week
Self-catered: £95–£192 per week
First-years guaranteed accommodation
www.accommodation.leeds.ac.uk/

Where do the students come from?

State schools (non-grammar)	71.8%	First generation students	33.8%	White working-class males	3.9%
Grammar schools	10.5%	Low participation areas	8.9%	Black achievement gap	-15.1%
Independent schools	17.7%	All ethnic minorities	21.9%	Mature (over 21)	6.8%

Social inclusion ranking: 99

Leeds Arts University

A research culture is emerging at Leeds Arts, the north of England's only specialist arts institution. For the first time, the former Leeds College of Arts showcased its work in the latest Research Excellence Framework (REF 2021). It enters at the foot of our research rankings in 131st place but is proud to have some work recognised as world-leading. The best results were in history of art, design and architecture.

Having gained full university status only in 2017, the former Leeds College of Arts was ineligible for the previous national research assessment in 2014 and now hopes to improve its research pedigree as time goes by. Leeds Arts made clear its commitment to developing practice-based research in the arts by including all teaching staff in its REF 2021 submission – rather than just those with a significant responsibility in research.

The past five years has been a period of expansion all round, with enrolments almost double what they were a decade ago. Demand is increasing: applications rose 14% year-on-year in the 2021 cycle. Yet the student community remains at about 2,000 undergraduates. University life is based on the Blenheim Walk campus, a 10-minute walk from the centre of Leeds. At Vernon Street, the original base in the city centre, further education courses are taught.

Professional-standard equipment includes large-format digital printers, 3D scanners and industrial-grade machinery for working with wood, metal and plastics. Acoustically insulated sound booths can be used to create radio or television advertisements.

Students appear to like what they see. In our analysis of the latest National Student Survey, published in summer 2022, Leeds Arts has risen an impressive 63 places to rank 35th for satisfaction with teaching quality – returning to the top third of universities in the country for this measure. Only two years ago it was in the top 20, until the pandemic hit student satisfaction rates hard. As the university tells us: "The dominant, social mode of learning is hugely important in creative subjects and this cannot be replicated remotely."

Now that in-person teaching has returned, the university – up 44 places to rank =67 for student satisfaction with the wider undergraduate experience – should be on track to continue to regain lost ground.

When it was still Leeds College of Art, the institution was rated silver in the Teaching Excellence Framework. The panel was impressed that a significant number of teaching staff were active artists and designers, enhancing the students' exposure to the creative industries, and praised the level of support for mature students and those with disabilities.

The sculptors Henry Moore and Dame Barbara Hepworth, who were contemporaries,

---

Blenheim Walk
Leeds LS2 9AQ
0113 202 8039
admissions@leeds-art.ac.uk
www.leedsartsunion.org.uk
www.leeds-art.ac.uk
Open days: see website

The Times and The Sunday Times Rankings
Overall Ranking: =71 (last year: =103)

Teaching quality	77.1%	35
Student experience	71.7%	=67
Research quality	6	131
Entry standards	149	=30
Graduate prospects	62.4%	=125
Good honours	80.1%	48
Expected completion rate	93.1%	=23
Student/staff ratio	16.1	=62

are among the institution's long list of famous alumni. More recently, its former students Damien Hirst and Marcus Harvey were leading lights of the YBA (Young British Artists) scene. Guest speakers at the university's Creative Networks events have included the artist and cartoonist David Shrigley, the designer Jimmy Choo and the late film-maker Jamal Edwards.

Skin – the lead singer of Skunk Anansie, DJ, fashion icon, actress and activist – initially came to Leeds Arts as a guest speaker and became the university's first chancellor in early 2021. She has a scholarship in her name: Skin's Chancellor Scholarship, which awards £3,000 per year for three years to two UK students and one international student.

In our social inclusion survey, 92.9% of students attended non-selective state schools, 9.5% are from an ethnic minority and 41.6% are the first in their immediate family to attend university. The university improves by 13 places to rank =51 in our overall social inclusion index.

Leeds Arts, our 2019 University of the Year for Student Retention, continues to keep its dropout rate low at 3.1%. Its performance on completion rates earns a top-25 place in this section of our analysis.

Easter and summer schools are among activities aimed at widening participation at Leeds Arts University. All students receive two £55 payments in their first year to help with the cost of materials, and an extra £75 in the third year.

Students build their portfolios through paid external projects, forging industry links through live briefs and opportunities to show their work at trade fairs, studios and in galleries. Hyundai, AON and John Lewis are among the organisations that have awarded prizes and commissions to Leeds Arts students in recent years. Graduates can access university facilities and a support network, and can also apply for funded studio and project spaces in Leeds.

Graduate prospects are always a challenge for art and design specialisms. According to our analysis of the Graduate Outcomes survey, tracking those in highly skilled work or postgraduate study after 15 months, Leeds Arts has lift-off from the bottom of our table but remains in the bottom 10.

University accommodation is owned and managed privately: there are places for about 70% of students who want to live in. If accommodation is full, the students' union provides links to private rental companies around Leeds city centre. Buoyed by students from its four universities, Leeds offers a vibrant social scene.

Tuition fees

» Fees for UK students	£9,250
» Fees for International students 2023–24	£16,000–£17,100
» For scholarship and bursary information see www.leeds-art.ac.uk/apply/finance/	
» Graduate salary	£19,500

Student numbers

Undergraduates	2,184	(0)
Postgraduates	58	(52)
Applications/places	5,480/760	
Applications per place	7.2:1	
Overall offer rate	49.6%	
International students – EU	2.6%	
Non-EU	6.2%	

Accommodation

University provided places: 553
Self-catered: £129–£164 per week
First-years given priority
www.leeds-art.ac.uk/life-in-leeds/accommodation

Where do the students come from?

State schools (non-grammar)	92.9%	First generation students	41.6%	White working-class males	4.2%
Grammar schools	2.5%	Low participation areas	15.4%	Black achievement gap	-10.2%
Independent schools	4.6%	All ethnic minorities	9.5%	Mature (over 21)	10.7%

Social inclusion ranking: =51

Leeds Beckett University

Leeds Beckett's Lioness Lucy Bronze – a member of the England women's football team that claimed victory in the Euro 2022 championship – is not the university's only graduate with a glittering trophy cabinet.

Bronze, 30, who graduated in 2013 with a degree in sports studies, joins Commonwealth Games medallists Alex Yee, 24, who won gold for England in the men's triathlon sprint, and Keely Hodgkinson, 20, who won silver in the 800m in Birmingham in August 2022.

Hodgkinson is a criminology student while Yee graduated from Leeds Beckett with a degree in sports and exercise science. He was also part of a contingent of 18 Team GB athletes at the Tokyo Olympic Games who had graduated or trained at the university.

Behind them all the way was the university's world-class Carnegie School of Sport, which hosts the Leeds Talent Hub – an elite programme run in partnership with British Athletics. Based at the Headingley campus, the school's £45million facility opened in 2020.

As well as nurturing top athletes, the university has partnerships with clubs and associations including Leeds United Football Club, Leeds Rhinos rugby league contenders, and Yorkshire County Cricket Club.

However, there is more to Leeds Beckett than sport. Development is continuing to upgrade the site at Headingley and Leeds Beckett's City campus. The £80million School of Arts building has 11 floors of specialist facilities for more than 2,500 students taking 40 courses in creative technologies, fashion marketing, film, music and sound, and the performing arts.

The university has recently formed a School of Health by merging the School of Clinical and Applied Sciences and the School of Health and Community Studies. It has also launched an Obesity Institute – bringing together its expertise on obesity and weight management.

A biomedical sciences laboratory opened for the 2022 academic year and by January 2023 facilities for law will include a new courtroom, lecture theatre and social space within refurbished buildings. A virtual reality lab is joining the Carnegie School of Education.

Leeds Beckett has improved access to student support services at both campuses. One-to-one interview rooms for confidential support have been installed as part of a drive to improve wellbeing services. Students can also self-refer for consultations.

Such efforts have yet to translate into better rates of student satisfaction, however. In our analysis of the outcomes of the latest National Student Survey, published in summer 2022, Leeds Beckett ranks =71 for satisfaction with teaching quality (falling seven places) and =77 for the wider experience (falling nine places). Just two years ago it ranked in the top 25 for how students feel about the wider experience.

City Campus
Leeds LS1 3HE
0113 812 3113
admissionenquiries@
leedsbeckett.ac.uk
www.leedsbeckettsu.co.uk
www.leedsbeckett.ac.uk
Open days: see website

The Times and The Sunday Times **Rankings**
Overall Ranking: 113 (last year: =112)

Teaching quality	74.9%	=71
Student experience	70.8%	=77
Research quality	26.8%	98
Entry standards	107	=119
Graduate prospects	69.7%	=87
Good honours	75.2%	86
Expected completion rate	79.9%	103
Student/staff ratio	21.7	120

A suite of new degrees in applied sports launched in September 2022 in five pathways: athletics, cricket, football, netball and rugby league.

A silver rating in the Teaching Excellence Framework (TEF) brought commendation for Leeds Beckett's employability strategies for students, who can learn real-world skills through live project briefs, case studies, practice-related assessments and placements. Students were stretched, the panel said, and developed transferable and personal skills.

External partnerships with more than 2,000 organisations support the university's ambition to provide graduate talent to the local, regional and national labour markets. The School of Events, Tourism and Hospitality Management has opened its Jet2Suite, giving access to interactive seminars and a base for recruitment events for paid student and graduate roles. Our analysis of graduate prospects shows a four-place rise to =87 for the proportion in highly skilled work or postgraduate studies 15 months after the end of a degree.

From Leeds Beckett's beginnings in its predecessor institutions – the Leeds Mechanics Institute (1824) and the City of Leeds Training College (1913) – the university has been known for widening access to higher education. A contextual offers scheme supports this mission today and in 2021 benefited 57% of eligible entrants.

In the latest Research Excellence Framework (REF 2021), sports sciences produced some of the university's best results, while the allied health professions, dentistry, nursing and pharmacy and building also did well. Overall, 53% of the university's submission was rated world-leading or internationally excellent, the top two categories. Leeds Beckett edges into the top 100 in our research quality index, rising three places to 98th.

You don't have to be an England Lioness, or an Olympian, to take part in sport at Leeds Beckett. The university's fitness app allows students to manage bookings. The Athletic Union has 38 sports clubs with more than 80 teams, many of them offering the chance to compete in the British Universities and Colleges Sports (BUCS) league.

Leeds Beckett guarantees accommodation to all first-years who make the university their firm choice and apply by the deadline. Lively and relatively affordable, Leeds nightlife is a big draw for the city's students.

Tuition fees

» Fees for UK students	£9,250
» Fees for International students 2023–24	£12,500–£14,000
Foundation courses	£11,000
» For scholarship and bursary information see	
www.leedsbeckett.ac.uk/undergraduate/financing-your-studies/	
» Graduate salary	£22,000

Student numbers

Undergraduates	16,798	(1,315)
Postgraduates	3,016	(2,560)
Applications/places		27,925/5,625
Applications per place		5.1
Overall offer rate		79.4%
International students – EU		1.4%
Non-EU		3.7%

Accommodation

University provided places: 2,156
Self-catered: £144–£245 per week
First-years guaranteed accommodation
www.leeds-beckett.ac.uk/accommodation/

Where do the students come from?

State schools (non-grammar)	92.4%	First generation students	42.1%	White working-class males	7.7%
Grammar schools	2.7%	Low participation areas	18.8%	Black achievement gap	−20.2%
Independent schools	4.9%	All ethnic minorities	21.3%	Mature (over 21)	16%

Social inclusion ranking: =66

Leeds Trinity University

Leeds Trinity makes a virtue of its relatively small size and a personalised approach to study. At Leeds Trinity, "you're a name, not a number," the university vows.

With its sights set on being a top career-led and applied university, Leeds Trinity has put its 2021-26 strategy into action. The academic structure has changed, now encompassing a Faculty of Business, Computing and Digital Industries, a Faculty of Social and Health Sciences, and an Institute of Childhood and Education. A new executive team is also in place, tasked with guiding the university to achieve growth targets.

According to the stellar rates of student satisfaction expressed in the latest National Student Survey, published in summer 2022, Leeds Trinity is on the right track. The university is 18th for satisfaction with the wider undergraduate experience (a giant leap of 100 places), and joint 24th for satisfaction with teaching quality (up 89 places, year-on-year).

The massive rises show how significantly student satisfaction at Leeds Trinity were affected by the pandemic, when its scores fell out of the top 100. Teaching has returned to an in-person model of delivery, with online resources provided to complement face-to-face sessions.

The university has its roots in two Catholic teacher-training colleges established in the 1960s, while today it welcomes students of all faiths or none. Recent developments on campus include new psychology teaching facilities and a 3G football pitch. They follow other upgrades such as a fitness and sports therapy suites and a new motion-capture analysis lab for use by students on sport and media courses. Photography students have gained two studios and a modern darkroom.

The first business management and law students started their courses in September and three new degrees begin in 2023: professional policing, physiotherapy and biomedical science. Applications were up by 12% in the 2021 admissions cycle and new student enrolments rose by 20%, year-on-year. The rise looks likely to continue, according to a snapshot at the end of March 2022 that showed an increase of 8% rise compared with the same point a year before.

All Leeds Trinity degrees include professional work placements without students needing to take a sandwich year. Volunteering, at home or abroad, is also credited as a placement. All graduates leave with at least three months' work experience relevant to their degrees on their CV and references from employers. The university's network of industry partnerships means students are placed at local, national and global organisations.

Graduate prospects slipped slightly in our rankings, by four places, to =115, based on the proportion in highly skilled work

Brownberrie Lane
Horsforth
Leeds LS18 5HD
0113 283 7123
admissions@leedstrinity.ac.uk
www.ltsu.co.uk
www.leedstrinity.ac.uk
Open days: see website

The Times and The Sunday Times **Rankings**
Overall Ranking: 100 (last year: 124)

Teaching quality	78.2%	=24
Student experience	76.2%	18
Research quality	15.1%	122
Entry standards	107	=119
Graduate prospects	65.5%	=115
Good honours	79.7%	52
Expected completion rate	78.3%	111
Student/staff ratio	21.5	=118

or postgraduate study 15 months on from finishing a degree course.

The placement scheme contributed to a silver rating in the Teaching Excellence Framework (TEF). Assessors highlighted high-quality support mechanisms for employability, including professional placements, as well as excellent use of technology and innovative assessment and feedback.

The Centre for Apprenticeships, Work-based Learning and Skills co-ordinates Leeds Trinity's earn-as-you-learn programmes and has specialist tutors and support staff. The university offers seven programmes, including digital marketing, business-to-business sales, and children, young people and families practice. A police constable programme is run in partnership with the West Yorkshire force. A total of 670 student apprentices were enrolled at the last count but Leeds Trinity forecasts significant growth in numbers by 2023, to 1,200.

Theology produced by far the best results for Leeds Trinity in the latest Research Excellence Framework (REF 2021). Its submissions in sport and exercise sciences, leisure and tourism were also strong. Overall, Leeds Trinity has almost maintained is position in our research quality rankings (122nd, down just one place year-on-year).

Leeds Trinity succeeds in attracting the eighth-highest proportion of students from non-selective state schools (97.6%), while almost six in 10 are the first in their family to attend university, and nearly seven in 10 students are aged over 21 when they enrol.

Initiatives to widen participation include contextualised admissions, foundation years, pre-16 support, and, for local Year 12 students, taster days and a summer school. Most successful course graduates enrol at Leeds Trinity the following year. The university was also the first in Yorkshire to receive the Race Equality Charter bronze award in recognition of its work to improve representation, progression and success of black, Asian and minority ethnic students.

A spin studio and two floors of gym equipment feature in the campus fitness suite, with free weights and a training rig. Bookings and online classes are available via an app. Other facilities include 3G and grass pitches, an athletics track and outdoor hard courts for netball and tennis.

Halls of residence have been upgraded, doing away with part-catered provision and creating bigger kitchens to suit self-catering. There are 783 rooms, allocated on a first-come, first-served basis, and all students who apply by the UCAS deadline can be accommodated.

Tuition fees

» Fees for UK students	£9,250
Foundation degrees	£5,000
» Fees for International students 2023–24	£11,500–£12,500
» For scholarship and bursary information see www.leeds-trinity.ac.uk/study/fees-and-finance	
» Graduate salary	£20,488

Student numbers

Undergraduates	6,358	(367)
Postgraduates	527	(454)
Applications/places	7,120/3,480	
Applications per place	2.1	
Overall offer rate	85.9%	
International students – EU	1%	
Non-EU	0.1%	

Accommodation

University provided places: 783
Catered costs: £100–£143 per week
www.leeds-trinity.ac.uk/accommodation/

Where do the students come from?

State schools (non-grammar)	97.6%	First generation students	59.8%	
Grammar schools	1.4%	Low participation areas	19.1%	
Independent schools	1%	All ethnic minorities	23.1%	

Social inclusion ranking: =40

White working-class males	3.1%
Black achievement gap	-20.1%
Mature (over 21)	69.8%

University of Leicester

Leicester has leapt 11 places to =26 in our research quality index based on results from the latest Research Excellence Framework (REF 2021). Clinical medicine, history, and sports and exercise science produced its best results. Overall, 89% of the university's submission was assessed as world-leading or internationally excellent, the top two categories.

As part of a £500million capital development plan, Leicester has opened the Brookfield satellite campus a few minutes away from the main site for the School of Business. There are teaching rooms, lecture theatres, a trading room and breakout areas for students.

Further enhancements include a £21million renovation of the Percy Gee students' union building that has resulted in a spacious food court and extra multi-use areas. Elsewhere, at Freeman's Common, the £150million redevelopment of student accommodation near campus has also added offices, a large lecture theatre and a multistorey car park, with landscaped gardens and tree-lined pathways.

The improvements should serve to lift rates of student satisfaction. In our analysis of the latest National Student Survey (NSS) published in summer 2022, the university fell 20 places to rank =94 for satisfaction with teaching quality and fell fell 17 places to rank =62 for how students for how students feel about their wider undergraduate experience.

Leicester was in a good position for the pivot to remote learning when university life changed shape during the pandemic, as it already had a suitable infrastructure. The Teaching Excellence Framework (TEF) assessors praised these resources when awarding Leicester silver, highlighting the university's system for filming lectures, which had been introduced in response to student feedback. The TEF panel also congratulated the university on engaging students with the latest research.

Leicester's main campus and much of the residential accommodation is in a leafy suburb a mile from the city centre. The university's first overseas venture opened in China in 2017. The Leicester International Institute/Dalian University of Technology, based in Panjin, offers degrees taught in English in chemistry, mechanical engineering and mathematics.

Building on a longstanding commitment to space research, the university recently opened its Space Park. Dedicated to companies developing space technology or using space-enabled data, students are welcomed into its collaborative community of academics and industry partners.

An expanding portfolio of degrees at home had triggered a 24% rise in applications in the 2022 admissions cycle by the end of March 2022, compared with the same point a year before. New offerings include finance, journalism and media, journalism and sociology, and sociology with criminology. From 2023, four more will be

University Road
Leicester LE1 7RH
0116 252 5281
study@le.ac.uk
www.leicesterunion.com
www.le.ac.uk
Open days: see website

The Times and The Sunday Times **Rankings**
Overall Ranking: 35 (last year: 37)

Teaching quality	73%	=94
Student experience	72%	=62
Research quality	53.6%	=26
Entry standards	129	=55
Graduate prospects	75.3%	54
Good honours	81.2%	42
Expected completion rate	91.4%	34
Student/staff ratio	13.7	=12

introduced: radiography, biological sciences with psychology, economics and data analytics, and English and translation. The university makes effective use of Clearing, recruiting 30% of new students via this route in 2021.

Leicester's provision of scholarships and bursaries is extensive, benefiting 38% of UK and 63% of international students among 2021-22's entrants. Awards include the Citizens of Change 100 scholarship, which sets applicants the task of recording an Instagram Reel, or a TikTok-style video of up to 60 seconds, responding to the question: What do you want to change? Students with the best videos are awarded fee discounts of £2,500 for the first three years of a course. Widening participation scholarships of £1,000 go to mature students aged 30-plus from low participation postcodes.

Nearly six out of every 10 students are from ethnic minority backgrounds (ranking 21) and Leicester has successfully reduced its black attainment gap (15.2%) to rank among the top third of universities. With only 82.3% of students recruited from non-selective state schools, however, Leicester is in the lower half of the sector. Its performance for social inclusion overall earns 76th place in our analysis.

To widen access, Leicester runs a range of progression programmes – such as Pathways to Law and its in-house scheme AccessLeicester: Medicine and STEM (science, technology, engineering and mathematics) – which target and support the progression of students from underrepresented backgrounds in the local area and London. Contextual offers two grades lower than standard may also be made to eligible applicants on most, but not all, courses. Leicester's dropout rate is lower than expected, given the university's course and student mix.

Graduate prospects are just outside the top 50 (54th) for the proportion in highly skilled work or further study after 15 months.

Both of the university's sports centres have a gym, swimming pool, spa, sauna and steam room, and studios. The campus centre also has a sports hall and there are floodlit tennis courts, all-weather courts and rugby pitches at the Stoughton Road playing fields in Oadby.

The university insists on compulsory training for new students on sexual consent and how to help a friend under threat.

Leicester's award-winning students' union is the only one in the country with its own O_2 Academy. Nights out in town benefit from Leicester's student-friendly size: not too big and not too small, and relative affordability. First-years who apply by September 1 are guaranteed a space in university-managed accommodation.

Tuition fees

»	Fees for UK students	£9,250
»	Fees for International students 2023–24	£17,500–£23,000
	Medicine	£23,000–£40,140
»	For scholarship and bursary information see	
	www.le.ac.uk/study/undergraduate/fees-funding	
»	Graduate salary	£25,000

Student numbers

Undergraduates	11,074	(226)
Postgraduates	3,560	(1,240)
Applications/places		20,995/3,690
Applications per place		5.7:1
Overall offer rate		69%
International students – EU		4.2%
Non-EU		11.7%

Accommodation

University provided places: 3,993
Self-catered: £70–£215 per week
First-years guaranteed accommodation
https://rooms.le.ac.uk/student_portal/

Where do the students come from?

State schools (non-grammar)	82.3%	First generation students	39.4%	
Grammar schools	11.3%	Low participation areas	9.8%	
Independent schools	6.4%	All ethnic minorities	58.2%	

Social inclusion ranking: 76

White working-class males	3.2%
Black achievement gap	-15.2%
Mature (over 21)	9%

University of Lincoln

The University of Lincoln has introduced flexible "bite-size" courses to give students the skills in demand from employers. The microcredential programme, run across Lincoln's academic colleges, is delivered mostly online. Credits can be stacked up to lead to postgraduate qualifications – or simply add breadth and depth to a student's CV.

The initiative is the latest curricular development at Lincoln, where a vastly broadened course offering has almost doubled student numbers in the past 13 years or so. Winner of our Modern University of the Year award in 2021, the university has kept up with the expanding register by investing more than £375million in its contemporary Brayford Pool campus in the medieval cathedral city of Lincoln.

A new home for the Lincoln Medical School is located at the heart of the campus. Its £21million dedicated building houses specialised teaching and learning facilities, supported by the latest technologies. Established in collaboration with the University of Nottingham, which confers the BMBS (Bachelor of Medicine, Bachelor of Surgery) degree on graduates, the Lincoln Medical School launched in 2018 and its first cohort of students started the following year.

A foundation year widens access to the school, which was awarded an extra 20 places in its second year of operation. Grounded in the university's civic role within England's second-largest county, its graduates will be encouraged to complete their junior doctor training locally and apply for jobs in the region.

Lincoln achieved a gold rating in the government's Teaching Excellence Framework. Assessors complimented the university on a strong approach to personalised learning through highly engaged personal tutors, with access to analytics to monitor students' progress proactively.

After years of buoyant rates of student satisfaction, Lincoln lost ground in last year's pandemic-affected National Student Survey (NSS) – in common with most universities. It now ranks =54 for students' assessment of teaching quality (down from =41 last year) and =40 for the wider undergraduate experience (down from 38th). Even so, Lincoln remains comfortably in the upper half of institutions nationally for student satisfaction. Teaching has returned to in-person delivery.

The first biomedical engineering students started courses in September, as did those enrolled on new degrees in human geography and physical geography; and in education and digital learning. From September 2023, the curriculum gains another two options: robotics; and psychology (sport and exercise psychology).

Lincoln's stable of 13 degree apprenticeships had 465 learners on programmes at the last count. The earn-as-you-learn roles range from social worker, nursing associate and food

---

Brayford Pool
Lincoln LN6 7TS
01522 886 644
enquiries@lincoln.ac.uk
www.lincolnsu.com
www.lincoln.ac.uk
Open days: see website

Edinburgh
Belfast
LINCOLN
London
Cardiff

***The Times and The Sunday Times* Rankings**
Overall Ranking: 53 (last year: 49)

Teaching quality	75.8%	=54
Student experience	73.5%	=40
Research quality	38.4%	67
Entry standards	120	=81
Graduate prospects	70.2%	=84
Good honours	77.6	=62
Expected completion rate	88.8%	49
Student/staff ratio	16.1	=62

industry technical professional to manufacturing manager and cultural heritage conservator.

More than three-quarters (79%) of Lincoln's research was judged to be internationally excellent or world-leading, the top two categories in the latest Research Excellence Framework (REF 2021). History produced some of the best results, along with social policy, the allied health professions and computer science.

Agricultural research was another strength. The university hosts the world's first Centre for Doctoral Training for agrifood robotics and the National Centre for Food Manufacturing. A building for Lincoln's Centre of Excellence in Agri-food Technology has been developed at the South Lincolnshire Food Enterprise Zone in Holbeach.

Lincoln is heading one of the country's first government-backed Institutes of Technology. Unified by a digital theme, it will specialise in agritech and food manufacturing, energy and engineering. Activities at the £20million Lincoln Science and Innovation Park (a joint venture between the university and the Lincolnshire Co-Op) include pharmacy students honing their skills in the science park's flagship laboratories, which feature a pharmacy clinical skills suite.

Lincoln has risen 27 places to rank 38th for social inclusion overall in our analysis of the latest data. Efforts to widen participation, which focus on Lincolnshire's higher education "cold spots", as defined by the Office for Students, are paying off, the results show. About half of new undergraduates qualify for some form of financial assistance.

The university's course completion rates are in the top 50. Lincoln's dropout rate is lower than its benchmark figure, based on the background of its students and the subject mix. Graduate prospects have fallen nine places to =84 in our analysis of the numbers in highly skilled work or postgraduate studies within 15 months.

The university manages more than 4,500 residential spaces across seven purpose-built accommodation developments. First-years who apply by September 1 are guaranteed a spot. Residential wardens are on hand round-the-clock to support those living in student accommodation, and organise social activities. The Engine Shed, operated on campus by Lincoln's students' union, is the county's largest music and entertainment venue.

A sports centre on campus includes a hall and outdoor pitches. There is a £6million performing arts centre, too, with a 450-seat theatre and three large studio spaces.

Tuition fees

» Fees for UK students	£9,250
» Fees for International students 2023–24	£14,700–£15,900
Medicine (see University of Nottingham)	£28,700–£46,500
» For scholarship and bursary information see www.lincoln.ac.uk/home/studywithus/undergraduatestudy/ feesandfunding/	
» Graduate salary	£21,829

Student numbers

Undergraduates	12,571	(1,811)
Postgraduates	1,547	(1,638)
Applications/places		15,535/3,745
Applications per place		4.1:1
Overall offer rate		84.5%
International students – EU		1.1%
Non-EU		3.71%

Accommodation

University provided places: 4,500
Self-catered: £93–£171 per week
First-years guaranteed accommodation
www.lincoln.ac.uk/accommodation

Where do the students come from?

State schools (non-grammar)	93.3%	First generation students	51.8%	White working-class males	9.3%
Grammar schools	4%	Low participation areas	19.8%	Black achievement gap	-20.7%
Independent schools	2.7%	All ethnic minorities	11.1%	Mature (over 21)	12.2%

Social inclusion ranking: 38

University of Liverpool

Liverpool's impressive results from the latest Research Excellence Framework (REF 2021) have triggered a 16-place rise in our research quality index, where it has gone from 40th to 24th place. A founding member of the Russell Group of universities, the REF results reinforce Liverpool's standing as a research-intensive institution.

The university's submission in the national assessment spanned 23 subjects and 91% of the work was rated world-leading or internationally excellent, the top two categories. The best results were in veterinary science; chemistry; psychology; and modern languages.

Established in 1881 on the principles of "the advancement of learning and ennoblement of life", Liverpool's original Victoria Building inspired the "redbrick university" term. The city campus at the top of Brownlow Hill and Mount Pleasant is about five minutes on foot from the city centre, while students of the School of Veterinary Science also have a base at the Leahurst campus on the Wirral Peninsula – near the university's 64-acre Ness Botanic Gardens.

Investment in the city-centre campus has created developments including the DIF (Digital Innovation Factory), a 1,530 sq m building on the north side of the campus. The university forecasts that the DIF will create about 400 jobs over a decade and boost the region's economy by £44.5million.

The Tung auditorium, Liverpool's new teaching and performance centre, opened in 2021 within the Yoko Ono Lennon Centre, housing a 400-seat auditorium.

Extending its global opportunities, Liverpool offers the option for students to spend an academic year studying at one if its 26 partner universities around the world. Unusually, the opportunity to go abroad is available in any year of study. The university also has a campus in the Chinese city of Suzhou, run in partnership with Xi'an Jiaotong University, and offers joint courses with the Singapore Institute of Technology.

Liverpool was upgraded from bronze to silver in the Teaching Excellence Framework. Having been one of the better-performing Russell Group universities in terms of student satisfaction before and during the pandemic, outcomes of the latest National Student Survey (NSS), published in summer 2022, revealed steep declines. It has fallen back in both of our NSS-derived measures, falling from joint 51st for student satisfaction with teaching quality in 2021 (and joint 62nd the year before) to 114th. For sections of the NSS relating to the wider undergraduate experience, our analysis shows a 63-place year-on-year drop to =100.

All teaching had returned to in-person delivery by the start of the 2022-23 academic year, which should help to lift rates of student satisfaction.

Liverpool L69 7ZX
0151 794 5927
ug-recruitment@liverpool.ac.uk
www.liverpoolguild.org
www.liverpool.ac.uk
Open days: see website

The Times and The Sunday Times Rankings
Overall Ranking: =33 (last year: =30)

Teaching quality	71%	114
Student experience	69%	=100
Research quality	55.6%	24
Entry standards	141	42
Graduate prospects	78.8%	38
Good honours	81.8%	39
Expected completion rate	92.5%	29
Student/staff ratio	13.8	=15

A third successive year-on-year rise in the numbers of new students starting courses brought them to record levels in the 2021 admissions cycle. The curriculum continues to expand. Liverpool is launching another seven degrees, in communication, media and politics; English literature with drama studies; English with world literature; media and culture; media, data and society; and screen industries and entertainment. All life science disciplines are gaining new integrated master's programmes.

In our annual social inclusion index Liverpool's strongest performance comes in recruitment of white working-class male students, the most underrepresented group (4.6%) and of students from areas with low participation in higher education (9.1%).

Long-term engagement with local disadvantaged schools and colleges underpins the university's widening participation agenda. The FastTrackers mentoring scheme for local Somali and Yemeni students was highlighted by the Office for Students for its good practice. In common with most of its Russell Group peers, however, Liverpool is near the bottom of our overall social inclusion ranking at =100.

About a third of UK undergraduates receive Liverpool bursaries. An £800 housing discount for those who receive the Liverpool bursary or other bursaries is a rare scheme among UK universities. It equates to about a quarter of students living in halls of residence receiving the saving, at a cost of about £920,000 to the university each year. Accommodation is guaranteed to first-years.

Industry partnerships include close links with AstraZeneca, HSBC, IBM, the Civil Service Fast Stream and CISCO. An interns programme and graduate scheme offers exclusive paid internships, placements and graduate opportunities offered by employers in the Liverpool City Region. The latest graduate prospects metric for Liverpool students is in the top 40.

The university has been investing significantly in its campus sport and fitness offering to enhance the free-to-use facilities. Off campus at the Wyncote Sports Ground, the university has 10 pitches for football and rugby, one for lacrosse, a floodlit all-weather pitch and 3G rugby facilities.

When it comes to student life, Liverpool is renowned as one of the UK's friendliest cities. It combines a booming and varied nightlife with relative affordability.

Tuition fees

» Fees for UK students	£9,250
Foundation courses	£5,140
» Fees for International students 2023–24	£18,500–£26,100
Medicine £34,500; Dentistry £37,100; Veterinary Medicine £34,500	
» For scholarship and bursary information see www.liverpool.ac.uk/study/undergraduate/finance	
» Graduate salary	£24,900

Student numbers

Undergraduates	21,919	(331)
Postgraduates	4,537	(2,400)
Applications/places		42,255/6,630
Applications per place		6.4:1
Overall offer rate		72.3%
International students – EU		2.5%
Non-EU		19.9%

Accommodation

University provided places: 4,800
Catered costs: £222–£223 per week
Self-catered: £145–£222 per week
First-years guaranteed accommodation
www.liverpool.ac.uk/accommodation/

Where do the students come from?

State schools (non-grammar)	74.8%	First generation students	39.2%	White working-class males	4.6%
Grammar schools	12.6%	Low participation areas	9.1%	Black achievement gap	-19.2%
Independent schools	12.6%	All ethnic minorities	16.4%	Mature (over 21)	8.7%

Social inclusion ranking: =100

Liverpool Hope University

Liverpool Hope has announced plans for several campus development projects. A proposed £6million IQ Building at the main Hope Park campus will house a simulation lab equipped with virtual reality hardware, while at the university's Creative Campus a multimillion-pound Motion Picture Factory, due to open in late 2022, is dedicated to film and television production, and comprises three studios. A further £500,000 investment at the site has added broadcasting equipment and enhanced drama studios.

The new facilities build on remarkably improved rates of student satisfaction at Hope year-on-year. In our analysis of the latest National Student Survey results, published in summer 2022, Liverpool Hope is =20 for satisfaction with teaching quality (up from joint 58th) and =42 for satisfaction with the wider undergraduate experience (a 48-place jump from =90 last year). The results are more in keeping with Hope's history of high rates of student satisfaction and appear to show that last year was a pandemic-induced blot on the landscape for the university.

Hope was the only higher education institution in Liverpool to achieve gold in the Teaching Excellence Framework (TEF). Assessors commented on "outstanding levels of stretch provided through judicious partnerships, good curriculum design and extracurricular activities".

The university is an accredited Duke of Edinburgh Gold Award provider and bases the expedition at its outdoor education centre, Plas Caeredon, in Snowdonia National Park. Hope's own Service and Leadership Award (SALA) extracurricular scheme credits hours spent volunteering by students, who also receive training in health, safety, leadership and diversity and inclusion. Those who achieve their SALA earn an additional reward on graduation day.

Formed by the 1980 merger of teacher-training colleges, Liverpool Hope achieved university status in 2005. Teaching is based at the main campus, Hope Park, in the leafy suburb of Childwall, four miles south of the city centre, and at the Creative Campus close to the heart of Liverpool.

At Hope Park the School of Social Sciences building features a simulation suite, where social work students can tackle common scenarios and assess their performance via video and audio recordings. The physiotherapy and sports rehabilitation clinic provides access to clinical teaching and training spaces. An £8.5million health sciences building houses laboratories for nutrition, genomics, cell biology and psychology, along with a 25m biomechanics sprint track.

Among resources at the Creative Campus are two theatres, an arts centre, studios for fine and applied art courses, a recording studio and dance studios.

Hope Park
Taggart Avenue
Liverpool L16 9JD
0151 291 3899
admission@hope.ac.uk
www.hopesu.com
www.hope.ac.uk
Open days: see website

The Times and The Sunday Times **Rankings**
Overall Ranking: =80 (last year: 81)

Teaching quality	78.5%	=20
Student experience	73.4%	=42
Research quality	22.3%	106
Entry standards	114	103
Graduate prospects	64.8%	=119
Good honours	74.3%	90
Expected completion rate	82.9%	=86
Student/staff ratio	16.3	69

Hope is in increasing demand. In 2021 more than 11,000 students applied to the university – an 11% rise in applications year-on-year and the third uplift in a row. After a bumper year in 2020, new student numbers returned to more usual levels.

The first students taking contemporary fashion design degrees began their courses in September 2022, as did those on new degrees in contemporary performance; digital creativity; human geography; and young work and community development. The curriculum gains a degree in creative business management in 2023.

The university remains in the lower reaches of our graduate prospects measure, however (=119). Work to boost employability is in hand through links between Liverpool Hope's academic schools and related industry partners, such as Tate Liverpool, Liverpool's Royal Court Theatre, Liverpool School of Tropical Medicine, Chester Zoo and Facebook Technologies-owned Oculus.

Hope recruits the fifth-highest proportion (10.2%) of white working-class males, the most underrepresented group in higher education, but its overall social inclusion ranking (69th) is affected by one of the wider black attainment gaps (97th).

In the previous Research Excellence Framework (REF) assessment in 2014, Hope submitted work from more eligible staff than most post-1992 universities. But as research standards rise across the sector, the latest REF 2021 round saw the university sink from =62 to rank 106th. Theology and education produced some of the best results in Hope's submission.

A flagship collaborative research project with Everton Football Club looks into brand loyalty and the socioeconomic impact of the club in the local community.

Facilities at the university's £5.5million Sports Complex were refurbished in March 2022. Access to all facilities and classes is £25 per year.

At the Aigburth Park residential campus, three miles from the Hope Park site, about £2.7million has been invested with a focus on reducing the university's carbon footprint. Accommodation is guaranteed for entrants who apply through the main cycle.

All resident students receive a compulsory welcome talk that covers issues of alcohol use and abuse, drug taking and sexual consent. Training to tackle bystander negligence is part of a new suite of domestic abuse and sexual violence prevention training offered to students. The students' union runs a buddy scheme and has produced a city guide for trans and non-binary students. Trained therapy dogs visit campus regularly to provide support.

Tuition fees

» Fees for UK students	£9,250
» Fees for International students 2023–24	£12,500
» For scholarship and bursary information see www.hope.ac.uk/undergraduate/feesandfunding/	
» Graduate salary	£22,000

Student numbers

Undergraduates	4,303	(57)
Postgraduates	873	(452)
Applications/places	11,030/1,695	
Applications per place	6.5:1	
Overall offer rate	88.5%	
International students – EU	3%	
Non-EU	1.1%	

Accommodation

University provided places: 1,145
Self-catered: £95–£126 per week
First-years guaranteed accommodation
www.hope.ac.uk/halls

Where do the students come from?

State schools (non-grammar)	91.2%	First generation students	49.5%	White working-class males	10.2%
Grammar schools	7%	Low participation areas	21.6%	Black achievement gap	-29.5%
Independent schools	1.8%	All ethnic minorities	11.9%	Mature (over 21)	21.4%

Social inclusion ranking: 69

Liverpool John Moores University

Students at Liverpool John Moores (LJMU) reported significantly improved rates of student satisfaction in the latest National Student Survey compared with the year before. In our analysis of the outcomes, published in summer 2022, LJMU has leapt 49 places year-on-year for student satisfaction with the wider undergraduate experience, from joint 83rd place to =34. For students' evaluation of teaching quality, the university has gone from joint 96th place in 2021 to 68th.

The prospering rates of student satisfaction have contributed to an impressive 22-place rise in our main academic league table this year.

Such positive results signal that LJMU's investment in the student experience appears to be paying off. The £64.5million Student Life Building and Sports Building opened on Copperas Hill in 2021. It houses the students' union, a chaplaincy, a café and a study area as well as general teaching spaces.

Next to it, the Sports Building provides access to a modern gym and two multipurpose halls. Another project has provided nursing and allied health students with an extension at the Tithebarn Building, adding six technology-enhanced simulation suites, two flexible-use 75-seat lecture theatres and three IT suites.

Other specialist learning facilities include the Liverpool Screen School, housed at the £37.6million Redmonds Building (along with the schools of business and of law), which has links with the region's creative industries such as the BBC in Salford and ITV Northern Lights.

Through the business faculty's Liverpool Business Clinic, students work in a consultancy team tackling real challenges presented by the region's businesses. Similarly, law undergraduates can gain real-world, pro bono experience at the university's Legal Advice Centre.

LJMU has a silver rating in the Teaching Excellence Framework. Assessors complimented its "highly effective institutional strategic drive to improve satisfaction with assessment and feedback", strong recognition of teaching excellence and a consistent commitment to student engagement.

One of the pioneers of degree apprenticeships, LJMU has reduced its portfolio of programmes from 17 options to 11, at the last count – although student apprentice numbers remain at about 2,000. The earn-as-you-learn options are registered nurse; social worker; chartered manager and police constable.

Undergraduate courses include work-based learning opportunities. Graduate prospects are improving, according to our analysis of the latest Graduate Outcomes survey, published in summer 2022, with LJMU rising 12 places year-on-year to joint 74th.

Student Life Building
Copperas Hill
Liverpool L3 5AJ
0151 231 5090
courses@ljmu.ac.uk
www.jmsu.co.uk
www.ljmu.ac.uk
Open days: see website

The Times and The Sunday Times Rankings
Overall Ranking: =71 (last year: 93)

Teaching quality	75.2%	68
Student experience	74.1%	=34
Research quality	32.8%	=76
Entry standards	139	=43
Graduate prospects	71%	=74
Good honours	75.4%	=83
Expected completion rate	83.8%	78
Student/staff ratio	18	=95

LJMU falls nine places in our research quality index to =76 against improvement across the sector in the latest Research Excellence Framework (REF 2021). However, the university furthered its burgeoning research reputation, submitting work from more than 600 academic staff (up from 242 in the previous national assessment in 2014). Nearly three-quarters (73.1%) of the submission to REF 2021 achieved the top ratings of world-leading or internationally excellent. Astrophysics; sport and exercise sciences; engineering; and English produced some of the best results.

Researchers and students use the university's robotic telescope in the Canary Islands, which is set to be joined by a second £24million, four-metre-diameter telescope built by an international consortium led by LJMU. Closer to home, the Football Exchange (FEX) at the School of Sport and Exercise Sciences has engaged in research and consultancy projects for several Premier League clubs and governing bodies such as UEFA.

Applications increased by about 10% in the 2021 admission cycle, year-on-year – taking them to a new high. The number of new students starting courses also increased, by about 5%. From September 2023, three new degrees launch: forensics, policing and investigations; policing and investigations; and environmental science.

With roots that can be traced to the Industrial Revolution, university status came in 1992 and with it the John Moores moniker,

in honour of the Liverpool entrepreneur and philanthropist who helped to fund LJMU's forerunner institutions.

The university's intake has a relatively high proportion of white working-class male students, the most underrepresented group in higher education (10.8%) – ranking fourth on our newest measure of social inclusion. Its outreach work has helped to recruit more students from Northern Ireland than any university outside the province itself. The proportion of students recruited from deprived areas (17.8%) is within the top 25 universities.

In the Times Higher Education's Young Universities Rankings 2022, which rate universities that are aged 50 years and under, LJMU took sixth place among the UK institutions and joint 109th globally.

Financial help includes the £500 LJMU Progression Bursary, paid automatically to eligible students for each year of study. The university endorses 4,000 residential spaces in privately operated halls of residence. All first-years are guaranteed a room.

Tuition fees

»	Fees for UK students	£9,250
»	Fees for International students 2023–24	£16,900–£17,400
	Foundation years	£11,000
»	For scholarship and bursary information see	
	www.ljmu.ac.uk/discover/fees-and-funding/	
»	Graduate salary	£22,600

Student numbers

Undergraduates	19,923 (1,705)
Postgraduates	2,484 (3,087)
Applications/places	36,110/7,855
Applications per place	4.6:1
Overall offer rate	81.6%
International students – EU	1.3%
Non-EU	4.4%

Accommodation

University provided places: 4,000
Self-catered: £80–£170 per week
First-years guaranteed accommodation
www.ljmu.ac.uk/discover/your-student-experience/accommodation

Where do the students come from?

State schools (non-grammar)	89.7%	First generation students	51.2%
Grammar schools	8.3%	Low participation areas	17.8%
Independent schools	2.1%	All ethnic minorities	13%

Social inclusion ranking: 65

White working-class males	10.8%
Black achievement gap	−26.4%
Mature (over 21)	19.1%

London Metropolitan University

Rates of student satisfaction are riding high at London Metropolitan University (London Met). Following impressive outcomes in the latest National Student Survey, published in summer 2022, the university is in the top 10 for how its undergraduates perceive teaching quality and their wider experience.

Teaching is in-person only for 2022-23, supported by lecture-capture technology that allows students to revisit the content at their own pace. Resources for students have been relocated into new offices for each school to enhance the wider experience, bringing together administrative, course and pastoral support.

Most of London Met life takes place at the university's largest campus, on Holloway Road in north London, where the angular, steel-clad graduate centre designed by Daniel Libeskind is a standout feature. The School of Art, Architecture and Design is nearly four miles east in Aldgate. The university was created by the merger of London Guildhall University and the University of North London in 2002, although its parent institutions date from the mid-19th century.

London Met's School of Art, Architecture and Design dropped "Sir John Cass" from its title in 2020 because of the 18th-century politician and philanthropist's early links to the slave trade. The university has also established an Education for Social Justice Framework which aims to reflect the diversity of London Met students and create an inclusive curriculum.

The Science Centre's Superlab on Holloway Road is among the largest teaching laboratories in Europe, with audiovisual systems that can transmit 12 practical lectures simultaneously for different groups of students. A social learning hub at the centre has high-spec classrooms and a café.

Responding to the capital's jobs market, the university is launching a School of the Built Environment, focusing at first on quantity surveying, building surveying and construction management. The university is also preparing to introduce nursing courses to the curriculum.

Such developments should improve the prospects for London Met graduates. It is fourth from bottom in our graduate outcomes measure, derived from the results of the 2022 Graduate Outcomes survey, which records the proportion of graduates in professional jobs or further study 15 months after finishing their degree. A Careers Education Framework has been set up to enhance employability, enabling students to find a work placement.

The low rates of graduate employment contribute to London Met's 28-place tumble in our overall academic league table this year, having risen to its highest rank yet – 100th – in 2021. In the Teaching Excellence Framework,

166–220 Holloway Road
London N7 8DB
020 7133 4200
courseenquiries@londonmet.ac.uk
www.londonmetsu.org.uk
www.londonmet.ac.uk
Open days: see website

The Times and The Sunday Times Rankings
Overall Ranking: 128 (last year: 100)

Teaching quality	81.4%	9
Student experience	77.9%	10
Research quality	29.2%	90
Entry standards	101	=130
Graduate prospects	60.2%	129
Good honours	64.5%	130
Expected completion rate	68.7%	128
Student/staff ratio	22.7	123

London Met was rated bronze in light of student achievement "notably below benchmark across a range of indicators". Assessors recognised a range of positive strategies to improve student satisfaction, but expressed concern that comparatively few students carried on to postgraduate study.

Completion rates are a sticking point for London Met, with more than two in 10 students (22.6%) projected to drop out – a higher rate than the 21.5% benchmark based on the social and academic backgrounds of the student intake.

There was much better news for London Met in the latest Research Excellence Framework (REF 2021). Sixty per cent of the university's research was assessed as world-leading or internationally excellent, the top two categories. The proportion of staff whose research was assessed increased by almost a third compared with the previous assessment in 2014. Maths produced the best results and the university gains 21 places in our research quality index to rank 90th, thanks to its REF 2021 improvements.

Cybersecurity is a strong subject and the university's research centre was the first of its kind in the UK when it opened in 2018, bringing together students and businesses.

Applications increased by 9% in 2021 but enrolments fell by about 18% to their lowest number yet. An architecture degree apprenticeship began in March 2022 and London Met also offers a teaching apprenticeship programme.

The university is in the top 40 overall for social inclusion, with almost all (96.8%) of its students drawn from non-selective state schools, and more than half (56.4%) from ethnic minority backgrounds. London Met also has the second-highest proportion of students aged over 21 when they enrol (78.4%).

Outreach programmes to support disadvantaged students from underrepresented groups include national Saturday clubs, which offer 30 weeks of workshops for 12- to 16-year-olds covering topics such as art and design, writing and talking, and developing confidence. The Upward Bound programme on alternate Saturdays targets Key Stage 3-4 pupils and aims to raise their GCSE attainment.

Membership of the university's modern gym and sports hall is free for students and staff. London Met does not own halls of residence but works with private accommodation providers to find new entrants somewhere affordable to live in the capital.

Tuition fees

- » Fees for UK students   £9,250
- » Fees for International students 2023–24   £13,200–£14,500
- » For scholarship and bursary information see www.londonmet.ac.uk/applying/funding-your-studies/undergraduate-tuition-fees/
- » Graduate salary   £24,000

Student numbers

Undergraduates	9,587	(688)
Postgraduates	1,287	(962)
Applications/places		13,985/2,425
Applications per place		5.8:1
Overall offer rate		86.2%
International students – EU		6.5%
Non-EU		2.4%

Accommodation

University provided places: 0
Self-catered: £155–£435 per week (linked external halls of residence)
www.londonmet.ac.uk/services-and-facilities/accommodation/

Where do the students come from?

State schools (non-grammar)	96.8%	First generation students	53.5%		
Grammar schools	0.9%	Low participation areas	7.1%		
Independent schools	2.4%	All ethnic minorities	56.4%		

Social inclusion ranking: 37

White working-class males	2.1%
Black achievement gap	-22.6%
Mature (over 21)	78.4%

London School of Economics and Political Science

The university's flagship Marshall Building opened in January 2022, capping a significant makeover at the London School of Economics and Political Science (LSE) campus in recent years. The development on the corner of Lincoln's Inn Fields houses co-curricular and academic facilities, featuring a new sports centre, café, arts and music rehearsal rooms alongside a teaching and learning hub.

The building is also home to some of LSE's leading departments and research centres, including the departments of management, finance and accounting and the Marshall Institute (for philanthropy and social entrepreneurship).

The building follows the addition of more open spaces around the Centre Buildings on Houghton Street off Aldwych, and improved student facilities.

Improving rates of student satisfaction have gone hand-in-hand with the heavy investment in resources, outcomes of the latest National Student Survey (NSS) show. In our analysis of the latest NSS, published in summer 2022, the LSE ranks =44 for satisfaction with the wider undergraduate experience, up from 65th in 2021 and 112th only three years ago. Students have marked the university down for teaching quality (=77). It is a fall of 16 places year-on-year, although it represents an improvement from 99th place in 2020.

The government's Teaching Excellence Framework rated the LSE bronze in 2017 in light of poor student satisfaction at the time. Post-pandemic, teaching has resumed to in-person delivery.

In the field of research, results of the latest Research Excellence Framework (REF 2021) reinforced the LSE's outstanding contribution to the social sciences. Fifty-eight per cent of the university's research was judged to be world-leading (4*) and 35% was rated internationally excellent (the top two standards). The best results were in economics; anthropology; social policy; healthy policy; and media and communications. Overall, the strength of the university's research in REF 2021 places it third in our research quality measure, which takes in the strength and breadth of submissions, behind only Imperial College London and Cambridge.

The stellar REF 2021 outcomes should soften the blow of dropping a place in the 2022 QS World Rankings, where after nine consecutive years of coming top in Europe and second in the world for social sciences and management (beaten by Harvard alone), the LSE finished second in Europe and third in the world in the latest rankings.

The LSE was founded in 1895 by the left-leaning Fabian Society members Sidney and Beatrice Webb, the political scientist Graham

Houghton Street
London WC2A 2AE
020 7955 6613
www.lse.ac.uk/ask-LSE
www.lsesu.com
www.lse.ac.uk
Open days: see website

The Times and The Sunday Times Rankings
Overall Ranking: 4 (last year: 5)

Teaching quality	74.5%	=77
Student experience	73.3%	=44
Research quality	68%	3
Entry standards	181	10
Graduate prospects	89.1%	6
Good honours	93.6%	2
Expected completion rate	96.7%	5
Student/staff ratio	13.4	11

Wallas and the writer George Bernard Shaw. Demand for places is competitive and reached new heights in the 2021 admissions cycle, when the university received almost 26,000 applications (a new record) for roughly 1,700 places. The LSE is one of only a few UK universities not to participate in Clearing.

The curriculum continues to evolve and the first politics and data science students started courses in September 2022, while from September 2023 a degree in mathematics and data science launches, and actuarial science gains the option of a placement year.

Promising graduate prospects are a perennial draw for students – as borne out by results of the latest Graduate Outcomes survey in summer 2022. The school ranks 6th (falling from second place last year), with 89.1% working in professional level jobs or furthering their studies 15 months after finishing their degrees.

Career-building opportunities are built into degrees via LSE's collaborations with more than 15,000 organisations, ranging from multinational corporates with UK offices; to small-to-medium size enterprises and start-ups; policy institutes; and government departments.

With 51.4% of the intake drawn from private or selective grammar schools, LSE has one of lower proportions of students from non-selective comprehensive schools (113th). However, it is 15th for the proportion of students from ethnic minority backgrounds (62.6%) and

the school is succeeding where others fail with regards to closing the black attainment gap, rising from fifth place last year to third this year on this measure of social inclusion.

Contextual offers one or two grades lower than standard have joined the school's initiatives to widen access. All academic departments are participating in the scheme, but any maths requirement still has to be met.

The Marshall Building sports centre has brought two squash courts and a heavy weights gym along with a sports hall, while the Saw Swee Hock student centre has a gym and dance studio and Old Building hosts a badminton court. The LSE's 23-acre sportsground is a train ride away in New Malden.

Accommodation is guaranteed to first-years who apply by the June deadline within 4,235 university-owned or endorsed rooms – almost half of them eligible to be catered. Prices vary considerably, from £120.05 per week for a bed in a triple room at Passfield Hall to £444.54 per week for a single studio at Urbanest Westminster Bridge.

Tuition fees

» Fees for UK students	£9,250
» Fees for International students 2023–24	£24,264–£35,856
» For scholarship and bursary information see www.lse.ac.uk/study-at-lse/undergraduate/fees-and-funding	
» Graduate salary	£32,577

Student numbers

Undergraduates	5,629 (12)
Postgraduates	7,311 (504)
Applications/places	25,845/1,715
Applications per place	15.1:1
Overall offer rate	21.9%
International students – EU	13.6%
Non-EU	40.3%

Accommodation

University provided places: 4,235
Catered costs: £120.05–£332 per week
Self-catered: £173–£444.54 per week
First-years guaranteed accommodation
www.lse.ac.uk/accommodation

Where do the students come from?

State schools (non-grammar)	51.4%	First generation students	32.1%	
Grammar schools	18.2%	Low participation areas	7%	
Independent schools	30.4%	All ethnic minorities	62.6%	

Social inclusion ranking: 105

White working-class males	1.8%
Black achievement gap	-3.2%
Mature (over 21)	1.4%

London South Bank University

True to its longstanding focus on the local community, London South Bank University (LSBU) is at the centre of a unique network offering secondary and further education, as well as a full range of university courses and commercial spinoffs.

The LSBU Group includes school academies – one specialising in engineering – and further education colleges in south London as well as the university and separate research, innovation and employment arms. The latest addition, the £100million South Bank Technical College opened in Nine Elms in September 2022, concentrating on science, technology and health.

Pathways between levels in the network are designed to improve social mobility and make the area more prosperous. Two thirds of LSBU's students are from ethnic minorities, most of them drawn from the surrounding boroughs, helping the university to feature in the top 30 of our social inclusion index. The university has been chosen to take over the leadership of the capital's main outreach network: London Uni Connect.

The university is firmly rooted in south London, where £65million has been spent in recent expansion. A campus opened last year in the centre of Croydon, focusing on business and healthcare, including a chiropractic clinic serving London's only undergraduate master's degree in the subject. The London Road building at the main campus in Southwark has been refurbished to add a library as well as computer rooms, catering facilities and a gym and sports centre.

Health students are based in hospitals in Romford, Leytonstone and Havering in east London, making LSBU one of the largest providers of healthcare professionals in the country. The university's Institute of Health and Social Care underpins its mission to become the university of choice for the NHS and the healthcare workforce in London. The LSBU Health Skills Centre opened in 2021 in partnership with Guy's and St Thomas' NHS Foundation Trust in a bid to encourage more local people into health and social care jobs.

The School of Health and Social Care was the institution's star performer in the latest Research Excellence Framework (REF 2021). Overall, however, LSBU has dropped 28 places in our research ranking to 92nd place, outpaced by the improvement of its peer institutions.

LSBU regards itself primarily as a university of technology, although the modern curriculum is much wider than that. Three sociology degrees, specialising in sustainability, black studies and social policy, took their first students in 2022-23. Courses in history and human geography closed in 2021 because of poor recruitment.

103 Borough Road
London SE1 0AA
0800 923 8888
course.enquiry@lsbu.ac.uk
https://www.lsbu.ac.uk/
student-life/students-union
www.lsbu.ac.uk
Open days:
see website

***The Times and The Sunday Times* Rankings**
Overall Ranking: 126 (last year: 127)

Teaching quality	72.8%	=97
Student experience	67.9%	=108
Research quality	28.8%	92
Entry standards	107	=119
Graduate prospects	66.4%	110
Good honours	74.1%	=92
Expected completion rate	78.5%	110
Student/staff ratio	17.5	=85

Student satisfaction improved in the latest National Student Survey, published in summer 2022, after a big drop in 2021 reflecting the impact of the Covid-19 pandemic on undergraduate experience. Satisfaction with teaching quality has returned to the top 100 (=97).

However, in our main academic league table, LSBU gained just one place overall and remains in the bottom 10.

Emerging from the pandemic, LSBU has returned to face-to-face tuition for undergraduates, retaining some elements of online provision.

Consultation with students showed support for the majority of teaching to be delivered in person but enthusiasm for the flexibility of online features in a blended system. The university's 2025 corporate strategy promises to reduce the volume of exam assessment but to hold those that continue to be required on campus.

A growing cohort of apprenticeships now involves a thousand employers, with earn-as-you-learn programmes operating from Level 4 (the equivalent of a foundation degree) to Level 7, equivalent to a master's degree. There are expected to be 3,500 students enrolled on more than 30 programmes by 2023, with 2,500 taking degree apprenticeships.

A tranche of healthcare programmes has been introduced for 2022-23 with others in management, engineering and surveying planned for 2023-24.

The university operates its own employment agency to help students to find part-time work while they study and provides strong support for start-up companies.

However, although LSBU was our University of the Year for Graduate Employment in 2018 and 2019, it has slipped out of the top 100 (110th) in our analysis of the latest Graduate Outcomes survey, tracking the proportion of graduates in highly skilled work or further study within 15 months.

Newly improved sports facilities include a multipurpose hall, therapy services and a fitness suite, dance studio and injury clinic.

There are 1,338 rooms in halls of residence, allowing 80% of students to live in if they want to do so. International students are guaranteed a place and UK students who are far from home have priority.

Tuition fees

» Fees for UK students	£9,250
» Fees for International students 2023–24	£15,400–£18,480
» For scholarship and bursary information see www.lsbu.ac.uk/study/undergraduate/fees-and-funding	
» Graduate salary	£27,000

Student numbers

Undergraduates	10,441 (3,635)
Postgraduates	2,121 (2,359)
Applications/places	22,915/4,340
Applications per place	5.3:1
Overall offer rate	63%
International students – EU	4.2%
Non-EU	7.6%

Accommodation

University provided places: 1,338
Self-catered: £139–£229 per week
www.lsbu.ac.uk/student-life/accommodation

Where do the students come from?

State schools (non-grammar)	96%	First generation students	52.8%	White working-class males	3.1%
Grammar schools	2.1%	Low participation areas	5.6%	Black achievement gap	-20.1%
Independent schools	1.9%	All ethnic minorities	67.8%	Mature (over 21)	41.8

Social inclusion ranking: 28

Loughborough University

Loughborough – renowned for its sporting success – proves once again that it has brains as well as brawn, ranking 11th in our academic table overall. Missing out on the top 10 spot it held last year by the narrowest of margins is likely to rankle at an institution where competitive spirit abounds. That it has outdone 16 of the 24 Russell Group universities (Loughborough's principal competitors for the most academically able students) in our league table may be some consolation.

In the academic arena, the university regularly tops our rankings for sports science and takes the top spot for sport-related subjects once again in the 2022 QS World University rankings. Academic excellence across subjects, coupled with sustained high levels of student satisfaction, has twice won Loughborough our University of the Year title. No university has been shortlisted for our main award more times in its 24-year history.

Students are contented with their overall undergraduate experience (=5) in our analysis of the latest National Student Survey. Although the university falls 40 places for student satisfaction with teaching quality, Loughborough remains in the upper half of universities in our comparison (58th) and is rated gold by the Teaching Excellence Framework for outstanding outcomes thanks to a culture of personalised learning and a comprehensive pastoral and academic tutorial programme.

It was Loughborough's research within architecture and the built environment; communication and media studies; and sport and exercise sciences that produced some of the best results in the latest Research Excellence Framework (REF 2021). Overall, 91% of the university's work was rated world-leading or internationally excellent (the top two categories). However, it slips four places to 34th in our research quality rankings against even bigger rises by other universities. Computer science also did well in REF 2021, and the subject is gaining a £1million Lovelace system.

Graduate employment is a consistent strong point. Loughborough is 12th in our analysis of the latest Graduate Outcomes survey. Talent Match, Loughborough's new internship programme, helps students and graduates to secure work experience, and for those wanting to start their own business, a Year in Enterprise placement is also available.

The 2022 Commonwealth Games in Birmingham prompted yet another "If Loughborough was a country…" medals table comparison. In this instance, athletes with a connection to the university (those who used its training facilities, current students or alumni) would have finished sixth in the overall medal table, ahead of South Africa, Jamaica and Nigeria.

Epinal Way
Loughborough LE11 3TU
01509 274 403
admissions@lboro.ac.uk
www.lsu.co.uk
www.lboro.ac.uk
Open days: see website

The Times and The Sunday Times **Rankings**
Overall Ranking: 11 (last year: 10)

Teaching quality	75.7%	58
Student experience	79.2%	=5
Research quality	52.5%	34
Entry standards	153	26
Graduate prospects	85.4%	12
Good honours	85.8%	21
Expected completion rate	93.4%	21
Student/staff ratio	13.8	=15

With 14 medals, including three golds, at the Tokyo Olympics in 2021, Loughborough would have ranked 23rd in the final medals table, ahead of Sweden, Switzerland and Belgium. At the Rio Olympics in 2016 it was 17th, with five gold medals in its total of 12.

The university is introducing a world-first Elite Athlete Management Qualification in partnership with the Wellbeing Science Institute in Australia. Work has also begun on a £9million eco-friendly expansion to SportPark, on the university's Science and Enterprise Park.

Our three-time Sports University of the Year, Loughborough is likely to be in the sights of any student serious about sport. Investment of £60million over the past 15 years means that the 440-acre campus on the edge of its small Leicestershire market town home has the resources to allow anyone already of national and international standard to flourish, while also developing raw talent.

The indoor Seb Coe High Performance Athletics Centre and the Paula Radcliffe Athletics Track pay tribute to two world-class alumni. Among a long list of medal winners to have made a splash in the 50m, eight-lane training pool (one of two British Swimming National Centres) is Adam Peaty, the triple Olympic champion and Commonwealth Games gold medallist. The triathlete Alex Yee, who won gold and silver in Tokyo, trained at the British Triathlon Performance Centre.

Loughborough's all-round strength on and off the sports fields is no secret in Britain's schools. In the past decade applications have soared by 58% and enrolments have climbed 45%, including a 5% rise in 2021, year-on-year. Significantly stiffer entry requirements for a number of the university's larger programmes triggered a 10% decrease in applications by the end of March 2022 compared with the same point in the admissions cycle a year earlier, figures showed. A degree in fashion design and technology will be introduced in 2023.

Loughborough remains just outside the top 100 for its intake from non-selective state schools (66.6%). The dropout rate compares well with other universities. In 21st place, it is below the university's benchmark figure. A revised contextual offer scheme began in 2022. It is expected to benefit more students than the previous scheme.

Most of student life takes place on campus and all first-years are guaranteed a space in halls of residence.

Tuition fees

» Fees for UK students	£9,250
» Fees for International students 2023–24	£22,000–£27,250
» For scholarship and bursary information see www.lboro.ac.uk/study/undergraduate/fees-funding/	
» Graduate salary	£27,014

Student numbers

Undergraduates	14,082 (264)
Postgraduates	3,175 (814)
Applications/places	34,255/4,980
Applications per place	6.9:1
Overall offer rate	74.4%
International students – EU	4.5%
Non-EU	8.7%

Accommodation

University provided places: 6,208
Catered costs: £159–£203 per week
Self-catered: £64–£195 per week
First-years guaranteed accommodation
www.lboro.ac.uk/services/accommodation/

Where do the students come from?

State schools (non-grammar)	66.6%	First generation students	32.3%	White working-class males	5.1%
Grammar schools	14.2%	Low participation areas	6.5%	Black achievement gap	-15.1%
Independent schools	19.3%	All ethnic minorities	24.8%	Mature (over 21)	1.8%

Social inclusion ranking: 103

University of Manchester

Students arriving at Manchester in September 2022 are the first to benefit from the largest construction project undertaken by any UK university. Four engineering schools and two research institutes will share the £400million Manchester Engineering Campus Development (MECD), connecting facilities along Oxford Road as part of a £1bn redevelopment to create a unified world-class campus.

With a floorspace roughly the size of 11 football pitches, the MECD can fit more than 8,000 students, researchers and staff who will have access to its blend of lecture theatres, makerspace and flexible teaching and learning facilities.

The extra room will not go to waste. The biggest university in our table, with more than 40,000 students, Manchester also attracts the most applications. And its popularity is growing: more than 88,000 students applied to the university in 2021 (an 11% year-on-year increase), while enrolments exceeded 11,000 for the first time in the same recruitment round. A snapshot of the latest recruitment cycle at the end of March 2022 showed another 4.5% rise in applications. The university also has four global centres in Dubai, Hong Kong, Shanghai and Singapore.

Seven courses will be added to the broad curriculum for 2023-24, six in Arabic with another language – including Russian, Portuguese and Spanish. A new degree in dental hygiene and therapy is also on the way.

Manchester maintains a top-25 position in our main academic league table despite recording falls in student satisfaction. Our analysis of the latest National Student Survey puts the university in the bottom 10 for how students view teaching quality (121st) and the wider undergraduate experience (=121).

Manchester's performance in British rankings, which take account of student satisfaction, has been variable, but the university places greater store in its success in research-focused international comparisons. It is in the top 30 in the QS World University Rankings 2022 and 35th in the Academic Ranking of World Universities, compiled in Shanghai.

Demonstrating its strength in research, Manchester has received a £17.4million increase in QR (quality-related) funding by Research England for 2022-23 – in third place behind the University of Oxford and Imperial College London. The boost to its research coffers follows an impressive showing in the latest Research Excellence Framework (REF 2021) across 31 subject areas.

Overall, 93% of the university's research was assessed as world-leading or internationally excellent, the top two categories. The results have propelled Manchester six places up our research quality index to reach seventh place – a significant step among the tightly bunched

---

Oxford Road
Manchester M13 9PL
0161 275 2077
study@manchester.ac.uk
www.manchester.ac.uk
www.manchesterstudentsunion.com
Open days: see website

The Times and *The Sunday Times* **Rankings**
Overall Ranking: 24 (last year: 23)

Teaching quality	69.5%	121
Student experience	66.3%	=121
Research quality	64.4%	7
Entry standards	162	=20
Graduate prospects	83%	22
Good honours	84.8%	24
Expected completion rate	93.9%	=17
Student/staff ratio	14.3	28

research-intensive universities. Manchester has had 25 Nobel laureates among its staff and students, most recently Sir Andre Geim and Sir Konstantin Novoselov, who shared the prize in physics in 2010 for discovering graphene, the strongest material to be measured. The university hosts the National Graphene Institute.

Jodrell Bank, the university's world-famous radio observatory, became a Unesco World Heritage Site in 2019 and a £21.5million refurbishment project was completed in June 2022, adding a visitor exhibition to aid public engagement with scientific research.

Facilities to help transform outcomes for cancer patients are being enhanced by the redevelopment of the former Paterson research building, destroyed by a fire in 2017. The centre, housing the university's collaboration with Cancer Research UK and the Christie NHS Foundation, is due to reopen in early 2023.

The university-owned Manchester Museum has been extended in a £15million refurbishment and the recently renovated Whitworth art gallery and the Alliance Manchester Business School are also part of the campus.

All undergraduates are set three "ethical grand challenges": sustainability, social justice and workplace ethics to reinforce social responsibility, a core aim at Manchester. The Stellify Award recognises extracurricular activities alongside degree studies and is designed to make Manchester students highly employable. The Times Top 100 Graduate Employers 2021-22 listing ranks the university's graduates as No 1 among those most targeted by the UK's top employers. In our analysis of graduate prospects, Manchester is steady in 22nd place.

Manchester is 91st in our social inclusion index, and fourth out of the research-intensive Russell Group universities. Efforts to widen participation include contextual offers. In 2021, nearly 4,000 applicants were made contextual offers (1,000 more than in 2020). The dropout rate has improved to be in our top 20 (=17) and is lower than expected in light of the university's course and student profile. About a third of undergraduates receive financial aid.

The city hosts about 100,000 students at a variety of institutions and Manchester's world-class reputation for diverse cultural life is well deserved. First-years who apply by the end of August are guaranteed a place in halls.

There are first-rate sports facilities and the university's teams frequently rank near the top of the British Universities and Colleges Sport (BUCS) league table.

Tuition fees

» Fees for UK students £9,250
» Fees for International students 2023–24 £20,000–£25,000
Medicine (clinical years) £48,000; Dentistry £29,000–£48,000
» For scholarship and bursary information see
www.manchester.ac.uk/study/undergraduate/student-finance/
» Graduate salary £25,000

Student numbers

Undergraduates	28,847	(141)
Postgraduates	11,457	(4,189)
Applications/places	88,330/11,070	
Applications per place	8.1	
Overall offer rate	60.2%	
International students – EU	8.2%	
Non-EU	25.3%	

Accommodation

University provided places: 7,244
Catered costs: £153–£212 per week
Self-catered: £110–£172 per week
First-years guaranteed accommodation
www.accommodation.manchester.ac.uk/ouraccommodation/

Where do the students come from?

State schools (non-grammar)	72.3%	First generation students	32.8%	White working-class males	3.1%
Grammar schools	11.5%	Low participation areas	8.8%	Black achievement gap	-14%
Independent schools	16.2%	All ethnic minorities	33.3%	Mature (over 21)	7.7%

Social inclusion ranking: 91

Manchester Metropolitan University

Already one of the biggest providers of undergraduate education in the UK, Manchester Met (MMU) attracted 14% more applications in 2021 than the year before and accepted record numbers.

The new intake will find an institution with plenty to celebrate. After a slump in student satisfaction during the pandemic, the latest National Student Survey, published in summer 2022, shows a dramatic recovery: satisfaction with the wider undergraduate experience makes a gargantuan leap of 73 places to reach =44 place. Satisfaction with teaching quality (=41) has recovered 59 places year-on-year.

The university has resumed face-to-face teaching since the pandemic and promises a "full, on-campus university experience" for the 2022-23 academic year. At undergraduate level, MMU has brought in block teaching in two 11-week semesters, with an assessment week at the end. Two-thirds of all assessments will take place online, either as full exams or quizzes.

The university had a bumper set of results in the latest Research Excellence Framework (REF 2021), when 30% of its work was considered world-leading, the top category. MMU entered 740 academics – double the number involved in the previous national assessment in 2014 – and is now among the top three post-1992 universities in our research ranking, with strength in art and design, English and sport, and leisure and tourism. In our overall league table, MMU has jumped 11 places and into the top 60.

Impressive facilities opened in 2021-22, including the £35million School of Digital Arts (SODA), where the first 1,000 students are studying film, animation, UX design, photography, games design and artificial intelligence.

In the centre of the sports-loving city, the Manchester Metropolitan Institute of Sport opened in 2022 to provide a world-class institute championing everything that sport can do – from strengthening communities and building a healthier society to inspiring the next generation and pushing the limits of human performance. The institute houses the Department of Sport and Exercise alongside leading researchers in musculoskeletal science, sports business experts plus specialists from the Faculty of Health, Psychology and Social Care.

The region's first public poetry library is based at the university and is proving popular with more than 10,000 books and recordings to explore. It is based in the new arts and humanities building, alongside the Manchester Writing School, where Carol Ann Duffy, the former poet laureate, is creative director.

The next development in prospect is a £45million extension and refurbishment for the Faculty of Science and Engineering.

All Saints Building
All Saints
Manchester M15 6BH
0161 247 6969
www2.mmu.ac.uk/contact/
course-enquiry/
www.theunionmmu.org
www2.mmu.ac.uk
Open days: see website

The Times and The Sunday Times **Rankings**
Overall Ranking: 60 (last year: 71)

Teaching quality	76.7%	=41
Student experience	73.3%	=44
Research quality	43.7%	51
Entry standards	126	62
Graduate prospects	67.9%	=100
Good honours	76.1%	79
Expected completion rate	86.1%	=59
Student/staff ratio	17.5	=85

MMU is also planning to pedestrianise more of the campus and provide more green spaces. The university topped the People and Planet Green League 2021 for all-round environmental sustainability.

MMU was among the pioneers of degree apprenticeships, taking its first students in 2015. It was the top university for the fourth year in a row at the 2021 RateMyApprenticeship Awards, based on student reviews. The university expects 2,400 trainees to start degree apprenticeships with about 500 employers in 2023, with programmes for laboratory scientists and digital design professionals starting in 2022-23.

Six degrees planned for 2023 include one in sport and youth leadership, and two in interpreting and translation (French and Spanish). Three new fashion degrees include one in fashion communications. Fashion is one of MMU's best-known fields. Another star attraction is the Manchester School of Architecture, run in collaboration with the University of Manchester, which climbed to seventh place in the worldwide QS 2022 subject rankings.

Employability is a key focus for traditional degree courses, too. Undergraduates are offered work placements and improved graduate prospects are in our top 100, based on the proportion in highly skilled work or postgraduate study 15 months after completing a degree.

MMU operates a variety of measures to broaden its intake, with about 40% of undergraduates qualifying for support worth £750 a year. Extra help is available for those in financial hardship. The Talent Match service, run in partnership with the Greater Manchester Chamber of Commerce, helps to pair skilled graduates with local employers' needs.

Named our University of the Year for Student Retention 2021, MMU is in the top 60 universities for its relatively low dropout rate. Its "whole student life cycle" programme, the First Generation Scheme, works with Year 12 pupils in local schools and colleges, and continues to offer support for those who take up a place at MMU, even after they graduate.

All first-years are guaranteed a room if they register by the end of July.

The Sugden Sports Centre, across the road from the All Saints campus, was redeveloped in 2018, and Manchester Aquatics Centre, with three gyms and a 50m pool, is also on the doorstep. The city's energy makes it a perennial student favourite.

Tuition fees

» Fees for UK students	£9,250
» Fees for International students 2023–24	£16,500–£18,500
Architecture	£26,000
» For scholarship and bursary information see	
www2.finance.mmu.ac.uk/students/	
» Graduate salary	£22,000

Student numbers

Undergraduates	25,906	(1,973)
Postgraduates	4,290	(3,773)
Applications/places		55,230/10,815
Applications per place		5.1:1
Overall offer rate		77.3%
International students – EU		2.1%
Non-EU		4.1%

Accommodation

University provided places: 5,132
Self-catered: £114–£189 per week
First-years guaranteed accommodation
https://www2.mmu.ac.uk/accommodation/

Where do the students come from?

State schools (non-grammar)	93%	First generation students	50%	
Grammar schools	3.3%	Low participation areas	14.7%	
Independent schools	3.7%	All ethnic minorities	39%	

Social inclusion ranking: 74

White working-class males	5.1%
Black achievement gap	-17.2%
Mature (over 21)	14.1%

Middlesex University

Middlesex is adopting a pioneering approach to mental health, making it "foundational" to all aspects of university life. By 2023, the university aims to be the first to incorporate University UK's Stepchange programme into all operations for its 44,000 students – most at its main campus in Hendon, northwest London, and the rest at satellite campuses in Dubai and Mauritius. The programme encourages self-belief and open discussion of mental health issues.

The university is moving towards an inclusive curriculum that is co-led, co-designed and co-created with students – a move likely to boost its scores further in the National Student Survey. Our analysis of the latest outcomes, published in summer 2022, show year-on-year improvements in student satisfaction, especially for teaching quality (up 19 places to 91st).

The biggest factor in its eight-place rise in our main academic league table is improving graduate outcomes. A rise of 13 percentage points in the proportion of students going on to highly skilled jobs or further study within 15 months has helped Middlesex to vault 54 places up our graduate employment index into 67th place. A branch of the recruitment service Unitemps is located on campus.

Applications dropped by almost 9% in the latest admissions round, following a similar decline in 2021. As a popular destination for European students for many years, the university blames Brexit, but is also feeling the effects of a revised curriculum aimed at better-prepared students.

The main campus has benefited from £200million of recent investment, including the consolidation of library services and two new academic buildings at the business school. Although the university's campus in Malta closed in September 2022, a Dubai outpost has opened for 4,500 students and there are 1,000 studying through Middlesex in Mauritius. A global strategy for the period up to 2031 aims to improve health and wellbeing and reduce inequality, use culture and creativity to enrich the lives of individuals and communities and help to protect the environment.

Middlesex has invested heavily in technology to facilitate its "learning through doing" approach, delivering practical courses with personalised support. The £24million StoneX Stadium in Hendon, which was set to open in late 2022, will provide access to virtual and augmented reality technology. It will house purpose-built facilities for the London Sport Institute, in partnership with Saracens Rugby Club, whose grounds will house the latest technology for motion capture, force sensing plates and full-body scanning.

New facilities for the natural sciences on the main campus will include diagnostic suites and laboratories, while nursing and midwifery

The Burroughs
Hendon
London NW4 4BT
020 8411 5555
enquiries@mdx.ac.uk
www.mdxsu.com
www.mdx.ac.uk
Open days: see website

The Times and The Sunday Times Rankings
Overall Ranking: =115 (last year: 123)

Teaching quality	73.5%	91
Student experience	70.2%	=83
Research quality	30.4%	=82
Entry standards	107	=119
Graduate prospects	72.2%	67
Good honours	72.6%	102
Expected completion rate	76%	123
Student/staff ratio	17.1	=79

students will have clinical skills facilities including wards, consulting rooms, birthing and sensory rooms, and skills labs to develop the confidence they need to practise safely during clinical placements. Middlesex led a project to develop an electronic practice assessment document (ePAD), introduced in nursing courses across London in 2021.

The university offers 14 apprenticeship programmes, with 1,800 students training for careers from broadcast and media engineer, sports coach and social worker to environmental health practitioner, police constable or risk and safety management professional. It expects to add 1,000 places by 2023.

Almost all British students at Middlesex are from non-selective state schools and the university has climbed six places to 21st in our overall social inclusion index. Nearly three-quarters are from black, Asian or ethnic minority backgrounds and more than half are the first in their family to go to university. A contextual admissions policy – taken up by about 3% of students in its year of introduction in 2021 – provides offers on average one grade lower than standard requirements for candidates facing the greatest barriers to study at Middlesex. The university offers a variety of schemes for students from low-income backgrounds, including a Summer Support Fund for those who need money urgently to cover living costs, and technology costs for online learning over the long vacation.

Middlesex submitted work in a dozen subject areas to the latest Research Excellence Framework (REF 2021), a broader range than the previous assessment in 2014. Business and management was the strongest area in the university's submission. But although REF 2021 recorded improvement, rival institutions did even better and the university has slipped more than 20 places down our research quality ranking to =82.

The university has 1,140 residential places on or close to campus, including 630 in a privately run development near Wembley Stadium. New entrants are guaranteed accommodation if they meet the summer deadline for applications.

Sports facilities are extensive and most are conveniently located. They include a bouldering wall and fitness pod and a real tennis court, although the latter is scheduled to close in four years' time because student usage is considered too low to justify the space it occupies. The West End and central London's many attractions are a Tube journey away.

Tuition fees

» Fees for UK students	£9,250
» Fees for International students 2023–24	£14,700
» For scholarship and bursary information see https://www.mdx.ac.uk/study-with-us/fees-and-funding	
» Graduate salary	£24,907

Student numbers

Undergraduates	14,172 (834)
Postgraduates	2,444 (2,707)
Applications/places	18,805/3,275
Applications per place	5.7:1
Overall offer rate	66.3%
International students – EU	10.2%
Non-EU	11.5%

Accommodation

University provided places: 1,140
Self-catered: £156–£196 per week
First-years guaranteed accommodation
www.mdx.ac.uk/student-life/accommodation

Where do the students come from?

				Social inclusion ranking: 21	
State schools (non-grammar)	97.8%	First generation students	57.1%	White working-class males	2.5%
Grammar schools	0.6%	Low participation areas	4.5%	Black achievement gap	-10%
Independent schools	1.6%	All ethnic minorities	73.5%	Mature (over 21)	46.2%

Newcastle University

Newcastle is No 1 in the UK for sustainable development in the Times Higher Education Impact Rankings 2022. The university, which adopted a climate action plan in 2021, is eighth in the world for its progress towards the United Nations' sustainable development goals. It promises investment of £15million a year on projects to decarbonise heat and power to reach net zero emissions by 2030.

Popular though these goals are among students, overall satisfaction has continued to decline according to the latest National Student Survey, published in summer 2022. Our analysis puts Newcastle towards the bottom of our table for satisfaction with teaching quality (123rd) and the wider undergraduate experience (=116).

The university's performance in other areas improved, however, moving it up nine places in our overall academic league table to =33. Graduate prospects, which are weighted more heavily this year, were the biggest factor. The proportion of students in highly skilled jobs or further study 15 months after graduation was up almost six percentage points, placing Newcastle in the top-25 on this measure.

There has been no shortage of investment by Newcastle. The £4.6million Farrell Centre marks the transformation of a nineteenth-century department store into a facility focusing on city life. It aims to be a new type of public institution – part research hub, part civic space, part gallery and museum.

The redevelopment of the Stephenson Building for engineering – due for completion in 2024 – is costing £110million. As well as a variety of student spaces, the complex will include facilities for research hubs in digital manufacturing, biomedical engineering and sustainable propulsion.

In 2020, the university opened the £350million Newcastle Helix (formerly Science Central), an urban regeneration project with the city council and Legal & General Capital. Its Catalyst building houses two national innovation centres for ageing and data as well as the National Institute for Health Research Innovation Observatory. The Helix also hosts the Frederick Douglass Centre, named after the American anti-slavery campaigner, with a 750-seat auditorium and 200-seat lecture theatre for the university's school of computing and business school.

Britain's ageing population will be the focus of a new £500million campus for research into dementia and frailty.

Newcastle's improvements in the latest Research Excellence Framework (REF 2021) compared with the previous assessment in 2014 promise a 20% increase in research funding. Ranking =26 in our analysis of research quality, a slight fall year-on-year

---

Newcastle upon Tyne
NE1 7RU
0191 208 3333
apps.ncl.ac.uk/contact-us/general-enquiry
www.nusu.co.uk
www.ncl.ac.uk
Open days: see website

Edinburgh
NEWCASTLE UPON TYNE
Belfast
London
Cardiff

The Times and The Sunday Times Rankings
Overall Ranking: =33 (last year: 42)

Teaching quality	68.6%	123
Student experience	66.7%	=116
Research quality	53.6%	=26
Entry standards	145	=38
Graduate prospects	82.3%	25
Good honours	84.4%	27
Expected completion rate	94.5%	13
Student/staff ratio	14.7	=33

against sector-wide success, Newcastle achieved the top category (world-leading) in 42% of its submission to REF 2021, up from 31% in 2014. The academic team involved in the assessment was 54% larger. English language and literature produced the best results, with almost 80% of the submission placed in the top category.

Newcastle also has a gold rating in the Teaching Excellence Framework. In our analysis of course completion rates it has an excellent record, finishing 13th, and the university's dropout rate is below the level expected in light of the background of its students and the courses offered.

Like many Russell Group universities, however, Newcastle does less well in our social inclusion index (107th). About one third of its undergraduates are drawn from selective schools, leaving it outside the top 100 on this measure. Only one in 12 are drawn from areas with the lowest participation rates in higher education, despite its location in the northeast of England, which has the country's lowest take-up of higher education overall. In 2021, almost a third of applicants qualified for a contextual offer as a result of educational disadvantage.

The university is working with the Newcastle United Foundation on outreach, education and research programmes across the region. Students from low-income families and those with dependent children receive extra support, and 27.5% of students with household incomes under £35,000 qualified for financial assistance in 2021. Newcastle has been designated a University of Sanctuary for its support for refugees, pledging up to £1million for scholarships and support for academics and researchers in Ukraine and other war-torn regions.

About £30million has been spent in recent years on new and refurbished sports facilities, including a Sport and Fitness Centre at the heart of the campus. The outdoor pitches are a little further away, as is the Newburn Water Sports Centre. But the university's 63 sports clubs offer a broad range of opportunities for competition and there are 45 exercise and wellbeing classes every week.

The 4,500 residential places owned or endorsed by the university are enough to accommodate all full-time first-year undergraduates who want to live in. Places are allocated via a computer-generated number to ensure fairness. Private rents in Newcastle are relatively cheap and the nightlife has acquired legendary status.

Tuition fees

» Fees for UK students   £9,250
» Fees for International students 2023–24   £20,400–£26,400
  Medicine £38,400; Dentistry £40,500
» For scholarship and bursary information see
  www.ncl.ac.uk/undergraduate/fees-funding
» Graduate salary   £25,000

Student numbers

Undergraduates	21,331	(46)
Postgraduates	5,008	(1,391)
Applications/places		32,400/6,255
Applications per place		5.2:1
Overall offer rate		78%
International students – EU		4.7%
Non-EU		12.6%

Accommodation

University provided places: 4,554
Catered costs: £136–£182 per week
Self-catered: £96–£179 per week
First-years guaranteed accommodation
www.ncl.ac.uk/accommodation/

Where do the students come from?

State schools (non-grammar)	66%	First generation students	32.4%
Grammar schools	10.6%	Low participation areas	8.8%
Independent schools	23.4%	All ethnic minorities	13.5%

Social inclusion ranking: 107

White working-class males	4.6%
Black achievement gap	-13.5%
Mature (over 21)	5.3%

Newman University Birmingham

Newman University Birmingham's levels of student satisfaction suffered more than most when the pandemic threatened the friendly community atmosphere that is a trademark of the small Catholic institution. They have yet to recover to their top-10 position of 2020 – but Newman still outperforms the other Birmingham universities, according to our analysis of the latest National Student Survey, published in summer 2022. Satisfaction with the wider undergraduate experience has fallen 21 places to =54 but the students' view of teaching quality remains in the top 30 (=28). The resumption of in-person activities and expanded students' union facilities on campus can be expected to lift spirits.

The modern campus, eight miles southwest of the centre of Birmingham, has had £20million of investment in recent years. A mock law court, computer science laboratory, a careers and employability hub and new halls of residence for 200 students have all been added. Work is continuing to make the campus more environmentally sustainable.

Newman describes itself as a "teaching-led" university and does not employ staff for research alone, to ensure that students have regular contact with active researchers. In the latest Research Excellence Framework (REF 2021), Newman doubled the size of its academic team submitting work compared with the previous national assessment in 2014 – and also doubled the amount of its world-leading research. Ninety-four per cent of its work in English was assessed as world-leading or internationally excellent, the top two categories. Overall, however, Newman is in near the bottom overall in our research quality index (=126).

Newman's 11-place fall for research holds back its progress in our main academic table, where it has gained four places to rank 118th.

The university is one of the smallest in our guide, with fewer than 3,000 students at its leafy location overlooking the Bartley reservoir and Worcestershire countryside. Its strategy for 2020-25 envisages gradual growth, but the disruption of the last two years has delayed progress on this target. As a former teacher training college, degrees for both primary and secondary teachers have been relaunched this year, with an accent on post-16 enhancement at secondary level.

A new School of Nursing and Allied Health has been established to broaden the curriculum. Degrees in adult nursing, mental health nursing and physiotherapy will take their first students in 2023, making use of the new facilities.

Policing, sociology, and psychology with criminology are also being introduced in 2023 at degree level. Every full-time degree has

Genners Lane
Bartley Green
Birmingham B32 3NT
0121 476 1181
admissions@newman.ac.uk
www.newmansu.org
www.newman.ac.uk
Open days: see website

The Times and The Sunday Times Rankings
Overall Ranking: 118 (last year: 122)

Teaching quality	78.8%	=28
Student experience	72.4%	=54
Research quality	13.3%	=126
Entry standards	105	128
Graduate prospects	69.7%	=87
Good honours	67.7%	123
Expected completion rate	76.7%	120
Student/staff ratio	18	=95

a work placement module and Newman has risen 15 places to rank =87 in our analysis of the latest Graduate Outcomes survey, tracking the proportion of students in highly skilled work or further study 15 months after finishing their degree course.

The focus on employability helped to secure a silver rating in the Teaching Excellence Framework. Most teaching will be delivered in person in the coming academic year, although learning materials will be available online.

Newman has risen two places to reach the top 10 in our social inclusion index. Enrolments from non-selective state schools are the highest in the country (99%) and the university also has the biggest proportion of students who are the first in their family to experience higher education (72.2%). More than 45% come from black, Asian or ethnic minority backgrounds, although Newman has struggled to close the achievement gap between black students and others, ranking 102nd.

The institution is named after John Henry Newman, the 19th-century cardinal who wrote The Idea of a University in 1852. It claims to be a "different kind of university", driven by the belief that higher education should enable students to develop new ways of understanding the world and help make a positive impact within it. Students are recruited from all faiths and none.

Newman is part of the Aimhigher West Midlands consortium, with the other Birmingham universities and Worcester, which offers a range of activities, information, advice and guidance for young people aged 13-19, and the university runs its own outreach programmes.

No bursaries are available for students in the 2022-23 academic year, but the Newman University Support Fund provides up to £1,750 a year for those experiencing hardship having exhausted other forms of support. There are also six Sanctuary Scholarships for asylum seekers, four of them reserved for Ukrainians in a scheme introduced this year.

First-year students are guaranteed one of the 282 places in university-owned accommodation. There is a well-equipped fitness suite and performance room, as well as a 3G sports pitch, sports hall, gymnasium and squash courts. Birmingham city centre, with its cultural attractions and student-orientated nightlife, is within easy reach.

Tuition fees

» Fees for UK students	£9,250
» For scholarship and bursary information see www.newman.ac.uk/study/student-finance/	
» Graduate salary	£22,950

Student numbers

Undergraduates	1,828	(292)
Postgraduates	395	(328)
Applications/places		3,225/520
Applications per place		6.2:1
Overall offer rate		83.5%
International students – EU		0.5%
Non-EU		0%

Accommodation

University provided places: 282
Self-catered: £105–£195 per week
First-years guaranteed accommodation
www.newman.ac.uk/study/student-finance/

Where do the students come from?

State schools (non-grammar)	99%	First generation students	72.2%	White working-class males	3.8%
Grammar schools	0.5%	Low participation areas	21.4%	Black achievement gap	-31.9%
Independent schools	0.5%	All ethnic minorities	45.4%	Mature (over 21)	43.4%

Social inclusion ranking: 10

University of Northampton

Northampton has rationalised its undergraduate curriculum, removing a number of the options for joint honours, but still recorded a 5% rise in applications in a snapshot of the latest admissions round in March 2022. An 8% increase in 2021 suggests that the university has turned the corner in terms of student popularity after four years of decline. Demand has been high for foundation years and for new degrees in sport and exercise psychology, health studies, forensic psychology and business management. Interest from international applicants has been strong across the board.

Student satisfaction has rebounded, according to our analysis of outcomes in the latest National Student Survey, published in summer 2022. Northampton has returned to the top 100, up 17 places for satisfaction with teaching quality (=84), and up 19 for how students view the wider undergraduate experience (96th).

It is a welcome sign that the university's £330million development of the Waterside Campus, which opened in 2018, is finally paying off. A few minutes' walk from the town centre, the 58-acre campus has a four-storey Learning Hub, where most teaching takes place, as its centrepiece. Big lecture theatres have been replaced by classrooms for up to 40 people and smaller lecture spaces.

Overall, however, Northampton has dropped 17 places in our main academic league table and into the bottom 10.

Northampton had adopted a system of "active blended learning" before the pandemic struck, combining face-to-face and online provision in a "flipped learning" model where students prepare in advance for their teaching sessions and interact more with their peers and staff. The system was able to accommodate more online learning during the pandemic and has returned to more face-to-face learning since.

The university was rated gold in the Teaching Excellence Framework before the new campus opened, not least for its focus on social enterprise. Every student has the opportunity to develop entrepreneurial skills as part of their course to make them more employable.

The Northampton Employment Promise guarantees an internship of at least three months or a postgraduate course to any graduates who have not found full-time work within a year of graduating with at least a 2:2 degree or Higher National Diploma. The university also works closely with the Northamptonshire Growth Hub, assisting local businesses as well as providing opportunities for student placements and part-time jobs. In our analysis of graduate prospects, based on the proportion in highly skilled jobs or on postgraduate courses 15 months after leaving Northampton, the university ranks joint 84th.

Waterside Campus
University Drive
Northampton NN1 5PH
0300 303 2772
study@northampton.ac.uk
www.northamptonunion.com
www.northampton.ac.uk
Open days: see website

The Times and The Sunday Times Rankings
Overall Ranking: 125 (last year: =108)

Teaching quality	74%	=84
Student experience	69.3%	96
Research quality	13.8%	123
Entry standards	107	=119
Graduate prospects	70.2%	=84
Good honours	69.6%	117
Expected completion rate	81.5%	=95
Student/staff ratio	17.7	=89

Five new degrees are planned for 2023: in animation, artificial intelligence and data science, computer networks engineering, software engineering, and pharmacology. The university also expects some growth in the numbers taking its 10 degree apprenticeship programmes, which include provision for nursing associates, non-destructive testing engineers and occupational therapists.

More student placements will be available for arts, science and technology and health students through the creation of the University Hospitals of Northamptonshire NHS Group, a new alliance with the University of Leicester and hospitals in Northampton and Kettering.

The alliance will also open up research opportunities. The university increased the size of its submission to the latest Research Excellence Framework (REF 2021) but has fallen into the bottom 10 on this measure in our table (123rd).

Northampton fares much better in our social inclusion index (=33), admitting almost all of its undergraduates from non-selective state schools and featuring in the top 30 for the proportion of mature students. Professor Anne-Marie Kilday, who took over as vice-chancellor in 2022 after moving from Oxford Brookes University, has identified equality, diversity and inclusion as her top priorities, making higher education "a catalyst for positive social impact".

The university has a variety of schemes to encourage students from underrepresented groups into higher education, and awards a bursary of £400 in the second and third year of a degree to students with a household income of less than £25,000. Northampton also co-sponsors a University Technical College at the nearby Silverstone motor-racing circuit.

Northampton is one of few universities in the UK to offer all students free access to sports facilities, with the students' union providing the necessary kit. Leisure facilities are shared with the local community.

All new full-time students who apply by late May are guaranteed a room in halls, either on or close to the campus. Those who arrive through Clearing are guaranteed a room in the Scholars Green halls, four miles away. The town centre has a number of popular bars including the Platform, a students' union venue housing a nightclub, bar and café.

Tuition fees

» Fees for UK students	£9,250
» Fees for International students 2023–24	£14,000–£16,900
Foundation years	£14,000
» For scholarship and bursary information see	
www.northampton.ac.uk/student-life/fees-and-funding/	
» Graduate salary	£24,000

Student numbers

Undergraduates	9,174 (1,104)
Postgraduates	2,073 (1,689)
Applications/places	13,940/3,170
Applications per place	4.4:1
Overall offer rate	79.3%
International students – EU	3.2%
Non-EU	6.9%

Accommodation

University provided places: 2,344
Self-catered: £79–£155 per week
First-years guaranteed accommodation
www.northampton.ac.uk/student-life/accommodation

Where do the students come from?

State schools (non-grammar)	97.5%	First generation students	51.8%	White working-class males	4.4%
Grammar schools	1.2%	Low participation areas	16.7%	Black achievement gap	-21.6%
Independent schools	1.3%	All ethnic minorities	41.3%	Mature (over 21)	36.8%

Social inclusion ranking: =33

Northumbria University

Northumbria declares it is ready to "take on tomorrow" as a "research-intensive modern university". In 15 years, the university has transformed its research capacity and is celebrating improved results in the latest Research Excellence Framework (REF 2021) and a rise in our research quality index to 58th. The number of staff with work rated world-leading or internationally excellent has leapt from 58 in 2008 to 840 in 2021.

Professor Andrew Wathey had a triumphant send-off in May 2022 after serving as vice-chancellor throughout the period, ending with a 149% increase in research funding. Wathey has been replaced by Professor Andy Long, who moved from the University of Nottingham. He takes over an institution on the way up, jumping 13 places in our main academic league table into the top 50.

Student satisfaction has recovered – up 31 places to =85 in terms of the overall undergraduate experience, according to our analysis of the latest National Student Survey – after dipping more than most during the pandemic.

Graduate prospects is another metric that has shown year-on-year improvement, up 10 places to the top 40 in our analysis of the Graduate Outcomes survey, tracking the numbers in professional jobs or postgraduate study 15 months after leaving university.

The return to on-campus learning for the 2022-23 academic year has been welcomed and the university is providing weekly communications to guide students through their learning plan.

More than £250million has been invested in new and modernised facilities over the past decade at Northumbria's two campuses, one in the heart of the city and the other three miles away at Coach Lane, which houses the Faculty of Health and Life Sciences. Further afield, the university has a base in London, near Liverpool Street station, and also offers courses in Amsterdam in partnership with the Amsterdam University of Applied Sciences.

Northumbria has world-class teaching facilities for engineering funded by a £2million grant from the Office for Students. New facilities include a 120-seat microelectronics and communications laboratory with 100 individual workspaces, as well as space for group work with industry partners. More than 560 employers and 60 professional bodies sponsor or accredit Northumbria's programmes. The university is also a leader in successful start-ups. The latest Higher Education Business and Communities Interaction survey for 2020-21 placed Northumbria in the top five in the UK, with turnover for its graduate start-ups reaching £95.3million. It was the 12th consecutive year that Northumbria has been in the top 10.

Six degrees, in business, economics, and sport and exercise science, took their first

---

Sutherland Building
Newcastle upon Tyne
NE1 8ST
0191 406 0901
bc.applicantservice@northumbria.ac.uk
www.mynsu.co.uk
www.northumbria.ac.uk
Open days: see website

The Times and The Sunday Times Rankings
Overall Ranking: 49 (last year: =62)

Teaching quality	74.1%	=82
Student experience	70.1%	=85
Research quality	40.6%	58
Entry standards	137	47
Graduate prospects	78.2%	40
Good honours	80%	=49
Expected completion rate	83.4%	=81
Student/staff ratio	15.7	=52

students in September 2022. Another six will be launched in 2023 in computer science, data science, artificial intelligence, games computing, business computing, and networks and cybersecurity. The university offers 21 higher or degree apprenticeship programmes and expects trainees to exceed 2,000 in 2023. Apprenticeships range from nursing, policing and engineering to programmes for architects, chartered surveyors and academics.

Northumbria's relationship with neighbouring Newcastle University is much stronger than is often found between institutions elsewhere. The Collaborative Newcastle Universities Agreement is an innovative partnership to support the economic and social recovery of the region post-Covid. One example is NUdata, a centre for doctoral training in data-intensive science. The universities have teamed up with more than 40 industrial partners including Amazon Alexa, the BBC, Britishvolt, the Met Office and the National Audit Office, all of which rely heavily on big data to deliver their services.

Northumbria scores in the top 25 for recruitment from areas of low participation in higher education and has a wide range of scholarships and bursaries to encourage progression. It has the 12th-highest proportion of white working-class male recruits, the most underrepresented group. A 20% discount on postgraduate fees is an incentive to stick with the books.

As well as targeting local students, the university offers global scholarships of up to £3,000, which are taken up by 80% of international students.

The university has a strong record in competitive sport. The £30million Sport Central development at the City site was refurbished in 2019 and has a pool, sports science laboratories, sports halls and a 3,000-seat arena. Illustrious sporting alumni include the England rugby players Owen Farrell, Anthony Watson and Mako Vunipola. They all graduated with the business school's leadership and management distance-learning degree, which was designed with the Rugby Players' Association.

En-suite accommodation is guaranteed to all first-years from a stock of 2,769 rooms. Newcastle's nightlife is legendary and culture is thriving, too. Gallery North, part of the University Gallery, has been refurbished and relaunched as a public space, and Northumbria has forged a partnership with the Baltic Centre for Contemporary Art, in Gateshead, for teaching and research.

Tuition fees

» Fees for UK students	£9,250
» Fees for International students 2023–24	£16,500–£20,500
» For scholarship and bursary information see	
www.northumbria.ac.uk/study-at-northumbria/fees-funding/	
» Graduate salary	£24,000

Student numbers

Undergraduates	19,851	(1,538)
Postgraduates	6,718	(3,755)
Applications/places	23,890/6,055	
Applications per place	3.9:1	
Overall offer rate	88.9%	
International students – EU	5.6%	
Non-EU	6.4%	

Accommodation

University provided places: 2,769
Catered costs: £125–£126 per week
Self-catered: £86–£185 per week
First-years guaranteed accommodation
www.northumbria.ac.uk/study-at-northumbria/accommodation/

Where do the students come from?

State schools (non-grammar)	88.6%	First generation students	50.6%	
Grammar schools	5.1%	Low participation areas	18.4%	
Independent schools	6.3%	All ethnic minorities	11.1%	

Social inclusion ranking: 73

White working-class males	8.2%
Black achievement gap	-31%
Mature (over 21)	19.7%

Norwich University of the Arts

Norwich University of the Arts (NUA) is one of the biggest climbers in our research quality rating this year, rising 24 places from 86th to 62nd place. The steep improvement is driven by the university's results in the latest Research Excellence Framework (REF 2021), when 71% of its work in art and design was assessed as world-leading or internationally excellent, the top two categories. The REF 2021 judges praised two impact case studies on arts, health and wellbeing and public engagement in the Norfolk Broads.

Professor Simon Ofield-Kerr, who joined NUA as vice-chancellor in 2021 from the University of the Arts London, said the university would build on its REF 2021 success "as we embark on our new five-year university strategy". From 2022-27, NUA hopes to become the place where the debate about the future of creativity and the creative arts education is most passionately engaged.

The university's origins can be traced back to 1845, when the Norwich School of Design was established by the artists and followers of the Norwich school of painters, known for its landscape painting. Former tutors include Lucian Freud, Lesley Davenport and Michael Andrews.

University status was granted in 2012 and, with growth in its sights, NUA has developed a range of fine facilities. Duke Street Riverside opened in 2021, with 100 rooms for first-year students above a lecture theatre and teaching facilities beside the River Wensum.

The university's development programme has recently provided teaching facilities for film and moving image production, photography, and fashion communication and promotion. The Sir John Hurt Film Studio, named after the late actor and NUA chancellor, is in a grade II listed building that also houses the School of Architecture and won an award for the design of its renovation.

Next to come is Bank Plain, a 37,000 sq ft city centre site that will combine teaching, research, exhibition and public access spaces when it opens in early 2023. Student support services will also move to Bank Plain, as will the students' union, a café and social areas including a climbing wall.

The new focal point should help to boost rates of student satisfaction, which tumbled in the latest National Student Survey. Having done well to rank tenth for satisfaction with teaching quality in the pandemic chaos of 2021, our analysis of outcomes from 2022 shows a precipitous 35-place fall to 45th place. NUA has lost even more ground year-on-year in terms of its students' evaluation of the wider undergraduate experience, falling from 66th to =108.

Declining satisfaction has contributed to NUA dropping 14 places down our

Francis House
3-7 Redwell Street
Norwich NR2 4SN
01603 610 561
admissions@nua.ac.uk
www.nuasu.co.uk
www.nua.ac.uk
Open days: see website

NORWICH

The Times and The Sunday Times **Rankings**

Overall Ranking: 70 (last year: 56)

Teaching quality	76.6%	45
Student experience	67.9%	=108
Research quality	38.8%	62
Entry standards	130	54
Graduate prospects	65.6%	114
Good honours	72.2%	=106
Expected completion rate	84.5%	=74
Student/staff ratio	15.5	=49

main academic league table to 70th place. The university is committed to continuing with "flexible, digital learning" in 2022-23, combining digital teaching methods with practical skills sessions on campus.

Pre-pandemic teaching earned NUA a gold rating in the Teaching Excellence Framework (TEF). Course design and assessment practices encouraged experimentation, creative risk-taking and team working, the TEF panel found, providing "outstanding levels of stretch for students".

A degree in creative computing welcomed its first students in September 2022 and will be joined by one in creative technology from 2023. Short courses in creative coding and UX (user experience) design have also been introduced.

However, despite improving graduate prospects, the university remains in the bottom 10 in our analysis – partly because art and design graduates tend to have the lowest employment levels all over the UK. About two thirds of graduates are in high-skilled jobs or postgraduate study 15 months after leaving university.

NUA leads a regional outreach network in partnership with Cambridge, East Anglia, Anglia Ruskin and Suffolk universities and is in the top half overall for social inclusion (=51). The vast majority of its undergraduates come from non-selective state schools and the proportion drawn from deprived postcodes (16.9%) is among the top 30 nationally. Only

six universities have a higher proportion of disabled students (12.6%).

Applicants are offered a place on the strength of their portfolio and responses to questions in the admissions process, not solely on their predicted grades. The approach is successful, going by NUA's low projected dropout rate (8.9%) – 2.9% better than the expected level (11.8%) based on its students' backgrounds and the mix of courses. Up to half the entrants are expected to qualify for financial support in 2023.

In the absence of their own sports facilities, NUA students have access to the University of East Anglia's Sportspark, which includes an Olympic-sized swimming pool. The city of Norwich is popular with students and is one of the safest and greenest in the UK. All first-years can be housed in student accommodation.

Tuition fees

» Fees for UK students	£9,250
» Fees for International students 2023–24	£17,500
» For scholarship and bursary information see www.nua.ac.uk/study-at-nua/fees-funding/	
» Graduate salary	£20,000

Student numbers

Undergraduates	2,471	(0)
Postgraduates	82	(68)
Applications/places	3,290/1,005	
Applications per place	3.3:1	
Overall offer rate	77.9%	
International students – EU	3%	
Non-EU	3.2%	

Accommodation

University provided places: 900
Self-catered: £108–£165 per week
First-years guaranteed accommodation
www.nua.ac.uk/university-life/accommodation/

Where do the students come from?

State schools (non-grammar)	93.7%	First generation students	44.7%	White working-class males	8.3%
Grammar schools	2.8%	Low participation areas	16.9%	Black achievement gap	n/a
Independent schools	3.5%	All ethnic minorities	11.1%	Mature (over 21)	11.6%

Social inclusion ranking: =51

University of Nottingham

Prospective students attending Nottingham's open days receive what the university claims to be the world's first microprospectus. A QR code takes them to key resources online, saving an estimated 72 tonnes of paper and more than 18,000kg of CO_2. It reveals an internationally-minded university in the throes of a new phase of growth.

In the long run, that will include a new campus at the foot of Nottingham Castle in the city centre. The Castle Meadow site was bought in 2021 for the business school and Digital Nottingham, the university's civic, research and innovation hub.

There has been plenty of development at the main campus – most recently the modernisation of Nottingham's first female hall of residence, dating back to 1928, which was set to reopen in January 2023.

The 330-acre University Park is one of the most attractive campuses in the UK, winning 18 Green Flag awards for environmental quality.

For the past five years it has shared the environmental honours with the Jubilee Campus, a former industrial site with four lakes. The Power Electronics and Machine Centre opened there in summer 2022 with ambitions to become a world-leading hub for low-carbon aerospace innovation.

Students enrolling in 2023 will find new facilities at the expended School of Veterinary Medicine and Science at the Sutton Bonington campus, 12 miles south of the city, which now has two intakes per year. There is a new mock veterinary practice facility and refurbished teaching facilities for courses in food, nutrition and dietetics.

Applications and enrolments are running at record levels after four increases in a row. Only four British universities took more undergraduates in 2021 and there was another 3% increase in applications in a snapshot of the present admissions round at the end of March 2022.

Student satisfaction is yet to recover from the slump that afflicted most universities during the pandemic. Declining scores in the latest National Student Survey, published in summer 2022, have left Nottingham outside the top 100 for satisfaction with teaching quality (=107), and only just inside it for the broader student experience (95th). Its position in our overall table, where it shares 30th place with the University of Reading, is the lowest it has occupied for many years.

Results improved in the latest Research Excellence Framework (REF 2021) – but Nottingham has slipped two places outside the top 20 in our research quality index weighing up improvements across the sector since the previous national assessment in 2014. The university's submissions in pharmacy and

---

University Park
Nottingham NG7 2RD
0115 951 5559
www.nottingham.ac.uk/studywithus/enquiry.aspx
www.su.nottingham.ac.uk
www.nottingham.ac.uk
Open days: see website

The Times and The Sunday Times Rankings
Overall Ranking: =30 (last year: 28)

Teaching quality	71.9%	=107
Student experience	69.5%	95
Research quality	56.1%	22
Entry standards	148	=32
Graduate prospects	83.8%	=19
Good honours	85.3%	23
Expected completion rate	93.9%	=17
Student/staff ratio	15.8	=54

health sciences, and economics showed excellence and across all subjects, 90% of the work was rated world-leading or internationally excellent, the top two categories.

The university has always been among the favourite recruiting grounds of large employers. The latest High Fliers survey places Nottingham in the top two in 2021-22, and it is in our top 20 for the proportion of new graduates landing highly skilled jobs or going on to further study within 15 months.

Nottingham was rated gold in the Teaching Excellence Framework, with praise for high student engagement with advanced technology-enhanced learning.

Two new degrees in computer science with cyber physical systems began this year, and a BSc in health promotion and public health is planned for 2023. Numbers on the five degree apprenticeship programmes, which include architecture, data science and electro-mechanical engineering, are expected to rise from 300 to 400 by 2023.

Nottingham was the UK's main pioneer of overseas campuses, opening at scale in China and Malaysia. Undergraduates are encouraged to transfer between campuses and, with thousands of international students coming to Nottingham, the university markets itself as a global institution. It was our 2019 International University of the Year.

However, the university struggles in our social inclusion index, finishing in 106th place

this year. About 30% of UK undergraduates qualify for bursaries worth £1,000 a year because they have annual household incomes of less than £35,000 a year, and another £1,000 is available for those who meet a range of other criteria.

Nottingham is involved in a number of schemes designed to widen participation in higher education, but almost a third of its students still come from independent or selective state schools and the proportion of white working-class male students, the most underrepresented group in higher education and our newest measure, is among the lowest in the country.

First-year undergraduates are guaranteed one of the 11,200 residential places. Sports facilities are excellent at the £40million David Ross Sports Village and Nottingham was The Sunday Times 2019 Sports University of the Year.

The city is popular with students and the main campus offers a lively social life.

Tuition fees

» Fees for UK students	£9,250
» Fees for International students 2023–24	£11,600–£33,250
Medicine	£28,700–£46,500
Veterinary Medicine	£28,000–£46,500
» For scholarship and bursary information see	
www.nottingham.ac.uk/fees/tuition-fees-student-services.aspx	
» Graduate salary	£26,500

Student numbers

Undergraduates	27,506	(250)
Postgraduates	6,147	(1,882)
Applications/places		55,375/8,710
Applications per place		6.4:1
Overall offer rate		71.9%
International students – EU		2.8%
Non-EU		12.7%

Accommodation

University provided places: 11,208
Catered costs: £204–£265 per week
Self-catered: £112–£242 per week
First-years guaranteed accommodation
www.nottingham.ac.uk/accommodation

Where do the students come from?

State schools (non-grammar)	64.3%	First generation students	30.4%	White working-class males	3.1%
Grammar schools	15.9%	Low participation areas	8.3%	Black achievement gap	-18.2%
Independent schools	19.8%	All ethnic minorities	30.4%	Mature (over 21)	6%

Social inclusion ranking: 106

Nottingham Trent University

Nottingham Trent (NTU) is our Modern University of the Year, having recovered its popularity with its student body. The university notches up a top-20 ranking for satisfaction with the overall undergraduate experience in our analysis of the latest National Student Survey, published in summer 2022. For satisfaction with teaching quality, the university has overcome its pandemic blip, when it fell to joint 80th, to climb to 26th place. Students often find their experience impersonal in a large institution, yet NTU holds its own.

NTU appears to have got the balance right for its students between in-person and online learning. Most teaching is now delivered face-to-face, with assessment primarily online. More undergraduates started at NTU in 2021 than at any other university.

NTU has a gold rating in the Teaching Excellence Framework and is among the leading universities for the number of students on year-long work placements. A dedicated employment team can help students to find international opportunities to study or work and a specialist project officer helps with money management and budgeting. There is extra support for care leavers and estranged students, as well as mandatory consent awareness training for all new students.

Research has not been neglected as the university focuses on the student experience. NTU rises 26 places in our research quality index, based on improved results in the latest Research Excellence Framework (REF 2021). Eighty-three per cent of NTU's work was rated world-leading or internationally excellent, the top two categories. Law, engineering and allied health, dentistry, nursing and pharmacy were the top performers, each with at least 98% of their submissions rated in the top two categories.

The main City campus is close to the centre of Nottingham and is the academic base for about half of NTU's students. The Clifton campus, just outside the city, houses the arts and humanities, and science and technology, as well as the Nottingham Institute of Education, while the Brackenhurst campus is 14 miles from Nottingham, where environmental and agricultural courses are based. The Lyth Building, a new headquarters for the School of Animal, Rural and Environmental Sciences, won the Royal Institute of British Architects (RIBA) East Midlands Award in 2022.

NTU has been branching out across the East Midlands, with NTU in Mansfield offering foundation degrees and other qualifications in partnership with Vision West Nottinghamshire College. Subjects include

50 Shakespeare Street
Nottingham NG1 4FQ
0115 848 4200
ntu.ac.uk/askntu
www.trentstudents.org
www.ntu.ac.uk
Open days: see website

The Times and The Sunday Times **Rankings**
Overall Ranking: =42 (last year: 70)

Teaching quality	78.1%	26
Student experience	76.1%	19
Research quality	41.9%	54
Entry standards	121	=77
Graduate prospects	71%	=74
Good honours	72.1%	=109
Expected completion rate	88.9%	48
Student/staff ratio	15.3	=45

business, computing, education, and sport and exercise science. Construction and engineering courses took their first students from September 2022. The university also has plans to open a health campus in Worksop, run with Bassetlaw Hospital and the University of Derby. It is already offering a Higher National Certificate in future homes design and construction in the town.

In Nottingham, a new building for the School of Art and Design is scheduled to open in 2023. The university has already spent £23million on the new Medical Technologies Innovation Facility (MTIF), and the Dryden Enterprise Centre, which provided facilities and support to start-ups and more established companies, opened in 2021. At the Clifton campus, the Health and Allied Professions Centre opened in 2022, providing facilities for specialist courses such as adult and mental health nursing, paramedic science, and public health.

Six degrees that started in September 2022 include early childhood studies, criminal justice and climate change. Three more education degrees are due to follow in 2023, one focusing on special education needs, disability and inclusion. By then, the university expects to have 2,000 students on its 21 degree apprenticeship programmes, which include provision for hygiene specialists for the first time in 2022-23.

In our analysis based on the proportion of graduates in highly skilled jobs or on postgraduate courses 15 months later, the university has climbed 19 places to rank joint 74th.

NTU's system of contextual offers is beginning to have an impact on social inclusion on campus. Almost a third of all undergraduates benefit from a range of bursaries and scholarships. NTU co-leads the National Social Mobility Research Centre, although it remains in the bottom half of our social inclusion ranking for England and Wales (88th).

NTU has a strong sporting reputation, breaking into the BUCS (British Universities and Colleges Sport) top 10 for the first time this year. There are facilities on every campus, including a purpose-built equestrian centre at Brackenhurst and the multipurpose Lee Westwood Sports Centre at Clifton. Social life varies between campuses but the city's lively cultural and clubbing scene is in reach, wherever you are.

There is residential accommodation on every campus, and most of the 6,200 rooms owned or endorsed by NTU are reserved for new entrants.

Tuition fees

- » Fees for UK students £9,250
- » Fees for International students 2023–24 £15,600–£16,200
- » For scholarship and bursary information see www.ntu.ac.uk/study-and-courses/undergraduate/fees-and-funding
- » Graduate salary £23,000

Student numbers

Undergraduates	30,184	(1,592)
Postgraduates	4,008	(3,211)
Applications/places		47,685/11,150
Applications per place		4.3:1
Overall offer rate		90.1%
International students – EU		3.4%
Non-EU		5.7%

Accommodation

University provided places: 6,206
Self-catered: £111–£197 per week
First-years guaranteed accommodation
www.ntu.ac.uk/life-at-ntu/accommodation

Where do the students come from?

State schools (non-grammar)	87.2%	First generation students	41.5%	White working-class males	5.5%
Grammar schools	5.2%	Low participation areas	14.7%	Black achievement gap	-27.3%
Independent schools	7.6%	All ethnic minorities	28.8%	Mature (over 21)	10.5%

Social inclusion ranking: 88

The Open University

The Future is Open, as the latest advert for the Open University (OU) says. With no entry requirements and cheaper tuition fees (£6,456 a year), the original distance learning institution offers a port in the cost-of-living storm.

Founded in 1969 to promote educational opportunity for all, the Open University has brought in new financial aid to recruit students from all sections of society.

The Open Futures Scholarship for Black Students has been introduced for 2022-23, providing free tuition for UK residents with a household income lower than £25,000, plus a one-off grant of £500 towards study costs. There is also means-tested help available to cover the cost of Wi-Fi, travel, childcare and study materials.

The Open University offers a full range of undergraduate degree courses. All students are classified as part-timers, regardless of whether they study at full-time intensity or not, which allows them to complete their studies without any benefits being affected.

An honours degree in accounting and finance is being offered for the first time in 2022-23, as well as honours courses in public health and wellbeing, and geology. Sociology will join the curriculum from 2023.

The OU also offers eight degree apprenticeships and two higher apprenticeships in England and has more than 3,150 trainees on the books, studying for roles such as chartered manager; senior leader, digital and technology solutions; social worker; police constable; registered nurse; and advanced clinical practitioner. In Scotland, there are three graduate apprenticeships (covering BScs in cybersecurity, software development, and an MSc in cybersecurity) while in Wales the OU offers an applied software engineering degree apprenticeship.

Our rankings have never included the OU: it would be at a disadvantage in comparison with traditional universities which focus on teaching undergraduates on campus. Where comparisons are possible, however, the OU tends to perform well. In the latest Research Excellence Framework (REF 2021) more than three-quarters (76%) of the OU's research was rated world-leading or internationally excellent, the top two categories. The institution's research capacity had improved since the previous national assessment in 2014: 649 staff took part in 2021 compared with 396 in 2014.

Some face-to-face tutorials are returning at the university's headquarters in Milton Keynes, in Buckinghamshire. Teaching was largely unaffected by the pandemic. Thousands of part-time tutors are employed by the OU around the country to guide students through their studies. Its "supported open learning" system allows students to work

Walton Hall
Milton Keynes
MK7 6AA
0300 303 5303
general-enquiries@open.ac.uk
www.oustudents.com
www.open.ac.uk

The Times and The Sunday Times **Rankings**
n/a
No data available

where they choose: at home, in the workplace, or at a library or study centre. Tutorials, day schools, online forums and social networks provide contact with fellow students and students' work is monitored by continual assessment, examination or assignment.

More than 2million students in 157 countries have benefited from an OU education since its inception in 1969 and an enduring partnership with the BBC has allowed programming to reach an estimated 264million people over the past half-century. The age profile of OU students is steadily coming down and now stands at 27, with 70% of students continuing to work while they study.

The Personal Learning Advice (PLA) service was introduced in 2021, providing coaching and mentoring to students from underrepresented and disadvantaged backgrounds. The aim is to boost retention, completion, progression and satisfaction for students. In addition to its degree courses, the OU's half-price 30-credit access courses are designed to help those who have not studied for some time or who want to build their confidence or study skills. Access courses are free for applicants with an income below £25,000 to invite participation from disadvantaged groups.

Efforts to expand the university's reach continue. From its beginnings as a pilot scheme with a single Job Centre Plus office, the OU's Open Doors to Success programme of courses offers free training to jobseekers to increase their employability from more than 750 centres. Participants can earn digital badges to add to their CV.

Refugees arriving in Britain can study free of charge through the Open Futures Sanctuary Scholarship, also starting in 2022-23, if they have been displaced from their homeland for political, economic, ethnic environmental or human rights reasons.

In Scotland, a full-fee waiver is available for students with an individual income of up to £25,000. About 3,700 access students were expected to gain a free OU place in the 2021-22 academic year.

The university also has a Disabled Veterans' Scholarship Fund that provides full fee waivers for former members of the armed services. Under the Carers' Scholarship Fund, fee waivers are available for those who care for someone for an average of 15 hours a week, or have done so within the past two years until a bereavement.

Tuition fees

» Fees for England 2023–24	£6,456
Scotland, Northern Ireland, Wales	£2,616
Per two 60-credit modules. Full-time study represents two modules per year.	
Honours degree =360 credits	
» Fees for International students	£6,456
» For scholarship and bursary information see www.open.ac.uk/courses/fees-and-funding	
» Graduate salary	N/a

Students

Undergraduates	112 (102,765)
Postgraduates	251 (7,801)

Accommodation

Not applicable

Where do the students come from?

Not applicable

University of Oxford

Oxford is our leading university for the first time in 12 years after a shake-up at the top of our main academic rankings. It pips St Andrews to the No 1 spot and surpasses its ancient rival Cambridge after superb performances across all of our academic measures – and the lowest student-staff ratio of any institution (10.5:1) by a considerable margin.

Oxford's ratio of full-time students to academic staff (not including those purely engaged in research) is less than half of the highest figure – 27.4:1 at Bedfordshire. Even within the research-intensive Russell Group, the ratio reaches as high as 15.9:1 at Queen's University Belfast.

The university's league table ascent follows the global recognition of its groundbreaking work on the Covid-19 vaccine in partnership with AstraZeneca. Oxford was our University of the Year in 2021 as a result of its outstanding record during the crisis, and reached the shortlist in 2022.

Aside from the standard teaching through seminars, lectures, practical and fieldwork, it is the tutorial system that sets Oxford and Cambridge apart, and such individual attention from academic experts is taking place in person again.

However, Oxford's boycott of the National Student Survey means that student satisfaction with teaching quality or the wider undergraduate experience cannot be included in our analysis.

Exceptional facilities are a big selling point for undergraduates – and they keep getting better. The Biochemistry Building was completed in 2021 and the Institute of Developmental and Regenerative Medicine on the Old Road campus has opened since, housing about 240 scientists. A Centre for the Humanities is set to open in 2025 in the Radcliffe Observatory Quarter.

Oxford's strategic partnership with L&G (Legal & General) will provide up to £4bn of funding over 10 years to create world-class science and innovation districts at Begbroke and Osney Mead. Under the joint venture, work continues on the Life and Mind Building for psychological and life sciences, due to open in 2024.

Oxford has a gold rating in the Teaching Excellence Framework and claims fourth place in our research quality index following another stellar set of results in the latest Research Excellence Framework (REF 2021). Ninety-one per cent of the work submitted was assessed as world-leading, the top category. It is an improvement on the previous national assessment in 2014 (87%), yet Oxford falls one place in our research rankings against even bigger gains at peer universities.

University Offices
Wellington Square
Oxford OX1 2JD
01865 288 000
www.ox.ac.uk/ask
www.oxfordsu.org
www.ox.ac.uk/admissions/
undergraduate
Open days: see website

The Times and The Sunday Times Rankings
Overall Ranking: 1 (last year: 2)

Teaching quality	n/a	
Student experience	n/a	
Research quality	67%	4
Entry standards	198	5
Graduate prospects	91.6%	4
Good honours	94.5%	1
Expected completion rate	99%	=1
Student/staff ratio	10.5	1

How to get into Oxford remains a hot topic. In 2021, 68.2% of Oxford entrants arrived from state schools overall (including grammars) – slightly down on 68.6% in 2020 but up from 58.2% in 2017. However, our social inclusion figures count only admissions from non-selective state schools (52.2%). It is a huge leap from 45.6% in 2021 and an even greater improvement from 39.4% in our first social inclusion index, published in 2018. Even so, the university sits only one place from the bottom of our social inclusion index.

The proportion of first-generation students has risen from 14.8% to 16.3% year-on-year, however, and the number from ethnic minorities (23.7%) is in the upper half among English and Welsh universities. Oxford's efforts to reduce its black attainment gap put it in the top 20. The figure for students from low-participation areas has gone from 4.2% in 2021 to 6.4% in 2022, in 93rd place.

The Astrophoria Foundation Year is latest programme to improve opportunities for talented students. From October 2023, the fully funded subject-specific course will accept up to 50 UK state school students with high academic potential who have experienced severe personal disadvantage or disrupted education.

Oxford's financial support is among the most generous in UK higher education. About a quarter of all students receive some non-repayable bursary support, with those from families with household income of less than £27,500 per year receiving Crankstart bursaries of £5,000 a year.

The university places huge trust in its admissions process, with written tests for certain subjects and interviews for all shortlisted candidates. Picking one of the more than 30 undergraduate colleges is especially important for arts and social science students, whose tuition is based in-college. Science and technology subjects are mainly taught in central facilities.

Oxford has fallen two places year-on-year to be listed fourth in the 2023 QS World University Rankings, relinquishing the honour of being Britain's highest-ranked university to Cambridge, which is second.

One prize at the end of an Oxford degree is fine job prospects: the university is fourth in our analysis of the latest Graduate Outcomes survey.

Only eight weeks long, terms are intensive. Students pack plenty in, helped by high-class sports facilities and active JCRs (junior common rooms) that provide much of the entertainment.

Tuition fees
- » Fees for UK students £9,250
- » Fees for International students 2023–24 £28,950–£44,240
  Medicine £52,490
- » For scholarship and bursary information see
  www.ox.ac.uk/admissions/undergraduate/fees-and-funding
- » Graduate salary £30,000

Student numbers

Undergraduates	12,137 (3,537)
Postgraduates	8,458 (3,017)
Applications/places	24,338/3,298
Applications per place	7.4:1
Overall offer rate	19.1%
International students – EU	6%
Non-EU	10%

Accommodation
College websites provide accommodation details
First-years offered accommodation
www.ox.ac.uk/students/life/accommodation
See Chapter 13 for individual colleges

Where do the students come from?

				Social inclusion ranking: 115	
State schools (non-grammar)	52.2%	First generation students	16.3%	White working-class males	2%
Grammar schools	16.5%	Low participation areas	6.4%	Black achievement gap	-10.4%
Independent schools	31.3%	All ethnic minorities	23.7%	Mature (over 21)	2.5%

Oxford Brookes University

Oxford Brookes is running a rolling programme of "future-think" projects until 2035 to prepare its students to flourish in an uncertain environment. There is already an extensive programme of work placements and students will be among the first to benefit from the government's new Turing Scheme to provide opportunities to work and study abroad. The university won funding for up to 90 students – more than 30% of them from disadvantaged backgrounds – to go to Japan under the Turing Scheme in 2022-23.

Oxford Brookes has also promised "personalisation" of the learning experience, which has mainly returned to campus since the lifting of Covid restrictions. However, our analysis of the latest National Student Survey, published in summer 2022, shows that satisfaction with teaching quality has yet to recover: the university ranks outside the top 100 on this measure. It ranks =88 for satisfaction with the wider undergraduate experience.

Although the university remains among the leading post-1992 institutions in our overall rankings, its progress up the table has stalled.

A 19-place drop in our research quality index to =76 is one factor holding the university back. More than 400 researchers in 15 subject areas were entered for the latest Research Excellence Framework (REF 2021) – a 40% increase on the previous national assessment in 2014 – and the proportion of work judged to be world-leading or internationally excellent grew from 60% to 70%. However, in our analysis, Oxford Brookes was left behind by greater improvement across the sector.

Oxford Brookes has four campuses, although the engineering base at Wheatley, seven miles from Oxford, is to be redeveloped for housing. Courses are due to be transferred to the main campus in Headington, but the move has been delayed. Harcourt Hill, three miles from the city centre, houses education, English, communication, philosophy and sport students, while nursing is based in a business park in Swindon. The university also shares education, clinical practice and research in nursing, midwifery and allied health professions with two NHS trusts: Oxford University Hospitals NHS Foundation Trust and Oxford Health NHS Foundation Trust.

The degree system was streamlined during the pandemic, introducing more interdisciplinary courses favoured by employers, such as information technology for business. Partly as a result of the changes – and despite rising applications – in 2021 enrolments on undergraduate courses fell to their lowest level since 2012. Six new degrees are planned for 2023, three of them in hospitality and events management. The

---

Headington Campus
Oxford OX3 0BP
0345 350 3699
admissions@brookes.ac.uk
www.brookesunion.org.uk
www.brookes.ac.uk
Open days: see website

The Times and The Sunday Times Rankings
Overall Ranking: =57 (last year: 54)

Teaching quality	72.5%	102
Student experience	70%	=88
Research quality	32.8%	=76
Entry standards	117	=93
Graduate prospects	74.6%	=57
Good honours	79.1%	=55
Expected completion rate	90.8%	37
Student/staff ratio	14	23

others will be in economics, digital marketing, and liberal arts.

Expansion is also under way in the degree apprenticeship programme at Oxford Brookes. Two new nursing programmes and one for chartered planners have been added in 2022-23, and by 2035 the university hopes to increase the number of "employer-led" students by 25%.

Oxford Brookes is building its international profile. Since 2020, some of its courses have been delivered in Athens and Thessaloniki through a partnership with Metropolitan College Greece. The first 100 graduates emerged with a dual-award accountancy degree from Oxford Brookes and Chengdu University of Technology, in central China, that same year. A global partnership with the Association of Chartered Certified Accountants ensures that Oxford Brookes has far more students taking its qualifications in other countries (more than 200,000) than any other British university. The university's long-term strategy calls for a 30% increase in the numbers studying through partnerships at home and abroad.

On campus, Oxford Brookes has become the first British university to install an advanced geo-exchange heating system, predicted to reduce carbon emissions by 20%. A £220million investment programme, continuing until 2025, has already provided specialist computing equipment for the Faculty of Health and Life Sciences at Headington.

The university is working with more than 120 schools in an outreach programme to widen participation, yet Oxford Brookes still fares relatively poorly in our social inclusion index (104th). More than a third of its students come from independent or grammar schools – by far the biggest proportion among post-1992 universities – and only 35.8% are the first in their family to go to university (91st). It is in the top 40 for its course completion figures, however.

Applicants who make Oxford Brookes their firm or insurance choice are guaranteed one of the 4,376 rooms owned or endorsed by the university. It now has permission to add another 600 places to the 1,300 already available in its student village.

Oxford Brookes is especially strong in rowing, while the cricketers join those from the "other" university in town in a Centre of Cricketing Excellence. The students' union runs one of the biggest entertainment venues in Oxford. The city has plenty of student-oriented activities, although it can be expensive.

Tuition fees

»	Fees for UK students	£9,250
	Foundation courses	£7,570
»	Fees for International students 2023–24	£15,200–£17,200
	Biomedical Science & Medical Science	£16,100
»	For scholarship and bursary information see	
	www.brookes.ac.uk/studying-at-brookes/finance/	
»	Graduate salary	£24,900

Student numbers

Undergraduates	12,499	(681)
Postgraduates	2,157	(2,458)
Applications/places		20,015/4,050
Applications per place		4.9:1
Overall offer rate		79.5%
International students – EU		4.7%
Non-EU		8.7%

Accommodation

University provided places: 4,376
Self-catered: £120–£178 per week
First-years guaranteed accommodation
www.brookes.ac.uk/studying-at-brookes/accommodation/

Where do the students come from?

						Social inclusion ranking: 104	
State schools (non-grammar)	65.6%	First generation students	35.8%	White working-class males	3.7%
Grammar schools	4.6%	Low participation areas	6.9%	Black achievement gap	-23.6%
Independent schools	29.8%	All ethnic minorities	17.1%	Mature (over 21)	17.9%

Plymouth University

The biggest rise in admissions for more than a decade last year – over 12% – has greeted expansion of Plymouth's curriculum. Ten new courses began in 2021 and the range continues to grow with 24 beginning this year, from musical theatre to artificial intelligence. Five more are planned for 2023 including e-sports, and dental surgery with a foundation year.

Plymouth's priority is to recruit more UK undergraduates and degree apprentices before carrying out plans for substantial increases in both postgraduate and international students by 2030. The university expects to have 1,000 students taking higher or degree apprenticeships by 2023, with new programmes in engineering, nursing, computing, planning and psychology. Across all the qualifications offered at Plymouth, about 12,000 students undertake work-based learning or placements each year.

Plymouth's 16-place slide overall in our academic rankings can be attributed in part to the loss of nine places in our research quality index. More than three-quarters of Plymouth's submission to the national Research Excellence Framework (REF 2021) was rated world-leading or internationally excellent, the top two categories. However, the scale of improvement elsewhere left Plymouth adrift in our new measure calculating grades as a proportion of the maximum possible score.

Environmental research is the university's best-known feature. It won a Queen's Anniversary Award in 2019 for its research on microplastics and marine litter, and Times Higher Education magazine ranks it among the top five universities in the world for the impact of its marine research in relation to the United Nations Sustainable Development Goals. Plymouth has formed an international partnership with University College Cork in Ireland to work on the critical climate and sustainability challenges facing coastal areas.

More than 7,000 people, in addition to the university's 18,000 students, are taught in partner colleges, mainly in the southwest and the Channel Islands. Plymouth is one of the partners in the South West Institute for Technology, established by the government to train students in technical subjects. International partners include Peninsula College in Penang, Malaysia.

Undergraduates in 2022-23 will be taught face-to-face most of the time, with support available for a small remaining proportion of online learning.

Before the pandemic, Plymouth's scores for student satisfaction with teaching quality lay just outside the top 20 – but the university has fallen 25 places to =66 in the bottom half of our table in our analysis of the latest National Student Survey.

Drake Circus
Plymouth PL4 8AA
01752 585 858
admissions@plymouth.ac.uk
www.upsu.com
www.plymouth.ac.uk
Open days: see website

The Times and The Sunday Times Rankings
Overall Ranking: 74 (last year: =58)

Teaching quality	75.3%	=66
Student experience	72%	=62
Research quality	38.6%	65
Entry standards	127	=60
Graduate prospects	77.7%	=43
Good honours	76.5%	=75
Expected completion rate	85.3%	66
Student/staff ratio	17.3	=83

Plymouth has a growing reputation in medicine and other health subjects. It is still the only post-1992 university with a medical and dental school. With a school of nursing in Exeter as well as courses in Plymouth and Truro, it is the largest provider of nursing, midwifery and health professional education and training in the southwest of England.

The new Brain Research and Imaging Centre (BRIC) opened last year on Plymouth Science Park and a centre for nursing and health education is under construction at the 11-storey InterCity Place, at the railway station, which is being converted and refurbished as a teaching and clinical skills space.

A new engineering and design building is also on the way on the western edge of the city-centre campus, providing a new home for the School of Engineering, Computing and Mathematics, and additional space for the School of Art, Design and Architecture. It will include specialist equipment aligned to staff research and expertise, easing collaboration with regional industrial partners.

Plymouth has one of the country's leading business incubation facilities, focusing on small and medium-size enterprises in the southwest. The Cube business service works with more than 1,000 students a year, giving them the opportunity to discuss business ideas, attend workshops, work with peers, access specialist business advice and build up the skills they need to work in a small business or start up their own.

Plymouth is 22nd for its recruitment of white working-class males, the most underrepresented group in higher education, and in the top 40 for the proportion drawn from deprived areas. It has risen 11 places to 49th in our social inclusion index, well within the upper half of universities in England and Wales, though far behind its neighbour Plymouth Marjon. The university won a gold award this year from Stonewall for its work promoting LBTQ+ equality and inclusion.

There are 1,754 residential places in Plymouth, with 235 in Truro. Applicants holding Plymouth as their firm choice are guaranteed a place in one of the managed halls or in an accredited private hall if they apply by early June. On campus there is a sports hall, fitness centre, dance studio and squash courts, while upgraded facilities for water sports are a 10-minute ferry ride away. Plymouth city centre has plenty of student-orientated nightlife.

Tuition fees

» Fees for UK students	£9,250
» Fees for International students 2023–24	£14,600
Medicine & Dentistry	£22,100–£41,100
» For scholarship and bursary information see www.plymouth.ac.uk/fees	
» Graduate salary	£24,000

Student numbers

Undergraduates	14,152 (1,047)
Postgraduates	1,876 (1,832)
Applications/places	21,325/4,625
Applications per place	4.6:1
Overall offer rate	71.9%
International students – EU	3%
Non-EU	7.1%

Accommodation

University provided places: 1,989
Self-catered: £104-£192 per week
First-years guaranteed accommodation
www.plymouth.ac.uk/student-life/services/accommodation

Where do the students come from?

State schools (non-grammar)	86.4%	First generation students	45.1%	White working-class males	7.5%
Grammar schools	7.4%	Low participation areas	15.2%	Black achievement gap	-17.3%
Independent schools	6.2%	All ethnic minorities	15%	Mature (over 21)	32.5%

Social inclusion ranking: 49

Plymouth Marjon University

Having started life as a teacher training college, Plymouth Marjon long ago diversified into arts and business courses. Its latest strategy is to go for growth as the number of 18-year-olds rises, focusing strongly on health and social care courses. Three of the five new degrees this year and three of the six planned for 2023 are in health and social care, including psychotherapy, counselling and physiotherapy.

The university has climbed 21 places in our rankings overall to reach =80. Extensive new teaching rooms and clinical environments will open to accommodate growing numbers of health students. In addition to the new degrees, Marjon is planning short courses and professional development programmes, including a bridging programme into degree-level study for talented individuals from the health and care workforce who do not meet the traditional entry criteria.

The mix is proving popular with Marjon's undergraduates and applicants alike. The university was top in England in 2021's National Student Survey (NSS) for satisfaction with the "learning community" and in the top 10 in both our measures derived from the NSS. It has not quite held on to those rankings, but is still =7 for satisfaction with teaching quality and 11th for satisfaction with the wider undergraduate experience.

Marjon benefited in our rankings from its decision to enter the Research Excellence Framework (REF 2021), having chosen not to be part of the national assessment in 2014, although it finished 119th, towards the bottom of our table. For course completion, Marjon ranks =101, with a dropout rate higher than expected in light of the mix of courses and the background of its students.

Applications to study on the attractive campus on the north side of Plymouth grew by more than 10% during the pandemic and have maintained that level in the latest admissions round. Overall recruitment is down because the university has closed some of its franchise programmes in colleges elsewhere in the southwest of England. A number remain open in Cornwall and Devon in subjects ranging from business management to professional golf.

Teaching is back on campus but Marjon's post-pandemic version of blended learning has retained some online activity. Spared the need to travel, commuting students – of which Marjon has many, some travelling long distances – have increased their attendance rates at one-to-one meetings. The new system ensures that interactive and practical learning sessions take place on campus, with remote learning for information and background theory. Almost all courses include some form of work placement.

Derriford Road
Plymouth PL6 8BH
01752 636 890
www.marjon.ac.uk/msu/
admissions@marjon.ac.uk
Open days: see website

The Times and The Sunday Times **Rankings**

Overall Ranking: =80 (last year: =101)

Teaching quality	81.6%	=7
Student experience	77.3%	11
Research quality	17.4%	119
Entry standards	119	=86
Graduate prospects	68.8%	=94
Good honours	75.8%	82
Expected completion rate	80%	=101
Student/staff ratio	19.2	=108

Originally the College of St Mark and St John, which was established in London in 1840 and moved to Plymouth in 1973, Marjon retains Church of England control but welcomes students of all faiths and none. The university takes second place in our social inclusion index in England and Wales, up from third place in 2021. It has the joint highest proportion of white working-class males in the UK and is in the top four for the recruitment of disabled students. More than half of the undergraduates are the first in their family to go to university. Marjon has long-term progression agreements with 12 local schools and colleges, and makes lower offers to promising applicants from disadvantaged backgrounds.

Investment is planned for the already impressive sports facilities, all of which are available to the public. The tennis courts are to be redeveloped and an artificial pitch rebuilt by 2024. Other facilities include a climbing wall, 25m indoor swimming pool and gym. There is also a rehabilitation clinic and sports science laboratory with a climate chamber and an anti-gravity treadmill, for use by the thriving sports science courses.

The university is also spending £3.5million to replace its gas boilers with ground-source heat pumps, as part of an effort to cut carbon dioxide emissions by 80% by 2023.

A new health and wellbeing programme launched in September 2022 within the Sport and Health Centre, encouraging student physical activity and sport for all.

Marjon was one of the first 41 universities to join the Student Minds Mental Health Charter framework last year, and is actively working towards gaining Mental Health Charter status.

Future building plans include a £12million hall of residence and the demolition of some existing accommodation blocks. Marjon has 459 residential spaces in seven halls of residence and 38 village houses. In 2022, for the first time, new entrants on the main campus were guaranteed either a room on campus or in off-site accommodation approved by the university. The lively city centre is a short bus ride away and the region's beautiful countryside and coastline is easily accessible.

Tuition fees

» Fees for UK students	£9,250
Foundation courses	£6,000
» Fees for International students 2023–24	£13,000
» For scholarship and bursary information see	
www.marjon.ac.uk/courses/fees-and-funding/	
» Graduate salary	£21,000

Student numbers

Undergraduates	2,221	(78)
Postgraduates	389	(367)
Applications/places		3,165/855
Applications per place		3.7:1
Overall offer rate		86.8%
International students – EU		0.8%
Non-EU		0.6%

Accommodation

University provided places: 459
Self-catered: £95–£145 per week
First-years guaranteed accommodation
www.marjon.ac.uk/student-life/accommodation/

Where do the students come from?

State schools (non-grammar)	95.4%	First generation students	56.4%	White working-class males	11.9%
Grammar schools	3.1%	Low participation areas	16.1%	Black achievement gap	n/a
Independent schools	1.5%	All ethnic minorities	6.8%	Mature (over 21)	34.3%

Social inclusion ranking: 2

University of Portsmouth

The return to campus helped Portsmouth to jump more than 50 places on our two measures of student satisfaction this year, contributing to a 26-place rise in the overall table. The university is now in the top 35 in the sections of the National Student Survey focused on teaching quality. In 2023-24, Portsmouth is continuing with its "blended and connected approach", with most teaching delivered in person, but up to 20% of learning taking place online.

The university earned a gold award in the Teaching Excellence Framework, with assessors praising high levels of student engagement and commitment to learning. Yet applications have dropped by a third since 2014, after seven successive declines. The numbers taking up places were down by a fifth in 2021, despite Portsmouth dropping out of the top 100 for average entry grades.

A £400million campus development programme may help to boost applications. The striking new £57million Ravelin Sports Centre at the heart of the campus was ready for the start of the 2022-23 academic year, and the university is spending another £135million on a 12-storey academic building in the city centre with large, flexible spaces for teaching, research and collaboration, which is due to open in 2024. A new £7million Centre for Creative and Immersive Extended Reality (CCIXR) opened in 2022, bringing together an unprecedented variety of XR technologies, and enhancing the work of the Future Technology Centre, which opened in 2019.

Much of the university's recent investment has been on simulated facilities to give students hands-on experience to prepare them for careers. Students on healthcare courses, for example, learn to dispense medicines in a pharmacy and to treat NHS patients at a dental clinic. The ability to develop creative solutions of benefit to society and the economy is one of the 10 "hallmarks of a Portsmouth graduate" that will apply to the new intake.

A good performance in the 2021 Research Excellence Framework has moved Portsmouth into the top half of our research quality index. More than three-quarters of its work was considered world-leading or internationally excellent, the top two categories. Portsmouth entered more than 600 academics, twice the number involved in the previous national assessment in 2014.

The university has been branching out in the south of England. A University Centre in Basingstoke will offer professionally focused higher-education courses in partnership with the University of Reading, and a partnership agreement was signed this year with Ryde town council on the Isle of Wight. There have also been talks with Waltham Forest council

University House
Winston Churchill Avenue
Portsmouth PO1 2UP
023 9284 5566
admissions@port.ac.uk
www.upsu.net
www.port.ac.uk
Open days: see website

The Times and The Sunday Times Rankings
Overall Ranking: 62 (last year: 88)

Teaching quality	77.2%	=33
Student experience	73.2%	=46
Research quality	39.1%	61
Entry standards	112	=108
Graduate prospects	73.7%	=62
Good honours	76.3%	78
Expected completion rate	84.9%	=71
Student/staff ratio	16.8	75

on the establishment of a London campus in the borough in the northeast of the capital.

Three new degrees have been launched, in primary education, global communication, and criminology and environmental justice. Portsmouth's 19 degree apprenticeship programmes have seen considerable growth recently, but were expected to stabilise at 1,000 apprentices in 2022-23.

More than a third of the undergraduates qualify for financial support, which includes a £750-a-year bursary for all students with a household income of less than £25,000. There are also scholarships to encourage progression to postgraduate courses where this will help a student's career plans. Portsmouth Football Club contributes one scholarship of £3,000 a year for students from low-income homes in the city and the Isle of Wight.

Nine out of 10 undergraduates are from non-selective state schools and Portsmouth is in the top 20 for the proportion who are white working-class males, the most underrepresented group in higher education. The university set up a multi-academy trust in 2022, bringing together two primary schools in the city and one in nearby Gosport.

The university has pioneered new approaches to student wellbeing. Academic staff, including personal tutors, are trained in mental health awareness and how best to support their students. Portsmouth was the first university to use WhatsUp?, a mental health app that promotes better communication between students and pastoral services. A student leadership programme develops resilience and community-building skills.

Most of Portsmouth's residential accommodation is close to the central Guildhall campus, although many students live in neighbouring Southsea. The university has 3,500 residential places – enough to guarantee accommodation to all new students who apply by the deadline and make Portsmouth their firm choice.

A £6.5million student centre includes alcohol-free areas. Facilities at the new sports centre include an eight-lane 25m swimming pool, an eight-court sports hall, a 175-station fitness suite, squash courts and a ski simulator, while outdoor provision is at the Langstone Sports Village, three miles from the city centre and reached via the university bus service. The university's seaside location provides an excellent base for water sports and other leisure activities, while the city's nightlife is lively.

Tuition fees

- » Fees for UK students   £9,250
- » Fees for International students 2023–24   £16,200–£18,300
- » For scholarship and bursary information see www.port.ac.uk/study/undergraduate/undergraduate-fees-and-student-finance
- » Graduate salary   £24,000

Student numbers

Undergraduates	20,109 (2,059)
Postgraduates	3,955 (2,156)
Applications/places	22,110/4,410
Applications per place	5.1
Overall offer rate	84.3%
International students – EU	5.1%
Non-EU	11%

Accommodation

University provided places: 3,512
Catered costs: £135–£175 per week
Self-catered: £100–£165 per week
First-years guaranteed accommodation
www.port.ac.uk/student-life/accommodation

Where do the students come from?

State schools (non-grammar)	91.4%	First generation students	45.6%
Grammar schools	5.1%	Low participation areas	17%
Independent schools	3.4%	All ethnic minorities	31.7%

Social inclusion ranking: =40

White working-class males	7.6%
Black achievement gap	-19.4%
Mature (over 21)	15.6%

Queen Margaret University Edinburgh

Having moved into a new, award-winning campus only 15 years ago, Queen Margaret University (QMU) has traded partly on its surroundings. Now QMU is planning a special addition to its facilities in the shape of an outdoor learning hub that will support "sustainable access" to the natural world for staff, students, the local community and teachers.

Other universities have inherited separate sites that specialise in outdoor pursuits, but QMU will be the only one with specially designed all-weather outdoor space on its main campus. The hub will include a digital element to connect learners from all over the country with QMU academics and other groups. The university's strategic plan promises to address sustainability in all courses, so graduates leave with a "rounded understanding of the sustainability challenges facing the world and the tools to contribute to solutions".

QMU has been growing in popularity among prospective students, although its small size, at fewer than 5,000 full-time students in Edinburgh, encourages fluctuations in recruitment statistics. It attracted its largest ever volume of applications in 2021, but ended up with a smaller intake than the record numbers it took the previous year. Entry standards have been rising, taking the university into our top 20 on this measure in our latest guide and helping it to maintain a mid-table position overall.

The university is planning five years of growth and already has more than 3,000 students taking its qualifications in partner institutions outside Scotland. One obstacle to its ambitions will be the loss of free tuition for European Union students, who previously accounted for a fifth of admissions. Business management will be one area of expansion, with two new degrees launched this year and two more planned for 2023, one specialising in digital marketing and the other in human resources.

QMU hosts the Scottish Centre for Food Development and Innovation, and a Food and Drink Innovation Hub is scheduled to open in 2025. The restaurateur and Great British Bake Off host Dame Prue Leith is the university's chancellor. Three-quarters of the undergraduates are female, as befits an institution that started out in 1875 as a cookery school for women and was named after St Margaret, the 11th-century wife of King Malcolm III of Scotland. A new degree in food science and innovation is planned for next year.

Queen Margaret has the broadest range of allied health courses in Scotland and is one of only three universities north of the border to offer paramedic science. Health and rehabilitation is regarded as one of the three "flagship areas", together with sustainable

University Way
Musselburgh
Edinburgh EH21 6UU
0131 474 0000
admissions@qmu.ac.uk
www.qmusu.org.uk
www.qmu.ac.uk
Open days: see website

The Times and The Sunday Times Rankings

Overall Ranking: =67 (last year: 66)

Teaching quality	76.8%	=37
Student experience	73.1%	48
Research quality	27.3%	97
Entry standards	162	=20
Graduate prospects	68.3%	97
Good honours	79.9%	51
Expected completion rate	83.7%	=79
Student/staff ratio	21.9	=121

business and creativity and culture. Scotland's first BSc in public health took its first students from September 2022.

The university does well in our social exclusion index (third in Scotland) and has committed to recruiting greater numbers from disadvantaged groups. About half of QMU's undergraduates qualify for university bursaries of up to £2,000 a year and there are fee reductions of £3,000 for some international students. QMU has trained nearly a quarter of its workforce in mental health first aid.

Most teaching has returned to campus, although larger lectures and 70% of assessment took place online in 2021-22. QMU's dramatic rise up the rankings for student satisfaction, which took the university to the verge of the top 20 in our last analysis of the National Student Survey, has gone into reverse in our new guide. It remains in the top 40 for satisfaction with teaching quality (=37), and the top 50 for the wider undergraduate experience (48th).

QMU has also fallen in our research ranking, falling 18 places to 97th, although some world-leading or internationally excellent work was identified in each of the seven research areas included in its submission. Communications, cultural and media studies, speech and language science, and global health and development produced the best results for the impact of their research.

A successful employer mentoring scheme matches third and fourth-year students with professionals who have relevant experience. QMU is aiming to be Scotland's top modern university for graduate employment. In our national graduate prospects measure, however, it has fallen nine places to 97th, based on the proportion of graduates in highly skilled work or further study 15 months after leaving. The university has appointed its first Entrepreneur in Residence, with a particular brief to advance female entrepreneurship.

QMU has 800 residential places and good sports facilities on its campus in the seaside town of Musselburgh, 10 minutes by train from the centre of Edinburgh. Its accommodation won awards for the top booking experience and best student community at the most recent National Student Housing Awards. Priority for a place goes to students from outside the Edinburgh area, as well as those who have disabilities or have been in care.

Tuition fees

» Fees for Scottish students	£0–£1,820
» RUK fees	£9,250
» Fees for International students 2023–24	£7,000–£15,500
» For scholarship and bursary information see www.qmu.ac.uk/current-students/current-students-general-information/fees-and-charges/	
» Graduate salary	£24,000

Student numbers

Undergraduates	3,363	(501)
Postgraduates	834	(1,217)
Applications/places		7,255/945
Applications per place		7.7:1
Overall offer rate		70.5%
International students – EU		17.7%
Non-EU		1.8% %

Accommodation

University provided places: 800
Self-catered: £121–£146 per week
www.qmu.ac.uk/campus-life/accommodation/

Where do the students come from?

State schools (non-grammar)	95.3%	First generation students	41.7%	White working class males	n/a
Grammar schools	1.7%	Low participation areas	13.1%	Black achievement gap	n/a
Independent schools	3%	All ethnic minorities	7%	Mature (over 21)	43.4%

Social inclusion ranking (Scotland): 3

Queen Mary, University of London

Rising three places to 16th in our research quality index, Queen Mary University of London (QMUL) is proud of its excellent results in the latest Research Excellence Framework (REF 2021), when 92% of its submission reached the top two categories: world-leading and internationally excellent.

QMUL's research results have helped the institution to climb four places in our main academic league table, too (36th). Drama produced some of the best results, followed by film, politics and international studies, engineering, economics and history. Another leading research area is computer science and informatics, which will be boosted by the new Digital Environment Research Institute (DERI), launched in March 2022. The university's centre for digital, data science and artificial intelligence is based in Whitechapel, close to the main Mile End campus in east London.

Queen Mary joined the elite Russell Group of research-intensive universities in 2012 and is its most socially inclusive member, according to our analysis. Its strong record for recruiting students from underrepresented groups made QMUL runner-up for our University of the Year award in 2020.

More than three quarters of QMUL students (77%) are from black and minority ethnic backgrounds: only four UK universities have a higher proportion. The university's black achievement gap is among the five narrowest (best) in the country. With 46.1% of students who are the first in their family to go to university, QMUL is well within the upper half of universities on this measure.

Graduate prospects are just outside the top 50 (52nd) in our analysis of the Graduate Outcomes survey. Most QMUL undergraduates are taught and housed on the self-contained campus in Mile End. Its large medical school, Barts and the London School of Medicine and Dentistry, is based in Whitechapel. Facilities have benefited from £100million of investment in recent years.

An £18million project at the School of Mathematical Sciences has provided seminar and workshop teaching rooms and a new lecture theatre. The university has spent £30million remodelling undergraduate teaching space at the School of Engineering and Materials Science, developed a graduate centre and new dental school, and added the Neuron Pod, an extension of the award-winning Centre of the Cell science education centre. The Art Deco People's Palace, built to bring culture, entertainment and education to Victorian-era East Enders, has been restored to host events.

The university was rated silver in the Teaching Excellence Framework (TEF), impressing assessors with the quality of its coaching and mentoring schemes which help

327 Mile End Road
London E1 4NS
020 7882 5511
admissions@qmul.ac.uk
www.qmsu.org
www.qmul.ac.uk
Open days: see website

The Times and The Sunday Times **Rankings**
Overall Ranking: 36 (last year: 40)

Teaching quality	70.3%	117
Student experience	68.4%	107
Research quality	58.7%	16
Entry standards	146	=35
Graduate prospects	75.9%	52
Good honours	88.3%	=13
Expected completion rate	93%	25
Student/staff ratio	14.6	=31

students to find good jobs. The QMUL Model accounts for 10% of a student's degree, covering work experience, volunteering in the community, overseas travel, project work with local businesses and other organisations, learning a language, or taking modules from other subjects.

Post-pandemic feedback has been used to refine QMUL's learning approach – Active Curriculum for Excellence (ACE) – in light of which elements of remote learning worked best for students. All students on London-based programmes have had timetabled in-person activities since September 2022.

ACE may help to turn around the disappointing rates of satisfaction expressed by QMUL students in the latest National Student Survey, published in summer 2022. The university has lost ground in student satisfaction with teaching quality (falling from =102 to 117th) and the wider experience (=70 in 2021 and 107th in 2022).

Student numbers are established at QMUL, following another record year for applications and enrolments in 2021. Degrees in digital and technology solutions (data analyst), and accountancy (Flying Start) began in September 2022, while the option of a year in industry has been added to a range of degrees. A programme in business management (social change) will be available in 2023-24.

QMUL is adding four degree apprenticeship programmes – in systems engineering, financial services, investment operations, and physician associate – to the five that already have 583 students enrolled. Degree apprentice numbers are expected to increase by 150-200 in 2023.

About a quarter of admissions in 2021 received a contextual offer and about half of undergraduates tend to receive financial help from the university. The undergraduate scholarship programme helps local students from households with incomes up to £42,875 and there is support for students from forced migrant backgrounds.

QMUL students can use the Queen Elizabeth Olympic Park sports facilities in Stratford, including the Copper Box indoor arena and the Aquatic Centre's swimming pool. There are sports grounds at Chislehurst, southeast London and the Mile End campus has a refurbished students' union.

Drapers Bar and Kitchen offers an on-campus social hub while fashionable east London enclaves are on the doorstep. Accommodation is guaranteed to first-years who apply by June 30.

Tuition fees

» Fees for UK students	£9,250
» Fees for International students 2023–24	£21,200–£26,250
Medicine & Dentistry	£44,250
» For scholarship and bursary information see www.qmul.ac.uk/undergraduate/feesandfunding/	
» Graduate salary	£28,000

Student numbers

Undergraduates	16,247	(0)
Postgraduates	5,694	(1,930)
Applications/places	37,695/6,385	
Applications per place	5.9:1	
Overall offer rate	64.5%	
International students – EU	8.4%	
Non-EU	14.7%	

Accommodation

University provided places: 3,121
Self-catered: £132–£183 per week
First-years guaranteed accommodation
www.qmul.ac.uk/study/accommodation

Where do the students come from?

State schools (non-grammar)	82.9%	First generation students	46.1%		
Grammar schools	9.4%	Low participation areas	3%		
Independent schools	7.7%	All ethnic minorities	77%		

Social inclusion ranking: =58

White working-class males	2.5%
Black achievement gap	-5.5%
Mature (over 21)	9%

Queen's University Belfast

Queen's University Belfast (QUB) attracted 10% more applications in 2021 compared with the year before and they edged up almost 4% in a snapshot of the current admissions cycle in March 2022. But the university has warned that cuts in government funding may mean hundreds fewer places for students from Northern Ireland and the Republic of Ireland over the next three years.

At the upper end of the cuts Queen's was asked to model, 1,575 of the 11,600 places for Irish students would have to go – a reduction of 15%.

The threat of budget cuts comes as QUB has been stepping up its efforts to recruit disadvantaged students from the province and redoubling its research links with universities in the Republic of Ireland. Queen's and University College Dublin have signed a memorandum of understanding to enhance co-operation in research and innovation in areas of mutual strength, and Queen's is involved in 43 of the 62 projects to be funded by the Irish government's £33million Shared Island North-South Research Programme, announced in 2022.

Queen's had already been increasing its recruitment of international students and plans to double their numbers. The appointment of Hillary Rodham Clinton as chancellor has raised the university's global profile.

The university has been rising steadily up our league table in recent years, but falls in student satisfaction and research quality scores have halted its progress. QUB remains in our top 30 overall, however, despite sliding four places.

In our analysis of the latest Research Excellence Framework (REF 2021), QUB has tumbled 21 places to 35th place, having failed to keep pace with improvements among its immediate rivals.

The results of the latest National Student Survey show that students have somewhat lost faith in teaching quality, leading to a fall of 20 places to =94. In terms of the wider undergraduate experience, QUB has slipped even further: 39 places, to =74.

Student facilities were set to improve dramatically after the opening of a new students' union and guidance centre in 2022. It is the latest in a string of developments over the past 10 years worth £350million, including new buildings for law, biological sciences and computer sciences.

Most undergraduates come from Northern Ireland – two-thirds from grammar schools, which educate a much larger proportion of the population there than elsewhere in the UK. Because of that feature of the Northern Irish school system, the university does not appear in our social inclusion ranking, where it would be disadvantaged by the focus only on non-

University Road
Belfast BT7 1NN
028 9097 3838
admissions@qub.ac.uk
www.qubsu.org
www.qub.ac.uk
Open days: see website

The Times and The Sunday Times Rankings

Overall Ranking: 28 (last year: 24)

Teaching quality	73%	=94
Student experience	71.3%	=74
Research quality	52%	35
Entry standards	148	=32
Graduate prospects	84.5%	15
Good honours	85.5%	22
Expected completion rate	92.3%	=30
Student/staff ratio	15.9	=57

selective state school recruitment.

QUB has stepped up its efforts to broaden its intake, and about 30% of undergraduates received some financial support in 2021-22. The Pathways Opportunity Programme guarantees Northern Irish students living in disadvantaged areas a conditional offer that may be two grades lower than the norm for their chosen course.

Civic responsibility and economic prosperity are among the main pillars of the university's strategy for the rest of the decade. Queen's plays a leading role in the Belfast City Region Deal, a 15-year programme to boost growth. It has been awarded £170.8million towards an Advanced Manufacturing Innovation Strand, £52.4million towards a Global Innovation Institute and £39.7million towards an Institute for Research Excellence in Advanced Clinical Healthcare.

A member of the Russell Group, the university won a seventh Queen's Anniversary prize for higher education in 2020 for its pioneering work to facilitate collaboration between schools of different faiths. For more than a century the university's own charter has guaranteed non-denominational teaching as well as student representation and equal rights for women.

The campus, on the south side of the city, has a cinema, an art gallery and theatre, all of which are open to the wider community as well as students. Belfast city centre has plenty of nightlife but the social scene is mainly concentrated on the students' union and the surrounding area.

Most of the residential places are at the Elms student village, close to the university, but a recent development of 1,200 rooms with its own services, including pastoral care, security and social activities, has added the option of living in the city centre. First-years, including those taking foundation degrees, are guaranteed a place, as are those with disabilities, care leavers and students who are estranged from their family.

The university's sports facilities, which include a cottage for climbers in the Mourne Mountains, also boast an international-standard hockey pitch, an arena pitch that can host football, rugby or Gaelic sport, and a recreational trail. The Physical Education Centre has two swimming pools and there is a boathouse on the River Lagan.

Tuition fees

» Fees for Northern Ireland students £4,530
  Students from England, Scotland and Wales £9,250
» Fees for International students 2023–24 £18,800–£34,450
  Medicine £34,450; Dentistry £35,800
» For scholarship and bursary information see
  www.qub.ac.uk/Study/Undergraduate/Fees-and-scholarships/
» Graduate salary £24,000

Student numbers

Undergraduates	16,530	(996)
Postgraduates	5,037	(2,801)
Applications/places	28,355/5,065	
Applications per place	5.6:1	
Overall offer rate	67.9%	
International students – EU	3.2%	
Non-EU	9.6%	

Accommodation

University provided places: 4,428
Catered costs: £90–£189 per week
Self-catered: £85–£175 per week
First-years guaranteed accommodation
www.qub.ac.uk/accommodation

Where do the students come from?

State schools (non-grammar)	34.2%	First generation students	35.3%	White working class males	n/a
Grammar schools	64.1%	Low participation areas	8.7%	Black achievement gap	n/a
Independent schools	1.7%	Ethnic minorities	4.3%	Mature (over-21)	14.5%

Social inclusion ranking: n/a

Ravensbourne University, London

Ravensbourne remains in the bottom three of our league table, despite moving up one place in our latest Good University Guide. But that is not putting off prospective students going by the 30% increase in applications to Ravensbourne by the end of March 2022, compared with the same point in the admissions cycle a year earlier. An expanded portfolio of courses, particularly in the areas of business and computing, accounts for much of the growth, but increased recruitment and outreach activity has contributed to rising demand across the board.

Digital content creation, digital marketing, business management and computer science were among the degrees introduced for 2022-23. The university has also launched three-week online courses in brand strategy, strategic design, influencer marketing and creative communication with the FutureLearn platform, as an introduction to the respective fields.

A striking building next to the O2 Arena on the Greenwich Peninsula is one obvious attraction to applicants. But, like some other specialist arts universities, Ravensbourne is held back by poor student satisfaction. Although its ratings improved in the latest National Student Survey, Ravensbourne remained in the bottom three for satisfaction with the wider undergraduate experience (129th)

and only 11 places higher for how students evaluate the teaching quality (=118).

However, the university has a silver award in the Teaching Excellence Framework, praised by assessors for close collaboration with industry. Ravensbourne hosts more than 100 creative technology businesses that utilise its technology and media resources, while also collaborating with students.

The Institute for Creativity and Technology, which opened last year, markets itself as an "ecosystem of professional partnerships, industry networks, business incubation and an internationally recognised transdisciplinary team". Its aluminium-clad building houses the university's postgraduate provision and the CreativeLab in-house creative agency, as well as incubation and research activities.

Ravensbourne also fares well in our social inclusion index, with relatively high proportions of white working-class males (6.6%, 34th) and students from ethnic minorities (49.6%, 30th). All new students receive a £100 voucher towards course materials, rising to £500 for those from low-income households, who receive cash awards of the same value in the second and third years.

The official entry requirement at A-level is a modest two Cs, but candidates on most courses are judged primarily on their portfolio or showreel and on performance at interview. Most successful applicants comfortably exceed the minimum requirement – Ravensbourne is not in

6 Penrose Way
Greenwich Peninsula
London SE10 0EW
020 3040 3500
hello@rave.ac.uk
www.ravesu.co.uk
www.ravensbourne.ac.uk
Open days: see website

The Times and The Sunday Times Rankings
Overall Ranking: 130 (last year: 131)

Teaching quality	70%	=118
Student experience	58.6%	129
Research quality	13.5%	125
Entry standards	113	=106
Graduate prospects	64%	122
Good honours	81.5%	40
Expected completion rate	79.5%	=104
Student/staff ratio	24.6	128

the bottom 20 on this measure in our table. Most also thrive on their course – the measure of good honours is by far the university's strongest suit in our league table. It has jumped more than 30 places and into this year's top 40 for the proportion awarded firsts or 2:1 degrees.

Ravensbourne achieved university status only five years ago. Established in 1962 from the merger of Bromley, Beckenham and Sidcup art schools, its degrees were validated by the University of the Arts London until 2018. It moved to the Greenwich peninsula in 2010 and is an important part of the developing Greenwich design district.

Describing itself as a specialist creative university, designed for industry and majoring in design and digital media, Ravensbourne wants to be recognised as a national and international leader in creative industries education and training. A partnership with Berghs School of Communication, in Stockholm, began in 2019, bringing Swedish students to the university, although the process was inevitably interrupted by the pandemic.

The university entered the Research Excellence Framework for the first time in 2021. Almost 40% of its submission in art and design was rated world-leading or internationally excellent, although it enters our research quality index, comparing improvements across institutions, in the bottom 10.

Ravensbourne's best-known alumni include the fashion designers Clare Waight Keller of Givenchy, who designed the dress that Meghan Markle wore for her wedding to Prince Harry, and Stella McCartney, who studied for her foundation degree at Ravensbourne College of Design and Communication (as the university was formerly named). Jay Osgerby, co-designer of the Olympic 2012 torch, and comedian Andi Osho studied at Ravensbourne, too.

The university does not own or manage halls of residence but works with private providers and host families to arrange accommodation and secure discounts for those on low incomes. There are no university-owned sports facilities either but the students' union signposts which local facilities offer deals.

A renowned market and plenty of pubs, bars and restaurants provide local entertainment, while the Jubilee line brings central London within easy reach. On the cultural side, Maritime Greenwich has World Heritage status, with the Royal Observatory, the Cutty Sark and National Maritime Museum all on the doorstep of the campus.

Tuition fees

» Fees for UK students	£9,250
» Fees for International students 2021–22	£16,500
Foundation courses	£12,100
» For scholarship and bursary information see www.ravensbourne.ac.uk/information/prospective-students/fees-and-funding/	
» Graduate salary	£23,000

Student numbers

Undergraduates	2,470	(34)
Postgraduates	61	(4)
Applications/places		3,235/885
Applications per place		3.7:1
Overall offer rate		95.1%
International students – EU		7.4%
Non-EU		6.1%

Accommodation

University provided places: 100
Self-catered: £169-£408 per week
www.ravensbourne.ac.uk/information/prospective-students/accommodation/

Where do the students come from?

State schools (non-grammar)	93.7%	First generation students	47.8%		
Grammar schools	1.9%	Low participation areas	6%		
Independent schools	4.4%	All ethnic minorities	49.6%		

Social inclusion ranking: 21

White working-class males	6.6%
Black achievement gap	-18.1%
Mature (over 21)	18.7%

University of Reading

A record number of students started undergraduate degrees at the University of Reading in September 2022, following the third successive rise in applications. Clearing had to be closed earlier than planned, such was the demand for places. Firm acceptances were up by an impressive 9%.

One welcome aspect of these successes is that, while arts and humanities degrees continued to struggle (or even close) at other universities, they saw some of the strongest recruitment at Reading. Fine art, typography, humanities and archaeology, as well as computer sciences, all attracted sharp increases in applications. Six of the 13 new degrees beginning in 2022-23 combine modern languages with another subject.

A rise of four places overall on the back of a significant recovery in student satisfaction takes Reading back into the top 30 in our league table and may help the university to achieve its growth and sustainability goals by the time of its centenary in 2026. Up a gargantuan 49 places year-on-year to rank =31 for student satisfaction with the wider undergraduate experience, Reading also records a 36-place improvement for satisfaction with teaching quality, according to our analysis of the latest National Student Survey.

Reading's £200million campus development programme, some of which is selected from projects put forward by the students' union, must have helped. Larger developments have included the new £55million Health and Life Sciences Building, which was completed last year and includes one of the largest teaching labs in the UK.

Previous developments included the £40million refurbishment of the main campus library. The 320-acre Whiteknights campus on the outskirts of Reading, which in 2022 won its 12th consecutive Green Flag award for the quality of its parkland, has been given traffic-free walking, cycling and running routes.

The university has a second campus in town and 2,000 acres of farmland are at nearby Sonning and Shinfield for its highly regarded agricultural degrees. The other main site houses its business school, formerly Henley Management College, which has an attractive position on the banks of the Thames. It offers postgraduate and executive programmes, while business undergraduates are taught on the Whiteknights campus.

Ranked in the top 230 universities in the QS World University Rankings, despite a 27-place decline in 2022, Reading draws about a fifth of its undergraduates from outside the UK. Its global engagement strategy includes a target for one student in three to have some experience of studying abroad by 2026, beginning with summer schools at the

---

Whiteknights
PO Box 217
Reading RG6 6AH
0118 378 8372
www.reading.ac.uk/question
www.rusu.co.uk
www.reading.ac.uk
Open days: see website

The Times and The Sunday Times **Rankings**
Overall Ranking: =30 (last year: 34)

Teaching quality	75.1%	=69
Student experience	74.5%	=31
Research quality	51.1%	=39
Entry standards	124	=70
Graduate prospects	77.4%	47
Good honours	83.6%	=32
Expected completion rate	92.3%	=30
Student/staff ratio	16.6	=73

university's branch campus in Malaysia, as well as at a longstanding partner institution in Nanjing, China.

The student welfare team is integrated with an academic tutor system to address personal problems and enhance students' professional development. There is also a wide range of scholarships and bursaries, including 10 new Sanctuary Scholarships for Ukrainians, offering free tuition and a bursary of £5,000 a year.

All undergraduates are offered work placements, as well as career management skills modules that contribute five credits towards their degree classification. Second-year students have access to the award-winning RDGgrad programme over the summer vacation and into the autumn of their final year to prepare for graduate job applications. In our analysis of graduate prospects, based on the Graduate Outcomes survey headcount of those in highly skilled work or further study 15 months after finishing a degree, Reading is 47th.

The Reading Experience and Development (RED) award certificates extracurricular activities that might be of interest to employers. Two new award programmes have been added this year, focusing on global activity and sustainability, aiding students' personal development while helping to deliver the university's strategy. Reading is one of the leading universities for the study of climate change and won the Queen's Anniversary Prize for its research and teaching in the area in 2022. The university derives all its electricity from renewable sources and is committed to "genuine carbon neutrality" by 2030.

Reading's grades improved in the 2021 Research Excellence Framework compared with the 2014 exercise, but it has still dropped 10 places in our research table to =39 because increases were more substantial elsewhere. Archaeology, earth systems and environmental sciences, architecture and art and design were among the top performers.

Almost 5,000 residential places are either on or within easy walking distance of the Whiteknights campus, so all new entrants are guaranteed a hall place. The SportsPark, on the edge of the campus, has extensive indoor and outdoor facilities. There are also boathouses on the Thames and a sailing and canoeing club nearby.

Almost £3million was spent upgrading the student union's popular 3sixty nightclub. Reading has plenty of nightlife and is within easy reach of London, although rents are high in the private sector.

Tuition fees

» Fees for UK students   £9,250
» Fees for International students 2023–24   £19,500–£24,500
» For scholarship and bursary information see
   www.reading.ac.uk/ready-to-study/study/fees-and-funding
» Graduate salary   £25,000

Student numbers

Undergraduates	12,190	(493)
Postgraduates	3,131	(4,164)
Applications/places		20,920/4,185
Applications per place		5:1
Overall offer rate		87.1%
International students – EU		6.5%
Non-EU		13.8%

Accommodation

University provided places: 4,982
Catered costs: £140–£211 per week
Self-catered: £138–£281 per week
First-years guaranteed accommodation
www.reading.ac.uk/ready-to-study/accommodation

Where do the students come from?

				Social inclusion ranking: 90	
State schools (non-grammar)	76.4%	First generation students	35.9%	White working-class males	3.3%
Grammar schools	10.2%	Low participation areas	6.9%	Black achievement gap	-9.3%
Independent schools	13.4%	All ethnic minorities	33.1%	Mature (over 21)	10.1%

Robert Gordon University

The close relationship between the university authorities and students at Robert Gordon (RGU) paid off during the pandemic and has produced further dividends since restrictions were lifted. The university, in Aberdeen, is now in the top 10 for satisfaction with the quality of teaching and top 20 for the wider graduate experience, according to our analysis of the National Student Survey. With extensive new space for student union activities opening up across three floors of the Georgina Scott Sutherland Centre, the trend may well continue.

An annual partnership agreement with the students identifies a set of objectives to enhance the student experience. Not surprisingly, these have focused recently on RGU's response to the pandemic and the promotion of mental, physical and social health. A welcome package for new students that emerged from these discussions during the pandemic, involving professional and academic staff as well as students, won a national prize for its longer-term impact.

RGU was also the first university in the UK to provide Schwartz Rounds for all students, creating a structured forum to discuss the emotional and social aspects of work and study. They are licensed by the Point of Care Foundation and run in more than 130 healthcare organisations.

Despite its excellent satisfaction scores (the best at any of Scotland's modern universities), RGU has slipped three places in our overall league table. It remains close to the top 20 for entry standards and graduate prospects have improved, but staffing levels have declined and the university has dropped further down our research ranking. The best results in the 2021 Research Excellence Framework came in the Allied Health Professionals category.

The university has a gold award in the Teaching Excellence Framework, with the panel commenting favourably on the range of opportunities for students to develop knowledge, understanding and skills that are most highly valued by employers. Students were said to engage "consistently and frequently" with developments at the forefront of professional practice. Undergraduates interact with employer partners from early in their studies and, depending upon their degree, will have access to industry projects, placements and insight days.

Six degrees were launched in 2022-23, in subjects ranging from digital marketing and business analytics to applied sociology and psychology. There are also seven graduate apprenticeship programmes, mainly in business and engineering. More than 250 businesses and public sector organisations are involved, and the university expects to have more than 700 active students by September 2023.

Garthdee House
Garthdee Road
Aberdeen AB10 7AQ
01224 262 728
admissions@rgu.ac.uk
www.rguunion.co.uk
www.rgu.ac.uk
Open days: see website

The Times and The Sunday Times **Rankings**
Overall Ranking: 65 (last year: =62)

Teaching quality	81.2%	10
Student experience	76%	20
Research quality	20.8%	113
Entry standards	156	24
Graduate prospects	77.6%	=45
Good honours	72.9%	100
Expected completion rate	85.2%	=67
Student/staff ratio	20.8	116

Entrepreneurial students on all types of course have the opportunity to solve global challenges on a five-month Innovation Accelerator programme. Teams working on innovative projects receive mentoring, city centre office space and access to £2,000 seed funding as part of the programme, which is run in partnership with North East Scotland College and open to staff and alumni. There is an eHub jobs board and a creative entrepreneurship short course for graduates to turn their ideas into a business.

Although there is a small research presence on Orkney, the Garthdee campus, overlooking the River Dee on the south side of Aberdeen, is the hub of all teaching. A Vibrant Campus Group has been formed to encourage and support activities that inspire people to explore the picturesque riverside location more often. Named after an 18th-century philanthropist, RGU has more than 250 years' history in education. Its landmark green glass library tower symbolises its future ambitions after a £120million capital programme.

On-campus activity has returned fully, but RGU promises a blend of online and in-person learning. It intends to move towards "increasingly creative and impactful" use of in-person contact time, carefully balanced with online learning, allowing students to play an active role in their learning and enhancing their capabilities as independent and lifelong learners.

Full-time undergraduates who come from Scotland's most deprived postcodes can apply for free accommodation in standard single rooms at RGU's Woolmanhill flats. There are discounted options elsewhere. Students who have been in care qualify for a 20% accommodation discount in their first year. For everyone else, nearly half of the 912 residential places cost less than £100 a week to rent and there is usually space for all who want a room, although there is no formal guarantee. Another 20 rent-free rooms for students from disadvantaged backgrounds have been added for the new academic year after a donation by Ardmuir, an Aberdeen-based provider of student accommodation.

Scotland's third largest city offers a student-friendly atmosphere with excellent transport links. Three gyms, a swimming pool, badminton courts, bouldering and climbing facilities and a sports hall are available on RGU's campus. All students are entitled to free RGU Sport membership throughout their time at the university.

Tuition fees

» Fees for Scottish students	£0–£1,820
» RUK fees	£9,250
» Fees for International students 2023–24	£14,00–£17,270
» For scholarship and bursary information see www.rgu.ac.uk/study/courses	
» Graduate salary	£24,995

Student numbers

Undergraduates	8,630	(1,503)
Postgraduates	1,940	(2,169)
Applications/places	10,520/2,250	
Applications per place	4.7:1	
Overall offer rate	61.1%	
International students – EU	9.2%	
Non-EU	4.2%	

Accommodation

University provided places: 912
Self-catered: £85–£162 per week
www.rgu.ac.uk/life-at-rgu/accommodation

Where do the students come from?

State schools (non-grammar)	94.9%	First generation students	34.9%	White working-class males	n/a
Grammar schools	0.1%	Low participation areas	6.1%	Black achievement gap	-32.8%
Independent schools	5.1%	All ethnic minorities	10.1%	Mature (over 21)	38.5%

Social inclusion ranking (Scotland): 12

University of Roehampton

Roehampton has embarked on a controversial restructuring of its portfolio of courses, dropping some arts and humanities degrees and introducing more "career-focused" degrees. The first phase, which expanded nursing and computing provision, has boosted the demand for places, with 25% growth in applications for undergraduate programmes at the official deadline in 2022. But the second phase, which requires more than 100 academics to reapply for their jobs while degrees such as classics, drama, creative writing and philosophy are removed from the curriculum, has been the subject of protests by staff and students.

The university says it is responding to "evolving student demand" and growing financial challenges, aiming to provide an excellent student experience and deliver successful graduate outcomes in a sustainable way. There were 17 new degrees introduced in 2022-23, from computing web development and cybersecurity to English language and linguistics, children's nursing and a BA in liberal arts, which allows students to create their own degree programme from a range of options in humanities, social sciences and the arts before specialising.

Children's nursing will be taught in a £1million clinical simulation centre at Croydon College, which already offers adult nursing as part of a strategic partnership with Roehampton. The university also has study centres in central London, Birmingham and Manchester, where business and computing degrees are taught by staff from QA Higher Education, a private company.

Roehampton's main location, however, is an attractive 54-acre campus on the edge of Richmond Park, in southwest London, which blends historic buildings with modern facilities in a woodland setting. A Bloomberg trading room launched in September 2022, as did a healthcare hub to accommodate the growing provision in this area. A business laboratory also opened in 2022, providing space for students to develop their entrepreneurship activities.

Another recent addition was the £13million Sir David Bell Building, which houses Roehampton's digital media hub. Students have access to industry-standard film studios, editing suites and newsrooms, and can use resources for media, photography and sound production. There is a cinema and computing facilities, with study spaces and a gallery area for student displays and creative industry events.

The university has dropped 36 places in our league table, despite improving its rankings for student satisfaction and performing well in the latest Research Excellence Framework (REF 2021). Its research quality is in our top 50, making it the highest-placed non-specialist modern university. Three-quarters of the research across 11 different areas was rated as world-leading or internationally excellent,

Grove House
Roehampton Lane
London SW15 5PJ
020 8392 3232
ug.information@roehampton.ac.uk
www.roehamptonstudent.com
www.roehampton.ac.uk
Open days: see website

The Times and The Sunday Times **Rankings**

Overall Ranking: 101 (last year: 65)

Teaching quality	74.9%	=71
Student experience	72.4%	=54
Research quality	45.9%	48
Entry standards	102	129
Graduate prospects	62.4%	=125
Good honours	70.6%	=112
Expected completion rate	78.6%	=108
Student/staff ratio	18.3	102

the top two categories. However, Roehampton remains outside the top 100 for entry standards, graduate prospects, good honours and course completion.

Roehampton does much better in our social inclusion index, where a seven-place rise has brought it up to 23rd. Almost all the undergraduates are from non-selective state schools or colleges, nearly two-thirds from ethnic minorities, and more than half are the first in their family to go to university.

The university was upgraded to silver in the Teaching Excellence Framework in 2019. The panel was impressed by the reduction in the attainment gap for black, Asian and minority ethnic students, and for support to find work experience.

Roehampton is based around four historic constituent colleges – Digby Stuart, Froebel, Southlands and Whitelands, which pioneered the training of women as teachers. Education courses remain a significant area for Roehampton. The colleges all have religious or humanist origins but have long been open to students of all faiths or none.

Each college has a student wellbeing officer and the university's Mental Health Network runs a peer-mentoring scheme that pairs students with a trained colleague. A free, confidential short-term counselling service is offered to all students, in tandem with therapeutic groups and workshops.

The sports facilities, which include four dance studios, are excellent. Gym Roehampton, on campus, is run by Nuffield Health. The university is also a leader in e-sports and has a dedicated room for multiplayer video game competitions.

Roehampton offered the UK's first e-sports scholarships, worth £1,500 a year for talented students, as well as Europe's first Women in Esports scholarships, offered with the aim of increasing diversity in the field. The subject's popularity is not limited to those studying related degrees — e-sports has become the largest of the university's many student societies.

Within easy reach of central London but offering a campus community environment, Roehampton claims to offer a best-of-both-worlds experience. All first-years are guaranteed accommodation in one of the 1,676 on-campus hall rooms if they make Roehampton their firm choice and apply by mid-June. The same guarantee is offered to second and third-year students. Bus services between the campus and local stations at Barnes and Wimbledon, e-bikes and "college kitchens" support commuting students.

Tuition fees

» Fees for UK students £9,250
» Fees for International students 2023–24 £13,705–£17,295
» For scholarship and bursary information see www.roehampton.ac.uk/undergraduate-courses/tuition-fees/
» Graduate salary £23,300

Student numbers

Undergraduates	9,179	(226)
Postgraduates	2,074	(953)
Applications/places		7,730/1,585
Applications per place		4.9:1
Overall offer rate		87%
International students – EU		3.6%
Non-EU		8%

Accommodation

University provided places: 1,676
Self-catered: £131–£194.25 per week
First-years guaranteed accommodation
www.roehampton.ac.uk/accommodation

Where do the students come from?

State schools (non-grammar)	97%	First generation students	52%	White working-class males	5.6%
Grammar schools	0.7%	Low participation areas	4.4%	Black achievement gap	-18.4%
Independent schools	2.3%	All ethnic minorities	64.8%	Mature (over 21)	36.4%

Social inclusion ranking: 23

Royal Agricultural University

The Royal Agricultural University (RAU) is branching out from its secluded Cotswolds setting in a big way. It has entered into a long-term partnership with the Uzbekistan Ministry of Agriculture to launch the International Agriculture University (IAU) in Tashkent, while at home it plans to turn part of its land into an innovation village, containing commercial, academic and residential space, as well as a hotel. The University Gate project will be funded privately and is intended to house a "global community of influencers, practitioners, researchers and entrepreneurs".

The RAU was already making the most of its international reputation as the first high-level agricultural college in the English-speaking world, leading a global group of agricultural universities researching sustainable business models to reduce food poverty, decrease the carbon footprint of agriculture, and protect the livelihoods of farmers. As well as launching the first undergraduate programmes at the IAU at the start of the 2022-23 academic year, the university has twinned with Sumy National Agrarian University, in Ukraine, to support its day-to-day operation after the Russian invasion.

Big increases in student satisfaction have helped the RAU jump 14 places in our league table, although it remains outside the top 100. It has recovered from pandemic woes to be among the top 10 universities for student satisfaction with the wider undergraduate experience, and ranks =54 for satisfaction with teaching quality, according to our analysis of the latest National Student Survey outcomes.

Applications have been booming, rising 30% in 2021. The addition of foundation years on all BSc courses has been one reason for the growth in demand for places, as well as assisting the efforts to widen the intake.

Based in 25 scenic acres outside Cirencester, the RAU has been visited by every monarch since Queen Victoria. Established in 1845, it has acquired the nickname of "Oxbridge of the countryside" owing to its high proportions of privately educated students. It remains close to the bottom of our social inclusion index for England and Wales, with only 55.9% from non-selective state schools and just 1.4% from ethnic minorities.

In an effort to widen the intake, applicants from particular low-performing schools and colleges, students from areas with low participation in higher education, care-leavers and those from ethnic groups underrepresented at the RAU were guaranteed a conditional offer this year. The university intends to make this a contextual offer for 2023 entry, reducing the standard offer by one A-level grade or its equivalent

Stroud Road
Cirencester GL7 6JS
01285 889 912
admissions@rau.ac.uk
www.rau.ac.uk/university-life/
social/student-union
www.rau.ac.uk
Open days:
see website

The Times and The Sunday Times Rankings		
Overall Ranking: 102 (last year: 116)		
Teaching quality	75.8%	=54
Student experience	78.7%	8
Research quality	24.2%	102
Entry standards	114	=103
Graduate prospects	67.6%	=102
Good honours	66.9%	124
Expected completion rate	90.4%	=38
Student/staff ratio	21.5	=118

for students in the target groups. In addition, a new Ethnic Minority Excellence Scholarship gives full remission for tuition fees.

The RAU was awarded silver in the government's Teaching Excellence Framework, winning praise for its specialist facilities. Assessors were impressed by the employer-informed course design, work placements and extracurricular opportunities for students to develop skills and attributes valued by employers. Hands-on learning takes place at Coates Manor Farm next to the campus, at Kemble Farms dairy complex and at Leaze Farm. A recent partnership with the neighbouring Bathurst Estate also gives students access to 15,000 acres of farmland, forestry, environmentally managed land, real estate and heritage properties, along with a range of rural enterprises for teaching, research and knowledge exchange.

Students may spend a sandwich year in industry as part of their degree, and entrepreneurial activity is encouraged by schemes such as the RAU's programme for student start-ups, which offers access to local business mentors. The RAU is one of only six universities – and the only specialist provider – to be made a Centre of Excellence by the Institute of Enterprise and Entrepreneurs.

Results improved in the 2021 Research Excellence Framework, although the university did not quite break into the top 100 in our research ranking. Half of the work submitted was considered world-leading or internationally excellent. The RAU has six research clusters concentrating on applied work in the natural world and with links as far afield as China, Brazil and sub-Saharan Africa.

On campus, a new student hub opened in 2019 housing all student facilities, including the students' union. There are facilities for a number of sports, from lacrosse, hockey and rugby to tennis, croquet and netball. Polo is played at a club about 12 miles from campus, rowing at Gloucester Rowing Club and shooting at Hollow Fosse.

Three-quarters of the 339 rooms in eight halls of residence on campus are catered. They are enough to accommodate about 80% of first-year students, and the university works with local providers to satisfy those who live off campus. The university's small numbers and countryside location encourage a collegiate atmosphere, with the campus the centre of social activity. There are ample opportunities to explore the Cotswolds and London is only 90 minutes away by train.

Tuition fees

» Fees for UK students	£9,250
» Fees for International students 2023–24	£13,500
» For scholarship and bursary information see www.rau.ac.uk/study/undergraduate/ funding-your-time-at-university	
» Graduate salary	£24,000

Student numbers

Undergraduates	941	(33)
Postgraduates	146	(55)
Applications/places		1,450/415
Applications per place		3.5:1
Overall offer rate		n/a
International students – EU		2.7%
Non-EU		6.7%

Accommodation

University provided places: 339
Catered costs: £208–£266 per week
Self-catered: £197–£205 per week
www.rau.ac.uk/university-life/accommodation

Where do the students come from?

State schools (non-grammar)	55.9%	First generation students	36.7%	White working-class males	3.6%
Grammar schools	7.5%	Low participation areas	2.8%	Black achievement gap	n/a
Independent schools	36.6%	All ethnic minorities	1.4%	Mature (over 21)	30.1%

Social inclusion ranking: 110

Royal Holloway, University of London

Improving research quality has helped Royal Holloway to retain its top-30 position in our overall rankings. In an excellent performance in the latest Research Excellence Framework (REF 2021), 88% of the university's research was assessed as world-leading or internationally excellent, the top two categories.

Royal Holloway moves up four places in our analysis of research quality (=26) led by success in music, communication and media studies, and geography.

The university has been named by the government as one of eight academic centres of excellence in cybersecurity research. It hosts 52 research centres in total, across wide-ranging academic fields from the Centre for Algorithms and Applications to the Centre for Workplace Research in Asian Societies.

Royal Holloway is in increasing demand, with applications exceeding 20,000 for the first time in the 2021 admissions cycle. A growing curriculum offers more options to applicants. After the introduction of 22 new degrees in the 2022-23 academic year, another five will welcome their first students in 2023-24 including geography, culture and identity; and geography, geopolitics and global affairs.

Degrees in health studies, and health studies and social care are also on the way at the new Department of Health Studies, where the focus is on advancing teaching and research allied to communities, the wellbeing of people and the environment and the challenges of living sustainably.

When rating Royal Holloway silver in the Teaching Excellence Framework, assessors praised the level of investment in e-learning facilities and said students were engaged with developments from the forefront of research, scholarship and professional practice.

Undergraduates on all Royal Holloway's courses may take an additional year to complete their degree. The Optional Placement Year scheme allows them to spend their third year gaining work experience related to their course or in an area that interests them. Alternatively, they can opt to spend it volunteering, studying abroad – or a combination of all three. The university has also expanded partnerships with overseas institutions, to allow students to gain access to more global opportunities.

A new employability framework, CVstac, has been introduced to support students in identifying and building the 12 key meta skills (the permanent talents that enable people to achieve things) required by employers. Embedded into teaching and the student experience, CVstac is intended to get students thinking about graduate employability skills from their first year and ultimately to give them an edge in securing employment.

Responses to the latest national Graduate

Egham Hill
Egham TW20 0EX
01784 414 944
study@royalholloway.ac.uk
www.su.rhul.ac.uk
www.royalholloway.ac.uk
Open days: see website

The Times and The Sunday Times Rankings
Overall Ranking: 29 (last year: 26)

Teaching quality	74.1%	=82
Student experience	72.7%	52
Research quality	53.6%	=26
Entry standards	129	=55
Graduate prospects	73.8%	61
Good honours	84.2%	29
Expected completion rate	92.7%	27
Student/staff ratio	16.2	=65

Outcomes survey place the university in the upper half (61st) for the proportion of graduates in professional-level jobs or further study 15 months after finishing their degrees.

Royal Holloway stays steady in 52nd place for student satisfaction with the wider undergraduate experience, according to our analysis of the latest National Student Survey. However, it drops eight places to rank =82 for their evaluation of teaching quality.

The palatial redbrick Founder's Building, modelled on a French château and opened by Queen Victoria, is often likened to Harry Potter's Hogwarts. The latest developments on campus include the SuperFab world-class "cleanroom" in the physics department, which has advanced electronic nanofabrication equipment for research and development of the technology needed for medical imaging and quantum computers.

The Beatrice Shilling Building, named after the pioneering British aeronautical engineer and amateur motor racing driver, houses the Department of Electronic Engineering. One of its aims is to attract more female engineering students – fittingly for an institution formed from the merger of two colleges (Royal Holloway and Bedford) that were among the first British institutions to educate women. Bedford's early students included Sarah Parker Remond, the first African-American woman to carry out a lecture tour around Britain (about slavery), and the novelist George Eliot.

Royal Holloway has improved its course completion ranking to 27th with a dropout rate lower than the expected level in light of the university's course profile and the background of its students.

More than a quarter of 2021's intake qualified for some sort of financial award. Some awards credit broader abilities than A-level grades alone, such as the Reed Innovation scholarship, worth £15,000 over three years, awarded to undergraduates studying any degree who have proven innovative and creative problem-solving skills and who are expected to achieve AAA at A-level or equivalent.

Royal Holloway is one of the University of London's top sporting colleges, with more than 80 teams and good facilities. The university also has the use of a boathouse on the Thames.

New entrants are guaranteed a room in halls (of which almost three in 10 are catered), as long as they make Royal Holloway their firm choice and apply in time. The self-contained campus, close to Heathrow airport and Windsor, is 40 minutes from central London.

Tuition fees

» Fees for UK students	£9,250
» Fees for International students 2023–24	£20,000–£25,200
» For scholarship and bursary information see	
www.royalholloway.ac.uk/studying-here/fees-and-funding	
» Graduate salary	£23,000

Student numbers

Undergraduates	9,265	(69)
Postgraduates	2,123	(838)
Applications/places	20,070/3,495	
Applications per place	5.7:1	
Overall offer rate	84.9%	
International students – EU	7.1%	
Non-EU	11.7%	

Accommodation

University provided places: 3,349
Catered costs: £122–£185 per week
Self-catered £139–£194 per week
First-years guaranteed accommodation
www.royalholloway.ac.uk/student-life/accommodation/

Where do the students come from?

State schools (non-grammar)	80.3%	First generation students	40.3%	White working-class males	3.4%
Grammar schools	9.1%	Low participation areas	4.6%	Black achievement gap	-16.8%
Independent schools	10.6%	All ethnic minorities	52.9%	Mature (over 21)	4.7%

Social inclusion ranking: 82

University of St Andrews

Our Scottish University of the Year is the leading Scottish university in our academic rankings – although Oxford has bumped it off the No 1 spot. St Andrews continues to shake up the time-honoured order of our institutional table by outperforming third-place Cambridge once again. Its position is fuelled by remarkably – and consistently – high rates of student satisfaction. The university has the second-best results in the two National Student Survey-derived measures included in our league table: teaching quality and student experience. Last year it came top in both.

Confirming its academically elite reputation, St Andrews' entry standards are only one percentage point lower than the highest in the country at Cambridge. And once enrolled on degrees its students succeed: the proportion of firsts and 2.1s achieved at St Andrews puts the university in the top five nationally. The university is in the top 10 for graduate prospects and staff-to-student ratio, and remains the top-performing university in Scotland.

The small coastal town of St Andrews, located to the northeast of Edinburgh on Scotland's east coast, is dominated by its university – perhaps more than any other location in the UK. A fundraising appeal for its 600th anniversary in 2013, led by the Prince of Wales, an alumnus, successfully raised £100million to improve the university's physical facilities.

A recent development, the £12.5million Laidlaw Music Centre, opened in spring 2022 and is named after one of its philanthropic donors, Lord Laidlaw. The first building to be dedicated to music in the long history of St Andrews, its first-rate facilities include an oak-lined recital room and a chamber hall with moveable floor, along with rehearsal and practice rooms, a recording suite and a library.

Construction began in early 2022 on one of the first new colleges for three centuries at the third-oldest university in the English-speaking world. Bringing together the schools of International Relations, Management, and Economics and Finance, the new hub for Social Sciences aims to create space for expanding student and research numbers and to encourage interdisciplinary work. Building on the university's strength in the student learning experience, St Andrews has begun offering all academic staff engaged in teaching the opportunity to boost their skills by taking a postgraduate certificate in academic practice.

St Andrews is in high demand. More than 21,400 students applied to the university in 2021 for a little over 1,800 places. Since 2011 applications have soared by more than 75%. The curriculum gained Chinese studies degrees in 2021, taken in combination with a

College Gate
North Street
St Andrews KY16 9AJ
01334 462 150
admissions@st-andrews.ac.uk
www.yourunion.net
www.st-andrews.ac.uk
Open days: see website

ST ANDREWS
Edinburgh
Belfast
London
Cardiff

The Times and The Sunday Times Rankings
Overall Ranking: 2 (last year: 1)

Teaching quality	84%	2
Student experience	80.5%	=2
Research quality	53.8%	25
Entry standards	204	2
Graduate prospects	86.9%	8
Good honours	92.6%	=4
Expected completion rate	95.9%	=7
Student/staff ratio	11.8	6

wide variety of other subjects as part of a joint honours programme.

When the Prince of Wales met his future wife, Kate Middleton, at St Andrews at the start of the century, it helped to put St Andrews on the global map. Today it has one of the most international student populations of any British university. Two-fifths of the student population comes from abroad, with 16% recruited from Scotland (a number capped by the government) and the remainder from the rest of the UK. Another of Queen Elizabeth II's grandchildren, Lady Louise Windsor, begins her studies at the university in 2022-23.

More than 88% of the work submitted by St Andrews to the latest Research Assessment Framework (REF 2021) was assessed as world-leading or internationally excellent. Other universities did even better, however, hence St Andrews drops from 11th to 25th place in our research quality index.

Unlike some other Scottish universities, St Andrews does not discount tuition fees to mirror three-year courses south of the border for UK students who are not from Scotland. This means the standard four-year undergraduate course costs £37,000 at present. However, there is an extensive bursary and scholarship programme, funded by more than £1million each year, that makes awards worth £1,500 to £4,000 a year to UK-domiciled students with household incomes of up to £40,000.

Professor Dame Sally Mapstone, principal and vice-chancellor of St Andrews, led the Scotland-wide work on contextual admissions that is now Scottish government policy. The university moves off the foot of our Scottish social inclusion ranking for the second time in 2022. Its intake is more ethnically diverse than any other university in Scotland. After a spate of sexual misconduct allegations, St Andrews is one of very few to require all students to undertake compulsory training in sexual consent, equality, diversity and inclusion.

Sports fans can take part in everything from football and rugby to shinty, ultimate frisbee and lacrosse, and the sports centre at Hepburn Gardens, a 10-minute walk from the historic town centre, has undergone a £14million redevelopment and extension.

Six halls of residence encircle University Park, where all first-years are guaranteed a place if they apply by the end of June. Pubs and societies are to the fore of St Andrews' social scene.

Tuition fees

»	Fees for Scottish students	£0–£1,820
	RUK fees	£9,250
»	Fees for International students 2023–24	£28,190
	Medicine	£35,920
»	For scholarship and bursary information see www.st-andrews.ac.uk/study/fees-and-funding/	
»	Graduate salary	£27,000

Student numbers

Undergraduates	8,347	(669)
Postgraduates	2,087	(382)
Applications/places		21,405/1,820
Applications per place		11.8:1
Overall offer rate		25%
International students – EU		5.8%
Non-EU		34.4%

Accommodation

University provided places: 3,665
Catered costs: £178–£209 per week
Self-catered: £146–£229 per week
First-years guaranteed accommodation
www.st-andrews.ac.uk/study/accommodation/

Where do the students come from?

State schools (non-grammar)	56.5%	First generation students	18.1%
Grammar schools	6.6%	Deprived areas	10.2%
Independent schools	36.9%	All ethnic minorities	15.8%

Social inclusion ranking (Scotland): 14

White working-class males	n/a
Black achievement gap	-15.2%
Mature (over 21)	3.8%

St George's, University of London

St George's, the University of London's specialist health university, is third in our analysis of graduate prospects. Soaring applications and enrolments reflect an institution at the forefront of Britain's drive to train more doctors and other medical staff to fill vacancies.

The latest Graduate Outcomes survey showed that 91.7% of those leaving St George's were in highly skilled work or postgraduate study within 15 months. The university was No 1 for graduate prospects in 2021.

Stimulated by Covid-19's spotlight on the health professions, applications to St George's full range of courses increased enormously in 2021, by about 58% year-on-year. Out of 9,500 applicants, the university placed 1,050 new students – more than it has welcomed ever before.

The number of places to study medicine in England is strictly regulated by the government at 7,500, but the cap was lifted in 2021 because of a surge in students achieving high grades. Never an easy subject to get into, at St George's applications to study medicine rose again in 2022. Professor Jenny Higham, the university's vice-chancellor, told The Times on A-level results day in August: "We've seen a 20% increase in applications at St George's." Asked if some candidates with three A*s would be rejected, Higham said: "Yes. They might not have done well in the BMAT [BioMedical Admissions Test] or might not have shown empathy in the interview."

St George's, founded more than 250 years ago, is based in Tooting, south London, and was the second in the country to award medical degrees. Today, course options include biomedical science and healthcare science degrees covering respiratory and cardiac physiology and sleep physiology, among others. Paramedic science and radiography degrees are taught in a partnership with Kingston University.

For the 2022-23 academic year, the prevalent teaching model at St George's is hybrid, combining online and in-person lectures. Outcomes of the latest National Student Survey (NSS), published in summer 2022, suggest that students feel there is room for improvement in teaching quality (129th), however, and the wider undergraduate experience (128th).

The poor NSS outcomes have contributed to the university dropping to =82 in our main league table, falling four places in a year and 33 since 2020, when it was 49th.

St George's is one of only 11 universities in our rankings rated bronze (the lowest grade) in the government's Teaching Excellence Framework. Although the panel gave the university credit for an "embedded institutional culture that rewards excellent teaching, and promotes inclusivity among staff and students", it was held back by low levels of student

Cranmer Terrace
Tooting
London SW17 0RE
020 3897 2032
study@sgul.ac.uk
www.sgsu.org.uk
www.sgul.ac.uk
Open days: see website

The Times and The Sunday Times Rankings
Overall Ranking: =82 (last year: 78)

Teaching quality	65.5%	129
Student experience	60.9%	128
Research quality	48.8%	=42
Entry standards	144	41
Graduate prospects	91.7%	3
Good honours	80%	=49
Expected completion rate	93.7%	20
Student/staff ratio	13.1	10

satisfaction with assessment and feedback, and comparisons with other predominantly medical institutions with even higher employment rates.

St George's also achieved success in the latest Research Excellence Framework (REF 2021), nearly doubling the number of staff who contributed, compared with REF 2014.

Thirty-six per cent of the submission was rated world-leading, the top category. Consequently, the university moves 10 places up our research quality index, to joint 42nd. Historic developments in cardiac pacemakers and IVF are among St George's research achievements. Recently, the institution's expanding range of Covid-19 research projects has included work on a rapid antibody test.

St George's was the first UK institution to launch the MBBS graduate entry programme 22 years ago. The four-year fast-track degree in medicine is open to graduates in any discipline and has become an increasingly popular route into the medical profession. St George's also offers a four-year graduate-entry Bachelor of Surgery degree at the University of Nicosia in Cyprus.

Applicants are interviewed for entry to all undergraduate courses except biomedical science and clinical pharmacology. A shadowing scheme offers sixth-formers from state schools in Wandsworth and Merton the opportunity to spend time with a consultant at St George's Hospital or a local GP.

More than three-quarters of students come from ethnic minority backgrounds (the seventh-highest proportion in England and Wales). However, the university's overall performance on social inclusion (=85) is affected by its large contingent of recruits from fee-paying or selective state schools (nearly one quarter).

To help to widen participation, St George's makes contextual offers up to two A-level grades lower than the standard requirement to students who meet criteria for widening participation. The university does a good job of retaining the students it recruits, featuring in our top 20 for course completion. More than a third of entrants tend to qualify for financial help, including bursaries.

Applicants who have accepted St George's as their firm offer and apply by July 1 are guaranteed one of Horton Hall's 486 self-catering rooms.

An active students' union offers 120 clubs, societies and community projects. Students have the use of a rowing club on the River Thames and can take advantage of University of London facilities for sport.

Tuition fees

- » Fees for UK students   £9,250
- » Fees for International students 2023–24   £18,250–£20,250
  Medicine   £40,500
- » For scholarship and bursary information see www.sgul.ac.uk/study/undergraduate-study/fees-and-financial-support/
- »Graduate salary   £29,988

Student numbers

Undergraduates	3,174	(576)
Postgraduates	347	(1,086)
Applications/places		9,500/1,050
Applications per place		9.1
Overall offer rate		35.3%
International students – EU		1.3%
Non-EU		4.8%

Accommodation

University provided places: 486
Self-catered: £176–£186 per week
First-years guaranteed accommodation
www.sgul.ac.uk/study/life-at-st-georges/accommodation

Where do the students come from?

State schools (non-grammar)	73.9%	First generation students	35.5%	White working-class males	1.5%
Grammar schools	17.3%	Low participation areas	3.3%	Black achievement gap	-14.1%
Independent schools	8.8%	All ethnic minorities	76.5%	Mature (over 21)	35.1%

Social inclusion ranking: =85

St Mary's University, Twickenham

St Mary's University is on the cusp of the top 50 this year, after a 16-place rise in our league table. Its upward trajectory is powered by stellar rates of student satisfaction, our analysis of the latest National Student Survey shows. For students' evaluation of teaching quality St Mary's ranks fifth in the country, and for their feelings about the wider undergraduate experience it is seventh. The outcomes show consistency; the university was in the top 10 for both measures in our previous edition, too.

Clearly, St Mary's "face-to-face plus" model of teaching delivery is going down well with students. Under the strategy teaching is predominantly in person, supported by online learning and lecture-capture technology. Where exams are used, some are taking place in exam halls while others are online, according to strict protocols.

At the height of the pandemic, to ensure digital equality for students, the university provided wi-fi-enabled laptops, noise-cancelling headphones and 4G wi-fi dongles via a long-term equipment loan scheme. It now provides detailed guidance on what new students require pre-arrival.

The university has recently opened the Dolce Vita development, linking three existing buildings with a new open-plan social and study space. The renovation of existing buildings has added a new bar, private study rooms, four classrooms, meeting rooms and social seating areas. Founded in 1850 to train teachers for a growing number of poor Catholic children, St Mary's is the largest of the UK's three Catholic universities and these days admits students of all faiths or none. About a third of the 5,000-strong undergraduate community are enrolled on teacher-training programmes.

All undergraduate provision is based in Twickenham, where St Mary's occupies an attractive 35-acre campus featuring gardens, parkland and the shimmering white gothic fantasy Strawberry Hill House near the River Thames – 30 minutes from central London. The university also has a community building in the centre of Twickenham.

St Mary's was awarded silver in the Teaching Excellence Framework and assessors commended its high-quality resources and good staffing levels, which allowed personalised and small-group learning. Every student has an academic tutor and a team of learning and development lecturers provide further support. Students can apply for extensions to deadlines via an extenuating circumstances form.

The latest data shows that such efforts are not entirely paying off, however. More than two in 10 (22.6%) of its students are projected to drop out – more than twice as many as the expected benchmark (10.5%) based on the social and academic backgrounds of St Mary's

Waldegrave Road
Strawberry Hill
Twickenham TW1 4SX
020 8240 2394
apply@stmarys.ac.uk
www.stmaryssu.co.uk
www.stmarys.ac.uk
Open days: see website

The Times and The Sunday Times **Rankings**
Overall Ranking: 51 (last year: 67)

Teaching quality	82.4%	5
Student experience	78.9%	7
Research quality	29.4%	88
Entry standards	109	=117
Graduate prospects	68.8%	=94
Good honours	77%	=70
Expected completion rate	78.8%	107
Student/staff ratio	16	=59

students and the university's course profile.

The university has launched 11 new courses with a placement year in the areas of business management, communications, English, film, history, liberal arts and sports management. New degree courses in law with politics and law with sports business (offered as either an LLB or BA qualification) are also being introduced.

St Mary's has a postgraduate facility in Edinburgh, at the Gillis Centre, where master's programmes in theology and education are being delivered. Granted research degree-awarding powers in 2021, the university plans to expand postdoctoral programmes across a number of specialisms, starting with two options in strength and conditioning in 2021.

Industry collaborations include two courses run with the Chelsea Football Club Foundation. There is a partnership with the Royal Ballet in London's Covent Garden and St Mary's is also London Irish rugby club's official educational partner. With 69% of graduates in high-skilled jobs or further study 15 months after finishing their degrees, St Mary's ranks in the top 100 of our graduate prospects measure this year (=94).

Sport is a well-established strength at St Mary's: Sir Mo Farah, a former student, won a scholarship to its renowned Endurance Performance and Coaching Centre and trained at St Mary's for 10 years in the run-up to his gold medal-winning performance in the 5,000m and 10,000m events at the London 2012 Olympics.

Sport scholarships are awarded in gold,

silver and bronze ratings. Packages worth up to £2,000 include financial support with free gym membership, and access to the strength and conditioning suite and massage clinic.

Academic scholarships include the Vice-Chancellor's Excellence Scholarship of £3,000 per year of study, awarded to students who arrive with at least ABB at A-level or equivalent, and who come from households with incomes under £25,000.

Indoors sports facilities include a performance hall, studio, tennis centre, and fitness and conditioning suite at the main campus. Outdoors, there are two rugby pitches and the 2022-resurfaced Sir Mo Farah Athletics Track. The Teddington Lock campus is home to floodlit all-weather pitches.

All of St Mary's 600-plus self-managed halls of residence are catered – a highly unusual feature among UK universities – and on campus. These factors are likely to contribute to the university's buoyant rates of student satisfaction.

Tuition fees

»	Fees for UK students	£9,250
	Foundation courses	£6,620–£9,250
»	Fees for International students 2023–24	£13,650
	Two-year degrees	£11,100
»	For scholarship and bursary information see	
	www.stmarys.ac.uk/student-finance/undergraduate/	
	tuition-fees.aspx	
»	Graduate salary	£24,000

Student numbers

Undergraduates	**3,368**	**(149)**
Postgraduates	**1,233 (832)**	
Applications/places	**5,620/1,180**	
Applications per place	**4.8:1**	
Overall offer rate	**88%**	
International students – EU	**3.8%**	
Non-EU	**11.7%**	

Accommodation

University provided places: 650
Catered costs: £170–£255 per week
First-years guaranteed accommodation
www.stmarys.ac.uk/student-life/accommodation/overview.aspx

Where do the students come from?

State schools (non-grammar)	92.9%	First generation students	45.6%	White working-class males	6.4%
Grammar schools	2.8%	Low participation areas	5.4%	Black achievement gap	-15.5%
Independent schools	4.3%	All ethnic minorities	32.7%	Mature (over 21)	26.6%

Social inclusion ranking: 62

University of Salford

Students at Salford this term will be the first to access the new £65million Science, Engineering and Environment (SEE) Building on the university's main Peel Park campus. The 100% electric-powered building features open spaces to promote collaborative working between students, staff and industry. Hands-on learning facilities include a wind tunnel and the Morson Maker Space for manufacturing and digital fabrication.

The building is part of an ambitious £2.5bn, 240-acre Salford Crescent masterplan to regenerate the city. The 20-year development will link the centre of Manchester with MediaCityUK, where Salford has another campus in the same development as the BBC and ITV. Courses in nursing, midwifery, psychology, social sciences, sports and health are based at the Frederick Road campus, 10 minutes from Peel Park.

Salford moves up 10 places in our main academic rankings this year, helped by a 16-place rise for student satisfaction with teaching quality (=89). Students' feelings about the wider undergraduate experience also improved – but only by two places – to =103 in our analysis of results of the National Student Survey.

The university received much-improved results in the latest Research Excellence Framework (REF 2021) compared with the previous national assessment in 2014, and moves up three places in our research quality index against even steeper gains at other universities. Overall, 78% of Salford's research was rated world-leading or internationally excellent. Some of the best results were produced by social work and social policy; earth systems and environmental science; music drama, dance, performing arts, film and screen studies; communications and media studies; and engineering.

New facilities are launching that will further enhance Salford's research, such as the £16million North of England Robotics Centre. The Z House, constructed by housebuilder Barratt, is a zero-carbon home designed to represent the future of UK housebuilding. Salford students are living in the Z House this year to emulate the experience of the customer in the transition to net-zero living. At Peel Park, the £55million New Adelphi teaching centre houses the latest facilities for art, performance, and design and technology students.

Founded in 1896 as the Royal Technical Institute to provide for the workforce that powered the Industrial Revolution, the University of Salford continues to foster industry links that benefit its students. An agreement with the BBC Philharmonic, for instance, has allowed students first access to technology that turns classical concerts into immersive musical experiences, while free virtual events run with the BBC Academy

---

Maxwell Building
43 The Crescent
Salford
Greater Manchester
M5 4WT
0161 295 4545
enquiries@salford.ac.uk
www.salfordstudents.com
www.salford.ac.uk
Open days: see website

The Times and The Sunday Times **Rankings**
Overall Ranking: 88 (last year: 98)

Teaching quality	73.6%	=89
Student experience	68.7%	=103
Research quality	37.8%	68
Entry standards	125	=63
Graduate prospects	71.4%	73
Good honours	76.6%	74
Expected completion rate	81.3%	97
Student/staff ratio	17.9	=93

over the past year have covered topics from scriptwriting to location management.

Salford prioritises real-world education for students. For example, a partnership with Harvey Nichols facilitated more than 30 fashion design graduates to present in excess of 150 one-off garments for display and retail at the company's Manchester store. Siemens partners with the university to offer an engineering qualification.

However, Salford was awarded bronze in the Teaching Excellence Framework (TEF) and an appeal to upgrade the assessment was rejected in 2018. Despite its good links with employers and a commitment to learning by students, the TEF panel found progression to employment or further study remained "exceptionally low" – a position now countered by results of the latest Graduate Outcomes survey, which showed that 71.4% of graduates were in high-skilled jobs or postgraduate study 15 months after finishing their degree. The proportion puts Salford just outside the top half in our comparison.

At the last count, Salford's portfolio of 14 degree apprenticeships in business, construction, health and science had 765 student apprentices enrolled on programmes. Two new undergraduate degrees joined the curriculum in 2022: nursing (adult), taught at Bury College; and business with supply chain and project management. From next year an e-sports management course will welcome students, as will a degree in creative computing.

Salford is in the upper half of universities in our social inclusion index and the top 25 for its proportion of students from non-selective state schools (96.1%). Outreach work aims to raise aspirations among young people. Among widening participation initiatives are contextual offers, currently made only to students who have been in care, but eligibility is likely to broaden by 2023 entry.

Financial support includes the Salford Inspire fund for UK and EU students. Scholarships for UK students target those from low-income backgrounds, while Salford's international scholarships award high-achievers from overseas.

Completion rates hold Salford back in our main academic ranking, as more students are projected to drop out (13.3%) than the benchmark proportion (11.4%).

A swimming pool, five fitness suites and a multiuse sports hall are among Salford's facilities. For most students, the university's proximity to Manchester's bright lights is a big selling point.

Tuition fees

»	Fees for UK students	£9,250
	Foundation courses	£8,250
»	Fees for International students 2023–24	£15,120–£17,580
»	Foundation	£12,960
»	For scholarship and bursary information see www.salford.ac.uk/undergraduate/fees	
»	Graduate salary	£24,000

Student numbers

Undergraduates	17,503	(641)
Postgraduates	3,502	(2,309)
Applications/places	25,795/5,645	
Applications per place	4.6:1	
Overall offer rate	77.6%	
International students – EU	2.2%	
Non-EU	4%	

Accommodation

University provided places: 2,111
Self-catered: £105–£167 per week
www.campuslivingvillages.co.uk/salford/

Where do the students come from?

State schools (non-grammar)	96.1%	First generation students	46.5%	White working-class males	6.2%
Grammar schools	2.5%	Low participation areas	15.7%	Black achievement gap	−21.9%
Independent schools	1.4%	All ethnic minorities	34.4%	Mature (over 21)	28.8%

Social inclusion ranking: =56

University of Sheffield

A raft of academic facilities are opening at Sheffield, dedicated to further augmenting the Russell Group university's research-led teaching and learning. Leading the way is the new Faculty of Social Sciences building, due to open in the spring of 2023, where a range of disciplines will be housed under the same roof, enabling students to benefit from collaborative teaching and social spaces.

The social sciences development follows the completion of a building for the university's Gene Therapy and Manufacturing Centre, where scientific discoveries into treatments for patients with life-threatening diseases are being advanced. Elsewhere, a new building in the university's renowned Faculty of Engineering houses the Royce Discovery Centre, whose aim is to develop the next generation of materials for UK manufacturers.

At Sheffield's Advanced Manufacturing campus, situated on the former Sheffield Business Park, the Translational Energy Research Centre (TERC) has begun working on the latest carbon capture technologies. The university is developing a neighbouring facility and partner to the TERC that will focus on research, innovation and commercial testing of sustainable aviation fuels – the first of its kind in Europe.

The university's renowned Advanced Manufacturing Research Centre (AMRC) provides work experience opportunities for students with industry giants such as McLaren, BAE Systems, Boeing and Rolls-Royce and is extending its footprint across the north. The £20million AMRC North West opened on the Samlesbury Aerospace Enterprise Zone in Lancashire in 2021.

Sheffield's strength in research was evidenced in the 2021 Research Excellence Framework (REF), in which 92% of its work was rated in the highest two categories of world-leading or internationally excellent. The university entered all of its independent researchers and submitted work to 25 different REF units of assessment.

The REF outcomes have triggered an eight-place rise in our research quality index for Sheffield, helping to propel the university into the top 20 of our main league table this year. Sheffield is in the top 100 of the 2023 QS World University Rankings, where it ties for 96th place with St Andrews.

In tandem comes impressive rates of student satisfaction. Based on the latest National Student Survey, Sheffield ranks 28th for the wider student experience (it was 27th last year) and 47th for students' evaluation of teaching quality (joint 48th last year).

Teaching is in-person this year and the university has an internal system for lecture-capture that has been operating since pre-pandemic times. "We are a campus-based

---

Western Bank
Sheffield S10 2TN
0114 222 8030
study@sheffield.ac.uk
http://su.sheffield.ac.uk
www.sheffield.ac.uk
Open days: see website

The Times and The Sunday Times **Rankings**
Overall Ranking: =20 (last year: 22)

Teaching quality	76.3%	47
Student experience	75%	28
Research quality	59.1%	15
Entry standards	150	=28
Graduate prospects	80.1%	=32
Good honours	84.7%	25
Expected completion rate	93.1%	=23
Student/staff ratio	14.9	=36

university and we will use digital methods to enhance in-person teaching," Professor Mary Vincent, vice-president for education, said.

Sheffield's main university precinct stretches for a mile, ending near the city centre. Among its resources is the Engineering Heartspace – home to renowned Faculty of Engineering and the £23million Information Commons, which is live 24-hours throughout the year. The university also operates at the Advanced Manufacturing Research Centre/Campus East and provides student accommodation at Endcliffe and Ranmoor.

Rated silver in the Teaching Excellence Framework, assessors commended "high levels of stretch and challenge" that help students to develop skills valued highly by employers.

More than four in five graduates were in high-skilled work or further study 15 months after finishing their degrees according to the latest figures, ranking Sheffield just outside the top 30 of our graduate prospects measure. The university is one of Siemens's leading UK suppliers of graduates. A longstanding relationship with Rolls-Royce is the source of an active apprenticeship.

Sheffield offers nine degree apprenticeships in total, across a range of engineering disciplines, and also in nursing and in psychology. There were nearly 370 student apprentices, at the last count.

The first PPE (politics, philosophy and economics) students started courses at Sheffield in 2022-23. Four options in quantitative social sciences also launched, offering specialisms in criminology, management, politics or sociology, and the landscape architecture master's course welcomed its first students. From 2023, the curriculum gains another two degrees, in global sustainable development and data science.

Between 45% and 50% of 2021's intake received some form of financial help, a proportion the university expects to be much the same for 2023. Sheffield is the second-highest ranked Russell Group member in our social inclusion index. It has moved up to 75th place this year, closing the gap on 58th-ranked Queen Mary, University of London. Ten per cent of applicants in 2021 received a contextual offer.

Sheffield has one of the biggest programmes of internal leagues at any university, while scholarships for elite student athletes contribute to the university's flourishing high-performance sports.

The university guarantees accommodation to first-years who apply by the deadline. Students can look forward to a student-centric city.

Tuition fees

- » Fees for UK students £9,250
- » Fees for International students 2023–24 £21,000–£26,950
- » Medicine £39,950; Dentistry £42,770
- » For scholarship and bursary information see www.sheffield.ac.uk/undergraduate/fees-funding/
- » Graduate salary £25,295

Student numbers

Undergraduates	19,275	(289)
Postgraduates	8,846	(2,195)
Applications/places	39,350/5,980	
Applications per place	6.6:1	
Overall offer rate	75.6%	
International students – EU	5%	
Non-EU	19.3%	

Accommodation

University provided places: 6,005
Self-catered: £80–£147 per week
First-years guaranteed accommodation
www.sheffield.ac.uk/accommodation

Where do the students come from?

State schools (non-grammar)	77.3%	First generation students	32.6%		
Grammar schools	11.2%	Low participation areas	10.3%		
Independent schools	11.5%	All ethnic minorities	22%		

Social inclusion ranking: 75

White working-class males	5%
Black achievement gap	-6.9%
Mature (over 21)	10.3%

Sheffield Hallam University

One of the country's largest universities, Sheffield Hallam is digging deep to make vast campus improvements for its student community – which includes about 25,000 undergraduates. Breaking new ground in the city centre campus, the university has three buildings under construction to the latest sustainability standards. Due for completion in 2024 and carbon zero ready, they will provide teaching and learning environments for the business school and the social sciences and humanities departments. A university green is also being added.

Part of a 20-year campus development framework, Hallam's city centre developments will have £220million invested over five years. The development follows the £27million Heart of the Campus teaching and learning building on Hallam's Collegiate campus. The £30million Charles Street Building houses education courses. Hands-on learning resources include the largest PlayStation teaching lab in the world, in partnership with Sony, and a 3D virtual radiography room for healthcare students to practice cancer treatment.

The campus upgrades should help to improve Hallam's rates of student satisfaction, which having suffered among the 30 biggest declines over the pandemic have dropped further again this year. In our analysis of the latest National Student Survey, the university places outside the top 100 for teaching quality and the wider experience. The declines have contributed to Hallam dropping 10 places to sit joint 82nd in our main league table this year.

The university has developed a "new way of delivering learning" it tells us, which includes: in-person on campus; remote online; learning by doing (in labs, studios, simulated environments and workshops) and through working in placements, internships and volunteering.

The campus developments chime with Hallam's mission to transform students' lives and give everyone the chance to reach their full potential. Among widening participation initiatives, 38% of applicants for September 2022 received a contextual offer. At the time of writing the scheme was under review, however, so this proportion may change.

Hallam succeeds in recruiting almost 12% – the largest proportion in England and Wales – of white working-class boys (the most underrepresented group), which contributes to a nine-place rise in the overall social inclusion index, bringing Hallam into the top 15.

There was more good news for the university when the 2021 Research Excellence Framework published its results this year – rating 72% of Hallam's biggest and most diverse submission to date as world-leading (4*) or internationally excellent (3*) and triggering an impressive 20-place rise in our research quality index. Sport; art and design;

City Campus
Howard Street
Sheffield S1 1WB
0114 225 5533
admissions@shu.ac.uk
www.hallamstudentsunion.com
www.shu.ac.uk
Open days: see website

Edinburgh
Belfast
SHEFFIELD
London
Cardiff

***The Times and The Sunday Times* Rankings**
Overall Ranking: =82 (last year: 72)

Teaching quality	72.3%	=104
Student experience	66.4%	120
Research quality	36%	69
Entry standards	116	100
Graduate prospects	75.1%	56
Good honours	77.6%	=62
Expected completion rate	85.5%	64
Student/staff ratio	17.7	89

and the built environment and planning produced some its best work.

Undergraduates are promised work experience and Hallam works with employers on its course design. With the latest figures showing three-quarters of graduates employed in high-skilled jobs or further study 15 months after finishing their degrees, Hallam is in the top half of UK universities for graduate prospects.

Hallam's employability initiatives helped earn a silver award in the government's Teaching Excellence Framework (TEF), of which the university's vice-chancellor was chairman. He was not involved in the decision. The TEF panel complimented the institution on an exemplary commitment to the region and support for students to be retained in the area. Almost half of undergraduates come from the Yorkshire and Humber region, and an even larger proportion stay and work in the area after graduation.

More than 2,000 Hallam students are enrolled on degree apprenticeships linked with about 600 employers. The institution is a leading provider of the earn-as-you-learn higher education route, offering 32 programmes in 11 study areas including policing, digital and technology, food and drink, management, and architecture and chartered planning. With the addition of seven more courses (including district nursing; dietetics; and medical ultrasound) this year and next, apprentice numbers should reach 3,000.

The first economics and finance students began courses in 2022, while from September 2023 Hallam will offer degrees in computing (smart technologies); computer science with artificial intelligence; and accounting and finance for sport industries. There will be no new English literature students joining from 2023 however, because the university made the controversial decision to drop the subject.

Applications to Hallam have declined steeply over the past decade, by more than 40% between 2011 and 2021. New student enrolments have decreased much less sharply over the same period, but after a 10% year-on-year dip reached their lowest in 2021.

Accommodation is guaranteed to first-years who apply by the August 1 deadline. Sports facilities at the Collegiate and City campuses include sports halls, and fitness suites while the City Athletics Stadium two miles from the City campus hosts an eight-lane track among its resources. The Sports Park at Bawtry Road (five miles away) has grass and synthetic pitches as well as an indoor cricket hall.

Tuition fees
- » Fees for UK students £9,250
- » Fees for International students 2023–24   £14,415–£15,860
  Foundation   £10,880, two terms; £14,370, three terms
- » For scholarship and bursary information see
  www.shu.ac.uk/study-here/fees-and-funding
- » Graduate salary £24,000

Student numbers

Undergraduates	22,146 (2,389)
Postgraduates	4,375 (4,358)
Applications/places	28,965/6,890
Applications per place	4.2:1
Overall offer rate	73.7%
International students – EU	1.3%
Non-EU	2.2%

Accommodation
University provided places: 5,000
Self-catered: £87–£162 per week
First-years guaranteed accommodation
www.shu.ac.uk/study-here/accommodation

Where do the students come from?

				Social inclusion ranking: 15	
State schools (non-grammar)	95.8%	First generation students	52.1%	White working-class males	11.9%
Grammar schools	1.9%	Low participation areas	24.4%	Black achievement gap	−25.3%
Independent schools	2.3%	All ethnic minorities	21.2%	Mature (over 21)	23.3%

SOAS, University of London

A small university of fewer than 6,000 students, SOAS has a global reputation for its focus on Asia, Africa and the Near and Middle East, and is seeking to showcase its appeal with the launch of a new website in June 2022.

Soaring success in the latest Research Excellence Framework (REF 2021) has given SOAS even more to boast about. Law, anthropology and music did especially well and, overall, 87% of the research submitted was ranked world-leading or internationally excellent, the top two categories. The REF 2021 outcomes have sent SOAS 10 places up our research quality index to rank 36th overall. The university is also second in the world for development studies in the 2022 QS World University Rankings, up from fifth in 2021.

The school moved into the five-storey north block of Senate House, the imposing Bloomsbury headquarters of the University of London, in its 2016 centenary year – consolidating facilities around Russell Square for the first time in many years.

Undergraduates can select from wide range of degree combinations across law, politics, economics, finance, business, management, the arts, humanities and languages – all with the specialist international focus for which SOAS is renowned. More than 40% of undergraduate programmes offer the opportunity to spend a year studying in another country. All students have the option to study a language alongside their degree programme, choosing from an unparalleled range of non-European languages available from beginner level.

The university gained a silver award in the Teaching Excellence Framework, upgraded from bronze after an appeal process. The panel praised a strong institutional emphasis on personalised learning and small-group teaching, as well as a comprehensive student engagement system and outreach initiatives to widen participation.

Outcomes of the latest National Student Survey (NSS), published in summer 2022, paint a less positive picture from the perspective of SOAS undergraduates. Having fared better than most in the pandemic-hit NSS of 2021, the university drops to 125th place (from =102) for student satisfaction with teaching quality. It has fallen from =101 to 127th for how students assess their wider experience.

Blended online and in-person learning is the prevalent model for 2022-23. "Students have a good mix and a varied experience, including plenty of time on campus, whilst also experiencing a timetable that is effective, efficient and designed to promote student success," the university says.

A third consecutive rise in the number of new students starting courses in 2021 brought enrolments to a new high, although

10 Thornhaugh Street
Russell Square
London WC1H 0XG
020 3510 6974
study@soas.ac.uk
http://soasunion.org
www.soas.ac.uk
Open days: see website

The Times and The Sunday Times **Rankings**

Overall Ranking: 37 (last year: 33)

Teaching quality	68.5%	125
Student experience	62.7%	127
Research quality	51.9%	36
Entry standards	145	=38
Graduate prospects	74.6%	=57
Good honours	84%	30
Expected completion rate	84.9%	=71
Student/staff ratio	14.6	=31

applications dipped a little for the third year running. Almost three in 10 (28.7%) first-years gained their places via Clearing in the same admissions round. A combined degree entitled *Africa and Black Diaspora* welcomed its first students in September 2022.

Drawing more than eight in 10 (81.7%) of students from ethnic minority backgrounds, SOAS has one of the most ethnically diverse undergraduate populations in the country, the highest percentage in London and behind only Bradford and Aston universities on this measure of social inclusion.

SOAS has pioneered moves to decolonise the curriculum and committed itself to challenging Eurocentrism. The university has developed a toolkit for making teaching more inclusive and redressing disadvantage through racism and colonialism. There has been a student working group on the subject since 2016, prompted in part by SOAS' colonial origins.

SOAS moves into the upper half of universities in the country for graduate prospects (=57) after strong results in the national Graduate Outcomes survey, which tracks graduates 15 months after finishing their degrees and records the proportion in highly skilled jobs or postgraduate study. The university fosters relationships with organisations from the public sector, charities, NGOs, law firms, consultancies and the cultural and creative industries – and counts

PwC, HM Treasury, Sotheby's and Linklaters among its industry partners. A paid internship programme, launched in 2022, is co-funded by SOAS, SMEs and charities.

The university offers a free, week-long bridging course to prepare applicants who are the first in their family to go to university, or are over 21, or from a low-participation neighbourhood. Those with household incomes below £25,000 receive a cash bursary of £4,500 over the duration of their degree.

Students have their own bar, social space and catering facilities. The former University of London Union, now a student centre, is close at hand. While SOAS does not own sports facilities, it is well placed for University of London and public amenities.

All new students are required to take part in Enough is Enough, a students' union initiative that aims to tackle potential gender-based violence on campus through consent training workshops, events and online campaigns. There are 1,002 residential places available, enough to guarantee a space for all first-years in 2021-22.

Tuition fees

» Fees for UK students   £9,250
» Fees for International students 2023–24   £10,175–£20,350
» For scholarship and bursary information see
www.soas.ac.uk/study/student-life/finance/tuition-fees
» Graduate salary   £25,000

Student numbers

Undergraduates	2,994	(65)
Postgraduates	1,514	(1,294)
Applications/places		5,300/1,395
Applications per place		3.8:1
Overall offer rate		89.1%
International students – EU		11.9%
Non-EU		18%

Accommodation

University provided places: 1,002
Catered costs: £166–£302 per week
Self-catered: £156–£290 per week
First-years guaranteed accommodation
www.soas.ac.uk/accommodation

Where do the students come from?

State schools (non-grammar)	86.1%	First generation students	47.2%	White working-class males	1.8%
Grammar schools	4.8%	Low participation areas	2%	Black achievement gap	-10.7%
Independent schools	9.1%	All ethnic minorities	81.7%	Mature (over 21)	13.7%

Social inclusion ranking: 64

Solent University

An immersive learning experience with specialist facilities that include Europe's largest maritime simulation centre awaits at Solent. Based at sites across the centre of Southampton, the university formed in 2005 via mergers between Southampton College of Art, the College of Technology and the College of Nautical Studies at Warsash.

Maritime education remains a special focus, and the university provides tuition for Merchant Navy senior officers, yacht certification, maritime safety management, leadership and security courses. Solent is unique in having its own fleet of 11 manned model ships, based at a training centre on Timsbury Lake. It offers the UK's only three-year officer cadetship training leading to a full honours degree approved by the UK Maritime and Coastguard Agency. Most cadets are sponsored by shipping companies such as Maersk, Carnival, Princess and Aramco. The university's superyacht academy is also renowned within the industry.

Elsewhere, courses are arranged under faculties of creative industries, architecture and engineering; sport, health and social sciences; and business, law and digital technologies. The university's £33million Spark building featured educational technology including lecture-capture facilities even before the pandemic hit.

Technological advances of late include free access for all students to the entire suite of Adobe creative software, while physical developments have added an attractive new quad with outdoor space and a replica law court. A new student services hub (located within the teaching and learning spaces) is planned for 2023. Allowing easy access to student-facing supports should further improve Solent's rates of student satisfaction, which took a big hit in during the pandemic but have risen to enter the top 40 for teaching quality (up 13 places) this year and the top 70 for the wider experience (up eight places).

The uplift in students' evaluation of teaching quality suggests that Solent's blended approach is being reasonably well received. As the university emerged from lockdown in September 2021 Solent adopted a new teaching model based on three pillars – of collaborative, guided and directed learning. Directed learning is Solent's new term for lectures, which happen mainly online.

Building industry connections into courses, Southampton's newly established Business Advisory Boards have placed senior leaders from organisations such as NatWest, Sunseeker and Pinterest at the heart of the university.

There is also a 2021-launched strategic partnership with Southampton FC ("Saints") that gives students real-world industry experience with Southampton FC. Football studies degree students receive more than 20 hours of professional development from the team's coaches.

East Park Terrace
Southampton SO14 0YN
023 8201 5066
admissions@solent.ac.uk
www.solentsu.co.uk
www.solent.ac.uk
Open days: see website

The Times and The Sunday Times Rankings
Overall Ranking: 114 (last year: =112)

Teaching quality	76.8%	=37
Student experience	71.7%	=67
Research quality	12.6%	128
Entry standards	112	=108
Graduate prospects	63.3%	123
Good honours	73.1%	98
Expected completion rate	77.8%	115
Student/staff ratio	17.5	=85

The university's portfolio of higher and degree apprenticeships encompasses 19 programmes, with about 650 student apprentices on courses at the last count. Options span subjects within business and administration; marketing; health and science; digital; construction; engineering and manufacturing; and transport and logistics. Courses in cybersecurity and advanced clinical practice are being offered from 2023, in line with Solent's plan to grow its earn-as-you-learn options.

The university's employment-boosting initiatives have yet to lift its ranking in our graduate prospects measure, however, where it places 123rd this year (down one place on last year), based on the latest figures showing 63.3% of graduates in high-skilled jobs or further study 15 months on from their degrees.

Solent was upgraded to silver in the Teaching Excellence Framework. Assessors were impressed by students' high levels of engagement and commitment to learning, and by the substantial investment in learning resources and successful integration of research and professional practice into the curriculum.

In the 2021 Research Excellence Framework (REF) 34% of the work submitted for assessment by Solent achieved the top ratings of world-leading or internationally excellent, moving Solent off the foot of our research quality index ranking to fourth from bottom. Two new research centres – the Centre for Maritime Sustainability and the Maritime Autonomy research centre – strengthen the university's commitment to building its research profile.

Among the eight indicators included in our social inclusion index, Solent excels in its recruitment of white working-class boys, which at 9.3% of entrants is among the top 10 proportions in England and Wales. A fifth of students are recruited from underrepresented areas (a top-15 measure) and more than four in 10 are aged over 21 when they enrol. Contextual offers are among the initiatives supporting the university's widening participation ambitions and are worth a 16-point or 32-point reduction on the standard UCAS tariff for entry.

The sports complex on the main campus is a recent addition and students have access to the Coalporters Rowing Club near campus and Spinnaker Sailing Club 18 miles away, among other local pursuits. Team Solent Sailing teams compete successfully in national competitions.

First-year students are guaranteed a residential room if they apply by July 1. Along with student-friendly pubs and clubs in the East Park area, Southampton offers sea air, beaches nearby and the New Forest.

Tuition fees

» Fees for UK students	£9,250
» Fees for International students 2023–24	£14,250
Foundation	£11,500
» For scholarship and bursary information see www.solent.ac.uk/finance/tuition-fees/	
» Graduate salary	£21,00

Student numbers

Undergraduates	9,562	(514)
Postgraduates	865	(400)
Applications/places		8,460/1,870
Applications per place		4.5:1
Overall offer rate		87.4%
International students – EU		15%
Non-EU		6.7%

Accommodation

University provided places: 1,200
Self-catered: £109–£156 per week
First-years guaranteed accommodation
www.solent.ac.uk/studying-at-solent/accommodation

Where do the students come from?

State schools (non-grammar)	96.2%	First generation students	48.1%	White working-class males	9.3%
Grammar schools	0.7%	Low participation areas	20.2%	Black achievement gap	-35.7%
Independent schools	3.1%	All ethnic minorities	17.3%	Mature (over 21)	44.2%

Social inclusion ranking: 42

University of South Wales

Hands-on teaching facilities at the University of South Wales (USW) mean that students starting in 2022-23 can make the most of an in-person, on-campus experience. Lecture-capture technology allows students some flexibility too, which supports the many who balance work and/or caring responsibilities with their studies. The approach meets the approval of students, as evidenced by student satisfaction with teaching quality USW is comfortably in the top half of universities nationally.

The wider undergraduate experience received less positive reviews than teaching quality in the latest National Student Survey, however, and USW loses 14 places in our analysis of this measure. USW – formed by a merger between Glamorgan and Newport universities – has two campuses in Pontypridd, Treforest and Glyntaff. The Pontypridd sites are the focus of developments for chiropractic students, who now have use of a new teaching and learning hub and will soon gain a new clinic. These join a £6million Learning Resource Centre, acute care simulation suites for nursing and midwifery students, upgraded laboratories and a law school.

USW's Cardiff campus in the city centre is home to its creative industries courses – which benefit from industry-standard equipment for advertising, television and film set design, and fashion – as well as dance studios, rehearsal spaces and photographic studios. Cardiff is also the base for Startup Stiwdio, an incubation space. Operations moved from the Caerleon campus outside Newport to the Newport City Campus in 2011, where courses include cybersecurity, education, and psychology.

USW's first aerospace engineering students began their courses in the 2022-23 term, as do those on new degrees in biomedical sciences; operating department practice; music producing; and an accelerated professional policing course. The new perfformio, theatre a'r cyfryngau degree (performance, theatre and the media) is taught entirely in Welsh.

An improved performance in the 2021 Research Excellence Framework, compared with the 2014 exercise, has triggered a nine-place rise for USW in our research quality ranking. Sport and exercise sciences; social work and social policy; music, drama, dance, performing arts, film and screen studies; and allied health subjects produced some of the university's best results. As with many universities in Wales, USW has not entered the Teaching Excellence Framework.

A Personal Academic Coaching scheme provides students with support through a series of conversations with a dedicated coach regarding their overall academic and professional progress. Such provision may improve completion rates at USW, which are among the bottom third nationally at present.

1 Lantwit Road
Pontypridd CF37 1DL
03455 76 77 78
admissions@southwales.ac.uk
www.southwales.ac.uk
www.uswsu.com
Open days: see website

The Times and The Sunday Times **Rankings**
Overall Ranking: 103 (last year: 99)

Teaching quality	75.8%	=54
Student experience	69.6%	=92
Research quality	27.5%	95
Entry standards	119	=86
Graduate prospects	66.5%	=108
Good honours	72.3%	105
Expected completion rate	81.7%	93
Student/staff ratio	16.1	=62

The university offers eight degree apprenticeship programmes in Wales: including cybersecurity; data science; and mechanical, manufacturing, electrical and electronic engineering. A police constable degree apprenticeship operates in England.

The proportion of mature students aged over-21 is approaching four in 10 and 95.9% of USW undergraduates went to non-selective state secondary schools, evidence of USW's effective outreach activities. It ranks =33 overall for social inclusion. Degrees in music producing, applied engineering, biomedical science, and sport and exercise science welcomed their first students this term. Applications declined for the seventh consecutive year in 2020, as have the number of students starting courses – though less sharply. Maintaining entry standards, South Wales still turns down about three in 10 applications.

Partnerships with the Welsh Rugby Union (WRU), Football Association of Wales Trust and BBC Wales, as well as close relationships with police forces across England and Wales, the Celtic Manor Resort and Health Education Improvement Wales are among tie-ins that boost experience and opportunities for USW students. In other initiatives, cybersecurity students engage in live projects with real companies while courses within USW's School of Engineering benefit from industrial advisory boards.

However, for graduate prospects USW falls outside the top 100 this year, to rank =108. Only two-thirds of students are employed in high-skilled work or further study 15 months on from their degree, the latest Graduate Outcomes survey found.

USW succeeds in recruiting the ninth highest proportion of students from deprived areas in England and Wales, and more than four in 10 are aged over 21 when they enrol on their degree. Contextual offers were introduced for 2022 entry, which should help widen participation further still.

Welsh-medium scholarships are available to students who study at least 40 credits of an eligible degree in Welsh.

The purpose-built USW Sport Park has a 3G pitch and 270-seat stand used by student teams as well as Pontypridd FC. The Sport Park includes specialist equipment for sports degree studies and a full-size 3G indoor football pitch, the only one in Wales and one of five in the UK. Laboratories at the Glyntaff campus provide a scientific background for sports degrees.

First-years are guaranteed a room in halls of residence. Surrounded by coast and countryside, all USW sites are either within striking distance of – or in – Cardiff, renowned as one of the UK's leading student cities.

Tuition fees

» Fees for UK students	£9,000
» Fees for International students 2023–24	£13,700–£15,500
» For scholarship and bursary information see www.southwales.ac.uk/study/fees-and-funding/	
» Graduate salary	£22,000

Student numbers

Undergraduates	13,890 (3,084)
Postgraduates	2,737 (3,440)
Applications/places	11,130/2,555
Applications per place	4.4:1
Overall offer rate	77.8%
International students – EU	3.7%
Non-EU	6.1%

Accommodation

University provided places: 1,372
Self-catered: £94–£180 per week
First-years guaranteed accommodation
www.southwales.ac.uk/student-life/accommodation

Where do the students come from?

State schools (non-grammar)	95.9%	First generation students	42.9%		
Grammar schools	1.3%	Low participation areas	22.6%		
Independent schools	2.7%	All ethnic minorities	10.4%		

Social inclusion ranking: =33

White working-class males	6.8%
Black achievement gap	-25.5%
Mature (over 21)	42.8%

University of Southampton

Applications to study at Southampton are rising (up 16% in 2022) as would-be undergraduates increasingly cotton on to its quality education. The research-intensive university, a founding member of the Russell Group, maintains its position in our elite top 20 this year, buoyed by high rates of student satisfaction with the wider experience and the eighth-best student-to-staff ratio in the UK – among other qualities.

At the main Highfield campus, two miles from Southampton city centre, the Centenary Building features teaching and learning facilities have been designed to enhance the student experience. Independent study spaces come with views across the campus and the city, seminar rooms are bookable and private study pods are plentiful.

Facilities for chemical engineering have benefited from a £5.3million upgrade, with specialist and design laboratories and an immersive virtual control room that simulates industrial facilities among resources. Research within chemistry has also benefited from a £1.1million upgrade to crystallography equipment, bringing a new goniometer and high-powered focusing optics.

The Avenue campus houses most humanities departments, and clinical medicine is based at Southampton General Hospital. Winchester School of Art and the National Oceanography Centre are among the university's other sites. Overseas, the university has a campus in Malaysia – originally dedicated to engineering, it also offers business courses.

Southampton is leading from the front on issues of student welfare, having made consent training mandatory for all students. Many other institutions offer advice to undergraduates but few have made such guidance a formal requirement. Active bystander training is also offered, while the *Welcome to Southampton* module supports academic transition for new students. An anti-spiking campaign run with local clubs included "stop tops" and drink testing kits.

The student-friendly initiatives are paying off. In our analysis of the latest National Student Survey outcomes Southampton is up eight places to rank joint 34th for students' assessment of the wider undergraduate experience. Conversely, it has lost ground for their evaluation of teaching quality but remains in the upper half of UK universities on this measure.

Southampton holds a silver award in the Teaching Excellence Framework (TEF), whose assessors highlighted the support it provides all new undergraduates, as well as a strategic commitment to enhancing teaching quality. Investment in resources, excellent student progression rates and effective employability initiatives also came in for praise by the TEF panel.

The first neuroscience students began their courses this term, as did those on the

University Road
Highfield
Southampton SO17 1BJ
023 8059 9699
enquiry@southampton.ac.uk
www.susu.org
www.southampton.ac.uk
Open days: see website

SOUTHAMPTON

The Times and The Sunday Times **Rankings**
Overall Ranking: 16 (last year: 16)

Teaching quality	75.4%	=62
Student experience	74.1%	=34
Research quality	60.1%	14
Entry standards	152	27
Graduate prospects	80.7%	31
Good honours	87.2%	18
Expected completion rate	93.2%	22
Student/staff ratio	12.6	8

chemistry and medicinal sciences course. From 2023, degrees in population sciences and a suite of biomedical engineering and medical engineering degrees will be offered.

The university ranks 78th in the 2023 QS World University rankings and secured another strong performance in the 2021 Research Excellence Framework – an assessment conducted every six to seven years to evaluate the quality of research across UK universities. Engineering; allied health subjects; and computer science produced some of Southampton's best results. Overall, about 90% of its work was rated world-leading or internationally excellent. Southampton sits 14th in our research quality index, a seven-place drop in the face of rising research standards elsewhere.

The National Infrastructure Laboratory houses the latest teaching and research facilities for geomechanics, heavy structures, solid mechanics and infrastructure engineering. The laboratory is located at the £140million Boldrewood Innovation Campus, which is dedicated to marine engineering and engineering sciences, and was developed jointly with Lloyd's Register.

Most Southampton degrees offer a year in employment and undergraduates are encouraged to spend time studying abroad. The university does well in our measure of graduate prospects, with four in five graduates in high-skilled jobs or postgraduate study 15 months on from finishing their degrees.

Southampton is only just inside the top 100 in our social inclusion ranking, although this represents a more diverse intake than all but five other Russell Group universities. Just under a quarter of students are from ethnic minority backgrounds and about seven in 10 went to non-selective state schools. Bursaries of £1,000 or £2,000 per academic year are based on UK students' household incomes of less than £30,000. A number of merit-based scholarships are offered, too.

A 10-year investment in Southampton's estate is launching with more than £40million committed to new and improved sports facilities. Existing facilities include a 25m pool. Flying Formula is the university's Sigma 38 yacht, available for taster sessions or bareboat charter.

The university guarantees accommodation for all new entrants who apply by the deadline. Its proximity to sandy beaches and the New Forest adds to Southampton's kerb appeal, while the local nightlife has a lively reputation.

Tuition fees

» Fees for UK students	£9,250
» Fees for International students 2023–24	£20,340–£28,902
Medicine	£26,352–£51,648
» For scholarship and bursary information see	
www.southampton.ac.uk/courses/fees/undergraduate.page	
» Graduate salary	£25,714

Student numbers

Undergraduates	14,291	(36)
Postgraduates	5,839	(1,231)
Applications/places	37,580/5,315	
Applications per place	7.1:1	
Overall offer rate	63.9%	
International students – EU	8.3%	
Non-EU	10.3%	

Accommodation

University provided places: 6,428
Catered costs: £159.25–£214.41 per week
Self-catered: £121.03–£192.01 per week
First-years guaranteed accommodation
www.southampton.ac.uk/student-life/accommodation

Where do the students come from?

State schools (non-grammar)	72.1%	First generation students	33.1%	White working-class males	4.5%
Grammar schools	14.8%	Low participation areas	8.1%	Black achievement gap	-17.3%
independent schools	13%	All ethnic minorities	24.2%	Mature (over 21)	8.3%

Social inclusion ranking: 96

Staffordshire University

In a busy year of developments, the Catalyst building has been added to Staffordshire's main Stoke-on-Trent campus. The facility provides students with apprenticeship and skills training across four storeys of digitally enabled space – a boon for Staffordshire, which delivers more than 20 higher and degree apprenticeships with more than 200 employers, including the NHS, BT, Merlin Entertainments and Bentley Motors. The university expects to have 3,100 student apprentices by September 2023. A nursery and forest school has joined the facilities at Stoke, too.

At the Stafford campus there has been investment in simulation facilities at the new Centre for Health Innovation, used by students taking nursing and allied health degrees. Further south, the university has doubled the size of its Here East London campus, near Queen Elizabeth Olympic Park, with a £3.5million extension catering for a growing course portfolio that encompasses gaming and e-sports, computer science, and cybersecurity.

The upgrades and expansions are in keeping with Staffordshire's ambition "to become the UK's best modern university". However, a 30-place decline in our main academic league table suggests room for improvement in some areas.

The high rates of student satisfaction enjoyed at Staffordshire before the pandemic, when the university ranked 15th in the country for teaching quality in the National Student Survey (NSS), have yet to return – thus contributing to its league table tumble. The university falls 28 places for how students view the quality of their teaching (51st) and drops 38 places for satisfaction with the student experience, now ranking =90.

The prevalent teaching model for the present academic year is in-person across all locations (other than for distance learning degrees). The university's modern facilities, such as The Catalyst, the London campus, and the Centre for Health Innovation, allow for more flexible and hybrid teaching across modules and courses.

The university has strong links with employers such as the NHS, police forces, Airbus, Amazon and Bet365. However, Staffordshire has fallen outside the top 100 of our graduate places this year. A 26-place drop to =106 reflecting only two-thirds of students being in high-skilled jobs or further study 15 months on from their degrees.

But when awarding Staffordshire the highest rating (gold) in the government's Teaching Excellence Framework (TEF), after an upgrade in 2019, assessors said students from all backgrounds achieve outstanding outcomes and complimented the university on high rates of progression to high-skilled

College Road
University Quarter
Stoke-on-Trent ST4 2DE
01782 294 000
enquiries@staffs.ac.uk
www.staffsunion.com
www.staffs.ac.uk
Open days: see website

The Times and The Sunday Times Rankings
Overall Ranking: 106 (last year: 76)

Teaching quality	76%	51
Student experience	69.9%	=90
Research quality	30%	=85
Entry standards	118	=89
Graduate prospects	66.6%	=106
Good honours	74.8%	88
Expected completion rate	78.2%	114
Student/staff ratio	17.7	=89

employment or further study. The TEF panel also praised its strong commitment to supporting students' personal and professional development, and noted the effectiveness of initiatives that help students into university and support them during their studies.

Staffordshire's efforts to promote social mobility are demonstrating more success. White working-class boys (the most underrepresented group in UK higher education) represent more than one in 10 of the student intake. Only two universities in England and Wales have more. Almost a quarter of students come from deprived areas and six in ten are the first in their family to go to university.

Nevertheless, completion rates remain a sticking point, with 14.4% of students projected to drop out of their degrees, almost a percentage point above the benchmark 13.5% based on the academic and social mix.

Sixty-eight per cent of Staffordshire's submission to the 2021 Research Excellence Framework was rated world-leading or internationally excellent – a big leap from the 37% that achieved these top standards in the previous 2014 REF. While the university increased the number of staff submitted to the 2021 exercise, it still entered just 109 academics. Against bigger improvements elsewhere it loses 30 places in our research quality index this year, to rank =85. Art and design produced the best results.

A new partnership with Wilkes Academy of Performing Arts in Swindon contributed to an 11% rise in applications in the 2021 admissions cycle. Since then the university has ended another partnership (with Liverpool Media Academy) and noted an 8% decline in applications by the end of March in the 2022 recruitment cycle. A growing curriculum gained six new degrees this term, among them honours degrees in working with children, young people and families; security and intelligence; forensic and criminological psychology; and a foundation degree in rehabilitation and manual therapies.

The Hanley area is known for clubbing and nearby Newcastle-under-Lyme for its pubs. The Sir Stanley Matthews sports centre on the Stoke campus is close to university accommodation and the campus itself is close to the city and transport links. Accommodation is guaranteed for students at the Stoke and Stafford campuses who meet the end of August deadline and other eligibility criteria, and who accept their offer of a room within three days.

Tuition fees

- » Fees for UK students $£9,250$
- » Fees for International students 2023–24 $£14,500–£19,000$
- » For scholarship and bursary information see www.staffs.ac.uk/courses/undergraduate/fees-and-funding
- » Graduate salary $£23,000$

Student numbers

Undergraduates	9,732 (5,535)
Postgraduates	904 (1,675)
Applications/places	13,390/3,730
Applications per place	3.6:1
Overall offer rate	79.2%
International students – EU	1.1%
Non-EU	1.3%

Accommodation

University provided places: 1,000
Self-catered: £95–£127 per week
First-years guaranteed accommodation
www.staffs.ac.uk/student-life/accommodation

Where do the students come from?

State schools (non-grammar)	96.3%	First generation students	60.9%		
Grammar schools	1.8%	Low participation areas	24.6%		
Independent schools	1.9%	All ethnic minorities	16.5%		

Social inclusion ranking: 9

White working-class males	10.8%
Black achievement gap	-32.8%
Mature (over 21)	39.1%

University of Stirling

The university at which Sir Andy Murray and his brother Jamie began to build their tennis careers has created a new £20million sports complex. Stirling's facilities now include fitness studios, a gym, a three-court sports hall and an indoor cycle studio plus strength and conditioning areas. The university already hosts the National Swimming Academy and National Tennis Centre. The new resources are intended to support its elite athletes as well as students more widely, staff and the community. The curriculum has also gained sporting breadth, with the first students of new degrees in sport development and coaching, and in sport psychology starting courses this term.

The new facilities befit a former winner of our Sports University of the Year award, a trophy lifted by Stirling in 2020 in recognition of its world-class facilities and excellence across sports performance, research and education.

Stirling's 330-acre campus, centred on a loch beneath the Ochil hills, is arguably the UK's most beautiful. The 1960s Pathfoot Building, an architectural masterpiece by John Richards, sits among modern buildings that include the £23million Campus Central. A three-storey extension to the refurbished atrium at the heart of the campus, the development has increased study and social spaces. It also houses the student services hub, the Macrobert Art Centre's box office and the Institute for Advanced Studies.

Such investment in the student experience should help to boost scores for Stirling in future National Student Surveys, after its 2022 outcomes that have triggered declines in our NSS-derived measures for teaching quality and the wider experience. But improved completion rates at Stirling and the 16th-highest entry standards in the UK have helped propel the university three places up into the top 40 of our main academic ranking.

Stirling's significant investment to innovate on teaching practice and learning infrastructure helped see it through the pandemic with less of a downturn in student satisfaction than felt at most other universities. The university has new software, a library of digital resources and is providing a "digital-ready and flexible learning experience", it tells us, in which in-person teaching delivery is supported by aspects of online learning.

The first institution in the UK to pioneer an academic year of two 15-week semesters, Stirling places ninth in our Scottish social inclusion ranking. It works with local schools in low-participation areas and has a joint degree programme with Forth Valley College, whose students can enter Stirling's second or third year in programmes such as adult or mental health nursing.

Stirling
FK9 4LA
01786 467 044
admissions@stir.ac.uk
www.stirlingstudentsunion.com
www.stir.ac.uk
Open days: see website

The Times and The Sunday Times Rankings
Overall Ranking: =38 (last year: 41)

Teaching quality	76.2%	=48
Student experience	72.8%	=50
Research quality	43.8%	50
Entry standards	169	16
Graduate prospects	73.7%	=62
Good honours	76.9%	72
Expected completion rate	85.9%	62
Student/staff ratio	18.6	104

A contextual approach to admissions assesses UCAS applications in conjunction with personal and educational circumstances, resulting in Stirling dropping a grade in offers to eligible students. Of the 2,000-plus entrants in 2021, 100 receivedd a contextual offer, a proportion which may change as sixth-form exams have returned to pre-pandemic methods of assessment. A widening-participation officer is on hand to offer support during the admissions process.

Stirling offers one graduate apprenticeship, in data science, and expects student apprentice numbers to reach around 80 by September 2023. Applications were up 7% in 2021.

Stirling's proud research record was upheld in the new 2021 Research Excellence Framework (REF) assessment, in which almost 80% of the work submitted was judged to be world-leading or internationally excellent (up from almost three-quarters in the previous 2014 REF). Against even bigger uplifts in research quality across UK universities the university slips eight places to rank 50th in our research index this year, however. Some of the best results were in agriculture, veterinary and food science; geography and environmental science; and social work and social policy.

Stirling's Institute of Aquaculture was awarded the Queen's Anniversary Prize in 2019 for its pioneering work in the world's fastest-growing food production sector in a bid to tackle global hunger. The university is now targeting its research on the government's "grand challenges" such as Scotland's aim to reach net zero greenhouse gas emissions by 2045.

Stirling has a global network for students, staff and alumni to share advice and seek mentorship, while the University of Stirling Innovation Park is a key hub for start-ups and established businesses, research collaboration and potential jobs. With almost three-quarters of graduates in high-skilled jobs or further study 15 months after their degrees, Stirling ranks in the upper half of UK universities in our graduate prospects measure.

As well as the new sports complex, Scotland's designated university for sporting excellence also has facilities including fitness studios, a gym, three-court sports hall, indoor cycling studio, strength and conditioning areas and a high-performance suite, which opened in 2020.

There are also artificial pitches for hockey, football, rugby, Gaelic football, lacrosse and American football and an all-weather athletics track. The National Tennis Centre includes six indoor, two outdoor clay and two synthetic courts.

Tuition fees

- » Fees for Scottish students   £0–£1,820
  RUK fees   £9,250 (capped at £27,750 for 4-year courses)
- » Fees for International students 2023–24   £16,400–£20,300
- » For scholarship and bursary information see
  www.stir.ac.uk/study/fees-funding/
- » Graduate salary   £24,000

Student numbers		
Undergraduates	8,731	(373)
Postgraduates	2,972	(2,333)
Applications/places	16,790/2,425	
Applications per place	6.9:1	
Overall offer rate	57.9%	
International students – EU	12.4%	
Non-EU	6.2%	

Accommodation
University provided places: 2,894
Self-catered: £86–£183 per week
First-years guaranteed accommodation
www.stir.ac.uk/student-life/accommodation

Where do the students come from?				**Social inclusion ranking (Scotland): 9**	
State schools (non-grammar)	90.3%	First generation students	38.5%	White working-class males	n/a
Grammar schools	5%	Low participation areas	13.4%	Black achievement gap	n/a
Independent schools	4.7%	All ethnic minorities	5.9%	Mature (over 21)	30.4%

University of Strathclyde

Scotland's third-largest university is ploughing £1bn into campus developments over 10 years. Strathclyde students gained access to a £60million Learning and Teaching building in 2021, which houses student-facing services and extra study spaces at the university's John Anderson campus in Glasgow city centre.

The university has also begun its transformation of the site of the former Rottenrow maternity hospital and surrounding streets into a Heart of the Campus learning and teaching environment, which will feature electric bike charging points. Facilities for biomedical engineering have also been upgraded at the £15.5million Wolfson Building.

The advances should go down well with students. At Strathclyde, rates of student satisfaction held up better than most in the pandemic-affected National Student Survey of 2021. A year on, the latest results show some ground has been lost. However, for a research-intensive university such as Strathclyde, its top-25 rank for satisfaction with the wider undergraduate experience is especially commendable. The university is joint 41st for satisfaction with teaching quality. For the 2022-23 academic year teaching is on campus.

Strathclyde has committed to net zero carbon emissions by 2040 (or sooner). Its targets include a 70% reduction target by 2025 and 80% by 2030. The university is creating "climate neutral districts" – operating on 100% renewable heat, power, transport, climate resilience, and health and wellbeing solutions – aligned with city and regional partners. The first of these projects, the new National Manufacturing Institute Scotland building, opens near Glasgow airport this year.

More developments are on the way. Thanks to a £50million donation from Dr Charles Huang, an alumnus and entrepreneur, Strathclyde is creating a new building at its Technology and Innovation Zone as well as funding entrepreneurship awards and a scholarship programme.

The Hunter Centre for Entrepreneurship, a unit endowed by the Scottish businessman and philanthropist Sir Tom Hunter, is one of Europe's leading centres for the study of entrepreneurship, innovation and strategy, and offers degrees in business enterprise.

With 83.8% of graduates in highly skilled jobs or postgraduate study within 15 months of finishing their degree, the university confirms its strong record on graduate prospects, in the top 20. Students benefit from Strathclyde's well-established links with business and industry, which include partnerships with organisations such as Rolls-Royce, GSK (formerly GlaxoSmithKline) and the Fraunhofer Centre for Applied Photonics.

The university delivers Scotland's graduate apprenticeships as well as degree apprenticeships validated in England. Its growing portfolio

McCance Building
16 Richmond Street
Glasgow G1 1XQ
0141 548 4400
study-here@strath.ac.uk
www.strathunion.com
www.strath.ac.uk
Open days: see website

The Times and The Sunday Times Rankings
Overall Ranking: 18 (last year: 17)

Teaching quality	76.7%	=41
Student experience	75.1%	=25
Research quality	53.1%	30
Entry standards	202	4
Graduate prospects	83.8%	=19
Good honours	84.6%	26
Expected completion rate	91.1%	=35
Student/staff ratio	19.1	=106

includes seven options such as senior leadership; civil engineering; and information technology. More are planned – under both the English and Scottish programmes – which should bring the number of trainees to more than 900 by September 2023.

Like most Scottish universities, Strathclyde did not enter the Teaching Excellence Framework, but the university performed strongly in the latest Research Excellence Framework (REF 2021). Almost 90% of its research was rated world-leading or internationally excellent, the top categories. The submission by Strathclyde's School of Government and Public Policy achieved the university's best results, while work within allied health subjects; and architecture, built environment and planning also did particularly well. But against rising standards elsewhere Strathclyde drops nine places to rank 30th in our new research quality index.

Given its high entry standards (in the UK top five) and the mix of courses offered, Strathclyde does well to occupy eighth position in our Scottish social inclusion index (up two places year-on-year in 2022). With almost 14% of students from ethnic minority backgrounds, Strathclyde is more ethnically diverse than all but three other Scottish universities. The university became the first in Scotland to sign a commitment to support access to higher education for the Gypsy, Traveller, Roma, Showman and Boater communities.

Strathclyde is in demand. Nearly 4,500 new students enrolled in 2021, the largest number of entrants to date, and applications crested 29,200 – also a record. Contextual offers (lower than the standard requirement) are made to eligible applicants from under-represented groups. The Strathclyde Accommodation Bursary, provides £1,000 towards rent in halls of residence for students from England, Wales, the Republic of Ireland and Northern Ireland.

The recently opened £31million sport centre has a six-lane, 25m swimming pool; two sports halls; squash courts; a café and specialist health facilities. Outdoor pitches are at the Stepps Playing Fields, five miles from the university's Cathedral Street headquarters.

Accommodation is guaranteed in one of Strathclyde's 1,355 rooms as long as applications are received before the August closing date. Named the world's friendliest city by the Time Out Index 2022, Glasgow combines legendary nightlife, a student-centric vibe and plenty of culture.

Tuition fees

» Fees for Scottish students £0–£1,820
  RUK fees £9,250 (capped at £27,750 for 4-year courses)
» Fees for International students 2023–24 £16,750–£24,950
» For scholarship and bursary information see
  www.strath.ac.uk/studywithus/feesfunding/
» Graduate salary £27,000

Student numbers

Undergraduates	14,325	(1,431)
Postgraduates	5,983	(2,712)
Applications/places		29,265/4,460
Applications per place		6.6:1
Overall offer rate		44.9%
International students – EU		3.7%
Non-EU		6.8%

Accommodation

University provided places: 1,355
Self-catered: £104–£141 per week
First-years guaranteed accommodation
www.strath.ac.uk/studywithus/accommodation/

Where do the students come from?

State schools (non-grammar)	90.4%	First generation students	37.4%	White working-class males	n/a
Grammar schools	2.2%	Low participation areas	21.6%	Black achievement gap	-18.4%
Independent schools	7.4%	All ethnic minorities	13.9%	Mature (over 21)	18.7%

Social inclusion ranking (Scotland): 8

University of Suffolk

Results of the latest Graduate Outcomes survey showed that 81% of Suffolk's graduates were in highly skilled work or further study 15 months after finishing their degrees – a top-30 performance nationally for one of the UK's youngest universities. Founded in 2007 as University Campus Suffolk and a satellite of the University of East Anglia (UEA) and Essex University, Suffolk began awarding its own degrees in 2015.

Helping to pave the way from an undergraduate degree to a career is Suffolk's Knowledge Exchange Academy. Students can try their hand at real-life project briefs and are guided towards internships, placements and graduate positions. The university has links with industry partners including BT, which collaborated with the university on its DigiTech Centre at BT's Adastral Park, which opened in 2021.

At the Ipswich waterfront campus, 10 minutes from the town centre, a new Health and Wellbeing building has opened, featuring clinical simulation facilities. Students also have access to a recently renovated library. The Hold, Suffolk's 2020-opened £20million heritage research centre, houses the region's historic treasures alongside learning spaces.

Suffolk's Integrated Care Academy is its latest venture. An alliance between the university, NHS Integrated Care System and Suffolk county council, it aims to provide co-ordinated and collaborative care to local communities, reducing health inequalities.

Student numbers are growing. In the 2021 admissions round new student enrolments increased by 7%, year on year. The university has far surpassed its 2020 goal of between 6,000 to 7,000 students and now reached more than 12,000. Just over a quarter of the 2021-22 intake entered their degrees via Clearing. An expanding curriculum launched seven new courses this term, among them physiotherapy; crime, justice and society; and a foundation degree in biomedical science.

Two more foundation degrees are due to start in 2023: in web technologies; and network development and cybersecurity. Both will be delivered at University of Suffolk East Coast College, which is based in the coastal towns of Great Yarmouth and Lowestoft.

Suffolk succeeds at recruiting around two in 10 students from areas most under-represented in higher education and the proportion who are the first in their immediate family to go to university (57.8%) is the 11th highest nationally. Such diversity in the student community often translates to student retention issues, as it does at Suffolk, where almost three in 10 students are projected to drop out, resulting in a bottom 10 ranking for Suffolk on completion rates.

The university is launching a suite of international scholarships for undergraduates enrolling in 2023-24, which will range in value

Waterfront Building
Neptune Quay
Ipswich IP4 1QJ
01473 338 348
admissions@uos.ac.uk
www.uosunion.org
www.uos.ac.uk
Open days: see website

IPSWICH

Edinburgh
Belfast
Cardiff
London

The Times and The Sunday Times Rankings
Overall Ranking: =115 (last year: 105)

Teaching quality	74.4%	=79
Student experience	66.2%	123
Research quality	21.8%	108
Entry standards	113	=106
Graduate prospects	81%	30
Good honours	70.3%	116
Expected completion rate	65.6%	129
Student/staff ratio	15%	=39

from £1,0000 to £4,000 per year of study. About three in 10 UK students will qualify for Suffolk's means-tested bursary of £500 per year of study. A digital technology support fund is available to successful applicants, worth £300 towards IT equipment to support blended learning.

The university made its first submission to the Research Excellence Framework in 2021. Although it only submitted work in social work and social policy, 68% was rated world-leading or internationally excellent (the top two categories), and Suffolk ranks above 23 universities in our research quality index in its first year of entry.

However, the university was awarded only bronze (the lowest level) in the Teaching Excellence Framework. Assessors said it was "substantially" below its benchmarks for student satisfaction and graduate employment, although they acknowledged the contribution of employers to course design and found a "developing approach to the creation of research and practice-based communities of staff enabling students to benefit by exposure to scholarship, research and professional practice".

Graduate employment rates are now buoyant, but student satisfaction has tumbled this year. In our analysis of the latest National Student Survey, Suffolk ranks 123rd for the wider undergraduate experience (down 40 places) and sits in joint 79th for teaching quality (a fall of 31 places).

A hybrid teaching model of in-person and online content is the prevalent mode of delivery for this academic year. Degree programmes at Suffolk are taught via a "block" learning model. Each block includes assessment completed in Brightspace (a virtual learning environment) where appropriate. The university tells us that students find this approach helps them to manage their time and focus on topics individually.

Eight degree apprenticeships are offered in digital and technology; nursing; and social work. There were 384 student apprentices enrolled at the last count.

There are plenty of sports facilities near the campus, although Suffolk does not have its own. Lots of students live at home and Suffolk's 756 student rooms are usually enough to go around.

The modern Waterfront development around Ipswich's marina is a popular hub of bars and restaurants. For exploring the region, students could take inspiration from local singer-songwriter (and honorary Suffolk graduate) Ed Sheeran, whose song *Castle on the Hill* about Framlingham Castle describes some of the county's simple pleasures.

Tuition fees

» Fees for UK student	£9,250
Foundation courses	£8,220
» Fees for International students 2023–24	£13,992–£16,497
» For scholarship and bursary information see www.uos.ac.uk/content/undergraduate-tuition-fees	
» Graduate salary	£24,500

Student numbers

Undergraduates	11,406	(637)
Postgraduates	109	(472)
Applications/places		3,925/3,265
Applications per place		1.2:1
Overall offer rate		72.7%
International students – EU		10.8%
Non-EU		0.8%

Accommodation
Available places: 756
Self-catered: £95–£189 per week
www.uos.ac.uk/accommodation

Where do the students come from?

State schools (non-grammar)	97%	First generation students	57.8%		
Grammar schools	2%	Low participation areas	20.1%		
Independent schools	1%	All ethnic minorities	18.6%		

Social inclusion ranking: 11

White working-class males	1.7%
Black achievement gap	-27.5%
Mature (over 21)	86.6%

University of Sunderland

Medical and allied healthcare students at Sunderland may hone their skills in the university's new Anatomy Centre, which was opened in March 2022 by Professor Neil Mortensen, president of the Royal College of Surgeons of England. Its facilities support cadaveric anatomy (considered the gold standard for anatomy education as digital resources cannot reproduce the variability and complexity of the human body). The norm for medical students, such provision is less common for allied healthcare students and characterises Sunderland's strong track record in healthcare provision.

The Anatomy Centre joins Sunderland's other simulation facilities that include a £1.4million midwifery suite with a full maternity ward. The Living Lab reflects care settings from mock hospital wards and pharmacy dispensaries to an immersive simulation suite, while Helen McArdle House facilities include child and mental health settings.

A former winner of our University of the Year for Social Inclusion title, Sunderland is one of higher education's leading lights in offering university opportunities to those that might not be given them elsewhere. The university moves three places up our social inclusion index to rank sixth and draws almost three in 10 students from deprived areas. Around six in 10 students are the first in their immediate family to go to university and nearly seven in 10 are aged over-21 when they enrol.

The university's inclusive outlook extends to the School of Medicine, which is teamed with Keele's. One of five recently opened medical schools around the country, it is helping to address regional shortages of doctors and an imbalance of provision. There is a contextual offer for applicants from low-participation postcodes in the northeast and Cumbria, and a medicine summer school for Year 12 students. This guarantees participants who meet widening participation criteria a Multiple Mini Interview (MMI), subject to meeting the GCSE, A-level and UCAT requirements.

Across all subjects, the university works with more than 40 schools in the northeast, targeting middle-achieving children who have the capability to consider higher education. Successful completion of the First Choice progression scheme is worth 16 UCAS tariff points, should they then apply to an eligible course at Sunderland.

There are two campuses in Sunderland, one in the city centre and the other, the Sir Tom Cowie site, on the banks of the River Wear, built around a seventh-century abbey described as one of Britain's first universities and incorporating the National Glass Centre. A campus in Canary Wharf, London, offers business, healthcare, tourism and hospitality courses and first opened in 2012. Numbers

Edinburgh Building
City Campus
Chester Road
Sunderland SR1 3SD
0191 515 3000
student.helpline
@sunderland.ac.uk
www.sunderlandsu.co.uk
www.sunderland.ac.uk
Open days: see website

The Times and The Sunday Times Rankings
Overall Ranking: =98 (last year: 77)

Teaching quality	78.5%	=20
Student experience	73.5%	=40
Research quality	30.5%	81
Entry standards	120	=81
Graduate prospects	66.1%	112
Good honours	66.7%	=125
Expected completion rate	78.3%	=111
Student/staff ratio	15.9	=57

swelled in 2020 when the London site introduced four new degree programmes. Overseas, Sunderland has a Hong Kong campus, which deliver business and tourism courses.

Sunderland rose in our previous edition's academic ranking, owing to outstanding results in the National Student Survey (NSS) at a time when most other institutions lost considerable ground in areas such as learning opportunities and course organisation and management. Its rankings have dropped back this year in our two NSS-derived measures: teaching quality (down eight places) and student satisfaction (down 23 places). In spite of the losses, Sunderland remains in the top-20 for teaching quality and the top-40 for student experience, although the declines have contributed to its fall in our overall league table.

The university has a silver rating in the Teaching Excellence Framework. The panel praised the exposure of students to professional practice through engagement with industrial and community partners. Among an extensive list of business partners regionally and nationally are GSK, Delphi Powertrain Systems, Tata Steel and five northeast NHS Trusts.

The university offers 15 degree apprenticeships with more than 900 on programmes that include two options within teaching – primary or secondary; four in nursing – adult, learning disabilities, mental health, or district nursing; and social work.

When the most recent Graduate Outcomes survey took its census just over two-thirds of Sunderland graduates were in high-skilled jobs or further study 15 months after finishing their degrees, a proportion that ranks the university 112th in our graduate prospects measure.

The university performs better in our research quality indicator where it has gained two places to rank 81st this year. More than 70% of the work it submitted to the 2021 Research Excellence Framework was rated as either world-leading or internationally excellent (the top standards). Some of the best results were produced by the arts and creative subjects; engineering; health sciences; social work and English.

Sunderland's leisure facilities span the northeast's only 50m swimming pool and dry ski slope, as well as Europe's biggest climbing wall, and a theatre that shows West End productions. And while Sunderland is fiercely proud of its identity, a short Metro or bus journey brings students to neighbouring Newcastle's arguably brighter lights.

Tuition fees

» Fees for UK students	£9,250
Foundation courses	£8,200
» Fees for International students 2023–24	£13,000–£13,500
» For scholarship and bursary information see www.sunderland.ac.uk/about/your-finances/	
» Graduate salary	£24,000

Student numbers

Undergraduates	12,405 (1,396)
Postgraduates	3,139 (1,552)
Applications/places	9,085/3,680
Applications per place	2.5:1
Overall offer rate	69.4%
International students – EU	6.2%
Non-EU	10%

Accommodation

University provided places: 1,055
Self-catered: £78–£154 per week
www.sunderland.ac.uk/about/accommodation/

Where do the students come from?

State schools (non-grammar)	96.1%	First generation students	61.9%	White working-class males	7.5%
Grammar schools	1.5%	Low participation areas	29.9%	Black achievement gap	-26.3%
Independent schools	2.4%	All ethnic minorities	16.7%	Mature (over 21)	68.6%

Social inclusion ranking: 6

University of Surrey

Shortlisted for our 2022 University of the Year award, Surrey has been charging up our league table recently. The university ranked 39th only two years ago and has risen to 22nd this year.

Positive feedback from students is among the factors behind its ascent: Surrey was one of only two UK universities that avoided a decline in student satisfaction throughout the pandemic. In our latest guide it has improved its ranking on both measures derived from the National Student Survey. For satisfaction with the wider undergraduate experience, Surrey enters the top five (up four places) and for teaching quality it is in the top 20 (up 17 places).

Much-improved research quality, as demonstrated by excellent results in the latest Research Excellence Framework (REF 2021), has also contributed to Surrey's 10-place rise up our main academic table. Surrey submitted work from more than 660 researchers, 41% of which was assessed as world-leading, the top standard.

From beginnings in London in 1891 as Battersea Polytechnic Institute, the university was founded in its present form in Guildford in 1966. Surrey's two campuses, Stag Hill and Manor Park, just over a mile away, are 10 minutes' walk from the centre of Guildford. The £36million

Surrey Sports Park is at Manor Park. Among modern resources are Surrey's £45million School of Veterinary Medicine and the £14million Kate Granger building, which opened in 2020 at Surrey Research Park, and houses the School of Health Sciences' clinical simulation suites for training nurses, midwives, physicians' associates and paramedics. Specialist resources at the newly upgraded £5million psychology facility include virtual and augmented reality suites, and soundproof neuropsychology laboratories.

From this term, the Department of Music and Media has fresh equipment to enhance students' learning – including audio and computer labs, a TV studio and a Dolby Atmos surround sound recording studio – as well as improved sound recording equipment.

A food innovation unit has been added to complement Surrey's expertise in food science, nutrition and dietetics. Physics facilities have had a £2.7million upgrade, with refurbished laboratories, and the School of Mechanical Engineering's Design Centre has been modernised. For sport and exercise science, the human and physiology laboratories at Stag Hill have been enhanced. A moot court is now available for law students, replicating a courtroom and providing virtual-technology experience.

Teaching has returned to in-person delivery this year but Surrey is keeping the aspects of provision that worked best during

---

Senate House
Guildford GU2 7XH
01483 682 222
admissions@surrey.ac.uk
www.ussu.co.uk
www.surrey.ac.uk
Open days: see website

The Times and The Sunday Times **Rankings**

Overall Ranking: 22 (last year: 32)

Teaching quality	78.6%	=18
Student experience	79.2%	=5
Research quality	53.3%	29
Entry standards	138	46
Graduate prospects	84.4%	16
Good honours	81.1%	=43
Expected completion rate	90.4%	=38
Student/staff ratio	16	=59

the pandemic, such as lecture recordings and adapting spaces to suit social learning.

Rated gold in the Teaching Excellence Framework, Surrey gained a glowing reference from assessors for "innovative and personalised provision", "high levels of teaching excellence" and an effective approach to the development of professional skills and employability".

Professional training placements of up to 12 months are offered on most degree programmes. Taken in between the second and third years in the UK or overseas, the placements mean that many students spend four years at university.

Surrey has built a network of more than 2,300 national and international businesses where students can learn on the job, including Microsoft, Unilever, and Sky. The connections are paying off for its graduates: 84.4% were in highly skilled jobs or postgraduate study 15 months after completing their degree, the latest Graduate Outcomes survey found. Surrey ranks 16th in our analysis of graduate prospects.

The first cohort of professional international hotel management students began courses this term at Surrey, which ranks 14th in the world for hospitality and leisure management in the QS World Rankings 2022. New for 2023 are degrees in environment and sustainability, and in criminology with forensic investigation. Applications are being taken for a new graduate entry medicine programme (Bachelor of Medicine, Bachelor of Surgery), with a start date of February 2024.

Surrey has moved 10 places further up our social inclusion ranking this year to sit 81st. It is among the country's more ethnically diverse institutions, with more than a third of students from black, Asian or minority ethnic backgrounds. Surrey's black attainment gap is among the 21 narrowest nationally. About four in five students went to non-selective state schools (87th).

Under the Team Surrey banner there are more than 45 sports clubs for all abilities. Students can earn rewards for keeping active through the SurreyMoves+ app. Extensive facilities are up to standard for elite athletes and teams including Harlequins rugby union, Surrey Storm netball and Guildford City swimming club.

Surrounded by green countryside, commuter-belt Guildford is known for being a safe and unintimidating town. First-years are guaranteed a place in halls of residence – as long as they apply by the deadline – and a network of wardens and peer supporters provide support around academic and non-academic issues. Warden talks are compulsory for all new starters, covering alcohol, drug taking and consent.

Tuition fees

» Fees for UK students	£9,250
» Fees for International students 2023–24	£19,100–£35,500
Veterinary Medicine	£36,900
» For scholarship and bursary information see	
www.surrey.ac.uk/fees-and-funding	
» Graduate salary	£26,400

Student numbers

Undergraduates	12,423	(448)
Postgraduates	2,820	(875)
Applications/places		29,125/3,300
Applications per place		8.8:1
Overall offer rate		64.5%
International students – EU		9.1%
Non-EU		11.4%

Accommodation

University provided places: 6,000
Self-catered: £73–£244 per week
First-years guaranteed accommodation
www.surrey.ac.uk/accommodation

Where do the students come from?

State schools (non-grammar)	79.9%	First generation students	40.8%	White working-class males	4%
Grammar schools	10.6%	Low participation areas	7.9%	Black achievement gap	-11%
Independent schools	9.5%	All ethnic minorities	37.1%	Mature (over 21)	16.9%

Social inclusion ranking: 81

University of Sussex

Sussex has opened a £28million Student Centre, providing a welcoming focus for undergraduate life on the university's leafy campus in Falmer, near Brighton.

The development features flexible spaces for workshops and collaboration, confidential rooms for student support services – and from September 2022, a coffee tuk-tuk, international grocer and optician.

There were excellent results for Sussex in the latest Research Excellence Framework (REF 2021), which have triggered a five-place rise for the university in our research quality index. Psychology, sociology, education, English, history, art and design, and communication, cultural and media studies produced some of the best work. Overall, 89% of Sussex's work was assessed as world-leading or internationally excellent (the top categories). In the 2022 QS World University Rankings by subject, Sussex tops development studies for the sixth consecutive year.

Sussex celebrated its 60th anniversary in 2021. Occupying acres of rolling parkland on the edge of the South Downs National Park, it features listed 1960s architecture by Sir Basil Spence. The university has transformed its 1970s East Slope accommodation into terraced townhouses, featuring common rooms and communal laundry rooms as well as bookable study spaces and secure cycle parking.

Sussex must be counting on the Student Centre and improved accommodation to mark a sea change in student satisfaction. In our analysis of the latest National Student Survey, Sussex is once again 110th for satisfaction with teaching quality – quite a tumble since it appeared in our top 20 six years ago. The university falls seven places to =92 for satisfaction with the wider undergraduate experience. The faltering scores continue to hold the university back in our main academic rankings.

Teaching is predominantly in-person for 2022-23, although Sussex continues to make use of online platforms and activities to some extent.

Sussex gained silver in the Teaching Excellence Framework, winning praise for its "outstanding" employment strategy, designed to help students develop transferable employment skills. Mentoring, internships and graduate opportunities are available and the university has more than 10,000 registered employers of all sizes and sectors on its careers database.

There is also support for student start-ups, freelance careers and social enterprises via the Sussex Entrepreneurship programme. However, with 70.6% of graduates in high-skilled jobs or postgraduate study 15 months after finishing their degrees, Sussex drops three places to rank 80th for graduate prospects this year, following a 25-place fall the year before.

Sussex House
Falmer
Brighton BN1 9RH
01273 876 787
ug.enquiries@sussex.ac.uk
www.sussexstudent.com
www.sussex.ac.uk
Open days: see website

The Times and The Sunday Times Rankings
Overall Ranking: 50 (last year: 47)

Teaching quality	71.6%	110
Student experience	69.6%	=92
Research quality	52.9%	=32
Entry standards	136	=48
Graduate prospects	70.6%	80
Good honours	78.4%	59
Expected completion rate	92.3%	=30
Student/staff ratio	17.3	=83

The university does better at keeping students on track with their courses. Winner of our University of the Year for Student Retention award in the previous edition of our guide, Sussex continues to have a dropout rate far lower than the benchmark figure based on the social and academic background of the intake.

A successful joint medical school is shared with the neighbouring University of Brighton, and students split their time between the Royal Sussex County Hospital and the two universities' Falmer campuses.

Six degrees are due to begin in 2023 – in automotive engineering; applied social science; computing for digital media and games; geography, sustainable development and climate change; creative writing; and English and creative writing. Applications were up by 19% in 2021, returning them to their usual levels following a dip the year before. Entry standards remain in the top 50.

To address inequality, Sussex has welcomed its first pro-vice-chancellor for culture, equality and inclusion and has set targets to halve the gender pay gap, hold a Race Equality Charter and become a Disability Confident Leader by 2025. Sussex became a University of Sanctuary in 2020 in recognition of its welcoming culture and has pledged to further develop its support for forced migrants.

Sussex's new sustainability strategy aims to make it one of the most sustainable universities in the world. Its energy is drawn entirely from renewable sources. The university has risen to seventh place in the UK and 37th globally in the 2022 Times Higher Education's World Impact rankings, which recognise universities' achievements on delivering the United National Sustainability Development Goals (SDGs).

Sussex is 87th in our social inclusion index. With 9.6% of the intake registered disabled, the university is 31st on that measure. The Sussex Bursary, which awards £1,000 in the first year to students from low-income households and £500 in subsequent years, helps about 25% to 30% of the intake. A range of academic scholarships are available for those studying music, business, sport or the environment.

On-campus sports facilities can be used via memberships or on a pay-and-play basis. Sussex has 5,055 residential spaces for students, almost all on campus – enough to guarantee a room to all first-years who apply by the deadline. A few minutes away by public transport, Brighton's nightlife, diversity and seaside stretch are hard to beat.

Tuition fees

» Fees for UK students	£9,250
» Fees for International students 2023–24	£19,050–£23,175
Medicine	£39,158
» For scholarship and bursary information see www.sussex.ac.uk/study/fees-funding	
» Graduate salary	£24,000

Student numbers

Undergraduates	14,869	(1)
Postgraduates	3,483	(1,062)
Applications/places	21,185/5,020	
Applications per place	4.2:1	
Overall offer rate	91.8%	
International students – EU	8.2%	
Non-EU	18.4%	

Accommodation

University provided places: 5,055
Self-catered: £116–£177 per week
First-years guaranteed accommodation
www.sussex.ac.uk/study/accommodation

Where do the students come from?

State schools (non-grammar)	81.6%	First generation students	38.4%	
Grammar schools	7.4%	Low participation areas	8.9%	
Independent schools	11%	All ethnic minorities	28.2%	

Social inclusion ranking: 87

White working-class males	4.5%
Black achievement gap	–17.4%
Mature (over 21)	12.6%

Swansea University

A five-mile curve of sandy beach separates Swansea's original Singleton Park campus from its £450million, 65-acre Bay Campus, which doubled the size of the university when it opened in 2015. King George V laid the university's foundation stone at Singleton Park more than a century ago: his great-grandson, King Charles III, helped to develop the Bay Campus via the Prince's Foundation for Building Community.

Along the way, developments at the original parkland campus include the Hillary Rodham Clinton School of Law, named after the former US secretary of state and presidential candidate who received an honorary doctorate from Swansea in 2017. Students can learn career skills in the new facility's courtroom and law clinic.

A gold rating in the government's Teaching Excellence Framework adds to the appeal of Swansea's seaside location. Assessors praised the university's clear employability strategy and strong staff-student partnerships.

The university has had glowing reviews over the years in the National Student Survey (NSS). The latest results from summer 2022, however, reveal a less contented student community than usual as Swansea's undergraduates grapple with the ongoing impact of the pandemic on university life.

The university has dropped out of the top 30 for our NSS-derived measures for teaching quality (down 56 places) and the wider student experience (down 51 places. In-person teaching only is the prevalent model for the coming academic year – which should help to return student satisfaction to its former high levels.

With 78.1% of graduates in high-skilled jobs or postgraduate study 15 months after finishing their degree, the university ranks only just outside the UK top 40 on our graduate prospects measure. It has more than 500 key industry partnerships across 53 countries with organisations such as Rolls-Royce, Tata Steel, Ospreys Rugby and Pfizer. Many of Swansea's business partners have research bases at the Bay Campus.

Career-boosting support includes the Swansea Employability Academy, which provides paid internships and co-ordinates programmes for career development. At the last count more than 600 organisations were advertising 43,000 jobs.

Swansea has shifted its academic structure in the past year from seven colleges to three faculties: Medicine, Health and Life Science; Humanities and Social Sciences; and Science and Engineering. A broadening curriculum gains degrees in biomedical engineering; criminology and sociology; leadership for global challenges; and computer science and artificial intelligence. A BSc in environmental science and the climate emergency is another

Singleton Park
Swansea SA2 8PP
01792 295 111
admissions@swansea.ac.uk
www.swansea-union.co.uk
www.swansea.ac.uk
Open days: see website

The Times and *The Sunday Times* **Rankings**		
Overall Ranking: =42 (last year: 39)		
Teaching quality	74%	=84
Student experience	70.4%	=79
Research quality	47.5%	46
Entry standards	131	53
Graduate prospects	78.1	=41
Good honours	80.3%	47
Expected completion rate	89.9%	=41
Student/staff ratio	16.2	=65

recent addition and, like many of Swansea's degrees, it can be taken as a four-year course with a year spent in industry or abroad.

Applications boomed in 2021, rising by about 16% to surpass 20,000 for the first time. New student enrolments went up much less steeply but also hit a record, while about one in five of 2021's new entrants gained their places via Clearing.

A research profile in the upper third of universities enhances Swansea's academic reputation. In the latest Research Excellence Framework (REF 2021), 86% of the university's work was rated world-leading or internationally excellent (the top categories). Medicine and life science; allied health subjects; mathematics; and geography produced some of the best results. The university's research income has increased by 160% since the previous national research assessment in 2014, up from £148million to £286million.

Research facilities are being developed all the time. A Centre for Integrative Semiconductor Materials opened in 2021. It follows the £35million Institute for Innovative Materials, Processing and Numerical Technologies (known as Impact).

The £20million Sports Village beside the Singleton campus has an athletics track, grass and all-weather pitches, squash and tennis courts, plus an indoor athletics training centre and 80-station gym. There are 50-metre and 25-metre pools at the Wales National Pool next door.

Bay Campus is gaining a World Rugby and Fifa-compliant 3G surface. At Singleton Park, the No 1 hockey pitch has been resurfaced with the same international-standard material that was used at the Tokyo Olympics.

The university's grass and 3G pitches at Fairfield, five miles away, were built in partnership with Swansea City Football Club. As well as the Ospreys, the university also has links with the Scarlets professional rugby club.

Swansea offers a lively social scene at wallet-friendly prices. Mumbles seaside resort nearby is also popular for nights out. Further west, the Gower Peninsula has some of the UK's finest beaches including Rhossili and Three Cliffs Bay.

The university has more than 4,300 residential spaces – enough to guarantee accommodation to all first-years who apply by June 30. Bay Campus has direct access to the beach and houses about 2,000 students in on-site halls of residence – some of them designated for Welsh speakers.

Tuition fees

»	Fees for UK students	£9,000
	Foundation courses	£7,500
»	Fees for International students 2023–24	£16,800–£21,700
	Medicine	£ 41,750
»	For scholarship and bursary information see	
	www.swansea.ac.uk/undergraduate/fees-and-funding	
»	Graduate salary	£24,210

Student numbers

Undergraduates	15,997	(694)
Postgraduates	3,378	(1,394)
Applications/places	20,675/5,355	
Applications per place	3.9:1	
Overall offer rate	74.4%	
International students – EU	4.6%	
Non-EU	8.8%	

Accommodation

University provided places: 4,326
Catered costs: £164–£170 per week
Self-catered: £139–£167 per week
First-years guaranteed accommodation
www.swansea.ac.uk/accommodation/

Where do the students come from?

State schools (non-grammar)	92.1%	First generation students	37%	White working-class males	7%
Grammar schools	0.9%	Low participation areas	12.4%	Black achievement gap	-15.7%
Independent schools	7%	All ethnic minorities	18.8%	Mature (over 21)	20.5%

Social inclusion ranking: 77

University of Teesside

A 32-place leap up our league table returns Teesside resoundingly into the top 90 in 2022, where it last appeared two years ago. The university has improved on all but one of the measures included in our academic ranking – only the proportion of students attaining "good honours" of 2.1s and firsts is a non-mover. This achievement is crowned by some of the biggest improvements in student satisfaction seen in 2022. In our analysis of the latest National Student Survey, Teesside rises 79 places for teaching quality into a top-25 position. For the wider undergraduate experience, the Middlesbrough-based university ranks 38th this year – on the strength of an 80-place rise.

Evidently, the challenges faced by Teesside students during the pandemic that triggered huge falls in student satisfaction last year have been consigned to history, as healthcare students have returned to work placements and the university's hands-on learning facilities across academic departments have reopened. All teaching is on campus this year. The university also launched Your Voice Matters, a feedback scheme for students to suggest improvements.

Almost two-thirds of Teesside's research submitted to the 2021 Research Excellence Framework (REF 2021) was classed as world-leading (4*) or internationally excellent (3*).

The proportion of four-star world-leading work almost doubled compared with the university's REF 2014 submission. The upswell in research excellence has boosted Teesside 16 places up our research index.

Teesside's campus masterplan, which has already turned £275million investment into new developments, continues. A £13.1million Net Zero Industry Innovation Centre is under way – thus delivering on the carbon neutral ambitions of the northeast region and UK more widely, while creating "hundreds" (the university tells us) of clean energy jobs.

A £15million Digital Life Building is next in Teesside's sights, with plans already in place that will enhance facilities for the School of Computing, Engineering and Digital Technologies. The university is also spending £30million on installing the latest in science laboratories.

The university's Future Facing Learning model was in place pre-pandemic and helped to earn Teesside the status of Adobe Creative Campus (the first to be designated in Europe) giving students and staff access to Adobe Creative Cloud apps. It has since been recognised as an Apple Distinguished School. Addressing digital poverty during the pandemic, the university increased the range of equipment available to students through its Advance Scheme to include mobile data.

Job-specific and vocational degree programmes help to keep Teesside's graduate employment rates within the upper third of

Middlesbrough
TS1 3BX
01642 218 121
enquiries@tees.ac.uk
www.tees-su.org.uk
www.tees.ac.uk
Open days: see website

The Times and The Sunday Times **Rankings**
Overall Ranking: 86 (last year: 118)

Teaching quality	78.3%	23
Student experience	73.7%	38
Research quality	28%	94
Entry standards	117	=93
Graduate prospects	78.1%	=41
Good honours	73%	99
Expected completion rate	77.1%	119
Student/staff ratio	17.1	=79

UK universities. Teesside was offering 32 higher and degree apprenticeships, at the last count, with more than 1,750 student apprentices enrolled on programmes in fields including engineering, forensic science and midwifery. Ten more options are joining the portfolio of courses over the coming two years. Broadening the curriculum further, a School of Law is being introduced by the university.

Our previous edition's University of the Year for Social Inclusion, in honour of the outstanding role it plays in making higher education an option for teenagers in a region with the lowest participation rate in England, Teesside continues to succeed in our social inclusion index, placing third overall and with the highest proportion of students (31.1%) drawn from deprived areas. The university also succeeds in recruiting the sixth-highest proportion (10%) of white working-class boys – the most underrepresented group in higher education and its numbers from non-selective state schools (99%) are the highest in the country.

A high dropout rate is often the price to pay for such diversity, but Teesside's students are strongly supported in their studies from the outset, so the dropout rate is almost on track with the expected level.

Foundation years are offered as a route into university and levelling up is assisted by the Teesside University Advance scheme, which provides all students beginning a full-time undergraduate degree with a new iPad and separate keyboard, and up to £300 of credits to buy learning resources.

A strong culture of partnership with students was acclaimed by the Teaching Excellence Framework, which awarded Teesside silver. Our analysis of the latest Graduate Outcomes figures positions the university on the cusp of the top 40 in the UK for its proportion of students in high-skilled jobs or further study 15 months after completing their course. Teesside has a programme of more than 200 internships each year.

Sports facilities are available with the Olympia sports complex on campus and the Saltersgill Pavilion two miles away. The university is also a stakeholder in the River Tees Watersports Centre.

The £21million Cornell Quarter for student residences has opened its doors, housing 300 students in the 2021-22 academic year and increasing the university's accommodation stock by nearly a third to about 1,300 places – an important step towards broadening Teesside's appeal beyond the local region it serves so well.

Tuition fees

» Fees for UK students		£9,250
Foundation courses		£6,150
» Fees for International students 2023–24		£9,750–£14,000
» For scholarship and bursary information see www.tees.ac.uk/sections/fulltime/fees.cfm		
» Graduate salary		£24,100

Student numbers

Undergraduates	10,143	(5,364)
Postgraduates	3,823	(1,946)
Applications/places		12,215/3,460
Applications per place		3.5:1
Overall offer rate		73.8%
International students – EU		1%
Non-EU		4.3%

Accommodation

University provided places: 1,300
Self-catered: £65–£125 per week
www.tees.ac.uk/sections/accommodation

Where do the students come from?

State schools (non-grammar)	99%	First generation students	57.3%		
Grammar schools	0.2%	Low participation areas	31.1%		
Independent schools	0.8%	All ethnic minorities	14.7%		

Social inclusion ranking: 3

White working-class males	10%
Black achievement gap	-14.6%
Mature (over 21)	47.9%

Ulster University

Ulster is on the up and up in our league table, having outdone last year's best-ever performance by ranking higher again in our guide's latest edition and breaking into the UK top 40. From September 2022, students have had access to the full breadth of facilities at Ulster's expanded campus in Belfast's Cathedral Quarter.

The 75,000 sq m development, which has been built to last more than 300 years, began with a phased opening in September 2021 that completed 12 months on. The project resulted in the closure of most undergraduate provision at the Jordanstown site seven miles outside the city, where a multimillion pound extension to the existing High Performance Sport facility is planned.

Designed to be a "campus community within a building", the Belfast site has space for more than 15,500 staff and students (equivalent to the population of Armagh) within its teaching, learning, research and operational facilities, all digitally smart and socially connected. A student-run restaurant and training kitchens feature among the latest openings at the Belfast campus, which cost nearly £400million and is one of the biggest university capital investments in Europe.

Ulster welcomed its first graduate-entry medicine students in 2021 to the Magee campus in Londonderry. Run in partnership with St George's, University of London, the four-year MBBS programme is open to graduates from science and non-science backgrounds and is intended to fulfil a shortfall of doctors in Northern Ireland. Specialist facilities for the new medical school have been added. They join provision for other health-related courses at Magee, including a nursing and paramedic skills suite. The School of Health Science has relocated its undergraduate programmes to Magee from Jordanstown – bringing in 800 students.

Ulster was shortlisted for our University of the Year award last year, on the strength especially of its improved rates of student satisfaction, which held up better than most under the pandemic's challenging conditions. In our analysis of the latest National Student Survey, published in summer 2022, Ulster has entered the top-25 for teaching quality (up four places) and retained a top 25 position for the wider experience, too, even after losing four places on this measure.

Helping to drive these high rates of student satisfaction is Ulster's history of blended learning for more than 20 years. While an in-person teaching model is the prevalent method, the curriculum is continuing to be informed by relevant and engaging digital content.

More than three-quarters of Ulster graduates were in high-skilled work or further study 15 months after finishing their degrees, according to the Graduate Outcomes survey,

Cromore Road
Coleraine BT52 18A
028 9036 6565
study@ulster.ac.uk
http://uusu.org
www.ulster.ac.uk
Open days: see website

The Times and The Sunday Times Rankings
Overall Ranking: =38 (last year: 44)

Teaching quality	78.2%	=24
Student experience	75.7%	23
Research quality	47.8%	45
Entry standards	128	=57
Graduate prospects	75.6%	53
Good honours	80.6%	45
Expected completion rate	88.2%	52
Student/staff ratio	20.3	115

which positions the university comfortably in the upper half of UK universities.

Ulster's degree programmes often feature a work-based learning component. More than 2,000 students annually undertake a professional practice placement or a placement year.

Thirteen degree apprenticeship programmes are offered within areas such as business technology; computing systems; and accounting and finance. The university expects to have about 600 student apprentices enrolled by September 2023.

Building on Northern Ireland's emergence as a leading film and television centre, Ulster opened a £6.5million media centre in Coleraine on the Atlantic coast five years ago. It has a BBC television studio at its heart, with a multimedia newsroom and editing suites. Courses in the environment, hospitality and communication are also based at the Coleraine campus.

Eighty-seven per cent of Ulster's research submitted to the 2021 Research Excellence Framework was judged to be either world-leading or internationally excellent, with some of the best results in allied health subjects. Connected by the themes of social renewal, sustainability, healthy communities, and creativity and culture, 97% of the university's research was assessed as having "outstanding" or "very considerable impacts" in terms of its reach and significance.

Almost all the undergraduates are from state schools, but the university does not feature in our social inclusion ranking because the education system in Northern Ireland is radically different from the rest of the UK, with selective grammar schools making up a significant proportion of state secondary schools.

The High Performance Sports Centre, which houses the Sports Institute of Northern Ireland, has cameras installed in the sports hall and three outdoor pitches, enabling performance analysis and live-streamed matches. Jordanstown's outdoor and indoor sprint tracks, sports science and sports medicine facilities remain available to students. The Coleraine and Magee campuses also have sports facilities, and the Belfast site is opening a new gym and studio.

A place in one of the university's 2,445 rooms in university accommodation is guaranteed for all first-year students who apply by the August 14 deadline. Social scenes vary by campus location, but rumour has it that smaller Coleraine can keep pace with the nightlife of Derry and Belfast.

Tuition fees

» Fees for Northern Irish students £4,630
  RUK fees £9,250
» Fees for International students 2023–24 £15,840–£19,620
  Medicine £37,000, plus from 2023 an obligatory clinical placement levy of £10,000
» For scholarship and bursary information see www.ulster.ac.uk/student/fees-and-funding
» Graduate salary £23,000

Student numbers

Undergraduates	16,077	(7,878)
Postgraduates	4,595	(4,495)
Applications/places	30,175/6,315	
Applications per place	4.8:1	
Overall offer rate	78%	
International students – EU	3.2%	
Non-EU	22.3%	

Accommodation

University provided places: 2,445
Self-catered: £88–£134 per week
First-years guaranteed accommodation
www.ulster.ac.uk/accommodation

Where do the students come from?

State schools (non-grammar)	60.6%	First generation students	48.2%	White working class males	n/a
Grammar schools	39.4%	Low participation areas	12.8%	Black achievement gap	n/a
Independent schools	0%	All ethnic minorities	2.3%	Mature (over 21)	23.8%

Social inclusion ranking: n/a

University College London

University College London (UCL) opens its new campus on Queen Elizabeth Park in Stratford, east London, in 2022-23 – the biggest expansion in the history of the university, founded in 1826. UCL East has ambitions to match its size, underpinned by the aim "to find solutions to the biggest challenges facing people and the planet".

The campus will provide extra teaching, learning and research space as part of East Bank, the education and cultural legacy of the London 2012 Olympics, alongside partners the BBC, V&A, Sadler's Wells and UAL London College of Fashion.

From September 2022, students have had access to UCL East's One Pool Street building, a multi-use facility with a centre for Robotics and Autonomous Systems among the academic provision, as well as space for the School of Creative and Cultural Industries and a "living lab" for investigating biodiversity loss and climate change. UCL's Global Disability Innovation Hub is also moving to One Pool Street.

The campus's Marshgate building is set to open in 2023. Predominantly for academic purposes, it will also include student accommodation and some shops and community areas.

All degrees based at UCL East allow for collaboration across disciplines. The university will launch seven degrees in 2023, including heritage; creative arts and humanities; population health sciences with study abroad; robotics and artificial intelligence; and science and engineering for social change.

UCL has recorded a remarkably consistent set of results in the measures included in our academic rankings, staying steady year-on-year in seventh place. The university has also maintained fifth position in our new research quality rating based on the latest Research Excellence Framework (REF 2021). Ninety-three per cent of an outstanding submission was graded 4* (world-leading) or 3* (internationally excellent), the top two categories. Law; medicine; area studies; and social sciences were among UCL's highest-scoring subject areas.

With 30 Nobel laureates among its staff, researchers and graduates, UCL's immense strength in research also stimulates undergraduate life. Every student gets the opportunity to engage in research. Its strength in research contributes to the university's position in eighth place for the second consecutive year in the QS World University rankings.

Graduate prospects are once again in the top 10 (ninth). The latest Graduate Outcomes survey shows that 86.4% of the most recent UCL graduates found highly skilled work or returned to postgraduate study within 15 months.

Our analysis of the latest National Student Survey, published in summer 2022, shows a big shift in how students feel about the wider

Gower Street
London WC1E 6BT
020 8059 0939
undergraduate-admissions
@ucl.ac.uk
http://studentsunionucl.org
www.ucl.ac.uk
Open days: see website

The Times and The Sunday Times Rankings
Overall Ranking: 7 (last year: 7)

Teaching quality	73.8%	88
Student experience	73.8%	37
Research quality	66.8%	5
Entry standards	178	=11
Graduate prospects	86.4%	9
Good honours	91.4%	8
Expected completion rate	94.8%	12
Student/staff ratio	11.1	2

undergraduate experience: UCL climbs an impressive 25 places into the top 40 on this measure. Only two years ago UCL was =99 for satisfaction with the wider experience. The university has improved two places to 88th for satisfaction with teaching quality.

The university headquarters are in Bloomsbury, central London, and UCL is comfortably the biggest of the University of London colleges. Its medical school, with several associated teaching hospitals, is among the largest in Europe. UCL was a founding partner in the Francis Crick Institute (named after one of its Nobel laureates), which undertakes leading research in health and disease.

The demand for places reached new heights in the 2021 admissions cycle, when more than 68,000 students (up 16% year-on-year) applied for about 8,100 places (down 11% on the previous admissions round – which was a bumper one affected by the Covid-19 pandemic). Applications were up by another 11% by the end of March 2022, compared with the same point the year before.

While entry is highly competitive, the university does operate a contextual admissions scheme, Access UCL. In September 2021, about 13% of new undergraduates received a contextual offer, a proportion UCL expects to rise to 20% for the 2023 intake. Investment of £13.5million in bursaries and activities to support students from diverse backgrounds also helps to widen participation.

UCL achieves the lowest black attainment gap, the latest data shows, the best result in England and Wales. It does less well on other measures of social inclusion, drawing just over half of students from selective state or independent schools, for example (51.7%, ranking 112th on this metric).

Close to the West End, UCL also has its own theatre and recreational facilities. The college owns or endorses more than 7,000 residential places and guarantees accommodation for those who apply by the end of May. Indoor sports and fitness facilities are close at hand, but the main outdoor pitches are a (free) coach ride away in Hertfordshire.

Student advisers help first-years to settle in. The new campus, within easy reach of Hackney Wick, opens up the fashion-forward East End enclaves to UCL students, while literary the Bloomsbury site is in the heart of London — named by QS as the Best Student City globally in 2018, 2019, 2022 and 2023.

Tuition fees

» Fees for UK students	£9,250
» Fees for International students 2023–24	£24,000–£35,100
Medicine	£47,000
» For scholarship and bursary information see www.ucl.ac.uk/students/fees-and-funding	
» Graduate salary	£30,450

Student numbers

Undergraduates	21,702	(72)
Postgraduates	17,911	(6,028)
Applications/places	68,085/8,140	
Applications per place	8.4:1	
Overall offer rate	42.8%	
International students – EU	15.5%	
Non-EU	38.5%	

Accommodation

University provided places: 7,252
Catered costs: £193–£284 per week
Self-catered: £131–£397 per week
First years guaranteed accommodation
www.ucl.ac.uk/accommodation

Where do the students come from?

State schools (non-grammar)	51.7%	First generation students	27.4%	
Grammar schools	15.9%	Low participation areas	4.3%	
Independent schools	32.4%	All ethnic minorities	58.2%	

Social inclusion ranking: 98

White working-class males	1.6%
Black achievement gap	-2.1%
Mature (over 21)	6.5%

University of Wales, Trinity St David

The university once known as St David's College, Lampeter celebrated its bicentenary in August. The original Lampeter institution is the third-oldest university in England and Wales after Cambridge and Oxford – with an original royal charter dating from 1822. Two hundred years and a series of mergers on, today's University of South Wales, Trinity St David (UWTSD) celebrated its history by laying a foundation stone to mark the beginning of higher education in Wales.

Created in its present form by the 2010 merger of Trinity University College Carmarthen with University of Wales Lampeter, the multicampus university is based in Carmarthen, Lampeter, Swansea and Cardiff after a subsequent absorption of Swansea Metropolitan University in 2013. A campus in London opened in 2012, where courses in computing, business management, accounting, and health and social care are offered. In Birmingham, UWTSD's courses focus on workplace skills.

The university does well to feature in the top 30 for student satisfaction with teaching quality, although this represents a 15-place decline year-on-year that is among the factors that have caused the university to fall outside our league table's top 100 this year.

UWTSD offers both in-person and distance learning degrees. It was one of six Welsh universities to enter the Teaching Excellence Framework (TEF) in 2017. An initial bronze rating that year was upgraded to silver in 2019, with the panel praising "optimal" contact time, leading to outstanding personalised provision. The panel also approved of UWTSD's strong sense of regional and civic mission.

While Lampeter is the home of humanities courses, the Carmarthen site (established in 1848 to train teachers) offers programmes in the creative and performing arts, as well as a growing portfolio within the School of Sport, Health and Outdoor Education. A mile from the campus, the university has a refurbished centre for outdoor education on the Wales Coast Path at Cynefin, which offers direct access on to the River Towy.

The original Swansea campus began as a college of art, but its automotive engineering courses – especially those focused on motorsport – have become its best-known. Automotive engineering students work as part of a race team involved in UK motorsport events. The university has good links with Aston Martin, Jaguar Land Rover and McLaren Automotive.

The Construction Wales Innovation Centre is another feature of the Swansea campus. Home to construction course undergraduates, it provides laser measurement and surveying equipment for hands-on learning.

New at Swansea will be the Innovation Matrix, an addition to the SA1 Swansea

---

Carmarthen Campus
College Road
Carmarthen SA31 3EP
0300 500 5054
admissions@uwtsd.ac.uk
www.tsdsu.co.uk
www.uwtsd.ac.uk
Open days: see website

The Times and The Sunday Times **Rankings**

Overall Ranking: 104 (last year: =83)

Teaching quality	77.8%	=28
Student experience	71.6%	70
Research quality	23.8%	103
Entry standards	136	=48
Graduate prospects	62.6%	124
Good honours	76.5%	=75
Expected completion rate	77.7%	116
Student/staff ratio	21.1	117

Waterfront Innovation Quarter which is due to be completed in time for the start of the 2023 academic year. The low-carbon building is designed to provide a platform for UWTSD's collaboration with businesses and entrepreneurs to boost Wales' digital economy.

New degrees are broadening the curriculum, in subjects including: digital media production; cruise ship management; and human resource management. After four years of declining admissions numbers the university had noted an increase in applications of about 15% in 2022 at the end of May, compared with the same point in the cycle the year before.

UWTSD had more than 1,200 degree apprentices on 16 programmes, at last count, across fields that include engineering, policing and ordnance, munitions and explosives. The university expects 1,400 degree apprentices by September 2023.

The university's graduate prospects remain rooted to the lower reaches of our ranking, however, with UWTSD among the bottom 10 universities, with 62.6% of graduates in high-skilled jobs or postgraduate study 15 months on from their degrees. This is in spite of opportunities to gain professional qualifications, work placements and internships with partner organisations such as Jaguar Land Rover, South Wales Police, H&M and Keir.

There was better news for the university when the 2021 Research Excellence Framework published its results this year. An improved performance has prompted a 13-place rise in our research quality index, where UWTSD now sits only just outside the top 100. Art and design; education; Celtic languages and literature; theology; and psychology produced some of the best results.

Having broken into the top 10 of our social inclusion ranking last year, UWTSD drops to 14th in England and Wales this year. Almost all (97.8%) of its students attended a non-selective state school (the sixth-highest proportion). Nearly three-quarters are aged over-21 – only four universities have more mature students.

Sports facilities are available at the Carmarthen, Lampeter and Swansea campuses. A 40ft climbing wall at Carmarthen is a good place to practice before students scale the nearby crags of Pembrokeshire – or leap off them, coasteering-style – into the Irish Sea.

Accommodation is split between Carmarthen (288 spaces), Lampeter (260 spaces) and Swansea (80 spaces), and the university is "committed to offering 100% of first-year full-time undergraduates a place in accommodation" it tells us.

Tuition fees

» Fees for UK students	£9,000
» Fees for International students 2021–22	£13,500
» For scholarship and bursary information see www.uwtsd.ac.uk/student-finance/	
» Graduate salary	£20,000

Student numbers

Undergraduates	10,880	(1,554)
Postgraduates	1,370	(993)
Applications/places		3,000/1,085
Applications per place		2.8:1
Overall offer rate		88.7%
International students – EU		2.2%
Non-EU		1%

Accommodation

University provided places: 628
Self-catered: £89–£140 per week
First-years guaranteed accommodation
www.uwtsd.ac.uk/accommodation

Where do the students come from?

State schools (non-grammar)	97.8%	First generation students	49.7%	White working-class males	4.1%
Grammar schools	0.2%	Low participation areas	12.5%	Black achievement gap	-13.8%
Independent schools	2.1%	All ethnic minorities	5.2%	Mature (over 21)	73.6%

Social inclusion ranking: 14

University of Warwick

The FAB – Warwick's new Faculty of Arts Building – makes a commitment to interdisciplinary collaboration within the university's arts and humanities departments. An architecturally striking addition to the university's 750-acre campus, its light-filled teaching and learning spaces are designed to inspire creativity and innovation. Specialist resources cater for the different disciplines housed under the development's roof. Among them is an antiquities room for classics and ancient history, creative writing and film screening rooms along with theatre studios, rehearsal rooms, a media lab and an edit suite.

Warwick's extraordinary record as a top-10 university in every edition of our league table to date remains unbroken this year. Research-led since its 1965 foundation, Warwick reaped impressive results in the 2021 Research Excellence Framework, whose panel of global experts rated 92% of its submissions as world-leading (4*) or internationally excellent (3*). Economics; classics; computer science; and business and management produced some of the best results.

Research in the fields of neuroscience, microbiology and infection, cell biology and disease models benefits from Warwick's new Interdisciplinary Biomedical Research Building. Life sciences and medical students are also gaining from being taught within its dedicated facilities. The university places 64th in the 2023 QS World Rankings.

Another arts-focused project – the university's expansion of its Warwick Arts Centre – opened last year, bringing a concert hall, theatre and café. Its opening coincided with nearby Coventry's investiture as European City of Culture. The market town of Warwick is a longer seven-mile journey from the university's campus, despite its name.

The university (winner of our previous edition's Teaching Quality award) is delivering all teaching and learning in person only this year, supported by lecture-capture. In our analysis of the latest National Student Survey (NSS) outcomes, Warwick ranks 36th for students' evaluation of teaching quality – although a 20-place drop, year-on-year, it still places the university higher than all other Russell Group members on this measure.

NSS scores for the wider undergraduate experience have held up better, with Warwick slipping only five places slipping only five places into the top 25.

In the government's 2017 Teaching Excellence Framework (TEF), though, Warwick was restricted to silver, in spite of consistent high achievement by its students and staff, excellent completion and employment rates, and exceptional employer feedback – criteria suitable for a gold award.

The TEF panel was impressed by the

Admissions Office
University House
Coventry CV4 8UW
024 7652 3723
ugadmissions@warwick.ac.uk
www.warwicksu.com
www.warwick.ac.uk
Open days: see website

The Times and The Sunday Times Rankings
Overall Ranking: 9 (last year: 8)

Teaching quality	77%	36
Student experience	75.1%	=25
Research quality	60.9%	13
Entry standards	170	=14
Graduate prospects	86.3%	10
Good honours	88%	16
Expected completion rate	95.6%	9
Student/staff ratio	14.2	=26

culture of research-stimulated learning that challenged students, but said Warwick had missed its benchmarks for student satisfaction and continuation rates among some groups of students. Our findings differ, with student satisfaction now firmly on track and Warwick placing in our top 10 for completion rates – with just over 2% of students dropping out, significantly below the expected level.

Graduate prospects are in the top 10 nationally and Warwick was the among the 10 most targeted universities by leading graduate employers in 2021-22, according to the High Fliers Graduate Market report.

The university's large business school has a London base in the Shard. Further afield, Warwick partners with universities across Europe, North America, South America, Australasia and east Asia to offer study-abroad opportunities for undergraduates, with availability varying by department.

Global sustainable development students spend part of their second year at Monash University – in Melbourne, in Australia, or Kuala Lumpur, in Malaysia. The history department takes students to Venice in the autumn in a partnership with the University of Venice Ca'Foscari that gives students access to its libraries and other facilities.

Warwick's portfolio of degree apprenticeships comprises 27 programmes – including five strands of engineering; social work; and senior leadership. Student apprentice numbers are expected to reach about 1,200 by September 2023.

Warwick edges two places further inside the top 100 of our social inclusion ranking this year and sits seventh among the 21 Russell Group universities of England and Wales. The university admits more students from selective state and independent schools than most. But with 43.1% of students from ethnic minority backgrounds its diversity ranks in the upper third of universities and Warwick's black attainment gap is among the top 10 narrowest.

A £49million sports and wellness hub includes a 230-station gym, a 25m pool, fitness studios, bouldering and climbing walls, a sports hall and 4G outdoor pitches.

First-years who apply by the end of July are guaranteed accommodation. All students must complete the *Warwick Values Programme*, which covers support around alcohol, drugs, sexual consent and racial, LGBTQ+ and social tolerance.

Tuition fees

- » Fees for UK students   £9,250
  Foundation courses   £6,750
- » Fees for International students 2023–24   £23,390–£29,830
  Medicine   £27,290–£47,580
- » For scholarship and bursary information see:
  www.warwick.ac.uk/services/wss/studentfunding/funding
- » Graduate salary   £29,060

Student numbers

Undergraduates	17,617	(1,196)
Postgraduates	6,306	(2,989)
Applications/places	42,260/6,000	
Applications per place	7.1	
Overall offer rate	65.1%	
International students – EU	11.7%	
Non-EU	17.8%	

Accommodation

University provided places: 7,500
Self-catered: £85–£218 per week
First-years guaranteed accommodation
www.warwick.ac.uk/services/accommodation/

Where do the students come from?

State schools (non-grammar)	63.4%	First generation students	31.7%	White-working-class males	3.2%
Grammar schools	17.3%	Low participation areas	5.7%	Black achievement gap	-6.5%
Independent schools	19.3%	All ethnic minorities	43.1%	Mature (over 21)	7.8%

Social inclusion ranking: 97

University of the West of England Bristol

A 12-place rise brings the University of the West of England, Bristol (UWE Bristol) to the cusp of our top 60 this year. The university has been the focus of increasing demand – attracting more than 34,200 applications for entry in 2021-22 – its highest numbers for a decade. More new students (over 7,500) began courses than ever before. The trend is continuing, going by the 6% uplift in applications the university had noticed at the end of March this year.

Some much-needed student accommodation is under construction at the Frenchay campus. It will house an extra 2,250 students when fully complete; the first 900 of them by September 2023. The development is being built to low-carbon certified standards and will yield a 54% reduction in running costs and carbon emissions compared with typical "good practice" buildings – a valuable saving considering the current cost-of-living increases.

Frenchay is one of three campuses, all accessible by bus from each other and within easy reach of the city centre. UWE holds a gold rating from the government's Teaching Excellence Framework (TEF). Assessors noted the above-benchmark levels of student satisfaction with academic support and rates of progression to high-skilled employment.

The latest figures from the national Graduate Outcomes survey support the TEF panel's findings. With more than three-quarters (76.3%) of UWE graduates in high-skilled jobs or further study 15 months after finishing their degrees the university secures a top-50 rank in our graduate prospects measure.

As part of efforts to help students on to the career ladder, UWE Bristol's careers systems host 17,000 employer contracts across more than 10,000 organisations. More than 2,000 vacancies were being advertised, a recent snapshot showed. Volunteering is well supported and employer events attract high rates of student engagement.

The university offers 25 higher and degree apprenticeships which have more than 2,000 student apprentices on programmes in diverse fields including aerospace engineering, occupational therapy, architecture, diagnostic radiography, and junior animator. UWE's police constable degree apprenticeship has the advantage of newly remodelled and refurbished teaching spaces at the Frenchay campus that now include two 60-seat lecture theatres.

A School of Engineering building joined the Frenchay campus in 2020 – to meet a predicted increased in demand for engineering graduates in the region. More recently the university has created a "restorative walled garden" for students and staff.

Such care for student wellbeing may help life rates of student satisfaction – which although still in the top half of UK

Frenchay Campus
Coldharbour Lane
Bristol BS16 1QY
0117 328 3333
admissions@uwe.ac.uk
www.thestudentsunion.co.uk
www.uwe.ac.uk
Open days: see website

The Times and The Sunday Times **Rankings**
Overall Ranking: 61 (last year: 73)

Teaching quality	75.5%	=60
Student experience	72.4%	=54
Research quality	35.7%	70
Entry standards	123	=72
Graduate prospects	76.3%	50
Good honours	77%	=70
Expected completion rate	83.4%	=81
Student/staff ratio	15.7	=52

universities for teaching quality and the wider undergraduate experience after declines in both – have yet to return to their pre-pandemic high levels. Teaching this year is following a hybrid model of delivery, mainly face-to-face but with some online lectures.

At the City campus in Bower Ashton, modern design studios are part of a £37million investment in facilities for creative industries. They also house the Fabrication Centre and the Centre for Fine Print Research.

The £5million optometry and clinical skills centre on the Glenside campus is housed in a Grade II listed former NHS laundry. It is the base for trainee paramedics, occupational therapy students, nurses as well as undergraduates on the optometry programme.

More than three-quarters (76%) of the work submitted for assessment in the 2021 Research Excellence Framework was rated as world-leading or internationally excellent. Architecture, built environment and planning; allied health subjects; communication and media studies; engineering; and law produced the best results.

UWE Bristol occupies a middling position in our social inclusion ranking, drawing 92.1% of students from non-selective state schools. About one in five students (19.5%) are from ethnic minority backgrounds. The university's recruitment of students from under-represented areas and of white working-class boys falls within the upper third nationally.

The Frenchay campus has fitness suites next to student residences as well as a sports hall, indoor climbing wall, squash courts and an all-weather pitch. Sports teams including soccer, American football and rugby are based at the £4.5million Hillside Gardens facility a few miles away. The MOVE programme provides free access to students on more than 80 sporting opportunities — from intramural leagues to wellness and fitness classes.

With the boom in student numbers creating pressure on UWE Bristol's halls of residences, the university had 485 students waiting to be housed in September 2022, according to news reports. The university says it is not able to guarantee accommodation for first-years and allocates rooms on a first come, first served basis. Housing applications opened on June 10 for the present academic year and new entrants are advised to keep abreast of 2023's application deadline on the UWE website.

Students tend to love Bristol, so much so that many never leave.

Tuition fees

» Fees for UK students	£9,250
» Fees for International students 2023–24	£14,250–£15,250
» For scholarship and bursary information see www.uwe.ac.uk/courses/fees	
» Graduate salary	£24,000

Student numbers

Undergraduates	22,885 (1,732)
Postgraduates	4,538 (5,225)
Applications/places	34,230/7,555
Applications per place	4.5:1
Overall offer rate	73.8%
International students – EU	3.8%
Non-EU	9.8%

Accommodation

University provided places: 5,208
Self-catered: £96–£226 per week
www.uwe.ac.uk/life/accommodation

Where do the students come from?

State schools (non-grammar)	92.1%	First generation students	41.8%	White working-class males	6.8%
Grammar schools	2.9%	Low participation areas	15.2%	Black achievement gap	-30.6%
Independent schools	5%	All ethnic minorities	19.5%	Mature (over 21)	27.7%

Social inclusion ranking: 70

University of West London

  Boasting the highest rates of student satisfaction in Britain, the University of West London (UWL) wins our University of the Year for Student Experience award – for the second time. In our analysis of the latest National Student Survey outcomes, UWL comes top for students' evaluation of teaching quality and their wider undergraduate experience.

In common with almost all universities, UWL lost ground on student satisfaction during the pandemic – but has bounced back in style. The university, based in Ealing and in Brentford, is underpinned by a commitment to the student experience that has helped transform it from the former Thames Valley University (which finished bottom of our league table in 2001) into today's top-40 institution, after an impressive 34-place rise this year.

Guided by the principles of the right to educational enhancement, inclusion and participation, Professor Peter John, the vice-chancellor, put student experience at the heart of recent campus developments.

"You've got to design your campus system for the students rather than the opposite way round," he commented when UWL won its Student Experience award in 2020. The student support building in Ealing is the first thing anyone entering sees, its "street" of services running right through the campus.

At the Brentford campus, which occupies an 11-storey building, student services occupy a whole floor. Also enhancing student wellbeing is the university's new £13.8million leisure centre in Gunnersbury Park, a partnership with two local councils that is now one of London's largest outdoor facilities.

A campus in Ealing is opening in September 2023 next to a new cinema development. It will provide modern teaching rooms and social spaces, redoubling UWL's commitment to on-campus teaching, which is the prevalent model of delivery this year.

UWL has also been investing in research, creating more than 20 research centres and groups around the themes of problems faced by society today and creating solutions that will transform lives tomorrow. Two research centres opened last year: the Centre for Inequality and Levelling Up and the Institute for Policing Studies, which draws on UWL's experience in police training in research that aims to help to shape the future of policing worldwide.

The focus on research has translated to a huge 29-place leap into the top 100 of our research quality rating for UWL this year, based on results of the 2021 Research Excellence Framework. Nearly 80% of the university's work submitted for assessment

St Mary's Road
Ealing
London W5 5RF
0208 231 2220
www.uwlsu.com
undergraduate.admissions
@uwl.ac.uk
www.uwl.ac.uk
Open days: see website

The Times and The Sunday Times Rankings
Overall Ranking: 40 (last year: 74)

Teaching quality	84.3%	1
Student experience	81.4%	1
Research quality	28.7%	93
Entry standards	119	=86
Graduate prospects	69	=90
Good honours	77.3%	66
Expected completion rate	77.2%	118
Student/staff ratio	12.9	9

was rated world-leading or internationally excellent (the top standards).

UWL's specialist learning facilities are designed to prepare graduates for the world of work. Among them is a Boeing 737 flight simulator with commercial airline software and a flight management system. In addition, there is a mock courtroom and replica hospital wards. The new School of Biomedical Sciences has benefited from £1.5million investment.

The latest figures showed that 69% of UWL graduates were in high-skilled work or postgraduate study 15 months after finishing their degree – resulting in a 19-place rise in our graduate prospects measure. Helping to lift these figures, graduates are given lifelong access to UWL's careers service, which offers placement opportunities, industry workshops and careers counselling among its supports.

At UWL's Brentford campus, the landmark Paragon building is the headquarters of one of the largest healthcare faculties in Britain. The university also has a Reading outpost, housing the Berkshire Institute for Health, and nursing and midwifery students.

UWL achieved silver in the government's Teaching Excellence Framework (TEF). The panel complimented the university on its investment in high-quality physical and digital resources, with students fully involved in the design of the new facilities. It also commented favourably on peer mentoring and targeted financial support programmes to improve the engagement of those most at risk of dropping out. Even so, UWL's high dropout rate remains above the predicted level, based on the academic and social mix. Ranking 13th in our social inclusion index overall, at UWL seven in 10 students are aged 21 or over when they enrol (the eighth-highest proportion of mature students) and more than half are the first in their immediate families to go to university (ranking UWL 22nd on this measure). Nearly all (94.7%) students went to non-selective state schools and 52.6% of students come from ethnic minority backgrounds. About half of full-time students qualify for some form of financial assistance.

Applications were 16% higher in the 2021 recruitment cycle, year-on-year. From the present academic year, the curriculum gains nine degrees in subjects including biomedical informatics; human genetics; and popular music performance.

Most students "live out", so the 450 rooms endorsed or managed by the university provide enough space for all first-years to be guaranteed a spot. UWL has an on-campus sports centre as well as the new development at Gunnersbury Park.

Tuition fees

- » Fees for UK students — £9,250
- » Fees for International students 2023–24 — £13,250–£14,250
- » For scholarship and bursary information see www.uwl.ac.uk/study/undergraduate-study/fees-and-funding-undergraduates
- » Graduate salary — £25,000

Student numbers

Undergraduates	11,335	(846)
Postgraduates	1,670	(1,316)
Applications/places	16,360/2,995	
Applications per place	5.5:1	
Overall offer rate	59.1%	
International students – EU	17.4%	
Non-EU	7%	

Accommodation

University provided places: 550
Self-catered: £185–£240 per week
www.uwl.ac.uk/student-life/accommodation

Where do the students come from?

State schools (non-grammar)	94.7%	First generation students	55.7%	
Grammar schools	1.4%	Low participation areas	7.4%	
Independent schools	3.9%	All ethnic minorities	52.6%	

Social inclusion ranking: 13

White working-class males	2.5%
Black achievement gap	-20.5%
Mature (over 21)	70.4%

University of the West of Scotland

The University of the West of Scotland (UWS) – founded in 2007 with bases in Paisley, Lanarkshire, Dumfries, Ayr and London – is of Scotland's youngest universities as well as one of its largest, with about 22,000 students. UWS is one of Scotland's most successful universities in widening access and far exceeds the Scottish government's access targets. Its exemplary record on widening participation continues, the latest figures show.

UWS recruits the highest number of students in Scotland from non-selective state schools (98.7%) and the most who are the first in their immediate family to go to university (48.3%). Almost three in 10 (29.9%) come from the most underrepresented areas in higher education and almost six in 10 students were aged over-21 when they enrolled (59.6% and the highest proportion in Scotland again). Overall, UWS ranks second only to Abertay in our Scottish social inclusion index.

At UWS, a contextualised approach to applications is the norm. Financial assistance supports the widening access agenda. UWS budgets £1.1million in childcare funds to help eligible student parents meet childcare costs. Another £1.1million is budgeted for "discretionary funds" to help students meet their basic costs of living.

In the Times Higher Education (THE) Impact Rankings for 2022, which measure universities' progress in delivering against the United Nations' Sustainable Development Goals (SDGs), UWS places second in Scotland and tenth in the UK for its success at reducing inequalities (SDG 10). It is first in Scotland and fourth in the UK for SDG 8: decent work and economic growth.

Headquarters are at the Paisley campus, while at the Ayr site £81million of investment has added facilities including a prizewinning library shared with Scotland's Rural College. The Dumfries campus shares an 85-acre parkland site with the University of Glasgow and Dumfries and Galloway College.

The UWS School of Health, Nursing and Midwifery is the largest in Scotland and the launch of a healthcare simulation centre at the Lanarkshire campus has boosted provision. There has also been an expansion to the London Docklands base.

A 19-place rise in our National Student Survey-derived measure for teaching quality shows improvement in some areas of student satisfaction – at a time when UWS moves to a hybrid model of on-campus learning activities together with flexible online resources. Yet UWS has dropped further outside the top 100 for students' assessment of the wider undergraduate experience. An increase in the staff-to-student ratio has also contributed to its 12-place fall down our academic ranking this year.

Paisley Campus
Paisley PA1 2BE
0800 027 1000;
+44 141 849 4101 (international)
ask@uws.ac.uk
www.sauws.org.uk
www.uws.ac.uk
Open days: see website

PAISLEY
Edinburgh
Belfast
London
Cardiff

The Times and The Sunday Times **Rankings**
Overall Ranking: =122 (last year: =110)

Teaching quality	74.9%	=71
Student experience	67%	=112
Research quality	19.2%	117
Entry standards	139	=43
Graduate prospects	70.7%	79
Good honours	74.2%	91
Expected completion rate	78.3%	=111
Student/staff ratio	23.5	125

With 70.7% of graduates in highly skilled jobs or further study 15 months on from their degrees, UWS places in the top 80 UK universities for graduate prospects. In a new employability-focused initiative, the university has rolled out academic, professional and personal development (APPD) modules across undergraduate programmes. The university has also appointed an entrepreneur, Yekemi Otaru, as its new chancellor.

Students on the university's music programmes are being given opportunities to develop their careers via UWS's new record label, Damfino Records, which is backed by Jim Prime from Deacon Blue and Paul McGeechan from Love and Money, who are lecturers on the music courses.

UWS also offers five graduate apprenticeships (known as degree apprenticeships in the rest of the UK), spanning business and management; civil engineering; early learning and childcare; engineering design and manufacture; and software development. It hopes to increase the number on courses to 400.

The university's Institute of Clinical Exercise and Health Science is responsible for some of its leading research spanning sport and exercise science nationally and internationally. UWS became Celtic Football Club's first Youth Academy sports science partner in 2020. Since then it has announced a new partnership with Celtic Football Club's

Women's first-team as well as made ties with Motherwell and Hamilton Academical women's teams.

Sport and exercise sciences, leisure and tourism led the way for UWS in the 2021 Research Excellence Framework, with 71% of the work in this area judged as world-leading or internationally excellent. Research within physics was another of the university's strongest suits. Overall though, other universities performed better, resulting in a 19-place decline for UWS in our research quality index this year.

Students have free membership to UWS-operated fitness facilities. The students' union was crowned University Students' Association of the Year at the NUS Scotland awards.

Most students live at home, which means the university's 196 student bedrooms at the Ayr campus and 491 at the Paisley site are usually enough for all first-years who want to live in to be allocated a space. If UWS properties are full students are referred to nearby accommodation providers such as Craigie House at Ayr and MyPad Paisley.

Tuition fees

» Fees for Scottish students   £0–£1,820
  RUK fees   £9,250 (capped at £27,750 for 4-year courses)
» Fees for International students 2023–24 £14,500–£17,250
» For scholarship and bursary information see
  www.uws.ac.uk/money-fees-funding/
» Graduate salary   £24,900

Student numbers

Undergraduates	12,686	(1,336)
Postgraduates	2,777	(1,137)
Applications/places	20,475/4,115	
Applications per place	5.1	
Overall offer rate	52.95	
International students – EU	3.6%	
Non-EU	1.6%	

Accommodation

University provided places: 687
Self-catered: £97–£164 per week
www.uws.ac.uk/university-life/accommodation

Where do the students come from?

State schools (non-grammar)	98.7%	First generation students	48.3%	
Grammar schools	0.2%	Low participation areas	29.9%	
Independent schools	1.1%	All ethnic minorities	10.7%	

Social inclusion ranking (Scotland): 2

White working-class males	n/a%
Black achievement gap	-30.5%
Mature (over 21)	59.6%

University of Westminster

Plans to restore an iconic London theatre in Westminster's Riding House Street building are being put into action by the university. The Soho Poly venue was recognised as a leader in radical "lunchtime theatre" throughout the 1970s and 1980s – dedicated to widening democratic access to the arts and giving voice to underrepresented groups. Renovations to the basement venue will add disability access and create new exhibition space as well as restoring its professional performance facilities.

Founded as the UK's first polytechnic in 1838, Westminster occupies some of the capital's most central locations. Headquarters are on Regent Street in the West End. At Titchfield Street around the corner, home to law courses, the university's Legal Advice Clinic has launched a free service in partnership with the London Black Women's Project to support black women experiencing issues with the criminal justice system. The nearby Cavendish campus is the focus of programmes including engineering, psychology and biological and biomedical sciences.

Westminster's best-known feature – its School of Media, Arts and Design – is in Harrow, northwest of the city. Art and design produced the university's best results in the latest Research Excellence Framework (REF 2021), keeping pace with many of the top institutions in the country. Westminster's research within business and management; and politics and international studies also did especially well, helping the university to maintain its position in the upper half of UK universities in our research quality index.

Westminster's Marylebone campus, near Regent's Park, houses teaching and learning in a wide range of subject areas including architecture, data science, tourism and accounting — and is also the site of the university's central student support services.

Student satisfaction with the wider undergraduate experience has improved this year – contributing to Westminster's 14-place rise in our main academic league table to rank =115. The university was third from bottom overall in 2021.

However, its students' evaluation of the quality of their teaching remains a thornier issue – and Westminster slips one place to joint 118th on this measure. Most subjects have a hybrid model of teaching delivery for 2022-23.

The university is investing in modernising its estate. In line for upgrades are the School of Computer Science and Engineering at the Cavendish campus. At the Harrow campus, a new broadcast newsroom is being added, while at Marylebone the Bloomberg suite is being extended and the ground floor remodelled. At Regent Street, the gym changing rooms are being refurbished. In another initiative to improve the student

---

309 Regent Street
London W1B 2HW
020 7911 5000
admissions@westminster.ac.uk
www.uwsu.com
www.westminster.ac.uk
Open days: see website

Edinburgh
Belfast
Cardiff
LONDON

experience, Westminster has joined the Mental Health Charter, which brings together 32 universities to share good practice.

Westminster was rated bronze in the Teaching Excellence Framework, which takes account of the students' background at each institution. Assessors praised the consistent support for students at risk of dropping out and a strategic approach to improving employment and entrepreneurship.

With 64.8% of graduates in high-skilled jobs or postgraduate study 15 months on from their degrees, Westminster climbs seven places in our graduate prospects measure this year to rank =119, still a relatively low position in our table. The new Centre for Employability and Enterprise may help.

Westminster's recently-expanded degree apprenticeship portfolio offers 10 undergraduate programmes in areas including healthcare, property and project management. The university expects to have around 400 degree apprentices by September 2023.

With Britain's 16th-highest proportion of European Union students, Westminster maintains an international perspective. Its courses are taught in nine countries, from Sri Lanka to Uzbekistan, and UK students have the opportunity to gain experience abroad via exchange partnerships with more than 100 institutions in 26 countries. The Polylang programme offers free language tuition, including Arabic, French and Chinese.

Westminster is 55th overall in our social inclusion index, just inside the top half of universities. More than seven in 10 (73.1%) of undergraduates are from ethnic minority backgrounds, ranking the university in the top 10 on that measure. Among Westminster's initiatives to widen participation in higher education is the university's tie-up with Sony Interactive Entertainment, which is funding scholarships for black students and those from underrepresented groups.

Sports facilities include gyms at the Regent Street and Harrow campuses. By far its best sporting hub is Westminster's Quintin Hogg 45-acre sports ground overlooking the River Thames in Chiswick.

Westminster does not offer an accommodation guarantee so new students are advised to apply early for places. The university's halls of residence have their own vibes while the bright lights of London – named the world's best student city by QS in 2023 – are ripe for exploring.

Tuition fees

» Fees for UK students	£9,250
» Fees for International students 2023–24	£9,250–£14,800
» For scholarship and bursary information see www.westminster.ac.uk/study/fees-and-funding/	
» Graduate salary	£24,000

Student numbers

Undergraduates	14,614 (1,054)
Postgraduates	2,466 (1,546)
Applications/places	25,085/5,380
Applications per place	4.7:1
Overall offer rate	81.7%
International students – EU	10.9%
Non-EU	14.7%

Accommodation

University provided places: 1,150
Self-catered: £185–£315 per week
www.westminster.ac.uk/study/accommodation

Where do the students come from?

				Social inclusion ranking: 55	
State schools (non-grammar)	94.7%	First generation students	55.8%	White working-class males	3.3%
Grammar schools	2.4%	Low participation areas	5.2%	Black achievement gap	-20.6%
Independent schools	2.9%	All ethnic minorities	73.1%	Mature (over 21)	19.5%

University of Winchester

Vastly improved rates of student satisfaction at Winchester have prompted a 19-place rise for the university in our main academic league table to rank 87th. In our analysis of the latest National Student Survey results, Winchester is in the upper half of UK universities for satisfaction with teaching quality (up 33 places to =62). For satisfaction with the wider undergraduate experience it has made even bigger gains, up from 108th in 2021 to joint 57th in 2022 and far outdoing its pre-pandemic performance on this measure.

Teaching is now in-person only at Winchester. Its King Alfred campus occupies a wooded hillside overlooking the cathedral city, a 10-minute walk away. And while the university has extended its capacity for recording lectures, this does not replace the requirement for students to attend in real life.

The university's new facilities may also play a part in the upturn in student satisfaction. Winchester's flagship £50million learning and teaching building, the West Downs Centre, opened in 2021 – housing computer and digital-related degrees and business and management programmes. Clinical skills training facilities opened in April 2022 at the centre, too, thus bringing nursing (a fast-growing area for Winchester) onto campus. The striking building features a drum-shaped auditorium and won an architecture prize at the Civic Trust awards, whose judges said: "It enhances not just the university campus and teaching facilities but also the wider neighbourhood."

A packaging-free, zero-waste shop on campus is among the university's sustainability initiatives. A £3.1million grant from the Public Sector Decarbonisation scheme should make further inroads towards Winchester's goal of being one of the lowest carbon-emitting universities in the UK. Winchester's first nutrition students started their courses in September 2022, as did those on new degrees in biomedical science and in educational technology. From 2023, the curriculum will also offer midwifery and architecture as it continues to broaden.

With a growing choice of study options, applications to Winchester rose by about 6% in 2021, year-on-year, and were up by 5% by the end of March 2022, too.

Winchester has a silver rating in the Teaching Excellence Framework. The panel was impressed by its "appropriate" contact hours, tutorials and buddy schemes that produce personalised learning and high levels of commitment from students.

Winchester has improved its ranking in our graduate prospects measure for the second year running and now ranks inside the top 100, with 68.2% of graduates in high-skilled jobs or postgraduate study 15 months after finishing their degrees.

Sparkford Road
Winchester SO22 4NR
01962 827 234
admissions@winchester.ac.uk
www.winchesterstudents.co.uk
www.winchester.ac.uk
Open days: see website

The Times and The Sunday Times Rankings
Overall Ranking: 87 (last year: =106)

Teaching quality	75.4%	=62
Student experience	72.2%	=57
Research quality	22%	107
Entry standards	111	=112
Graduate prospects	68.2%	=98
Good honours	74.6%	89
Expected completion rate	85.4%	65
Student/staff ratio	18.1	=99

The university has a Centre for Apprenticeships and offers 15 programmes (a big leap up from six in our previous edition). The subjects covered span business; social work; and nursing and Winchester expects to have more than 500 student apprentices on programmes by September 2023 (almost double the 227 it had at the last count).

Winchester tripled the proportion of research rated 4* since the last REF in 2014. The volume of staff submitted also increased by 126%. But overall, its 2021 performance did not hold up as well as in 2014 and the university drops 24 places in our research quality ranking, to 107th. Theology was among the strongest subjects submitted by Winchester, which was first established as a Church of England foundation for teacher training and known as King Alfred College until 2004.

Professor Sarah Green, the university's vice-chancellor, took up her post in January 2022, and said she was "drawn to Winchester's values and ethos and its rich heritage of educational excellence and inclusion". The professor joins a university that sits comfortably among the top half of universities in our social inclusion ranking, its position boosted by having the tenth-highest proportion (12%) of disabled students in England and Wales. Most students (93.3%) went to non-selective state schools.

Widening participation focuses on increasing low progression rates to higher education and increasing the diversity of the student body. Targeted support packages are offered to care-leavers, estranged students, young adult carers, students seeking sanctuary and Gypsy, Roma, Traveller, Showman and Boaters (GTRSB), offering contextualised admissions, designated support staff, access to year-round housing, and financial help.

About 40% of entrants qualified for some form of financial support in September 2022, a proportion the university expects to remain the same for 2023 entry.

The two-floor university gym is at the heart of the £12million Burma Road student village and offers daily classes at no extra charge to members. On campus there is also a fitness studio, a sports hall and a multi-use games area. The Winchester Sports Stadium nearby is open to the public as well as students.

With 1,949 residential spaces, the university guarantees accommodation to all first-years who apply by the mid-June deadline. Students benefit from being able to get to know each other relatively quickly in compact, peaceful Winchester, home to Europe's longest medieval cathedral.

Tuition fees

» Fees for UK students	£9,250
» Fees for International students 2022–23	£13,800
» For scholarship and bursary information see www.winchester.ac.uk/accommodation-and-winchester-life/students-and-money/	
» Graduate salary	£22,000

Student numbers

Undergraduates	6,651	(231)
Postgraduates	693	(655)
Applications/places	10,730/2,455	
Applications per place	4.4:1	
Overall offer rate	87.1%	
International students – EU	1.7%	
Non-EU	3.4%	

Accommodation

University provided places: 1,949
Catered costs: £173 per week
Self-catered: £122–£165 per week
First-years guaranteed accommodation
www.winchester.ac.uk/accommodation-and-winchester-life/accommodation

Where do the students come from?

State schools (non-grammar)	93.3%	First generation students	49.1%	White working-class males	6.6%
Grammar schools	2.7%	Low participation areas	14.2%	Black achievement gap	-23.4%
Independent schools	4%	All ethnic minorities	9.4%	Mature (over 21)	20.6%

Social inclusion ranking: 48

University of Wolverhampton

Wolverhampton's creative course provision has gained new degrees in recent years – such as acting and theatre; dance and creative performance; and digital production arts for theatre. Multimillion-pound investment in the university's Screen School is keeping pace with the curriculum, with the aim of boosting skills in the digital arts and media industries. A new radio studio reflects local BBC station layouts, while Wolverhampton's emerging newsreaders also have access to a bulletin studio.

Also based at the Wolverhampton campus, the teaching of pharmacy has benefited from a dispensary and extended practice suite. The developments follow the university's £45million School of Architecture and Built Environment at the Springfield campus, which opened in 2020 and is part of a £120million regeneration of a 12-acre derelict brewery into a supercampus for courses in the built environment. The National Brownfield Institute has also opened at Springfield, focusing on modern methods of building.

The university has headquarters in its home city and an expanding regional footprint. At the Telford campus, a £5million health and social care training centre opened in May 2021. In Hereford, Wolverhampton's Midlands Centre for Cybersecurity occupies a 2,000 sq m site. The joint venture with Herefordshire council provides research and development resources out of three cyberlaboratories.

The university also has a site in Walsall, where the high-quality sports facilities include grass and 3G pitches, outdoor courts for tennis and netball, a gym and strength facility and a 200m running track. Sports scholarships of up to £4,500 over three years come with access to physiotherapy, strength and conditioning training and mentoring.

The skills-boosting equipment may further cement Wolverhampton's improved graduate prospects, which, having entered the top 100 last year at joint 99th, remains just inside it again. When the Graduate Outcomes survey took its latest census almost 68% of Wolverhampton graduates were in high-skilled employment or postgraduate study 15 months after leaving university.

Wolverhampton has embraced degree apprenticeships and has more than 1,000 students on programmes spanning a wide range of subject areas – with more to come within healthcare and other fields in 2023.

Wolverhampton was awarded silver in the Teaching Excellence Framework in 2018, upgraded from bronze. The university still missed its benchmarks for student satisfaction and progression to high-skilled employment, but the panel praised the commitment to enhancing students' learning experience, as well as the involvement of employers in the development and review of courses.

Student satisfaction with teaching quality

Wulfruna Street
Wolverhampton WV1 1LY
01902 323 505
admissions@wlv.ac.uk
www.wolvesunion.org/
www.wlv.ac.uk
Open days: see website

The Times and The Sunday Times Rankings
Overall Ranking: 127 (last year: 128)

Teaching quality	75.8%	=54
Student experience	71.2%	76
Research quality	21.6%	109
Entry standards	109	=117
Graduate prospects	67.9%	=100
Good honours	68.8%	120
Expected completion rate	71.8%	127
Student/staff ratio	16.5	=71

and with the wider experience have shot back up our rankings this year, having tumbled in the pandemic. In our analysis of the latest National Student Survey outcomes, Wolverhampton ranks joint 54th for teaching quality (up 24 places), while the university gains 16 places for students' evaluation of the wider undergraduate experience.

Wolverhampton ranks in the top 10 of the English Social Mobility Index 2022 (compiled by the Higher Education Policy Institute), which looks at how effective different universities are at delivering social mobility and is compiled by the Higher Education Policy Institute (HEPI) think tank. Almost all students (97.4%) are recruited from non-selective state schools and more than two in 10 come from underrepresented areas. Only one university in England and Wales succeeds in attracting a greater proportion of "first generation" entrants (almost seven in 10) – who are their first in their immediate family to go to university – than Wolverhampton.

A new Department for Work and Pensions pilot scheme to ease the transition from university to the workplace for disabled students is underway at Wolverhampton and Manchester Metropolitan universities.

Poor completion rates – often a by-product of a diverse intake – hold Wolverhampton back in our academic ranking. Almost two in 10 students are projected to drop out – higher the benchmark rate of 14.9%, based on the social and academic backgrounds of Wolverhampton students.

The majority of students are eligible for some form of financial help, such as the new student bursary for first time, full-time undergraduates that makes cash awards for each year that students progress to the next level – of £200 in year one and £100 thereafter. Access bursaries for care-leavers, the deaf or those with hearing loss, and estranged students are worth £1,000 in each of years one and two. There are also scholarships that reward academic merit.

More than half of Wolverhampton's research submitted to the 2021 Research Excellence Framework (REF) was judged as internationally excellent (3*) or world-leading (4*). The university entered 75% more staff than in the previous REF 2014 and included four new subject areas. But within the context of bigger improvements made elsewhere, Wolverhampton lurches 27 places down our research quality index.

Accommodation prices are among the UK's most pocket-friendly, with £108 per week the top whack. Students can make requests such as single-sex or quiet corridors, or to be housed with fellow first-years.

Tuition fees

»	Fees for UK students	£9,250
	Foundation courses	£8,400
»	Fees for International students 2023–24	£13,450–£16,000
»	For scholarship and bursary information see	
	www.wlv.ac.uk/apply/funding-costs-fees-and-support/	
»	Graduate salary	£24,000

Student numbers

Undergraduates	12,248	(2,581)
Postgraduates	2,213	(2,255)
Applications/places	18,565/3,645	
Applications per place	5.1:1	
Overall offer rate	90.8%	
International students – EU	0.7%	
Non-EU	6.4%	

Accommodation
University provided places: 1,081
Self-catered: £90–£108 per week
www.wlv.ac.uk/university-life/accommodation

Where do the students come from?

State schools (non-grammar)	97.4%	First generation students	69.5%	
Grammar schools	1.5%	Low participation areas	21.2%	
Independent schools	1.1%	All ethnic minorities	52%	

Social inclusion ranking: 8

White working-class males	4.4%
Black achievement gap	-18.1%
Mature (over 21)	48.1%

University of Worcester

Worcester's commitment to – and excellent facilities for – disability sport are getting even better. The university already has a 2,000-seat arena on its Severn campus that was designed to accommodate wheelchair athletes as well as the able-bodied. There is also a 10-acre lake at the Lakeside campus with a disability hoist for inclusive watersports and disabled wet/dry changing facilities. Cricket is the next sport to be given Worcester's inclusive treatment. In January 2022, city planners gave the go-ahead for an international inclusive cricket education centre, which is set to provide outstanding facilities for all forms of disability cricket – blind, deaf, learning disability and physical disability.

The new centre will be located at Worcester's new Health and Wellbeing campus overlooking the River Severn. The development is based in the former Worcester News building – which is being transformed to include an anatomy suite and simulation room. A therapies suite will allow physiotherapy and sports therapy students to practice clinical students and take part in student-led clinics.

The facilities will be used by students including those of the anticipated Three Counties Medical School, the opening of which has been postponed until 2023. The medical school has received funding for 20 UK medical students, having first launched with only international student applications. The school builds on Worcester's strong reputation for health-related courses – it has been shortlisted as Nurse Education provider of the Year (pre-registration) multiple times in the Student Nursing Times Awards. The new building will house its wide range of health disciplines, helping students to learn together.

Worcester's usually high rates of student satisfaction tumbled this year, leading to the university losing ground in our main league table. Only last year our National Student Survey analysis showed it was in the top 20 for students' evaluation of the wider experience and the top 25 for their assessment of teaching quality, but these have fallen to =64th and 81st respectively. In-person teaching only is the prevalent model of delivery in the present academic year, which may lead to more positive reviews next year.

Work placements of up to 12 months are offered within degree courses. The School of Sport and Exercise Science, for instance, has secured placements with local teams such as the Worcester Warriors rugby club and Worcestershire County Cricket Club. Industry initiatives at the School of Arts include monthly masterclasses and guest lectures, plus links with organisations that include the Writers' Guild, Channel 4 and ITV Central.

The focus on employability translates into Worcester ranking in the top 60 for graduate

Henwick Grove
Worcester WR2 6AJ
01905 855 111
admissions@worc.ac.uk
www.worcsu.com
www.worcester.ac.uk
Open days: see website

The Times and The Sunday Times Rankings
Overall Ranking: =110 (last year: 86)

Teaching quality	74.2%	81
Student experience	71.9%	=64
Research quality	15.3%	121
Entry standards	117	=93
Graduate prospects	74.6%	=57
Good honours	66.7%	=125
Expected completion rate	85.2%	=67
Student/staff ratio	17.5	=85

prospects this year (as it did in our previous edition). The university's three teaching campuses are all close to the city centre. The attractive City campus incorporates the former Worcester Royal Infirmary and the striking and contemporary Hive library.

The business school, health and wellbeing centre and the Jenny Lind law building are also at the City site.

Just opposite is the Art House, opened in 2019, which has modern facilities for art and illustration courses in a Grade II listed Art Deco building, complete with clock tower. St John's campus, the headquarters, is 15 minutes from the city centre and houses science facilities, the National Pollen and Aerobiology Research Unit, the digital arts centre and drama studio.

The curriculum gained nine new degrees this year in subjects including: criminology with politics; professional policing; data science; and digital business. From September 2023, nutrition and dietetics joins the roster.

Having made big gains in the previous Research Excellence Framework (REF) 2014 compared with previous assessments, based on the new REF 2021 Worcester drops 23 places in our research quality ranking this year. A third of its work was classified as world-leading or internationally excellent (the top standards) with some of the best results produced by art and design; history; and sport and exercise sciences.

As well as the Worcester Arena at the Severn campus there are sports facilities throughout the university sites. The Lakeside campus has 50 acres of open grass and woodland for bushcraft. University rowing benefits from amenities at Worcester Rowing Club on the River Severn.

The university moves five places up our social inclusion ranking this year, recruiting 97% of students from non-selective state schools (only 10 universities have fewer entrants from selective state or independent schools). More than one in 10 students is disabled, the 12th highest proportion in any university. Contextual offers, foundation years in science and health and links with further education colleges and schools all help to improve access and participation at the university.

One in 10 Worcester residents is a student, creating a student-friendly atmosphere amid the Tudor buildings, riverside scenery and the nearby Malvern Hills. Clubs and societies play an active role in the social scene and accommodation is guaranteed to first-years.

Tuition fees

» Fees for UK students	£9,250
» Fees for International students 2023–24	£13,400
Medicine	£45,100
» For scholarship and bursary information see www.worcester.ac.uk/study/fees-and-finance/	
» Graduate salary	£24,000

Student numbers

Undergraduates	7,212	(595)
Postgraduates	1,152	(1,151)
Applications/places		9,415/2,540
Applications per place		3.7:1
Overall offer rate		84.7%
International students – EU		5.1%
Non-EU		2.2%

Accommodation

University provided places: 1,200
Self-catered: £111–£189 per week
First-years guaranteed accommodation
www.worcester.ac.uk/life/accommodation

Where do the students come from?

State schools (non-grammar)	97%	First generation students	51.1%	White working-class males	6%
Grammar schools	1.3%	Low participation areas	14.4%	Black achievement gap	−22.6%
Independent schools	1.8%	All ethnic minorities	12.2%	Mature (over 21)	40.8%

Social inclusion ranking: =45

Wrexham Glyndŵr University

Wrexham Glyndŵr continues to blaze a trail in our social inclusion ranking – leading the field as the most socially inclusive university in England and Wales for the fifth consecutive year. Recruits from non-selective state schools account for all but 1.5% of the student population (ranking the university =4 on this measure) and 28.2% come from low-participation areas (also =4). The university ranks eighth for the proportion of students whose parents did not go to university (59.6%), and almost seven out of 10 students are aged over 21 when they enrol (also eighth). Nearly two in every 10 students have a registered disability – the highest proportion.

Named after Owain Glyndŵr, the fifteenth-century Welsh prince who championed the establishment of universities throughout Wales, the university does less well on completion rates – perhaps a price to pay for its achievements in widening access.

A £1million upgrade to teaching facilities at the main Plas Coch campus and the Regent Street art school site are part of a £60million Campus 2025 programme to improve its sites. One of them, Glyndŵr University Racecourse Stadium, is shared with Wrexham football club, with interest peaking after an investment in the club by the Hollywood stars Ryan Reynolds and Rob McElhenney.

The university gained silver in the Teaching Excellence Framework (TEF), scoring well for part-time courses. The TEF panel was impressed by the high levels of interaction with industry, business and the public sector and praised the quality of work-based learning that matches the region's priorities.

The Centre for the Creative Industries on the Wrexham campus features high-quality studios used by students on television production degree courses, and is the regional home of BBC Cymru Wales. Other specialist facilities include a complementary medicine clinic, laboratories for computer game development and for the study of crime scenes. There is also a flight simulator and supersonic wind tunnel.

The rural Northop campus in Flintshire specialises in animal studies and biodiversity courses, and has a small animal unit and an equine centre. The St Asaph campus in Denbighshire is a research centre for the opto-electronics industry, focusing on technology to make high-resolution telescopes. The campus incubator offers a programme for space industry start-ups.

Wrexham Glyndŵr has introduced six new degrees within nursing and health. The first mental health nursing students started their courses in September 2022, as did those on degrees in children's nursing, paramedic science, speech and language therapy, nutrition and dietetics, and operating practice.

Mold Road
Wrexham LL11 2AW
01978 293 439
enquiries@glyndwr.ac.uk
www.wrexhamglyndwrsu.org.uk
www.wgu.ac.uk
Open days: see website

The Times and The Sunday Times Rankings
Overall Ranking: 120 (last year: =110)

Teaching quality	81.6%	=7
Student experience	74.6%	=29
Research quality	13.3%	=126
Entry standards	115	=101
Graduate prospects	69%	=90
Good honours	71.6%	111
Expected completion rate	74%	125
Student/staff ratio	24.9	129

The courses had triggered a huge 40% increase in applications by the end of March 2022 compared with the same point in the application cycle the year before, building on a small rise in applications in 2021 that halted four years of decline. Fewer first-years started courses in 2021 than have done before, however, with enrolments falling by 12%, their fifth consecutive decline.

The university continues to adapt and expand its curriculum. From 2023, degrees will be offered in canine behaviour, training and performance, practical wildlife management, and veterinary physiotherapy.

In our analysis of the results of the latest National Student Survey, published in summer 2022, the university ranks =7 for satisfaction with teaching quality – proof that the hybrid model of online and in-person lectures offered at Glyndŵr is popular with its students. It ranks =29 for how students feel about the wider undergraduate experience. The results follow stellar student satisfaction scores during the pandemic, which lifted the university to second place behind only St Andrews for satisfaction with teaching quality.

In partnership with Airbus, which has a large plant nearby, Wrexham Glyndŵr's Advanced Composite Training and Development Centre in Broughton carries out research to help improve the efficiency of aircraft, and feeds into the university's engineering courses.

Social work and social policy produced some of Glyndŵr's best results in the latest Research Excellence Framework (REF 2021), with some world-leading research. The accolade will be a boon to staff setting up a new Social Inclusion Research Institute at the university. However, the university has fallen to =126 in our research quality index against improved performance across the sector compared with the previous national assessment in 2014.

Graduate prospects improved by 11 places in our latest analysis of the numbers in highly skilled work or postgraduate study 15 months after leaving Wrexham Glyndŵr.

The university's Racecourse stadium, which hosts journalism, business, history and sport students, features the world's oldest international football ground in use. The campus also has a modern sports centre. Many students live at home, allowing all first-years who required a room to get one in 2021.

Tuition fees

- » Fees for UK students £9,000
- » Fees for International students 20223–24 £11,750–£16,000
- » For scholarship and bursary information see www.glyndwr.ac.uk/fees-and-funding/
- » Graduate salary £24,000

Student numbers

Undergraduates	2,600	(2,552)
Postgraduates	747	(1,584)
Applications/places	1,880/585	
Applications per place	3.2:1	
Overall offer rate	72.5%	
International students – EU	3.9%	
Non-EU	4.1%	

Accommodation

University provided places: 385
Self-catered: £115–£168 per week
www.glyndwr.ac.uk/accommodation

Where do the students come from?

State schools (non-grammar)	98.5%	First generation students	59.6%	White working-class males	6.3%
Grammar schools	0.5%	Low participation areas	28.2%	Black achievement gap	-19.4%
Independent schools	1%	All ethnic minorities	6.1%	Mature (over 21)	69.5%

Social inclusion ranking: 1

University of York

York has risen eight places to rank ninth in our research quality index after an impressive performance in the latest Research Excellence Framework (REF 2021). It occupies the same position among the 24 Russell Group universities. Overall, 93% of York's research was rated world-leading or internationally excellent (the top two categories) in the national assessment. Language and linguistics; education; philosophy; and sociology produced some of the university's best results.

The rise in its research rating has contributed to York's two-place rise in our elite top 20 in our main academic rankings. The university is moving its academic structure to a semester model in 2023-24 and each semester will consist of one week's induction, 11 weeks of teaching and four weeks for assessments. There is some reshaping of academic areas, too – with related departments being brought together under three schools, of Business and Society; of Digital Creativity and Performing Arts; and of Physics, Engineering and Technology.

The new School of Business and Society (which encompasses York Management School, and social policy and social work) has a new home to match in the university's recently completed Church Lane building, and investment in facilities at the original Heslington West campus and the linked Heslington East campus continues. The Hull York Medical School has been redesigned and has new clinical skills spaces nearby.

Pushing the boundaries of research towards innovations such as driverless cars, the £45million York Institute for Safe Autonomy has opened. Another recent launch, the Eleanor and Guy Dodson Building, provides cutting-edge research facilities for determining protein structure.

Occupying a 200-acre parkland campus, York is one of only a handful of UK universities to operate a collegiate system. Anne Lister (York's tenth college) opened in 2021 with 348 student bedrooms. Newer still is David Kato College, which opened in September 2022 on Campus East to host about 700 students. Applications to York increased by about 11% in 2021 while enrolments rose by roughly half as much.

The university maintains a top-40 position for satisfaction with the wider undergraduate experience. It has lost some ground regarding its students' assessment of teaching quality, but remains comfortably among the upper half of universities nationally. For the 2022-23 academic year, York is ensuring that all students have in-person teaching.

Career planning begins early for undergraduates via a number of employability initiatives. The York Strengths programme kicks off in the first year, providing opportunities for students to work out what careers suit

Heslington
York YO10 5DD
01904 324 000
ug-admissions@york.ac.uk
www.yusu.org
www.york.ac.uk
Open days: see website

The Times and The Sunday Times **Rankings**
Overall Ranking: 17 (last year: 19)

Teaching quality	75.9%	=52
Student experience	73.6%	39
Research quality	62.8%	9
Entry standards	149	=30
Graduate prospects	82%	=26
Good honours	83.9%	31
Expected completion rate	93.9%	=17
Student/staff ratio	15.1	=41

them. Another initiative, Your Career Journey, highlights the opportunities available throughout university life. Students have the opportunity to take a placement year and host organisations have included Amazon, Warner Brothers and the Foreign and Commonwealth Office – as well as smaller digital and creative businesses.

Such efforts are paying off in high rates of graduate employment. The latest figures show that more than four in five (82%) York graduates were in highly skilled jobs or further study 15 months after finishing their degree. The university's performance in the Graduate Outcomes survey earns joint 26th place in our graduate prospects ranking.

York's efforts to develop employability skills and careers support were among the factors behind its upgrade to gold in the Teaching Excellence Framework in 2018. The panel found excellent academic support and a research-strong environment that engages students and provides outstanding levels of stretch.

York, founded in 1963, became a University of Sanctuary in 2020 to demonstrate its commitment to offering a safe place for refugees, asylum seekers and other forced migrants. The university ranks above all but four of its fellow Russell Group members in our social inclusion index and it was the first of its research-led peers to sign the Social Mobility Pledge.

The proportion of students recruited from non-selective state schools is approaching three-quarters (73.9%) and almost 10% of students are drawn from deprived areas (ranking York in the top half of UK universities on this measure). At 5.3%, York's proportion of white working-class boys – the most underrepresented group in higher education – is just outside the top 50 nationally. About a quarter of British undergraduates and about 5% of undergraduates from the European Union qualify for some form of financial assistance.

The £9million York Sport Village features a 25m pool, trainer pool, 120-station gym, 3G pitch and five-a-side pitches. The university has the only outdoor velodrome in Yorkshire, a 1km cycling track and an athletics track, as well as its own boathouse on the River Ouse.

Legend has it that York's historic cobbled streets have a pub for every day of the year, while the city also has its share of student-friendly nightclubs. Leeds is within easy reach for bigger nights out.

First-years who apply by the deadline are guaranteed accommodation – much of it catered (breakfast and dinner, five days per week) depending on the college.

Tuition fees
- » Fees for UK students   £9,250
- » Fees for International students 2023–24   £19,600–£24,000
  Medicine (Hull-York Medical School 2022, annual increases capped at 2%) £38,500
- » For scholarship and bursary information see www.york.ac.uk/study/undergraduate/fees-funding/
- » Graduate salary   £25,000

Student numbers

Undergraduates	14,589	(277)
Postgraduates	5,424	(2,404)
Applications/places		27,625/5,295
Applications per place		5.2:1
Overall offer rate		83.6%
International students – EU		3.9%
Non-EU		10.8%

Accommodation
University provided places: 6,633
Catered costs: £136–£217 per week
Self-catered: £99–£263 per week
First-years guaranteed accommodation
www.york.ac.uk/study/accommodation/

Where do the students come from?

State schools (non-grammar)	73.9%	First generation students	31.6%	White working-class males	5.3%
Grammar schools	11.5%	Low participation areas	9.8%	Black achievement gap	-17.8%
Independent schools	14.6%	All ethnic minorities	15.7%	Mature (over 21)	7.4%

Social inclusion ranking: 95

York St John University

Based at an 11-acre campus on Lord Mayor's Walk near York city centre, students at York St John (YSJ) report consistently positive reviews of their university in the National Student Survey. Our analysis of the latest results, published in summer 2022, ranks YSJ 13th in the UK for satisfaction with teaching quality (up 18 places) and joint 25th for the wider experience (up 20 places).

Lectures, seminars and workshops have returned to face-to-face delivery for the 2022-23 academic year. For a university that markets itself on knowing its students by name, YSJ is likely to be delighted with the return to campus. The pandemic swivel to remote learning brought to light the importance of maintaining a sense of community – online as well as in real life, the university says.

Such is the YSJ campus atmosphere that 2022's 16% increase in applications by the end of March is thought by the university to be driven by its reintroduction of in-person open days.

There is a growing estate for prospective students to explore. A new Creative Centre opened in 2021 as a teaching base for drama, music, media production and computer science degrees. Geography facilities are next in line for an upgrade, while nursing and allied health facilities are being extended and refurbished.

YSJ's 2018-opened London campus caters for postgraduate courses. It has recently moved from a site in the Barbican to the Export building at East India Dock near Canary Wharf.

The curriculum also continues to evolve at YSJ, which was founded in 1841 as a teacher training college. The first cybersecurity and forensic psychology students began courses in 2022 and from 2023 the university will welcome students of new degrees in music technology; sport journalism; and radiography.

Low rates of graduate employment in high-skilled jobs contributed to a bronze rating in the Teaching Excellence Framework but the panel was impressed by a scheme that involves undergraduates in research and by the innovative measures to support vulnerable students, including those experiencing mental health difficulties.

Progression to high-skilled jobs continues to hold York St John back in our league table also. With just over two-thirds of graduates in high-skilled work or postgraduate study, the university drops outside the top 100 of our measure for graduate prospects, down eight places on last year. It does better on completion rates, with less students projected to drop out than the projected rate based on the social and academic mix.

Psychology produced the best results in the 2014 research ratings, when the 30% of research regarded as world-leading or internationally excellent represented a big improvement on

---

Lord Mayor's Walk
York YO31 7EX
01904 876 598
admissions@yorksj.ac.uk
http://ysjsu.com
www.yorksj.ac.uk
Open days: see website

The Times and The Sunday Times Rankings
Overall Ranking: 79 (last year: =83)

Teaching quality	80%	13
Student experience	75.1%	=25
Research quality	19.6%	115
Entry standards	110	=115
Graduate prospects	66.6%	=106
Good honours	76.5%	=75
Expected completion rate	85.1%	70
Student/staff ratio	18	=95

the 2008 assessments. The research strategy promotes interdisciplinary research, building on current areas of expertise and targeting further improvement in the 2021 exercise.

YSJ expects to have about 850 learners on its seven degree apprenticeships by 2032, up from 560 apprentices at last count. The professional areas covered by the suite of degree apprenticeship programmes include senior leadership, data science, project management, healthcare science and policing.

Fifty-eight per cent of YSJ's research submitted for the Research Excellence Framework 2021 was judged as world-leading (4*) or internationally excellent (3*), an increase on the REF in 2014, and the number of academic staff with significant responsibility for research submitted more than doubled. But against even bigger improvements elsewhere YSJ loses 14 places in our research quality ranking this year. Sport science; education; psychology; and music and performance were the university's strongest areas.

A revamped financial assistance package introduced for 2021 entry benefited 36% of new students. Awards include £800 per year scholarships for students from low-income households, for those estranged from their families and for those who have left care. A scholarship of the same value for students from ethnic minorities is based on household incomes of up to £42,000. Once enrolled on courses students can apply for £500 funding to help with work experience, internship or volunteering opportunities.

YSJ features in the lower half of UK universities in our social inclusion index overall (84th), although the proportion of students educated at non-selective state schools (96.7%) is in 17th place in England and Wales. YSJ is 20th for recruitment of white working-class boys – the most underrepresented group in higher education – at 7.5%. Helping to widen access, a contextual offers scheme makes 80 UCAS tariff point reductions to around a quarter of entrants.

The students' union (SU) hosts more than 50 clubs and societies, but if there's nothing that suits, students are invited to start their own. Quiz nights, karaoke, live sport and live music are among the entertainments hosted at the SU campus venue.

The Lord Mayor's Walk campus has a sports hall, climbing wall, basketball, netball, indoor football and cricket nets, while a 15-minute walk brings students to the sports park's extensive facilities.

Tuition fees

»	Fees for UK students	£9,250
	Foundation degrees	from £4,200
»	Fees for International students 2023–24	£13,000
»	For scholarship and bursary information see www.yorksj.ac.uk/students/your-finances/	
»	Graduate salary	£21,000

Student numbers

Undergraduates	5,557	(114)
Postgraduates	1,406	(501)
Applications/places	8,910/1,995	
Applications per place	4.5:1	
Overall offer rate	90.8%	
International students – EU	1.5%	
Non-EU	2.9%	

Accommodation

University provided places: 1,488
Self-catered: £104–£193 per week
First-years guaranteed accommodation
www.yorksj.ac.uk/study/accommodation

Where do the students come from?

State schools (non-grammar)	96.7%	First generation students	47.2%	White working-class males	7.5%
Grammar schools	1.5%	Low participation areas	17%	Black achievement gap	-35.5%
Independent schools	1.7%	All ethnic minorities	6.8%	Mature (over 21)	22.1%

Social inclusion ranking: 84

Specialist and Private Institutions

1 Specialist colleges of the University of London

This listing gives contact details for specialist degree-awarding colleges within the University of London not listed elsewhere within the book. Those marked * are members of GuildHE (**www.guildhe.ac.uk**). Fees are for a single year of study.

Courtauld Institute of Art
Somerset House Strand
London WC2R 0RN
020 3947 7711
www.courtauld.ac.uk
Fees: £9,250 (Overseas £24,000)

London Business School
Regent's Park
London NW1 4SA
020 7000 7000
www.london.edu
Postgraduate only

London School of Hygiene and Tropical Medicine
Keppel Street
London WC1E 7HT
020 7636 8636
www.lshtm.ac.uk
Postgraduate medical courses

Royal Academy of Music
Marylebone Road
London NW1 5HT
020 7873 7373
www.ram.ac.uk
Fees: £9,250 (Overseas £27,300)

Royal Central School of Speech and Drama*
Eton Avenue
London NW3 3HY
020 7722 8183
www.cssd.ac.uk
Fees: £9,250 (Overseas £21,000-£27,500)

Royal Veterinary College
Royal College Street
London NW1 0TU
020 7468 5000
www.rvc.ac.uk
Fees: £9,250 (Overseas £15,350-£41,500)

University of London Institute in Paris
9-11 rue de Constantine
75340 Paris Cedex 07, France
(+33) 1 44 11 73 83
https://ulip.london.ac.uk
Degrees offered in conjunction with Queen Mary and Royal Holloway colleges
Fees: £9,250 (Overseas £12,000)

2 Specialist colleges and private institutions

This listing gives contact details for other degree-awarding higher education institutions not mentioned elsewhere within the book. All the institutions listed below offer degree courses, some providing a wide range of courses while others are specialist colleges with a small intake. Those marked * are members of GuildHE (**www.guildhe.ac.uk**). Fees are the latest available for a single year of study.

Arden University
Business, finance, health and others
Arden House,
Middlemarch Park,
Coventry CV3 4FJ
   Campuses in London, Birmingham,
   Manchester & Berlin
0800 268 7737
www.arden.ac.uk
Fees vary – blended learning

BPP University
Mainly law, business & health
Aldine Place, 142-144 Uxbridge Road,
London W12 8AW
   Campuses in Abingdon, Birmingham,
   Bristol, Cambridge, Doncaster, Leeds,
   Liverpool, London, Manchester,
   Maidstone, Milton Keynes, Newcastle,
   Nottingham, Reading, Southampton
03300 603 100
www.bpp.com
Fees vary by subject and course

Conservatoire for Dance and Drama
Comprised of:
   Bristol Old Vic Theatre School, Central
   School of Ballet, London Academy of
   Music and Dramatic Art (LAMDA),
   London Contemporary Dance School,
   National Centre for Circus Arts,
   Northern School of Contemporary
   Dance, Rambert School of Ballet and
   Contemporary Dance, Royal Academy of
   Dramatic Art (RADA)*
14-16 Great Chapel Street,
London W1F 8FL

020 7387 5101
www.cdd.ac.uk
Fees: £9,250 (Overseas: contact school)

Dyson Institute of Engineering and Technology
Tetbury Hill Malmesbury
Wiltshire SN16 0RP
01285 705 228
dysoninstitute@dyson.com
www.dysoninstitute.com
Paid degree courses – no fees

Glasgow School of Art
167 Renfrew Street, Glasgow G3 6RQ
0141 353 4500
www.gsa.ac.uk
Fees: Scotland, £1,820 annual fee
RUK £9,250 (Overseas £19,440-£29,340)

Guildhall School of Music and Drama
Silk Street, Barbican,
London EC2Y 8DT
020 7628 2571
www.gsmd.ac.uk
Fees: £9,250 (Overseas £23,545-£24,970)

The University of Law*
Birmingham, Bristol, Guildford, Leeds,
London (Bloomsbury and Moorgate),
Manchester, Nottingham
0800 289 997
www.law.ac.uk
Fees: £14,750 – two-year course
(Overseas £17,750)
£9,250 – three-year course
(Overseas £14,150)

Liverpool Institute for Performing Arts*
Mount Street,
Liverpool L1 9HF
0151 330 3084
www.lipa.ac.uk
Fees: £9,250 (Overseas £18,500)

**The London Institute of Banking
and Finance***
4-9 Burgate Lane
Canterbury, Kent CT1 2XJ
01227 818609
   Student campus:
   25 Lovat Lane, London EC3R 8EB
   020 7337 6293
www.libf.ac.uk
Fees: £9,250 (Overseas £13,000)

Northeastern University London*
Devon House,
St Katharine Docks,
London E1W 1LP
020 7637 4550
www.nchlondon.ac.uk
Fees: £9,250 (Overseas £21,000-£25,000)

Pearson College*
Business, law & video games
190 High Holborn,
London WC1V 7BH
020 3944 8529
www.pearsoncollegelondon.ac.uk
Fees: £9,250 (Overseas £17,995)

Plymouth College of Art*
Tavistock Place,
Plymouth PL4 8AT
01752 203402
www.plymouthart.ac.uk
Fees: £9,250 (Overseas £16,500)

Regent's University London*
Business, design, media & psychology
Inner Circle,
Regent's Park, London NW1 4NS
020 7487 7700
www.regents.ac.uk
Fees: £20,500-£22,500

**Rose Bruford College of Theatre
and Performance***
Lamorbey Park,
Burnt Oak Lane,
Sidcup, Kent DA15 9DF
020 8308 2600
www.bruford.ac.uk
Fees: £9,250 (Overseas £18,900)

Royal College of Music
Prince Consort Road,
London SW7 2BS
020 7591 4300
www.rcm.ac.uk
Fees: £9,250 (Overseas £19,000-£28,900)

Royal Conservatoire of Scotland
100 Renfrew Street,
Glasgow G2 3DB
0141 332 4101
www.rcs.ac.uk
Fees: Scotland, £1,800
RUK £9,250 (Overseas £19,314)

Royal Northern College of Music
124 Oxford Road,
Manchester M13 9RD
0161 907 5200
www.rncm.ac.uk
Fees: £9,250 (Overseas £17,500-£34,900)

**Royal Welsh College of Music
and Drama**
Castle Grounds, Cathays Park,
Cardiff CF10 3ER
029 2034 2854
www.rwcmd.ac.uk
Fees: £9,000 (Overseas £20,790-£30,000)

St Mary's University College*
Teaching & liberal arts
191 Falls Road, Belfast BT12 6FE
028 9032 7678
www.stmarys-belfast.ac.uk
Fees: £4,530; RUK £9,250
(Overseas contact college)

Scotland's Rural College
Agriculture, environment & land
management
Peter Wilson Building,
The King's Buildings,
West Mains Road,
Edinburgh EH9 3JG
  Campuses at Aberdeen, Ayr, Cupar,
  Dumfries, Oatridge, West Lothian and
  Edinburgh
0131 535 4000
www.sruc.ac.uk
Fees: Scotland, £700-£1,008
RUK £7,500 (Overseas £16,000-£33,000)

Stranmillis University College
Teaching courses
Stranmillis Road, Belfast BT9 5DY
028 9038 1271
www.stran.ac.uk
Fees: £4,530;
RUK £9,250 (Overseas £17,900-£18,200)

**Trinity Laban Conservatoire of
Music and Dance**
King Charles Court
Old Royal Naval College,
Greenwich, London SE10 9JF
020 8305 4444
www.trinitylaban.ac.uk
Fees: £9,250 (Overseas £14,480-£23,390)

University Academy 92
Business, media & sport
UA92 Campus,
Brian Statham Way, Old Trafford,
Manchester M16 0PU
0161 507 1992
www.ua92.ac.uk
Fees: £9,250 (Overseas £14,466-£21,699)

University College, Birmingham (UCB)
Further and Higher Education courses
Mainly hospitality, tourism, business, sport
and education
Summer Row,
Birmingham B3 1JB
0121 604 1000
www.ucb.ac.uk
Fees: £9,250 (Overseas £14,500-£15,000)

**UCFB (University Campus of Football
Business)***
Wembley Stadium
London HA9 0WS
Etihad Campus, Manchester M11 3FF
0333 241 7333
www.ucfb.ac.uk
Fees: £9,250 (Overseas £16,450)

Writtle University College*
Land management
Lordship Road,
Chelmsford, Essex CM1 3RR
01245 424200
www.writtle.ac.uk
Fees: £9,250 (Overseas £13,335-£14,445)

Index